D1299867

The SCULPTURE REFERENCE *Illustrated*

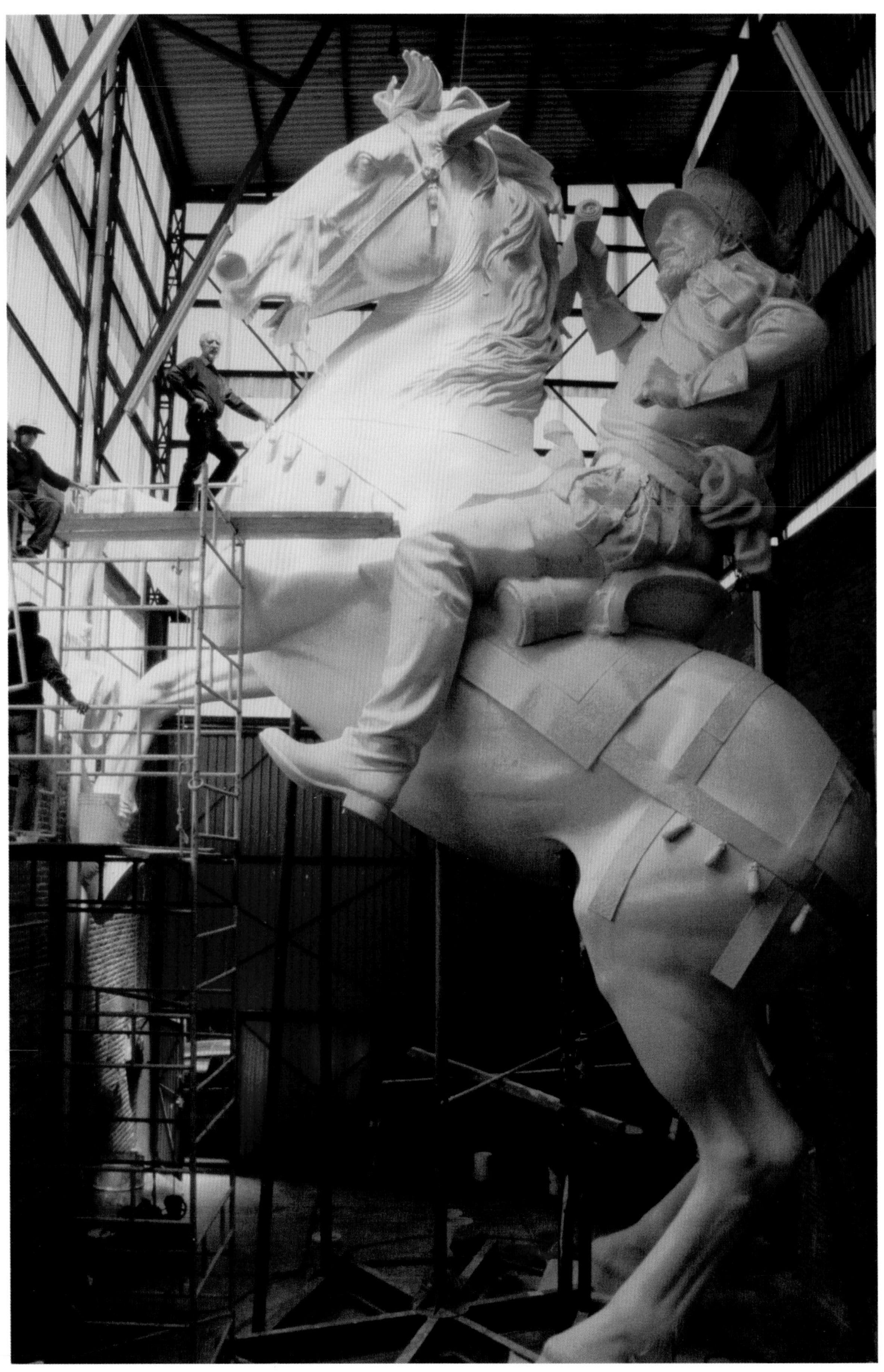

Don Juan de Oñate, Founder of the Hispanic Southwest, 1598. by **John Sherrill Houser**, Photographer: Ethan Houser. *see Enlarging.*

The

SCULPTURE REFERENCE *Illustrated*

Contemporary Techniques, Terms, Tools, Materials, and Sculpture

Arthur Williams

Sculpture Books Publishing

SculptureBooks.com

Acknowledgements

Many people have helped contribute to this manuscript. To all of the contributing artists, I am pleased to share your works with the rest of the world. Your images bring to life the written material. I know that all readers using metrics will thank Dr. Martin Ehde, who spent long hours translating the English measurements into metrics. I especially appreciate Susan Sasenick McCreary, who not only encouraged me to write this book, but proofread and offered many valuable suggestions. A special thanks goes to Amber Goodwin, graphic designer, for the advice and assistance in translating my work into a useful book.

What would I do without my wife and best friend, Jacqueline Williams? I do not type; she does. Translating a stack of handwritten material over eight inches (20.3cm) thick into accurate computer type took a lot of time and dedication. Her helpful comments were necessary to the completion. I am a sculptor with rough edges who happens to understand many things; Jacqueline is the polish that makes this information presentable.

Arthur Williams

Published by **Sculpture Books Publishing**
PO Box 7888, Gulfport, MS 39506 U.S.A.

SculptureBooks.com

ISBN 0-9755383-0-6

Library of Congress Control Number: 2004093578
Printed in China by C & C Offset Printing Co., Ltd.
Editor: Tucker Lee

Foreword

I have always desired a comprehensive sculpture reference book where all aspects of sculpture were alphabetically arranged, visually demonstrated and easily readable, with images furnished by living, practicing sculptors from diverse backgrounds. This is that book.

The terms are first defined and then expounded upon, some in more detail than others, depending on the volume of use. All entries are described in sculptural terms. If the reader is unsure of exactly what she/he is looking for, a cross reference can be located with a tool, technique, material or known term. The cross-reference should lead into what is needed. From a multitude of contemporary sculptors furnishing more than 16,000 images, 1,187 were chosen for quality sculptures, demonstrations, tools and materials. These photographs, charts and drawings are supplied alongside the informational entries. All measurements are in English and metric terms rounded out to make the text more readable.

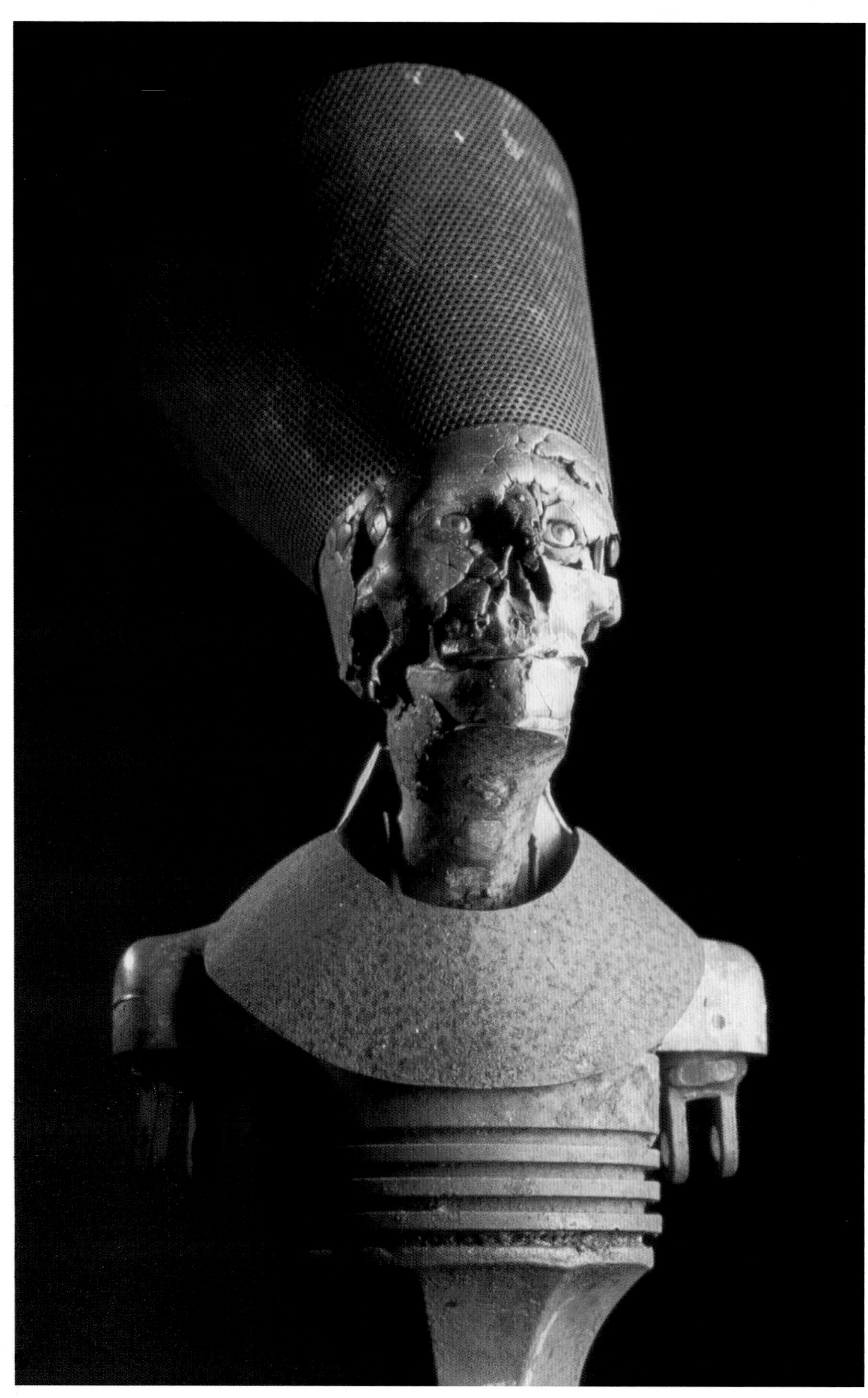

Bruce Larsen, *Pharaoh's Favorite*. Mixed media (Assemblage), 15"x72"x15" (38.1cm x 182.9cm x 38.1cm).

Jack Ransom Arvin uses an abrasive cutting disk to rough out a marble work.

Abrading tools Designed to remove part of the sculpture's surface by friction or scraping at the point of contact. Examples are files and rasps. *See **Files**; **Grinders**; **Rasps**.*

Abrasives Substances rubbed against a surface to grind, scratch or uniformly cut an irregular shaped surface into a smoother or textured surface. The abrasive materials consist of tougher substances than the actual surface. To achieve the optimum finish, one grade of abrasive grit follows another until the surface has been thoroughly worked. Each grit scratches down the coarser surface mark into smaller marks. After several grits, the marks can become so subtle they are not be seen by the naked eye; hence, a "smooth" surface.

Abrasives include all kinds of materials from nature, like diamonds, to synthetics, such as silicon carbide. Some abrasives (flint for example) are not very tough, while aluminum oxide is considerably stronger. Common forms of abrasives are sandpapers, pumice stones, rubbing compounds and polishing compounds. All have a purpose and work particularly well with certain materials. *See **Sandpaper**; **Polish**; **Flap wheels**; **Wire brushes**; **Grinders**; **Rubbing compound**; **Buffing compound**.*

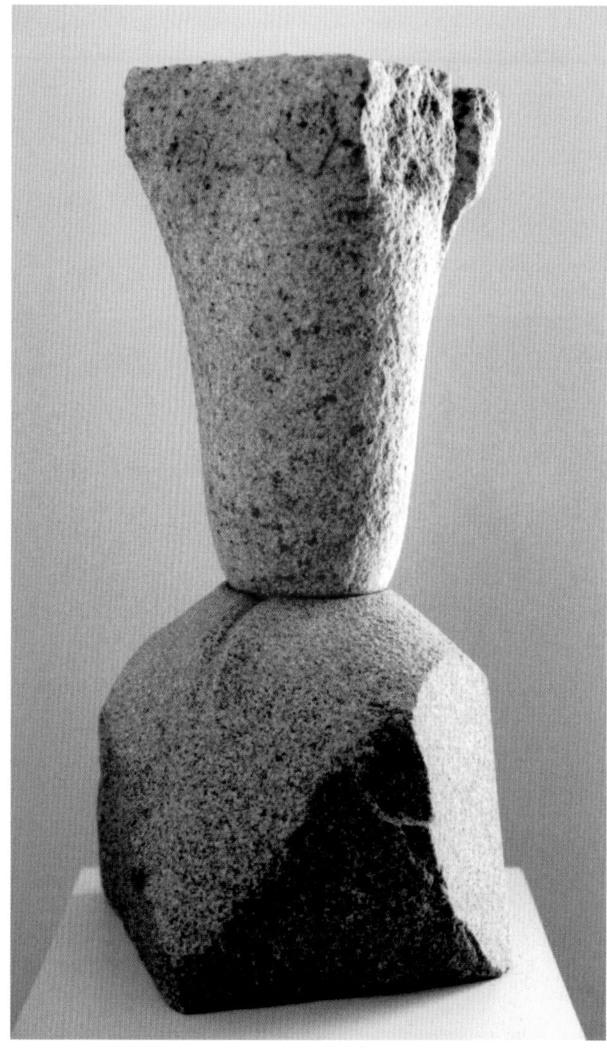

Enzo Torcoletti, *Maithuna Torso.* Pink and gray granite, 20" (50.8cm) tall.

Abstraction A work of art in which the subject is expressed in shapes or forms other than a copy or close representation of the object. The subject or content is often stylized, minimized or demonstrated as an essence of the object, thought or subject, but not necessarily as a recognizable or naturalistic shape. Formal design is favored over subject. When the work is without a meaningful title or subject or any form of representation, it is called nonrepresentational. *See **Nonrepresentational**.*

AC Abbreviated term for alternating current or the electricity that periodically reverses the electron flow used in welding. *See **Arc welding**.*

Academic art Art that is considered mediocre, undistinguished or conforming to acceptable standards. It does not attempt to add new ideas or reach beyond the commonplace. A contrasting meaning is art that is created purely for experiment without any commercial value.

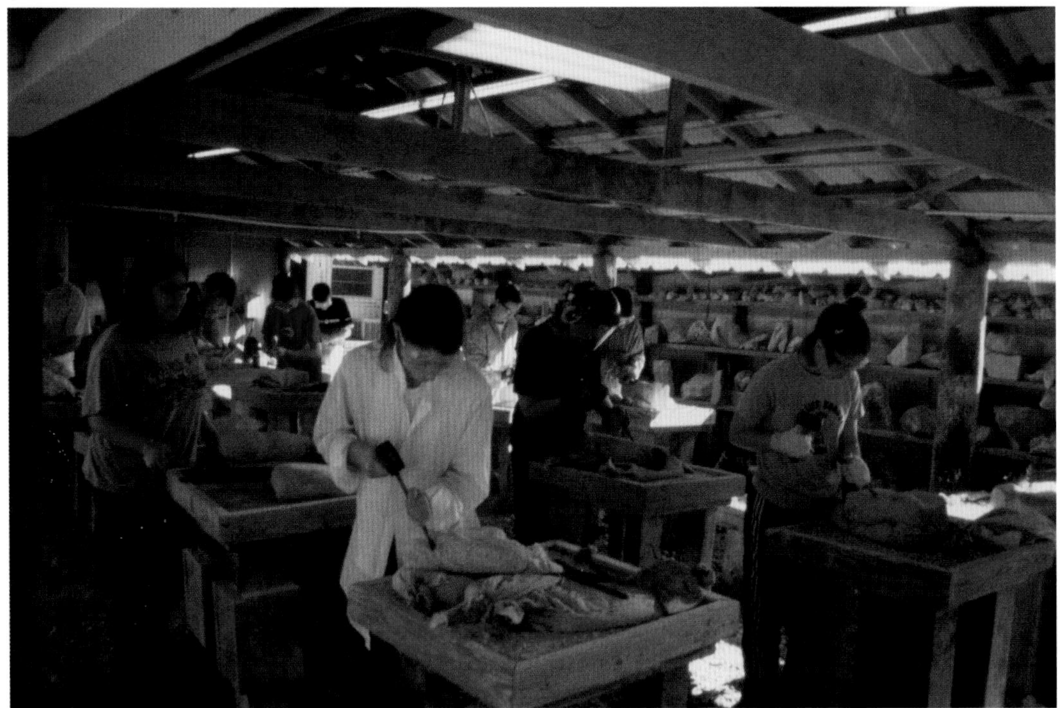

Academic credentials are required to teach college courses. A beginning sculpture class at William Carey College on the Coast in Gulfport, Mississippi, learns to carve.

Academic degrees (of art):

- **B.A.**: Bachelor of Arts, four-year liberal arts degree.
- **B.F.A.**: Bachelor of Fine Arts, four-year studio art degree, considered the professional undergraduate art degree.
- **M.A.**: Master of Arts, graduate degree, one or more years beyond undergraduate work, can specialize in art, usually requires a thesis.
- **M.Ed.**: One or more years beyond undergraduate work, intended for teaching in elementary or secondary schools, no thesis is required.
- **M.F.A.**: Master of Fine Arts, the terminal or final studio arts degree obtainable, two or more years beyond undergraduate work, usually an exhibition and brief thesis are required. It is the accepted degree for teaching studio.
- **Ph.D.**: Doctor of Philosophy, seldom given in studio arts, usually for art history or a combination of arts (music/art), two or more years beyond an acquired Master's degree, dissertation required.
- **D.A.**: Doctor of Arts, depending upon the institution, can be for the studio arts in application to teaching, two or more years beyond the M.A. or M.F.A. degree, dissertation required.

Acajon Another term for mahogany wood. *See **Mahogany**.*

Accelerator Catalyst, an ingredient combined with substances to increase the reaction speed of a process. Examples are organic peroxide used to harden resins or even common table salt (sodium chloride) added to plaster to increase the setting time. *See **Plaster** (additive); **Plastics** (resin); **Glue** (epoxy).*

Accidental form A form that is fortuitously discovered from the natural beauty or character of a material or the combination of materials. It was not planned, though it was recognized by the artist.

Acetone Dimethyl ketone, a volatile, flammable, colorless liquid used as a strong solvent or paint remover. It emits strong vapors that can result in flash fires. *See **Solvents**.*

Acetylene A colorless gas contained in a pressurized cylinder; highly flammable; combined with oxygen in a welding/cutting torch, it produces high temperatures in excess of 6000° F (3316°C) capable of melting metals. *See* ***Oxyacetylene cutting; Oxyacetylene welding; Cylinder***.

Acetylene cylinder A strong pressurized container often referred to as a bottle or tank because of its shape; used to store acetylene. *See* ***Oxyacetylene cutting; Oxyacetylene welding; Cylinder***.

Acetylene regulator A valve mounted on top of an acetylene cylinder that is designed to reduce and automatically keep acetylene gas pressure constant as it is supplied to the work. *See* ***Oxyacetylene cutting; Oxyacetylene welding; Cylinder***.

Acid A fast acting compound that reacts with a base to form salts (new compound). It can be used to clean a surface, etch a design, or be part of the metal patination process resulting in a new surface color. Depending upon the acid, it can be corrosive and hazardous, requiring special handling. *See* ***Patina; Concrete***.

Acid bath Immersing an object into a chemical bath to clean or etch. *See* ***Patina***.

Across the grain/Against the grain. Terms generally associated with wood or stone to designate carving or sanding at a perpendicular direction to the natural grain as opposed to working parallel or along the grain. *See* ***Wood*** *(carving);* ***Stone*** *(carving)*.

Acrylic (liquid) A polymer liquid that can be cast into a clear, transparent, solid, hard mass. An autoclave is needed for any work of size. Precise control keeps the liquid from boiling during the casting of larger, thicker forms. Molding is designed for the shrinkage involved. Even with an autoclave, annealing, sanding, compounding, polishing and buffing are essential. *See* ***Acrylic*** *(sheet plastic);* ***Autoclave; Acrylics*** *(paint)*.

Acrylic (sheet plastic) A sheet plastic known for its transparency by various trademark names, such as Plexiglas™ and Lucite™. Though it can be opaque, it is commercially available in various thicknesses and colors. It is manipulated by bending, press molding or folding when hot. It can be heated with household cooking ovens, heat lamps, handheld heat guns (used for paint stripping), as well as butane and gas torches and homemade gas burners.

Technique

Too much heat can result in a completely limp sheet that is uncontrollable. Extreme heat or flame can cause the material to ignite, bubble, discolor and run, giving off noxious and sometimes lethal gases. It is easier to precut before heating, though it can be cut once it is removed from the heat source. The protective backing, commonly made of flammable materials, must be removed before heating. However, it is good to keep the backing on as long as possible during cold cutting and sanding to avoid scratches, which so readily appear. Once heated, the plastic can be handled with tools and heat resistant gloves. If it is to be heated more than once, it is likely that the first shape will be partially, if not completely, lost to a limp state. Temperatures beyond 275°F (23.9°C) can result in unusable plastics.

Most sandpapers will work on plastics, especially wet-or-dry and aluminum oxide. Sculptors choose wet-or-dry papers to achieve an accurate grit size. Wet sanding prevents fine dust particles from floating in the workplace. Aluminum oxide is a good paper to use for earlier, coarser sanding purposes. *See* ***Sandpaper***.

Michael Wilkinson, *Journey*, Acrylic, 40'' (102cm) height. ©2002 MNW.

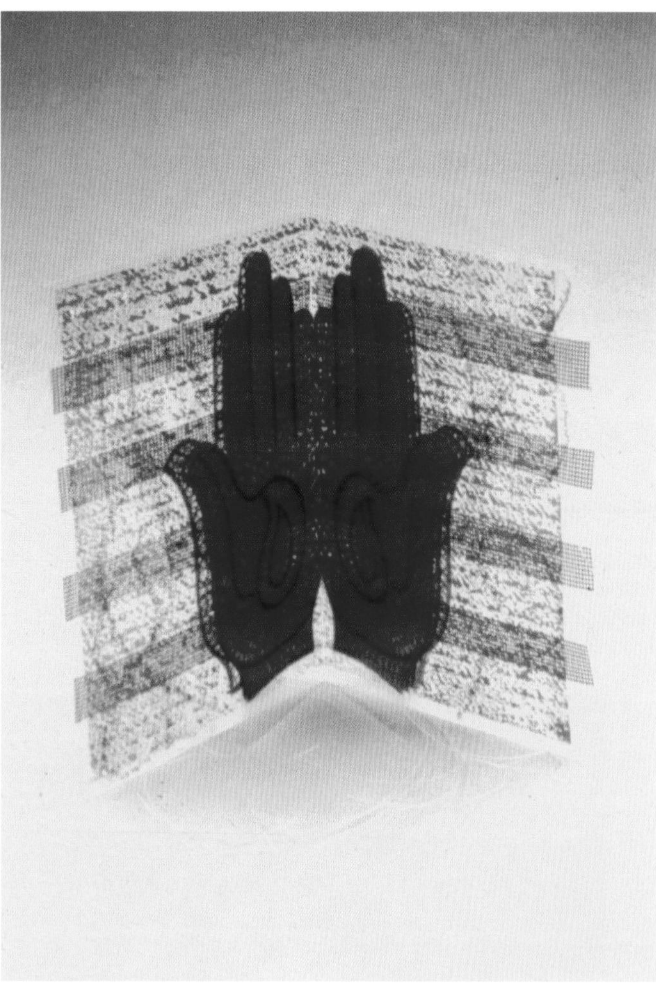

Claire Jeanine Satin, *Pentimento/mehndi (Red Book I)*. Multi-printing on acetate, fiberglass screen, ink/handwritten text, monofilament, glass beads, 8½"x 6½" (21.6cm x 16.5cm).

Plastic fabrication or forming is accomplished by thermoforming (with heat) or cold-forming (bolting, cutting and cementing without warmth) or a combination of both processes. *See* ***Thermoforming***. The plastic can be riveted and sheared, as well as welded. Sheet acrylic can be drilled, cut, broken, shaved, filed, sanded and polished depending upon the tool and speed, blade or bit and thickness of the plastic.

Tools need to be sharp, and the blades should not have coarse or rough teeth. Buffers that rotate higher than 2500 rpm will cause the surface to overheat and distort. Tripoli (rubbing and polishing compounds) are used to achieve a completely smooth or transparent surface. *See* ***Buffing compound***.

Sheet plastic (acrylic) can be cemented with ethylene dichloride applied by a simple syringe or hollow needle. Capillary action aids the process. Sometimes stresses, cracking or fractures for example, appear in works that have been laminated. To prevent this, the work needs to be annealed before machining to eliminate any stress that the machinery could cause if it heats the sheet. Annealing requires the acrylic to be slowly heated in an oven (or electric kiln), then heat soaked and slowly cooled at about the same rate that the temperature was originally raised.

Some processes for thicker plastics take days, even weeks to anneal in specially designed ovens. Annealing is needed if waves of color or color bands are sighted when the sculptor looks at the work through polarized eye lenses. If there is no stress, few, if any of the waves will appear. *See* ***Annealing; Capillary action; Ethylene dichloride***.

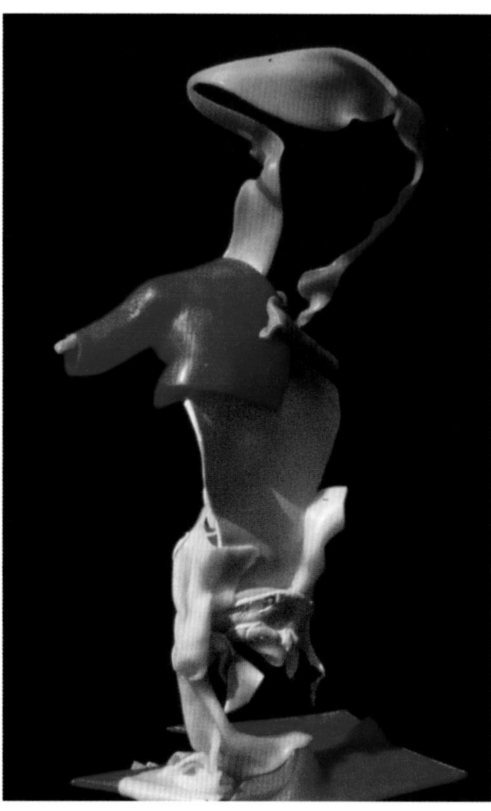

Renè Joseph, *Torso/Flower*. Acrylic, 13"x 9" x 9½" (23cm x 24cm).

Acrylic resin A synthetic, thermosetting resin that can be cast, machined or heated to shape. *See* ***Plastic***.

Acrylics (paint) Colors prepared with pigments placed in polymethyl methacrylate with mineral spirits. The resulting paint is made and packaged for the artist. It is often confused with polymer colors or pigment placed in an acrylic polymer resin water solution that is a fast-drying water based artist's paint. *See* ***Polymer*** *(paint)*.

Addition Process of adding a sculptural material, or building up a form, to achieve volume. Manipulative (malleable) materials, such as modeling clay or ceramic clay, are the most widely used sculptural media for addition.

Adhesion wax A wax, when heated, is formulated with properties designed to adhere two or more wax pieces together. It is primarily used when adding the metal pouring system to the wax artwork

Duda Penteado, *Engauis.* Oxbones, acrylic, 20"x21" (51cm x 53cm).

in preparation for casting. It melts at a higher temperature than the body wax and holds firm as it hardens. If the temperature of either the adhesive wax or the runners and form are decreased, the expansion rates of the waxes vary, resulting in a joint without adhesion unless the adhesion wax has been blended into the other wax pieces.

The best joints are those in which both waxes are melted together by means of a hot wax melting tool, whether it is commercially made for the purpose, a wood burner or an inexpensive constant heat soldering rod. If the waxes completely fuse and then return to the same temperature, the joint will be good. Adhesion wax is not a high-quality filler wax, since it dries harder than the surrounding wax, creating a clean-up problem. It is also called sticky wax. *See* ***Casting; Metal pouring system; Wax.***

Adhesion wax is added to the casting by brush.

Using a heated soldering iron, the adhesion wax is blended into the casting.

Adhesive (glue) A mixture or substance applied in the form of cement, resin, glue, etc., which has the ability to join or bond materials. The adhesive is selected based on the materials to be glued, the strength required, the life expectancy of the joint, the climatic conditions, the time allowed for the joint to set, as well as color, flexibility, etc.

ADHESIVES IN COMMON USE*

TYPE	METHOD	STRENGTH	WATER RESISTANCE	SETTING TIME	USES*
Carpenter's Glue	Squeeze bottle or brush	Good	Poor	1 hr. to overnight	Wood, Variety
Contact Cement	Brush or roller to both surfaces	Good	Good	30 min. +	Variety, Counter topping
Epoxy Cement	Two containers to mix, then brush	Excellent	Good	1 min. to 24 hrs.	Variety, Stone, Metal
Glue Stick	Glue gun that heats to use	Good	Excellent	As cools	Variety, Cloth
Polyurethane	Squeeze bottle or brush	Good	Good	4 hrs.	Variety
Silicone Rubber	Caulk tube	Good	Excellent	Overnight +	Variety, Glass
Super Glue™	Drops	Excellent	Good	Instant	Variety, Ceramics

**Uses are much broader than displayed; however, the most common are listed.*

Adobe Sun dried brick, or coating, consisting of earth and straw, or the structure made from the bricks. Sometimes used as a sculptural building material.

Adz (adze) A large curved blade mounted at a right angle on a wood handle used single handedly for quick wood removal. It resembles a hatchet or small ax, but is primarily used for heavy roughing and shaping wood. The gouge shape is the most common. Some adze heads are configured with a second blade.

Aerosol A suspension of particles or liquid such as paint, oil or cleaner, in a solution packed with a gaseous propellant under pressure in a container. It is released by pressing a valve designed to spray directly onto an object or into the atmosphere. The term also refers to the type of container itself.

Adze designs by **Mac McAllister.**

Agate Chalcedony. An extremely hard semi-precious stone.

Aggregate The inert ingredient that gives strength, consistency, body and sometimes beauty, to concrete, cast stone and other casting materials. Many particles from natural mineral materials, such as stone or sand, to manmade glasses are used as aggregates. In concrete, an aggregate is the source of strength; whereas, in cast stone, the aggregate is most often the source of design or color. Aggregates can be as coarse as boulders added to the mix or as fine as powder that allows exacting details. *See* ***Concrete; Cast stone.***

Coarse aggregates. Left to right: marble chips, light pea gravel, dark pea gravel, lavastone; normal 3/4″ (1.9 cm) mix concrete.

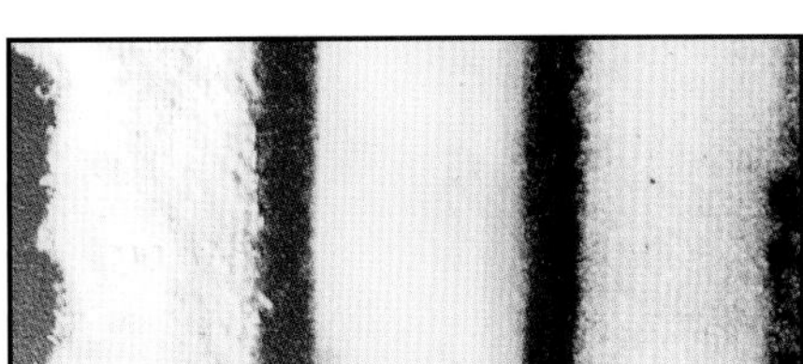

Fine aggregates. Left to right: marble dust, fused silica 50-100 grit, silica 30-50 grit.

Aggregate particles are graded through wire mesh sieves with specific measured holes per lineal inch (2.54 cm). An example of this would be to line up 100 particles of silica, touching each other in a straight row for one inch (2.54 cm). Sifting through a mesh screen designed for that size would result in 100 mesh sand. The sieve size of 50 mesh is coarse, while 200 mesh designates fine silica. The best aggregate mix for strength is one with a range of particle sizes from the smallest to the largest in several grades to avoid any gaps in size (spaces) between the aggregates to prevent air pockets or excess cement mix.

Aggregate particles that have sharply cornered, jagged or granular edges result in a stronger mix. Sands or pebbles that are rounded result in a weaker concrete. Less strong aggregates, either manmade or natural, such as glass, Vermiculite or other objects can add to the design, reduce the weight or make the mix easier to carve. Extremely hard aggregate is not easily ground without breakage of or resulting in holes where the unworkable particle breaks out of the casting.

The sculptor may choose to use crushed marble or granite for aggregate and sometimes crushed ceramic pieces. Depending upon the design, flat particles should be avoided, since they could cause voids in the final mix. Some

Carole A. Feuerman, *The Winner*. Cast marble, 57″x50″x20″ (145cm x 127cm x 51cm). Photographer: David Finn.

materials can be too weak or porous for out-of-door weathering and would cause the mix to eventually erode or fracture as moisture enters and freezes. Larger aggregates result in a rough-textured crude finish. In the construction industry, a quarter inch (0.635 cm) aggregate is considered fine, but for a small sculpture, it would be deemed coarse. Thus the size of the work is relative to the size of the aggregate.

While the aggregate may be chosen for aesthetic or hardness reasons, it must not interfere with the chemical properties of the (cement) mix. The aggregate should be clean and free of salt or other properties that would weaken the mix. If metals, such as lead, are used, a reaction to the mix results in a loose aggregate or weakening of the concrete.

Aging A natural or induced process on various substances resulting in a physical change in the material or its surface. Aged clay results in a soft, pliable body becoming hard and brittle. Aged patinas change colors.

Air-acetylene A gas welding rig that uses air from the surrounding space to mix with bottled acetylene gas. Air and gas are mixed in the tip of the torch to achieve a flame of no more than 2500°F (1371°C). It is used only for thin metals.

Jack Thompson air brushes *La Rosa Del Cardinal.*

Jack Thompson, *La Rosa Del Cardinal.* Ceramic, 38″x18″x13″ (97cm x 46cm x 33cm).

Air brush A small, handheld, cylindrical-shaped spray painting device with a trigger designed to control the fluid released for detailed painting and touch-up. It operates from 15 to 45 psi (103.4kPa to 310.2kPa) using a small air compressor. Airbrushes may have a small cup mounted for gravity feed or a siphon feed for easier handling or larger volume.

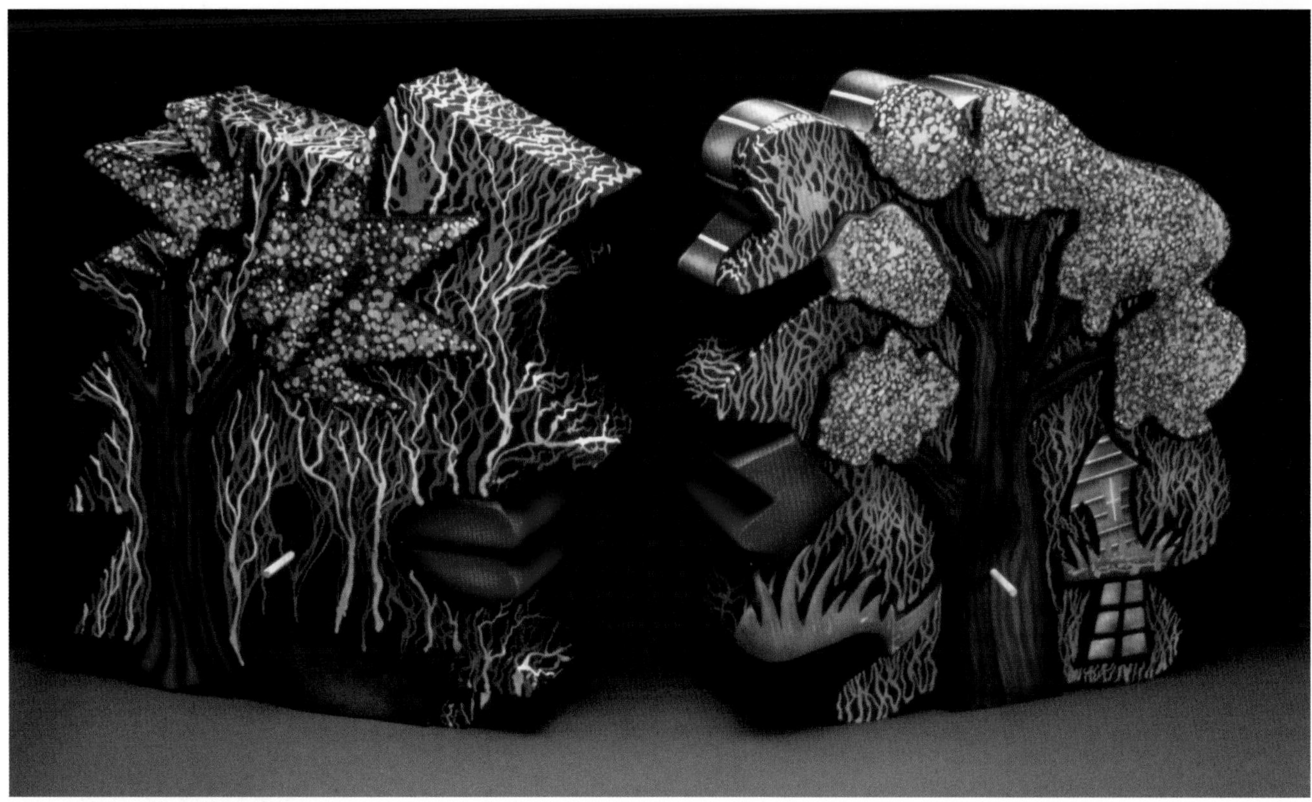

Pamela M. Segers, *Fraternal Ten*. Air brushed underglaze on lowfire clay, 23″x20″x6″ (58.4cm x 50.8cm x 15.2cm) each. Photographer: Bart Kasten.

7½ hp electric air compressor with 80 gallon (302.9L) tank.

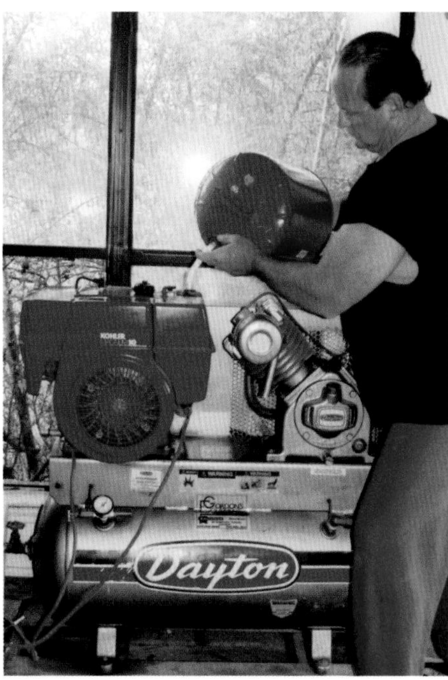

Jack Ransom Arvin adds gas to his gasoline powered compressor. Gas units of the same HP as electrical units are not as powerful as the electrical ones. While an exact difference is impossible to state, it could be as much as 50% less power. Gasoline engines operate continuously to keep the compressor ready to fill the tank.

Air compressors Motorized pumps designed to draw air from the surroundings, compressed into a smaller volume and delivered for use. As the air is released, it has force due to the compression. A high pressure steel storage tank holds the compressed air and then releases it in measured amounts as it is needed. Depending on the force and volume, the air can power tools.

Air compressor operation is simple. As an internal piston moves down, the air is drawn into the air chamber. As it pushes upward, it compresses the air and releases it into the line or storage tank or additional piston (two-stage). When the maximum prearranged tank pressure is reached, a pressure switch automatically shuts the machine off. As the air supply is used, the tank pressure is reduced. At a prearranged setting, power is once again added to the compressor and the pressure setting cycle is repeated. Pressures are kept constant to the work/tool by a second lower pressure setting, either at the exit of the air storage tank or the tool.

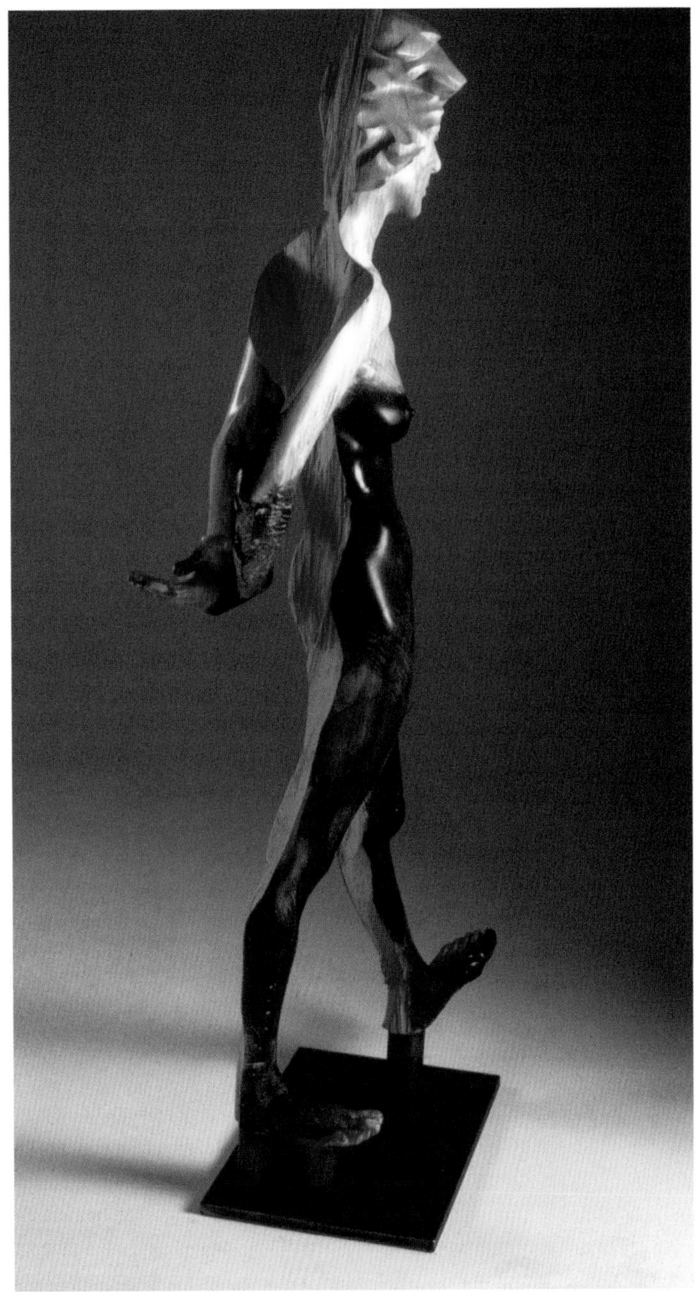

Michael J. Cooper, *Anne in Black.* Sugar pine, lacquer over oil paint, 65"x31"x17" (165.1cm x 78.8cm x 43.2cm).

Air compressors are listed by HP (horsepower), power source (gas or electric), air tank holding size, duty cycle, PSI (pounds per square inch) pressure of air, CFM (volume of air measured in cubic feet per minute), single or dual stage, oil or oil-less, piston or stationary, portable or stationary. To determine the best design and size, the sculptor needs to know if it is for portable or stationary use, the air requirements of the task and the power supply.

The **power source** can be electricity, gasoline or diesel. Electrical voltage includes 110, 220 or three-phase 200, 230, 440. The common household current is 110 volts. Compressors up to and including 6 hp are available that use 110. They need a 20 amp fuse and are rated by peak horsepower, as compared to running HP. Peak is when the maximum output is needed, especially during start-ups. The running HP is needed to fulfill the CFM and PSI stated for the compressor. Compressors less then 5 hp are used for portable construction and paint spraying duties. 220 volts produce more power, but the electrical outlets are less common and tailored for specific tools.

Compressors up to 7.5 hp are found with this voltage. The capacity is much greater and can power most of the hand tools used in industry. Three-phase electrical power requires specific electrical installation. Depending upon the location, it may not be feasible, because the installation expense may outweigh the need. Several 220 hp units can be powered at the same location when three-phase is not available.

Cubic feet per minute (CFM) measures the pump's air output. There are many factors that determine this, including the HP rating, as well as single or dual stage, etc. A higher HP rating with two stage compressors furnish the highest CFM. When securing an air compressor, the CFM must be studied to ensure that enough air is available for all the tools that will be used at the same time. Continuously used compressors should have a high CFM rating so that the compressor can cool and not constantly run. An compressor designated at a continuous duty cycle while under load

means that it can run full time. Rotary screw compressors are in this category. *See* ***Duty cycle***.

Pressure per square inch (PSI) is important. Most sculpture tools run at 90 psi. The compressor must be able to maintain this constant PSI or the tool's power will drop and the compressor will overload. A higher CFM machine is desirable, since it has a

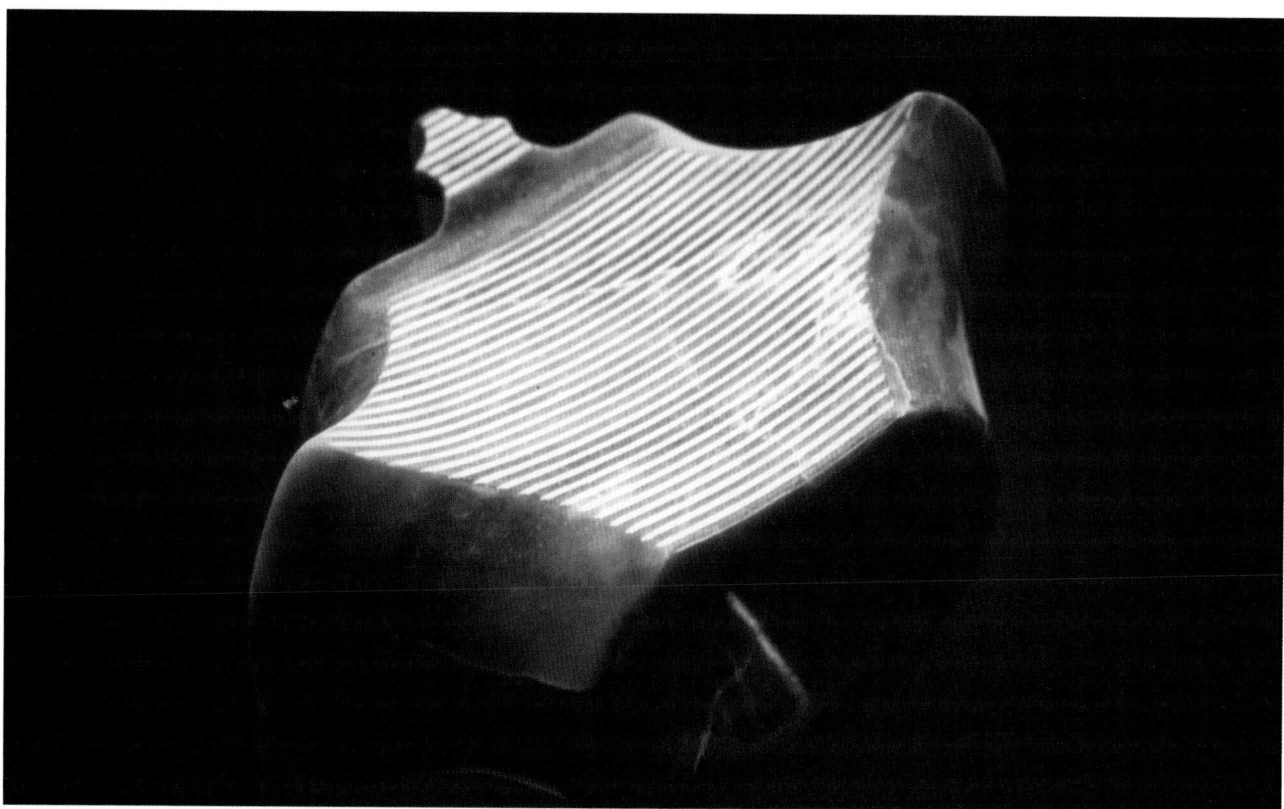

Andrès Hill, *Silent Lucidity*. Alabaster, 7½"x 9½"x ½" (19cm x 24cm x 19cm). This work was completed using an air compressor as the power source.

reserve of power available.

The air line system includes everything that is fastened to the air valve leaving the compressor, ending in a connection to the air tool. The system begins with a shut-off valve, known as a main gate valve that shuts off the air supply from the compressor tank. Then a short, but strong, steel reinforced flexible hose is attached, leading into a dryer or a large air line filter that cleans the air prior to entering the pressure regulator. Regulators are designed to control the air pressure from the compressor to the work. With the use of a gauge, they list from 0 to 150 pounds (68.1kg), 0 to 200 pounds (90.8g), etc. *See* ***Dryer***.

The main **pressure regulator** can service all lines without other regulators or can simply decrease the pressure before later regulators for specific pressure use. After the pressure regulator, a quick disconnect is added on small machines for a flexible air line hose. With larger machines, there may be several air regulators, each for a specific purpose.

Inline filters, called **water traps**, are placed directly into the line to eliminate water, oil and other contaminates from the compressed air. Depending upon the design and size, some are made of metal (usually with a visible gauge) or of a clear glass or plastic bowl that displays water and contaminants within the filter. They are manually drained by bending or twisting a drain cock to allow the trap to relieve itself using existing air pressure to force the liquid and/or debris out. However, some drains are automatic,

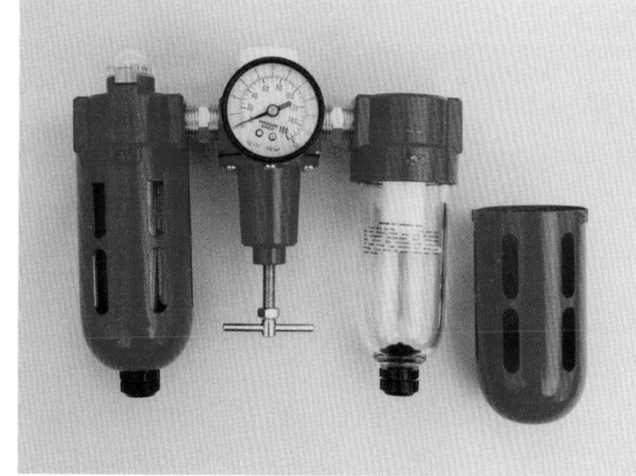

A combination installation including an air line filter, pressure regulator and lubricator with a metal cover removed.

using a water sensor to activate them. Generally, the visible filter is a separator type that noticeably produces a whirlpool of water as it separates from the air. It is easily drained from the bottom drain valve. Mechanical filters have absorption materials in a cartridge that must be replaced periodically before they become useless.

An **inline lubricator** is a permanent oil lubricator placed on the stationary air line (though small portable ones can be placed on tools) to add constant and adequate oil supply to air tools. It is adjustable with the amount of oil displayed in a clear bowl and easily controlled as to how many drops of oil are added to the air over a period of time. As the oil enters the line, it is blown into the tool to keep it lubricated. A lubricator should not be added to a line that will be used for paint sprays or a patina air source or it will contaminate the project.

Flexible air work hoses are essential to take the air to hand tools. Hoses come with male threaded ends of one-fourth inch (0.635cm) or three-eights inch (0.953cm) NPT threads that match for tool or connection fittings. General duty hoses are at least 200 psi (1378.6kPa), while heavy duty hoses are 250 psi (1723kPa) or more. Hoses with lower PSI tend to burst, tear or cut easily. Quick connect fittings are designed to allow air tools to be easily and quickly disconnected from the air lines without turning off the air supply. *See* ***Quick connect couplings***.

Air dried A material that has become equal to the outdoor atmospheric humidity. Wood is seasoned and dried in open air to reach the same humidity content as the atmosphere (12% moisture content is the assumed amount when working with wood). Referring to other forms of surface treatment, it usually means allowing a complete drying cycle while exposed to the air. *See* ***Kiln*** *(dry)*.

Air hammer (handpiece) A tool operated by an air compressor designed to control the number of blows or hits directed to a chisel or other tool that comes into direct contact with the work. They are of various dimensions and weights determined by their use and the size of the interior moving piston. Common sizes include one inch, (2.54cm) three-fourths inch (1.91cm) and one-half inch (1.27cm). All of these use interchangeable chisels that have a shaft of one-half inch (1.27cm). The one inch (2.54cm) handpiece is about eight inches (20.32cm) long and weighs approximately three and one-fourth pounds (1.48kg). This is the tool of choice among professional sculptors. It uses six cubic feet (0.18m^3) of air at 90 psi (620kPa) and can be feathered down (air supply turned down) to match the work requirements. The three-fourths inch (1.91cm) tools weigh about two pounds (0.91kg) while the one-half inch (1.27cm) tool is only one and one-fourth pounds (0.57kg). Larger handpieces are available for granite while smaller tools are available for fine finishing. The chisel shafts are made to accommodate these tools. *See* ***Air (pneumatic) tools***.

Enzo Torcoletti carves with an air hammer.

Carving air hammers. Right to left: ¼″ (0.635cm), ½″ (1.27cm), ¾″ (1.91cm), 1″ (2.54cm). These hammers have been dipped into a cold rubber compound for a softer grip.

Airless spray gun A spray painting system that is powered without the use of an air compressor. They are convenient portable pump/siphon units that can siphon spray from large or small containers. Though they can rapidly spray thick paints with less overspray, they do not coat with the quality of conventional sprayers.

Air (pneumatic) tools Tools operated by compressed air exerting force upon the inner mechanics. They are considerably lighter than comparable electric tools since they have a smaller mechanism with the power source (air) a distance away. They do not require the heavy windings, gears or shafts that are needed in electric motors. The compact design results in a more user-friendly tool that is easier to hold. There is not an electrical current, so it is safer to use since electrical shocks are not possible; it is ideal for wet cutting, sanding or operation in wet conditions not advised for electrical tools.

Also, instead of running hot because of the electrical current and function of electrical tools, air tools often run cold due to rapid air circulation. Most air tools have variable speed easily controlled by the trigger for air flow. If air tools bog down in the work, they will not overheat and burnup as electrical ones do; they temporarily cease to operate. But once pulled away from the work, they fully operate without any special treatment and are ready to re-enter the work. The disadvantage of air tools is the hose from the tool to the air supply and the expense of the air source (compressor) itself.

The tools are referred to by the air venting system. Air that escapes or is fed out of the front of the tool is called front exhaust. This serves to clean and clear the work area, making it easier to see the exact cut or work being done. Rear exhaust tools keep the air away from the work. This, too, is handy if the air could cause unnecessary airborne scattering of dust or material particles.

Most hand tools require 90 pounds (40.9kg) of pressure and can be operated with fairly small compressors (4 to 5 hp). However, the CFM determines the amount of air for use. While a paint sprayer requires minimal use, a jack hammer requires much more. *See* ***Air compressor***; ***Air hammer***.

Michael J. Cooper works with an air operated orbital sander with quick connect fittings to the compressor by a flexible work hose.

Alabaster A fine grained gypsum stone known for its beauty. It is easily carved with a fine finish similar to marble. It appears translucent even in an opaque form. It is available in single and multiple colors. *See* ***Stone*** *(chart)*; ***Stone***; ***Marble***.

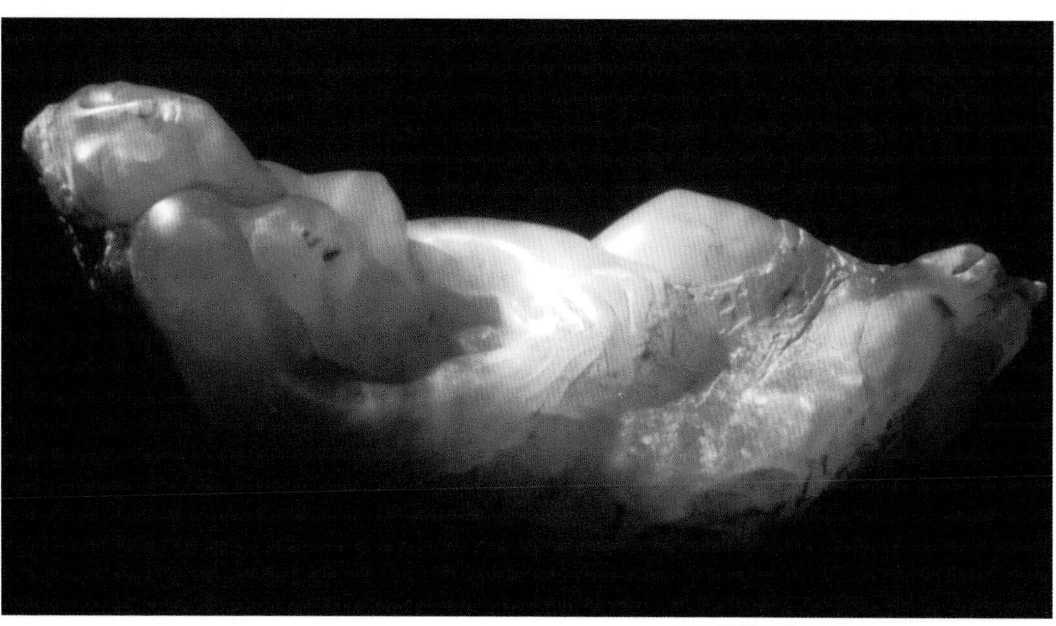

Patricia L. Verani, *Sleep*, Alabaster, 5" x 12" x 4" (12.7cm x 30.5cm x 10.2cm).

STAGES OF CARVING ALABASTER
by T Barny

A boulder of Italian alabaster is selected.

The initial roughing of a stone with a handheld hammer.

The roughing out is continued with an air hammer.

The design is constantly redrawn.

As the work progresses, a die grinder with a stone abrasive is used.

Nearing completion, small webs of stone keep the stone intact.

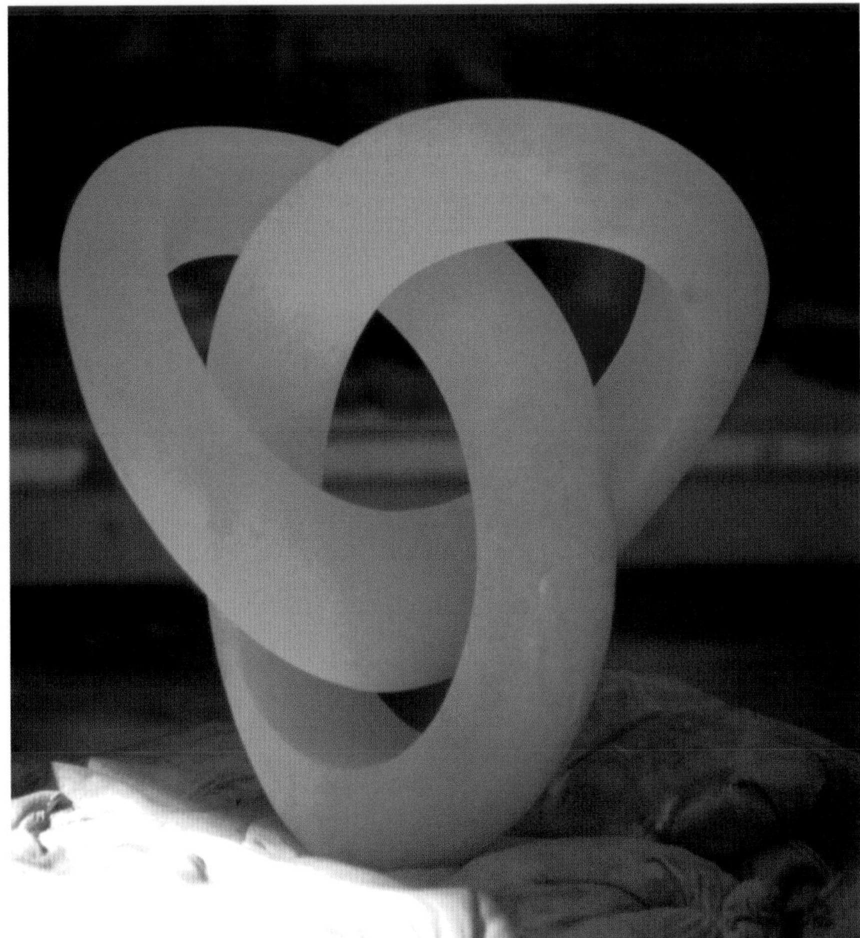

T Barny, *Fontanelle*. Italian alabaster, 18″x16″x9″ (46cm x 41cm x 23cm).

Albany slip A clay, from the region of Albany, New York, used for slip glazes. It is known for producing browns, black and, sometimes, yellow colors when used in glazes.

Alcohol A volatile, colorless, flammable liquid created by fermenting sugar and starches. It is used for solvents and fuel, as well as for drugs. It is also a thinner for shellac.

Alcohol lamp A small, wick burning lamp that uses alcohol for fuel. It is often used for smaller wax working, as well as for heating laboratory chemicals.

Alginate A manufactured form of algae primarily used for dental molding, because of its accuracy and quick drying properties. Adapted for molding sculpture, it is used for human body part casting. Appearing the same as plaster, it is a fine powder that is mixed with water. It dries quickly, is at first rubbery and tears easily, then hardens with characteristics like plaster. The setting time is extremely fast, being about two minutes. Afterwards, it can be immediately removed. Some commercial mixes, such as Algiform Slo-Set™ allow more working time. The longer the curing time, the harder it becomes and after about twenty-four hours, is similar to a brittle plaster. It can be used only once and after it sets, it does not adhere to itself.

The sculptor can encase a hand or head into an alginate mix if the work can be done quickly enough. However, since additional layers do not adhere, it has to be a one-time operation. It usually needs a mother mold for support. Some additives, such as Styrofoam™ beads or Vermiculite, can help strengthen and extend the mix, though they can cause slight impressions in the castings. The additives are dry mixed with the alginate. The new mixture can have tremendous body, and, if cast in a larger mass, may not require a mother mold. Petroleum jelly is the best separator for human skin. The alginate is "torn off" once the casting material (plaster) has properly set and is strong. *See **Body casting**.*

ALGINATE (Algiform Slo-Set™) Casting a hand holding a modeling tool.

Algiform Slo-Set™ is mixed with a drill and mixing paddle.

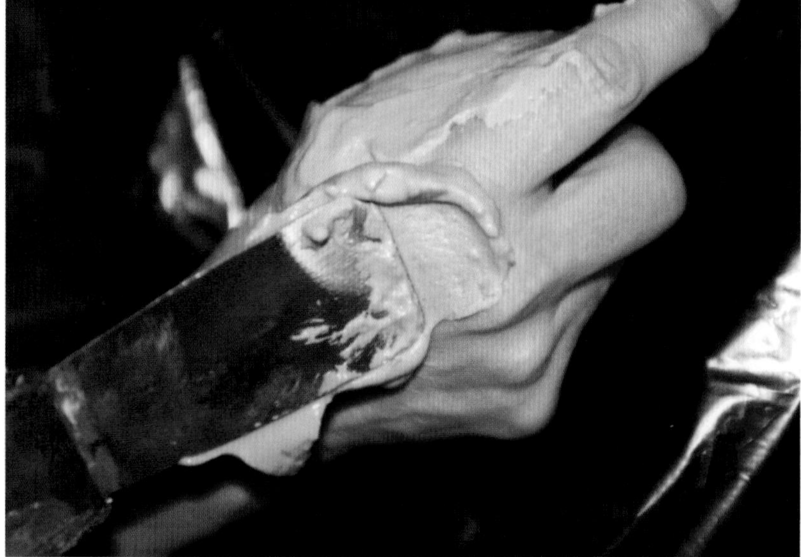

Algiform Slo-Set™ is applied by a metal spatula to the model's hand holding the tool.

The hand is encased with Algiform Slo-Set™.

A mother mold of plaster gauze is added. The first half is completed and readied for the other (top) half. A water-based clay slip is added to the seam to avoid adhesion by the second coat.

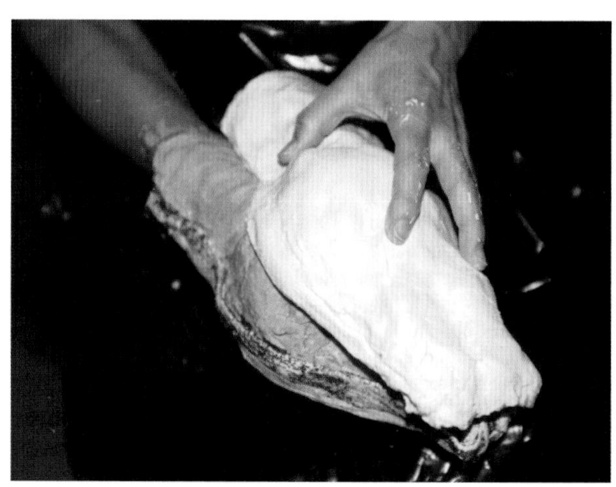

The completed mold is removed.

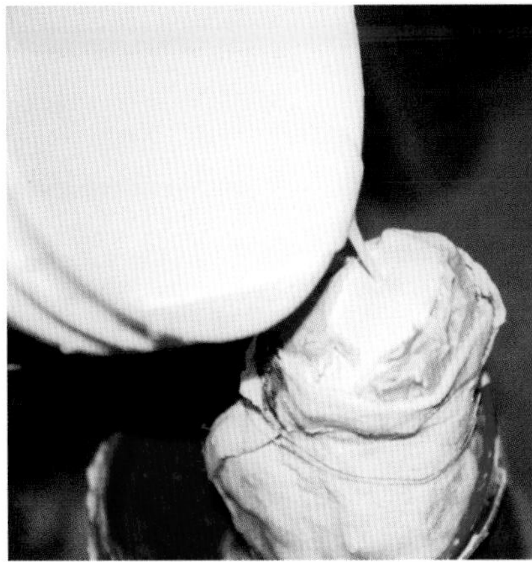

After the mother mold is removed and the model's hands are withdrawn, the mold is placed back together and plaster is added for a one-time casting.

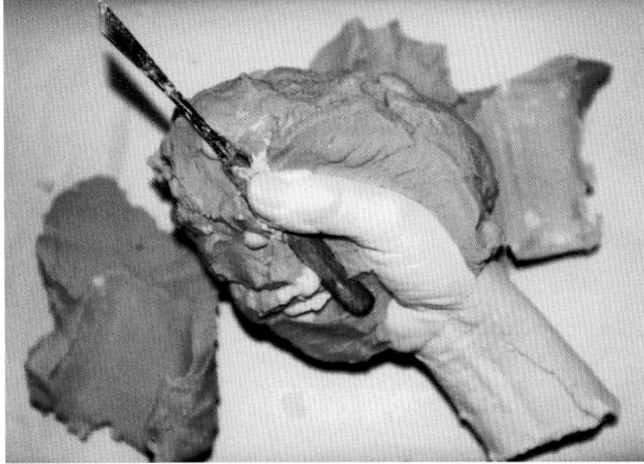

The Algiform Slo-Set™ is gently torn off after the plaster hardens.

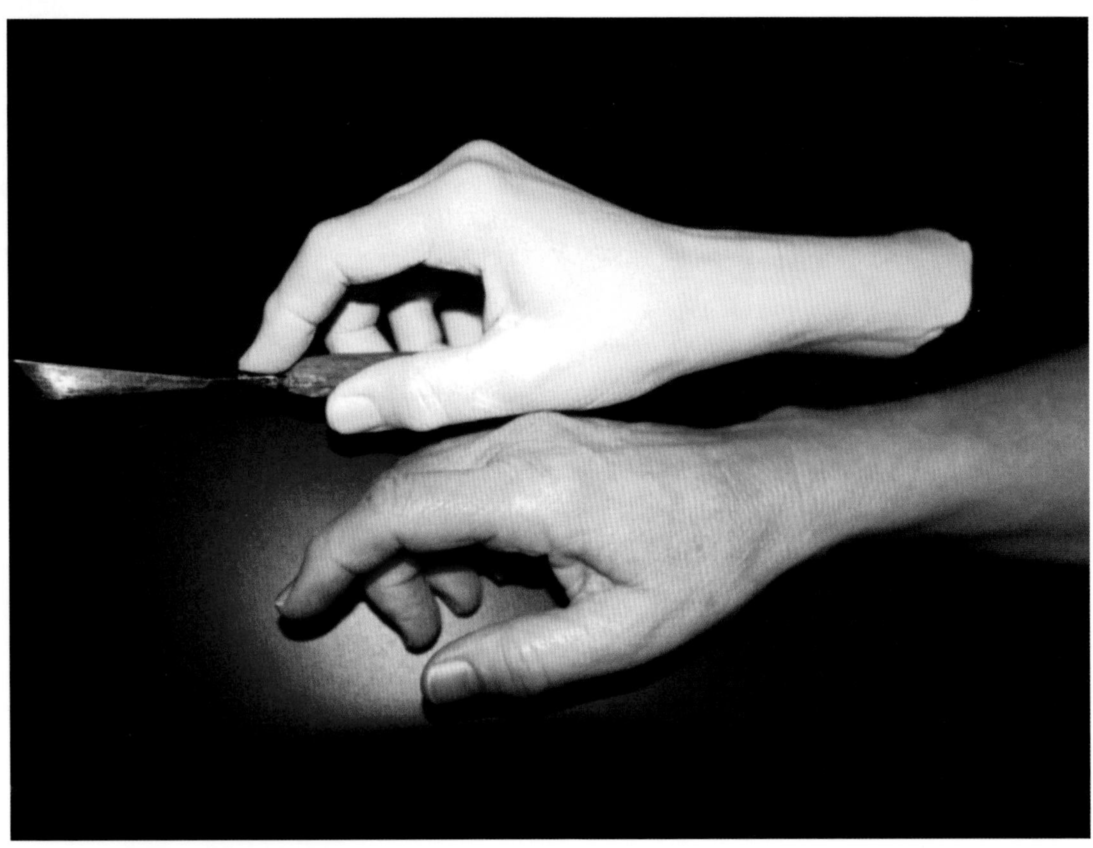

A comparison of the model's hands to the final casting.

Alloy Blending of metal to create a new mixture. It is a composite with new properties, usually less malleable but more corrosion resistant, providing a new color of metal. *See **Metals** (chart).*

Alumina A corundum used in abrasives and refractories. *See **Sandpaper**.*

Bruce Gray, *Big Cheese*. Welded aluminum, 20"x43"x28" (50.8cm x 109.2cm x 71.1cm).

Aluminum (Aluminium, British variant for aluminum). A silver colored, lightweight metallic element found in the earth. The metal is known for its corrosion resistance. Aluminum is often used in casting because of its lightweight and chasing properties. However, it is difficult to weld without the exact welding rod match, and the patina possibilities are limited. *See* ***Metals*** *(chart)*.

Aluminum oxide Hard abrasive used in sanding, especially mounted on sanding papers. Other than a diamond, it is the toughest mineral. *See* ***Sandpaper***.

Aluminum powder A pigment of metallic aluminum powders mixed into an aluminum paint that does not tarnish. It is sometimes used to create a faux silver paint.

Aluminum wire A pliable wire used for sculpture armatures. Available in many sizes, the most common sizes are from one-eighth (0.318cm) to one-fourth inch (0.635cm).

Arthur Silverman, *Gate*. Aluminum, 21'x6'x6' (6.41m x 1.83m x 1.83m).

Ammonia A strong, sharp-smelling, piercing gas used in assorted combinations as a cleanser and sometimes in patina formation. The fumes are toxic. *See* ***Patina***.

Amorphous Without definite form, shapeless.

Anatomy The actual structure or body of a human, animal, plant, etc., even sculpture. A study of anatomy would be to examine the structure in parts or the whole in detail. *See **Figure**.*

Anchors Devices used to permanently mount sculptures. Considerations when anchoring a work include vandalism, foundation and weather.

Angle iron A mild or high carbon steel, not iron, with a 90° angle that runs in long lengths. It comes in a variety of sizes and thicknesses.

Animal glue A sticky substance used for glue that is produced from animal bone and skins by boiling them. *See **Glue** (chart).*

Anneal(ing) Process of heating and prolonged slow cooling to strengthen, harden, temper or minimize the brittle aspects of the material. It removes inner stress, resulting in a strong final form that avoids cracks or breakage. It is used for many materials, including glass, metals and plastics. Glass is annealed by heating in a kiln; plastic is annealed in an oven; whereas, metal is heated by torch or in a forging hearth. *See **Forging**; **Glass**; **Plastics**.*

Annual ring Growth ring; a layer of wood (or bark) that is added each year as the tree grows.

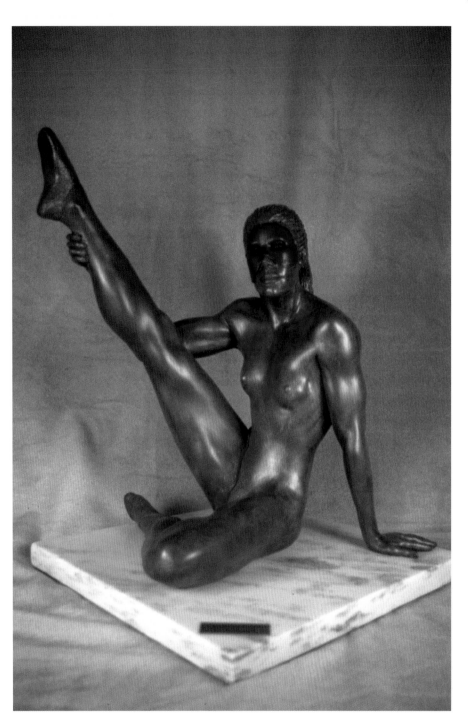

B. P. Barwick, *Masquerade*. Cast polyurethane, marble, 15″ (38cm) high.

Annular Refractory lined oven (kiln) that is used to slowly cool a substance, particularly glass, in a controlled manner. Glass workers sometimes refer to this oven as "the box." *See **Glass**.*

Anode A positively charged electrode used to electroplate substances, usually metal. Also, it is the negative pole of a battery that supplies the current. *See **Electroplating**.*

Anodize To surface coat a metal with a color or protective oxide to avoid corrosion. It is an electrochemical procedure that can result in several colors including browns (bronze), gold (brass) and blacks. *See **Electroplating**.*

Anti-foaming agent A liquid substance added to ceramic shell slurry to keep air from being mixed into it. *See **Slurry**.*

Anvil A specially shaped solid block of steel or iron that has a flat space on top and formed shapes upon which to bend or strike metals. It is often mounted on a large log end to help sustain the blow and sound. The height and type are determined by the operator's physical needs and the purpose or type of work to be done. A hammer is used in conjunction with the anvil for the striking device. *See* ***Forging***.

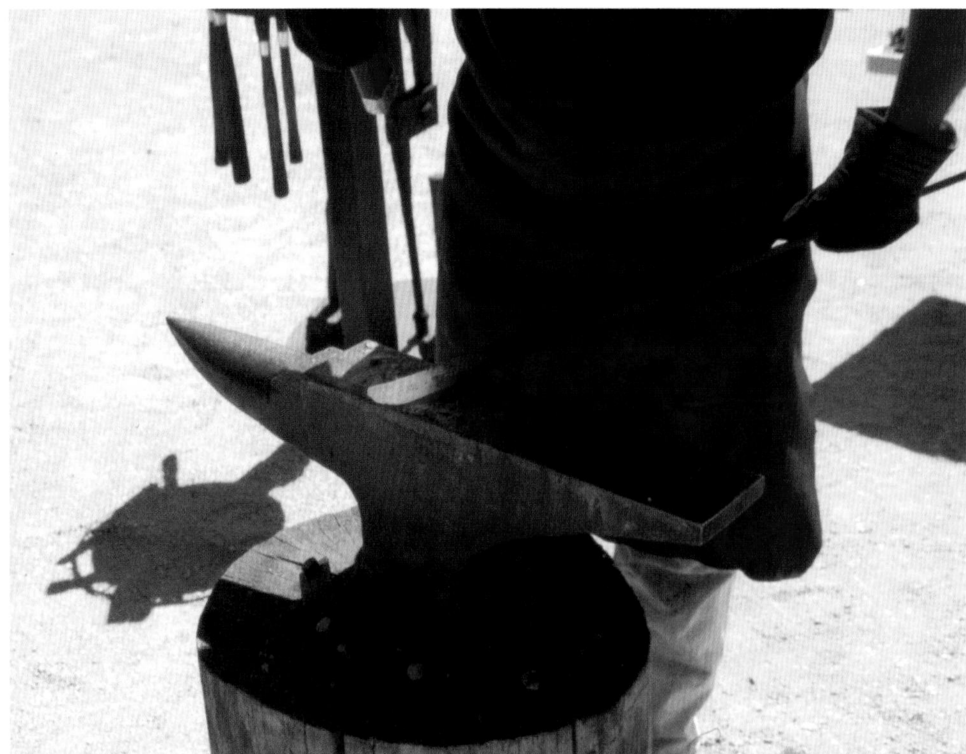

A blacksmith uses an anvil. An apron is worn for protection from the hot metal.

Appendage Part of a sculpture that protrudes, or is otherwise attached to the major mass. An extended arm becomes an appendage when it is placed out from the body, as compared to being next to the body, such as folded arms. In mold making, these parts create problem undercuts and are oftentimes cast separately and re-attached to the main mass.

Apron A cover worn over all or some of the frontal part of the human body as protection from stains, dirt, oils or heat depending on the apron material and purpose. The blacksmith wears a leather apron to prevent hot sparks from burning clothing and skin. It is also a term that describes an extended stage for a tool or work area. *See* ***Safety dress***.

Arbor A shaft, spindle or axis used to support or hold the rotating part of machinery such as a lathe or drill chuck. The term can also be used for the bar that supports tools.

Arc Electrical discharge or flow from an electric current across a gap to another object. To "create an arc" is to begin the welding process. *See* ***Arc welding; Welding***.

Arcair torch A handheld tool designed to cut into metal with an arc. It resembles the normal electrode holder but it is larger and has an attached air hose with a control that directs compressed air from the tip in the same direction of the carbon arc rod that it holds. *See* ***Carbon arc; Plasma cutting***.

Arc cutting Special carbon rods used with an ordinary arc welder in a common electrode holder can make rough cuts into ferrous and nonferrous metals. The sizes and types (AC, DC) vary, but generally can produce a sufficient cut. However, because of the ragged edge, it requires clean up if it is to be used for further welding. *See* ***Arcair torch***.

Architectural sculpture Sculpture designed to become part of the architecture, in contrast to sculpture displayed as autonomous, individualistic work. Being specifically planned to adorn or embellish a building, architectural sculpture is considered an essential component of the overall structure.

Arc length The empty space from a welding electrode to the work surface. *See **Arc welding**.*

Arc welding Welding produced by a controlled electrical current of intense strength passing from a wire or rod electrode to a metal surface or from the surface to the electrode material. This produces an arc of such concentrated energy that the joint instantly melts, resulting in the desired fusion. Preheating is not necessary.

The three most common forms of arc welding are **TIG** (tungsten inert gas) using a filler rod, the **MIG** (metal inert gas) using a wire rod electrode, and shortened fluxed electrode, **STICK**. The traditional arc produced by the fluxed STICK electrode is primarily used for ferrous metals. Both TIG and MIG discharge a gas (argon or helium) at the point of fusion that prevents contamination with the atmosphere and creates a strong weld with less metal distortion. TIG and MIG are chosen for all metals, but especially for nonferrous metals, such as bronze, brass, aluminum and stainless steel, because of the ease with which these metals can be welded.

Bruce H. White, *Crustaceans*. Welded aluminum, 15′x17′6″x8′ (4.6m x 5.3m x 2.4m).

A light duty arc welder with the electrode holder and ground clamp in the foreground.

All arc machinery consists of a transformer with two lead lines long enough to reach the working area. They are usually connected to the welding transformer (box) by a simple plug into sockets or jack-plugs. Twenty foot leads are common. One is a ground line (work) ending with a strong exposed metal ground clamp for temporary attachment to the metal or metal base (table) where the work is being done. The other is the line lead ending with an electrode holder that is designed with a handle and strong hand grip lever that controls the clamp holding the electrode. The holder is insulated except for the immediate clamp with the electrode. *See **Electrode; Electrode holder; Bead; TIG; MIG**.*

Voltage for welders ranges from 115v to 3-phase 440v. While 110v is lightweight, inexpensive and portable, it is designed for thin metals seldom exceeding three-sixteenths of an inch (0.476cm) in thickness. Expensive, large three-phase industrial welders can do almost any task rapidly because of the powerful penetration and duty cycles. The most common power source for electrical welding is 230v or about 50 amps. While power is generally available, special wiring may be required from the fuse box to the welder to have enough amperage to power the machine. Before any machine is purchased, the sculptor needs to be certain that it can be installed within the parameters of power and finances.

Gene Koss, *River Dam Run Gizmo Contraption.* Welded steel, cast glass, 70″x26″x26″ (177.8cm x 66cm x 66cm).

A less common arc electrical source is the **diesel** or **gasoline driven portable transformer**. They are self-contained and can furnish enough power to accomplish almost any welding task. They are placed on trucks or trailers to easily transport, allowing large scale sculpture in areas not otherwise accessible.

Within arc welding, there are AC, alternating current; DC, direct current; and combination AC-DC welders. Direct current offers a larger variety of rods and welding techniques and produces a smoother weld with less effort. Direct current, using straight polarity causes the electrons to move from the electrode to the metal, creating a deep penetration into the work. Direct current, using reverse polarity to reverse the flow from the metal into the rod, results in the rod melting quickly for less penetration but wider coverage. With the correct polarity, aluminum and bronze can be welded using a DC machine. Alternating current produces a stable air flow, but it does not allow for good welding of thin metals without burning holes or burnt edges due to the penetration characteristics. On a DC welder, the polarity can easily be altered by changing the leads into the proper sockets, according to machine and manufacturer instructions.

All welding machines have **duty cycles**, or a duration of time in which they can be productively operated without injury to the machine or decrease in intensity to the weld at a certain current amperage (amp). The cycle is listed in a percentage of time that a machine can operate within an amperage. Since higher amperages require more energy, lower amperages have longer duty cycles. Large, strong machines have excellent duty cycles. *See **Duty cycle**.*

Welders have high and low ranges of **amperage**. The low range uses smaller rods with less intensity allowing welding on thin metals, while the high range allows a greater thickness of weld with layer rods. The amperage control on a welder is simple, and the sculptor should be familiar with how the machine operates. Too high of a setting results in excessive rod melting, puddling and spattering. Too low of a setting does not allow penetration, resulting in a stringy, elevated bead. *See **Electrode**.*

The operator should be familiar with the particular machine to operate it properly. The off/on welding controls must be firm and absolute, so that there is no doubt when the machine is operating or not. With the amperage set, the ground clamp firmly in place, the lines properly connected, and the holder with an electrode, the electrode

is struck like striking a match. A bead of weld is carefully maintained.

Thick metals are often V-grooved for multiple welds. The groove between the joints is filled by successive passes of weld. Between each pass the flux is removed (chipped out). Three passes are not uncommon for large grooves. *See **Carbon arc**.*

Safety dress for welding is necessary. This includes clothing to protect the skin from burns because of the intense light. A full face mask with lens opening supporting a dark colored lens is always worn. Leather gloves protect the hands. All shop visitors must be protected, even from the reflected light. *See **Safety dress**.*

Argon An inert, odorless and colorless gaseous chemical element bottled under pressure to be used as a gas shield while welding, especially with the use of TIG (tungsten inert gas) welding. *See **TIG** (welding).*

Ark Slip storage tanks that are automatically stirred. *See **Slip** (ceramic).*

Arkansas stone A natural sharpening stone, as compared to a manmade stone. Mined in Arkansas, USA, it is also known as novaculite by geologists. These stones are graded by hardness. The softer stone is streaked and mottled in muted gray colors. The white or translucent Arkansas stone is most desirable for achieving extremely sharp tool edges. *See **Sharpening**.*

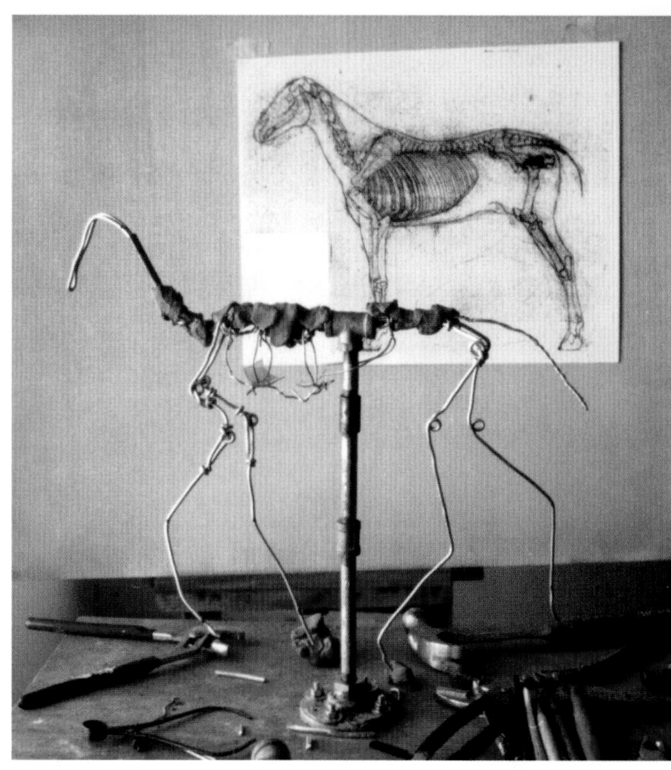

The metal armature as a study for the *Don Juan de Oñate Monument* by **John Sherrill Houser.**

Armature The internal or skeletal framework used to support the skin or outer surface of a form. An armature allows an otherwise thin, weak, runny or sloughing material to be reinforced to gain size, strength or desired form. It should be strong enough to temporarily hold the work in place. Though it may be removed after the work is completed, it may remain as a permanent support and becomes part of the finished sculpture.

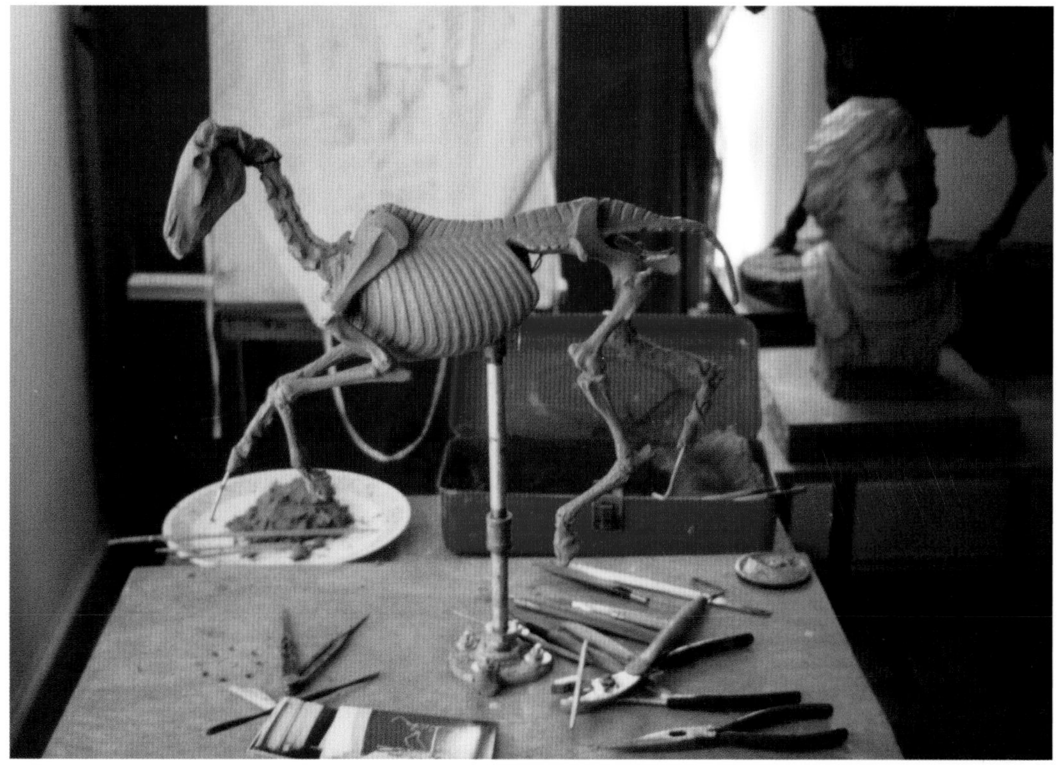

John Sherrill Houser's clay armature using exacting bone structure for the *Don Juan De Oñate Monument.*

Armatures can also save the sculptor expense and work, since armatures can reduce the quantity of the coating material. This is done by using solid bulky armature materials. *See* ***Expanded polystyrene; Portrait***.

There are two types of armatures: 1) A **self-supporting**, interior self-contained support, usually anchored to a base, or 2) an **externally-supported** armature, rigid and usually inflexible, so that the armature will not fall or move while sculptural material is added to it.

While some designs require unmovable rigidity, others are not only designed to be strong, transportable and flexible, but adjustable. This allows more experimentation in form, changes, direct finish or modeling as the work progresses. The larger the armature, the stronger and more complex it becomes. This is to insure that it will not collapse and will require only minor readjustments (if any) as the sculpture material is being affixed.

Technique

Depending upon the outer covering, the armature could be made of almost anything, including empty plastic or cardboard containers, rocks, tree limbs, toys, PVC, tools, machinery, soft foam rubber, hard steel, wire, Styrofoam™, paper, etc. All sorts of material combinations are used, such as plaster soaked cloth wrapped around wood or Styrofoam™ for mass with wires extending out for linear details. When using concrete, metal rebar and metal lathe are often used to hold the concrete in place. The concrete hardens about the armature, adding structural strength to the finished work. *See* ***Concrete; Plaster; Styrofoam.***™

In ceramics, an armatured form is used when a temporary interior brace is necessary. The support can be made of crushed paper or other items that can compress as the clay shrinks. Although some combustible substances can remain to be consumed during the kiln firing, many are removed prior to the dry shrinkage.

Armatures

The design of the armature for busts or smaller standing figures may use use the same construction materials: a shellacked plywood mounting base or one covered with counter topping. Two wooden planks across both sides of the bottom allow space to pick up the armature, which can become heavy when loaded with clay or other materials. Standard plumbing pipe fittings of steel pipe from one-fourth inch (0.635cm) and up may be used. Externally supported figures need to extend from the rear of the figure. A sealer is used to prevent corrosion. *See* ***Plaster; Mold; Papier machè; Concrete; Clay; Enlarging***.

Enlargement of the threaded "T" connection with a finger grip bolt to easily adjust height.

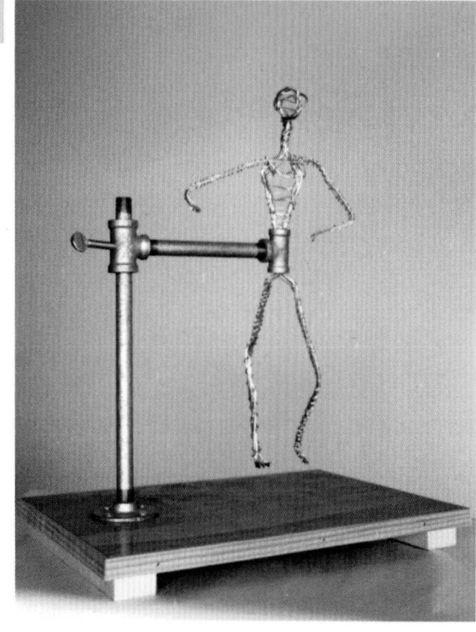

A pipe figure armature from hardware plumbing supplies.

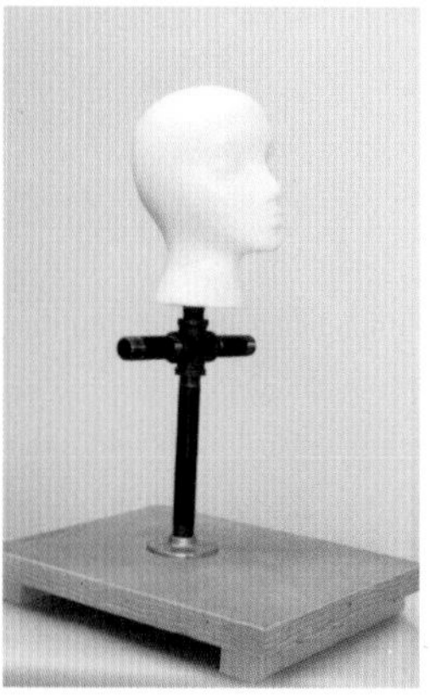

A pipe portrait/torso armature with a Styrofoam™ head used for construction bulk. The "cross" fitting provides a connection for the shoulders.

A pipe armature covered with crushed newspaper that will compress as ceramic clay dries around it.

ARMATURES

by Rich Muno

Rich Muno with a steel armature in the shape of a horse. Notice the Styrofoam™ body parts on the ground.

The armature with the Styrofoam™ for bulk. A rigid armature for the rider has been placed into position. Surface clay is now added.

The modeling is almost complete on the armature for *Young at Heart* by **Rich Muno**.

Rich Muno, *Young at Heart*. Bronze, life-size. The model, Johnny Kelly, poses beside the sculpture of himself.

Artist's proof The first casting(s) of an edition. Often one-of-a-kind and retained by the sculptor. The designation was originally intended as a work in progress to correct artistic or casting problems. To be authentic, it must have the artist's signature and AP (artist proof) legible on the work. *See* ***Foundry proof; Edition***.

Asbestos Noncombustible material used as a wall of protection from combustion, especially with welding. Resulting health problems have almost eliminated its use. It may be found in some carving stones, such as serpentine.

Asbestosis Lung disease resulting from inhaling asbestos particles. *See* ***Asbestos***.

Assemblage A sculpture created from gathering and arranging discarded articles that are manmade, from nature or a mixture of both. The work may be visually pleasing, of personal meaning or a combination of these elements. *See* ***Found object; Junk art; Mixed media***.

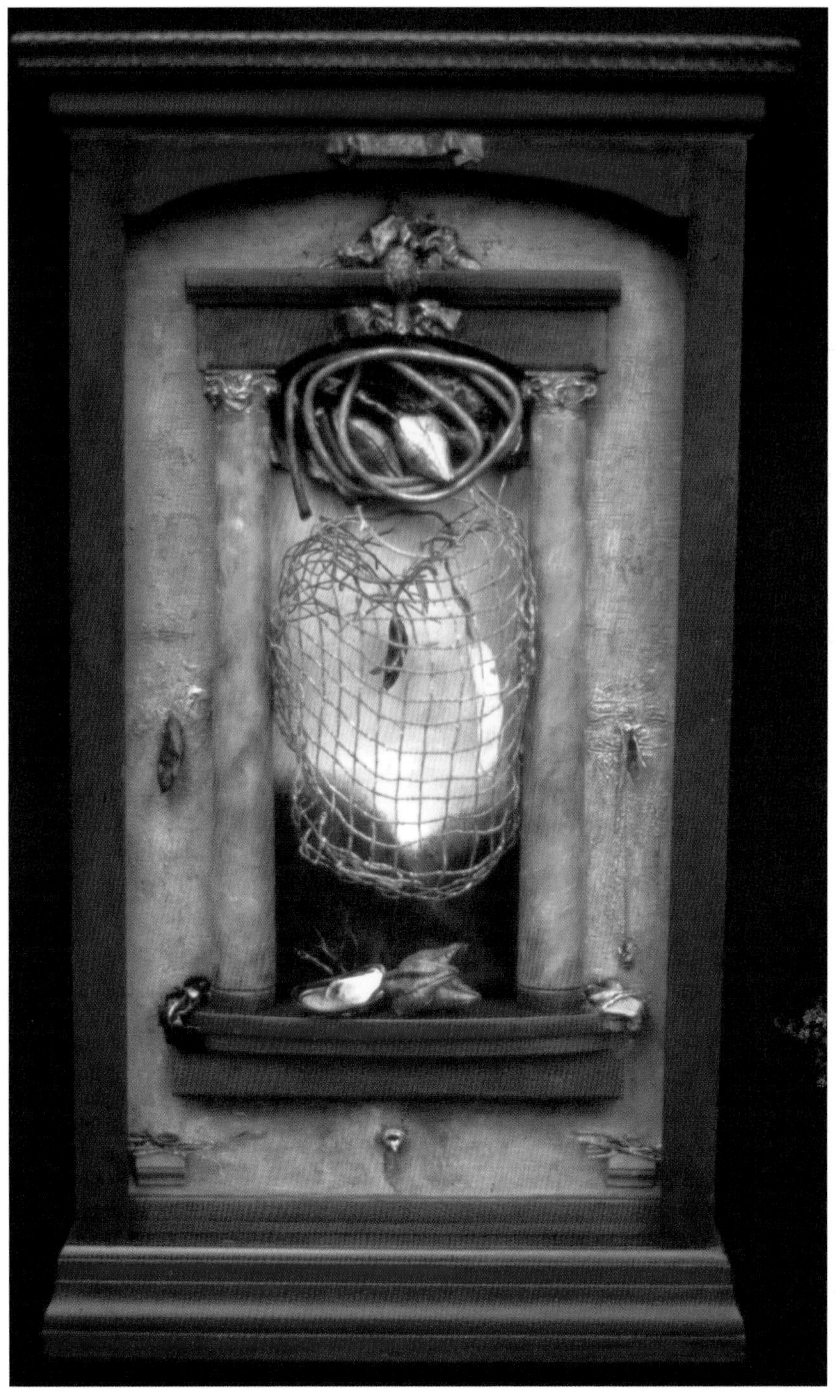

Joe Muench, *Hindsight/Foresight: Reflections of the 20th Century*. Steel, brass, mirror, wood, disabled handgun, 3"x8"x18" (7.6cm x 0.3cm x 45.7cm).

Joyce Blunk, *Deep Autumn, Ashville.* Wood, paint, metal, cloth, seed pods, shells, 15"x25¾"x3" (38.1cm x 65.4cm x 7.6cm).

Asymmetry (asymmetric) Not to be symmetrical, not to be balanced or without visual balance or symmetry. Some sculptors prefer asymmetrical forms to maintain a longer interest or hand-crafted appearance.

Atelier A sculptor's workshop (artist or craftsman). A designation for a teaching studio with apprentices or students receiving guidance from a master teacher. *See* ***Studio***.

Atlantis Male standing carved figure, such as Atlas, the Greek god. *See* ***Telamon; Caryatid***.

Atomizer A simple device that mixes air with liquids to form a fine mist. It is often used to apply surface coatings of ceramics or patinas of metal. Paint sprayers and aerosol sprays have almost eliminated the use of atomizers. *See* ***Sprayer***.

Auger bit A drill bit designed like a cork screw or with a rotation that enters the work in a spiral manner as it grasps the work. It is the term for older style bits used by carpenters with manual handheld drills in woodwork. *See* ***Drill***.

Autoclave A pressurized container of great strength combined with high temperatures for steam heating sculpture. It is used primarily for: 1) dewaxing ceramic shell molds, 2) casting acrylic, or 3) steam cleaning articles, used for sterilization in hospitals. When dewaxing ceramic shell molds, the autoclave works by providing pressure with heat and steam to remove the wax from the shell. The pressure offsets the heat swelling of the wax to keep the mold from collapsing or cracking. The pressure must be in excess of 100 psi (689.3kPa) to remove the wax rapidly. A plus is that the wax is saved intact, and the environment is not abused. *See* ***Burnout furnace; Dewaxing; Ceramic shell; Acrylic (liquid)***.

Auto-darkening lens Lens that automatically allow clear vision until a bright arc light flashes and then the lens immediately darkens to protect the eyes. They are used for vision protection while welding. *See* ***Welding lens***.

Avant-garde Art that is new, experimental or a departure from prevailing art techniques or forms. Artists who practice or advocate this may be termed avant-garde.

AWS Abbreviated term for American Welding Society.

Ayr stone A smooth, toothed whetstone primarily used in Britain for sharpening tools or polishing marble. Also termed scotch stone or snake stone. *See* ***Sharpening stones***.

Autoclave used in acrylic casting. Fine Art Acrylic, New York.

Jane B. Armstrong, *Tandem*. Cast bronze, 5½′ (1.7m) tall. Rock Resorts, Manchester, Vermont. Photographer: Mario Novak.

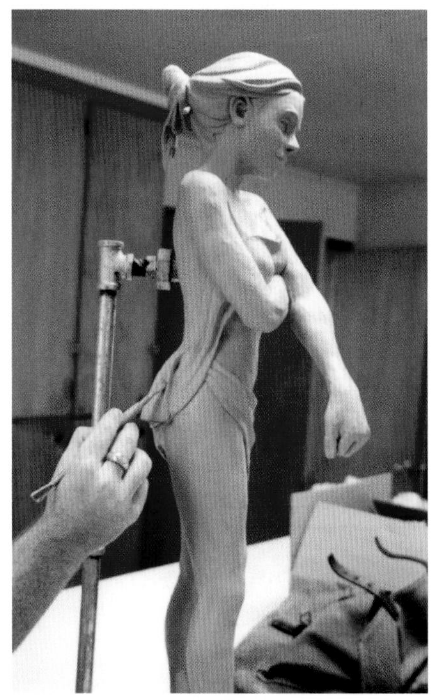

A back iron supports the armature as **Tim Kinard** models his work.

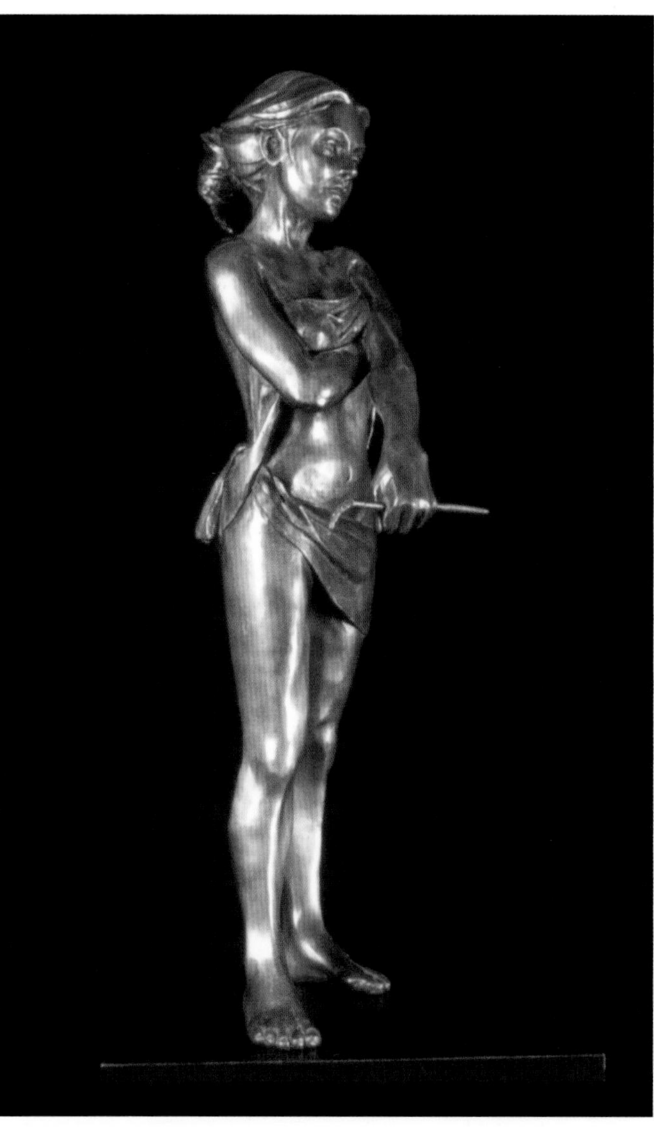

Tim Kinard, *Self-Portrait*. Cast bronze, 37″ (94cm) tall.

Backfire The momentary ignition of fuel inside the welding torch tip. It is usually brought about by too little fuel as the flame searches for combustible material. Afterwards, the flame will continue or extinguish. *See **Welding** (torch).*

Back iron The visible support that remains on the outside of an armature to keep it erect and in a stable location. It is a strong, stiff support, usually pipe, and placed in the lower back of a standing armature. It is anchored to the armature base. The drawback is that it presents an area that cannot initially be modeled over. *See **Armature**.*

Bag wall A kiln wall that isolates the interior flame from the sculpture. *See **Ceramics** (kiln).*

Baked enamel Paints or synthetic resins that are oven baked as high as 350°F (177°C) after application to the work. The process results in stronger adhesion and tougher wear.

Balance As relating to sculpture or design, a completeness of form, usually pleasing. It can be visual or actual. If visual, the work will have equal proportions or appear to have good visual proportions or possess a design of visual stability or symmetry. Actual balance requires stability and will not tip over even though it could be visually off-balance. Formal balance is commonly symmetrical.

The unique aesthetic aspect about balance (when referring to gravity) is that if the same building material is used throughout, and it balances due to gravity, it usually has a better visual appearance. If it is not gravity balanced, it has a disturbing look or a look of tension. *See* ***Symmetrical; Asymmetry***.

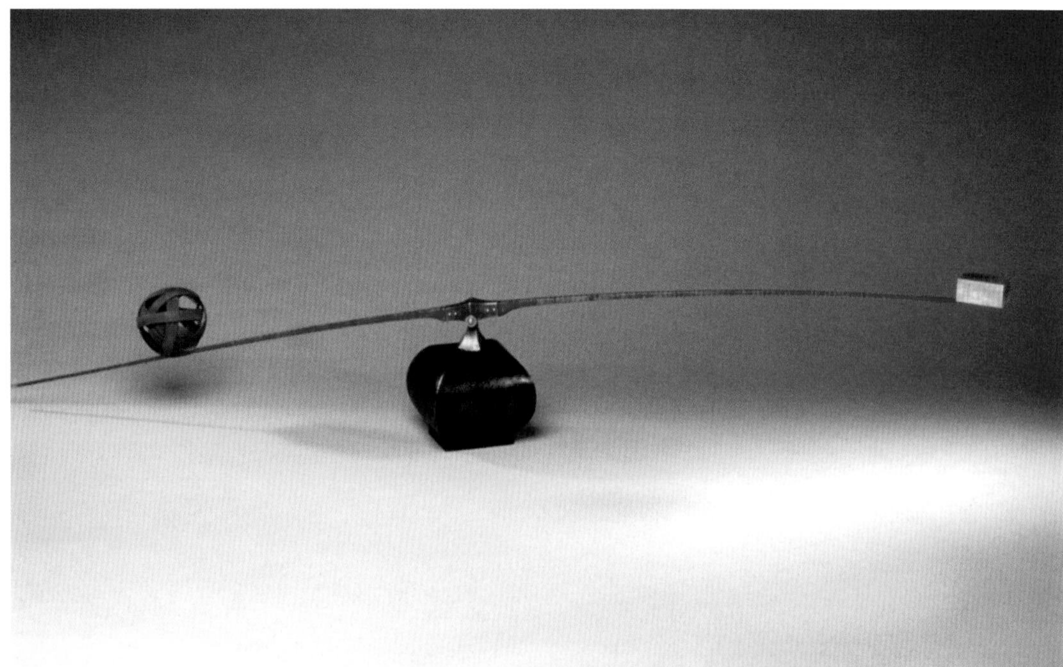

Joe Muench, *Delicate Balance*. Steel, brass, nickel, bronze, maple, paint, 6"x 8"x 42" (15.2cm x 20.3cm x 106.7cm).

Ball clay Highly plastic, fine clay due to the small particle size. Usually in light brown or buff color, it is added to clay bodies to increase the "slickness" of the body. Because of its high water content, it shrinks about 10% as it dries from a plastic state and an additional 10% or more during firing. *See* ***Clay***.

Ball mill A motorized revolving cylindrical tank containing pebbles (balls) for grinding or mixing a liquid. The process refines and blends glazes. *See* ***Ceramics*** *(glazes)*.

Ball peen hammer A steel headed hammer with a round, flat head on one end and a round, hemi-spherical head on the other. It is used in metal work, especially for shaping it.

Balsa A lightweight, porous and soft wood that is used as a substitute for cork. Easily carved, it is known for its use in model airplane making.

Banding wheel A turntable with a round top (wheel) that is used for deco rating (banding) centered pot tery with the use of a col orant (glaze, etc.). The col orant is usually painted with a brush that is held as the rotating piece touches it. *See* ***Turntable***.

Lin Emery cuts metal with a bandsaw.

Band saw A stationary, power operated saw with a thin lin ear blade in a continuous band about the circumferences of two or more wheels that are

Band saw with the upper and lower blade cover doors open to display the band wheels.

mounted on a rigid frame. The cutting height and distance is determined by the size and placement of the wheels. It is used for larger work in wood since the cutting area can be large and wide as compared to the smaller jig saw. *See **Jig saw.***

Banker (carving) A structure designed for wood or stone to rest upon while being carved. It is strong, usually made of wood to help cushion the blows. It may be in a turntable configuration so that the sculpture can be worked and viewed from different angles.

Bas (relief) Low relief in sculpture in which all parts are completely attached to the background without undercuts. Coins are a good representation of the process. *See **Relief**.*

Basalt Hard volcanic (igneous) rock colored in black or dark green or a combination. It is extremely difficult to carve. *See **Stone** (chart).*

Michihiro Kosuge, *½ Circle*. Basalt, stainless steel, 12″x75″x54″ (30.5cm x 190.5cm x 137.2cm). Photographer: Aaron Johanson.

Base The lowest part of a sculpture, the bottom or footing on which the sculpture rests; the supporting structure of a sculpture. Also used as a term for a "block" or object that the sculpture will sit upon for stability or enhanced display. Wood and stone are the most common bases. It is not a stand or pedestal; they are used for display and not support. *See **Stand; Display** (base).*

Barbara Diduk, *Untitled*. Ceramic rubber mounted on steel as an integral base part of the sculpture, 9″x12″ (22.9cm x 30.5cm).

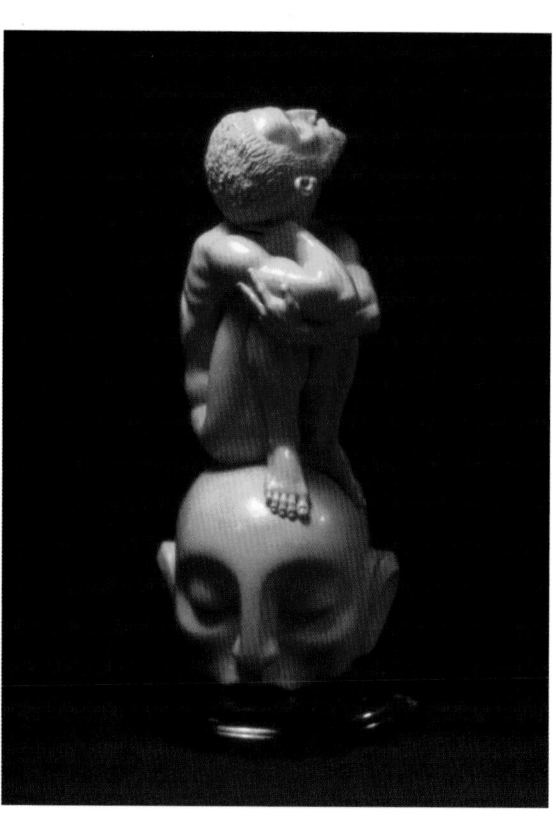

Alexander Tsalikhin, *Thinker*. Cast bronze mounted on a marble base, 12″ (30.5cm).

Baseboard The support base or board that the armature is firmly fastened to for support of clay, etc. *See* ***Armature***.

Base metal The main mass of metal or material that is being worked on. Sometimes called the "parent metal."

Basket The structure, or container, that molding material (plaster investment) is placed into that surrounds the work to be molded. It may be called a cage. *See* ***Cage; Plaster investment***.

Basswood A plain, soft, light-colored wood that is easily carved.

Bastard file A coarse toothed file.

Bat For ceramic sculpture, a portable, smooth, level surface used for a wheel head, sculpture support or drying of the clay. A common bat material is hardened, dry, porous plaster. *See* ***Clay*** *(bat)*.

Batch A chemical blend (glass formula) is brought to a liquid form by heat and becomes useable glass. *See* ***Glass***.

Bat wash (kiln wash) A mixture of refractory substances applied to kiln shelves and furniture to prevent fusion of the sculpture or surface material (glaze) during firing. *See* ***Kiln; Kiln wash***.

Bead The appearance of fused metal rod or wire on the base metal. The demeanor may vary from good to bad depending upon the worker's technique. A good welding bead is smooth with small uniform ripples formed from the molten metal as it fuses with the base metal. The size, height and depth depends upon the machine settings, type and thickness of metal. *See* ***Electrode; Welding; Arc welding***.

WELDING BEADS

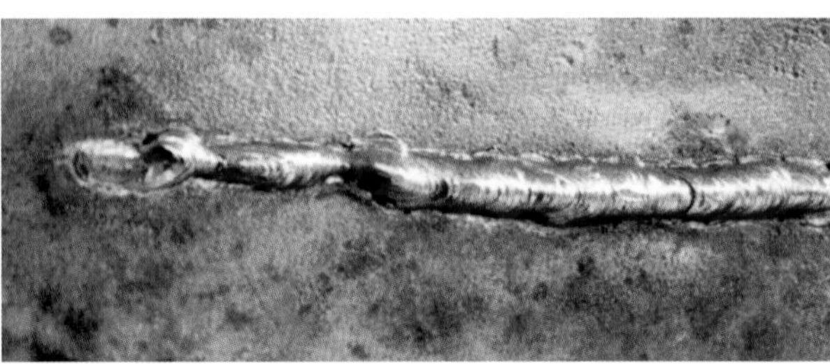

A welding bead with too little heat.

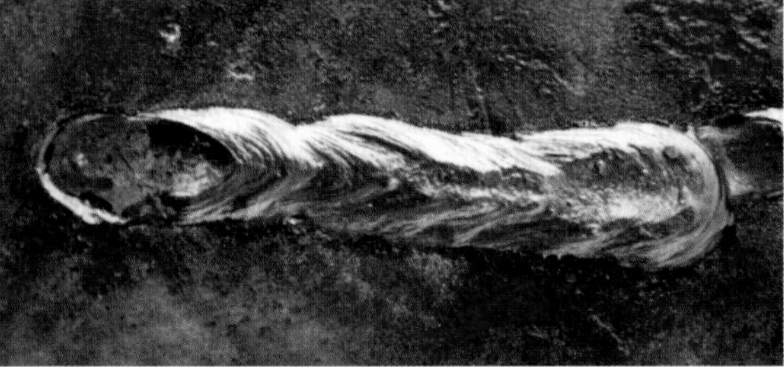

A welding bead with too much heat.

Welding bead with correct heat.

Beeswax A natural wax found in honeycomb made by bees, yellow to white in color. Taken and processed for commercial purposes, it is used for candles, polishes and sculpture modeling. *See* ***Wax; Patina***.

Belgian black A dense, black marble from Belgium. It is valued for carving because of its deep dark color without flaws or noticeable grain.

Melissa Kretschmer, *Powellspoint*. Glass, beeswax, ink, silicone, 7"x7"x3¼" (17.8cm x 17.8cm x 8.3cm). Photographer: Ace Gallery Louisiana.

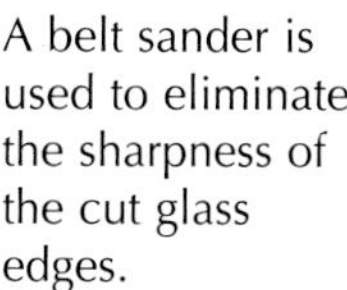

A belt sander is used to eliminate the sharpness of the cut glass edges.

Bench grinder with fine and coarse grinding disks.

Belt sander A power operated sander that has an abrasive belt in a continuous band. It can be an upright model or handheld.

Bench grinder A motorized configuration with a grinding wheel mounted on a shaft protruding from both ends of the motor. The wheels are usually coarse and fine; one is used for roughing and one for clean up. Designed for various sizes of wheels, the machine is mounted on a bench (work table) or individual stand. *See* ***Sharpening; Grinder***.

Bench screw A large, double-ended screw (threads on both ends) used to anchor a piece of wood. It is twisted (screwed) into the center of wood stock and into the carving table (bench) or stand to hold the work firm as it is being carved. Afterwards, it is removed. *See* ***Wood carving***.

Benchstone A stone specifically for sharpening tools. It is handheld, as opposed to a grindstone or grinding wheel on a machine. Oilstone, honing stone and whetstone are also terms used interchangeably with benchstone. The stone itself can be natural or manmade. *See* ***Sharpening***.

Benchstrop A strop (strap) of leather or canvas used for polishing (sharpening) metal tools. When stroked with a tool, it completes a fine finish. *See* ***Sharpening; Hone; Stropping***.

Bender Machine or device for bending metal.

Bentonite An extremely plastic clay found in nature that is exceptionally fine. It is used for flexibility (plasticity) in clay bodies and in glazes to help hold particles in suspension. *See* ***Clay***.

Bevel To finish the edge of a material by eliminating the sharp edge with a remaining angle, usually at about 45°. To grind metal butt edges into a groove (bevel) in order to fill with a weld for more strength. *See* ***Carbon arc***.

Binder An agent (liquid substance) added to dry substances to draw together and maintain a uniform consistency. In mold making for metal casting, a liquid colloidal silica is used as a binder by adding dry silica to create a slurry mold material. Methylcellulos (CMC) is a binder for paper pulp when making paper sculptures. *See* ***Paper; Slurry***.

Birchwood Casey™ A commercially designed liquid product used to achieve dark patina base coats. It is also used for metal gun bluing. *See* ***Patina; Patina*** *(chart)*.

Bird's-eye A natural, small, re-occurring rounded eye-like design in wood. It is common in sugar maple. *See* ***Wood*** *(chart)*.

Bismuth nitrate A chemical used in the patina process to achieve an off-white, gray color. *See* ***Patina; Patina*** *(chart)*.

Jack Thompson bisque fires the sculpture *La Rosa Del Cardinal*, 38″x18″x13″ (96.5cm x 45.7cm x 33cm).

Bisque The initial firing of unglazed clay resulting in a porous, pinkish color of most clay bodies. Once the body has received the bisque firing (about cone 06), it can easily be glazed for a higher temperature firing. It is sometimes left in the bisque state for sculpture. *See* ***Cone (pyrometric)***.

Bisque firing is accomplished by placing the dried clay sculpture into the kiln, gradually taking the temperature up until the desired temperature is reached, and then allowing it to slowly cool. This firing is ordinarily done to harden the clay to a state where it can be handled, but remains porous enough to allow glaze to saturate it for an additional glaze firing at a higher temperature. If the clay is thick or uneven, the firing cycle is more gradually completed. It may take more than twice as long to finish.

The moisture should leave the clay as 400°F (204°C) is reached; however, it may take up to 1300°F (704°C) for the chemically combined water to escape. During this cycle, the clay is shrinking. At between 950°F (510°C) and 1300°F (704°C) most of the chemically combined water and other gases leave. At 1300°F (704°C), the clay has become a permanent, but delicate, material that cannot be reused as clay. Different clays mature at separate rates: earthenware at 2000°F (1093°C), stoneware at 2350°F (1288°C) and pure kaolin at 3000°F (1649°C). Most bisque firings do not exceed cone 06 or 1830°F (999°C). *See* ***Kiln***.

Blacksmith A metal worker who uses a forge to heat and an anvil and hammer to shape the metal. The term, black, refers to the dark metal involved. "Smithy" is an abbreviation for blacksmith. The term is sometimes applied to one who works with horse shoeing, though "farrier" is the correct term for that. *See* ***Welding*; *Forge***.

Blacksmith welding Heating solid metals to a state near melting and then fusing them by force, hammering the pieces into one new mass. The preferred term is forge welding. *See* ***Forge welding***.

Black Tuffy™ Trademark name for a flexible molding product identified by its black color. *See* ***Flexible mold***.

Blades The sharpened cutting part of a tool. It also describes the thin, fanned out parts of a mixing propeller.

Blanks Rough shaped materials ready for use, such as steel pieces ready for refining by grinding, etc., in order to make a tool or other object. *See* ***Forging***.

Blast furnace (operation) A high temperature metal casting furnace using forced air and a fuel designed to heat metals to temperatures high enough to liquefy them in preparation for casting. *See* ***Furnace***.

Depending on the furnace design, the liquid metal is transferred from the furnace by **liftout, dipout, tipout** or **tapout**. In **liftout**, the entire heated pot (crucible) of metal is removed from the furnace. In **dipout**, the molten metal is removed by dipping a large steel ladle (to pour it from) into a metal pot resting inside but on top of the furnace. In **tipout**, the furnace container is tipped or tilted to allow the hot metal to flow into another smaller pouring container. The **tapout** furnace has a tap hole with a plug on the lower part. The plug is dislodged, permitting the liquid metal to flow out by gravity into a pouring container (ladle).

Blacksmith **Shannon Wright** at work.

Leitha L. Thrall, *Thorny Rose*. Bronze, 9½"x30"x8" (24.1cm x 76.2cm x 20.3cm). Photographer: George Post.

Blast furnace

The blast furnace typically found in sculpture studios or art foundries is a liftout that has a round cylinder barrel shape lined with refractory material, so that the flame can easily encircle the crucible, which sits in the middle of the unit. The flame is enhanced by a centrifugal blower creating a powerful mixture of gas and air as it rapidly spins about the crucible evacuating through a center hole in the refractory lid. The total unit can be mounted on the floor or down into the floor for easier access.

Furnace size varies with the size of crucible as the designation. A number 30 crucible is the standard size for a two-person operation without a lifting hoist. (A number 30 means that it will hold 30 pounds (13.62kg) of aluminum or three times the weight in bronze, [90 pounds (40.86kg)].) Units larger than this are difficult, if not impossible, for two people to operate successfully (without a hoist), unless the metal is lightweight aluminum. (With properly designed molds, two portrait busts can be cast, including the metal pouring system with one pour, from a number 30 crucible.) Smaller versions of this furnace can be operated by one person such as a number 15. Larger furnaces of this type can hold several hundred pounds of metal but must be operated with an overhead hoist and three or more workers. *See* ***Metal pouring system***.

BLAST FURNACE
Operation

Using metal tongs, pre-warmed metal is added to a No. 30 blast furnace as the ingot molds are pre-warmed.

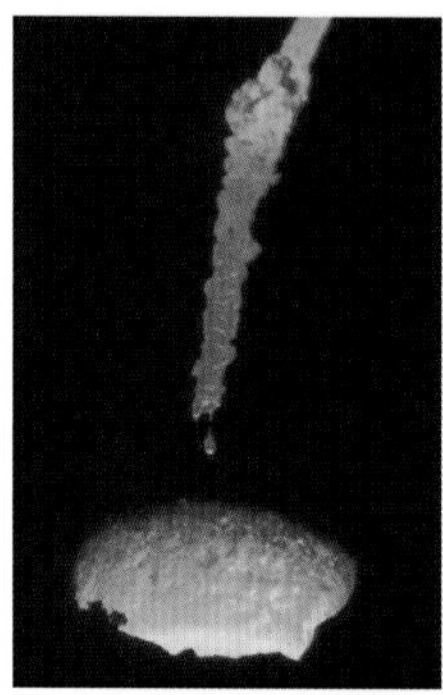

A pre-warmed steel rod inserted into the furnace verifies the correct heat.

The furnace lid is removed to reveal the hot crucible.

The molds that will be cast are pre-warmed and timed to the liquid metal's readiness.

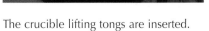

The crucible lifting tongs are inserted.

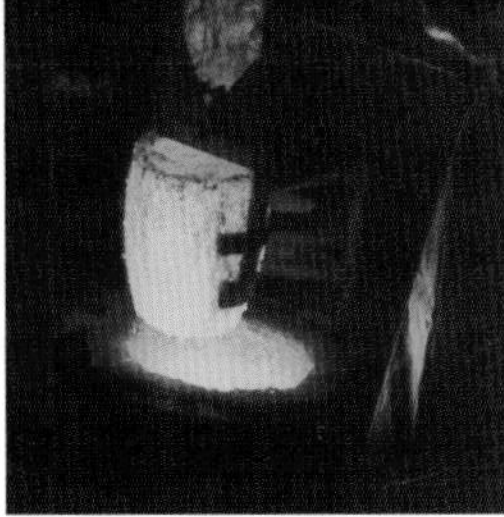

The crucible is raised from the furnace.

The crucible is placed onto a pouring block.

A pouring shank raises the crucible

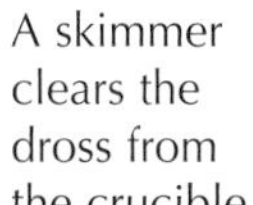

A skimmer clears the dross from the crucible.

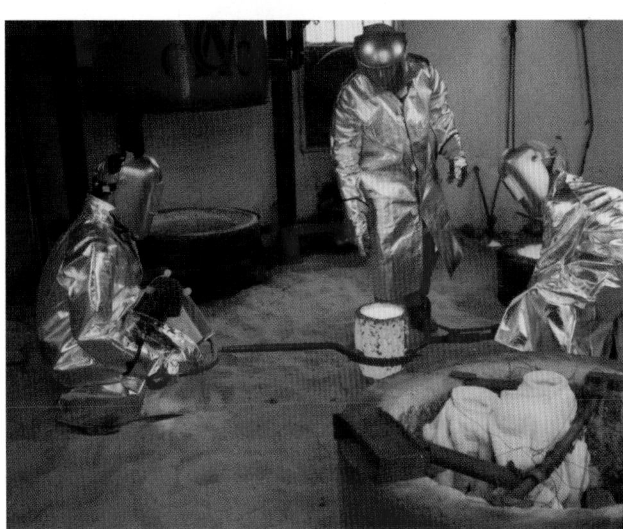

The hot molten liquid metal is poured with a two-person shank.

Technique

Furnace operation involves lighting the gas, adding metal to the hot furnace, degassing the liquid metal, measuring the temperature, removing the heated crucible from the furnace, pouring the metal and saving surplus metal.

A separate, small, **flexible gas line** with a long copper tubing on the end can contain a small flame to ignite the furnace for the initial start up. (Once hot, if the casting is done rapidly, the furnace can often reignite itself.) The furnace lid is open. The crucible is in place with starter ingots inside, and the gas is slowly turned on as the starting torch is placed into the gas flow. If the unit has an **automatic spark ignition**, a simple press of a button and control of gas makes the lighting easy. Manufacturers' instructions should be observed.

The air is added and adjusted and the lid is closed on the furnace. The mixture is readjusted to achieve a slow flame for preheating or slow warm-up of about ten minutes to expel any moisture that is in the furnace, crucible or on the metal. This avoids the possibility of thermoshock. Then the gas mixture is turned up, adjusting the flame to a mild oxidizing one that is a clear to a bluish-green color. Listening to the sound, adjust it to a loud regular blast, and notice the tip of the flame. Avoid a reducing flame color of yellow, which indicates excess fuel and a slow melting rate that will cause gas build-up in the metal.

Metal that is added to the hot crucible should be lifted with pick up tongs and never be allowed to drop in. All metal and tools must be preheated that come in contact with the hot molten metal; otherwise, it could result in an explosion or splashing out onto the wall of the furnace or onlooker. This is because of the immediate moisture that forms on cold objects as they come into contact with a hot flame or object. Never force or wedge an ingot into a crucible. It could result in a fractured or broken crucible. Metal should not be added to the top of the pot; rather, at least one inch (2.54cm) of space should remain to prevent overflow and oxidation.

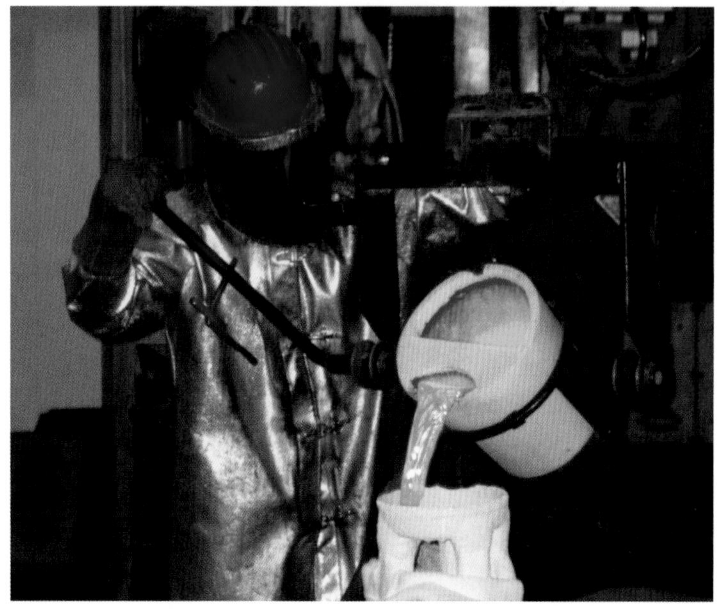

Pouring metal with a unique hoist operated, one person shank. Photographer: Dawn Weimer.

Metal has an accelerated cooling rate and will freeze onto the sides of a crucible in a matter of seconds once taken out of the furnace. For this reason, the pouring temperature is from 100°F (37.8°C) to 200°F (93.3°C) higher than the melting temperature. However, overheating can result in a burning off of some of the mixture alloys. The best pouring heat is the one that is near the melting point (higher heat for thin metal pours; colder for thick metal pours).

If a special metal mixture is desired, the alloy with the highest liquifying or melting point will be placed in the crucible first and allowed to melt before adding other alloys. Then the next highest melting point alloy is added until the last and lowest alloy is added to the final mix. An imperfect mix of metals can result in a sluggish pour of a brittle metal or a less than desirable color. Leftover scrap bronze or used bronze can be added to form a new batch, up to 50%, without noticeable difficulty in casting or metal working. Fresh metals should be used in uncontaminated crucibles, or the mix and resulting patina will vary.

Lifting tongs are necessary to remove the crucible from the furnace. They grip the hot crucible as it is lifted. When the metal is ready to take out of the furnace, the gas supply is closed off, then the furnace blower is turned off. After the crucible is removed, the lid is put back in place as soon as possible. *See* ***Lifting tongs***.

The **pouring block** provides a clean surface of a refractory material that is dry and can withstand instant heat without a reaction. It is a block made of fire bricks or silicone carbide. Prior to use, the block is covered with damp cardboard or a refractory sand to avoid a sticking crucible. A hot crucible should never be placed on concrete, since the gathered atmospheric moisture can cause a mild explosion that could result in a crucible fracture and breakage.

A **pouring shank** is used to firmly hold the crucible as the workers pour the hot metal from it. The pouring shank is in place surrounding the block or on it so that the hot crucible can be placed into the pouring shank after the crucible has been taken from the furnace. The common two-person pouring shank is designed for tilting control from only one operator to ensure accuracy without conflict. Of importance is that both operators hold the shank at the same height or the metal will fall from one side of the crucible lip and not the spout. Also, the distance from the mold to the crucible should be minimal to assure accuracy and create less pressure from the gravitational drop of the metal. A hard, sudden impact could cause a mold to fracture. *See* ***Pouring shank***.

Another foundry tool, the **skimmer,** is used to remove floating dross (trash) from the top of the hot liquid. It consists of a long handle with a spoon or half-cup-like perforated steel end to skim and hold the dross as it is removed. The skimmer must always be thoroughly pre-warmed to avoid bronze spit and to prevent a metal build-up.

The **plunger**, a small metal cup turned upside down and welded to a long shaft, is used to hold and plunge degassing pellets into the hot liquid. They are used to help eliminate excessive gas build-up, especially in re-melts. The process is called deoxidizing. It is completed at the end of the melt after the skimming but before the pour. It only takes about two ounces (56g) of pellets to degas a 90 pound (40.86kg) pot of bronze. However, virgin casting bronze ingots, especially silicon bronze, seldom need additives or other alloys for correction.

Reinhard Skoracki, *Ambivalence (Homage to Rene Magritte)*. Bronze, steel, 11.8″x11″x6.7″ (30cm x 28cm x 17cm).

The **pyrometer** is usually a long shafted tool with a heat sensor on one end and a reading gauge on the other. Accuracy is good, but the heat sensor can be melted off if held in the liquid metal too long. A smaller visual pyrometer is excellent for larger crucibles but is not commonly found in small foundries.

A plain, **long bent steel rod** is also used to test the metal for temperature and search the pot for unmelted metal ingots. The rod is allowed to pre-heat over the furnace and then thrust into the liquid metal and quickly removed. If metal adheres to it, then the metal is not sufficiently heated to pour. When the rod can be removed and all

Tim Kinard completes a one-person operation that is usually reserved for small sculptures and jewelry castings.

of the metal drips off it, then the metal is at the correct pouring temperature. If the metal cannot be lifted out on the rod before run-off, the metal is too hot for a good pour. If the rod detects an impediment in the pot (unmelted ingot), more time must be spent in heating. It is possible to use the rod to roll the solid mass around in the molten liquid to aid and expedite the melt. This results in a more rapid melt. If the metal begins to swirl, it may be overheating and should be immediately checked for temperature. It should be readied for a pour. If overheated, degassing is a consideration, even if the metal is virgin ingot, since cooling can cause gas problems.

Fluxes are used to cover the metal as it liquifies to keep out atmospheric impurities. Copper oxides or magnesium dioxide are commonly used for bronze. Broken bottles, especially old cola bottles, will work but create a messy build-up in the crucible. They are placed in the pot with the first hard metals and allowed to form an unbroken protective surface skim.

The mold must be able to sit flat and firm during the pouring. As the metal is poured, the liquid stream needs to be steady and uninterrupted until either the mold cup is filled or the metal flows out of the air vents. A swift or brisk pour is best but never so hurried that the target cup can be missed or overfilled. Depending on the mold and size, it is good to leave the cup completely filled, especially if it is on a large mold. This will serve two purposes: 1) to have a reservoir of metal to draw from as the metal shrinks and contracts, and 2) to use the weight to insure a complete fill of every section of the mold. If the mold breaks or leaks during a pour, the operator in charge must decide whether to stop, slowly fill the mold or take other action.

After the pour, if there is surplus liquid metal, it should be poured from the crucible into an ingot mold. Otherwise, the metal will contract as it cools and upon reheating, expand, possibly causing fractures in the crucible. After the pour, the crucible is returned to the furnace and placed on a coated (silica or other separator) base block. *See* ***Ingot mold***.

The unspent bronze is emptied into a pre-warmed ingot mold.

Bleaching Using an acid solution to remove natural or manmade colors and stains from wood.

Blistering Undesirable bubbles, burst or whole, on a glaze surface usually caused by immature glazes. *See* ***Glazes***.

Bloating A clay body with blisters or bubbles, allowing body gases to escape, sometimes bursting open.

Block(s) A hollowed wood tool that resembles a long handled pot or ladle that is used wet (with water) to shape gathers of glass. They are usually made of slow-burning cherry wood. Other definitions include stone made ready for carving or the pouring block inside a metal casting furnace. *See* ***Blast furnace; Glass molding***.

Blowers Designed with blades that may be enclosed or exposed for rapid removal of air or gases. The specific use depends upon size and configuration. They are measured by fan wheel diameter, outlet (air) opening, amperage (or electrical requirements), RPM (revolutions per minute) and CFM (cubic foot of air delivered per minute). Their uses include burner blowers for kilns, forges, fresh air, etc.

A small blower used on a pre-warmer furnace.

Blow holes A metal casting fault demonstrated by large visible holes in the surface of the metal that have thin metal edges about them, literally creating an impression of an interior explosion creating a hole in the side of the casting. These are caused by overheating metal, no degassing, a core releasing gas, or a lack of vents in the venting system.

Blow pipe The oxyacetylene torch and also the pipe used in blowing glass. *See* ***Welding torch; Glass; Blowpipe.***

Blowpipe (blowiron) A hollow pipe (tube) that is about five feet (1.53m) long, made of stainless or mild steel of various diameters, depending upon the size of glass work being done. Molten glass is gathered on the hot end. The glass blower blows on the opposite end into the pipe to create a hollow glass form. The blowpipe is also used as a tool to manipulate the glass in the air as well as on a marver. *See* ***Glass; Marver.***

Bluing A chemical mixture used to secure a patination or dark blue-black reaction to metal. The chemical Birchwood Casey™ is popular for this purpose. Bluing also describes the process to achieve the gun metal blue color. In addition, bluing is a laundry coloring agent that is used in the first layer (surface or face) of plaster in a plaster waste mold to visually alert the sculptor when the surface coat has been reached as the mold is being broken off. *See* ***Waste mold; Birchwood Casey™.***

Elisha Gold, *Siren.* Mixed metals from found objects and cast bronze, 24"x24" (61cm x 61cm).

Blunger A machine designed to keep a balanced mix of slip for use. It has a stirring propeller mounted on a motor shaft that keeps the heavier particles in suspension. At the bottom of the container is a spigot to conveniently pour the liquid. A larger tank, or ark, is used to keep greater quantities in preparation for the blunger. *See* ***Slip casting.***

Board foot A lumber measurement for volume in linear feet: one foot length by one foot width by one inch thickness, (1'x1'x1"), equals one board foot (30.48cm x 30.58cm x 2.54cm=2360cm^3). Any width or thickness can equal a board foot if the total volume of lumber equals a board foot. For example, a two foot long board by six inches wide by one inch thick equals one board foot. *See* ***Lumber.***

Body A combination of clays into a workable mixture, hence, "clay body." It may also refer to the major part of a structure or indicate the amount of artwork being displayed at an exhibit.

Body art The human body literally becomes the medium. It can be decorated or placed in special positions. Body art may be a form of conceptual art or performance art. *See* ***Tattoo; Body molding; Performance art.***

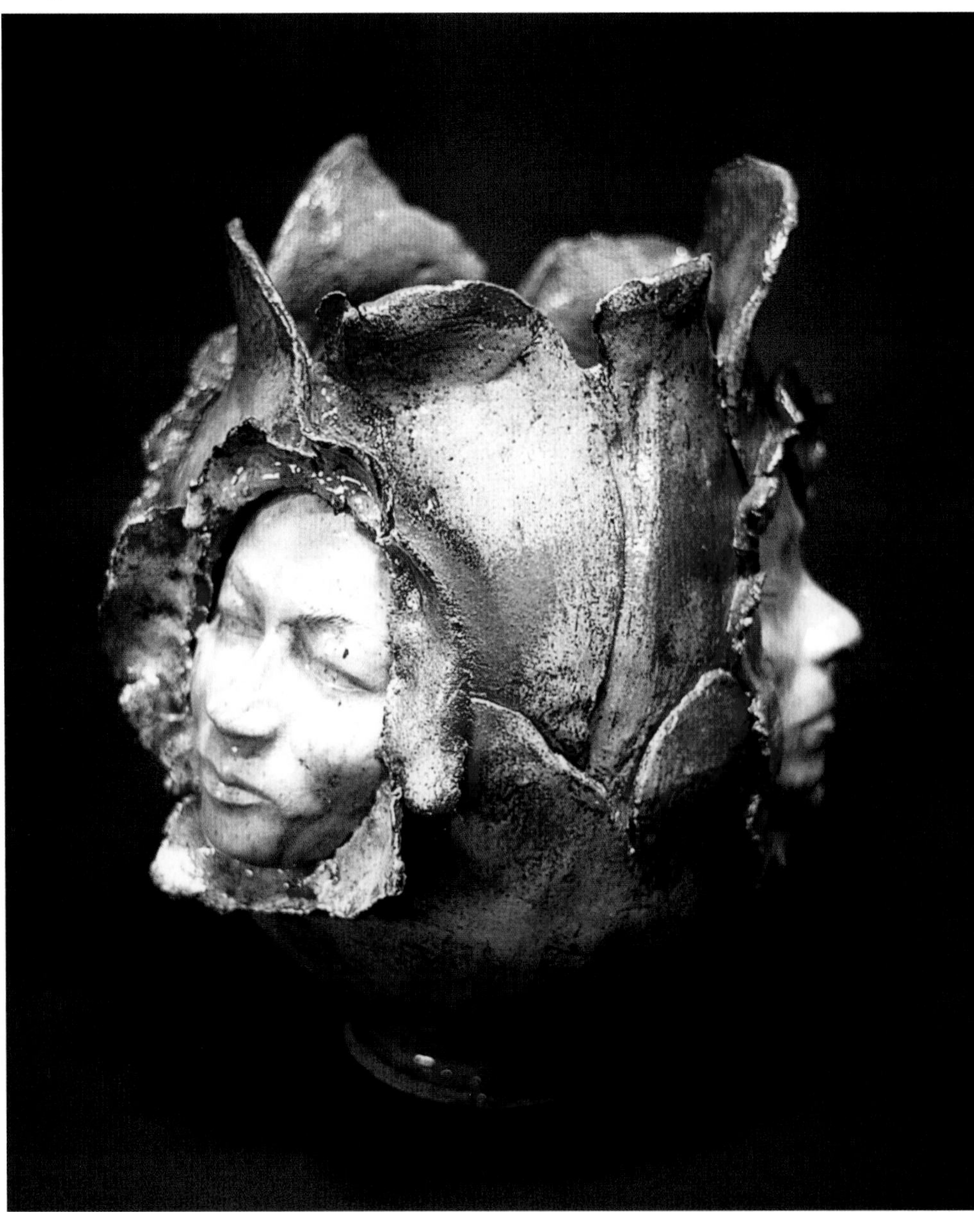

Kathy Vogler, *Twins*. Stoneware faces taken from a plaster mold, made from the artist's face, iron oxide stain, 15"x12" (38.1cm x 30.5cm).

Body molding Creating a mold from a live human body part and then making a positive casting of it. It is a good way to later study the human body when the model is not present. Plaster, plaster bandage, alginate and moulage are materials used for body casting. *See* ***Plaster gauze****;* ***Alginate****;* ***Life mask****;* ***Moulage***.

Plaster is frequently used for body/face casting, though it is not recommended because of potential health and safety hazards. Many sculptors, though, have reason to use plaster in body casting, since it is almost always on hand and can suffice for simple work. Only an artist that is well experienced with plaster should attempt this process. *See* ***Plaster***.

When plaster is used, petroleum jelly is the best release agent, since it coats and easily adheres. Hairy parts of the body either need to be shaved or covered (such as with a swim cap for the head) prior to using petroleum jelly. Unprotected hair will adhere to plaster. When making body/face casts, the work needs to be done with one mix or at one time, since the plaster setting heat can blister the model. Also, the plaster thickness needs to be slight to avoid an even greater heat. The model should be taken out of the mold as soon as it has set, prior to full heat cycle to avoid burns.

Technique

Face molds need precautions: Always apply a separator (usually petroleum jelly), always close eyes and mouth prior to placing plaster, do not place plaster into the ears and always prepare for breathing by adding soda straws (preferably paper to avoid discomfort when inserting or removing). An extra assistant is needed to reassure the model and keep the process moving as quickly as possible. The process:

1) The model should recline on a stiff surface where the head can be supported.

2) Use a single sheet of corrugated cardboard that can exceed the model's head at least four inches (10.16cm) on every side of the head. Cut the model's head shape from the cardboard. The shape is to be in front of the ears, beneath the chin and slightly over the crown of the head. Place the cut cardboard over the head with a good fit, but not too tight as to cause a circulation problem. The cardboard should rest on rigid objects on either side of the head to later support the weight of the plaster. The cardboard should be sealed around the face with soft ceramic clay to avoid drips down on the model.

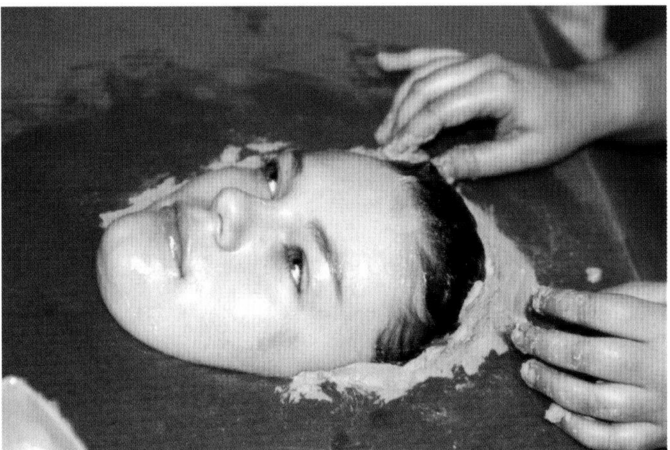

Face mold making: applying petroleum jelly for a release agent.

3) The model and cardboard need to be thoroughly coated with petroleum jelly. The hair needs a covering or shower cap to avoid plaster sticking. Eyebrows and eyelashes also need plenty of release agent.

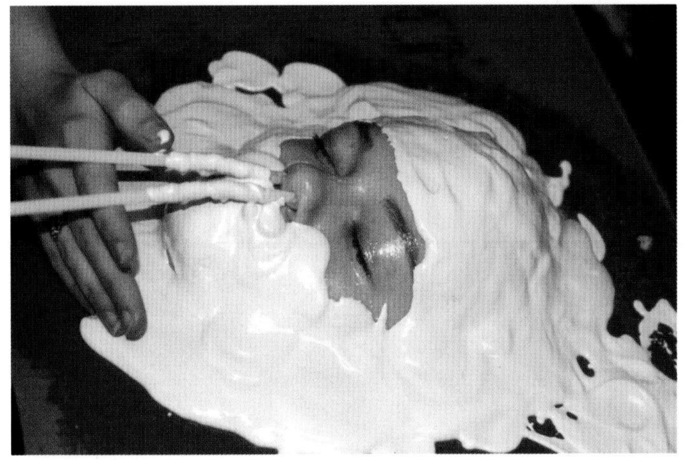

The breathing straws are in place as plaster is added.

4) Soda straws or flexible breathing tubes need to be inserted into the nostrils. Place a small amount of clay around the part in the nostril to form a seal that will keep the liquid plaster out and have the model and/or the assistant hold the straws in place until late in the modeling process.

5) Mix enough plaster in one batch to ensure that the mold can be completed. One half of a plaster bucket mix is ordinarily adequate. The water should be warm to hasten the setting and to keep the model from reacting to a cold or hot mix. The mix should be a thick liquid. Apply the plaster from the lower part of the mold upwards, working quickly but taking care to avoid air pockets. Do not place the mix over eyes or nostrils until the last moment to keep the model at ease as long as possible and to avoid unnecessary movement.

The face is completely covered.

6) Once the face is covered with a thin but even thickness, the mold begins setting. As the mold hardens and becomes warm, remove it as soon as it can retain its

strength to prevent a skin burn. Since the human face is soft and flexible, the mold is not easily broken when removed.

7) Remove the mold immediately after the nostril straws are taken out. The mold's withdrawal angle is achieved by pulling the mold from the top (of the head) forward and out over the face before pulling on the lower part. Set the mold aside to dry. Give the model clean towels and water to wash his/her face. Have a mirror handy so that the model can clean up while the plaster residue is still fresh.

8) Finish the mold by trimming, washing, and preparing it for casting. Some undercuts may need to be removed. Remember to fill the nostril holes before casting.

In use, this is an excellent mold for clay pressings when dry and wax casting when wet.

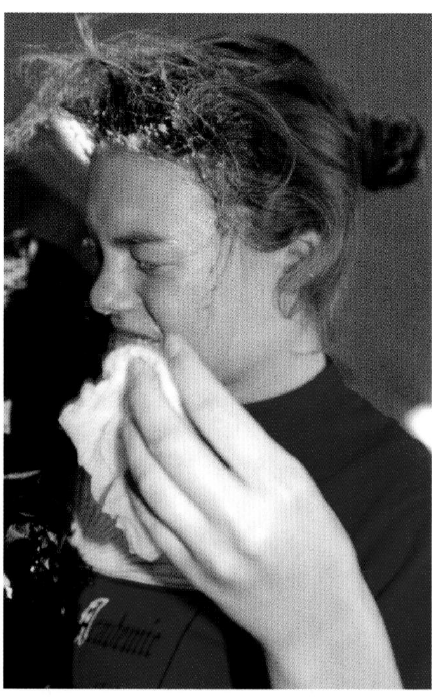

When the mold is removed, the model cleans her face.

A quick casting using wax in the damp plaster mold.

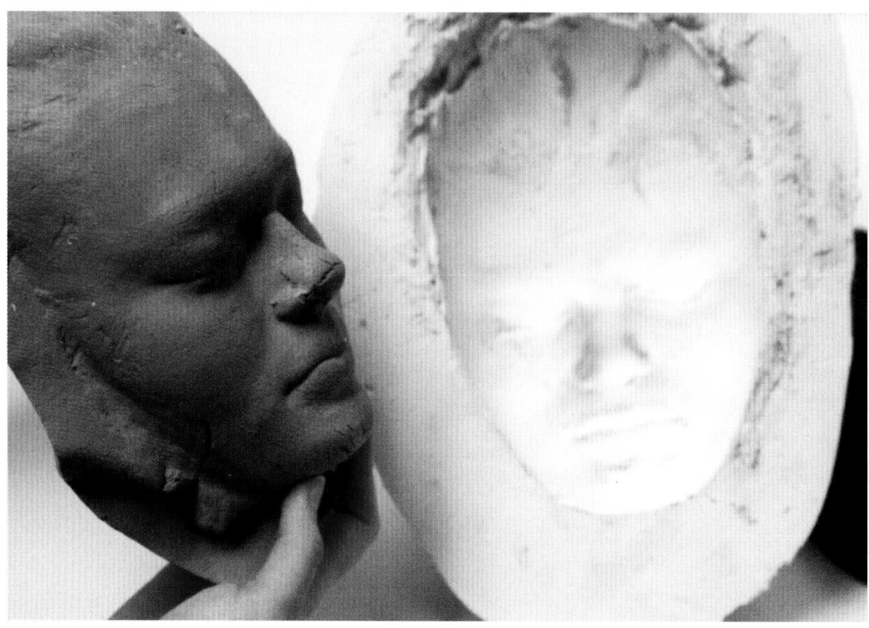

Once dried, the plaster is used as a press mold for ceramic clay.

Boiled linseed oil Production prepared linseed oil brought to a boil by heat with a dryer added. It may be mixed (thinned) with other ingredients such as turpentine to use in oiling woods for surface color and protection.

Bolt A shaft with a head on one end and threads on the other. A metal nut is screwed (rotated) around it to hold the fastening device in place. Bolts are designed for many purposes and strengths.

Bolt cutters Cutters (scissor-shaped configuration) designed to cut bolts, metal, padlocks, etc. The jaws are made with heat treated center cut blades. The toggle joints can take 50 pounds (22.7kg) of hand pressure that turn into 4000 pounds (1816kg) of cutting strength. The longer the handles, the larger and easier a piece of metal can be cut.

Bonded bronze Bronze powders combined with resin to form a simulated bronze look. *See* ***Cold cast***.

Four hundred steel segments were fastened with 2000 bolts in *Cornucopia 400* by **Aaron Royal Mosley**. Glass glazed steel, 65″x83″x83″ (165cm x 211cm x 211cm). Mission del Paso Campus, El Paso Community College, El Paso, Texas.

Patricia L. Verani, *Ferret*. Bonded bronze, 6″x8″x20″ (15.2cm x 20.3cm x 50.8cm).

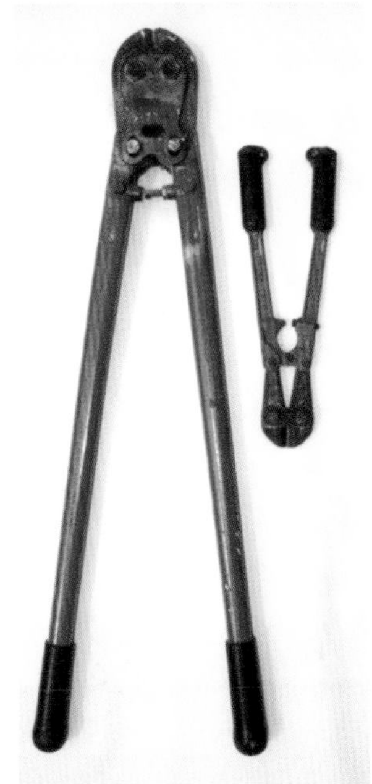

Bolt cutters, large and small sizes.

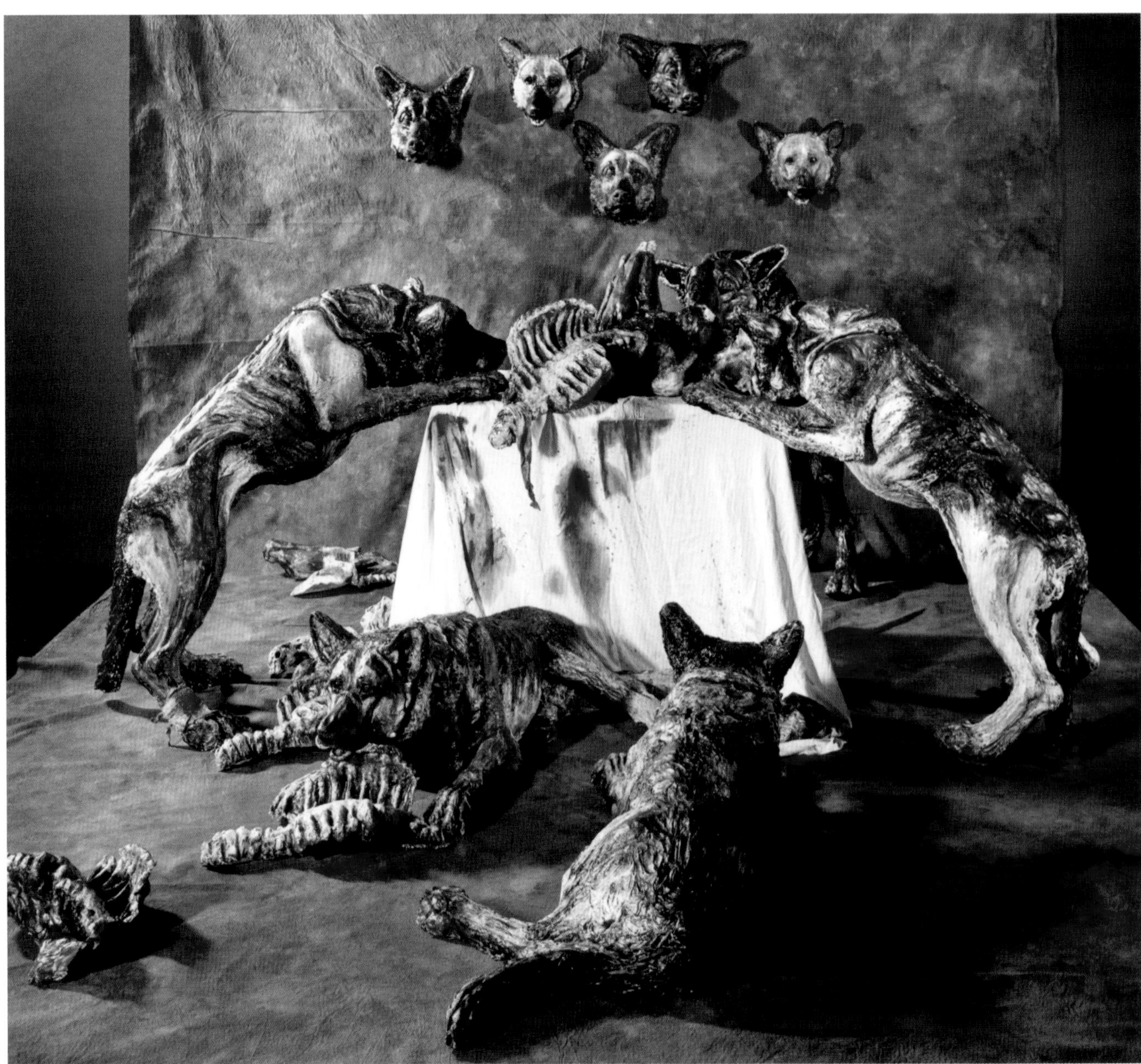

Doñalee Peden, *The Last Supper*. Bondo with painted surface, 10′x10′x12′ (3.1m x 3.1m x 3.7m); Individuals life-size, 4′ (1.2m) tall.

Bondo A two-part, epoxy/resin that is mixed together to form an of an extremely hard material. It can be successfully applied in thickness up to one-fourth inch (0.635cm) in a single setting (depending on the manufacturer). It is designed for car body repairs because of its strength and ability to take paint. Building up layers to achieve a rock-hard surface of thickness is sometimes used for sculptural shapes.

Bone china A porcelain fired to a translucent stage without glaze, then re-fired with glaze at a lower firing temperature. The fragile clay body is primarily made of bone ash. *See* ***Porcelain***.

Bonnet Buffing pads used to polish a surface made from sheepskin wool or a soft synthetic material; also, a removable hard cover protecting a machine part. *See* ***Polish.***

Booger Small unwanted fragments of metal clinging to the surface of a metal casting. Normally, it is the result of an air pocket in the investment located in a tight space that was inadequately covered or filled, such as a nostril in a portrait nose or an underarm pit.

Borax A soldering flux; also, a mineral used for low firing glazes. *See* ***Forge welding; Welding; Soldering***.

Bott A cone shaped, clay (fireclay) refractory, sand and Vermiculite or sawdust in equal parts that is used as a plug for metal casting furnaces. The bott is shaped so that it can easily be pushed into the tap and closed by compressing the form into the tap shape. It is placed on a specially prepared steel rod for support as it is forced into the tap. *See* ***Iron casting***.

Bottle A large cylinder of oxygen, acetylene, etc., when used in reference to metal work. *See* ***Cylinder***.

Bouchard Bushhammer. *See* ***Bushhammer***.

Boulder A rock mass of mammoth proportions. A boulder may be used for sculptural purposes but is probably not suitable for carving. *See* ***Stone***.

Bound water Absorbed water that is chemically combined with a substance that crystallizes. This is the process of forming plaster.

Bow saws A saw with a handle reminiscent of an archery bow configuration with a blade tensioned like an archery string. The saws are large with large-toothed replaceable blades designed for cutting green tree branches or green logs.

Boxwood (tools) A pale yellow hardwood with a dense grain. It is difficult to carve but excellent for sculpture modeling tools. *See* ***Modeling tools***.

Brake A heavy machine for working metal operated by hand or hydraulically. A brake is used to fold sheet metal, etc.

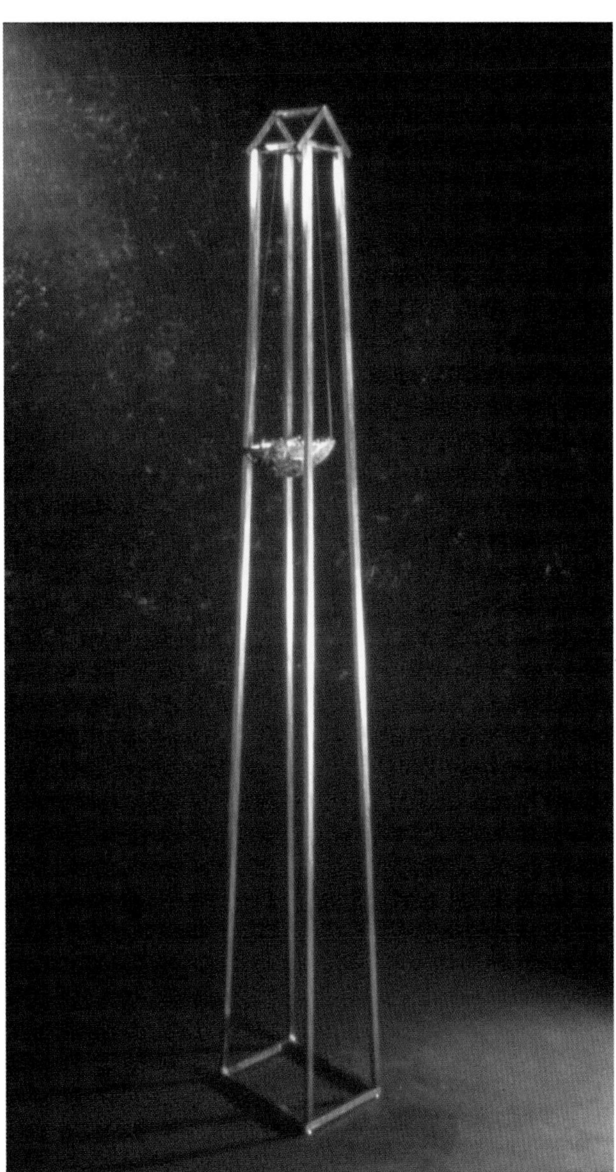

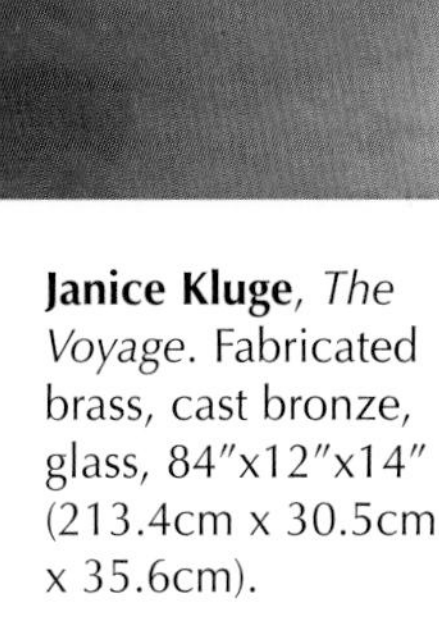

Janice Kluge, *The Voyage*. Fabricated brass, cast bronze, glass, 84″x12″x14″ (213.4cm x 30.5cm x 35.6cm).

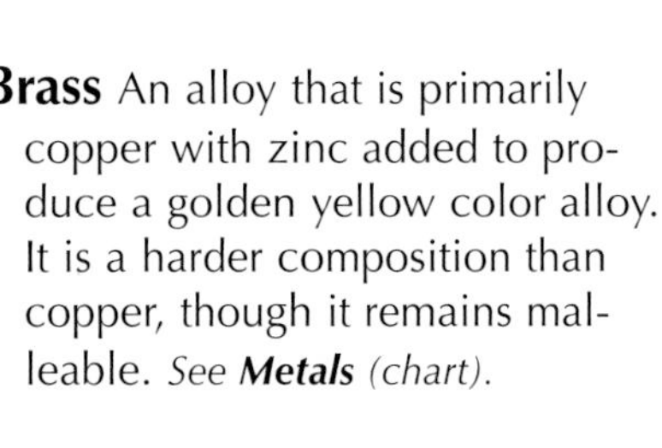

Brass An alloy that is primarily copper with zinc added to produce a golden yellow color alloy. It is a harder composition than copper, though it remains malleable. *See* ***Metals*** *(chart)*.

Maria Alquilar, *Tenderness of God*. Brass, 30'x15' (76.2cm x 38.1cm).

Braze welding (brazing) Soldering pieces of metal together using a high temperature solder. Brazing and braze welding are similar, but not the same. Both processes require that a filler metal have a temperature below that of the metals being welded. However, brazing filler metal is placed on a tight joint and drawn into it by capillary attraction. In braze welding, the filler metal is not dependent upon capillary attraction. Braze welding is also used for plating or decorative surface effects.

Technique

Brazing and braze welding require the base metals to be heated to temperatures above 800°F (427°C) and bonded with nonferrous filler metals (rods). The surfaces must be wire brushed, sanded or otherwise prepared to produce a clean surface. A flux is usually required to keep the joint clean by keeping atmospheric contamination or deposits from affecting the weld. Braze welding or brazing is used to attach copper, brass, bronze, aluminum, steel (including galvanized steel and stainless steel) and cast iron. These metals can be joined to each other, as well as to the same alloy.

A good braze weld is strong, rigid and permanent. Distinct fluxes are used for different metals, but the most common one is borax used with a brass rod. A method of applying flux to the weld is by dipping the heated rod into the flux and then applying it to the preheated base metal. Powder can be sprinkled on or more evenly applied if it has been mixed with water and brushed on. If the flux comes in a paste form, it is also brushed on. A pre-coated rod is more expensive but more desirable, especially for larger jobs. The rods are 24 inches (61cm) in length and range in numerous sizes from one-sixteenth inch (0.159cm) to over three-eighths inch (0.953cm). The thickness of the metals determines the size selected.

The joints should be clamped together or otherwise held steady. If clamps or wires are used to hold the parts together, they need to be at a distance from the weld, or they could be bonded with the base metal. When the flux is

Peter N. Cozzolino, *Reflection*. Bronze, 19″ (48.3cm) tall.

Gerald Balciar, *Wings of Power*. Bronze, 34½″x21x9½″ (87.6cm x 53.3cm x 24.1cm).

ready, it becomes like a melted glass transparent fluid material. (After the work is completed, the flux needs to be removed by a chipping hammer or wire brush.)

A **braze welding coating** can be grounded, sanded, polished and patinaed, depending on the embellishment or surface sought. The surfaces may exhibit a distorted surface or shape. However, if it is not desirable, it can be cancelled by hammering. *See* ***Capillary action; Borax***.

Bronze Alloys of copper and tin with traces of additional metals to form a strong metal with a predominate copper color. It is the standard for casting metal in sculpture. One of the most common bronzes is called 85-5-5-5, also known as red brass or European bronze, because it has been used for centuries in Europe. It can be polished to a pink color and readily takes a patina. It is 85% copper, 5% zinc, 5% tin and 5% lead. However, it is being used less because of the toxic aspects of lead. Most art foundries now use a silicon bronze because of its pouring qualities. Depending on the bronze, Everdur™ and other silicone bronzes are poured over 1850°F (1010°C), usually between 1950°F (1066°C) and 2050°F (1121°C). *See* ***Silicon bronze; Everdur™; Metal casting; Ingot; Blast furnace; Furnace***.

Glenna Goodacre, *Vietnam Women's Memorial*. Bronze. Vietnam Women's Memorial, Inc., Washington, D.C. Photographer: Greg Staley.

Bronze casting The process of pouring a hot liquid bronze metal into a mold or the casting itself. *See* ***Metal casting***.

Bronze disease The blemishes or pits on bronze brought about by the atmosphere, especially chlorides and their corrosive effects. It is sometimes referred to as bronze rot. The bronze has a texture made up of gas pits that can contain and hold moisture to keep the disease in continual action. Over a period of time, the bronze can literally fleck away. If properly diagnosed, it can be restrained by a washing and long soaking heat and then being completely encased with a wax coating to avoid moisture or the atmosphere.

Bronze powder Fine powders of bronze alloys that when enclosed in a varnish and applied to surfaces simulate cast bronze. It is used on plasters and ceramics to create a faux bronze. *See* ***Bronzing***.

Bronzing Applying a bronze powder or thin sheets of bronze to a surface to create a bronze look. Plaster is usually the surface that is used. *See* ***Bronze powder***.

Bronzing liquid A liquid with bronze powder and banana oil combined to create a metallic paint. Sometimes aluminum powders are used instead of bronze, but may still be referred to as bronzing liquid.

Bruise A surface injury brought about by a hard blow to a stone surface that does not change the surface level but does injure the under surface by crushing stone particles. It creates an undesirable lighter or white color beneath the surface that is easy to spot and cannot be removed without refinishing below the bruise. In wood, it creates a dent or compression, softening the wood by crushing the fibers. If oiled, it saturates, creating a noticeably darker spot on the surface.

Brush A tool used to apply a substance, usually liquid, to a surface. It consists of a handle with bristles or hairs attached to one end. It can also be made with sponges or other objects that can hold the substance being applied. In sculpture, dry brushing is a manner of cleaning a surface, such as a mold, with a soft bristle brush. A hard wire brush is used for removing surface refuse, rust, paint, etc. *See* ***Wire brush***.

Arthur Williams, *Birth of Woman*. Cast, buffed and polished resin on mirror surface, 36″x29″x36″ (91.4cm x 73.7cm x 91.4cm).

Brush-on The method of using a brush or spatula to apply a liquid substance to a surface. Brush-on mold material and brush-on paint are most common. *See* ***Flexible mold***.

BTU British Thermal Unit: 29307 kilowatt hours equal 1000 BTUs.

Buff To polish or clean an object with a softer material, sometimes with a polishing compound. Buff is also the term used for a polishing bonnet.

Buffer A tool with a wheel-mounted cloth pad used for surfacing, smoothing, or polishing. It is also the term used for the buffing wheel itself. *See* ***Buffing compound; Buffing wheel***.

Buffing compound A substance, either in liquid, paste, or a solid block that contains fine measured grit particles. It is applied to a surface or buffer in to polish the surface by abrasively rubbing. Abrasive polishing compounds in bar form include: Tripoli (orange/brown color) for buffing aluminum, brass, copper, pewter, plastics and wood, Red Rouge (red color) for gold, silver and other precious metals, White Rouge for stainless steel, aluminum, iron and chrome, and Emery Cake (black) for rust removal. They are applied to buffing wheels to polish the works. *See* ***Rubbing compound; Buffing wheel***.

Buffing wheel A rotating wheel composed of soft materials (e.g., cotton) that has a mildly abrasive buffing or polishing compound rubbed onto its surface. A hard object, such as metal or plastic, is pushed onto the spinning wheel to arrive at a highly polished, reflective finish. *See* ***Buffing compound***.

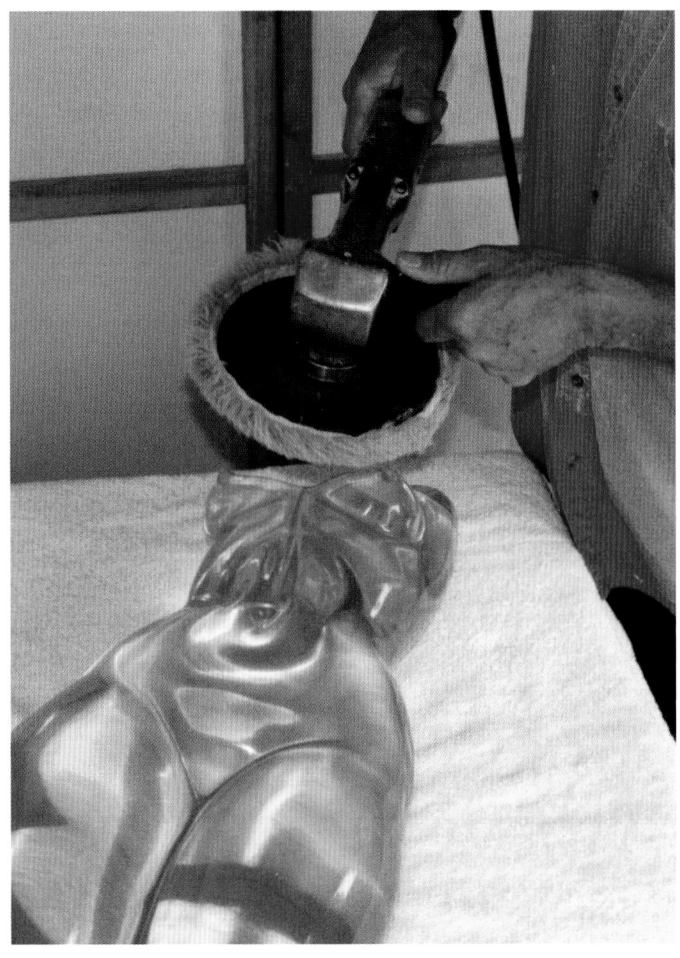

Arthur Williams buffs a cast resin.

Buffing compounds. Left to right: Red Rouge, Black Emery, White Rouge, Brown Tripoli.

A buffing compound is added to a buffing wheel.

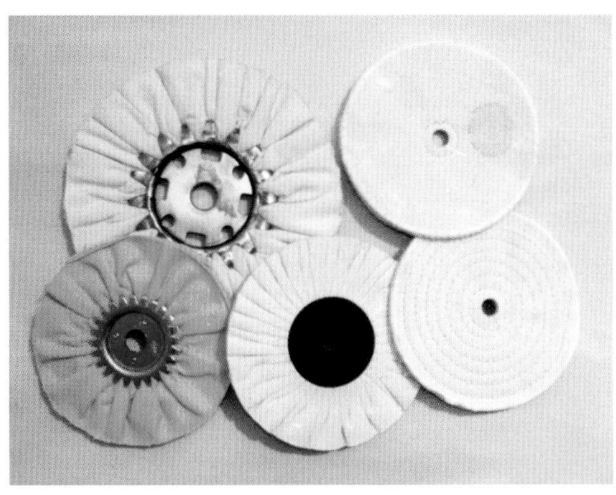

Buffing wheels. Those with center mounts are for buffing/polishing hard metals; top right is soft cotton center sewn for more delicate polishing; bottom right is spiral sewn for polishing/buffing all metals.

Buffing wheels and die grinder buffers/polishers. The larger ones have an obvious softness; the smaller buffers have a compact, firmer makeup.

Buildup Depending on what technique or product is being used, buildup can be a weld that extends above the surface of welded metals, adding clay to a model, or it can be a process of gradually adding mold materials to the surface when mold making.

Bumblebees Hot flying sparks resulting from welding or grinding metal.

Bung Insulated plug for an observation hole into a ceramic kiln or burnout furnace.

Bungee cord (strap) Rubber strap, often coated with an expanding cloth. It has hooks on each end to connect or be tied about an object. It is designed to tightly wrap around or over an object to hold it in place or together. *See **Molds; Waste mold**.*

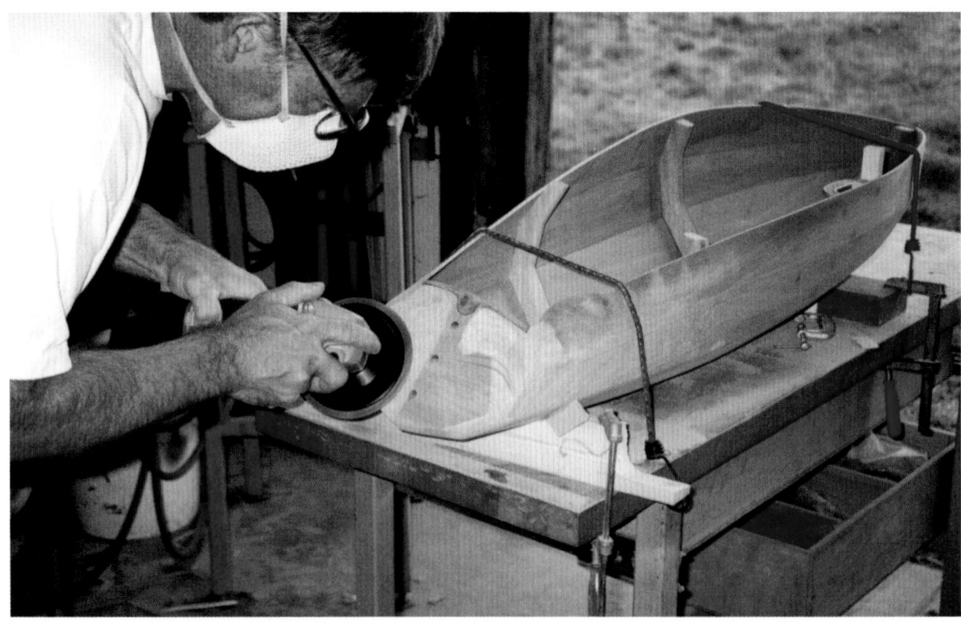

A bungee cord holds a form in place while **Michael J. Cooper** works.

Burl A spherical outgrowth, like a bulge, on a tree, usually cylindrical, though it may be irregular in shape. Frequently called a knot or gnarl, it is the result of bud cluster growths. It can be quite large, producing multi-color layers of wood displaying a unique, unpredictable swirl pattern. Roots may have many burls.

Burner Apparatus designed to create and disperse heat effectively. Burners usually have two air sources. Since the atmosphere only includes 20% oxygen, the burners must be designed to draw a large volume of air into the mix. The primary source is air that is mixed in a chamber with the gas prior to ignition. The secondary source is air that unites at the flame to ensure that all the fuel is used. A burner may also be an oxygen cutter when used for cutting metals.

Burners are designed to either rely upon fan forced pressure or atmospheric pressure to deliver air for the combustion to take place. Fan forced pressure is required when rapid heat buildup and control are necessary, such as with metal casting furnaces. Atmospheric pressure is good when electricity to operate the fan is not available or rapid warm up speed is not an issue such as with ceramic kilns. Gauges and ignition equipment are available from manufacturers as total packages. *See **Furnace; Oxyacetylene torch; Burnout furnace; Kiln**.*

Burnishing To refine or smooth a surface by rubbing a hard object on it. Burnishing is used for leather hard clay surfaces, although it can also be used for wood and stone. Burnishing tools are usually simple objects, such as smooth stones, glass or even strips of leather.

Burnout (furnace) The process of removing a substance (wax) by heat from a mold. It is also the term for the high heat furnace used for melting wax out of a mold in preparation for metal casting. The mold is made of a refractory material, such as ceramic shell or plaster investment, that can withstand heat as the wax is melted and later withstand the heat of hot metal.

Ceramic shell molds require a burnout furnace capable of up to 1750°F (954°C) rapid heat flash burns, while plaster investment is similar to ceramic kilns designed for slow heat in excess of 1500°F (816°C). A noticeable black smoke appears during this process with older style furnaces. However, a properly designed ceramic shell burnout furnace can recover almost all the wax in a completely reusable state with little, if any, pollution. The gas furnace is the most common method of de-waxing a mold, because it removes the wax and reaches heat to complete the maturation or tempering of the ceramic mold material all in one process. This will save time, as well as fuel.

The burnout furnace used for plaster investment casting is designed to withstand high temperatures with a strong floor that contains a drain for the hot liquid wax as it melts. The furnace resembles a ceramic kiln in structure and oftentimes is a ceramic kiln, though sometimes modified for the melting wax. The furnace eliminates all moisture from the mold, leaving a dry, but hot, mold ready to take the intensely hot fluid metal. The precision of ceramic kilns is good for this process, though the weight is hard on the floor system. Those with lower burners (updraft) may encounter problems if the melted wax is not directed away from the burners. One solution is to burn out the molds with the mold drains turned upward. But this causes problems since the carbon will enter the investment and molds must be burned out longer to ensure a complete wax removal.

Burnout Designs

There are six basic burnout furnace designs for ceramic shell that can also be used for plaster investment casting. However, if these furnaces are to be used for plaster investment, the flame needs to be buffered from the molds and a greater degree of temperature control for constant adjustments needs to be part of the design. Ceramic shell needs no adjustment after the furnace reaches full heat. The flames do not affect the shell molds. These burnout furnaces are: 1) **swing door**, 2) **drop floor**, 3) **overhead door**, 4) **raised furnace**, 5) **shuttle cart,** and 6) **holding furnace**. All are determined by the opening involved.

Norman D. Holen, *Girl with Leg Extended.* Bronze, 10 ½" x 5 ½" x 8 ½" (26.7cm x 14cm x 21.6cm). Photographer: Peter Lee.

The criteria for a good burnout furnace is to house enough insulation that it can achieve and hold heat rapidly, to easily and safely load and unload hot molds, to create the least environmental pollution and to save the wax, preferably without having to reprocess it. Round furnaces can be heated more quickly and in a more even fashion than rectangular or square furnaces. However, all of these furnaces can be designed to preserve the environment and save the wax in a usable state; some better than others.

BURNOUT FURNACE
Swing Door

A swing door burnout furnace is unloaded. Design by **Arthur Williams**.

View inside a swing door furnace.

1) The **swing door** furnace is popular since so many previously used and in-use ceramic kilns are available to the sculptor. The floor can be designed for use with a reusable basket. The burners should be on the sidewall aimed into the furnace, allowing the floor to be used for wax drainage and recovery. However, if the floor is not designed to avoid pollution and recover the wax, the furnace can cause environmental problems and promote a high reduction heat causing the molds to weaken or require longer burnout. A cart system for fast removal of the mold basket/floor must be designed. It works equally well for plaster investment.

Removal of de-waxed ceramic shell.

BURNOUT FURNACE

Drop floor

A drop floor burnout furnace is unloaded and reloaded. A tray of ceramic shell molds waits to be loaded. Design by **Arthur Williams**.

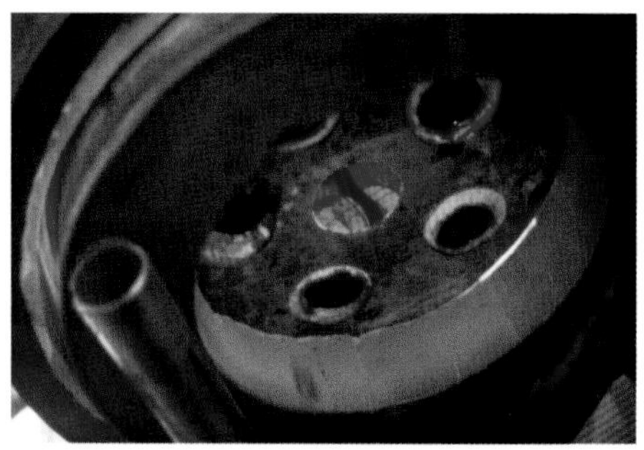

Looking up into the floor of a drop floor furnace.

Hot, dewaxed ceramic shell molds being lowered from the drop floor furnace.

2) The **drop floor** furnace is ideal for ceramic shell, but it must be custom built in place, because the floor needs to be hydraulically operated for heavy molds. The furnace will sit at least four feet (1.22m) off the ground and the hydraulic arm (piston) must be securely mounted into the ground. It can be air or oil operated. Oil may be preferred but is expensive. If a good compressor is available that can hold over 150 psi (1034kPa), then a hydraulic floor can be air operated. One of the unique benefits of the drop floor is that it gives off less heat to the workers, since the heat travels up and not out or down. If properly designed, all the usable wax is recovered, ready for use without pollution problems. It also will work with plaster investment, though a larger hydraulic system may be required for the oversized heavy molds.

Reusable wax from a drop floor furnace is recovered.

3) The **overhead door** furnace allows a manufactured square or rectangular furnace to be used. This furnace is built of high heat insulation bricks with a metal frame. The door is attached to the frame to easily slide straight up, being lifted either by a hoist or counterweight system. The advantages to this furnace are many. Size does not have to be a factor nor does wax or pollution if the floor/basket/cup system is correctly designed. The disadvantages are slight: the space tends to require a longer heat up period and much of it is unused. Safety checks for the door mechanism should be constant. It also works for plaster investment.

4) The **raised furnace** is popular, because it can be built with a simple 55 gallon (208L) metal drum and lightweight insulation material (blanket heat resistant material) attached to the inside. It can be removed by two people if it has handles on both sides, or it can be held up from the top by counter balance or hoist and removed by one operator. The gas can be applied from the floor or with a flexible gas cable into the drum itself. This furnace rapidly heats and with a proper floor/cup arrangement, it does not have to pollute. The wax can be recovered intact. The disadvantage is size limitation. With good controls, it works equally well for plaster investment.

5) Of these furnaces, the **shuttle cart** is the least used for ceramic shell, because it is difficult for the worker to load molds without losing the heat or being overcome by the escaping heat. At best, it is used for extremely heavy, large sculpture pieces that could not be placed into one of the other furnaces. However, this type furnace is excellent for large plaster investment molds, since the molds can be more easily maneuvered onto the cart floor from the open sides.

6) The **holding furnace** is one in which the mold is suspended in the furnace as the wax is being melted out. These furnaces are usually small makeshift operations. An example would be holding a mold (with the cup down) into a preheated metal casting furnace running at a lowered temperature as the wax is melted out. With some rigging, the holder (wire noose) on the mold can be held in place. Safety is a major consideration, especially since the lid is usually left open. Pollution is difficult to control, if not impossible, and usable wax recovery is impractical. These do not work for plaster investment.

When a burnout furnace is not available, an **acetylene torch with a rosebud tip** (several acetylene holes to help spread the heat out) can be used to dewax ceramic shell molds held in an outside furnace. However, the mold cannot be large, or the heat will not be applied quickly enough to avoid wax expansion and cracks. This method cannot be used for plaster investment.

Burnout floor-cup design

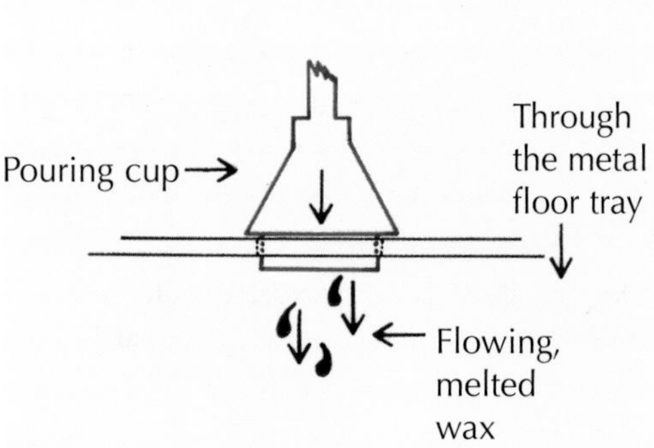

This floor/cup design avoids air pollution and toxic fumes. It saves the wax, keeping it intact for immediate reuse. It is the author's design and has been successfully used for several years (only two molds miscast out of the first one thousand casting). The wax for the metal pouring system is carefully attached to the pouring cup, and part of the cup is placed into or through the floor to allow the undamaged melting wax to run directly into a holding tank. The wax needs to run out from the hot furnace floor without hindrance. If the cup and floor are properly designed, the resulting wax pour off is excellent to use as is or with a harder wax intermixed with the melted runner and body wax. Older furnace floors can be modified to use this design.

Ceramic shell burnout process

All burnout furnaces used for ceramic shell molds must be able to heat to a minimum of 1750°F (954°C) and hold it to properly cure the mold. Preferably, the furnace could go to temperatures as high as 2000°F (1093°C) to compensate for the heat lost when inserting and removing molds. The better the heat range, the easier the molds can be dewaxed. However, molds heated too far or too long beyond 1750°F (954°C) can cause the surface to deteriorate into a soft refractory without details. When materials other than wax (such as Styrofoam™) are used with the wax, the burnout time must be high and of longer duration. If the furnace can initially be prewarmed rapidly (within an hour), then the energy costs are not too great a factor.

All furnaces need a bottom opening or removable floor with openings to allow wax to run out. Consequently, the furnace also needs some bottom height for the wax to drain and to be distant enough to avoid flames. If the furnace and draining wax must be in close proximity, then the wax should be drained into a pan of water covered with a fine mesh (screen door) of steel (preferably stainless steel) screen and removed as soon as possible. The screen keeps flames from flaring up. All furnace areas must be properly ventilated to prevent burning wax from becoming a health and safety problem. Some flames do escape, especially if the wax is allowed to burn into the atmosphere.

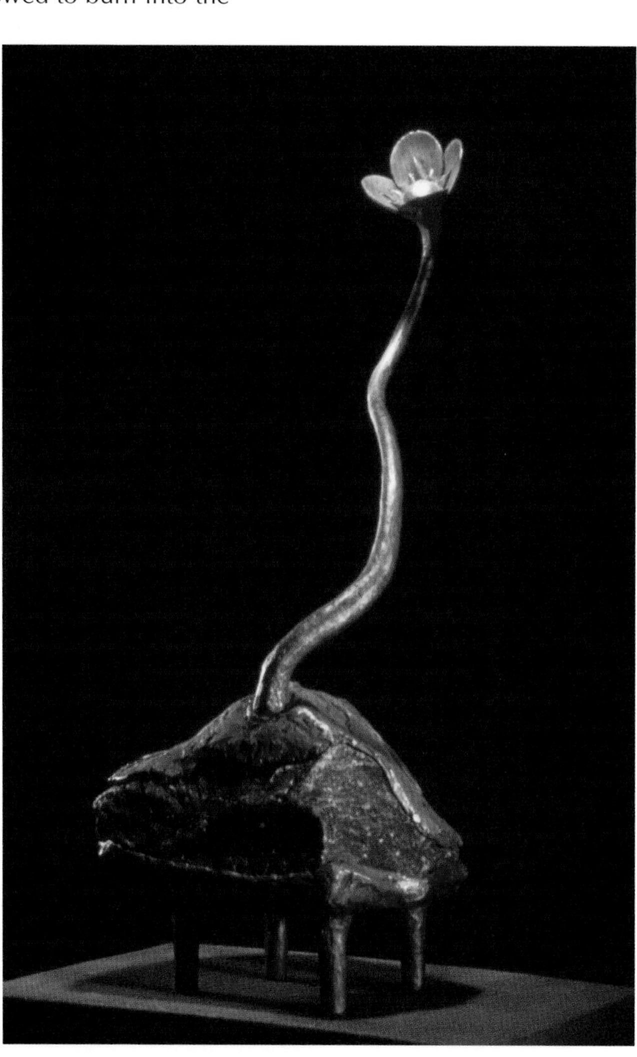

G. David Burch, *Tiresias*. Bronze and Granite, 34"x15"x12" (86.4cm x 38.1cm x 30.5cm).

The wax immediately swells (enlarges) as heat is applied. Though the shell is strong, it cannot withstand the total consistent pressure of the expanding wax, so the wax must escape. The mold must be able to withstand a shock heat by entering an extremely hot preheated furnace. The heat literally collides with the mold to instantaneously begin melting the wax closest to the surface before the main wax mass has a chance to swell from the heat.

The runners and the mold design have been created so that metal can easily enter them. Wax can also escape quickly by the same system if inverted with the cup down. To aid the wax removal in large molds, small holes are drilled in strategic locations, such as on the runners (for less chasing later), to allow the wax new escape routes. After the burnout is completed, the holes are plugged with heat setting cement or fiberglass dipped in slurry and then coated several times in slurry for strength. Also, the wax runners and sprues are frequently hollow for a more rapid wax draining.

The burnout (dewaxing) time varies with the mold, primarily depending upon the mold size. If Styrofoam™ has been used, then the temperature must be high and remain high during the burnout for at least thirty minutes longer to take care of carbon ash and the potential residue in the mold. Assuming that the burnout furnace is 1500°F (816°C) or higher, the time required to burnout a small mold (12 inches [30.5cm] or less) would be adequate in a thirty-minute period (this assumes several molds are in the furnace).

Larger molds (to 18 inches [45.7cm]) may take forty minutes, depending on the furnace and configuration. Very large molds (over 24 inches [61cm]) could take more than forty-five minutes, assuming that the heat can be maintained over 1500°F (816°C). This process should be continuous, without break or interruption, to make certain the wax does not shrink or expand within the unfinished mold causing cracks. As the mold is nearing completion, it glows with an even iridescent orange. If any flame, carbon or dark places remain, then the mold has not been completely dewaxed or brought to the temperature needed to harden the mold.

Once the burnout is completed, the molds can be removed into the cool air without fear of fracture. Even so, the molds should be visually examined for fractures, preferably while still hot since hairline fractures are easier to spot at this time. Assuming that the mold remains in a heat basket or is lifted by tongs, it is easy to handle while hot. Otherwise, it is dangerous to maneuver and, once removed, should be allowed to cool without handling for safety reasons. After dewaxing, the hardened shell is stored for future casting, made ready for immediate casting or placed into a prewarmer for a controlled mold temperature during metal casting. After casting, the molds are divested. *See* ***Divesting; Prewarmer; Metal pouring system; Pouring cup.***

Plaster investment burnout process

It is difficult to place the heavy molds into the furnace and then take them out while they are hot. Since investment molds are characteristically heavy, moving them into a confined space creates special problems. For this reason, some foundries have shuttle cart furnaces, overhead hoist systems above top loading furnaces, or use forklifts to handle the investment molds.

Tim Kinard loads a plaster investment mold for burnout. The pouring cup is turned down for the wax to melt out onto the floor drain.

The actual process, once the furnace is loaded, takes several hours, depending on the number and sizes of the molds, with the most massive mold determining the timeframe. While foundry operators vary in the exactness of the temperatures that the process goes through, all agree that the molds must be slowly soaked, eliminating as much wax and moisture as possible. Then the temperature is gradually raised until all trace of carbon is gone. The molds are allowed to slowly cool until a temperature is reached that allows the workers to move the mold using heavy insulated gloves, aprons and other equipment.

This is a suggested firing: Soak the molds for twelve to twenty-four hours at a very low temperature from 200°F (93.3°C) to 450°F (232.2°C). This allows the wax and moisture to escape. Then begin to take the temperature up at about 100°F (37.8°C) per hour until 1200°F (649°C) has been reached. Allow the molds to soak at this temperature or slightly higher, for an additional twelve to thirty-six hours, depending upon the size of the molds. Do not exceed 1500°F (816°C), or the molds can disintegrate. A pyrometer should be used to check the temperature. Once the molds have reached an even dull or dark cherry red (about 1175°F [635°C]) and have no carbon flame, the burners can be turned down, allowing the molds to cool slowly. With large molds, the furnace needs a more gradual decrease in temperature with the burners left on until toward the last six hours. Turn off the burners and close all furnace vents for several hours or until the molds reach below 500°F (260°C). They need to be removed and packed in supporting sand and poured before they are cooled below 250°F (121°C), or the metal will prematurely freeze up in the pouring. Because of all the mold material insulation, breakout of the metal from the mold cannot be done for several hours. *See* ***Plaster investment; furnace.***

Burns Created by exposure to excessive heat, radiation, friction or chemicals. Burns are ranked according to the severity as first, second or third degree. A first degree burn is considered minor and heals easily. A second degree burn results in blisters and swelling. A third degree burn is extremely serious, compelling immediate attention. Minor burns can be treated by immediately applying a fresh Aloe Vera plant's crushed leaves to avoid blisters and lingering pain. Cold water is good for most burns, followed by a dry dressing. Professional medical attention should be sought for chemical or extensive radiation burns.

Burr The loosely attached thin metal edge remaining after a tool is sharpened. It can be removed by sharpening on the opposite side with the same stone. Also, a washer, especially one fitting around a rivet, may be referred to as a burr.

Bushhammer (boucharde) A stone carving hammer with teeth in uniform rows of pyramid shapes on

Bushhammers.

each end of the two-sided head. It is used to remove fine particles by striking the stone with a series of blows that bruise or pulverize the surface causing it to turn to powder. They should not be used on softer stones to avoid deep internal bruising.

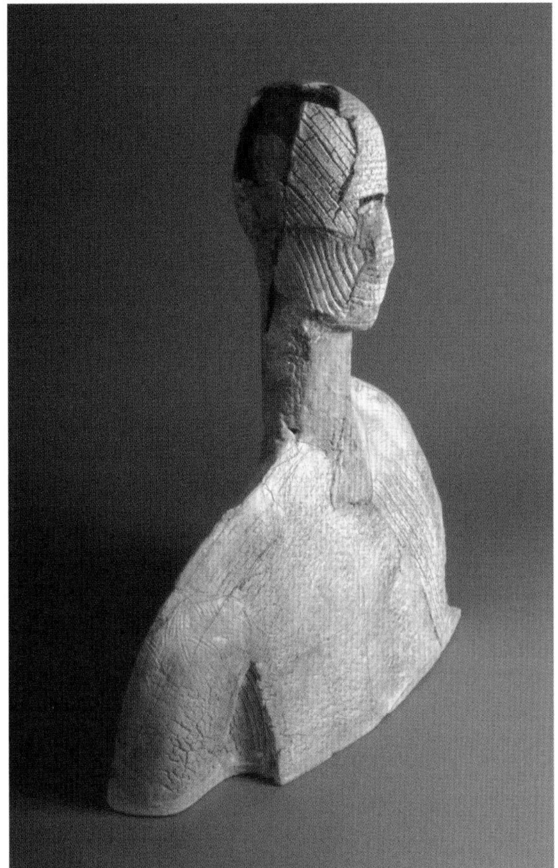

Marc Verbruggen, *To Speak in Silence*. Clay with grog, white color, 34.7"x28.4"x11.7" (88cm x 72cm x 29.7cm). Photographer: Hans Vulysteke.

Bushing tool The equivalent tool of a bushhammer for an air hammer with the additional ability to rotate in circular and semicircular movements during use.

Bush pick A bushhammer with a pointed pick shape on the back end. *See **Bushhammer***.

Bust (portrait) A sculpture portrait that usually includes all of the head and sometimes the neck, shoulders and/or breast, though it can embrace the body to the knees. If the entire body, or the majority of the body is included, it is considered a portrait figure. *See **Portrait bust; Armature***.

Bust peg (head peg) A strong, flat plank with a vertical center post for modeling a bust. *See **Armature***.

Butterfly A piece of wood, usually in a cross shape, hanging by wire within an armature to hold the modeling material. It supports modeling material while keeping it from moving or sagging. *See **Armature***.

Edward J. Fraughton, *Blending of the Races*. Bronze, 21"x12½"x2½" (53.3cm x 31.3cm x 6.4cm).

Butt joint When two materials, usually flat, are squarely pressed, touching each other on the edges (butting). The joint is completed by gluing, welding, etc. A joint made by placing two materials side-by-side without overlap.

Bruce Beasley, *Vitality*. Fabricated bronze, 30'x11'x9' (9.15m x 3.36m x 2.75), Oakland, California. One of the sculptor's works that began as part of a computerized program.

C

CAD (Computer Aided Design) Computer software designed for architecture and technical design applications. It is especially useful for architects and designers. *See **Enlarging** (digitized).*

Bruce Beasley, *Breakout*. Cast bronze, 28″x44″x12″ (71.1cm x 111.8cm x 30.5cm).

Assembling foam core sculpture parts in preparation for metal casting originating from a CAD program by **Bruce Beasley**.

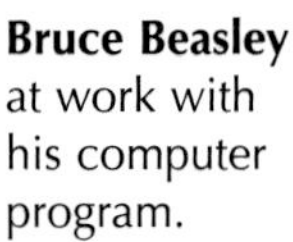

Bruce Beasley at work with his computer program.

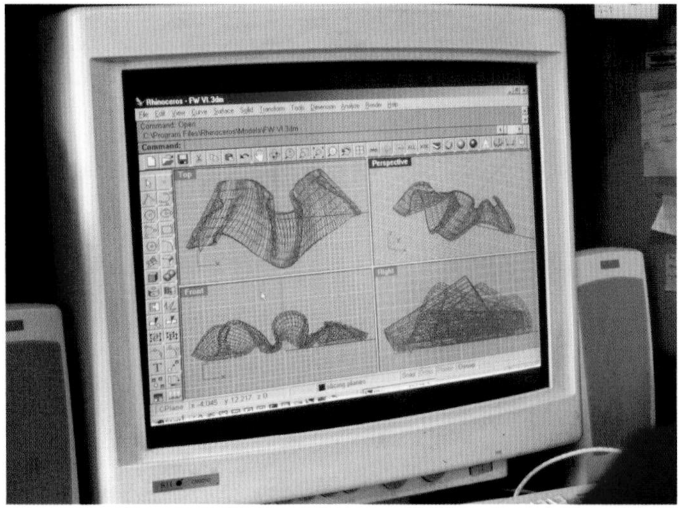

CAD
by Harry McDaniel

A CAD program is used to originate a sculpture.

The sculptor traces the drawings on wood.

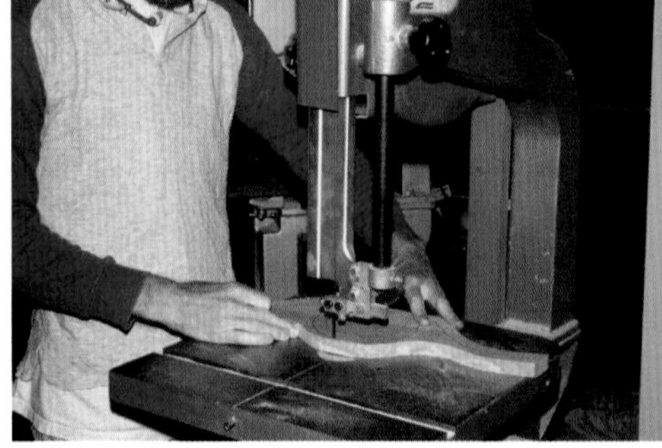

The wood is cut.

Glue and clamps are added to a stacked lamination.

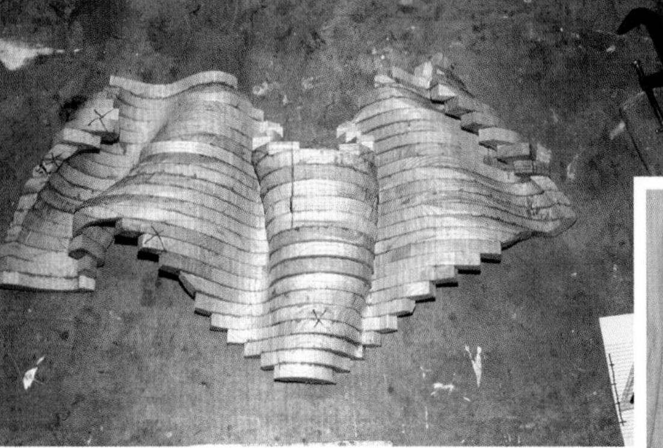

The work is ready to finish.

The sculptor rasps the shape.

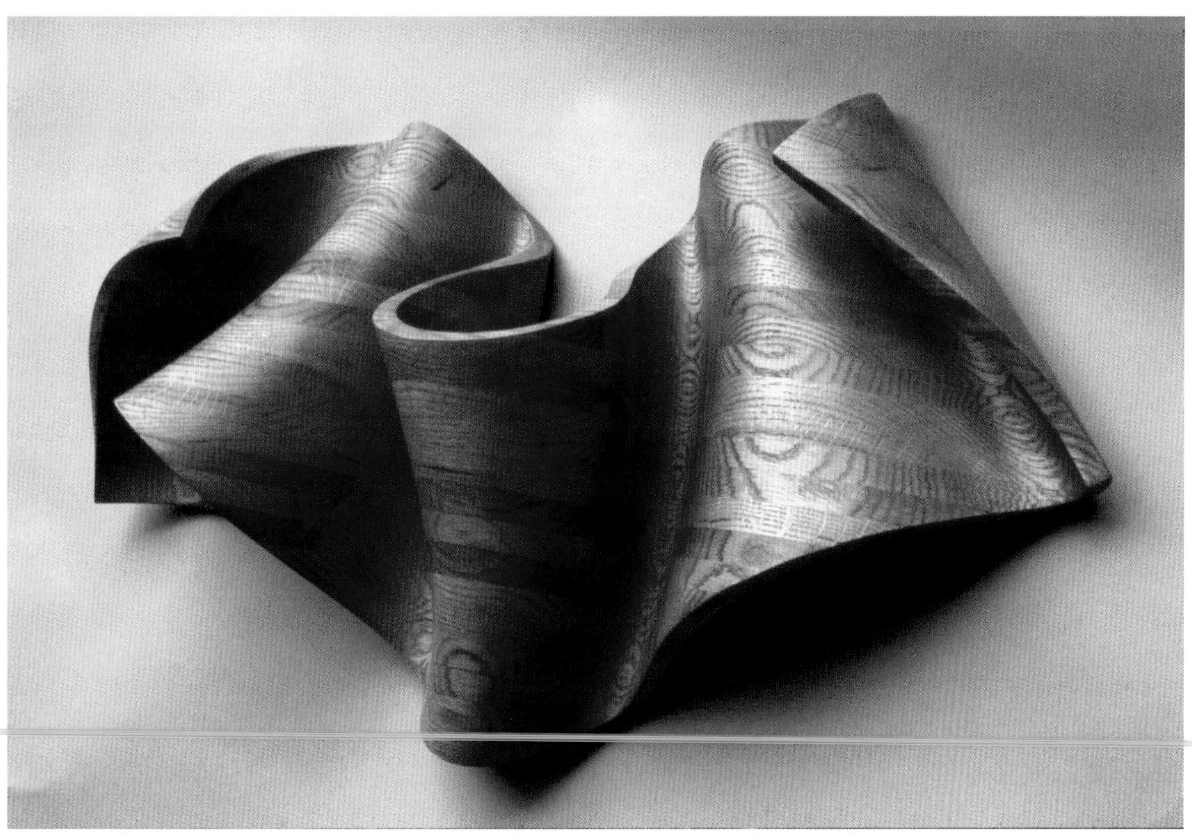

Harry McDaniel, *Folded Wood VI*. Oak, 18″x34″x8″ (45.7cm x 86.4cm x 20.3cm).

Cage A quick system for completing an investment mold. It involves using a container to enclose the wax artwork with the pouring system attached, suspended in the investment mix. The container can be anything from rolled roofing felt to a garbage can lined with metal lathe on all sides and the bottom. The prepared plaster investment is added to the suspended wax artwork to bring the mix to the top of the container where the vents and cup are visible. The system is also called the "basket system." *See* ***Plaster investment***.

Calcareous Chalky, composed of calcium carbonate or limestone.

Calcine Heating a solid substance to a high temperature, but not to the melting point, resulting in a moisture loss and some compound decompositions into a powdery residue. To heat at a controlled temperature in a furnace to purify a substance, cause reduction or oxidation. *See* ***Plaster***.

Caliper A measuring tool with two arm-like jaws held together by a wing nut. It can be opened to the distances that the size permits, then locked in place by tightening the wing nut. The jaws are then placed over the model or work to check the size for sameness. They can be reversed to measure the inside of an object. *See* ***Proportional calipers***.

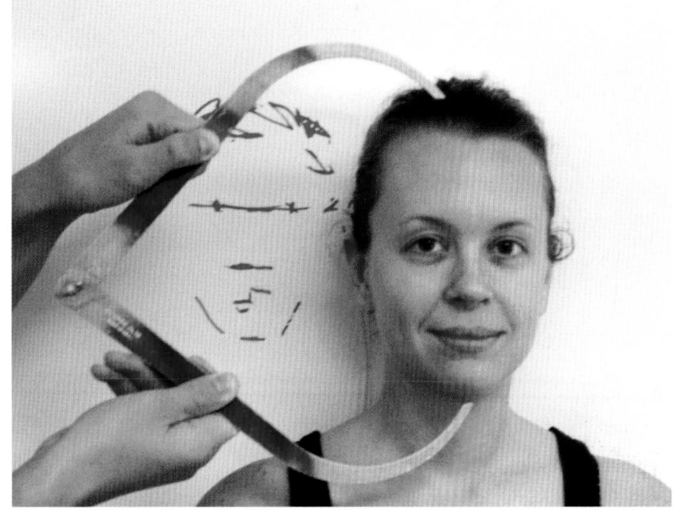

Calipers measuring the model in preparation for a portrait bust.

Cameo A relief carved from a shell, gemstone, etc., leaving a raised design, usually white against a traditionally darker background color. A cameo is usually carved as a medallion with a bust in profile view.

Candeilla wax A wax made from vegetables (weeds) added to other waxes for hardness. *See* ***Wax***.

Cap Smaller parts of piece or waste molds that, when removed, allow the original artwork to be detached and filled with castable materials. *See* ***Molds***.

Capillary action The interaction surfaces of a solid and a liquid that causes the liquid to rise and refashion itself around the solid, resulting in greater cohesion. *See* ***Soldering***.

Carbide An extraordinarily hard metal used in small quantities for tool tips because of its resistance to wear. The metal consists of compacted binary compounds of carbon with heavy metals. It is difficult to sharpen. A tool with a tungsten carbide end/tip brazed into or onto a larger steel part or shaft serves as an abrasive cutting or grinding tool.

Carbon A chemical element found in the majority of clays (especially fireclays) causing them to have a gray color. It is removed in the firing (oxidation), or the clay may bloat or bubble. It is also the partially burnt acetylene gas flame in welding and is visible in dark smoke emitted from an inefficient burnout. *See* ***Oxyacetylene welding; Oxyacetylene cutting***.

Carbon arc (Arcair) A tool designed to use an electrical arc and a carbon rod to cut through metal. A carbon arc rod is placed into the specially designed electrode holder that also has an air line connection into it. Compressed air is directed out around the rod, much like a high pressure air duster through the end of the holder in the direction of the arc rod tip. As the carbon rod heats the metal, the sharp hard air stream blows the melted metal away, leaving a gap slightly larger than the size of the carbon rod.

The air pressure is constant and the off-on air valve is controlled on the electrode handle. The actual air pressure is regulated at the air connection source and adjusted, depending on the size of the carbon rod and arc voltage. Ninety pounds of air will work, but sometimes the manufacturer recommends a different setting. The arc machine does not have to be high capacity unless a larger, heavier carbon rod is used; if so, more power is needed. A carbon arc is relatively inexpensive, assuming that an arc welder and strong air compressor are available. Having an airline moisture trap a short distance from the carbon air is important to ensure that no water is emitted into the cutting area. Since the air moves fast from the compressor and into the electrode handle, moisture builds up at a rapid pace and will periodically be expelled without a moisture trap to collect it. Because of the deafening roar of the air into the hot metal, ear protection is a must, especially if the process is continually repeated. A good welding helmet and strong heat resistant gloves are also necessary.

The carbon arc electrode connection is made by clamping the mainline to the connection on the electrode feed. The ground clamp is placed directly on the work or a ground that the work is resting upon. The air connection goes directly into the electrode. The air is first turned on, full blast, as the electrode is struck to create an arc, much like a regular welding arc.

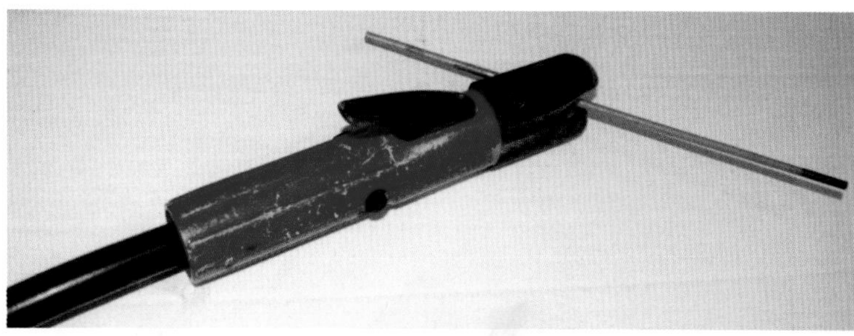

Carbon arc handpiece. Notice the black button trigger on the handle. When depressed, high pressure air is released around the carbon rod.

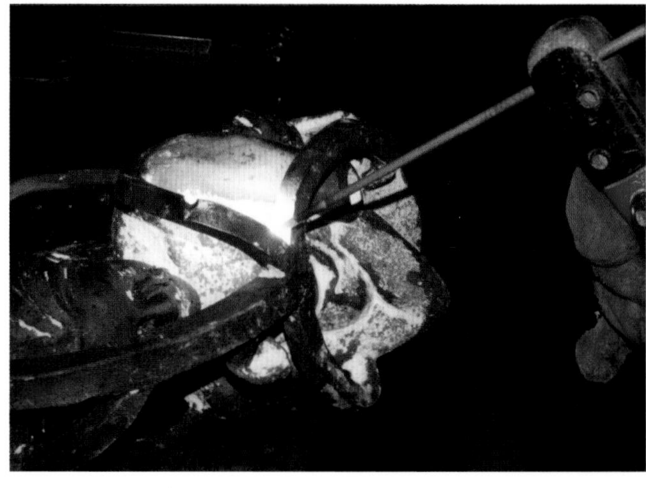
A carbon arc in use.

The carbon arc is ideal for removing the metal pouring system after casting. A small carbon rod is good for small runners, but it is slow or inadequate for larger sprues. Some back and forth movement is necessary for the best cut and any shell or investment left on the mold prevents the arc from cutting or doing a smooth job. The carbon rod will not stick. However, the flying liquid metal tends to coat and almost stick to the clean surface; whereas, a slightly dirty surface or unblasted surface allows easier removal of the splashing molten metal. Caution must be taken so that the direction of the hot blown off metal does not hit another worker or finished bronze, since it can cause severe damage including skin burns and fires on combustible materials. *See* ***Arcair torch***.

The carbon arc can cut or gouge a depression into two adjoining metals to allow a weld to later be added. This is needed when the weld is to be ground smooth or flush with the existing surface. *See* ***Gouger***.

The aftermath of carbon arc cutting on a bronze casting. The metal pouring system has been removed.

Carbon black A pigment created primarily from gas soot. It can be gathered, combined with other chemicals and used as patina material for almost all surfaces of sculpture.

Carbon monoxide A toxic, colorless gas produced from fuel that has not been fully combusted. It is expelled from kiln firings during reduction. It can cause headaches, dizziness and nausea, resulting in a loss of consciousness and even death, due to restricted oxygen to the brain.

Carbon steel Steel with carbon added to improve or increase the hardness. High carbon steel is from .60% to 1.50% carbon, while low carbon is less than .30% carbon.

Carborundum™ Trade name for silicon carbide as it is used for abrasive materials.

Carburize Flame with an excess of gas (acetylene) resulting in dark carbon on metal and excessively floating carbon in the air. *See* ***Oxyacetylene welding; Oxyacetylene cutting***.

Carnauba wax The hardest vegetable wax, manufactured from the waxy leaves of a Brazilian palm tree. Often called Brazil wax, it is used in mixtures with other waxes to increase their hardness. The trademark brand Trewax™, made with carnauba wax, is an excellent colorless polishing wax for many sculpture surfaces.

Carpenter's glue A popular liquid adhesive used by woodworkers primarily to fasten wood products together, though it is useful for many porous materials. It has two compositions, one termed natural and one synthetic. The natural is white and more transparent, while the synthetic is transparent yellow and stronger. *See **Adhesives** (chart); **Paper**.*

Carrara marble A fine, compact grained marble available in a pure white to creamy white color with streaks. It is found in Carrara, Italy. The finest grades appear translucent. *See **Stone** (chart).*

A marble quarry in Carrara, Italy. Photograph: Enzo Torcoletti.

Carriage bolt A bolt with a small square portion just beneath the round-headed top. It is sunk into wood or metal using the square segment to hold the bolt in place and to keep it from rotating as it is being tightened. *See **Fasteners** (chart).*

Carver's drill A power impact drill that both cuts (drills) and impacts at the same time for faster working results in stone.

Carving Method of removing parts of a material (usually wood or stone) to leave or create a form. The material to be carved determines the tools needed. The term is also refers to a carved work. *See **Stone carving**; **Wood carving**.*

Caryatid A female form, usually full figure, that is featured as an architectural support. Atlas is the male figure serving the same purpose. *See **Atlantis**; **Telamon**.*

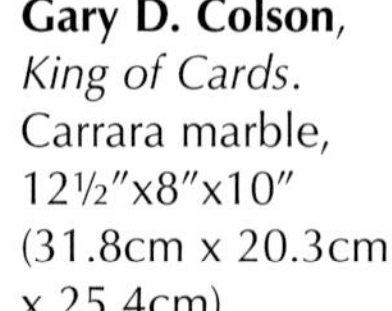

Gary D. Colson, *King of Cards*. Carrara marble, 12½″x8″x10″ (31.8cm x 20.3cm x 25.4cm).

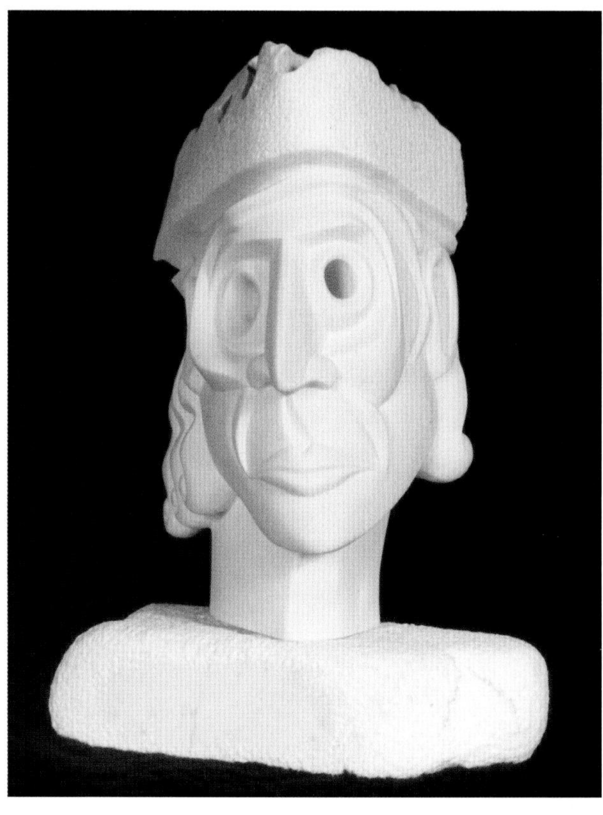

Case hardening Adding surface carbon to mild steel and then tempering it to develop an extremely hard surface. *See **Tempering**.*

Cast Sculpture extracted from a mold. Also, called a casting. *See **Mold**; **Casting**.*

Cast glass Glass that has been cast in a prepared mold to achieve a new form. *See **Glass molding**.*

Casting (in molds) The exact process of reproducing a work of art using a mold or the complete molding process. The final product is also called a casting or cast. *See **Mold making**; **Metal casting**; **Blast furnace**; **Cast**.*

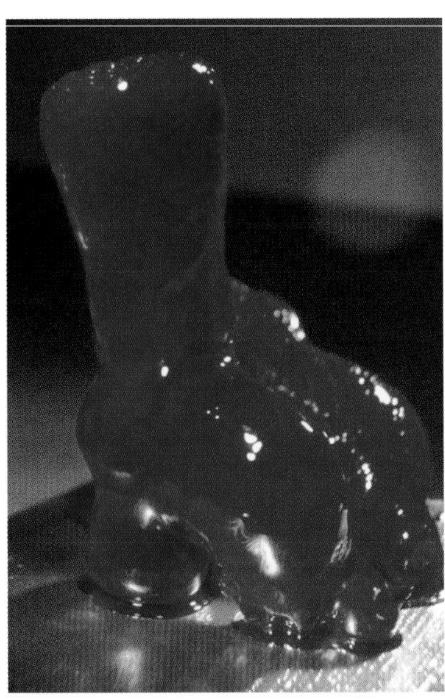

J. Jaia Chen, *Golden Lotus*. Cast lollipop candy and stool, 13″x5″x4″ (33cm x 12.7cm x 10.2cm).

Geoffrey Broderick, *Ceremonial Vessel*. Cast iron, 8"x3½" (20.3cm x 8.87cm).

Gene Koss, *Coulee Wagon*. Cast glass and metal, 4½′x8′x15′ (1.37m x 2.44m x 4.58m).

Casting plaster A plaster (gypsum) product especially designed for plaster casting in molds. U.S. Gypsum has a product with an additive that gathers on the surface as the plaster hardens. It has the qualities of an egg shell surface coating, with a slight sheen. *See* ***Plaster; Plaster*** *(chart).*

Carole A. Feuerman, *Remembrance*. Cast stone (marble), 18″x18″x10″ (45.7cm x 45.7cm x 25.4cm). Photographer: David Finn.

Casting slip A clay mixture with water added producing a smooth, easy, flowing, creamy slip. Ordinarily used with dry plaster molds culminating in a hollow casting. *See* ***Slip***.

Casting stone The aggregate used in cement, concrete, resin, etc., as part of the overall mix. *See* ***Aggregate; Cast stone***.

Cast iron A hard, nonmalleable metal cast from several iron base materials including carbon, silicon, phosphorus and sulfur. The metal is extremely brittle. *See* ***Iron casting; Metals*** *(chart).*

Cast paper Using pulp fibers (paper) to create a form from a mold. *See* ***Paper casting***.

Cast stone A mixture of cement, water and fine aggregate used for casting purposes and art design more so than strength, though it can be as strong as a normal concrete mix.

Commercial cast stone brands are Hydrostone™, Hydracal™, etc. Cast stone is also made with a Portland cement mixture using multi-colored aggregates of various shapes and sizes. All mixtures, once completed with water and cast, create a strong rigid mass that can be shaped and finished by carving, sandblasting, grinding, sanding, polishing or buffing to a high luster. Though frequently duplicating normal stone, that is not necessarily the intention of cast stone. *See* ***Cement; Aggregate***.

Catalyst A substance that produces a reaction when added to other chemicals. *See* ***Resin***.

Catenary arc (curve) The overall kiln design based on the curve created by hanging a flexible chain from two ends apart to equal to the depth (height) desired. Inverted, it produces a strong structure without buttresses. It resembles the arch noticed from a string of pearls loosely hanging around a woman's neck. *See* ***Kiln***.

Cathode The negative pole used in the process of electroplating substances, usually metal. *See* ***Electroplating***.

C-clamps A metal clamp in the shape of a C with a large threaded bolt that by twisting, opens or closes the clamp to release or apply holding pressure to a work. *See* ***Clamp***.

Celsius The metric temperature scale referred to as Centigrade where water freezes at 0°C and water boils at 100°C. This can be converted to the Fahrenheit temperature scale by multiplying the temperature by nine then dividing by five and adding 32. *See* ***Measurement*** *(chart).*

Cement It is defined in two ways: as an adhesive, i.e. glue, or a building material. When used as an adhesive, it serves as a binder or glue to hold two objects or surfaces together. *See **Adhesive** (chart); **Adhesive**.*

CEMENT FORM
by Lynn Olson

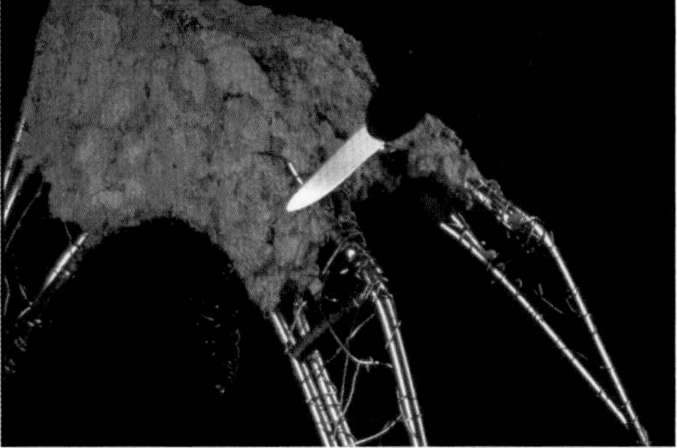

Stainless steel and wood are mixed with cement, silica, latex polymer and superplasticizer. The mixture is pressed in to cover the full armature.

A cement form is created by hand. A stainless steel armature is constructed.

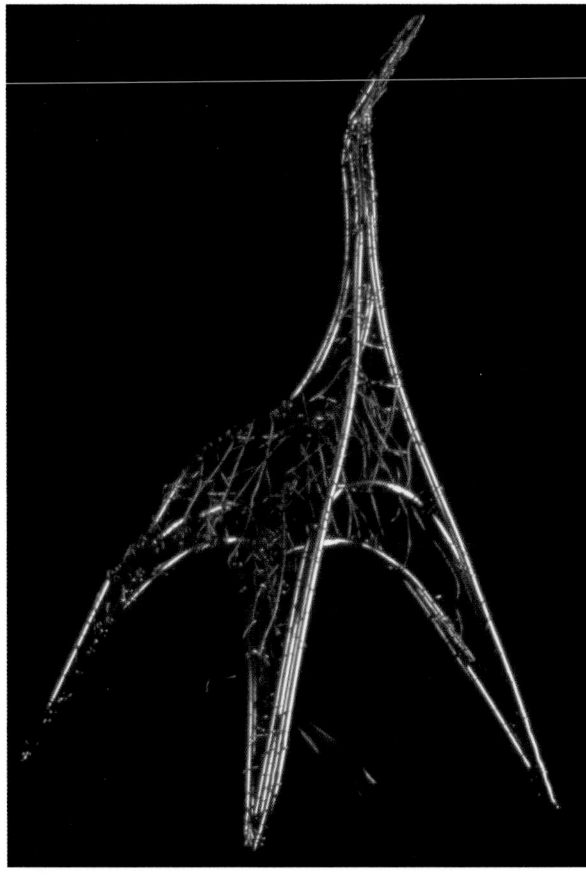

After the cement has set, a rasp trims the form.

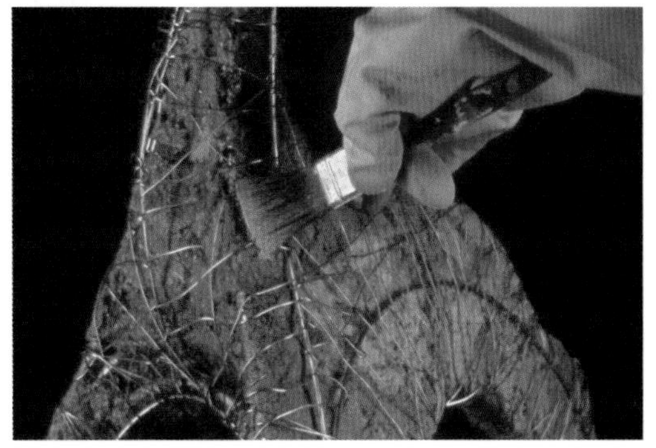

Additional stainless steel reinforcement is added. A latex polymer slurry is brushed on to help the bonding of the next application. More fiber cement is added.

Carbon fibers are mixed with white cement. Pigment is added but not mixed completely. After brushing a Latex polymer on for adhesion, carbon fiber-cement is applied. After setting, the work is once again trimmed with rasps and files.

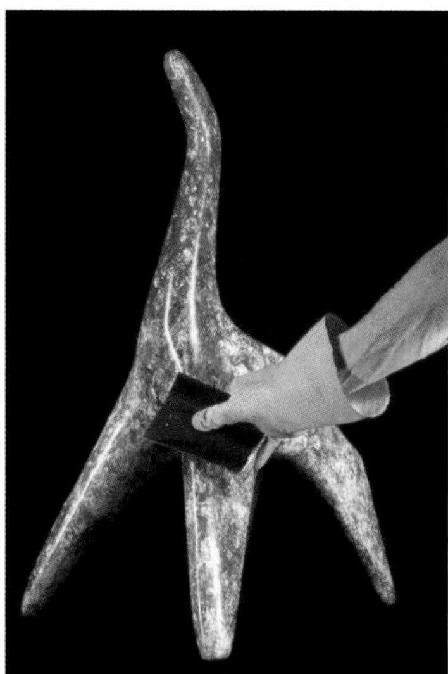

Wet-or-dry sandpapers finish the work. A 220 grit initially smoothes the wetter mix. After days of drying, finer grits to 600 are worked wet to achieve the finish. Two coats of methyl methacrylate are added and buffed.

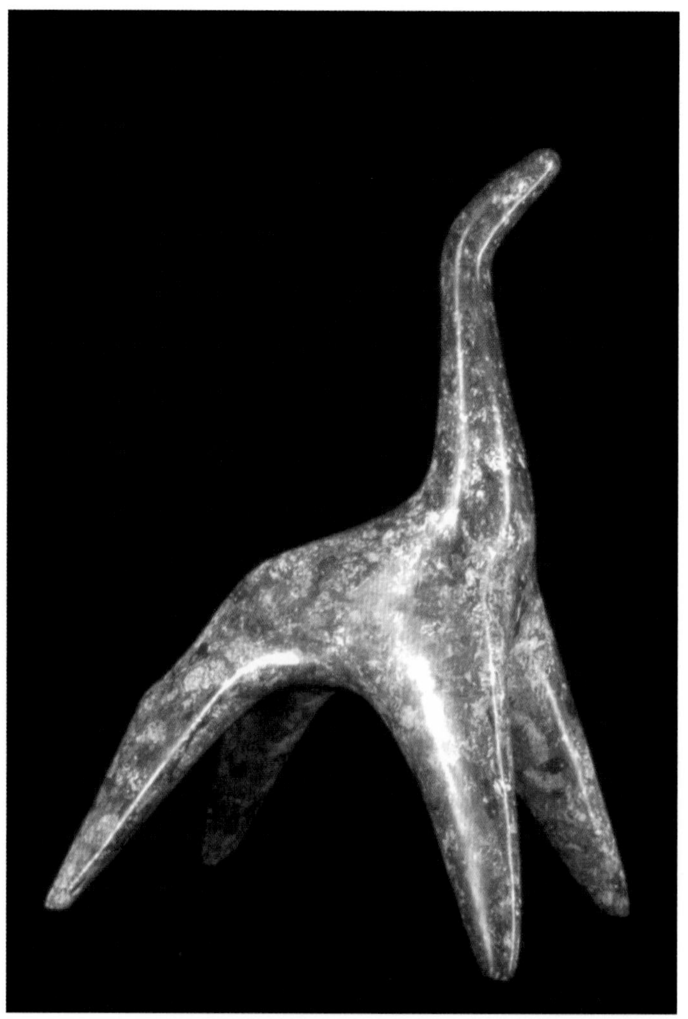

Lynn Olson, *Quadraped*. Hand modeled/armatured cement.

As a building material for sculpture, it is made of lime, silica and alumina sold in large quantities of 100 pound (45.4kg) sacks. It consists of finely ground powdered calcined limestone and clay. It is known as mortar when activated with water and strengthened with sand. It is an extremely durable, hard, building material. The term concrete is used when mixed with larger aggregates and sand. Portland cement is used in a mix as a casting material, though it can be carved and ground.

Cement is frequently prepared to be hand modeled using elementary modeling tools of a firmer, steel variety. Care should be taken when working with cement, as it can cause skin irritation, primarily because of the lime content. Repeated handling can weaken the skin, causing bleeding. Wear gloves and do not breathe the dust. Eyes can be damaged with wet or dry particles.

Cement will harden in sink drains, since it sets under water. Any residue or spill into a drain should be thoroughly flushed with running water for a long time to disperse the mix. Dry cement should be stored in a sealed container away from moisture.

Cements have three important time factors to consider:

1) **Setting speed** The time it takes to become settled, solid, but not necessarily rigid or with strength.

2) **Hardening speed** The interval of time necessary to acquire a rigid state of strength that can be handled and inflexible.

3) **Curing speed** The amount of time required to reach full strength for maximum use.

For sculptural uses, cement is not always used with building sand. For artistic purposes, many different substances for effect and/or strength are added. These include fiberglass, fibers from materials such as nylon or carbon or fine metal fibers from steel, bronze or wood. Marble dust or powders and other forms of silica can add a glisten to the final casting. To add extra design, objects such as stones, gems, glass or metal can be set into the surface while the cement is curing or placed into a mold. Sand itself may be replaced with ground marble or marble dust. *See **Concrete; Aggregate; Portland cement**.*

Aaron Royal Mosley, *Saint Me*. Cast bronze and cement on steel mesh, 14″x24″x54″ (35.6cm x 61cm x 137.2cm.)

Jodi Endicott, *What's Next*. Steel armature for cement.

Jodi Endicott, *What's Next*. Concrete, steel, ceramics, mesh, bronze; handbuilt of composite concrete with fiberglass and Vermiculite layered over the armature.

Center punch Resembling a chisel, though with a round sharp tip. The punch is struck to create a small center indentation as a starting location for a drill hole or other designation on metals.

Centigrade (C°) A metric measurement from 0 degrees freezing temperature to 100 degrees boiling. *See **Fahrenheit; Measurement** (chart).*

Centimeter (cm) One hundredth of a meter in the metric measuring system. *See **Measurement** (chart).*

Centrifugal casting A metal casting technique using the lost wax method by placing the mold on the end of a device with a wound-up center spring. The metal is poured into the center as the device springs, resulting in a centrifugal force filling every crevice of the mold. Because of the force involved, the process is used for small sculpture or jewelry.

Ceramic change The metamorphosis from usable clay to a permanent clay. Prior to the change, the clay can be reused. Afterwards, the clay is an inflexible substance; it is no longer a plastic material. *See* ***Clay***.

CERAMIC SHELL

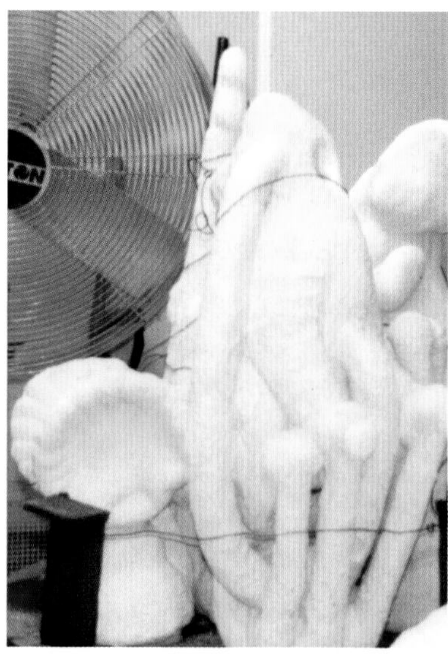

Dried ceramic shell ready for burnout.

The shell, covering the pouring cup, is removed with a thin disk grinder.

Burned-out, dewaxed shell molds ready for liquid bronze.

Shell molds (in pre-warmer) are filled with bronze.

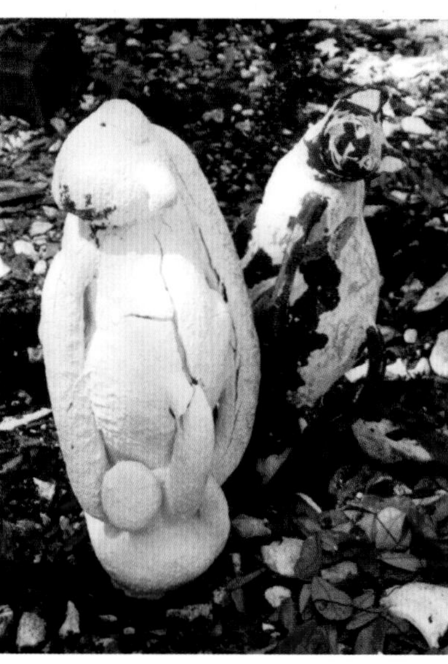

Shell molds are allowed to cool for divesting. The shell gradually fractures during this time.

Ceramics Clay items that are shaped and then fired at a high temperature to undergo ceramic change. This includes earthenware, tile, porcelain, terra cotta, etc.; items com posed of non-metallic minerals. The term is also used when a more academic/fine arts designation for clay work is sought. Pottery is the more limiting term applying only to functional items. *See* ***Pottery; Coil method; Slab; Wheel-throwing; Press-molding; Firing.***

Ceramic shell A hardened liquid slurry or refractory coating. In a liquid state, it is placed over a wax work to dry, hardened into a shell, and is then heated to create a heat resistant metal casting mold. The materials are normally associated with ceramics, though they are used for metal casting molds. They include silicas and a form of sodium silicate with most of the sodium removed.

The new binder is colloidal silica, a semi-transparent liquid with millions of microscopic particles that remain in suspension. By combining various sizes of refractory powders, a strong heat resistant mold material is produced with little thermal expansion, resulting in minimal or no distortion, even in large molds. The liquid ceramic material is called slurry, while the hard, or baked ceramic slurry is called shell. There are several manufacturers producing these materials, since the ceramic shell is one of the premier processes for precision casting of aircraft parts, as well as other industrial uses. *See* ***Metal casting; Colloidal silica; Slurry; Divest.***

Ceramic shell has many advantages over other mold systems for metal casting. Since the surface coating is finer and harder than other mold materials, the sculpture supports greater detail. The final mold is stronger and more rigid, producing a mold that is usually imperfection free. The pouring system is simpler since fewer runners are required and often the work can be top gated. Hollow castings can be created by coating the inner and outer surface at the same time with the same materials; thus, a core is seldom needed. The mold has a quick burnout time and can be easily repaired if a defect appears. Also, once the mold has been de-waxed, the mold can be reheated and stored indefinitely (away from moisture).

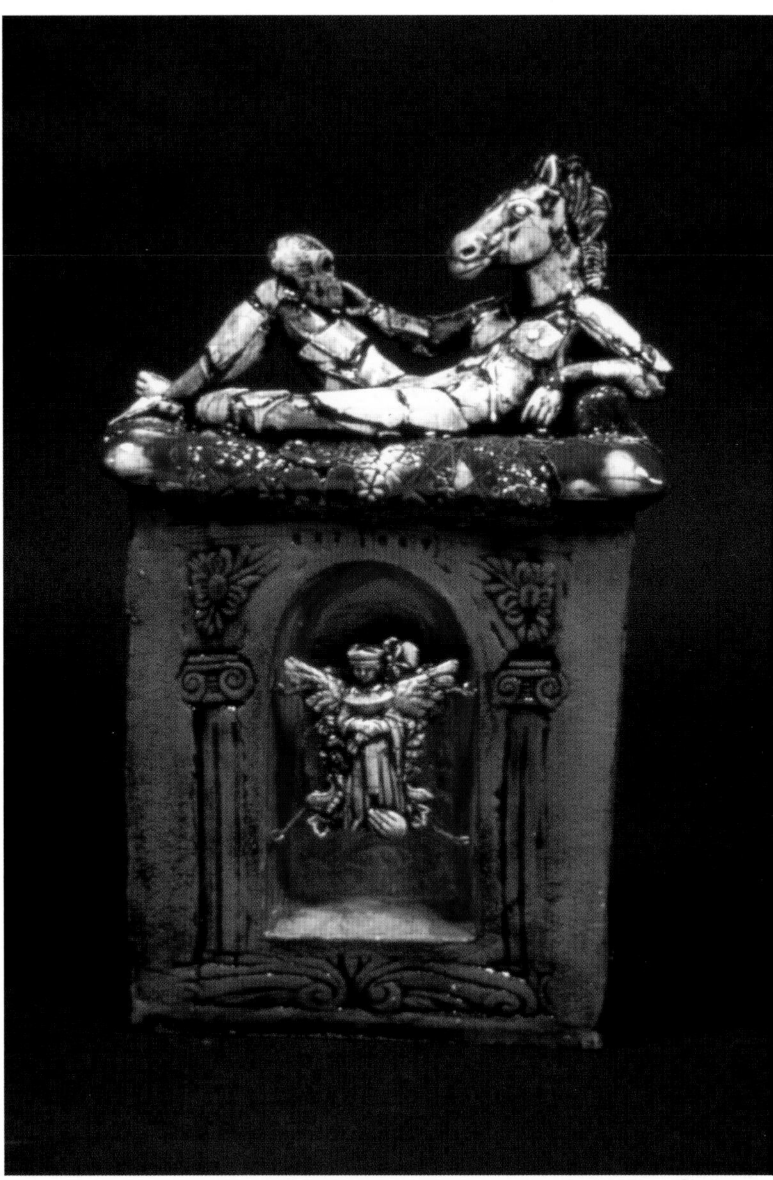

Cora Moczygemba, *Vanitas 2.* Ceramic, metal, wire, 16″x10″x4″ (40.6cm x 25.4cm x 10.2cm).

While the substance itself is not lightweight, the resulting mold is light due to its thinness and reduced size. For example: ceramic shell mold, as compared to a plaster investment mold, prepared for the same amount of liquid metal is approximately 15 times lighter in weight. It is easier to situate for metal pouring. It can be cast in a propped up position other than being packed in sand. Finishing a ceramic shell casting is quicker, since the surface is superior and there are fewer runners, sprues and vents to remove. *See* ***Slurry investing; Plaster investment; Burnout furnace.***

CFM Cubit foot per minute. A measure of air volume. It is associated with air compressors. *See* ***Air compressor; Air tools.***

Chainsaw A handheld portable saw powered by gasoline or electricity. It has a long continuous blade in a band form with chain-like links. The teeth are primarily used for cutting green wood, trees and logs in felling trees, and sawing or shaping logs for sculptural purposes. The gasoline models are the strongest and largest. However, the electrical models can be used indoors, creating a shape close to the desired finished sculptural form. Some sculptors have modified the saws for creating finished sculptures that are rough when compared to more traditional carvings. The saw, for example, is used for carving ice sculptures. *See **Ice sculpture**.*

CHAINSAW SCULPTURE
by Don Etue

A large log roughed out with a chainsaw.

The form progresses using only a chainsaw.

The final form with spear added.

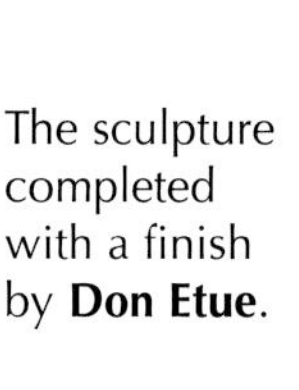

The sculpture completed with a finish by **Don Etue**.

Chalk Calcium carbonate, soft limestone, used as a marking tool.

Chamfer To bevel or to angle an edge.

Chamotte Another name for grog, a refractory clay that has been fired and then ground for use in clay bodies. *See* ***Grog***.

Charge Process of adding metal into a melting chamber or crucible for metal casting. It is also the term for adding other substances to a container, such as adding glass (cullet or batch) into a glass melting furnace. *See* ***Metal casting***.

Chasing (chase) The technique of completing the surface of a casting, usually a metal casting. Chasing begins after divesting the casting, but with the removal of the metal pouring system. The process may involve chiseling, sawing, grinding, sanding or polishing to obtain the surface quality that the sculptor desires. It involves removing mold seams, flashing, defects or flaws in the metal surface and core pins. It is also the term for the creating designs in metal work by hammering in a design. A hard faced punch or carbide tipped tool is struck with a hammer to determine the depth and angle of the engraved design.

Technique for metal castings

Once the mold material is dislodged, the hard metal sprues, runners and vents need to be removed by chisels, hack saws, metal grinders with abrasive cutting disks, handheld reciprocating saws, band saws, bolt cutters, plasma cutters or carbon arc. Each of these methods serves different needs of size, shape or economics. However, the most efficient in speed and ease is the carbon arc, sometimes known as the gouging whip. By the combined use of an arc welder and compressed air, the metal is heated and blown out of the cutting path. *See* ***Carbon arc***.

Brian McEneny uses a chainsaw to carve a large sculpture.

Though some foundries use plasma cutters, they are not very efficient for removing the metal pouring system, especially any large metal runner or sprue. Plasma cutters are designed for smooth, flat, thin metal cuts, *not* thick angular rods that are difficult to get to. They use expensive cutting tips and nozzles that need to be constantly replaced. *See* ***Plasma cutter***.

Chasing tools are individual to the person using them. Chasing punches, also called matting tools, are designed for a specific mark or design upon the sculpture. Professional chasers have carefully sorted punches for the size and shape of work. These punches literally stamp the shape into the surface. Simple tools, like tempered concrete nails, are shaped for unusual textures. Metal chisels are often sharpened to remove flashings and other unwanted metal. Hammers vary and some are used for direct blows to the metal in chasing. Hand sanding is usually required with wet or dry sandpaper. Wire brushes help blend the surface. Files, rasps and even hacksaw blades can serve the purpose. *See* ***Matting***.

Die grinders with carbide bits are commonly used for chasing. The higher the RPM, the smoother the cut, especially if it is combined with a fine tooth bit. Grinder chasing can save many hours of chiseling with a hammer and cold chisel. The most widespread commercial grinder available from local hardware or tool shops usually runs between 20,000 and 25,000 rpm and is designed to house a one-fourth inch (0.635cm) shaft bit. Using these grinders for flap wheels and sanding heads expedites chasing. Smaller, almost pencil-size 60,000 rpm or more, grinders with one-eighth inch (0.318cm) shank and fine toothed bits are excellent for fine detail. *See* ***Die grinder***.

A hammer and chisel are the most universally used chasing tools.

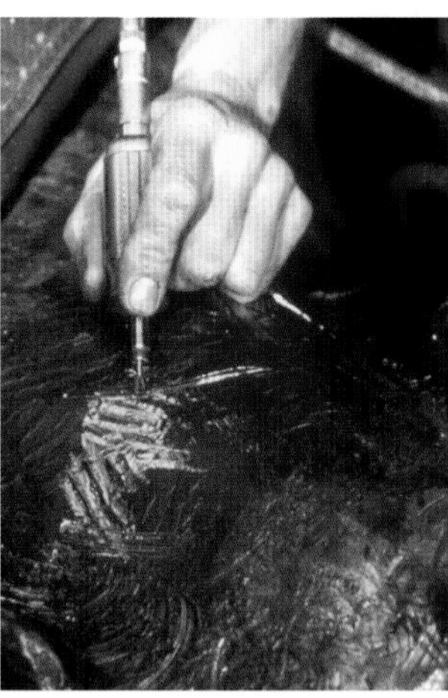

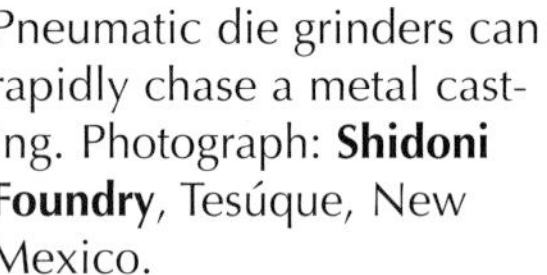

Pneumatic die grinders can rapidly chase a metal casting. Photograph: **Shidoni Foundry**, Tesúque, New Mexico.

Chatter mark Undesirable tool marks usually in a series (chattering). The marks are the result of tool misuse, cutting too deep or failing to complete the finish.

Checking (check) Perceivable stress and handling cracks; cracks or splitting in wood from the drying process. Rapid moisture loss intensifies the checking, while slow drying can thwart the process.

Cherry red The color of a metal when the correct temperature has been reached to forge metal. The term is also used to designate mold, glass and furnace heat. The temperature varies depending upon the surface but is associated with about 1375°F (746°C). *See* ***Welding***.

Cherry wood A hard, reddish wood from a fruit tree. *See* ***Wood*** *(chart)*.

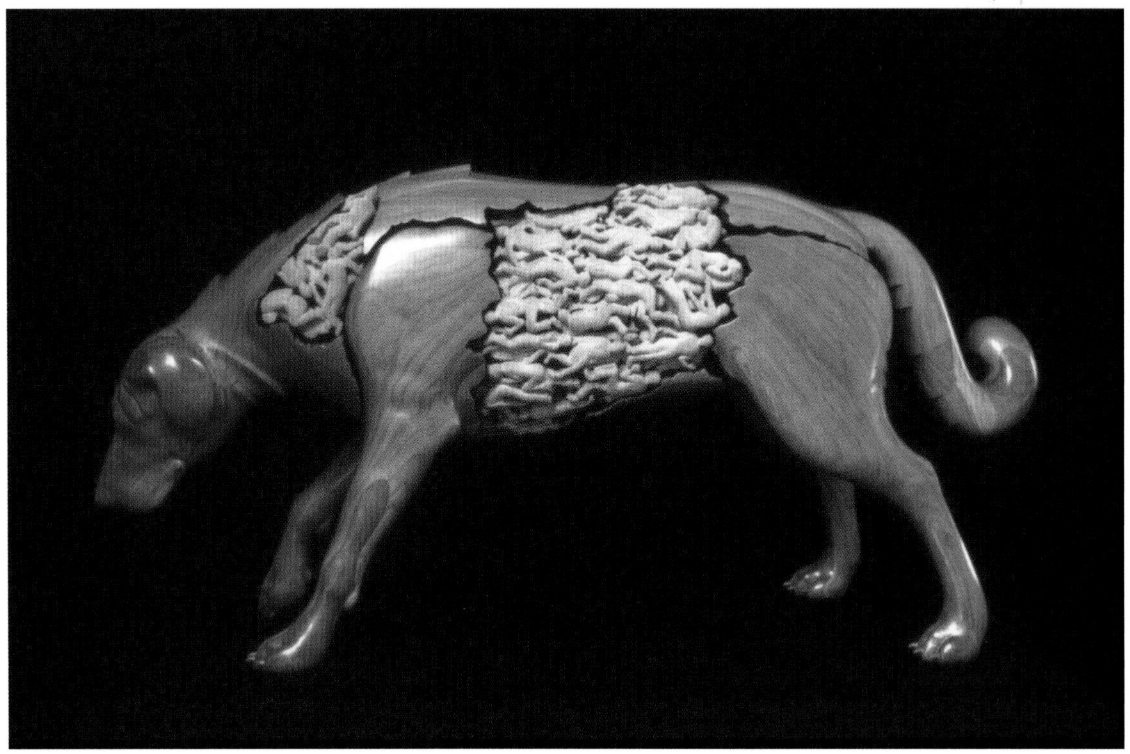

James Mellick, *Witness*. Cherry, white sand flocking, 24″x52″x21″ (61cm x 132.1cm x 53.3cm).

Cherub (or putto) A nude infant that is rather plump and large. A cherub is often pictured with wings and sometimes called Cupid.

Chill lines Layers or lines about a metal casting that resemble bath tub rings. They are caused in several ways: the metal is poured at too cold of a temperature, an irregular pouring technique, not enough sprues and runners or a poorly designed metal pouring system that does not allow an even filling of the mold. The metal is connected, even with chill lines.

Chill marks Marks (depressions) or cracks resulting from gloves, cold tools, etc., that remain on glass as it cools (chills).

China clay Kaolin, a hydrated aluminum silica known for its whiteness, especially good for making porcelain. *See* ***Porcelain***.

Chip carving The use of carving tools without mallets or hammers. The tools are called palm grip, because they fit in the palm of the hand, though small knives or pocket knives are also used.

Chisel Steel stone carving tools in the shape of a short rod with a cutting edge specifically shaped, tempered and sharpened for carving on one end. A mallet (hammer) strikes on top of the handle end. Chisels are designed specifically for wood, stone, metal, etc. *See* ***Wood carving; Stone carving***.

Chopsaw A wood cutting miter saw or metal cutting saw of a similar configuration. It has a motorized circular saw blade mounted over a base where the saw or base can be adjusted for different angles of cuts.

A chopsaw cuts steel.

Chrome (chromium) Metallic element used for electroplating metals to obtain an intense, bright silver shine and corrosion resistance. Chromium is also used in metal alloys. Care must be taken when oxyacetylene cutting with chrome metals, since the chrome coating burns back away from the heat. However, they are minimally affected by plasma cutter cuts. *See* ***Plasma cutter***.

Chromium oxide An oxide used to achieve bright greens. *See* ***Patina; Patina*** *(chart)*.

Chryseleplantine Sculpture made of ivory and gold, generally figurative.

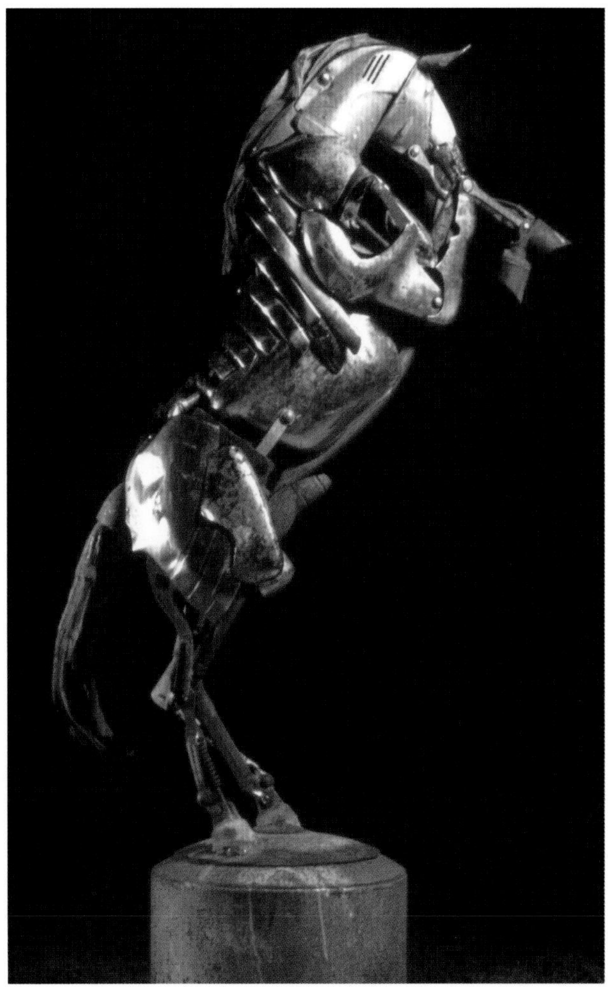

Bruce Larsen, *Rearing Horse*. Mixed media including metal with chrome, 24″x90″x36″ (61cm x 228.6cm x 91.4cm).

Chuck Clamping end of a tool that holds the cutting bit, such as a drill chuck. It may also be a reusable round form centered on a turntable or wheelhead to hold a round ceramic form for trimming. *See **Drill press**; **Collet***.

A chuck key tightens a chuck.

Ciment fondu An aluminous cement combined with sand used for cement work. When blended with fiberglass, it is used for tough, hard hollow castings of relative light weight. *See **Aluminum cement***.

Cirè perdu French term meaning "lost wax" casting by using heat resistant mold investment to achieve a metal casting. *See **Lost wax casting**; **Metal casting***.

CLAMPS

Clamp A device or configuration to hold objects in place while working with the object.

Left to right: pipe, bar, C-clamp, quick grip, spring, hardwood hand screw.

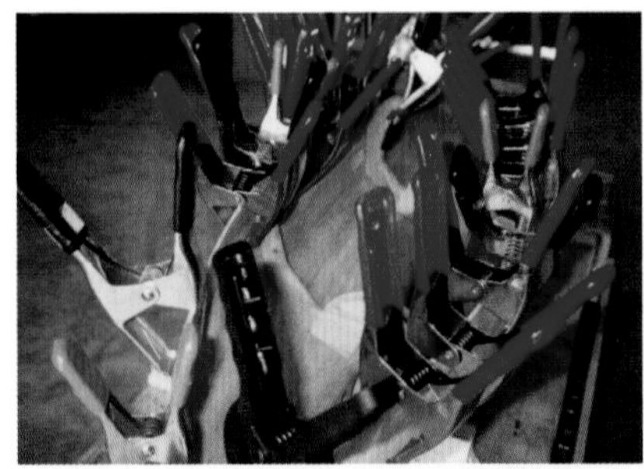

Spring clamps present quick tension and easy release. Photographer: Michael J. Cooper.

Bar (glue clamps) holding wood tightly as the glue sets. Photographer: Michael J. Cooper

Pipe clamps can be obtained in any length necessary to complete a work. Photographer: Michael J. Cooper.

Classical Art relating to the Hellenistic period, ancient Roman and Grecian art or the suggestion of the periods in the artwork.

Claw A carpenter's hammer with a head that has a striking end with the reverse end in the shape of a forked claw. It is used for pulling nails and sometimes a pry bar.

Clay (oil-based or modeling) A modeling substance that is completely plastic and reusable designed for sculptural use. When warmed or heated, it is soft as compared to a less pliable cold medium. It is composed of earth clay, oil, wax and grease mixed and heated to form the body. A typical formula for homemade clay proportions would be about ten pounds (4.54kg) of fine clay (ball clay), four pounds (1.82kg) of microcrystaline wax (common modeling wax), one pound (0.454kg) of non-fibered grease and one quart single weight motor oil (30kg). Heating the wax, grease and oil to a complete liquid state, the clay is added, stirred until smooth, then poured out onto plastic sheets. Varying the contents can create a more firm clay (add more earth clay) or soften (add more oil). *See **Armature**; **Portrait**; **Modeling clay**.*

Greg Polutanovich, *Neanderthal Man*. Cast bronze, 12″x18″x10″ (30.5cm x 45.7cm x 25.4cm).

Clay model for *Neanderthal Man* by **Greg Polutanovich**.

Clay (water-based or ceramic) Hydrated silicate of aluminum. A decomposed feldspathic rock substance made of earth materials. A mixture of earth substances (clay) designed for the plastic arts. When moist, it is plastic; when dry, it is brittle or powdery; when fired, it is permanent. Clay is used for ceramics or sculpture and sculpture modeling. The abundance of clay has made it one of the primary sculpture materials used throughout the centuries. Because of the permanency of the fired clay, shards or fragments of fired clay remain after more than 8,000 years of use.

Clays used in formulating bodies are taken from kaolin, a pure white high firing clay; ball clay, a clay used because of its plasticity or slippery smoothness; fire clay, for its capacity to withstand extremely high heat; stoneware, for its heat ability and color possibilities; earthenware clays, known for color variations brought about by the iron content; and bentonite, known for extreme plasticity. It is not difficult to find clay formulas. A mechanical clay mixer is needed to secure the best results. However, many clays are readily available mixed and pre-packaged from commercial suppliers. *See* ***Slab; Coil method; Pinching; Hollow out; Kiln; Firing.***

Dennis Amrhein, *Canteen, Bag, and Hat*. Clay, stain, glaze, life-size. Photographer: Robert Grosskreutz.

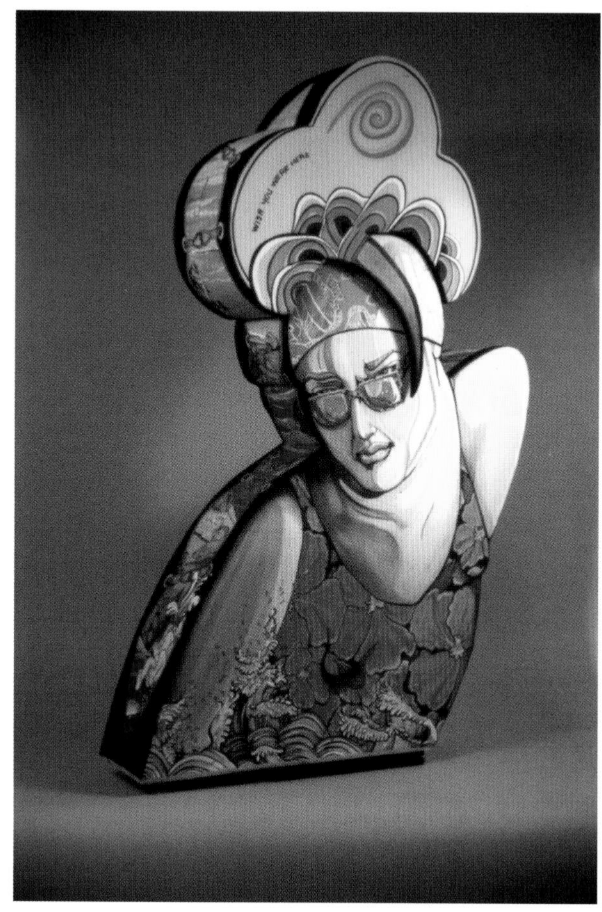

Jean Cappadonna-Nichols, *Postcard with El Niño and the Quick and the Dead.* White earthenware, underglazes, paint, 46″x31″x10½″ (11.8cm x 78.7cm x 26.7cm).

Patz Fowle models *Here Comes the Neighborhood.* Clay.

Patz Fowle, *Cool Cruising – Corvette.* Stoneware, 11½"x8"x6" (29.2cm x 20.3cm x 15.2cm).

Clay additives Materials added into the clay mix to achieve specific working or finished products. These include grog (the most common), fiberglass, nylon and other burnout additives, such as sawdust, vermiculite or sand.

Grog is a fired ground clay included in the clay body to provide strength when working with the moist clay and also during the firing. It aids in clay drying and reduces shrinkage. As an embedded substance, it creates a unique texture. *See **Grog**.*

Fiberglass is used to strengthen the body in a wet, working state. Only a small amount can be used and then not for wheel-thrown sculpture or hand formed bodies, since it can easily cause cuts. It does melt and become part of the clay body during high firings.

Nylon can add sturdiness to wet clay bodies. Also, it burns out in the firing leaving little effect, except for any surface area that may be encountered.

Sawdust, **vermiculite**, etc., completely burn out leaving small pours that the contracting clay partially displaces. The value of these burnout additives is for decoration and reduced breaks during the firing.

Bentonite is added for plasticity to the clay body. It is used in small proportions.

Clay body The mixture of earth clays and other ingredients to form a clay for a specific purpose, such as smoothness for wheel throwing, strength for sculpture, color, etc. *See **Clay** (water-based); **Terra cotta**; **Stoneware**; **Earthenware**; **Porcelain**.*

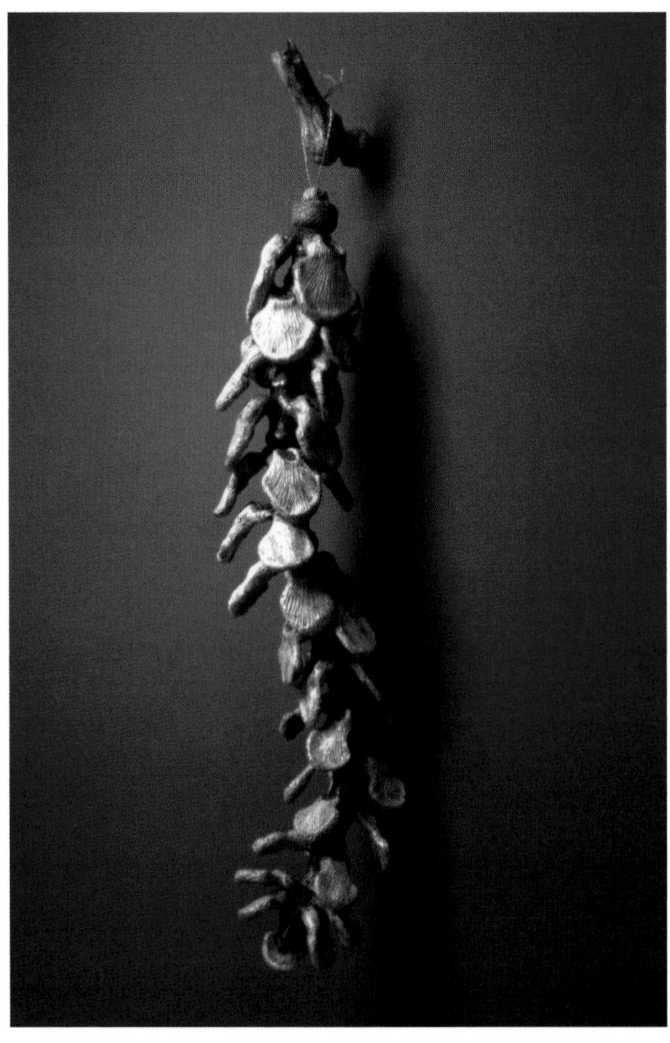

Debbie De Spain, *First Trimester*. Low fireclay, 30″x5″x6½″ (76.2cm x 12.7cm x 16.5cm).

Clay fence A parting substance made of modeling or moist clay that is used to separate parts of a mold. Designed like a thin fence, it must be removed prior to completing other sections of the mold. *See **Shims**; **Molds**; **Waste mold**; **Piece mold**; **Flexible mold**.*

Clay water A thin, runny composition of water and clay that is applied to surfaces as a separating agent in making molds. It is commonly used on plaster.

Clean-up tools Specifically designed tools that are used to scrape flashings and seams from molded works, particularly slip castings.

Clinker Limestone and clay that has been pounded into small stones with about 50% of the water removed by using a rotating kiln. It is used for Portland cement after it has been finely ground. Also, it is the term used for the fused residue remaining after the fuel coke has been thoroughly burnt. *See **Portland cement**; **Coke**.*

Cloisonné Surface adornment that consists of thin strips of metal that are fired on a surface as an outline of enamel paste. It is used both on metal and ceramic surfaces being fused in a kiln.

CMC Cold molding compounds. *See **Paper**; **Molds**.*

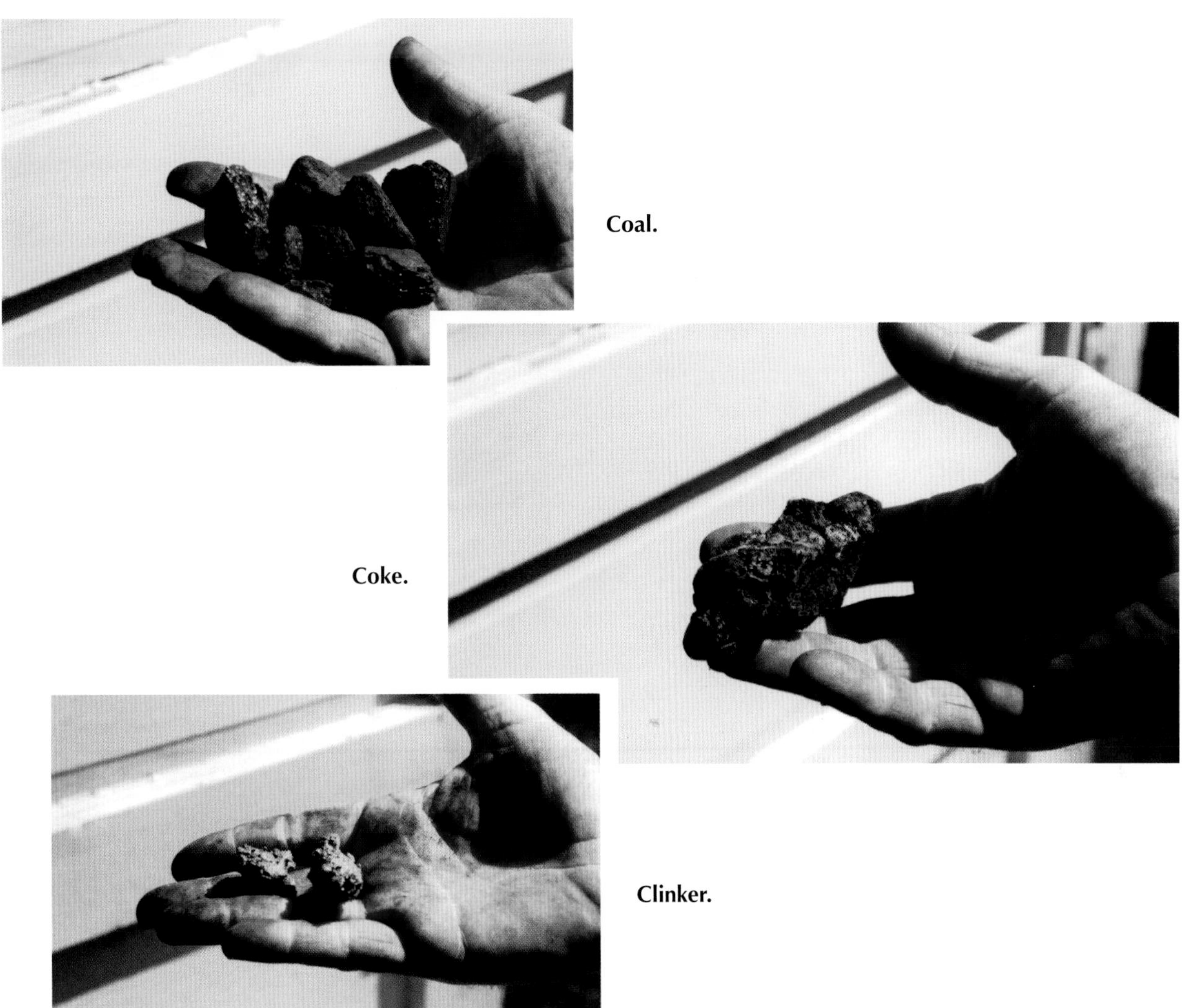
Coal.

Coke.

Clinker.

Coal A fuel formed from fossilized plants in a hard graphite-like rock form. It is known by its dark brown or black color and its ability to combust. *See* ***Coke***.

Coating Covering one material with another. The outer layer, such as a paint coat(ing) or metal coat(ing). Coatings provide strength, protection, color or a combination of these.

Cobalt (oxide) The most potent staining oxide to achieve a deep blue hue. The oxide is from a combination of oxygen and cobalt found in metal ore.

Coil method Process of creating a form using ceramic clay. Coils are rolled out by hand then incised (scratched) with slip added. The coils are mounted on top of each other to build up a shape. They are pinched together or smoothed out to leave a surface not usually reminiscent of coils. Sometimes they are paddled together with a small anvil (stone or wood stick) to form a solid wall. The size of coils depends on the size of the form to be created. It is used for round forms, especially pot shaped forms, and in primitive societies for smaller works, though the final works seldom reveal the coils. The size of a coil sculpture can be increased by allowing the lower coils to slightly dry as the upper coils are added. *See* ***Slab****;* ***Pinch****;* ***Hollow out****;* ***Kiln****;* ***Firing****;* ***Clay*** *(water-based);* ***Ceramics***.

Coin To fashion (strike) a flat circular piece of metal into money. *See* ***Relief***.

Coke A solid lightweight carbon fuel left after volatile elements from coal have distilled (burnt off). It is used for forging and iron casting. *See* ***Iron (casting)****;* ***Clinker****;* ***Coal***.

Cold cast Casting not done with heat added. The use of resins or gypsum cements to simulate another product, such as stone or bronze. Marketed as "cold cast bronze," for example, the public may be misled to believe that they have purchased a bronze casting. *See* ***Bonded bronze***.

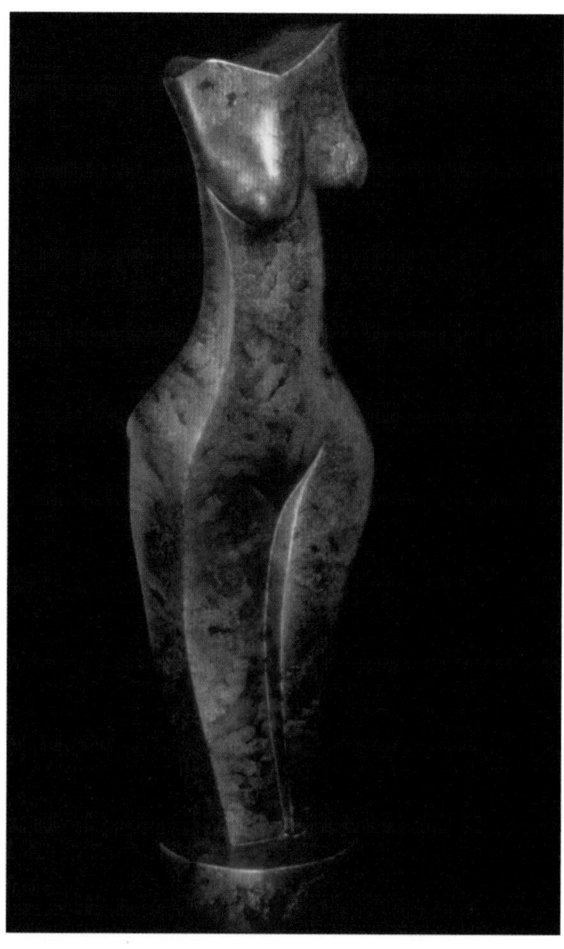

Joseph Rotella, *Roma*. Cold cast resin, 49″x12″ (124.5cm x 30.5cm).

Cold cathode light Often interchangeable with the term neon. It is a thin glass tube filled with neon (helium or argon) with an electrical current passing through, resulting in a bright light. It is regularly displayed and called neon light for business concerns. *See* ***Neon***.

Cold chisel A hardened, handheld tool in the shape of a rod, usually with a flat edge on the working end. It is tempered for working on cold metals that are struck with a metal hammer. *See* ***Chisel***.

Cold cracks Known as hot tears, demonstrated by ragged, broken or pulled apart edges in a metal casting. They are cracks caused by shrinkage. If the pouring temperature is too hot, it contracts more as it cools, causing the metal to pull apart. Also, if the metal, such as aluminum, is poured into a strong rigid mold material, such as normal ceramic shell or a hard unyielding core material, the metal will crack as it tends to shrink about undercuts in the mold. A poor quality of metal can also cause the problem. *See* ***Hot tears***.

Cold glass Glass that is precast and normally worked cold. This includes cutting, filing, etc. Although it can be heated, such as glass tubing and rods (cane), it does not lose its basic configuration; nor require annealing. *See* ***Glass***.

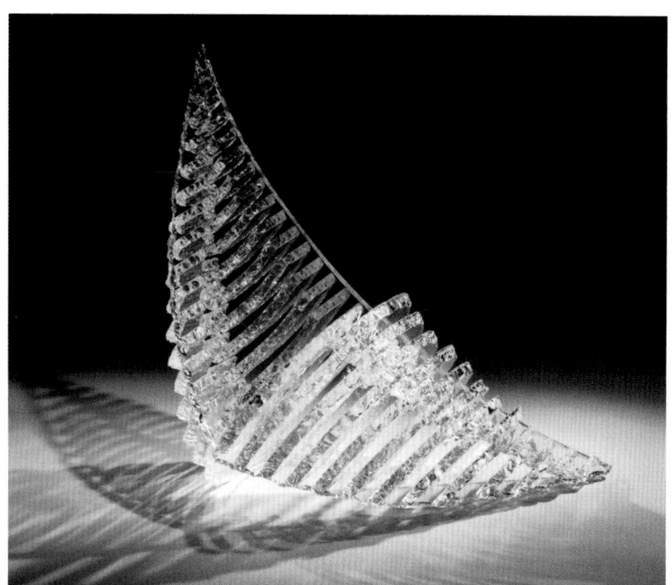

Henry B. Richardson, *Temporal Refraction*. Glass, 28″x24″x16″ (70.1cm x 61cm x 40.6cm).

Thomas H. Sayre, *World Wall*. Stainless steel, glass beads, 7500 square foot ($675m^2$) with 1.1 million marbles.

World Wall detail.

Gundi Viviani-Finch, *Natador Vessel*. Stacked plate glass, stained glass, 28″x14″x14″ (71.1cm x 35.6cm x 35.6cm). Photographer: Michel Proulx.

Cold pour Pouring metal with the lowest liquid temperature that will not freeze up to secure a quick firming. It is desirable for solid castings, because the metal will not shrink as much. The term is also used for casting materials that do not require heat or catalyst to promote the casting. *See **Cold cast**.*

Cold shut Two layers of metal that do not connect and are seen as a hairline crack on the metal's surface. It is caused by two streams of metal flowing into the mold that do not bond or fuse together, because of imperfectly placed runners, either in distance, height or isolated area. It can be avoided by a better metal pouring system design, increasing the mold temperature prior to pouring, and, possibly, increasing the metal's temperature for the pour.

Cold skinning (cold shot) Premature freezing of metal in smaller portions or thin surfaces that do not adhere to the total form's surface. It is the result of a poor runner system or inconsistent pouring in which the metal hits the cooler surface rapidly and splashes before filling.

Coldwork Working on annealed or cold glass, such as polishing, grinding, etc. *See **Engraving**.*

Two wrenches are required to tighten a collet.

Collaboration The process of constructing a sculpture with different artists involved. Each one contributes to complete the work.

Collet A quick release wrench tightened mechanism on the end of a die grinder used to hold bits or shafted tools. It is similar to a drill chuck, but designed for specific sizes. The term applies to other tools with the same mechanism. *See **Grinder; Chuck**.*

Colloidal (silica) Disjointed particles that remain in suspension within a liquid. The primary use is in a metal casting mold mix called slurry. *See **Slurry; Ceramic shell**.*

Colossal Sculpture that is greater than life-size. *See **Enlarging**.*

Commemorative (sculpture) Created in honor of a historical event or a person. *See **Medallion**.*

Commercial Artwork or an artist dealing with art in commerce. The creative or fine artist is sometimes incorrectly separated from the term. However, any art that is purchased or sold becomes commercial and that includes fine art of value. Art that is not bought or sold is usually for personal or therapeutic purposes and does not necessarily involve exhibition, profit or livelihood as the motive.

Commission Artwork that has been specifically selected in advance of creation. Sometimes the selection is made because of the artist's reputation; sometimes it is designated for a model or a certain type of artwork, design or location regardless of the artist.

Common wood Lumber classification designating some defects, being less than a select grade. *See **Lumber**.*

Compass A simple mechanism to draw circles. In an inverted "V" arrangement, the compass comprises a sharp point on one end (leg) anchored into the object being drawn upon with the other end (leg) holding a pencil or marking tools as it moves around, encircling the anchored leg.

Compound Combining two or more ingredients to form a new substance.

Concept model A model designed to present an idea for sculpture. It is not a finished work, is usually small, and is open to change or redesigning. *See* ***Mode; Maquette***.

Conceptual art Art in which the technique, skill, beauty, media or form is inconsequential to the idea or concept being presented. Materials can be any media, from steel to projected images. Substances do not have to be permanent. The creative act itself is of greater importance than the final product and often relies heavily on verbal explanation or on an understanding of the social or political context of the day. Sometimes called performance art, it is not traditional art. *See* ***Performance art***.

Dale Newkirk, *Meditations*. Cloth, dye, photo projection, steel, 7'x22'x6' (2.14m. x 6.72m. x 1.83m.)

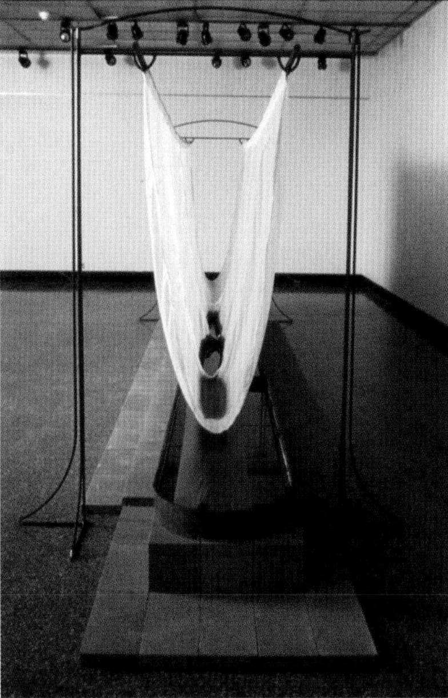

Meditations, additional view.

Concrete The combination of sand and hard aggregates, such as pebbles, stones, gravel, crushed marble, granite and metals, with a binder of cement, mixed with water that forms a strong hard mass. In industry, it is considered a basic construction material that is not always finished or exposed for visual purposes. Though it can be a construction material in sculpture, the finished product is prudently chosen more for visual appearance than for strength. In industry, concrete contains steel reinforcement, cement, sand for the smallest aggregate, and incremental grades of gravel and stones. It is important for strength that the sizes fill all voids in the final mixture. *See* ***Cement***.

CONCRETE
by Barbara Grygutis

Common Ground in progress.

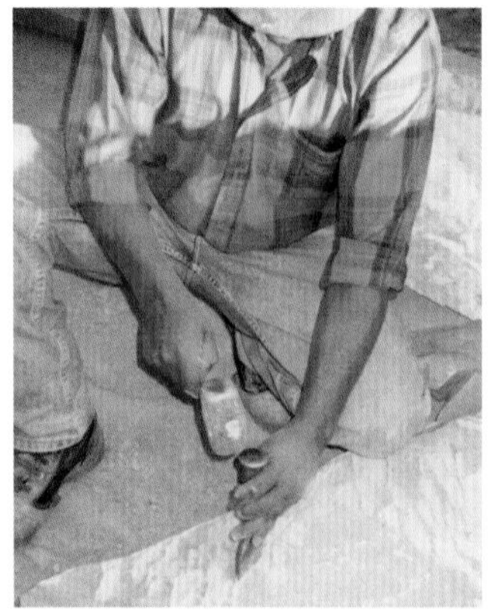

Stone mason shapes stones for *Common Ground,* Rock and Co. Construction. Photographer: Eddy Schuyler .

Barbara Grygutis, *Common Ground.* Stone and concrete, 18′x200′x50′ (5.49m x 61m x 15.25m). Gates Family Foundation. Photographer: Tim Fuller.

Technique

Mixing concrete properly is essential. Small batches can be dry mixed by hand while large mixes need to be carefully measured, especially if colorful aggregates and color pigments are used. Unlike plaster, water is added to the dry mix until the right amount is obtained. However, too much water results in a syrupy liquid with little strength, while too little water results in a flawed air infested structure. Small concrete sculptures can be hand-mixed with sand alone or a small aggregate. Hand mixing is easily accomplished with a trowel for small amounts.

For large works, a commercially premixed bag of concrete is available that needs only adding the recommended portion of water. These can easily be mixed in a wheelbarrow or in a mixing box. However, large mixes become tedious and may need to be poured rapidly. Renting a portable concrete mixer can solve many problems. For the very large work, a commercial mixture can be delivered by the yard (0.91m) in a concrete mixing truck (transit mix). If labor is figured in and tons (kilograms) of concrete are needed, transit mixes are the least expensive. If special aggregate is required, the commercial company can accommodate this and make further suggestions. *See* ***Yard***.

Mixes vary, but a good rule is to visually confirm the desired amount and size of aggregate from the dry mix in a small, clear plastic or glass container. If there is too much space between the large aggregates, then more small aggregates should be added. If more space is desired around the larger pieces, then more large aggregate needs to be added. Air pockets should not be present. The mix should tightly fill the space. Ideally, there should be an equal part of small, medium and large aggregate for strength. *See* ***Aggregate***.

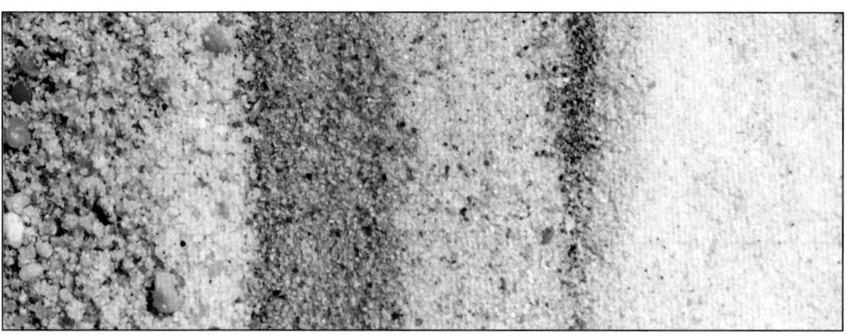

Concrete aggregates. Left to right: normal cement sand, mortar sand, fine white sand.

The mix of concrete depends on the size of the aggregate. The sculptor should avoid mixing aggregates with sieve sizes smaller than the cement. When aggregates measure the same as the cement sieve, then the mix should not exceed one to one (1:1). As the size of the aggregate gets larger, the concrete mixes actually decrease, because less is needed to coat it. Concrete mixes vary, but for non-critical mixes, one part cement to seven parts mixed aggregate is used. More structurally critical work may require a one to five (1:5) mix, and finer aggregates require additional cement in proportion to the aggregate.

Water should be added sparingly, depending on the amount of cement used. If too much water is used, the cement will literally be washed off the aggregates resulting in little adhesion and a weak structure. The mix itself should not be a runny liquid. If more water is added, cement has to increase proportionally to avoid a weak mix. It takes approximately six gallons (22.71L) of water for each 94 pound (42.7kg) sack of cement. Wet sand or aggregates will decrease the water needed.

Two good tests for the correct water proportion hand mixed concrete are the **hand test** and the **cup test**. 1) **The hand** test is the simplest for small amounts: Take an amount of concrete about the mass of a golf ball and with one squeeze compress the mass into a lump. If the concrete is correctly mixed, the lump will stay together in the compressed shape. If it sloughs or sags, it is too watery to stay in place. More mix is then needed. If it readily retains the shape but has a tendency to crumble or has a dry rough surface, then it needs more water. 2) **The cup** test requires a paper or plastic drinking cup. It is filled with the concrete mix and then inverted on a flat surface. If the mix is correct, it will stay in place with an ever-so-slight slump. If it is too dry, it will show surface air pockets or tend to crack; more water is needed. If it is too wet, it will slump and sometimes collapse. When adding water, it only takes a small amount at this stage to completely change the characteristics of the mix.

Additives include accelerators and retarders. Accelerators speed the setting time of concrete. Hot water is a natural accelerator. Calcium chloride in small amounts of no more than two pounds (907.2g) per 100 pounds (45.4kg) of dry cement can be added. Retarders allow the sculptor to work longer with the concrete since the setting time of the mix is slowed, preventing the rigid stage from taking effect as soon. Too much retarder could result in a mix not properly setting or becoming too weak.

Concrete cup tests. Left to right: too much water, adequate mix for casting, correct for working.

Concrete Molds

Using concrete as a castable material is common in sculpture. The most significant decision is the choice of mold material. **Styrofoam™** is a good mold material for concrete. Not only can it be used as a negative modeling material, but it can also be used as an interior or hump molding material, one that concrete can be hand laid up on. **Wood**, especially strong plywood, is good mold material for angular, geometric shapes; however, the wood needs to be thick enough not to warp, or it needs reinforcement to prevent warpage. A release agent, such as motor oil, needs to thoroughly saturate the wood prior to the pour to prevent the moisture from being drawn out of the concrete and for easier mold removal with less chipping or cracking. Wood forms can be removed once the concrete is hardened over a period of days. It is a mistake to remove it too soon, especially if the concrete is part of a large structure or over an expanse of space.

Sand molds can be used for a wetter mix of concrete. The mold needs to be moist and well packed. The sand will adhere to the surface unless a plastic covering is placed over it to pour the concrete on.

There are different ways to prepare a **plaster mold** for concrete. The primary consideration is the plaster mold for dryness. For dry plaster molds, a shellac is applied two or more times to ensure that the surface is sealed. Afterwards, a separator of motor oil is needed. Oils (separators) that are as clear as possible should be used to prevent staining. Coat the shellacked molds with a petroleum jelly. For damp plaster molds, a surface separator must be applied directly. Petroleum jelly is a good choice. Any severance or loss of separator that allows the plaster mold to touch the concrete will cause a moisture drain in the concrete, resulting in a different surface quality or sometimes a cracked powdery concrete. *See* ***Release agents*** *(chart).*

Prior to filling the plaster mold with concrete, the mold should soak in water before and after a separator has been applied. A generous amount of separator is applied. Reinforcement rods or wires are inserted as needed. The mold is fit together and securely tied and anchored on a surface. The mold needs a tight fit to keep the thin cement mix and water from draining off the aggregate, leaving a powdery weak mix.

Wire ties should be used to hold the mold together, so it cannot come apart during the casting. The mold must either be upright and self-supporting or tied in a way that will allow vibration to the mold without falling over. A uniquely designed mold may fill with a heavy weight that could change the balance of the mold, resulting in a tipped mold. Concrete is heavy. It will easily fracture a weak or poorly supported mold.

A vibrator can be used to eliminate the air pockets, though it can cause a weak mold to collapse as the cement settles. The vibrator helps to distribute the finer mixture into all areas of the mix and mold, for a superior surface. A ready vibrator (if the

Pouring concrete forms for **Barbara Grygutis**' *Four Rooms on Siringo.*

sculptor is also a stone carver) is an air hammer running at full capacity while touching the surface of the mold. If the mold is weak or not bound with a strong wire, it may break or fall apart; it is nearly impossible to repair one without washing it out and starting over. If the mold is to be thoroughly vibrated, it must be sealed to avoid leaks. Good vibration will allow a finer polish in the end. *See* ***Vibrator***.

Concrete can be poured into a mold, one bucket at a time, but the mix needs to be placed together or in a continuous setting to avoid layers of aggregate or a possible change in mix density or color. To compact the concrete, the fill needs to be tamped by forcing a thick rod into the mix when possible where it will not affect the mold. Packing can be done when the pour opening is large enough.

The mix will begin to set. The process must not be interrupted. While the mix may harden in a short period of two or more hours, the humidity and temperature play a great role in setting time. It should not be allowed to dry too fast. Covering the mix with a wet fabric and keeping it out of direct sunlight helps. Water should periodically be added to the surface and the mold, keeping it in a soaking state until the cast is removed. But, while plaster sets under water, it should not be poured in the rain because of mix properties and loss of strength. Concrete does not set well in cold weather. Freezing weather will result in an unusable mix or a fractured casting with no strength.

In 24 hours, the cast is set but not strong and not cured. After three days, the mold can be removed. In hot, arid climates, the mix will begin to set within minutes, so the sculptor has less time to work once it has been poured.

Barbara Grygutis, *Four Rooms on Siringo*. Stone, concrete, earth, landscape materials, 7'x30'x15' (2.14m x 9.15m x 4.58m). Park for City of Santa Fe, New Mexico, City of Santa Fe Arts Commission. Photographer: Christopher Harrington.

One way to decrease the setting time is by using cold water in the mix. It will continue to cure for more than 28 days, constantly gaining strength. It becomes stronger as it ages. Portland cement is about two and a half times as strong after 28 days of curing as compared to only three days after pouring. To prevent cracking and ensure good tempering, the set mix should remain wet or damp for the first month as it hardens. Repairs need to be made immediately after the mold is removed. Green concrete will still take repairs with less notice, especially if some of the original dry mix is available. It is good to saturate the repair surface and to use a commercial bonding agent. Depending on the surface quality desired, commercial sealers are designed specifically for concrete to retain smooth or glossy finishes.

Lay-up of concrete is practiced when the interior of the mold is open enough to be reached by hand and where a hollow form is desired, especially to cut down on the weight of the sculpture. The mold is prepared in the same manner, but concrete/cement mix is slightly drier, so that it can be padded into the form. The added benefit is that a reinforcement can be added for strength.

Modeling concrete mixes do not ordinarily contain large aggregate. They can be built up in thinner layers, allowing some setting time between each layer. However, cracking during any of these layers will result in a weak structure. The thinner modeling cement should be kept damp or covered with wet materials for the curing time.

A mortar mix or concrete does not model well without some sort of additive. A small amount of fireclay added to the mix will improve the plasticity, enabling the cement to be troweled and worked. However, it must be kept damp during the curing process to avoid the cracks caused by the fireclay prematurely hardening. (Fireclay shrinks as it hardens.) Plaster up to 50% can be added for a quicker set. The plaster will set in about 30 minutes while the concrete will continue to harden as normal. The final mix is concrete with plaster as an aggregate; it is not of maximum strength, but it is as waterproof as the plaster aggregate will allow.

Sculptors sometimes model over an armature. Size dictates the type of armature needed. Almost any armature used for plaster can be used for small scale concrete works. However, larger scale works require greater support. Metal lathe is a common reinforcement material used on an armature for applying cement and concrete. It anchors directly to the armature and is close to the inner surface. Modeling starts from the lowest parts and moves upward because of the weight and the looseness of the material. It will slump if it is not well applied into the armature. Effloresce will result if a surface application has been applied over a wet form, resulting in unsightly blemishes. *See* ***Effloresce***.

USE OF REBAR IN CONCRETE

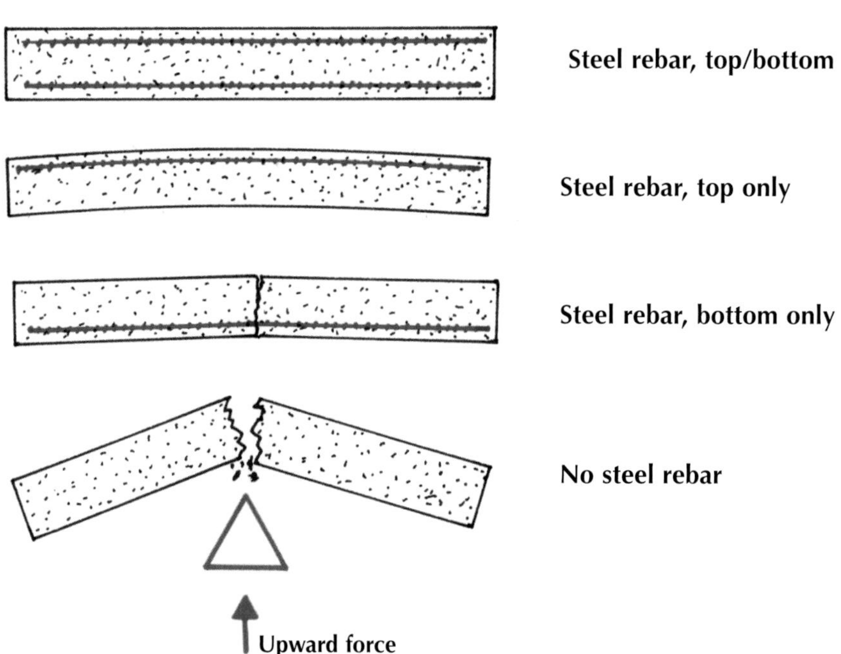

Reinforced concrete has interior steel rebar for additional strength, especially in construction. Wire mesh rebar is a good reinforcement, since concrete is not known for tensile strength. The reinforcement should be near the surface, in most cases, since the surface is under the greatest stress. Steel placed into a concrete mix greatly improves the ability of the concrete to hold together during stress. Steel stays in place, because the concrete shrinks around it, forming a tight grip. (Rebar has raised ridges to help hold the concrete in place.) Since the expansion and contraction rate are so similar, they form a good union.

Normally, the steel should not be coated with anything that will separate it from the concrete, since steel completely immersed or covered in concrete does not have a corrosion problem. However, if the steel protrudes out of the concrete or is exposed, then the steel rusts into the concrete, causing the concrete to weaken. Some sculptors use stainless steel at or near the surface to prevent this problem. A number of evenly spaced rods are stronger than one large steel rod. Some metals, such as bronze, brass or copper, slow the setting process of cement but seem to have no other effect on it. Lead will loosen in concrete. Aluminum will not only corrode, but it expands much more than steel when it is stressed. Fibers, such as fiberglass, can be added for strength, especially with finer aggregate mixes. If the sculptor does not want them to show, then an open mold can be coated with the mix having an inset layer of fiberglass. *See* ***Rebar***.

Stress on concrete is a force being placed on it. Temperature can cause stress, as the concrete heats and cools at different times from the outside to the inside of a large piece of sculpture. If the inside is warm and the outside rapidly cools, the work can crack, especially if a thin slurry coat is on the outside surface that cools and contracts faster than the inner core. As a result, the outside layer can flake off.

Normal **post-tension** and **pre-tension** allow additional flexibility and strength for thinner works or works for greater spans/expanse. Pre-stressed concrete is poured into a mold that contains steel reinforcement and then compressed to gain strength. It is especially useful for bridges or other construction that requires extended amounts of concrete. Tensile means to pull apart. Compression is to push together. Shearing is to sever. Pre-stress means prior. Post-stress means after pre-tension; post-tensioned.

There are different finishes for dry concrete. Stains and pigments can penetrate the concrete to permanently bond the color into the form. While concrete will take paint when cured, it will have to be repeated as often as any other painted product. Hardeners can be added directly into the mix or afterwards to help waterproof the surface and avoid a surface freeze. Concrete may be left as is when it emerges from the mold. It will remain unfinished and untreated to retain the natural color and texture of the material.

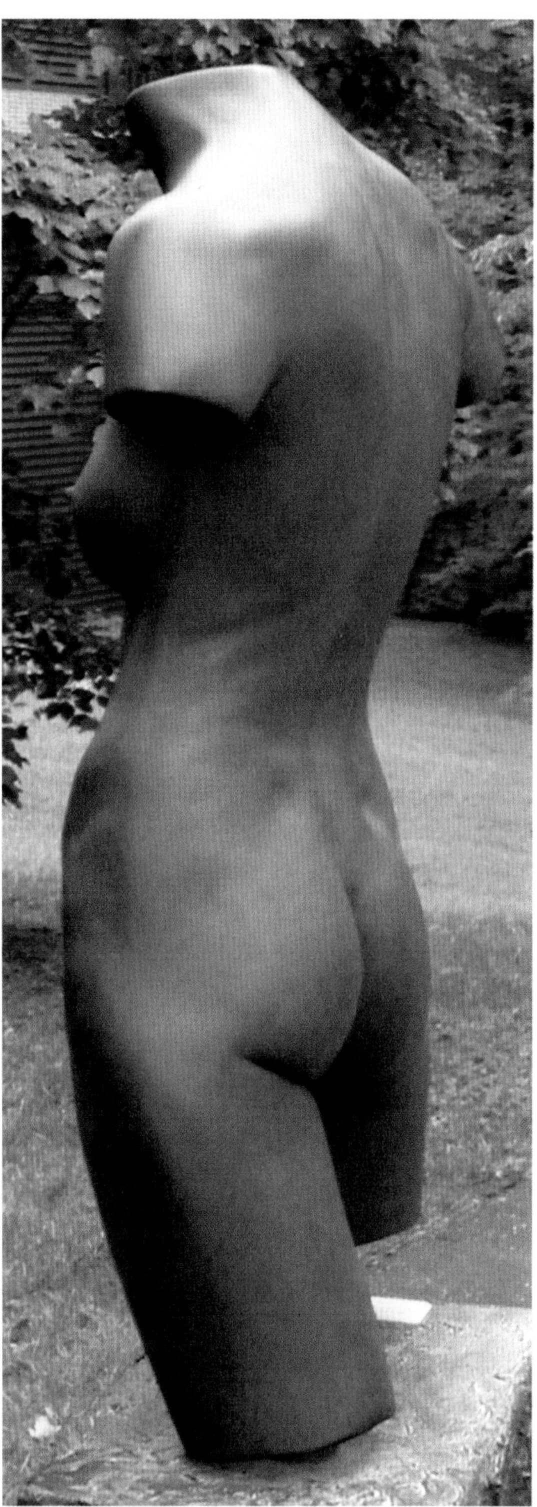

George E. Adamy, *Karen*. Polyadam concrete system, life-size casting, 36″x16″x9″ (91.4cm x 40.6cm x 22.9cm). This is only 5/8″ (1.59cm) thick.

Joe Muench, *Journeyman.* Fabricated and welded steel, concrete, 6"x6"x18" (15.2cm x 15.2cm x 45.7cm).

Concrete bit A carbide tipped metal bit for hard concrete or stone surfaces used to drill holes or shape the hardened substance.

Conduit (pipe) A lightweight aluminum pipe used to hold and protect electrical wire. It is used for sculptural purposes because of its rigidity and light weight, especially in large mold making. *See* ***Molds***.

Cone (gas) A flame that is cone shaped. It is the flame closest to the orifice tip of a torch, usually an oxyacetylene torch. *See* ***Oxyacetylene*** *(cutting).*

Cone (glass) A glass that has been stretched out to take the form of a rod of glass.

Cone (pyrometric) Disposable, small, extended triangular, heat measuring device for ceramic kilns. *See* ***Pyrometric cone***.

Connectors Devices used to join two objects, specifically pneumatic air joints on air lines to air tools or to connect two air hoses. The term is also used for a connector that electrical wire is inserted into and twisted to safely cradle and make tight electrical joints. *See* ***Coupler***.

Conservation The attempt to keep and restore artwork in the original state. Sometimes a simple cleaning is all that is required. However, if major conservation work is completed, the viewer needs to be aware of restoration conditions.

Construction Three-dimensional artwork made of raw materials placed into a final form. In contrast, assemblage is a form of construction using found materials, rather than raw (construction) materials if they should change the original artwork in any way. *See* ***Assemblage; Mixed media***.

Contact cement An adhesive that is deposited on both surfaces to be bonded to form a firm union on contact. It is initially flexible but hardens into a strong bonding agent as it cures. During curing, it can be highly flammable and toxic, depending on the manufactured form. *See* ***Adhesive*** *(chart);* ***Papier machè; Formica***™.

Content The important thought or idea of an artwork. The essence of the sculpture. The subject is a way of demonstrating content, while form is its package, and technique is the process of placing it all together. If successful, the content provides an aesthetic, even spiritual, sensation.

Continuos duty cycle A machine that can run continuously without damaging itself. *See* ***Duty cycle***.

Contract A formal binding agreement between two or more parties (people). A sculptor may have a contract with a buyer when a commission is being arranged. There can be pages of legal description or possibly a simple letter stating what is expected from both parties. Among the contents should be a reference to a model or drawing, size, material, delivery date, installation procedure and payment schedule. It is wise to seek advice when in doubt or confronted with a legal document.

Contrapposto A relaxed balanced pose of the human body. The majority of the weight is on one leg, and the hips are twisted in a direction different from the head and shoulders. The result is a gentle S-curve of the body.

Cope The top frame on a flask that is used in sand casting. *See* ***Sand molding***.

Juan Granados, *Edible Pair***.** Copper, clay, wood, 44″x36″x48″ (101.8cm x 91.4cm x 121.9cm). Photographer: Jon Q. Thompson.

Copper A reddish bronze (copper) colored, malleable, metallic element used in alloys to produce bronze or brass for sculpture purposes, especially casting purposes. Copper is an excellent conductor for electricity as well. Also, copper oxides and stains are used for ceramic work.

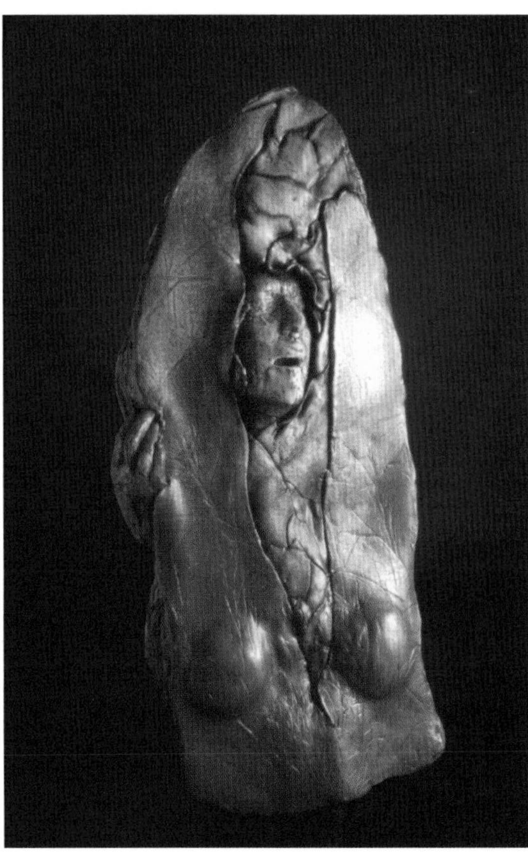

Nan Hoeting-Payne, *Untitled*. Clay, glaze, copper stains, oxides, 4″ (10.16cm) tall. Photographer: Bill Argall.

Copy The end product of a casting oftentimes referred to as a copy of the original, though most of the time it is of a stronger or more substantial material. For example: a bronze cast of a clay model.

Copyright A legally protected right for a creative artist to govern the use, image and reproduction of his/her work. Unless otherwise agreed, the artist retains the copyright to a fine artwork, even after the sale of it. A simple © with the artist's name and date will help establish many copyrights, although a more formal, officially entered copyright will ensure all rights to the artist in contested cases. Seek legal advice when in doubt.

Cordierite Glass annealing and ceramic kiln shelf composed of aluminum and mineral of silicate of magnesium.

Cordless Battery operated tools or tools that can be used temporarily without an electrical hook-up cord.

Core The solid investment mass placed into the center of a casting as a spacer. It is used between the surface walls to keep them from collapsing. Since it creates a thinner casting (walls only), it saves in cost and weight and solves technical problems associated with solid materials. *See **Core pin**; **Investment**; **Plaster investment**.*

Core pins The fasteners or spacers that hold the core an even distance from the outer wall of a mold. Usually made of ferrous metal, several are used, being placed in different locations and angles. They are removed after the casting. *See **Core**; **Core rod**.*

Core rod A metal rod covered by mold core material in preparation for metal casting. It serves two purposes: To keep the core (steel reinforcement) in one solid piece; and to keep the core in place, away from the outer mold. *See **Core pin**.*

CORE INVESTMENT

by Deresa Patrick

Preparing a hollow wax to add core investment. The core pins are added.

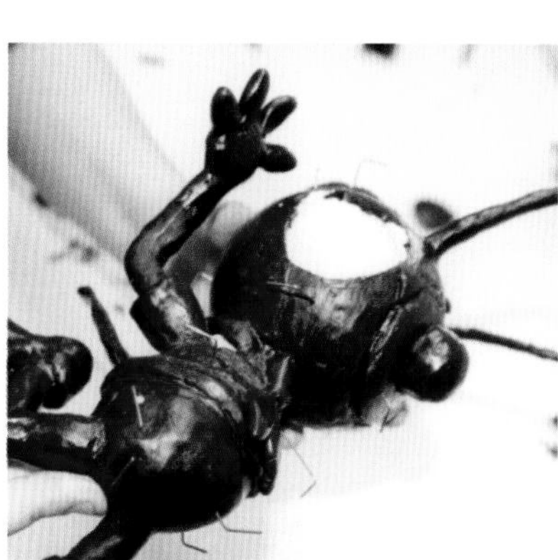

The core investment is added.

The core hole is sealed. The surface is matched to the rest of the wax.

Corns Clumps or gobs of removed finish materials that are snared onto the abrasive surface. This happens when the surface is either not properly cured or is wet, resulting in an ineffective abrasive that can damage the finish.

Corn left on the sandpaper.

Corrosion The product (such as rust) or the act of oxidation, disintegration or planned chemical reaction (such as patination) that changes the surface or object into a different color or texture. Though it can be planned (patination), it is usually not desirable.

Cor-Ten™ A steel that forms a protective rust coating (a patina) on the surface that stops the rusting unless the surface coat of rust is removed. Care must be taken to use the correct welding rod when working with this metal to avoid displaying seams. The result is an initial orange-brown rust that turns much darker brown with age. The work can be painted, but untreated surfaces for sculptural purposes are common.

Sam Spiczka, *Like Clockwork*. Cor-Ten™ and wood, 11½′x3′x4′ (3.55m x 0.915m x 1.22m).

Couching The transfer of a sheet of fresh paper pulp from one location (screen mold) to another (blotter). *See* ***Paper***.

Countersink Inserting a connecting device, such as a screw, nail or bolt, into a material deep enough to cause the head to be flush with the surface. The term may refer to increasing a hole at the surface enough to sink a part, so it may be level or below the material's surface. It may also refer to the cone-shaped drill bit that is used to create the hole or bevel.

Coupler The connector used to join pneumatic devices to hoses. They are designed to fit on the end of a hose and to be operated with one hand, resulting in a quick positive attachment or release. The coupler is female and accepts a male connector or plug. Safety exhaust couplers may be required, especially on larger or longer hoses, which allow air hose bleeding prior to disconnecting to eliminate air pressure that could result in airborne snaking hoses. They have matching plugs available. *See* ***Air compressor; Air tools; Connector; Quick connect couplings***.

Courtyard A specifically designed or controlled area enclosed by a building or alongside a building but protected by walls of trees, bushes or a fence. Courtyards are used for sculptural locations; sometimes designed specifically for sculpture. *See* ***Sculpture garden***.

Crackle A series of small craze lines found in glazes. Raku glazes display a reduced (dark) mark within lighter glazes. If it is uncontrolled, it is known as crazing. *See* ***Crazing; Raku***.

Crane A machine with a boom (beam/arm) that has a suspended, controllable cable system ending with a hook to attach to objects and lift or move them. When using a crane to install or move large sculptures, the weight and lift distance must be calculated to ensure the work can be safely lifted and moved without tipping the machine.

Crawling A glaze imperfection leaving lightly glazed or unglazed surfaces.

Crazing A network of thin fractures within a ceramic glaze. It is usually undesirable, but sometimes sought on raku surfaces. *See* ***Raku***.

Crosscut To saw or cut wood across the grain structure.

Crucible A container used to hold, melt and pour molten metals. It consists of a refractory material, such as silicone carbide, graphite or clay. Clay, being less strong, is rarely used. Graphite also does not have the strength or life of a more expensive silicon carbide. Graphite and clay require a thicker wall, resulting in a smaller supply of metal contained within.

Whichever crucible (pot) is used, a new pot must be annealed or tempered by slowly raising the temperature to about 500°F (260°C) and held for several minutes prior to using. This completes the process begun at the manufacturing plant. A crucible can also be a uniquely designed clay bodied pot with a large opening that houses melting glass.

The size of the crucible is a designation for how much metal it can hold. The size number matches the weight it will hold in aluminum. A number 30 crucible will hold 30 pounds (13.62kg), etc. The weight in bronze is figured at three times the same number. Thus, a number 30 crucible will hold 90 pounds (40.9kg) of bronze, etc. *See* ***Blast furnace; Glass; Metal casting***.

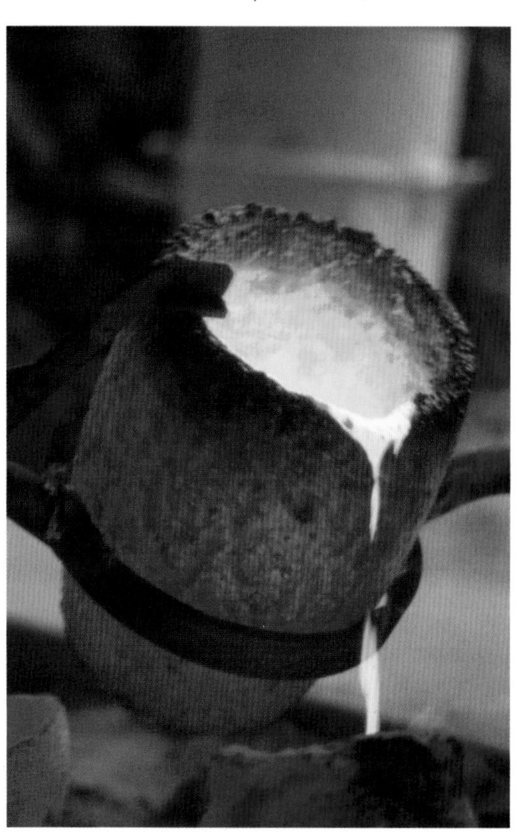

A crucible filled with hot liquid bronze.

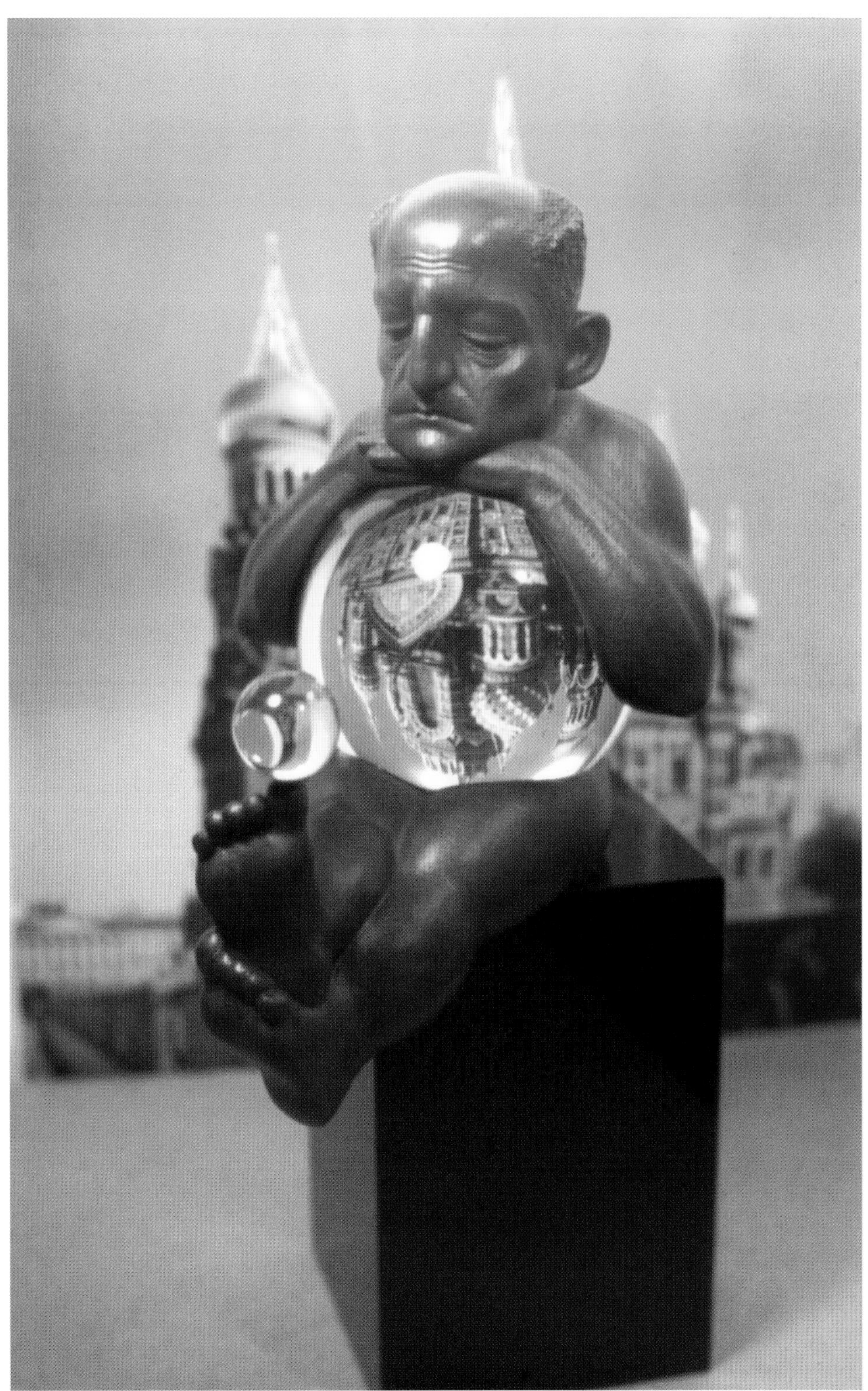

Alexander Tsalikhin, *Mind Games*. Crystal, bronze, marble base, 14″ (35.6cm) tall.

Crystal Quartz, a natural clear mineral or a lead crystal glass that is known for its clarity. A specific amount of lead is part of the makeup.

Cullet Reusable glass, fractured in particles suitable for charging. *See* ***Glass***.

Cup A container so called because of the shape and purpose. The pouring cup is used for molds, especially for the entrance of molten metal when metal casting. *See* ***Metal pouring cup; Metal pouring system***.

Cupola (and cupolette) Iron casting furnaces. They are steel jacketed, cylindrical containers lined with refractory materials, such as hard firebrick and refractory cement or cast refractory that can withstand heat exceeding 2700°F (1482°C). These furnaces have three interior sections: 1) **Stack,** where the metal is added/charged, 2) **Melt**, where the metal is introduced to air via the tuyeres surrounded by the wind box connected to the forced air supply, and 3) **Well,** where the melted iron is gathered.

These three main sections fit together with a temporary seal composed of one-third fireclay and about two-thirds riverbed sand. This allows the furnace to be disassembled to clean it, patch or reline it. The cupola is set on a platform stand designed to allow the bottom door to open or drop for clean-out.

Cupola

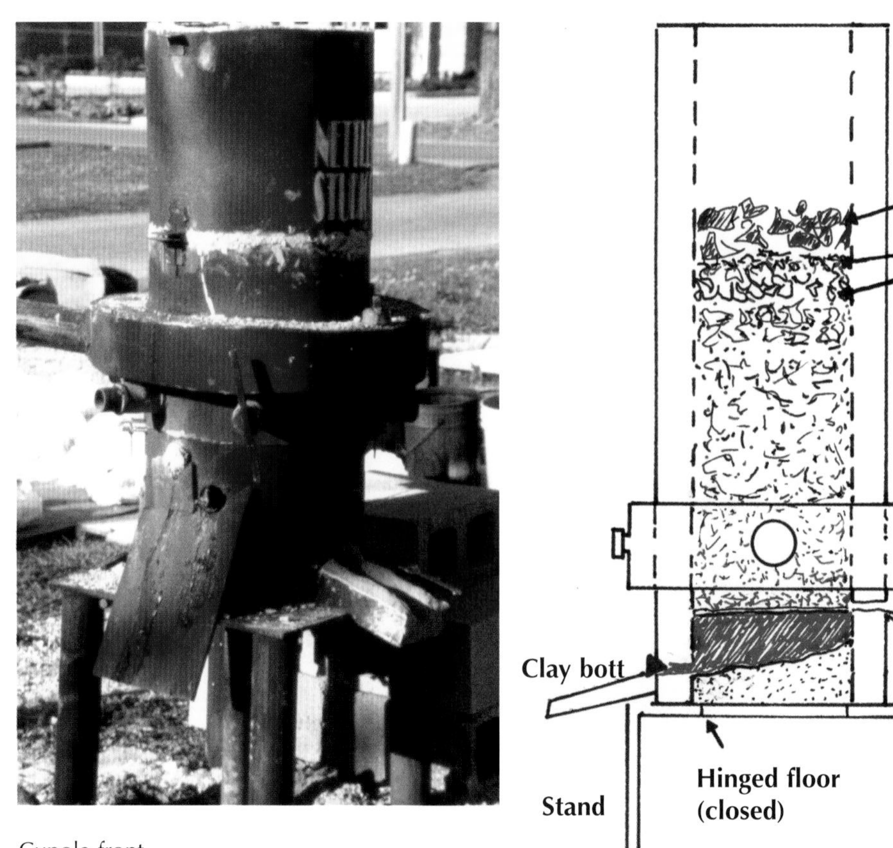

Cupola front view. **Nettles Studio**, Pass Christian, Mississippi.

The cupola and the cupolette are furnaces designed for the fuel and metal to literally be placed together. They use essentially the same construction, materials and have similar design, except the cupolette is usually shorter with a top cover while the cupola's height and open top allow fuel, metal and flux to be constantly added. Both are cylindrical containers lined with a hard refractory capable of extreme heat and physical strength enough to withstand the pressures of heavy metal and the fuel burned. As the fuel burns and the heat builds up, the metal melts and filters to the bottom of the furnace, where it is eventually discharged from a tap hole directly into a pre-heated crucible for further distribution.

The floor is firmly anchored, then it is slightly built up or rammed with either green sand or a mixture of approximately 90% river bed sand, 2% to 4% bentonite and about 5% to 6% vermiculite. It is shaped into a slight slope from the rear down to the tap hole. A temporary thin combustible plywood board is first placed on the front of the bed to keep the first introduction of the flame from igniting the coke. Also, it serves as an aid in the initial lighting.

Technique

The **basic operation** is to charge the furnace with coke (the solid form of carbon from coal, used as a fuel) and ignite it with gas. A white heat is secured and more coke is added. With iron (metal) and limestone (for flux), air is forced to promote faster and hotter heat. The metal is melted and drained through the hot fuel until the liquid metal drains from the furnace into a pouring crucible for filling molds. The cupolette limits the oxygen supply to the melt area, resulting in few impurities and, thus, no need for a flux or flux (slag) hole.

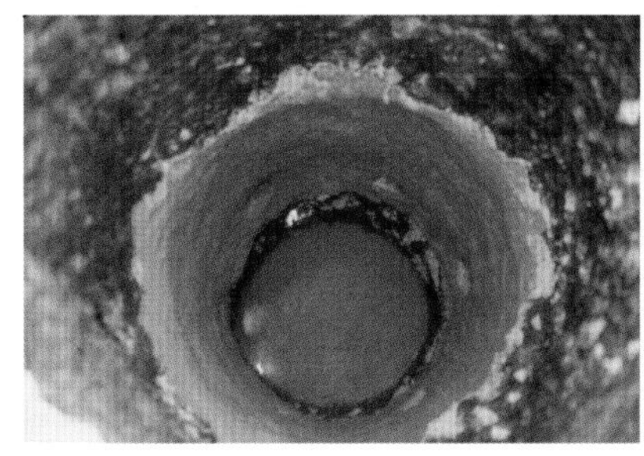
Cupola from top, viewing down, empty.

The charges consist of weighed amounts of coke, limestone and iron. The charge amounts, as well as the individual coke and iron fragment sizes, are determined by the inner diameter of the cupolette or cupola. The iron pieces and coke should ordinarily not exceed a tenth of the diameter involved. While the stack on the cupolette is not completely filled, the cupolette is filled, without any limestone, with just enough space for the lid to close. The furnaces are constantly charged as fan blown air keeps the fire hot. This air is added through the tuyeres. The iron and coke fall from the stack into the windbox where the coke is spent in a white hot heat. The limestone becomes slag, or flux, coating as it melts, and covers the top of the heavier liquid iron. This results in a metal that is kept from impurities.

Cupola with iron, limestone and coke added.

As the iron gathers into a reservoir at the bottom, it gradually rises until it begins to drain out of the slag hole. This designates the time to tap out or remove the clay bott from the lower drain, the tap hole. Once the bott is removed, the hot liquid metal gushes out in a strong stream to be captured in a preheated container used for larger pours or distributed into smaller preheated crucibles for final dispersion. *See **Coke**; **Tuyere**; **Bott**.*

This is a continuous operation if more than one melt is desired. After the pour, the tap hole is closed or plugged with the bott. The placement and size of the coke is important, especially near the tap hole where the flame is introduced into the cupola or cupolette. Larger pieces are arranged in a format resembling a cavern or cave towards the center of the chamber to allow good and rapid flame penetration. The coke bed height is primarily determined by the diameter of the wall. Before starting the firing, all hard floors beneath the furnace need preparation. Dirt or sand is spread around the working area and heavily under the furnace to be prepared for any spills.

Flame is introduced through the tap hole with a forced air gas torch. The flame remains in place until the coke bed reaches a white heat. The torch is removed, and the air supply is forced into the wind box and distributed by the tuyeres into the melt section. The iron begins to drip. This can be observed by looking into the tuyeres to see the dripping metal. The operator waits for a narrow course of continuous flowing metal and then plugs the tap hole. Once the bott is firmly in place, the metal rapidly melts and is soon ready for tap out, which takes approximately 20 minutes. The bott is loosed and dug out with a pick or similar tool. The liquid metal immediately flows into the preheated ladle or crucible. (The crucible and/or ladle may be preheated by the same blower that was used to introduce the flame into the furnace.) While the pouring container must be well heated, care should be taken not to overheat and destroy it. The forced air is always in effect until the last pour. The entire operation must be in constant motion to avoid a freeze-up.

Immediately after the last pouring, the furnace is drained, and the floor is loosened and allowed to drop or swing open. Then the floor mix and any remaining ashes and slag are removed from the furnace. A long handled, pick ax tool is used because of the extreme heat and danger of liquid metal that remains. This operation keeps the iron from solidifying into an unmanageable mass. This is called "dropping the bed."

After the furnace has been cooled, it requires repair and partial relining with refractory cement for upkeep.

CUPOLA OPERATION

by Brimmer Casting Inc.

Gulfport, Mississippi

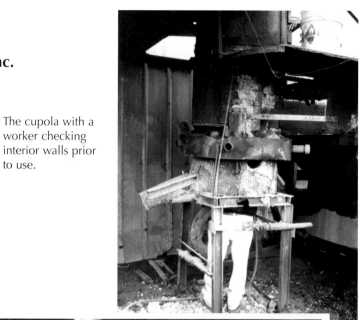

The cupola with a worker checking interior walls prior to use.

Iron, limestone and coke is added to a cupola.

The cupola is tapped out.

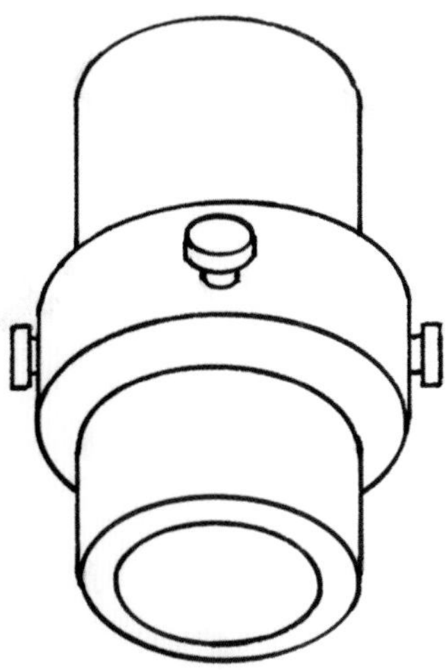

Cupolette A smaller and shorter form of a metal casting furnace than a cupola. The cupolette has a covered top. For this reason, it involves only an initial charge of metal and is known as a batch maker. It does not have a slag escape, since limestone is not in the charge.

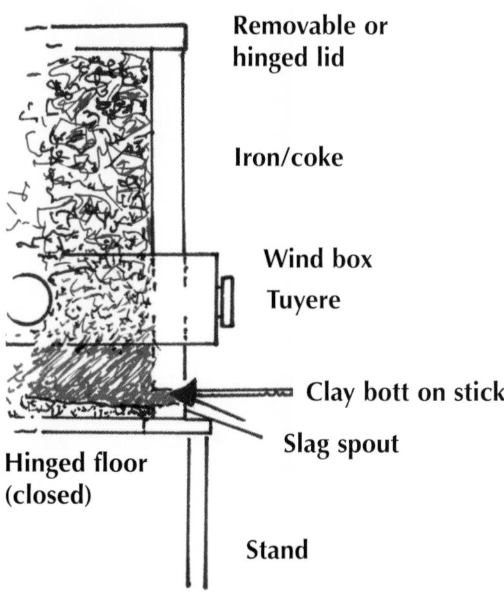

The cupolette with pouring crucible is pre-warmed at the top and on the ground below. Design by **Matthew Wicker**.

CUPOLETTE CASTING

Wayne E. Potratz, University of Minnesota, Minneapolis, Minnesota

The cupolette is lighted.

The coke is prepared for the cupoletta.

The cupolette is charged.

The cupolette with molds surrounding it in preparation for casting.

The crucible is pre-warmed.

Tapping out into a large crucible.

The iron is poured into sand molds.

Dropping the floor onto a bed of sand for clean-out .

Cupric nitrate This chemical produces a range of color from turquoise to baby blue. Because it reacts to heat, it is difficult to determine the exact color. *See* ***Patina; Patina*** *(chart).*

Cure To dry wood. Cured wood is stored for eventual use. To cure casting material is to allow it to set long enough to become strong (such as concrete).

Cut off blades Blades used in a chop saw or blades designed to remove appendages of materials, especially metals. They can be designed for and used in handheld grinders, etc. *See* ***Investment*** *(removal).*

Cutters Any type of cutting device, such as a cable cutter, rod cutter, bolt cutter, angle cutter, tile cutter, etc.

Cutting (metal) This can include several devices and substances, from metal shears to arc and gas cutting rigs. *See* ***Oxyacetylene; Arc; Arcair torch; Plasma cutter.***

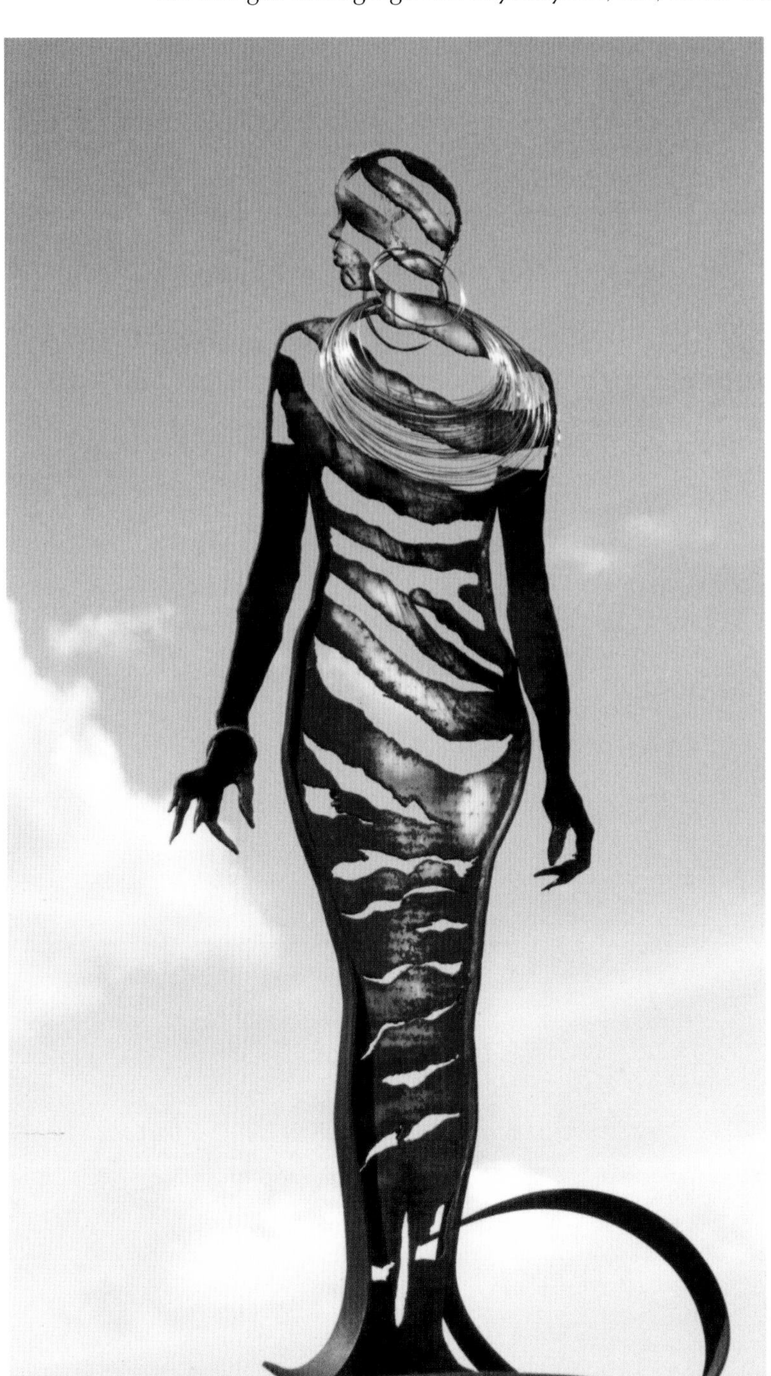

R. Mike Sohikian, *Mother Nature*. Steel, copper wire, acid finish and paints, 73" (185.4cm)

R. Mike Sohikian works on *Giraffe*. Cut and welded steel, glass, length 7' (2.135m)

Pressurized cylinders transported upright with tie-downs and caution signs

Cylinder A portable or pressurized steel container for industrial gases, storage and transporting. It is referred to as a tank or bottle because of its shape. *See* ***Oxyacetylene welding; Acetylene; Oxygen***.

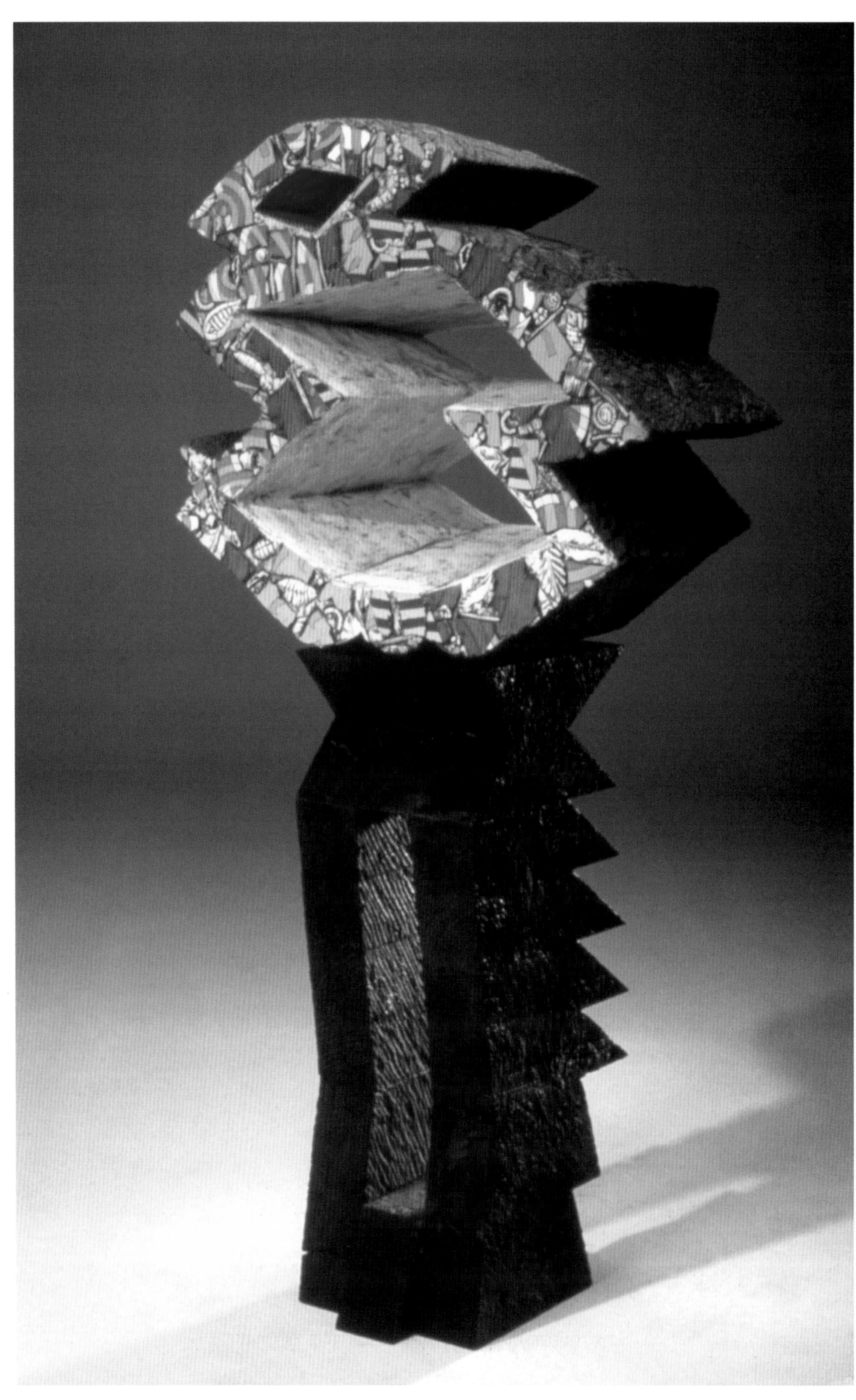

Aurore Chabot, *Eye Catcher.* Earthenware, slips, stains, wood, 56"x21"x24" (142.2cm x 53cm x 61cm). Photographer: Balfour Walker.

D

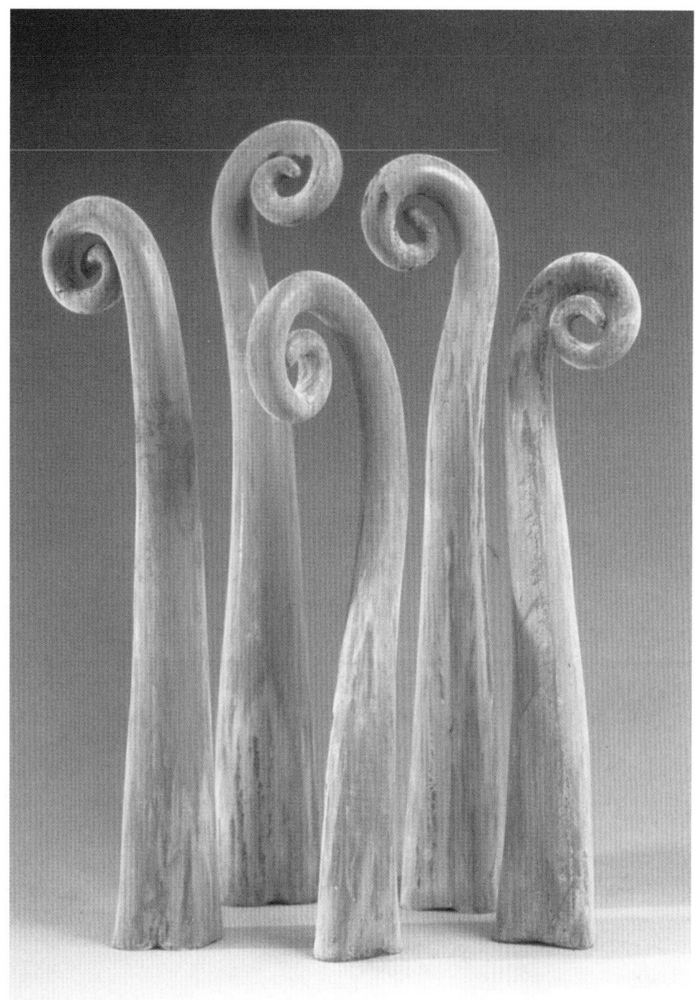

Leslie Eckmann, *Fiddleheads*. Terra cotta, sealant, copper patina, acrylic, 23" (58.4cm) high.

Damascene Inlaying metals into each other for strength and/or design. In design, a precious metal is usually hammered in, leveled and polished. Gold is often placed onto copper or iron, although many combinations of metal are used. In forging, it is the layering of metals to create a special look and feel that could create a stronger metal form.

Damp box (closet) An enclosed temporary storage area designed to allow ceramic clay sculptures to slowly and evenly dry. It is an environment that is air and temperature controlled for a uniform untouched drying cycle. A damp closet may also be used to keep moist clay stored for use. *See* ***Greenware***.

Damper A moveable refractory sheet or slab designed to control exhaust fumes from a kiln or furnace. It is usually located at the base of the flue near the firing chamber. *See* ***Kiln***.

Dead plaster Plaster that has absorbed moisture to the extent that it cannot set when mixed with water. Also, calcined plaster that has become worthless by being overheated with fire. *See* ***Plaster***.

Dead stone A stone that may have internal problems as determined by a dull sound when tapped by a hammer.

De-air To eliminate air in a material. Air can be eliminated from mold materials by placing them in a vacuum, resulting in a smoother, stronger mold. Wedging ceramic clay bodies will eliminate (de-air) clay. *See* ***De-air pug mill; Vacuum***.

De-air pug mill A pug mill used for ceramic clays that has a built-in vacuum system to eliminate air as the clay is pugged. It results in an easier use of the clay body that requires little or no wedging. *See* ***Pug mill***.

Death mask The taking of a mold from a cadaver's face and then casting a likeness (positive) from the mold. Traditionally, plaster has been the molding material, although alginate is now used. *See* ***Life mask; Body molding***.

Decay Rot brought about by fungi, causing decomposition of an object, such as wood.

Deciduous (tree) A tree that has new foliage each year with the leaves normally falling off after the growth period.

Deckle A frame made of wood that forms a wall around the screen mold while

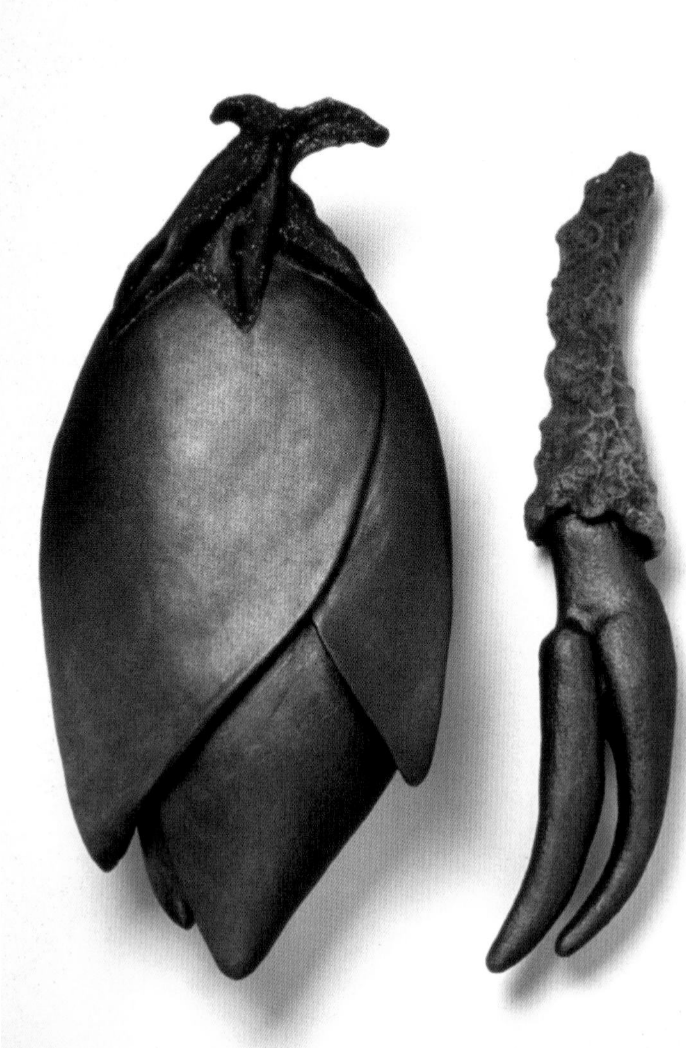

Juan Granados, *Germination*. Earthenware glaze, metallic oxide pigment, 29"x22"x8" (73.7cm x 55.9cm x 20.3cm).

making paper from pulp. When removed, a sheet of paper (pulp) remains. *See* ***Screen mold; Paper***.

Deep relief Also called high relief. Relief forms are nearly one-half their normal shape from the background surface. *See* ***Relief; Low relief***.

Deflacculation To disperse clay particles within a clay slip for more fluidity. Sodium silicate, a deflocculant, added to slip will promote fluidity. *See* ***Slip casting***.

De-foaming agent A substance used to eliminate excessive air retention or buildup in a liquid. A de-foaming agent is used in ceramic shell slurry mix to keep the liquid a tighter mix for a better, more even surface coating. *See* ***Slurry***.

Degasifier A compound inserted into hot liquid metal formulated to remove gases. *See* ***Blast furnace***.

Degrees A measurement unit on a temperature scale. Fahrenheit or Celsius is the common system of degree measurement. *See* ***Celsius; Fahrenheit; Measurements*** *(chart)*.

Dehydration The removal of encased water. Plaster is the result of partial dehydration.

Delamination Separation or coming apart of materials, such as laminated plywood or layered stone.

Denatured alcohol Alcohol with additives used as a chemical thinner and cleaner. It is unfit for drink or food. *See* ***Patina***.

Density Compactness of a mass; dense. The actual weight of a substance at a specific volume.

Dentist tools Stainless steel tools designed for dentists but readily adopted and adapted by sculptors for use in modeling fine details with oil-based molding clays.

Design The overall formal arrangement of an artwork or the plan of the arrangement. *See* ***Elements of design; Principles of order***.

De-waxing The technique of removing the wax from refractory molds that are used in metal casting for the lost wax process to leave a cavity to fill with hot liquid metal.

Plaster investment casting sometimes uses steam to remove wax from the mold to catch and retain the wax for future use. It can be weighed for an estimate of the bronze needed for the metal pouring. However, steaming out a plaster investment mold is not necessary, since the kiln burnout accomplishes the same task.

A flash heat de-waxing of the ceramic shell mold is essential to avoid wax swelling, resulting in mold breakage during the mold baking. Removing wax from ceramic shell can be done by steam, torch, autoclave or furnace. Steaming the wax out can be used on small molds, but it is dangerous and requires the mold to be heated to a mold maturation temperature. Torch de-waxing is acceptable for small single works but not for larger works. The torch flame is applied from the cup and up the runners and then to the main body. Care must be taken to work fast to avoid wax swelling which could fracture the mold. The shell must be heated to maturity. The autoclave works by pressure with heat resulting in steam to remove the wax. A variation of the autoclave is to place small molds into a kitchen pressure cooker with a pint of water and allow it to reach a pressure of 15 pounds (6.81kg). The resulting mold must then be taken out and reheated to achieve the mold maturation point. The burnout furnace not only melts out the wax, but also brings the refractory material to complete dryness and maturity in preparation for metal casting. If the burnout furnace is correctly designed, the wax can be recovered with no visible pollution. *See* ***Autoclave; Burnout; Ceramic shell: Plaster investment***.

Diamond blade (tools) A blade or surface with the cutting edge embedded with industrial quality diamonds used for cutting various materials and sanding surfaces. Tools include diamond coated die bits, diamond coated files, etc. One of the most common uses is in stone work, especially in cutting large stones for building and sculptural purposes.

DIAMOND BLADE CARVING
by Lothar Nickel

The sculptor uses a disk grinder with a diamond blade to carve stone. Photographer: Robert Bagley.

Evenly spaced cuts are made.

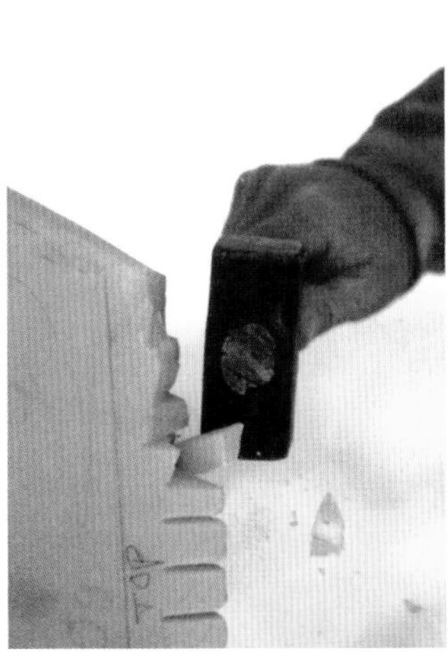

The cuts are hammered off.

Diamond cable blade for large stones. Photographer: Enzo Torcoletti.

Diamond blades.
Blades by color: Black, Segmented dry blade; Red, wet/dry blade; Yellow, Continuous wet blade.

Tools with dry-cut diamond blades.

Die A mold for forming, stamping or cutting material of a softer substance than the mold. An example is a die used to stamp coins.

Die-cast To force a casting liquid into a mold to create a sculpture.

Diecasting Pressure injecting a substance into an open mold to create a casting. A hard force or a hardened shape forces the image into softer material.

Die-forming A technique of forcing a material into a mold. It is associated with metal-working and the use of hammering copper sheet metal into wooden molds. *See **Repousse**; **Forging**; **Hammer**.*

DIE-FORMING
by Corrina Mensoff

A drawing for *Copper Dragons*.

Die-formed sheet copper uses wood molds.

Corrina Mensoff, *Copper Dragons*. Copper sheet metal, bar stock, tubing, patina, 3′6″x4′x2′ (106.7cm x 121.9cm x 61cm). Photographer: Jill Buckner.

Die grinder A handheld tool that holds a bit (die) for cutting or shaping a softer material. With the right bit, a die grinder can be used for almost any material.

Dimensional Spatial designation for a combination of height, width, length and depth. *See* ***Three-dimensional***.

Diorite A dark igneous, crystalline, granular rock not easily carved. It is generally crushed and found in materials used for coating roads. *See* **Stone** *(chart)*.

Dip coat The first coat of mold material used for surface detail. It is visually finer than the other subsequent mold layers of large coarser particles that are used for quickness in drying and strengthening the mold. *See* ***Slurry***.

Dipping Coating a surface by immersing the object (sculpture) into a substance. The term is used for coating sculptures' waxes with ceramic shell or silica afterwards (if a fluidizing bed is used). Dipping is also the process of coating a ceramic form with a glaze. *See* ***Ceramic shell; Slurry; Fluidizing bed; Glaze***.

Dipping tongs A clamping tool with handles used to hold objects as they are inserted into a liquid for cleaning or coating, such as glaze dipping tongs for ceramics.

Direct carving Carving a wood or stone sculpture directly into the final finished form without a duplication process. *See* ***Taille direct***.

Direct metal (sculpture) Working directly into the metal by processes such as welding, riveting and hammering. It involves creating a metal sculpture without casting. *See* ***Metal fabrication***.

Disclosing wax An extremely soft wax that is effortlessly placed into small wax sculpture imperfections as part of wax cleanup prior to molding for metal casting.

Display Exhibiting artwork, although "exhibit" is the better term. *See* ***Exhibit***.

James Mellick, *Get Out of Here!* Carved wood, copper; installed, 12′x8′x2′ (3.66m x 2.44m x 0.61m).

Distillation Refining a substance by heating, resulting in a liquid from vapors or condensation. Turpentine is produced by distillation.

Divest(ing) To remove the spent mold material from a metal casting to uncover the sculpture. With plaster investment, the bulk of the mold can easily be removed with a hard hammer, taking care not to hit the actual casting. If the mold is intricate, then high water pressure (car wash type) can rapidly clean the surface. Afterwards, sandblasting will complete the task. Dry plaster investment can be saved for luto to add to future investment mixes. *See* ***Investing; Luto***.

With **ceramic shell**, most of the material can be removed in large pieces by tapping the mold with a hammer. Striking the sprues helps vibrate the material from the bronze. (If iron or aluminum, it could cause a fracture.) Workers debate the use of water in mold removal, with most preferring to work on dry molds. Sandblasting is used to finish removing small traces of shell material. If chisels are used, they should never hit the casting or the chasing scars will require additional work.

Ceramic shell divested from a bronze casting.

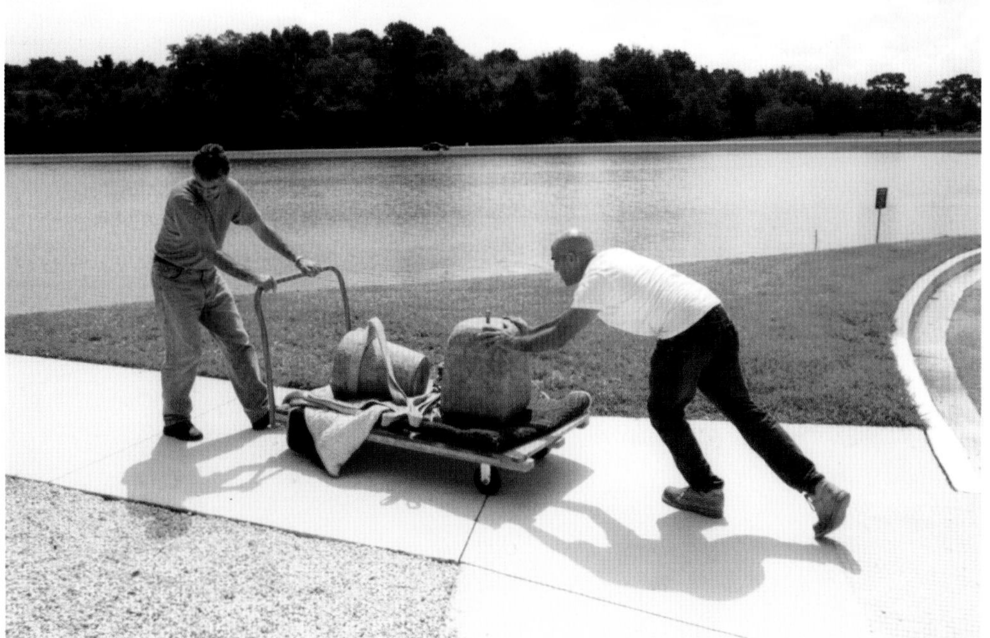

Enzo Torcoletti and **Joe Segal** move a stone sculpture with a dolly. Photographer: Walter Coker of *Folio Weekly*.

Dolly A platform with wheels (casters) that is used for moving heavy objects.

Dolomite Limestone containing magnesium carbonate and calcium carbonate in large quantities. It is finely ground and added to clay bodies for increased plasticity. *See* ***Clay***.

Double-cut file File with two rows of cross diagonal teeth. It cuts faster than a single cut file.

Double wire end tool A modeling tool with a wire loop on each end of the handle (shaft). The wire can be notched for better cutting (removal of material) or smoothing. It is used for water- or oil-based clays and wet plasters.

Dowel A cylindrical wooden rod used much like a nail to hold two parts together. It is usually made of a harder wood than the parts involved.

Down-draft (kiln) (down-draught) A kiln where the energy (flame) source can be anywhere from the front, back or sides with the heat directed upward by a baffle (bag wall). As the heat circulates, it is routed downward and out a rear opening and up a chimney (stack) until the desired temperature is reached. At this point, baffles will close off the lower part of the chimney, causing the heat to remain in the kiln for a slow cooling cycle. Characteristically, the hottest place in the kiln is at the top, though with careful loading and planning the heat can be balanced. *See* ***Kiln***.

Draft (angle) The angle of withdrawing a casting from the mold. *See* ***Mold***.

Drawing A preliminary sketch for a three-dimensional work usually accompanied with a model when presented for a commission. Sometimes a drawing is part of a sculptural form.

A finished part from the drawing of *Gunshy* by ***Michael J. Cooper***.

Michael J. Cooper's drawing for parts of *Gunshy*.

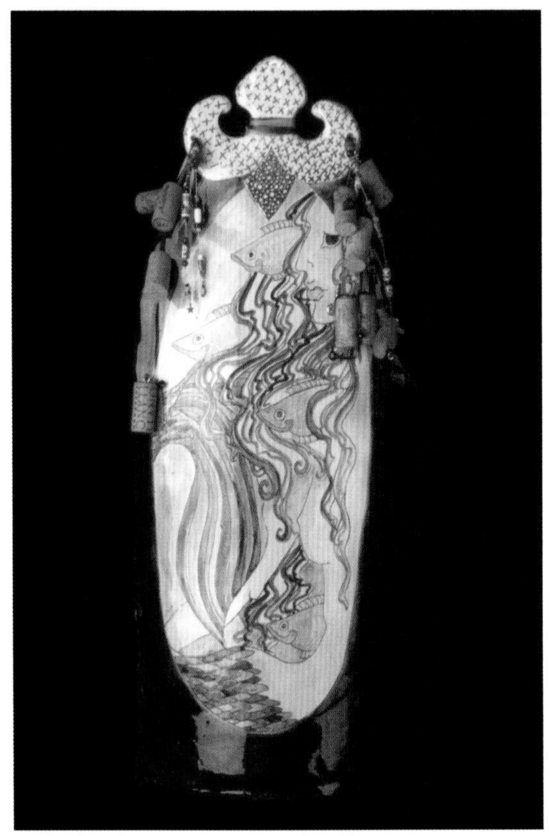

Angela Gallia, *Tabernacle with Mermaid*. Slab built earthenware, 28″x12″ (71.1cm x 30.5cm). Photographer: Luri Leigh Lawrence.

Draw knife A handled blade that is designed to be pulled toward the sculptor to remove wood in a carving. It is particularly used on logs for boat making.

Dremel™ (tools) Trademark name for small flexible shaft tools and bits. *See **Flexible shaft**.*

Dress To refine. To dress wood is to plane the surface in order to smooth it.

Dressed (board) Dry lumber that has been planed on at least one side (usually on all lengthwise sides). Also, dressed (size) is the remaining dimensions after the lumber has been surfaced or dressed with a planer. *See **Lumber**.*

A wheel dresser placed on a grinder wheel.

Dressed (stone) Quarried stone that has been "cleaned" or had extraneous, cracked or irregular appendages removed, resulting in a more compact and sometimes square or rectangular shape. It is easier to handle, ship and measure for work.

Dresser A handled tool with hardened, free-wheeling wheels with sharp points. Dressers clean and straighten bench grinder stones. They are pressed into the wheel as it turns until the wheel is straightened (dressed). A dresser is also a compound in hard form, such as a silicon carbide stick, that is used to fine clean and true grinding wheels.

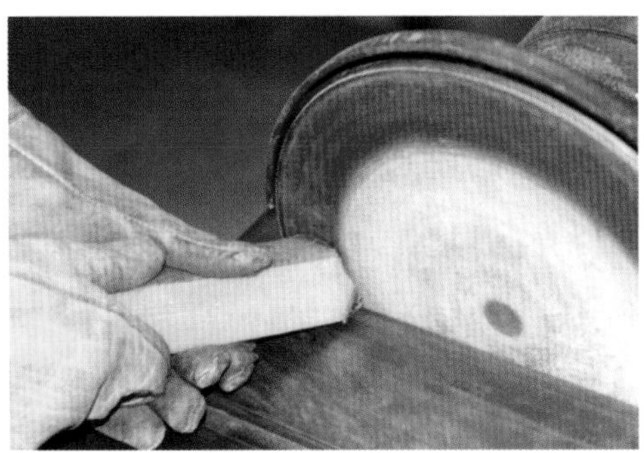

A hard rubber dresser cleans a sanding disk.

Dressing A dressing (stick) made out of silicon carbide. It is formulated to straighten bench grinder wheels. Also, substances, such as a hard rubber, are formulated to clean out other kinds of cutting-grinding and sanding disks. *See **Dressers**.*

Driftwood Wood found in or near water that has been aged and shaped by motion and/or saturation of water. Natural shapes and designs are found in driftwood that the artist may choose to take advantage of, with little or no modification. *See **Found object**; **Assemblage**.*

Bruce Larsen, *Triceratops*. Driftwood and acrylic, 10″x12″x27″ (25.4cm x 30.5cm x 68.6cm).

Drill A tool used for cutting a hole into diverse materials. It may be power or hand operated with a cutting bit held into place for the work. The word is also a verb for the act of drilling, creating a hole, as well as the bit (drill) itself.

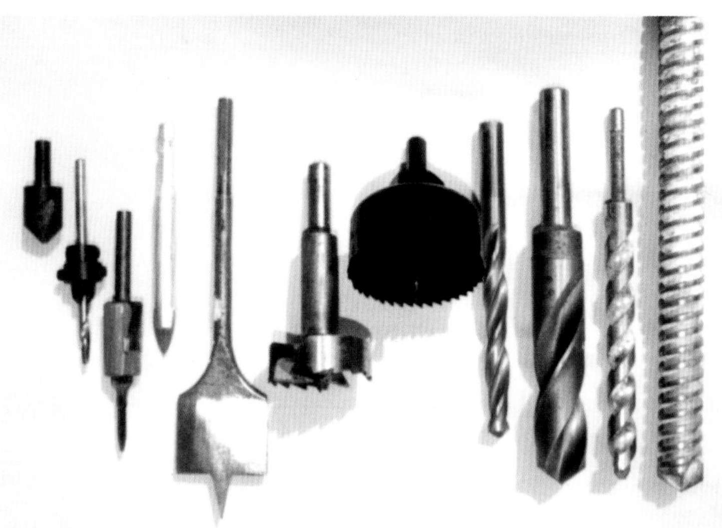

Assorted drills.

Drill press An upright vertical machine with a power drill system at the top that forces a drill bit into the material. It is designed so that the object to be drilled can be raised, lowered or angled on the strong drill shaft into the work by hand or automation. The cutting drill is held in place by an adjustable chuck.

Drill press.

Drop forging To shape or forge a piece of metal between dies by dropping a heavy weight or imparting force upon it. Sometimes known as a drop hammer. *See **Forging**.*

Dross Impure waste substance (slag) that surfaces (floats) on top of metal castings. Dross is the result of unclean casting metal and oxidation with the air. It is scraped off (removed) from the liquid metal prior to pouring. *See **Metal casting**.*

Drum sander Motorized sander with the abrasive coating placed on the outside of a rotating drum. Depending on the configuration, the drum can be in many sizes and shapes.

Dryers Machines designed for the air compressor to keep the air supply free from moisture and clean. It is not necessary for normal sculpture use, but preferred for scientific and paint or air coating operations that have stringent environmental/OSHA requirements. They are more efficient than a simple water tap bowl. A refrigerated unit is the standard. It condenses the moisture vapors and

Dross is removed in preparation for a metal pouring. **Inferno Foundry**, Atlanta, Georgia.

eliminates them from the unit, while allowing the water-free air to continue to the workspace. Larger, expensive units can cost as much as the compressor but may be required for extremely clean air. Less expensive, smaller, inline membrane dryers will suffice for most paint applications. *See* ***Air compressor***.

Dry rot Rot in wood that results in a severely weak wood that easily crushes into soft splinters or powder.

Duck's nest A spent fuel bin just below the hearth on a forge. *See* ***Forge***.

Ductile Easily shaped into another form; malleable. The ability to be worked, bent, molded or shaped with ease.

Ductility A property that allows metal to be worked without heat into a new shape without breaking.

Ducts A passageway for air or a substance to pass through. In sculpture mold making, a duct can be an air passage (channel) for escaping air and gasses, or it can be a pouring passage (duct) for receiving the liquid metal. *See* ***Metal pouring system; Investment casting***.

Handheld duster clears the workspace.

Dump mold A mold created in a container by dumping the mold material over the artwork. Afterwards, the artwork is removed by cutting it out to leave a useful mold. Also called pour-on. *See* ***Pour-on***.

Dust (mask) Airborne fine particles. All dust is a health hazard, some lethal. The sculptor should be aware of the dust involved. Dust masks (respirators) are designed to eliminate breathing dust into the lungs. Fumes may also be avoided. *See* ***Respirator***.

Duster Handheld air nozzle that disperses a hard, directed, high velocity stream of air by a pistol grip, top thumb operated lever. The actual nozzle end is shaped for a specific purpose, such as a rubber tip to provide a seal when placed tightly against a surface or a needle tip for tight places, etc. Also called a blow gun.

Duty cycle The percentage of time a machine should be run, as compared to the amount of time it should be idle during an hour's time. A 60/40 duty cycle designates that a machine should rest for 40% of the time and can be run 60% of the time. By observing the duty cycle, machines such as welders and air compressors will operate better with fewer problems over an extended life. A duty cycle that allows the machine to cool down will result in longer lasting parts, especially bearings (the first items to wear down). A continuous duty cycle rating, found on the most powerful commercial equipment, signifies that it can run full time. *See* ***Welder; Air compressor***.

Dye A coloring agent sometimes used for patina tion, wood stain, or for the initial plaster coating of a waste mold, etc. *See* ***Waste mold***.

Walter Zurko, *Sisters*. Wood, dyes, paint, 60″x16″x12″ (152.4cm x 40.6cm x 30.5cm). Photographer: Heather Protz.

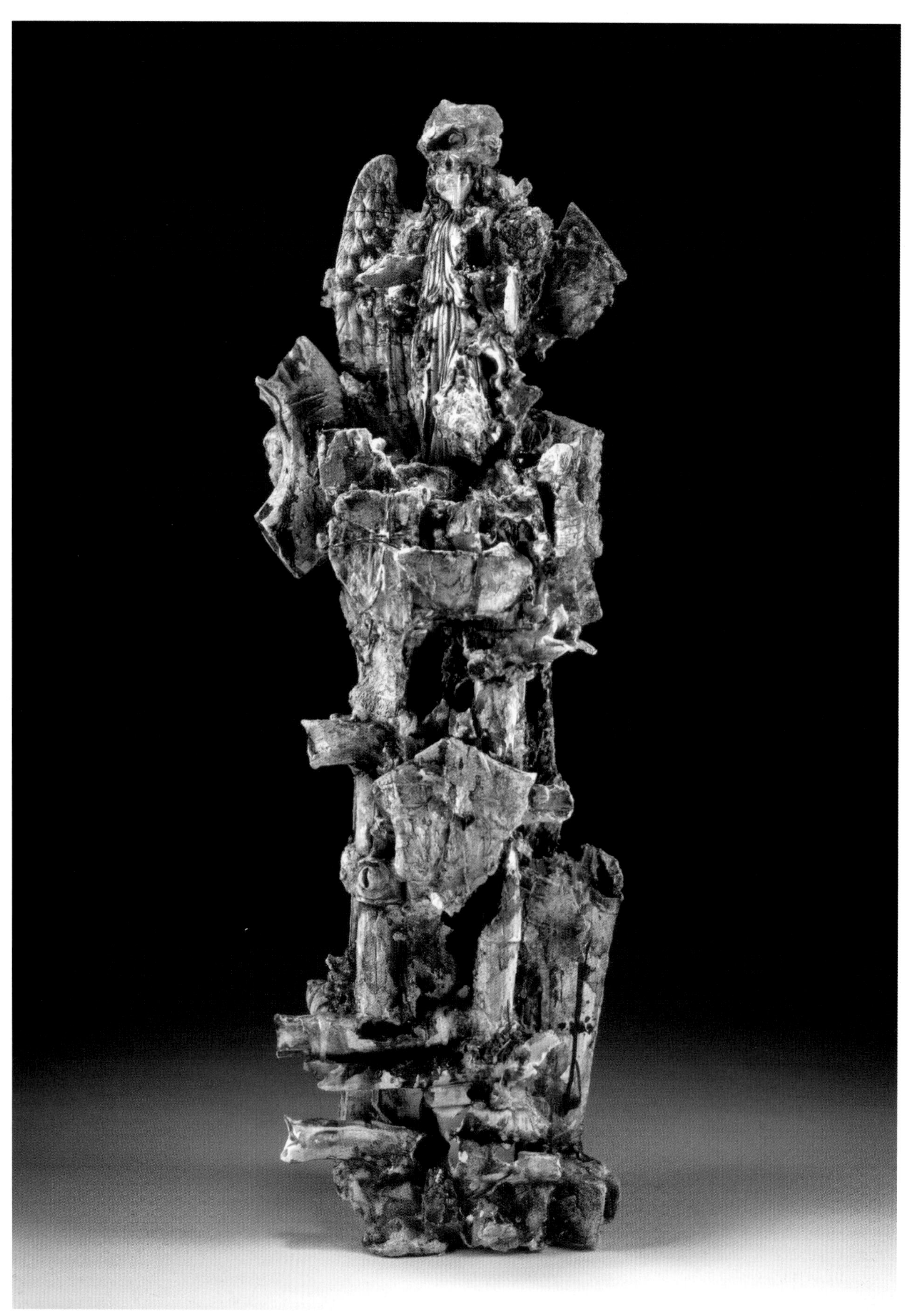

Christopher Vicini, *Earth Angel*. Earthenware, glass, steel, glazes, 47″x15″ (119.4cm x 38.1cm). Photographer: Mark Johnston.

Ear safety Ear plugs and muffs are for protection from machinery noise that could result in hearing loss. *See* ***Hearing protection***.

Earth cast concrete Concrete cast in a mold that is dug out in the earth. *See* ***Concrete; Sand mold***.

EARTH CAST CONCRETE
by Thomas Sayre

Heavy equipment prepares a ground (earth) mold for concrete.

Concrete with iron oxide for coloring is poured in the steel reinforced bare earth mold.

Concrete is allowed to set up and cure.

The sculpture is dug up and hoisted with a crane to the prepared location. It is anchored onto an engineered footing.

Thomas H. Sayre, *River Reels*. Earth cast concrete, iron oxide, 20′ (6.1m) diameter.

Aurore Chabot, *Malaprop*. Earthenware, slips, stains, 10"x23"x12" (25.4cm x 58.4cm x 30.5cm). Photographer: Chris Autio.

Earthenware Clay fired under 2012°F (1100°C) resulting in an absorbent, porous body usually of a coarse nature. Fire clay with 5% or more porosity is considered earthenware. While less porous than traditional terra cotta, it is used for thinner, hand formed pieces, especially with press molding. Clay bodies can be found in a broad range of colors and textures depending upon the addition of grog and the size of it. This is a good body for low fire glazes that are known for their bright colors. The firing range is from cone 08 to cone 02. *See* ***Clay*** *(water-based)*.

Earthwork An artwork created by modifying an outdoor area into a manmade environment or form, usually on a grand proportion with natural materials.

Tanya Preminger, *Balance*. Soil, grass. 29.5'x11.5'x31.2' (900x350x950 cm).

Interior of *Grosse Point Passage 2000.*

Herb Parker, *Grosse Point Passage 2000*. Rammed earth, sod, steel, neon, stone, mulch, 18′x22′x30′ (5.49m x 6.71m x 9.15m).

Ebony A black, fine grained hardwood. Because it is so dense, it is extremely difficult to carve. The purest blocks are from trees in Asia and Africa. The term is also used for a dark or black color. *See **Wood** (chart).*

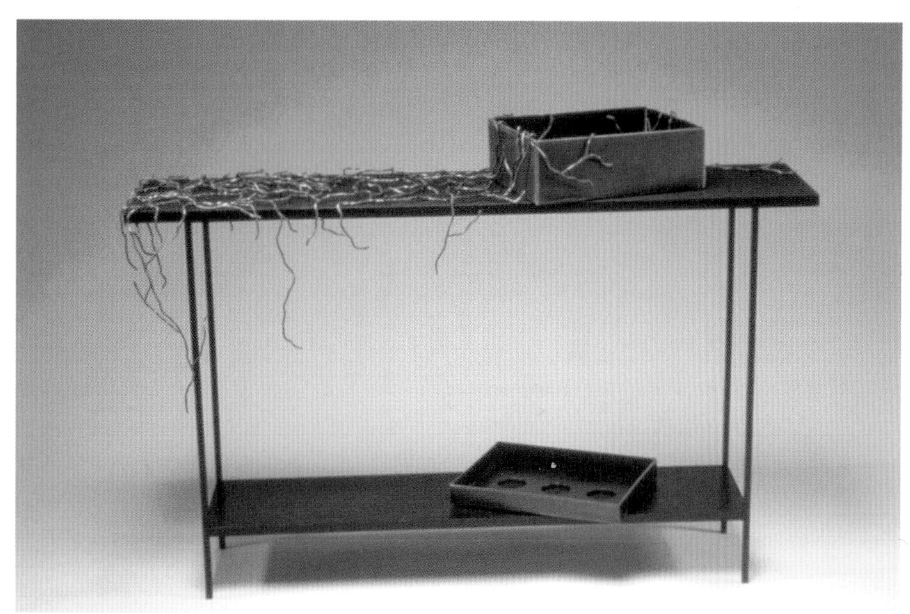

Lynden Cline, *Her Own Private Palimpset*. Ebonized mahogany, steel, 50″x14″ (127cm x 35.6cm).

Edition Artwork that has more than one casting from the same mold. A limited edition indicates that there is a limit to the number of works involved. The edition number is the exact individual number of a work. For example, edition number 2 is the second piece of a limited edition. If the total number of castings is five; the artwork is labeled: 2/5. The artist often retains one unnumbered artist's proof for his or her own purposes.

The quantity of edition pieces is determined by the artist. Edition sizes vary but seldom exceed 100 and are sometimes fewer than ten. The larger the edition, the less value the individual pieces possess, primarily since the work is less rare. The later (higher) numbers do not reflect the quality of the earlier numbers, due to the mold slowly wearing down, reducing the detail of the original artwork. All metal works are signed in the wax and numbered according to the sequence of casting. After the edition is completed, the mold is destroyed. *See* ***Limited edition; Foundry proof; Artist's proof; Original***.

Effloresce The result of a surface treatment that has been applied over a material, usually wet concrete. It is a flat white, uneven coating that inhibits paints and stains from adhering. It causes unsightly blemishes.

Electric Operated by electricity, as compared to gas, hand or air operated.

Electric kiln Insulated kiln (furnace) for firing clay bodies heated by electrical energy through the use of electrical elements encased into the surrounding wall. The electric kiln is preferred for bisque and low fire oxidation works. *See* ***Kiln***.

Electric wheel A ceramic wheel powered by electricity. It can be a very small machine (placed on a table) to an extremely powerful one able to hold hundreds of pounds of clay. *See* ***Throwing wheel***.

Electrode An electrical conductor used to initiate electrical current with another cell or medium. An electrode holder grips the electrode firmly in place as it is moved in a small, repetitious pattern held just above the metal surface during the arcing process. The electrical current melts and fuses the metals together. Drag electrode rods are available that need no motion while welding.

Electrodes, known as welding rods, are manufactured in two common lengths, either small diameter nine inch (22.9cm) long rods, used for thin metals, or larger 12 inch (30.48cm) diameter rods. The longer rod is the most common size. A smaller rod of one-eighth inch (0.318cm) diameter would be for thinner metals while a one-fourth inch (0.635cm) rod would be for heavy duty welding with a strong amperage machine and very thick metal. All are flux coated to form a shield about the weld to prevent oxidizing the metal. As the rod melts, a gas is formed that freezes into a hard, glassy surface on the finished weld. This slag must be removed by striking the weld with a chipping hammer. After the particles fly off, the weld can be finished. Rods include general purpose, deep-penetrating, hard-surfacing, vertical welding, etc., depending on the required use.

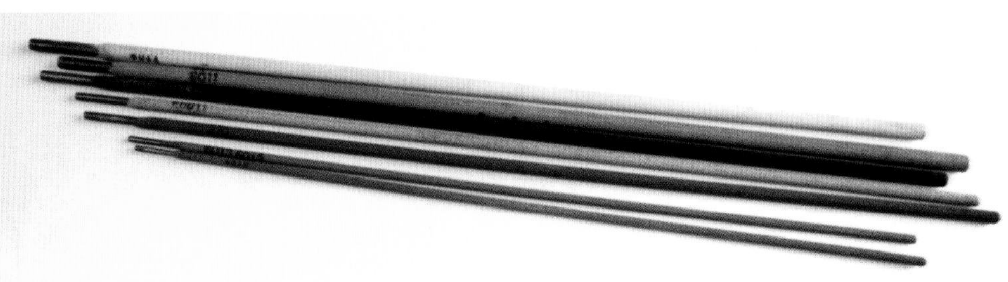

Electrodes with the electrode numbers near the holder end.

The AWS-ASTM (American Welding Society – American Society for Testing Materials) specifications are correlated into a set of four numbers printed on each welding rod by the manufacturers. Though the manufacturers vary, they furnish equivalent numbers for all the rods they produce. The number should begin with the letter E indicating arc welding or G for gas welding. *See* ***Electrode*** *(chart)*.

Rods deteriorate in wet conditions. The flux will flake off and the rod may rust. Using such rods will lead to weak, contaminated welds. Rods should be stored in air-tight containers. *See* ***Welding; Welding rod***.

ELECTRODE CHART

Electrode Numbering System *American Welding Society*

Example: **E 6010**

Reading the electrode numbers from left to right:

E = electrode

60 = strength in thousands of pounds per inch

1 = welding positions

1 = flat, horizontal, vertical, overhead
2 = flat and horizontal only
3 – flat, horizontal, vertical down, overhead

0 = type of coating and current needed

Digit	*Type of Coating*	*Welding Current*
0	cellulose sodium	AC or DCEP
1	cellulose potassium	AC or DCEP or DCEN
2	titania sodium	AC or DCEP
3	titania potassium	AC or DCEN or DCEP
4	iron powder titania	AC or DCEN or DCEP
5	low hydrogen potassium	AC or DCEP or DCEN
6	low hydrogen potassium	AC or DCEN
7	iron powder iron oxide	AC or DCEP or DCEN
8	iron powder low hydrogen	AC or DCEP

DCEP = Direct Current Electrode Positive *DCEN = Direct Current Electrode Negative*

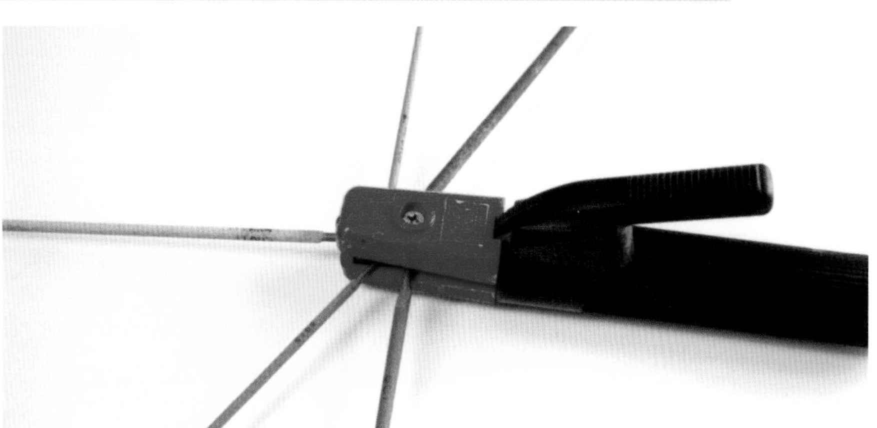

Electrode holder. Though this holder is displayed with various electrodes in different positions, only one electrode in one position is used at a time.

Electrode holder The insulated handheld device that grips the welding rod (electrode). It is designed with a firm built-in pressure spring that allows easy removal and placement of the electrode in multiple positions for different work requirements. Sometimes it is referred to as a stinger or torch. *See* ***Arc welding; Electrode***.

Electrolysis The problem that occurs when a metal, such as copper, is deposited on steel. It is a chemical change or decomposition of metals reaching to each other. If any steel, except stainless steel, comes into direct contact with bronze, a rust color appears. It can and does travel through metal, though the actual contact may be hidden and shielded from weathering.

Electrolyte A chemical compound, when dissolved, ionizes, producing an electrical conductor. *See* ***Metal plating; Slip casting***.

Electroplating The process involves electrical currents. The article to be electroplated is placed into a solution with a negative elective pole, the cathode. It is attached and suspended as electrical current moves throughout the solution, causing metal from a positive pole, the anode, to release. The current then moves to the negative pole, resulting in a thin deposit on the article.

Kelly Robinson, *Confession*. Electroformed copper, 6″x6″x6″ (15.2cm x 15.2cm x 15.2cm). Instructor: Nell Keyes. Photographer: Danny Grantham.

Metal plating on metal objects begins by thoroughly cleaning the sculpture so it is devoid of rust, dust, fingerprints or anything that could inhibit the coating. If the finish is to reflect smooth perfection, then the sculpture must be fine finished by polishing and buffing. Otherwise, the thin coating will display all the imperfections. To achieve maximum coating results some metals may be electroplated on the article before the chosen top coat. An example would be to first apply a coating of copper and nickel to steel before adhering chromium (chrome). This causes a stronger, more lasting bond. The resulting surfaces, such as copper, can be patinaed in the same way as a sculpture made of solid metal. Care must be taken to avoid unnecessary rubbing, especially on thin plates.

While materials and equipment for electroplating are not difficult to obtain, to create artwork of size causes several problems, especially of handling. Most sculptors elect to contact electroplating experts to finish their work to eliminate the problems of solutions, temperatures, tanks and coating materials.

Brush plating is used by sculptors on smaller objects or placed on specific locations within an object. The process is simple: A lead or connection is made to the article from the power source with the other power connection on the brush or on another instrument (stylus) covered with a clean cotton swab. The brush or stylus is plunged into the plating solution and rubbed onto the article. The resulting plating can be thin or thick depending upon the tank solutions. However, it is much more time consuming for larger objects.

Metal plating on non-metal objects requires more preparation. Non-metallic objects have to be especially clean and completely sealed; they cannot be porous. The surface has to have additional materials applied to allow the plating. Many non-metallic substances can be plated, such as plastic, wood or plaster. Plaster is the most common non-metallic substance to utilize, since it is the easiest to shape and is inexpensive. After it is thoroughly dried, it is coated with linseed oil, wax, shellac, lacquer or urethane paint to ensure that it is waterproof.

The surface quality must be maintained and treated with either a metallic or graphite powder. This is accomplished by either brushing on a coating of the powder and then gently wiping off the excess, or possibly immersing the sculpture into a bath of graphite and water mix. Afterwards, it can be electroplated. *See* ***Hot dipped metals; Metal cladding***.

Elements of design The visual thinking of sculpture expressed in terms for the physical appearance of three-dimensional objects. Terms include shape, texture, space, planes, value and color. *See **Principles of order**.*

Elephant's ear A small, flat, natural supple sponge in the shape of an elephant's ear. It is primarily used for finishing clay bodies, especially with wheel thrown pottery.

Embossing To make a slightly elevated design on a form's surface. *See **Low relief**.*

Emery An abrasive used like sandpaper. It can be in powdered form or attached to flexible cloth. Black carborundum is used, as well as aluminum oxide. *See **Sandpaper**.*

Emery stone An extremely hard, abrasive stone made of silicon carbide. It is used for smoothing and polishing. *See **Abrasives**.*

Enamel (baked) A vitreous coating for decoration and protection baked on metal or ceramic products. Being fused on, it forms a smooth, strong, hard finish. It can be a painted that dries resembling the baked-on enamel finish.

Nicole Fall, *Revolutions*. Welded steel, enamel, 17′x10′x8′ (5.2m x 3.1m x 2.4m).

Ronald Kostyniuk, *Never the Twin Shall Meet*. Enamel on aluminum, 34″x72″x8″ (86.4cm x 182.9cm x 20.3cm).

Encaustic A design technique using different colors of clay and inlaying them into the clay body.

End grain The grain as visible from the end of a cut across a tree trunk or the end of a long plank; a cross section of lumber displaying the growth rings.

Engaged Attached, joined or merged parts of sculpture within itself or to something else not independently supported. An example is an architectural sculpture (attached to a building) or engaged arms of a sculpture, meaning the arms attached join directly to the body without intervening space.

Engobe A mixture of color oxides, clays, silica and feldspar. It forms a thick fluid that is placed on top of a dry or leather hard clay body for design purposes.

Engraving A process of cutting a shallow decoration into a solid surface with a sharp instrument. This is done on many metals but especially silver and gold. It is also a method of working with glass. *See* ***Glass engraving; Etching*** *(glass).*

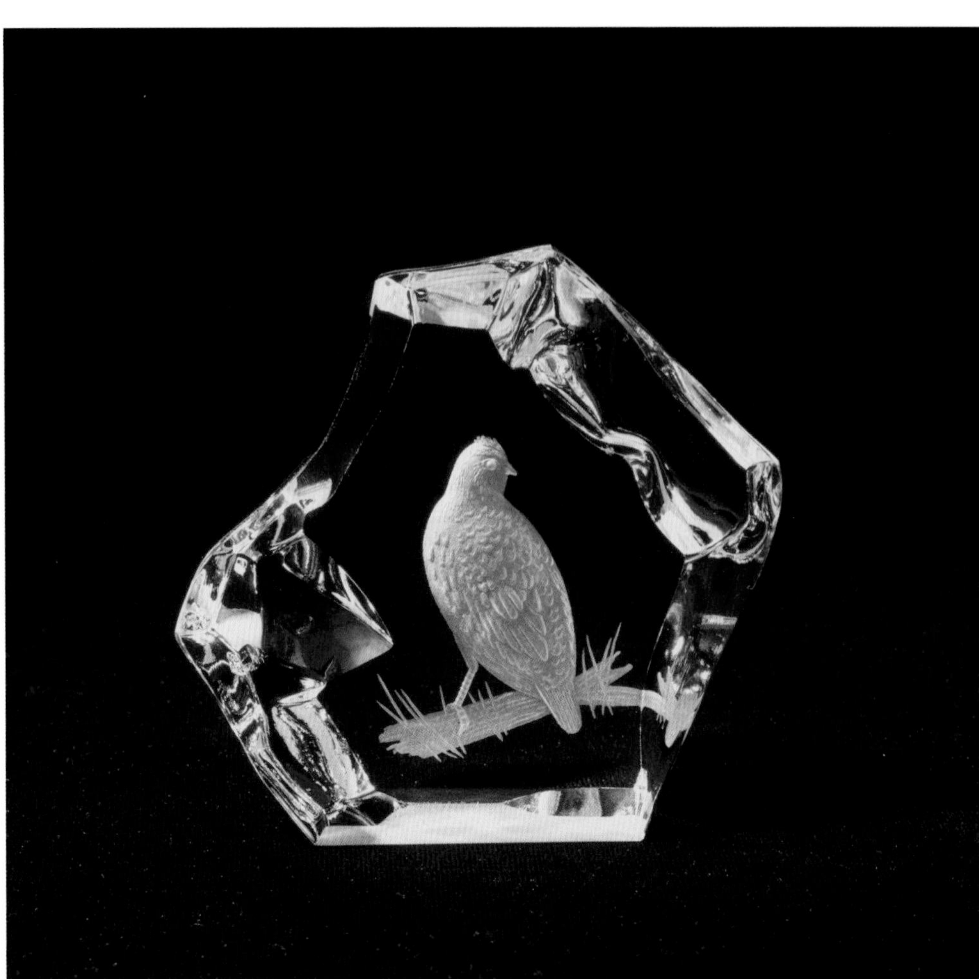

Boyd Graham, *Bobwhite Quail.* Deep engraved glass, 4″x4″ (10.2cm x 10.2cm).

Enlarging Increasing sculpture in scale. Sculptors have devised many methods to enlarge works. A small sculpture model is simply made larger by the use of proportional calipers. Templates taken from slices of the model are used, especially for large stone works that require several stones when precise stacking measurements are needed. Using a grid system is common.

Stone carvers may use a mechanical pointing machine. It is essentially a pantograph using several points for three-dimensional reference. Using fixed points from the model to the work, the artist can measure and calculate the increase in scale. *See* ***Pointing machine; Scale; Modeling (clay); Calipers.***

ENLARGING
by John Sherrill Houser

The artist prepares the armature for the enlargement of the 35′ (10.7m) tall *Don Juan de Oñate, Founder of the Hispanic Southwest, 1598,* Monument.

The selected model with the sculptor. Scale is demonstrated by placing a clay figure at the base of the model. Photographer: Jody Schwartz.

Even though the work is monumental in size, it is highly detailed. **Ethan Houser**, assistant sculptor, is working on details for the helmet.

Measuring points are required, as well as a strong steel armature and heavy scaffolding.

A plaster model stands in front of the work being completed.

Opposite page:

John Sherrill Houser pictured with his *Don Juan de Oñate Monument* in progress. Photographer: Ethan Houser

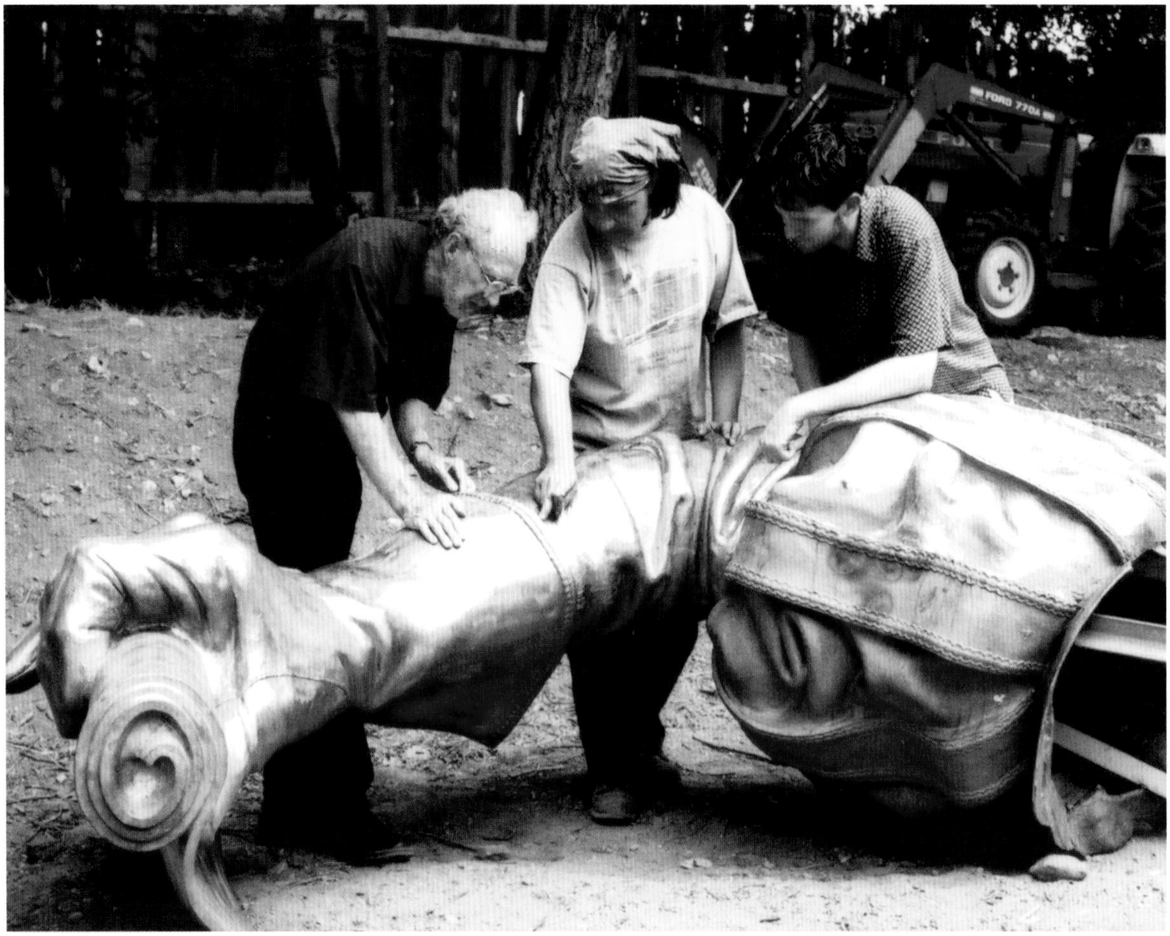

Sculptor **John Houser** (left) and foundry workers inspect the cast section of arm and hand holding La Toma. Photographer: Pres Dehrkoop.

Shidoni Foundry, Tesuque, New Mexico, completes the monument a section at a time.

A foundry worker TIG welds the cast sections of the head together.

Enlarging (digitized) A process of using computers with digital 3-D scanning and low density foam shaped by milling machines to achieve an enlargement. The resulting work does not require an internal support and is so lightweight that even a large work is easily transported and can be moved about in the studio by one worker. The process is extremely accurate, since the computer faithfully reproduces a model at an exacting scale requested by the sculptor. Enlargements have been completed to more than 50 feet (15.25m) in height and 25 times in scale. *See* ***Enlarging***; ***Mold***.

Model of *Chase the Wind* by **Joe Campbell** selected for enlarging.

DIGITIZED ENLARGING

by Kreysler and Associates Enlarging Service

American Canyon, California

A red laser scans across the model's surface to be captured as three-dimensional data.

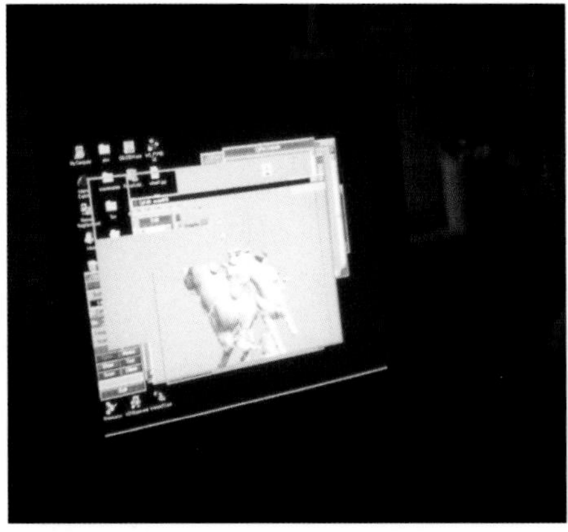

The captured image.

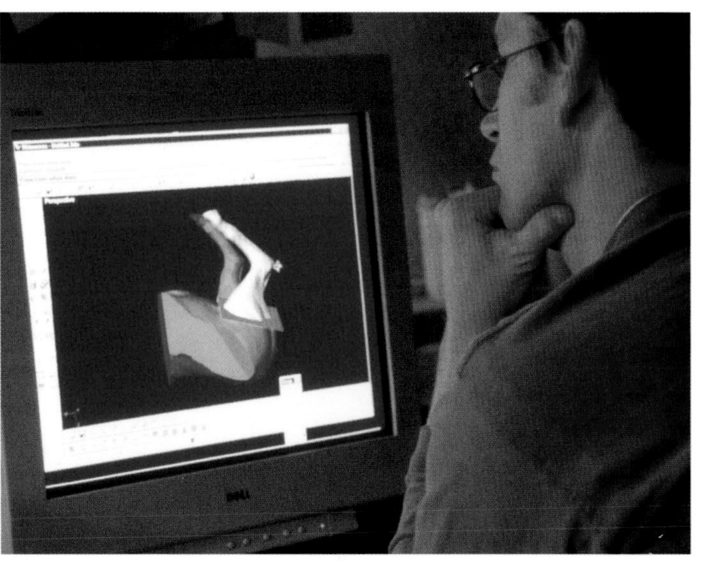

The scanned image is cut into shapes and sizes for machining.

The milling machine cuts the enlargement from a block of foam.

Completed parts to be assembled.

Different foam densities can be mounted together to produce a strong enlargement.

The parts are marked for reassembly by the sculptor.

Once packed by **Kreysler and Associates**, the parts are sent to the sculptor to assemble. The foam can be directly worked by the artist, or a surface coating of clay or wax can be added for finer details.

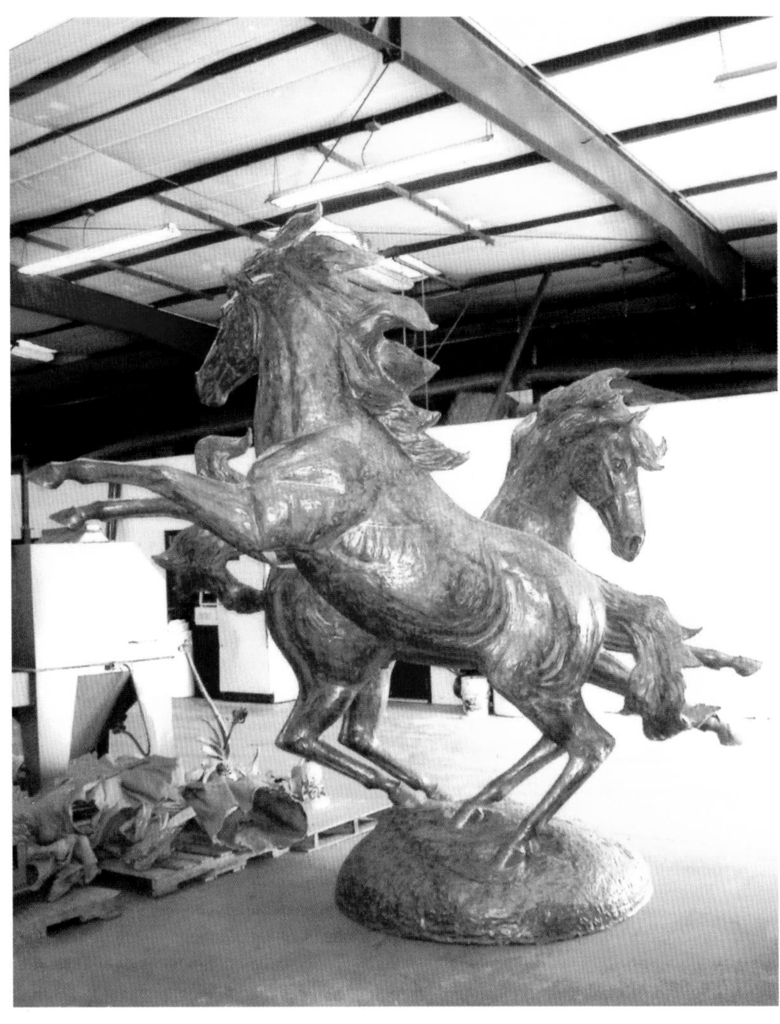

Finished sculpture ready to transport.

Joe Campbell, *Chase the Wind*, Cast bronze, 11.5'x11.5' (3.55m x3.55m), Commissioned by Superior, Colorado.

Environment Works of size, sometimes larger than a room; or referring to the location itself. The term installation explains the intent as well as the setting. *See* ***Installation***.

Environmental art Works that relate to the environment. The forms vary from full scale building processes such as using plants to walls to found objects. Taking the title environmental more seriously, the work would complement or readily be a part of the natural environment. *See* ***Sculpture garden; Site specific; Installation; Environment***.

Epoxy (casting) Using epoxy to create a hard surface casting. Epoxy is usually completed as a shell casting (hollow), as compared to resins, which are regularly done as a solid. (One of the primary reasons for this is cost; another is that epoxies do not cast well as solids.)

The same mold materials can be used for epoxies as for resins. If plaster, it must be sealed and waxed just as for resins. However, whatever molding process is used, PVA (polyvinyl acetate) needs to be brushed onto the mold surface since epoxy is an adhesive material. The mold is placed out in pieces and then each section is coated, frequently by means of a bristle brush.

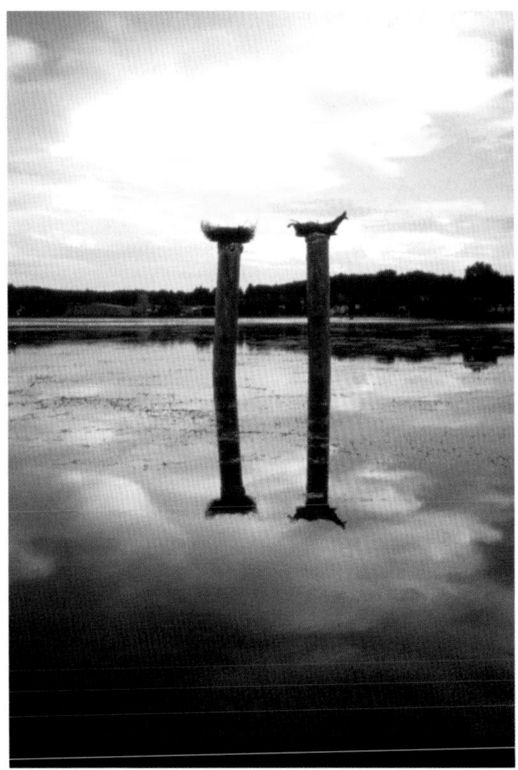

Hannah Franklin, *Time for Man and Bird*. Fiberglass, aluminum, grasses, 8'x2'x2' (2.4m x 0.6m x 0.6m).

Once the desired thickness is achieved, usually one-fourth inch (0.635cm), the sections are prepared to be placed together. They are now firm, so that they will not slough or sluff off from the wall. The outer seam top edges are coated with a bead of epoxy onto a slightly inner beveled surface. This squeeze seam will avoid air pockets and seal tightly since the epoxy readily adheres to itself. When the epoxy has set, the form is removed from the mold, and the seam is trimmed and all surfaces are cleaned. The benefit of hollow or shell casting is that the surface for epoxies and resins tend to be better with less finishing work required, except for cleaning seams in molds that cannot be done from just one opening. *See* ***PVA***.

Epoxy (glue) Thermosetting resins that are designed for adhesion purposes. The glue is in two parts, one being a catalyst. Once mixed, the thermosetting process begins. Some are designed to react within seconds, while others are more workable and take longer to set up. They form an extremely strong, hard bond with materials without the use of clamps or pressure. The catalyst can be toxic and should be handled carefully. *See* ***Adhesive*** *(chart).*

Epoxy putty A thickened form of epoxy adhesive. *See* ***Epoxy***.

Epoxy resins Resins that require a catalyst to become thermosetting. Being capable of achieving a rock-like hardness, they are used by sculptors for mold materials as well as molds. *See* ***Epoxy; Resin***.

Equestrian statue A public monument of a free standing horse and rider in celebration of a special event or for a public honor. The rider is a likeness or portrait of a leader. These statues are usually of bronze, though other materials have been used including wood and stone.

Etching (glass) A design on glass accomplished with hydrofluoric acid. The glass surface is prepared much like a metal plate is prepared for intaglio etching. A complete surface shielding coat of acid resisting substance is applied, then the design is scratched and scraped away leaving the area to be etched. The glass is dipped until the depth of the acid bite is obtained. The acid bath is neutralized, and the barrier shielding coat is removed to display the etched surface. Caution must be exercised when etching glass with acid. It is difficult to use, presents several safety problems and does not always render acceptable results. *See* ***Glass engraving; Glass; Engraving***.

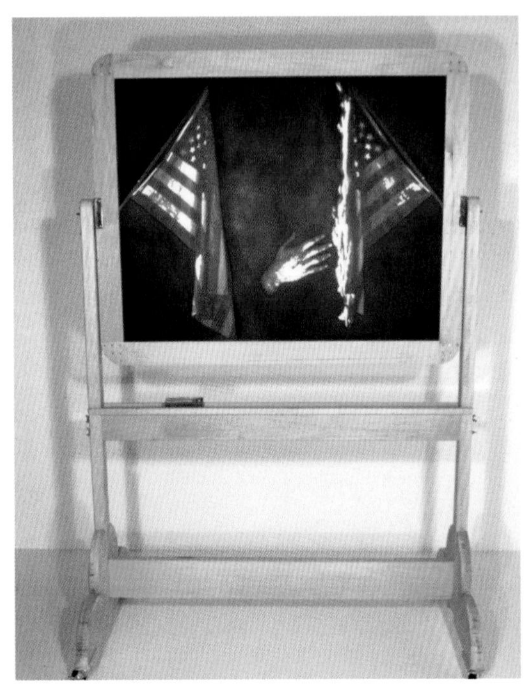

Jason Engelhardt, *Principal Parts*. Screen printed etched steel, 75″x52″x29″ (190.5cm x 132.1cm x 73.7cm).

Etching (metal) Creating surface designs in metal with the use of mordants (biting acids or other corrosive materials). The metal is first covered with a wax or substance that will resist the mordant, then the design is inscribed into the wax by scratching through it into the metal. The mordant is applied to bite the metal, deepening and sometimes widening the lines involved.

Ethyl acetate A volatile lacquer solvent.

Ethyl alcohol A thin, flammable liquid that is colorless, volatile and is used primarily for a solvent or cleaner for sculpture purposes.

Ethylene dichloride (EDE) A solvent, not a cement, that literally melts adjoining sheets of acrylic together. The dichloride is sparingly used and placed directly into the plastic joint, since capillary action aids the process. *See* ***Acrylic***.

Ethyl silicate A premixed ceramic shell slurry with an alcohol base. Because it dries rapidly, it decreases the production time in a foundry, though the mixture's vapors are flammable and potentially explosive. *See* ***Ceramic shell; Slurry***.

Everdur™ A quality brand of casting bronze with about 95% copper, 4% silicon, 1%

manganese and trace amounts of other metals, including zinc, tin, iron, lead and nickel with other trace metals. It is designed to pour easily, though the silicon makes it slightly difficult to patina. Matching silicon bronze welding rods are available. *See* ***Bronze; Silicon.***

Exhibit To show or display artwork, usually in a gallery or museum. *See* ***Exhibition.***

Exhibition The exhibit or show itself of a body of artwork. *See* ***Exhibit.***

Exothermic The generating and releasing of heat as a liquid solidifies. This is mainly noticed during the setting processes of plaster, cements and resins. A water-starved plaster mix will generate noticeable steam.

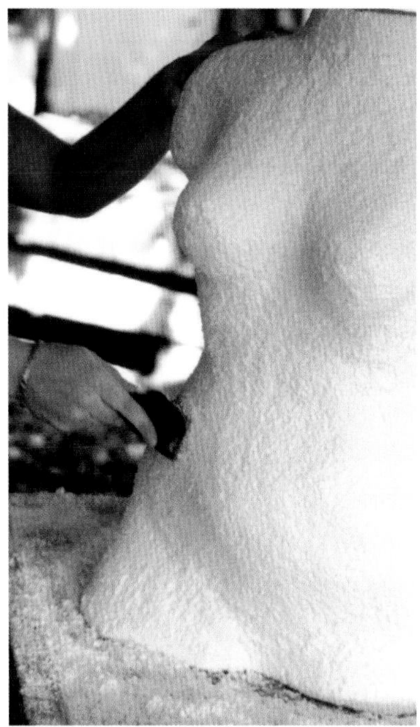

Expanded polystyrene is shaped by **Melissa Remel**.

Expanded polystyrene A thermoplastic better known by the trademark name, Styrofoam™. It is characterized by its expanded cell structure. Heat softens the material, literally melts it, but it hardens as it cools. Heated carving tools are not recommended because of the toxic styrene fumes emitted. Hot wire cutting should be kept to a minimum. The large cellular makeup does not react well with blunt or dull tools. While solvents can be used to melt it, they cause toxic fluids, vapors and gasses, as well as the loss of shape control.

Ventilation, respirators and eye protection are a necessity for working conditions. Expanded polystyrene is flammable, unless otherwise modified to be fire resistant. It can be obtained from boating and builders' suppliers, as well as from discarded packing containers.

Since many adhesives include chemicals that serve as a solvent for polystyrene, they need to be tested prior to use. Slow reactionary glues, such as carpenter's glue, may be used, but they need pinning or masking tape for temporary support. Plaster works well but may create a weight problem. *See* ***Adhesive*** *(chart);* ***Papier machè; Armature; Sand molding; Waste mold; Styrofoam™.***

Jeff Schmuki uses a clay extruder.

Extruder (clay) Device to force clay through a die in order to create a uniform shape or design. It is operated by placing the clay into the tube-like container and then pressing it with force created with an extended handle. The resulting extrusion may be hollow and of uniform thickness.

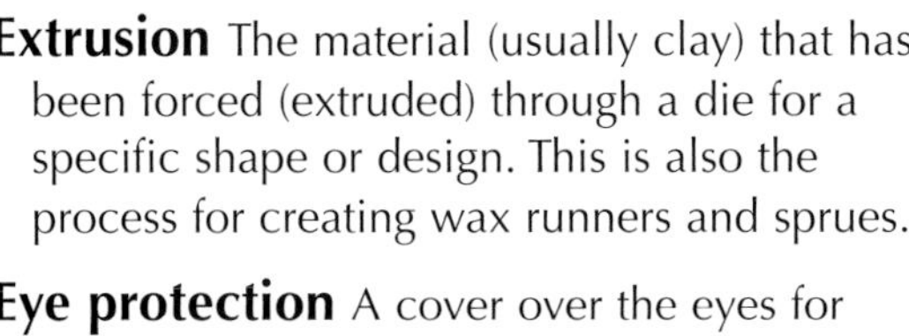

Extrusion The material (usually clay) that has been forced (extruded) through a die for a specific shape or design. This is also the process for creating wax runners and sprues.

Eye protection A cover over the eyes for protection from distinctive particles, chemicals or gasses. These can include safety eye glasses, goggles and face shields. The lens can be clear or colored depending upon the use. *See* ***Safety dress; Face shield; Welding lens.***

Eye protection.

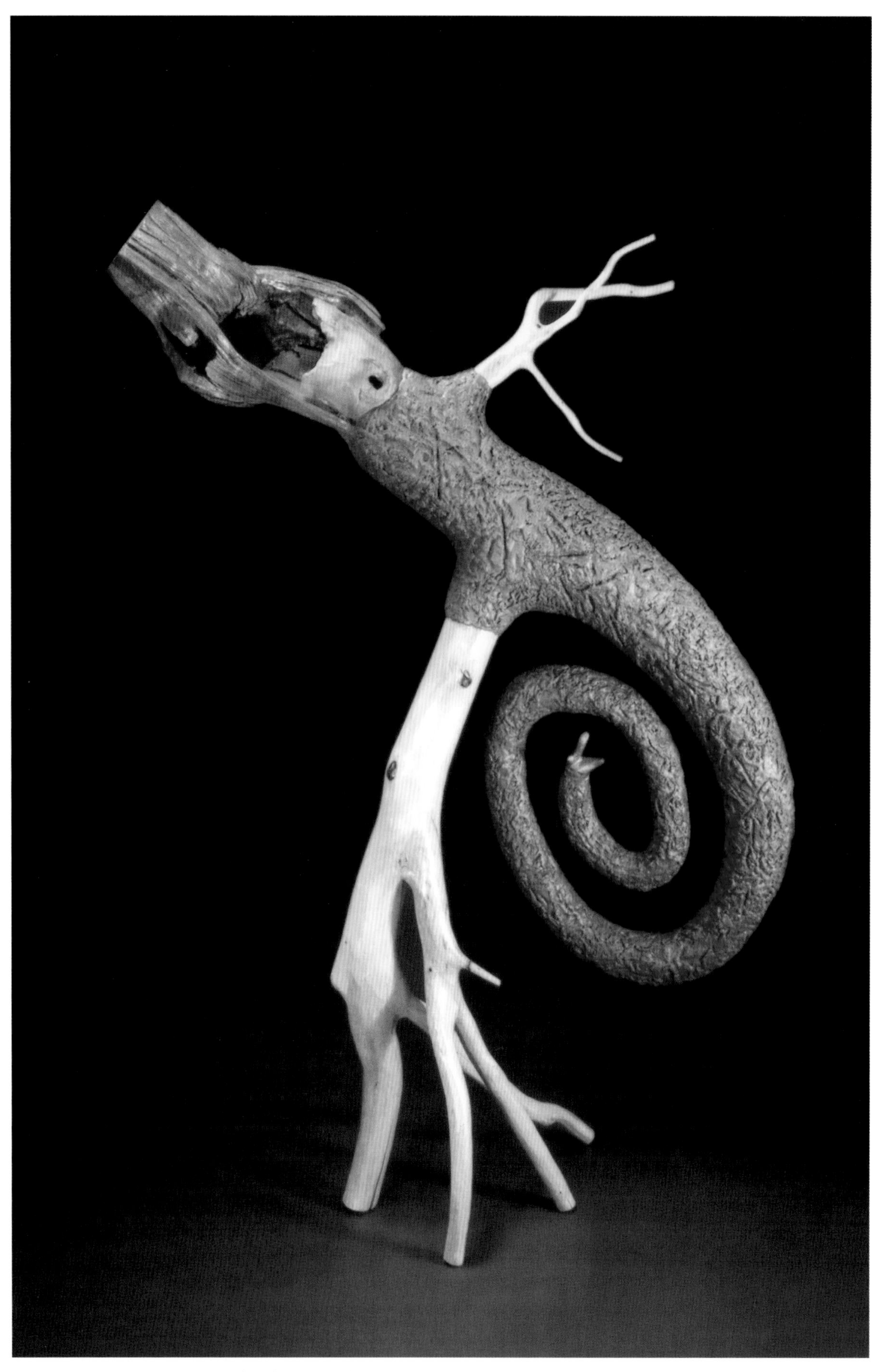

Duane Paxson, *Fossil Hunt*. Fiberglass, wood, ceramics, resin, acrylic, 82″x50″x24″ (208.3cm x 127cm x 61cm). Photographer: Moseley's Studio.

F

Fabric A material of woven cloth. It is associated with soft sculpture, since it can be stuffed and stitched into new forms. However, it can also be a very firm, hard material, especially if it is resin soaked cloth or combined with other substances. *See* ***Fiber***.

Catherine Jansen, *Parlor*. Fabric, scaled to life.

A detail from **Catherine Jansen's** *Parlor.*

Cynthia Harper, *When Hogs Fly*. Installation: corn sacks, wire, cable, cloth, paint, 2'x4'x3' (61cm x 121.9 cm x 91.4cm) each; site dimensions 20'x30'x20' (6.1m x 9.2m x 6.1m).

Fabrication Constructing or combining various parts of one or more materials into a sculpture. If one material is prominent, such as wood or metal, it is labeled as wood fabrication or metal fabrication. Sculptors who create large scale works sometimes rely on professional fabricators in part or total to manufacture their sculptures. Otherwise, the sculptor could not complete the work without additional skills, expertise or technique. *See* ***Metal fabrication***.

Paths to Greatness is fabricated by **William Baran-Mikle**.

William Baran-Mikle, *Paths to Greatness*. Brass, copper, nickel-silver, cast concrete, 7½'x7' (2.29m x 2.14m). State University of New York, Geneseo, New York. Photographer: Geoff Tesch.

Face coat The first layer of mold material that is placed onto a model or object to create a mold. The layer that captures the surface and significant details is the face coat. *See* ***Mold; Plaster investment***.

Face (top) The surface side of plywood or other lumber with the highest quality, as compared to the back or side that is usually not on display. The flat surface of a tool such as the top (face) of an anvil is another way the term is used.

Face (casting) Creating a mold from a human face and then completing a casting from it. The exposed surface of a work is also referred to as the face of a sculpture. *See **Body molding; Death mask**.*

Face shield A clear or tinted visor that is designed to protect the face and eyes from airborne debris and chemical splash. The face shield usually has a head mounted frame that allows the visor to be lifted or folded over the worker's head when not in use. It can be half, three-quarter or full face protection and is sometimes mounted to hard hats. *See **Safety dress; Welding lens; Eye protection**.*

Feathers and wedges with carbide tipped concrete drill, scored, drilled and inserted.

Fahrenheit A temperature scale with the water freezing point at 32°F and the boiling point at 212°F. The symbol is F. *See **Celsius; Measurements** (chart).*

Farrier One who forms horseshoes and then shoes (fits) the horse. The term comes from the word iron (ferrous in Latin). *See **Blacksmith**.*

Fastener Any device used to hold parts together, such as rivets, screws, nails and bolts.

Feathers and wedges Tools used for controlled splitting of stones. Several feathers (small shims) are placed into pre-drilled holes with a wedge in the center. The wedge is hammered down into the stone as it spreads the feathers. The result is an expected (split) break in the stone into a more useful size or edge. The splits should be planned for straight paths. Soft stones need deeper holes drilled than do hard stones. *See **Wedges** (shims).*

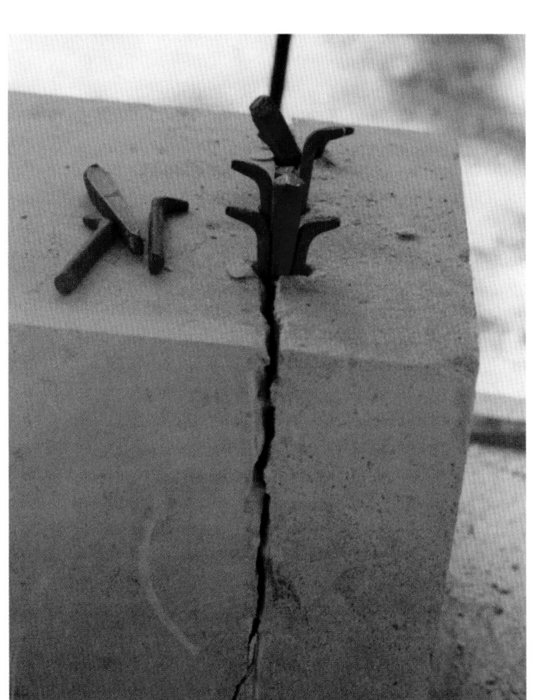

Feathers and wedges after striking even blows.

Feldspar Minerals used as a flux for glazes and clay bodies. *See **Glaze**.*

Female When used as a sculpture term, it indicates a negative, concave, depressed or typical mold shape that is hollow or empty. It is the intercepting or inner part of a mold, pipe, tool, etc., such as the female connector for an air line. *See **Male**.*

Fence The temporary wall or separator placed on a model used to divide or partition mold pieces. It can be made of any material. Aluminum or brass is commonly used when the fence is inserted into the model, and clay is used when the wall is placed on top of the mold surface. It is also the term for a rigid, but moveable, tool guide. *See **Mold making; Waste mold**.*

Ferric nitrate A chemical used in patina formulation especially for browns, oranges, and yellows. *See **Patina; Patina** (chart).*

Ferric oxide An iron oxide used in patinas to achieve a red color. Also used with ceramic clay and glazes for the dark red color. *See **Patina**; **Patina** (chart).*

Ferro cement A lightweight cement. Ferro concrete is a term used for concrete reinforced with steel. *See **Cement**.*

Mac Hornecker, *Prairie Fault*. Ferro concrete, steel, 9′x16′x18′ (2.75m x 4.88m x 5.49m).

Norma Minkowitz, *Sisters*. Wood, fiber, buttons, paint, wire, 43″x21″x19″ (109.2cm x 53.3cm x 48.3cm). Photographer: Joseph Kugielsky.

Ferrous Made of or containing iron.

Fettle To remove (trim) mold seams and other marks from castings. The knife used is a fettling knife, also called a potter's knife.

Fiber Elongated cells of wood or other materials that determine strength. When fibers are grouped, they become much stronger. Glass fibers are known as fiberglass and when grouped possess enormous strength. *See **Fiberglass**; **Fabric**.*

Fiber sanding pads Abrasive fiber sanding pads. They wear well, are very flexible and water resistant. Various grades can be obtained and are designated by color. *See **Patination**; **Scotch Brite**™.*

Fiberfrax™ A flexible refractory made of spun alumina-silica that resembles a roll of building fiberglass insulation. It is used to insulate kilns, forge heaters, annealers, metal casting furnaces, etc.

Fiberglass Filaments of thin, fine, glass fibers of high tensile strength. Extremely thin strands of glass fibers are spun together to form larger fiber strands, and these are often woven into sheets. Fiberglass does not distend. When fiberglass is saturated with liquid resin, the resulting form can be thin, strong and hard. Uses for sculpture are many from moldmaking to creating finished works. Strength can be gained in thin sheets. Two methods are used when working with fiberglass: lay-up and spraying. Lay-up is the most common method incorporated by sculptors.

Lay-up technique

Lay-up on molds involves a dry, non-porous mold sealed with lacquer or shellac; preferably two coats. It is waxed and buffed (if possible) at least twice with a final coat of PVA added for extra separation. Nonporous molds need only to be waxed. If waxing is not possible, two coats of PVA usually will do. *See **PVA**.*

All surfaces need to be about 70°F (21.1°C) to ensure good curing and also good working time. Being colder than 65°F (18.3°C) can initiate setting problems, while temperatures over 80°F (26.7°C) cause the chemical reactions to quicken, and decrease the working time, sometimes resulting in trapped air bubbles or poorly layered fiberglass.

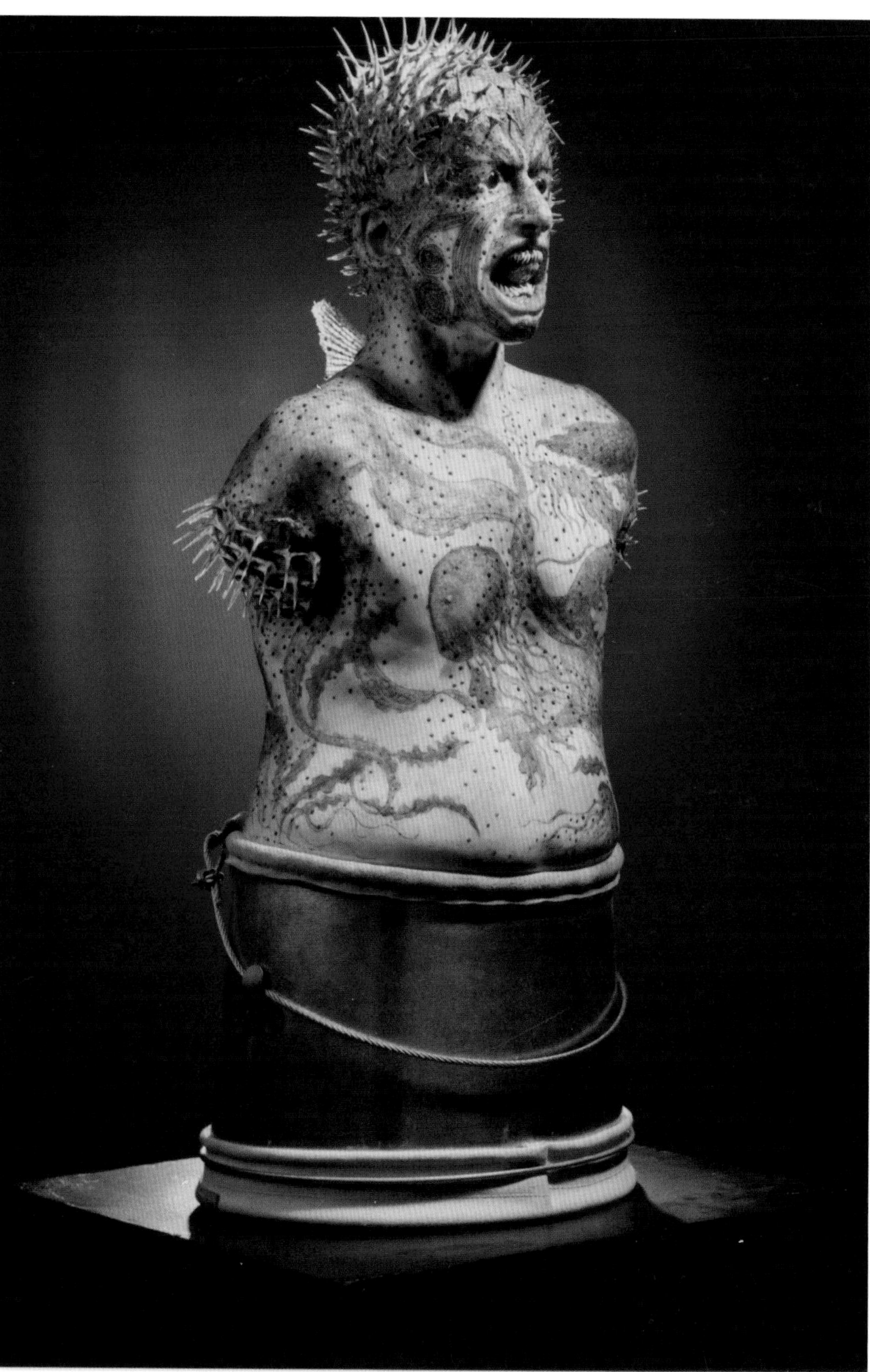

Mark Prent, *Ichthymorph*. Polyester resin with fiberglass; life-size casting and modeling. Photographer: Saltmarche.

The mixing container can be a plastic or paper paint mixing bucket, but not Styrofoam™ cups, which melt because of the resin. Unlike casting resin, the mixing container can be used after it dries (and it dries quickly unlike casting resins). Tools can be cleaned with acetone and even brushes can be reused if they have not been allowed to harden. The correct respirator and strong rubber gloves should always be worn.

Richard E. Prince, *Grecian Figures – Two Columns*. Fiberglass, muslin, 51″x16″x16″ (129.5cm x 40.6cm x 40.6cm). Photographer: Robert Keziere.

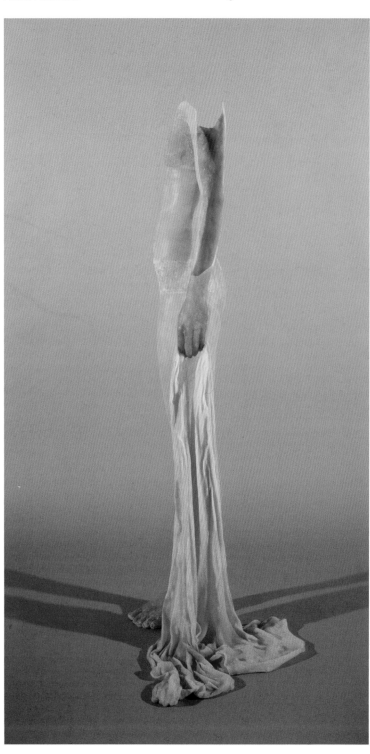

The first coat applied is the gel coat, which is available in a brilliant white to a jet black from manufacturers, but can also be mixed by the sculptor. The coat itself is necessary to keep the later layers of fiberglass from showing through. It can be sprayed on, as most commercial enterprises do on larger works, such as boats, but sculptors working with smaller, intricate molds frequently apply it by brush using two to three coats before proceeding. After the final coat has set, it is ready for the fiberglass to be applied.

The gel coat is brushed with a resin catalyst mixed according to the manufacturer's recommendations. The thick gel coat quickly dries, since it has a thickening agent. This helps to control the resin by avoiding a runny solution. It allows a faster build-up of resin. Immediately afterwards, a sheet-layer of fiberglass is added, spread out and pressed into the resin to be saturated and flattened without air pockets. Small hand rollers can be purchased for this purpose. They are designed with grooves to allow the air to escape while firmly pressing into the layer of fiberglass. Epoxy or resin can be used for fiberglass. Resin is a favored material, primarily because of the cost and ease of working with it. However, epoxies can be used in lower temperatures.

The size of the work determines the thickness needed. After the first layer of fiberglass has hardened, a second layer can be added. If the work is large, then a big weave fiberglass or a heavier fiberglass matt should be used. If the work is small, more layers may not be needed. However, if the work is to be built up, this process can continue, alternating matt and weave for strength. While the lay-up can continue over a long timespan, it is easier to remove the fiberglass after the last coat is laid up and hardened, but still warm. This allows the separator, especially if it is wax, to more readily release the gel coat. *See* ***Molds***.

Fiberglass can be draped or laminated over many objects, including Styrofoam™, cardboard, wood, steel, paper, chicken wire and plaster.

Spray molding technique

The spray or spray-up process is much the same as the hand lay-up method with the use of a spray gun for resin and chopped glass fiber instead of a woven fiberglass. Chopped fiberglass is shot or expelled from a feeder into a directed airborne surge of resin from a spray gun becoming one mix as it accumulates on the mold surface. A strand from the roll of roving is drawn into the chopper and chopped into shorter particles as it enters the airborne resin. The process is simple, if all of the controls are properly adjusted. The air compressor needs to be reasonably strong and able to deliver a continuous supply of 100 psi (689kPa). The sprayer needs to be immediately cleaned after use.

FIBERGLASS

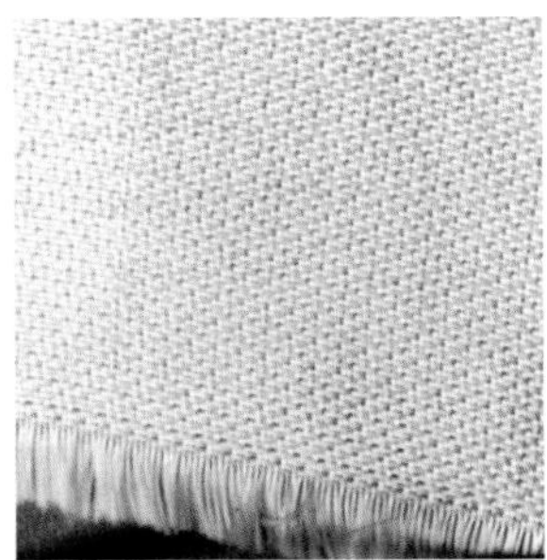
Lightweight fiberglass cloth.

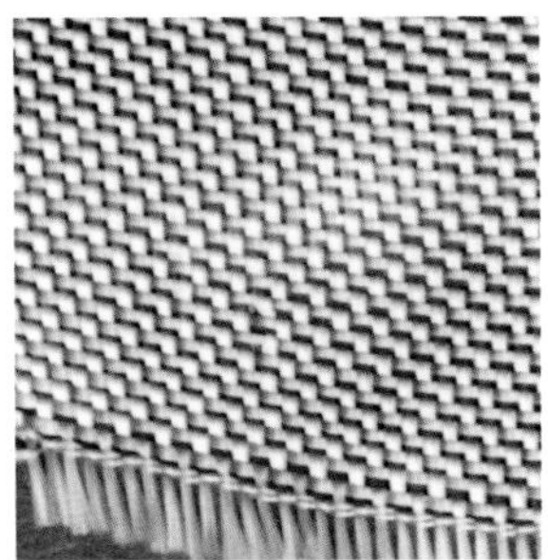
Medium weight fiberglass cloth.

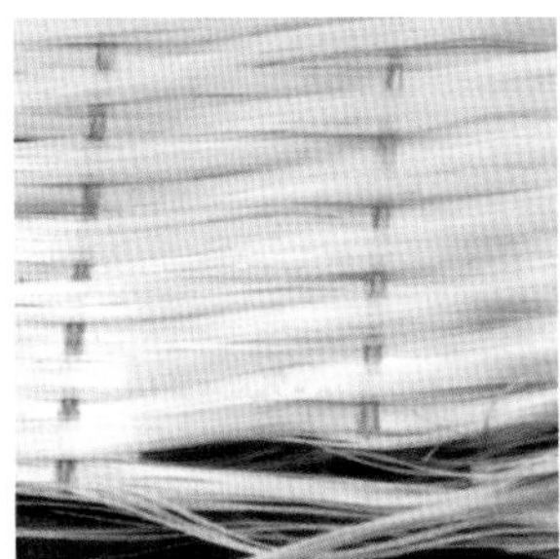
Unidirectional fiberglass cloth.

Fiberglass matt.

Fieldstone A stone found in a field or in locations other than quarries with various sizes and weights. They are very hard and not ordinarily carved. They are used in natural found shapes as part of a sculpture, usually without any attempt at reshaping.

Figurative Work that displays or represents the human body whether in total or part. Oftentimes, the term is used as the opposite of abstract, indicating recognizable subject matter (figurative versus nonfigurative).

Figure The human body. *See* ***Figurative***.

Figurine A small statuette or sculpted figure only a few inches (centimeters) in height. The term frequently refers to porcelain artwork.

File Hardened metal tool with sharp cutting ridges or straight teeth used to sharpen tools or to clean and shape works in wood, stone and other hard surfaces. Files are usually a long, narrow shape sometimes with handles. Popular shapes are flat, round or half-round.

Filigree A thin wire placed in detailed, involved designs as surface ornamentation. It can be made with a single wire or braided wires. Gold and silver filigree are regularly used in jewelry making.

Filler An additive to harden or soften, add embellishment or strengthen a mixture. Examples are stone used for concrete and grog used for clay. Also, a molding substance that is added to the mold material to replace parts of it to save expense, add strength, make it lighter or heavier, etc. A weld placed over the first weld, but not the last, may be a filler. It is used for strength when welding thick metals. *See* ***Filler rod; Welding***.

Filler rod A rod used for brazing or welding a metal. The rod is commonly brass melted with an acetylene torch to add to a joint seam or even to coat the base metal. *See* ***Welding***.

Fillet A thin substance placed into a gap or joint in a mold when it would not otherwise fit flush to ensure a continuous casting without leaks.

Dawn Stubitsch, *Jobie*. Polymer clay figurine 7½" (19.05cm) tall.

Filter A substance with minute pores that separates liquid, gas or particles for particular purposes. Examples are breathing filters to keep air impurities, dust particles or gasses from being inhaled. Filters are designed for specific purposes, such as airborne dust, as compared to chemical filters that are used for gas. *See* ***Respirator***.

Fine art Art made for aesthetic appreciation only, with no other function intended. Commercial transaction of the work has no bearing upon the definition of fine art. Applied art has other functions, but in time may become known as an aesthetic or fine art due to the fine craftsmanship involved.

Wendell Castle, *Friend.* Douglas fir, PC wood, 68″x29½″x29½″ (172.7cm x 74.9cm x 74.9cm). Photographer: Steve Lalouzetta.

Fine grain Close texture. The term is used to designate stones with a makeup of small particles or wood with smaller cells.

Fingerprint quality A superior casting of a surface, even to the extent that the sculptor's finger prints can be detected. Foundries use the term for excellent casting or high-grade metals used in casting.

Finish The final appearance, especially the surface, of a sculpture. This includes the coating, textures, patina, etc. A highly finished work means that the final form has been carefully detailed with high craftsmanship quality.

Finishing materials Substances (or tools) used in the final phases of completing a sculpture. These can be filing, sanding materials, buffing and polish ing compounds or any substance used to achieve the final appearance. *See* ***Abrasive*** *(chart);* ***Polish****;* ***Rubbing compound****;* ***Buffing wheel****;* ***Buffing compound***.

Fir (Douglas) A yellow-brown to pink colored wood better known for construction uses than sculpture. It is lightweight and easily splinters when carved. *See* ***Wood*** *(chart)*.

Firebox The heat chamber of a furnace, burnout furnace, forge or kiln.

Firebrick The hard refractory brick made of fireclay found in kiln or furnace walls. Though it can be used as an insulating brick, it is not the same as an art insulating brick of higher porosity. *See* ***Fireclay***.

Fireclay A high firing clay used for refractory products such as firebrick, chimneys and kilns. It is characterized by its high vitrification temperature. It can be fired and ground into smaller particles for grog.

Fire extinguisher A device designed to eliminate burning or fire by releasing a rapid flow of chemicals to quench the fire. Sculpture studios should keep an ABC dry chemical extinguisher that is wall mounted. It is designed to put out fires created by: A. dry materials (paper, wood, etc.), B. chemicals (paints, oils, gasoline, etc.), or C. electricity (operating motors, switches, etc.).

If a person is injured and sprayed with an extinguisher, then complete information from the extinguisher itself should accompany him/her to the emergency room. Treatment for sprayed extinguisher chemicals cannot be administered until the medical staff knows which chemical is on the skin.

Firing The procedure for heating clay thereby transforming it chemically and physically into a permanent hard state (above 1112°F [600°C]). In glaze firing the glaze and body maturing at the same time. *See* ***Kiln****;* ***Glaze***.

Technique

Loading the kiln for firing creates special problems for the sculptor, depending on the form and kiln configuration. Leather hard clay works should never be placed into a kiln for firing. They should be completely dried. If the work is heavy, it may require more than one worker or sometimes a fork lift to load it. In such cases, the kiln must be accessible by either a trolley cart system or large enough for the workers to enter with the sculpture. If the work is difficult to handle; precaution should be taken. If it is awkward to stack, it may need supports that shrink with the work. (These should have been made with the same clay body and cured at the same time.)

Because of weight, large sculptures are usually placed on the floor of the kiln to avoid crashing through the shelves. This may result in firing problems due to incorrect air circulation during the firing, etc. Every situation is different. The sculptor needs to exercise care at this point, since it is the time in which most clay sculptures are damaged. Though greenware can be stacked, sculpture is stacked to avoid breakage on unique protrusions.

The firing process begins by adjusting the kiln baffles to a more closed position, and in some cases, adding more gas to create more free carbon. Reduction is brought about by slowing the oxygen (air) supply, causing the fuel (gas) to remain unused as it circulates throughout the kiln. Reduction is generally performed late in the firing prior to reaching the high temperature. The resulting smoke will escape from the kiln anywhere. Since carbon monoxide is emitted, good ventilation is a safety necessity.

Pyrometric cones are used to determine the heat. They are periodically checked by looking through a peephole with a bung (replaceable plug) when not in use. The reduction does not have to go to the full firing term, but it can, if the temperature can be increased. (Over-reduced flames actually lower the firing temperature.) When the firing is complete, all openings to the kiln need to be closed for slow cooling. *See* ***Reduction****;* ***Slip casting****;* ***Damp box****;* ***Pyrometric cone***.

Abby Huntoon, *Elements*. Glazed earthenware, 9″x46″x11″ (22.9cm x 116.8cm x 27.9cm).

Firing cycle The sequence of time from the beginning to the end of firing and cooling clay. The term can also be used for the time it takes to achieve furnace metal melting for dewaxing a mold.

Firing range The extent that a clay can be heated without distortion.

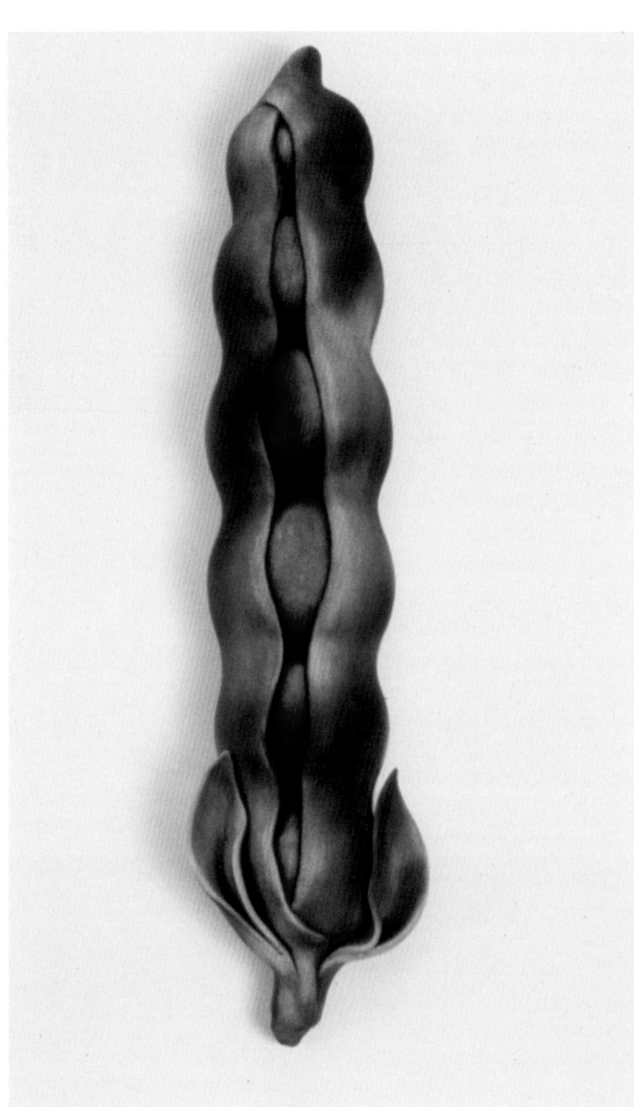

Whitney Forsyth, *Small Cathedral.* Ceramic, oil patina, 27″x8″x6″ (68.6cm x 20.3cm x 15.2cm). Photographer: Gene Johnson.

Firmer (tool) A wood chisel with an angled flat blade.

First aid kit A collection of items designed for medical treatment. Good kits have replaceable supplies of band-aids, creams, gauze, etc., that are designed for specific work areas, such as office, construction, welding, etc. The kit supplies are needed before more professional or thorough medical attention is available.

Fish tail (tool) A wood carving chisel in a similar shape to a fish tail, decreasing in size as it enters the handle.

Fissure A split or fracture in a bronze casting or a long fracture or crack in a stone used for carving.

Flame The burning gas at the tip of an oxyacetylene or propane torch. *See* ***Oxyacetylene***.

Flame cutting Cutting metal (ferrous) with an oxyacetylene torch. *See* ***Oxyacetylene cutting***.

Flap discs A hard backed disk with overlapping layers of abrasive sheets. As the abrasion wears away, new abrasive is uncovered. Different grits and sheets are designed for metal, wood, stone, etc. The diameters vary from under one inch (2.54cm) to over seven inches (17.78cm). *See* ***Abrasives***.

Flap wheel A replaceable abrasive wheel with numerous abrasive flaps designed with a small shaft for mounting in a die grinder. Sizes vary from several inches (centimeters) in diameter and width to extremely small. *See* ***Abrasives***.

Flash (de-waxing) Extreme heat with immediate application on a ceramic shell mold, usually in a burnout furnace. This allows the melting and liquefying of the interior wax surface to drain before the deeper interior wax can be expanded by the heat, thus avoiding mold fracture. *See* ***Burnout furnace***.

Various sizes of flap wheels for die grinders.

Flashing Thin seam-like protrusions on castings. They can be seen in cracks within molding surfaces. Flashings, sometimes called fins or runouts, are usually the result of defective molds. They can be found with the plaster investment type mold because of the fractures brought about by cracks in the mold materials being filled with hot liquid metals. Other reasons for flashing are poor mold materials or molds not properly reinforced. Ceramic shell molds rarely have flashings and then seldom thicker than tinfoil. If a flashing occurs on a ceramic shell mold, it is usually the result of improper dewaxing.

Flash point The lowest temperature that a liquid, vapor or substance will ignite. A flash fire results when the substance ignites.

Flask The container used for sand casting to hold the sand as it is rammed. The flask can be made of several products including metal or wood. The term is also used to designate any container used for holding metal casting investment. *See* ***Sand casting***.

Flat chisel A chisel with a flat tip. It can be a cold chisel, stone chisel, wood chisel, etc.

Flaw A blemish or imperfection in a material (such as stone) or a casting defect.

Flexible bowls Small rubber or pliable bowls used for small amounts of mixture, particularly plaster. After use, they are easily bent or twisted about the hardened residue allowing easy removal.

Flexible mold Molding material designed to bend repeatedly without breaking or losing its shape. It can be reused after removal from a cast object. Material such as latexes, silicones, polyurethanes and polysulphides are used for sculptural molds. *See* ***Molds***.

B. P. Barwick, *Quagmire*. Cast polyurethane, steel, 29" (73.7cm) tall.

Flexible molds have five significant properties: 1) They offer excellent details from the original. 2) They simplify otherwise difficult forms, allowing fewer mold pieces because of undercuts and the resilient quality of the mold. 3) They allow large editions. 4) With the correct separator, most casting materials can easily be used without destroying the mold. 5) They allow a very tight seam seal resulting in less clean up and fewer problems when using thin castable liquids.

Though many materials do not stick to flexible mold materials, a release agent is needed to ensure smooth removal and to prolong the life of the mold. Often, molding materials require separators unique to them. Shellacked surfaces will adhere to polyurethanes, thus, a separator is mandatory. The manufacturer will furnish a list of matching separators.

Flexible mold materials are usually one of three types: 1) **latex**, which is air dried in thin layers to secure the correct thickness, 2) **cold pour** rubber, polyurethanes, polysulfides or silicones that require a catalyst to complete the mix; various firmness and elastic properties are available, 3) **hot pour** rubbers, reusable vinyl materials of hard or soft ratings; the more pliable, soft vinyl may be preferred by the sculptor.

Flexible mold materials are furnished in two or more parts and require mixing before use. There are two major types of mixing processes. One type of compound requires scales for an exact ratio of catalyst to rubber compounds. Exact weights are necessary, or the mix may not set, or it could set too rapidly. The other kind requires a volume size to volume size, regardless of weight, to achieve the correct mixture. While care should be taken to secure the exact mix, this type will generally tolerate some guessing. Since no scales are involved, and it is a more forgiving compound to use, it tends to be the most popular mix to use in academic surroundings.

Jennifer Costa, *Bottoms Up. . . Bombs Away*. Cast aluminum, resin, 46"x12"x12" (116.8cm x 30.5cm x 30.5cm).

Several shore hardnesses are available from very flexible, limp materials to almost rock-hard compounds. Some blends have mixtures that are immediately thick for brush-on applications, while others may require a thickener or several coats to acquire a good thickness.

Consult the manufacturer for the correct separator. The most popular release agents are silicone spray and wax. Uncured CMC (cold mold compounds) should not come into direct contact with moisture or damp plaster molds, except for silicones. If a fresh plaster mother mold (supporting mold) is needed for a pour-on project, then it must be properly sealed prior to use or have a mold material that can work with damp plaster. Some manufacturers have products available to coat damp plaster molds, enabling them to be sealed enough for immediate use.

B. P. Barwick, *Precious*. Cast urethane, flexible silicone mold, plaster mother mold, 10" tall (25.4cm).

Mother molds are usually required when using CMC or RTV (room temperature vulcanizing) compounds, unless the mold itself is small and extremely thick or of the highest shore hardness available. When molds are made for use without the mother mold, they are formed in a pour-on container that allows a thicker mold. As a result, the greater volume of mold material drastically increases the strength and molding cost. This is seldom practical unless the mold is small, too delicate in detail to use shims or fences, or too much time is required to complete it using another process. The mother mold is also known as the supporting mold, a containing mold or an encasing mold.

Silicon rubber compounds are easy to use, though the two ingredients are generally weighed with scales, and de-airing with a vacuum is recommended. Depending upon the manufacturer's requirements, silicone rubber can be applied directly onto a damp plaster mold without a separator. Also, a separator is not necessary over most modeling materials, including modeling clays. This allows even finer details and ease of use not found in many molding substances. Silicone spray release should not be used, since it could cause the silicone mold to adhere to the mold surface, causing defects. Note the manufacturer's recommendations.

FLEXIBLE MOLD

by the Inferno Foundry, Atlanta, Georgia.

William N. Beckwith's *Mississippi 11th Monument* completed in clay is ready for molding.

The flexible mold is added.

Plaster is used as the reinforcing mother mold.

Requirements of rubber compounds

Though the material can be sprayed on, the most common methods of application are either brush-on or pour-on. The brush-on method is generally used and involves using a soft brush imparting a liquid mix to the form's surface with two or more layers of application. The mixtures after the first coat are of a thicker material or with a thickener substance added and applied with a spatula. Brush-on is used on larger works where the pour-on method cannot be completed because of size or expense.

The pour-on method involves pouring the flexible liquid material over an artwork that has been placed into a container or shaped mother mold.

Triple beam scales are suggested for materials that have to be weighed. They will register amounts with the accuracy that is needed, especially for smaller works. Throw-away brushes and plastic cups are ideal for small measuring and mixing needs. Mixing the brush-on only takes a few minutes, but higher room temperatures and high humidity can result in less working time.

Depending on the product, the average surface working time is about twenty minutes. However, once the mix begins to set, the initial face coat or surface coat should not be touched or moved until it is firm. Some mixes help in checking the thickness by providing a see-through surface, thus visually aiding the sculptor to an even thickness.

Mixing containers must be dry and clean enough to scrape the surface for excess mix. The mix should be removed from the sides and bottom and mixed back into the volume. Many inexperienced molders have problems with mold curing by not thoroughly mixing the substances and then using the unmixed material as part of the finished molds. It does not set. Unmixed mold material is an undying headache, sticking to anything within contact distance while cured material is easy to remove.

The components need to be 70° F (21.1°C) or above to ensure proper mixing and good setting. The humidity and room temperature is important. While manufacturer's requirements must be heeded, seldom does any flexible mold material set well in temperatures less than 65°F (18.3°C). Extremely high temperatures can decrease working time or have other adverse effects on the final product. High humidity can slow or even stop the curing process.

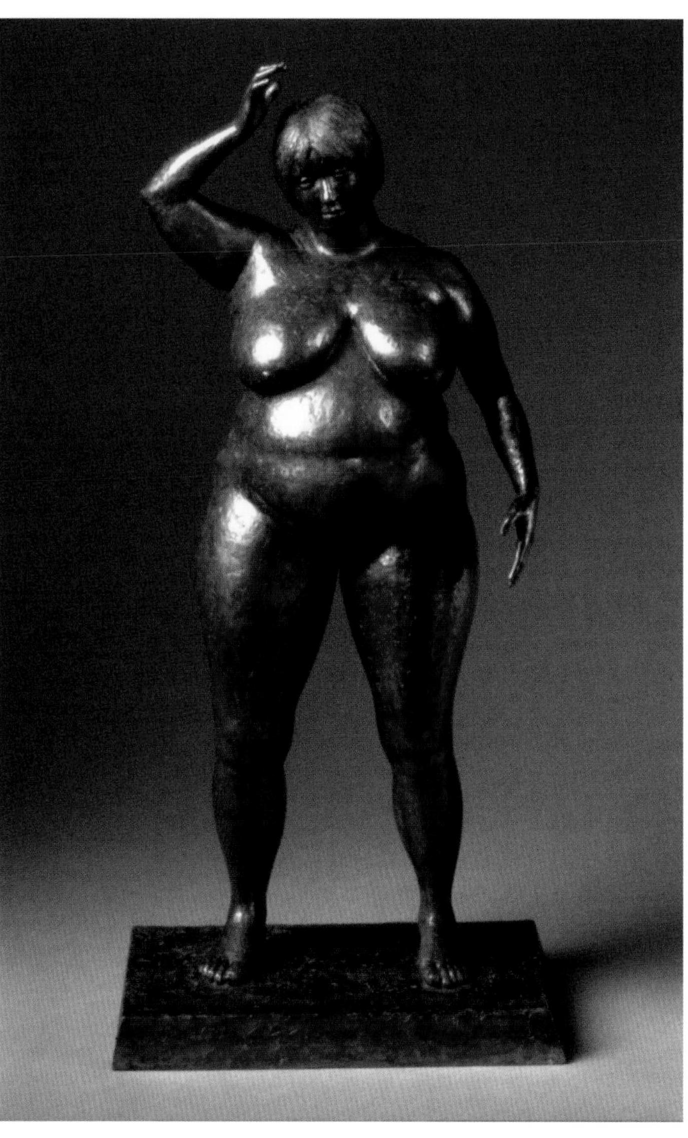

Norman D. Holen, *Early Morning*. Bronze, 9½"x6½"x20" (24.1cm x 16.5cm x 50.8cm) Photographer: Peter Lee.

Brush-on mold techniques

The sculptor needs to study the manufacturer's instructions, guidelines and safety cautions prior to preparing a mold.

Shims or fence material are used the same way as for any other type of mold. Once in place, the separator is applied if the manufacturer designates one. The brush-on material is proportionally mixed either by weight or volume per specifications. If the manufacturer requires a separate ingredient to be stirred prior to use, it must be done or the mix will not properly set. Many catalysts contain heavy substances that will settle out during shipping or storage.

Measure the components into two separate containers and then add to a third. The thinner or most liquid component is first added into the mixing container. (This keeps the thicker tacky material from adhering to the container.) Smaller mixes can be completed by hand with a stirring motion for three to five minutes, taking care not to whip or stir in unnecessary air. Once the mix is ready, it is easy to identify, since it is smoother and often a new color or shade. A stirring propeller, blade mixer or mixing shaft can be used on an electric or air drill. An egg beater can also be used, preferably in slow speeds to avoid air addition.

BRUSH-ON

by Lance Labadons

Brush-on silicone mold material is applied. Triple beam scales are used for exact weight measurements.

A simple soft throw-away bristle brush is the preferred applicator.

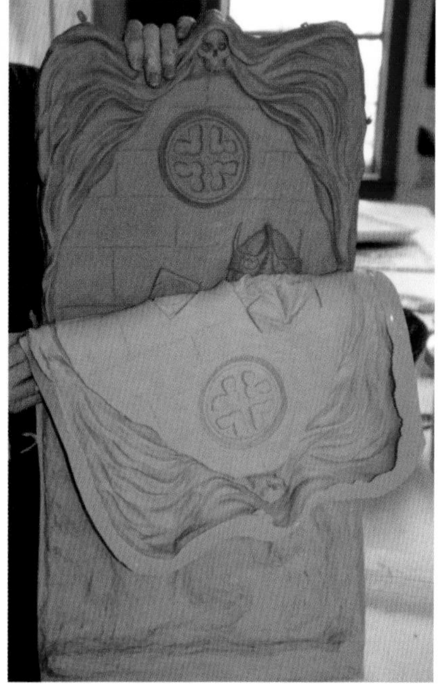

Once cured, a mother mold is added, then dislodged before removing the flexible mold. Notice the easy removal of this limp form by the sculptor.

To eliminate surface air bubbles, the first coat is brushed on using a soft bristle or sable hair brush. Also, the modeling compound can be distributed into small crevices with a spray nozzle of pressurized air directing its path. After it has hardened or set (see manufacturer's specifications) the next coat can be added with a thicker (thixotropic) mix brush-on applied with a spatula.

For smaller molds, an even three-sixteenth inch (0.476cm) in thickness will suffice. The shims or clay work need to also have the same thickness and extend to the end of the shim or fence. The mold should be allowed to cure, usually overnight. A separator is added.

The mother mold is placed on with a reinforcement (such as hemp) for strength to the completed mold. Afterwards, the shims or fences are removed. The separator is added to the shim or fence wall to prepare for the next half to be finished. The second side is finished as the first side was, but with a mother mold. Finally, the completed mold system is taken apart (a pressurized air supply from an air nozzle will greatly aid this) and cleaned. It is realigned and placed back together for use or storage.

One variation to this process is in using metal shims to do the complete job in one setting. This is accomplished by coating the entire artwork with the compound, including the shims, all at the same sitting. The mold is built up to one-fourth inch (0.635cm) on all sides, including the shims and allowed to set. Then the mold is encased in a mother mold, set, cleaned and placed together for use or storage. This does well for small objects or molds that do not require an absolute seal. However, once the shims are removed, there is an ever-so-slight gap or space left in the seam. Thin liquid materials (resins) can leak out, resulting in a seam line that has to be removed.

Larger artworks are done much the same way with more thickness and adjusting the fence or shims to be taller and have more reinforcement for better registration. Also, the rubber mold material not only needs the regular expected keys for registration but lock keys. These are set on the rubber mold wall held in place by the mother mold. They allow a larger expanse of rubber material without sagging away from the wall. Obviously, the mother mold needs additional reinforcement to guard against breakage or distortion of the mold. They are placed into the mold material just before it sets. They readily adhere, since dry compounds stick to the next mix with tight ease.

Techniques of pour-on

This is the process of designing an encasing or mother mold over the artwork with consistent space in between it and the artwork to fill with molding materials. An upper opening allows liquid material to be poured into the mold about the artwork. After the new mold hardens, the mother mold is removed. The new material is either taken off in one piece or cut open with a sharp blade to remove the artwork. This is a natural process for molds that have flat bottoms or a large base that will allow easy access for casting material to be placed back into the finished mold.

Gerald Balciar, *Staking Claim*. Cast bronze, 16"x12"x28" (40.6cm x 30.5cm x 71.1cm).

POUR-ON MOLD

by Ha Young Coffman

The clay artwork is ready.

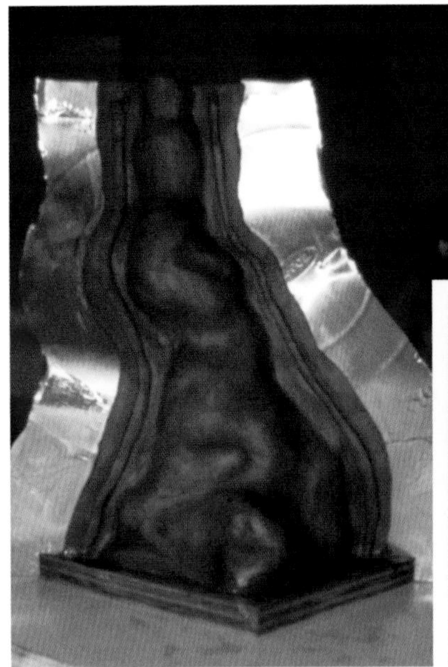

A soft, pliable ceramic clay is placed over the artwork to assure the correct mold thickness. Notice the clay and metal shims.

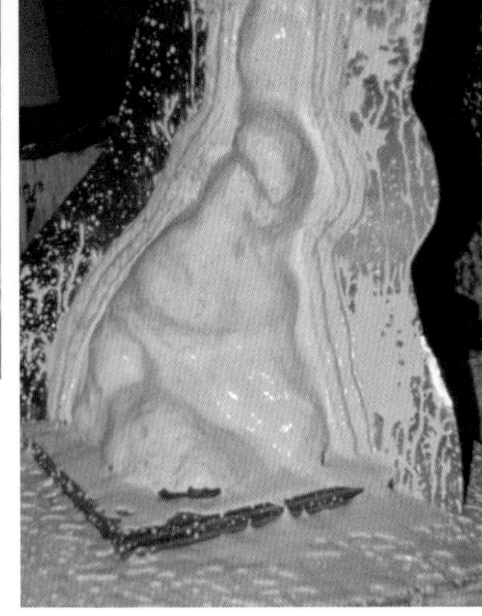

The plaster mother mold is added.

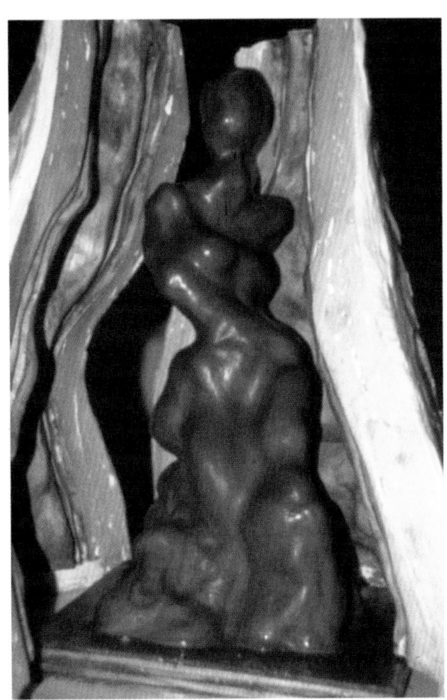

The mold and ceramic clay are removed revealing the original artwork.

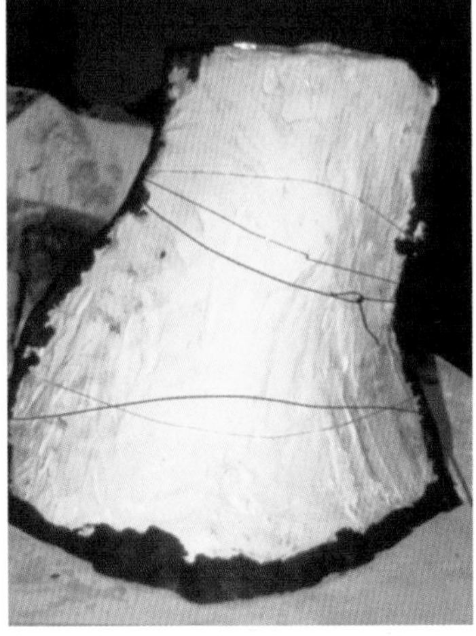

Reassembled, the mother mold is securely fitted. Any possibility of mold leakage is plugged with clay prior to filling.

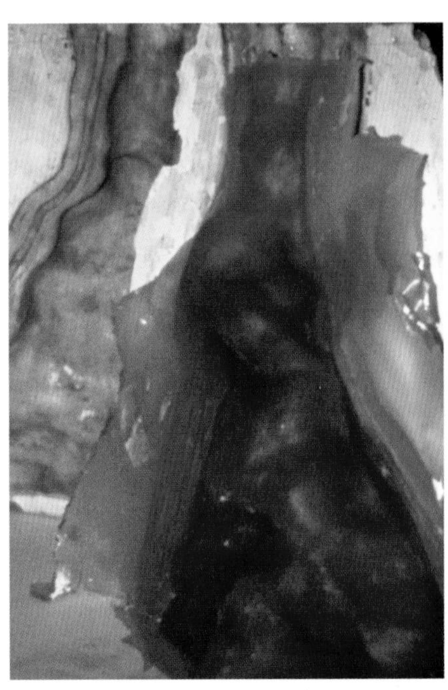

Once poured with mold material and cured, the mother mold is opened to reveal the pour-on mold. It will now be cut along the seam lines to make it usable.

The pour-on mold is best for CMC and RTV compounds, since both are set in motion by a catalyst and do not require air to aid in the curing process. Silicone mold materials are ideal, since they can be used in a freshly completed plaster mother mold without a separator, as long as surface water is not present, which causes bubbles to form in the silicone mold.

The artwork must be mounted in a fixed position on a base or platform that can be enclosed by the mother mold or easily registered to the mother mold. The mold must also provide an opening or duct placement that allows the mother mold to be completely filled with mold material. Sometimes this involves adding a separate air duct for the interior air to escape the liquid mold material that is being added. Once the artwork is mounted on a firm base for registration purposes, it is covered with a thin covering such as a flexible food plastic wrap to protect the artwork's details and surface from damage as the next step is completed.

To create the gap between the form and the mother mold, an even layer of something must be applied to the artwork prior to applying the mother mold. Soft ceramic clay is regularly chosen because it can easily be formed over the artwork. It is pliable and freely added to the surface of the form. Small molds need only a quarter inch (0.635cm) thickness of mold materials, while larger artworks may need thicknesses upwards to a half inch (1.27cm). The ceramic clay is rolled into sheets and applied by draping them over the artwork until it is fully covered, taking on the general shape of the original artwork, though not tightly pressed so as to not disturb the form's details. The top or high point of the artwork needs a funnel shape added as a pouring cup for the mold material. No ceramic clay can be higher than the pouring cup, and all high points must allow the air to escape from the mold.

A seam should be in the best location for the mother mold to later be separated. It should be thick enough to allow it to be cut down the middle into two equal supporting walls. A metal shim is placed directly into the center of the ceramic fence to separate the mother mold into two or more pieces when needed. Lock keys made of clay can be applied to the surface to later be dug out, or a die grinder with a rounded burr can be used to carve out the lock key shapes from the mother mold. (Lock keys are essential for larger works.) To remove the mother mold and accurately replace it, the artwork is securely anchored on a small wood base. The ceramic clay has been placed down to the top of the base but not around the outer edges. Only the mother mold can touch the outside edges for a tight fit, resulting in an accurate registration of the space between the mother mold to the artwork. The base needs waxing or a mold separator added before using the pour-on liquid.

Ha Young Coffman, *Figure*. Cast bronze, 12" (30.5cm) tall.

Another method of registration is for the base to have definite key indentations placed into it for the mother mold to be placed on. Again, it hinges on the artwork being anchored firmly to the base so that the form will not move during the molding process.

A third method is to apply small spacers of the same thickness as the ceramic clay wall. These spacers are placed in locations chosen to keep the mother mold from resting upon the artwork as the casting material is added. *See* ***Spacer.***

Ione Citrin, *The Rose*. Bronze, 23"x15"x13" (58.4cm x 38.1cm x 33cm).

Determining the amount of casting liquid is important to avoid waste and also to have enough liquid ready. When the ceramic clay is removed, it should be retained and placed into a measuring container to estimate the amount of pour-on needed. Additional mix will be needed to fill in small gaps created from the art surface to the clay material, especially undercuts that were not filled but covered over by the ceramic clay. Two methods are successful. One is to physically compress the ceramic clay into a measured mixing container. The other method is to submerge the spent clay into a container filled to the lip with water. Water will spill over and out. Afterwards, the clay should be removed. The volume of the water that remains should be measured. Subtract from the original amount to determine the pour-on that is needed. Make certain the proper separator is used, if one is necessary.

While the initial coat can be brushed onto the artwork prior to inserting the form into the mold, it is not necessary except on intricate surfaces or delicate details that appear to have severe undercuts.

Careful preparations should be made so that the mother mold will not leak and that the mold will be firmly anchored to a seated base or table top. Otherwise, the mold itself can and will float up from the working surface and the mold material will escape at the bottom. It can be strapped down with bungee cords, wires, etc., so that it will not move. All seams need either modeling or ceramic clay stuffed on top and into any visible cracks. Better yet, a heavy burlap or blue jean material in long strips that are about two inches (5.08cm) wide and saturated in plaster are added over the seams to ensure complete sealing of the mold. Plaster is slowly added about the base and allowed to set, sealing the bottom from potential leaks. The sculptor needs to be on hand for about 30 minutes or until the mold begins to set to ensure that there are no leaks, and if so, that they are plugged.

After the mold compound has set (usually overnight, depending upon the manufacturer's recommendations), the mold is removed. The new rubber mold is cut with sharp blades, such as X-acto™ knife blades, into the center of the seam to create two or more mold parts. The artwork is removed and the mold is cleaned. If it is to be stored, it needs to be filled with wadded newspapers or a fine silica sand to keep the mold material from collapsing. Whatever is used, care must be taken that the filler does not distort or stick to the mold material.

Container boxes, box molds, or dump molds are used for small delicate sculptures, or parts of larger sculptures. Basically, the pour-on method is used with pour-on molding materials being placed about the artwork in an ordinary box or a container designed to mold the liquid but not necessarily in the shape of the artwork. The artwork can be divided by a clay wall and cast one-half at a time, or it can be completely encased in the mold material and later cut into sections to remove the artwork. A pouring cup can be cut out (shaped) to add the casting material.

Clear or transparent pour-on liquids are best for this type of casting, since it is easier to place seam cuts on an artwork that is visible. Usually, the finished mold is strong enough to avoid retaining the mold container. However, occasionally the original container should be used for support if the mold is weak or thin enough to create distortions. Storing this mold is simple, since it is the container itself. *See* ***Latex molds; Vacuum pump; Lock key***.

Flexible shaft (flex shaft) Working tool attached to a flexible shaft with the other end connected to a motor that turns the shaft or drives the tool being held by the operator. The handheld tool is called a handpiece that holds various bits, wheels, etc., depending upon the design. The brand name Dremel™ is almost synonymous with small, flexibleshaft tools.

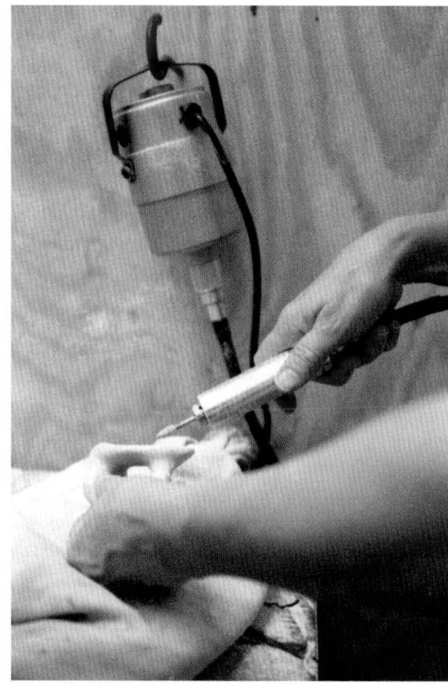

Small wall-hung flexible shaft handpiece in use.

Christine Federighi, *Red Foot Rider (wrapped)*. Bronze, stone base, 71"x7"x7" (180.3cm x 178.cm x178cm).

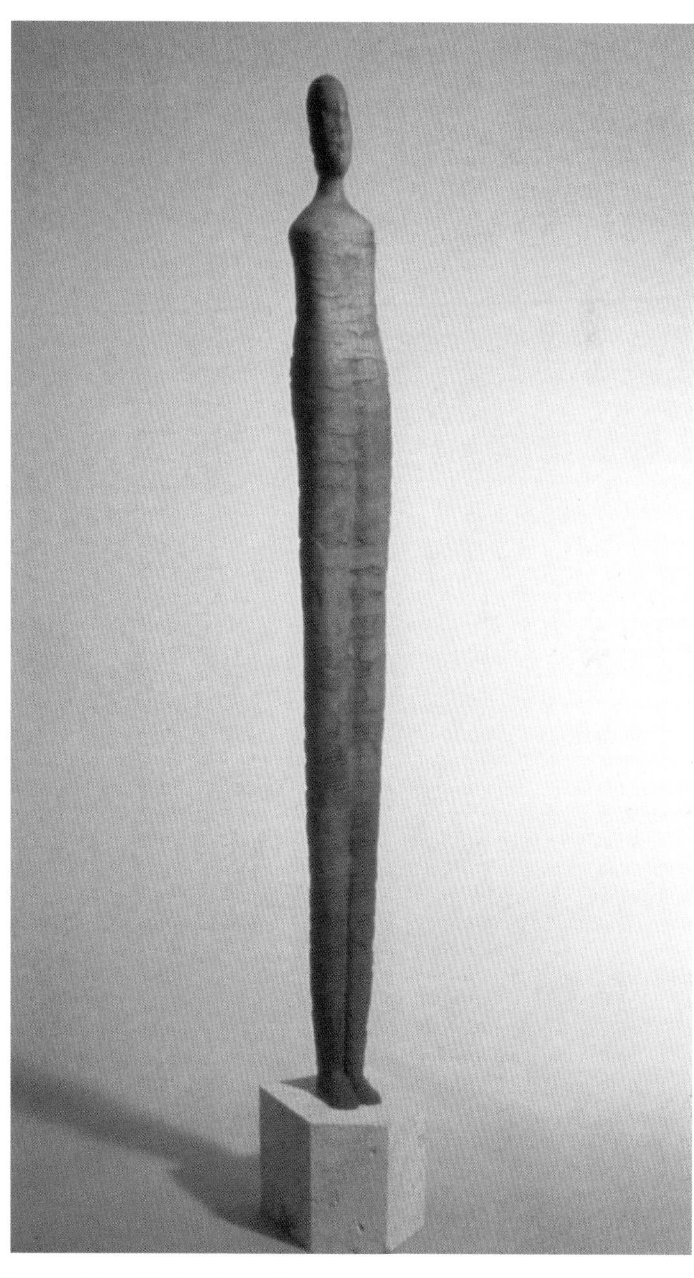

Flies Unevenly crushed sand mounds used to visually test the core spacing in sand cast molds. After a core has been shaped, it must fit correctly inside the mold without touching or coming too close to the inner mold wall. One way to ascertain the thickness is to place small mounds of sand evenly spaced throughout the wall, just enough to rise about three-sixteenth of an inch (0.476cm) with each mound being placed an inch (2.54cm) or two (5.08cm) apart. The core is delicately laid back on top with equal amounts of sand placed on top. Replace the top (cope) section. Look for unevenly crushed sand mounds. If any are crushed, it indicates that the core needs to be trimmed to ensure that it will not protrude into the poured metal. After the correct fitting, the flies are brushed away. *See **Sand casting**.*

Flint (silica) As a fine silica powder, it is mixed into clay bodies for whiteness and refractory strength. An almost invisible powder, it can become airborne and eventually cause silicosis.

Flocculation (flocculent) Process of aiding fine particles in suspension to join and become larger articles (flocs) and settle. Flocculation is primarily used for thickening slip mixtures. The flocculent is the added material (acid) that increases the particles' attraction and thickness. *See **Slip casting**.*

Fluidizing bed A uniquely designed container in which compressed air enters the bottom and is distributed beneath the lower floor. The porous floor allows the air to escape without the materials falling through. It is primarily used for ceramic shell mold-making. The compressed air rapidly rises to the upper part, where silica sand (stucco) particles are held in suspension by the air flow. When in use, the stucco evens out due to the air flow. If the operator can insert a hand without difficulty into the fluidizing bed, it is ready for use. Slurry coated mold works are easily dipped into the suspended silica particles. The hovering particles adhere all over the wet slurry for an even coating of silica. Ideally, the air supply is controlled by a foot pedal that can be adjusted for volume. The air pressure varies, but will generally be about 100 pounds (45.4kg) with a large enough air reservoir (tank) to maintain the flow until the work is completed.

Fluidizing beds can be made using specially designed porous tiles (ceramic) to evenly disperse the air throughout the sand. The tiles must be securely placed on base blocks to elevate them for the pressurized air to enter under them. With some experimentation, two fluidizing beds can be made, one for finer particles and one for coarser materials. Good ventilation, a dust mask, and eye protection are needed. *See* ***Ceramic shell; Slurry***.

FLUIDIZING BED
by Tim Kinard

Before using the fluidizing bed, the wax artwork is dipped into slurry.

The slurried wax is inserted into the fluidized bed.

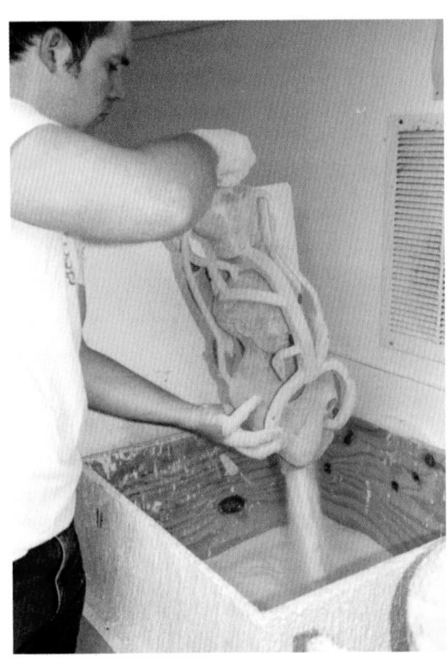

The artwork is immediately removed, completely coated. Notice the silica draining from inside.

Fluidizing a large mold held by an overhead hoist at **Shidoni Foundry**, Tesúque, New Mexico.

Fluorescent (lamp) A sealed glass tube with a coated inner wall that brightens (fluoresces) by an electrical current passing through it that discharges electrons. Many shades of white are available, as well as colors.

Jane Haskell, *Pittsburgh Biennial*. Fluorescent light, 25′x16′8″x8′ (7.63m x 5.08m x 2.44m). Photographer: Richard Stover.

Flux An ingredient that removes impurities within the welding, soldering or brazing areas. As a result, fusion between the two metals can occur. It is heat activated, such as the flux on a welding rod. In ceramics, an oxide (such as feldspar) interacts with other oxides to improve fusion. Feldspar mixed with the clay reacts at a lower temperature, hastening the vitrification. In casting, a flux is added to the molten metal in the crucible to keep gases from forming. *See* ***Soldering; Welding; Casting; Glaze***.

Foam (plastics) Lightweight, expanded plastics used for armature materials, molds and sculptures themselves. Solid Styrofoam™ or foamed urethanes are commonly used. Foam made of urethane can be coated with fiberglass, etc., for a hard surface, though it is especially useful as a core material for soft sculptures.

Solid foams, such as Styrofoam™ or polyurethane foam, do not create a permanent work, unless they are coated and/or used as a core with a more permanent material, such as fiberglass, epoxy or concrete. Each permanent coating reacts differently to the foam, so the manufacturer's suggestions need to be followed, as well as tested by the sculptor. The foam is easily shaped with saws, wire brushes, serrated knives and rasps. Styrofoam™ can be cut with a hot wire, while polyurethane produces deadly fumes if it is cut with a hot wire. The operator should wear a respirator and eye protection recommended by the manufacturer when using heat or burning tools on all foam products. *See* ***Armature; Styrofoam™; Expanded polystyrene***.

Liquid foam is a combination of two ingredients to create a rapid curing and expanding foam. It will stick to almost anything and expands many times its shape. PVA, wax and silicone spray can be used as separators. Foam is often used for packing, being expanded around a covered sculpture within a box for shipping purposes. It is a toxic material and should be handled with care. The fumes can damage unshielded eyes.

Liquid foam can briefly be troweled before it sets, and it can also be molded. Once set, it can be worked the same way as Styrofoam™. When mixed, it is considered a thermosetting plastic. Used in a closed mold, it forms a density based on the amount used in the required space. Liquid foam will find fine leaks and the expansion can fracture a weak mold. Foam blowing equipment is available that automatically does the mixing as it is sprayed onto the surface. *See* ***Soft sculpture****;* ***Urethane****;* ***Sand casting***.

Forge (structure) The open hearth area where the heat (fire) is for blacksmithing (forging). It is maintained by air from a tuyere (air pipe) at the bottom that directs the forced air into the firebox. The air is powered by a bellows, hand blower or electrical blower over the burning coal. The final product is customarily known as wrought iron.

While there is great diversity in design, all forges have the same components in some form of a large or small configuration. The forge is fueled by gas or coal with a forced air supply to intensify the heat. It consists of a hearth to contain the fire and heat, the **tuyere**, or delivery nozzle, where the air enters the hearth being conveyed to the fuel, and a blower, to deliver enough air with the force essential to not only maintain (fan) a fire, but to increase the rate of burn to make the fire extremely hot.

The Duck's nest just below the hearth hole that is used to collect spent fuel. The hearth container can be anything from a professionally cast iron rig to a cut off, metal barrel end. It must be able to hold heat and allow an air supply to enter. The air supply can be provided by anything from a bellows to a vacuum cleaner blower. It does not have to be powerful unless the hearth is large; however, it does need some form of control. Commonly, this is a damper, but it can be a speed rheostat control. The hearth is mounted on legs for a comfortable working height.

A hood with a chimney is required for indoor forges, since heat and fumes need to be directed away from the blacksmith or working space. An adjustable hood can be lowered at the start to gather smoke, then raised after heat to work under it. Outdoor forges will have a baffle or wind break on one side to help control the combustion and smoke. *See* ***Blacksmith****;* ***Forging***.

Greg Moran with his coke burning forge.

A gas forge.

The **gas forge** is simpler. It consists of a gas burner system with the hottest burner flame aimed directly into a small insulated chamber where the work is placed. Depending upon the design, the opening is large enough to contain the metal but small enough to keep the heat. The chief advantage is an exacting heat setting without smoke.

Forgery A work of art that is not the original or authorized by the artist; a counterfeit work. The most common forgery is among bronze castings, because it is easy to duplicate with a rubber mold. However, they can be spotted by the slight decrease in size or lack of quality in craftsmanship that forgers display. Most foundries now weigh individual bronze castings and furnish an authenticity certificate with each sculpture. *See* ***Limited edition; Original***.

Forging Shaping metal by heating, hammering or bending it. Basic forging requires few tools: a source for heating metal (a forge), a hard, solid surface to shape the metal (anvil), a hammer for beating out the shape and something to hold the hot metal (tongs). The senior forger possesses an array of specialized tools. A hydraulic power hammer can also "forge" or shape metal. The worker is often known as a "smithy." ***See Forge; Anvil; Power hammer***.

Technique

Coke is a preferred forging fuel. The most common way to start a forge fire using coke is to use newspaper for starter fuel. The paper is wadded into a small mushroom shape with the interior opening to the bottom to receive the air. The paper is placed into the hearth where it is surrounded by coke. As the smoke turns brown, the air is opened wide. It takes about 15 minutes after the flame leaves to have a fire ready to receive the metal. *See* ***Coke***.

Some forges operate with gas jets. Controlled gas fuel is good for production work. A gas flame is more localized, offering more penetration and less burn. Good gas combustion does not result in smoke, though confined burning of gas is hazardous.

Sculptors frequently use oxyacetylene torches to heat pipes and other metal to bend them. If the metal is brought to a cherry red at the bending point, a right angle bend is simple. To spread the bend or create a larger, more curvaceous shape, the heat has to be spread out further, and the sculptor has to take more care and probably use a hammer to even the shape. The oxyacetylene torch is held in a vise (cushioned by a supporting substance, such as wood). While the sculptor can make do for simple works or projects, repetitive works, processes and sizeable works need adequate tools. An oxyacetylene torch can serve for simple tasks, but it becomes impossible or tedious for large or repetitive works.

Greg Moran, *Surface*. Forged metal, iron, steel, aluminum, cast bronze, cherry wood, found objects. 60″x50″x12″ (152.4cm x 127cm x 30.5cm).

The design of the work area is important for ease, but fire prevention, air ventilation and lighting are also of concern. Natural ventilation is desirable, though not always possible. Many shops open to the out-of-doors with a complete wall or large door that opens to allow indirect sunlight and air ventilation. The tools, anvil and work bench are always near the forge. With careful arrangement, the blacksmith creates a clear, straight course from the anvil to the forge and the work. The most used tongs and hammers are located within easy reach about the anvil and worktable. Vises are mounted onto the workbench to securely hold the metal as it is formed. Tools are displayed in a rack strategically placed near the anvil. Time is of the essence, since the metal immediately begins to cool after removal from the heath, allowing a limited time to work.

To overheat the metal causes the metal to oxidize, resulting in an exaggerated slag buildup. Knowing the correct temperature to work the metal is essential. Dim light is best for judging heat. Metal heated to a bright yellow may be too weak to work properly, while a dull red heat is more rigid or unyielding. Cherry red is the ideal color. Non-ferrous metals, such as bronze and brass, are not worked with heat. Rather, they are worked at room temperature. Non-ferrous metals do not increase in plasticity with heat; they weaken and can fall apart, especially if struck. If they are worked, they need to be annealed afterwards to restore strength, especially if the work is to be reshaped by bending or hammering. Annealing involves heating bronze or brass to a dull red heat and then gradually cooling it. This realigns the molecular structure to regain its original strength. Working aluminum, especially hammering and heating, should be avoided. However, aluminum can be annealed but at a much lower temperature.

Bill Brown operates a power hammer in **Marvin Tadlock's** studio. The artist is looking on.

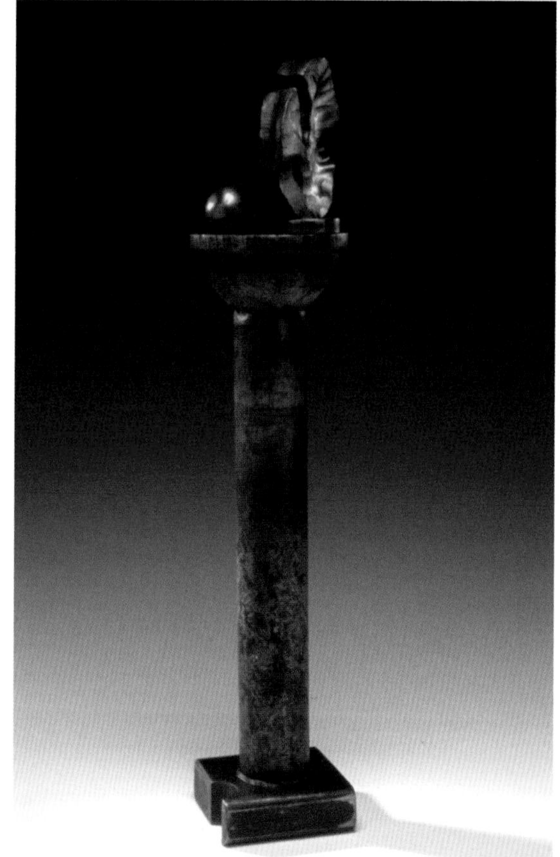

Marvin Tadlock, *Precipice*. Forged steel, 33″x8″x7″ (83.8cm x 20.3cm x 17.8cm).

LIGHTING A FORGE

Using Coke

The coke bed is prepared for use.

A small mushroom-shaped compressed newspaper is lit and then coke is placed over it.

The newspaper fire sets the coke ablaze.

The smoke clears up.

The forge is now in use.

Forge welding A welding (fusing metals) process using a forge to heat two pieces of metal to an extremely hot, almost liquid state. The metal is scarfed. Both metals are heated down in the coals out of the atmosphere without too much fire until sparks begin to fly. The metal is withdrawn and a flux (borax) is added to keep atmospheric impurities out. The metals are placed together and hammered on the intended welding area enough to impregnate (fuse) one metal into the other. *See* ***Forge***.

Ted Woods, *Kami-Kaze*. Forged, fabricated, painted steel, 54″x16″ (137.2cm x 40.6cm).

Form The total uniting mass or shape and structure of a sculpture resulting in a complete visual entity. Three-dimensional elements, arrangement, composition and manipulation of all of these result in the form. Form is the three-dimensional term for shape.

Formica™ (counter topping) Trademark name for hard, tough, high pressure laminated sheets of synthetic resin. It is used as a top sheeting cover for counters, sculpture stands and other surfaces that need heat and chemical resistant surfaces. It is applied with contact cement.

Formula A guide or complete set of materials and processes to achieve a particular result; a recipe. Patina, clay, glaze or slurry formulas are needed in sculpture.

Forton A casting system made up of several water-based components, including liquid polymer, dry powdered resin, dry powdered hardeners and Hydrocal™ (FGR95). Properly prepared and mixed, this system produces a strong, opaque, weather resistant casting material that has few drawbacks of similar resin mixes. Even though it is water-based, it can be layered with fiberglass in molds to produce rigid, lightweight, hollow castings. With metal powders, it is especially useful for cold-cast bronze. The major drawback is the accuracy

Harriet FeBland, *Moving On*. Formica over wood, 46″x27½x3¾″ (116.8cm x 69.9cm x 9.53cm).

required in measuring out the components. A gram scale is required. It cannot be cast clear. *See* ***Cold cast bronze***.

Found To heat metal into a molten state and then pour it into a mold. Foundries are places for completing such work. *See* ***Foundry***.

Found object An article or thing taken from the ordinary purpose and set aside for its artistic merit becomes a found object. Displaying it causes a new meaning, that of art. It can be natural, such as a bone, pebble, shell, etc., or man-made, such as a machine, bolt, etc. *See* ***Assemblage***.

Janice Kluge, *Stories*. Found objects and sound, 10′x7′x12′ (3.05m x 2.14m x 3.66m). Photographer: Lee Isaacs.

Thomas McDonald, *Aeroplane #6*. Found objects, steel, 20′x15′x45′ (6.1m x 4.58m x 13.73m).

Foundry A location or building where metal is melted or liquefied by heat and then poured into refractory molds to solidify into hard castings. The metal casting furnace is the most significant piece of equipment. Because of the intense heat needed, the building is fireproofed, a shed, or open area. The foundry layout is important to ensure good castings, as well as safety. The furnace must be near the pouring area or prewarmer but with adequate space to maneuver without tripping over or bumping into anything. It is good if the floor is a bed of sand, since any spill will not glance or explode out towards the operators. Onlookers need to be at a safe distance away and provisions need to be made for them. *See* ***Metal casting***.

Foundry. Background: left, wax burnout; right, metal melting furnace. Foreground: mold prewarmer. Design by **Arthur Williams.**

Foundry proof A first metal casting from a new mold that is carefully checked over and patinaed according to the sculptor's design. The foundry uses it as an example and guide for the remaining castings to ensure quality. *See* ***Artist's proof***.

Foundry returns (revert) Scrap metal parts, such as sprues, gates, pouring cups, etc., added to the melting pot for re-melt and use. Though former castings can be added, the metal should match. Re-melts without fresh metal can result in an alloy of poor composition that may not match parts of a previous section of casting.

Foundry sand Specially selected and bonded sand to sustain intense heat in a molded form. It is used in foundry castings. *See* ***Sand casting***; ***French sand***.

Fountain A structure with water protruding from it in some form. The structure consists of a large artificial basin or small pond, sometimes with sculpture within it that is designed to release water or to allow water to flow over it. The design of a fountain needs to consider the water source, the water movement, a circulating pump and a water-tight basin or container.

Fountain sculpture Sculpture designed specifically as, or for, a water fountain. Water is an integral part of the sculpture, though it may serve as only a small part. Through its volume, movement and design, it may become the total sculpture.

Jan Pearson, *Running Late*. Hand forged steel fountain with pearlescent finish. 9'x8' (2.75m x2.44m).

Todor Todorov, *Cascades*. Granite, concrete, 55,556 ft.^{2} (5000 sq.m.).

Andrè Harvey, *River Shadows*. Bronze, life-size manatees, 11' (3.36m). The sculpture and fountain were designed together.

Freehanding A process of creating a shape by hand, with acrylic being the most common material. A sheet of heated acrylic is twisted or bent into a new form using hands (with gloves). Ordinarily, this is done without the use of other tools. It is left to cool into the new shape. It could be draped over another form or even pushed into a negative form. This requires uniform heating of the plastic prior to the process to avoid fractures. The resulting sculpture is freeform, generally without symmetrical shape. *See **Acrylic** (sheet).*

Free standing Sculpture that is not being supported or does not rely on other objects to keep it upright. It is an independent form.

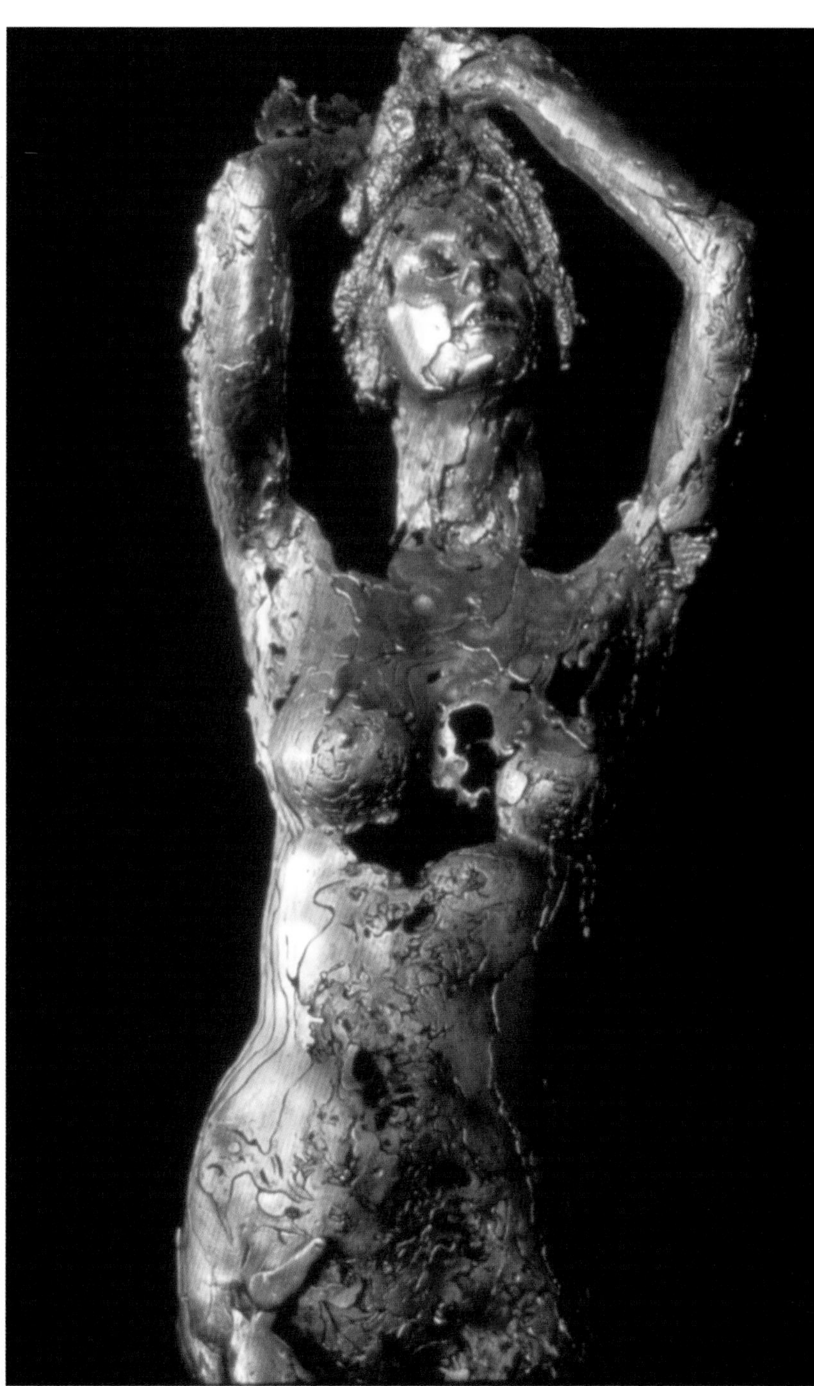

Carole A. Feuerman, *Thea.* Cast bronze from an open faced mold, 83"x31"x15" (211cm x 79cm x 38cm.

Freestone A stone easily carved in multi-directions with little tendency to flake or split or shatter. Soft limestone is a good example.

Freezing point The temperature when a liquid solidifies. *See **Measurements** (chart).*

French chalk A separator (release agent) made from talc.

French sand Same as foundry sand but traditionally formulated with alumina, silica and refractory clays to withstand the heat required of foundry molds. *See **Sand Casting**; **Foundry sand**.*

Frontal (depiction) The direct view or front of the figure or portrait. Also, the most common, obvious or best view in-the-round. *See **Sculpture-in-the-round**; **Full round**.*

Frosting tool A stone carving tool in the configuration of a hammer. The striking surface possesses a series of points equally spaced and sized. When used for decoration, the blows to the stone create uniform marks or bruises on a stone, producing a white texture. It looks like a bushhammer, but further refined.

Fruitwood Wood from fruit trees. The term is used for carving purposes when using wood from a pear or apple tree, for example. *See **Wood** (chart).*

Full round The complete object of sculpture as viewed from all angles or having access to all views. *See **Sculpture-in-the-round**.*

Full-scale Life-size or the exact size or dimensions of the original. *See* ***Life-size***.

Fume Vapor. Smoke, gas in a noticeable airborne quantity. It may be colorless without odor and poisonous, such as carbon monoxide, chlorine or lead oxide. A fumed patina depends on fumes (vapors) from select patina chemicals to determine the coloration. *See* ***Patina***.

Furnace An enclosure made of refractory materials to hold and sustain great heat while the inner object is being heated or melted as in a metal casting furnace or burnout furnace. Molds are dewaxed in a burnout furnace. Metal casting furnaces are determined by the type of metal to be cast.

Generally, ferrous casting (iron) is completed with a cupola or cupolette furnace, while the common blast furnace is used for non-ferrous metals, especially bronze and aluminum. Though there are other types of furnaces, such as the induction or high temperature electric furnace, most sculpture works are cast in an ordinary blast furnace.

Furnaces melt metal in different ways: 1) a liftout refractory container (crucible) that is heated inside the furnace with the metal in it, 2) a stationary container inside but above the heat (usually an iron pot) for dipping out; 3) inside the refractory lined combustion chamber itself (cupola type) for tapout; and 4) in a refractory container that swings down or tips out. The common type of studio or school metal casting furnace is the blast furnace powered by natural gas with a liftout crucible. It is primarily designed for nonferrous (bronze, aluminum) metals. *See* ***Blast furnace; Cupola; Burnout furnace; Induction furnace; Electric furnace; Kiln***.

An industrial tipout furnace by McEnglevan Industrial Furnace Manufacturing.

Fuse A total merging of materials usually brought about by heat or mixing. The welding arc melts metal, thereby liquifying and blending the metal together. Also an electrical circuit breaker. *See* ***Welding; Forge welding***.

Fusion Merging two substances to form one. In welding, two metals are simultaneously heated, blending into one liquid that solidifies. In ceramics, it is applying heat by a kiln to unite ingredients into one uniform substance, such as a glaze. *See* ***Welding; Glaze***.

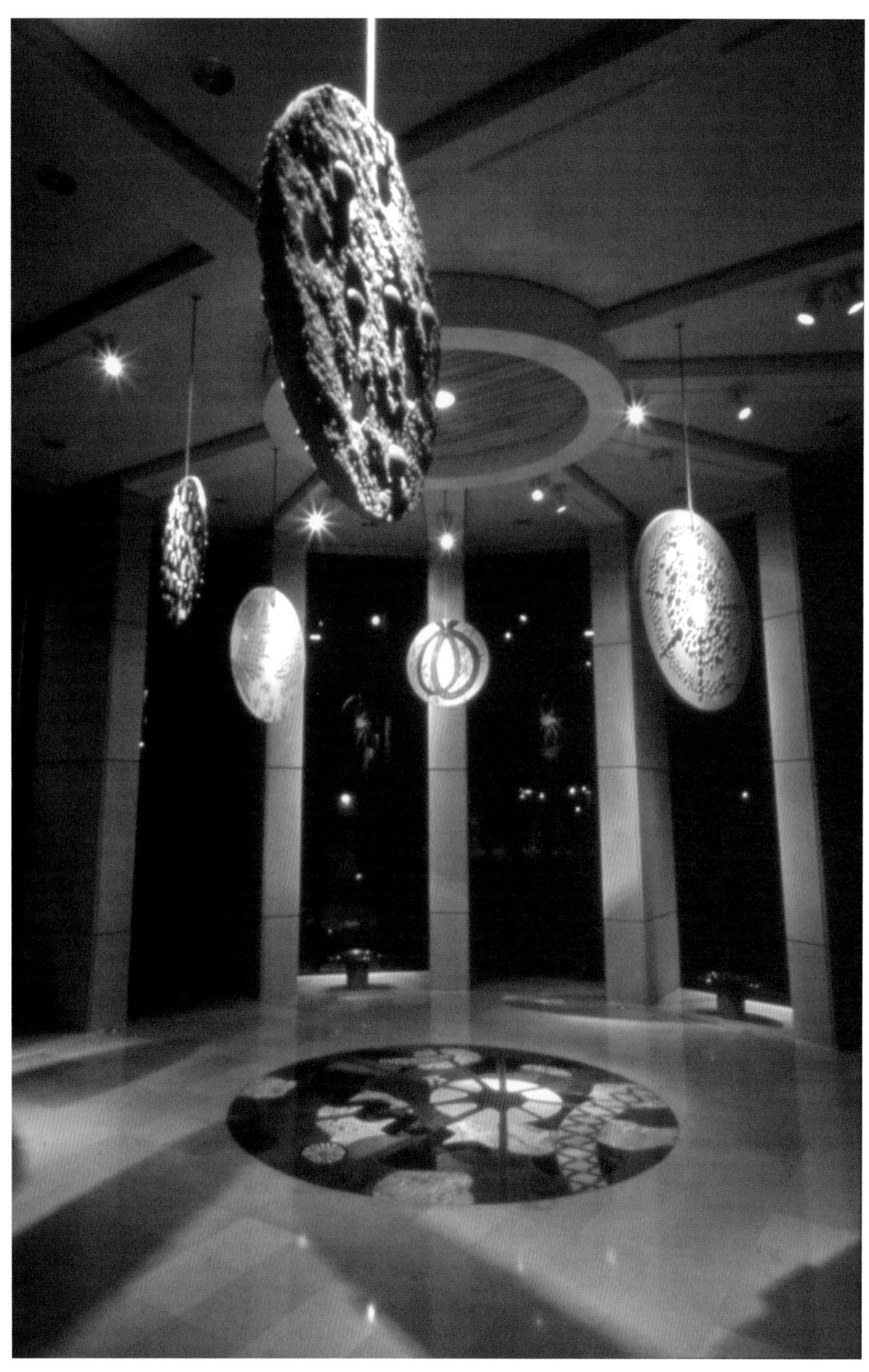

Jesús Moroles, *The Art of Life.* Granite, Commission for the Oklahoma Medical Research Foundation, Oklahoma City, Oklahoma.

G

Vernon Brejcha assists **Harvey Littleton** with a gather of glass.

Gaffer The foreman (boss) of a glass blowing team. *See **Glass blowing**.*

Gallery A location for display and sale of artwork. It can be a specific location in a building or the building itself. *See **Museum**.*

Galvanize (metal) Hot dipping or electroplating a zinc coating over steel to produce a rust or corrosion restraint coating. When welding, galvanized metals should not be cut or welded on without special ventilation and respirators due to the poisonous fumes emitted.

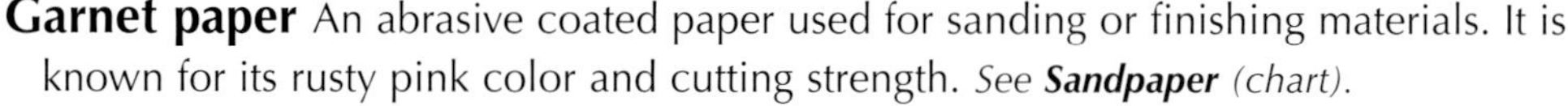

Garnet paper An abrasive coated paper used for sanding or finishing materials. It is known for its rusty pink color and cutting strength. *See **Sandpaper** (chart).*

Gas A fuel, such as acetylene, propane or natural gas. Some gasses, such as argon, are also used as a gas shield against atmospheric contamination while welding.

Gas defects Gas holes in cast metal resembling the porosity of a sponge. It is the result of overheated metal, excessive carbon in the mold not being consumed during the burnout, extreme turbulence in the pouring, or other gases formed in metal as it hardens. Generally, new silicon bronze, if not overheated, pours without gas problems. However, reused bronzes of all types need degassing with the proper products to eliminate problem gases.

Gasless wire feed Small portable arc welders that use a self-shielding flux core wire. While they are not very powerful, they can weld with a continuous wire feed and create various sizes of welds up to three-sixteenths inch (0.476cm) depending on the manufacturer. *See **MIG**.*

Gas Metal Arc Welding (GMAW) Known as MIG or flux cored arc welding with a gas shield. *See **MIG**.*

Gas Shield Metal Arc Welding Gas metal arc welding with shielding. *See **TIG**.*

Gas Tungsten Arc Welding (GTAW) Known as TIG (Tungsten Inert Gas) welding involves heating metals with a non-combustible tungsten electrode arc and shielding with a gas, such as argon. *See **TIG**.*

Gas welding Fusion brought about with gas and oxygen heat (usually oxyacetylene). *See **Oxyacetylene welding**.*

Gate (gating) Where the liquid metal enters from the runner to the body of the work being cast. This is an intricate part of the metal pouring system. The gating or gating system is the entire system or the total of gates to the work. *See* ***Metal pouring system***.

Gather The mass of molten glass at the end of the blowpipe. It is also the procedure of plunging a blowpipe or punty into a glass melting furnace to attach (gather) it to the instrument. *See* ***Glass blowing***.

Gauze (plaster impregnated) A thin strip of loosely woven cloth coated with plaster. Though it is flexible in the dry and the wet state, the plaster begins to set into a hard substance once it is dipped into water. Medically, it is used for covering human body parts to hold broken bones in place as they heal. The term is similarly used in sculpture when referring to body casts. *See* ***Body molding***.

Gelatin A glue processed by boiling animal hides and tissues. It was a flexible mold material once favored for sculpture use before the introduction of latex, polysulfides, slicones, etc.

Stephen Knapp, *Sentinel*. Glass and steel, 64″x28″x28″ (162.6cm x 71.1cm x 71.1cm).

Gel coat The surface, or visible coat, when working with polyester resins. When applying fiberglass and resins over a form, it is the top coat. The color pigment is part of the gel coat. *See* ***Fiberglass***.

Gemstone A stone, precious or semiprecious, qualified to be a jewel after appropriate cutting and polishing.

Georgia white (marble) A white marble with a large crystal formation; when used for stone carving, it retains a high polish. It is found in the state of Georgia (USA). Because of the structure, it is sometimes used for outdoor works. Though it holds up better than most marbles, it will still deteriorate over time in an outdoor environment. *See* ***Stone*** *(chart)*.

Gild (gilding) To add or cover with a thin layer of gold or a gold colored finish. Gilding is the technique of layering surfaces with thin metal sheets known as gold leaf. Also, it is a term for the coating of a surface with liquefied metallic powders. *See* ***Gold leaf***.

Glass A brittle hard substance that can be transparent or possess many degrees of opaqueness. Glass is primarily made of silica, which can withstand extremely high heat while resisting most chemicals. It is a permanent material but easily broken. It can be thin, such as glass used in window panes, or thick, like the glass used in large telescope lenses. Glass is available in sheets, rods (cane) and tubing. When working with these materials, they require delicate treatment, fracturing easily, especially when sudden heat or cold is applied. Glass can be molded, blown, cast, bent, cut, etched, engraved or broken into shape.

The hardness, transparency and color are determined by all the substances used in

the formulation. There are literally thousands of glass formulations to achieve specific results. An example would be Pyrex™ glass designed to withstand sudden heat changes.

The color in glass is created by adding chemicals to the formula, such as cobalt oxide for blue, ferric oxide for green, etc. Iron creates a color tint to glass. Manganese is added to neutralize the green into a clear appearance. Excessive manganese will cause a pink tint, etc. A decolorizer added to the formulation of glass is to counteract any existing impurity in the formula, rendering a neutral or colorless result.

Casting glass requires a heat resistant mold and the tools to work with hot glass.

Glass in the molten form is sluggish and placing it into a mold is more like lowering or dropping a globule into a container than pouring a liquid.

Kathleen Mulcahy, *Vapors*. Blown and etched glass, fabricated steel, 5′x15′x9′ (1.53 x 4.58m x 2.75m).

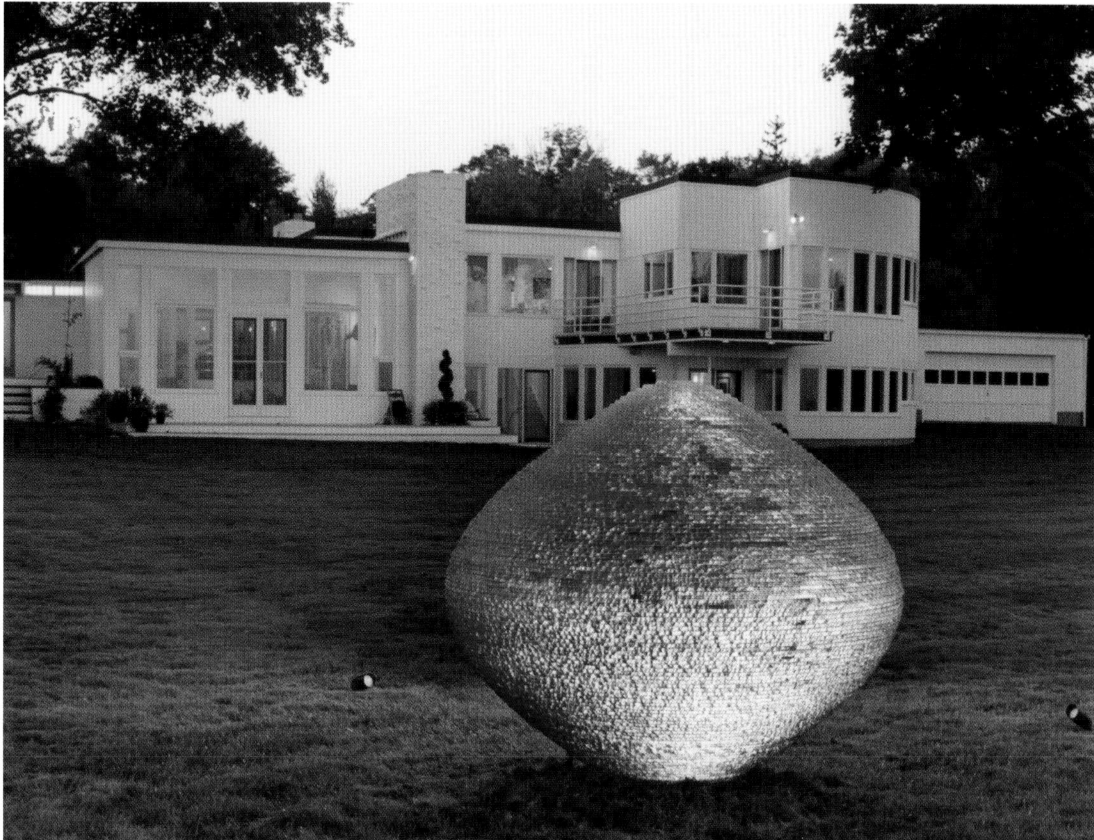

Henry B. Richardson *Coming of Age*. Solid glass, 5′ (1.53m) dia., 8000 lbs. (3632kg).

Glass needs to be annealed (slowly cooled) to avoid fractures or breaks due to the sudden strain brought about by temperature change. Special ovens for this process have heat resistant conveyor belts moving at slow pace, taking the glass through diminishing temperatures. It can take several hours to complete. Large telescope lenses can take months to cool to avoid stress.

Sandblasting glass is easy to do. The glass surface must have a protective coating placed on it to block the sand about the cut out design. If the blast is hard, then heavy rubberized protection is necessary. If the blast is short and gentle, even masking tape can be used. Factors that influence the final results are the size and kind of sandblasting materials, as well as the force applied. Normally, a fine etch is achieved with a fine grit and minimal force. Afterwards, the protective coating is removed to demonstrate the blasted surface.

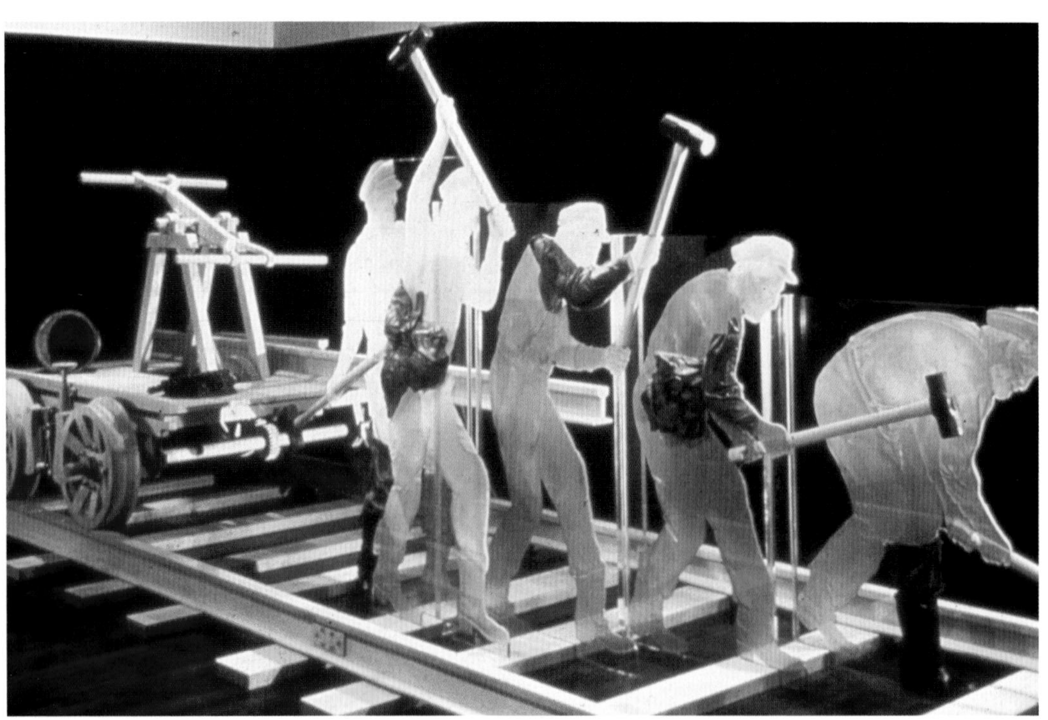

Steve Linn, *Candy Dancer*. Glass bronze, wood, 17.83' x49.16'x17.83" (5.44m x 15m x 5.44m).

Technique

Cold glass is working without heat or heating only one area of glass without liquifying or annealing it. Cold glass can be cut, drilled, etched, sanded, broken and engraved for effect. Drilling glass can be done with a carbide or diamond drill. The speed should be slow and well lubricated. Glass requires extreme care in handling; don't hit, bump or drop it onto or into a hard surface. It will fracture, break or shatter.

Glass sheet is cut with a **glass cutter**, which is a small, hardened steel wheel mounted on the opposite end of a steel handled shaft. The wheel freely turns, but very precisely and tightly. The handle has notches and a small solid metal striking ball. The notches are popular sizes for ordinary glass (window panes) and are used to grasp the glass for small breaks. Tapping the hard ball on the cut line helps the glass break in the correct location. A straight edge rule should be placed from end to end and held firmly. The glass cutter wheel should be sharp and pressed firmly down on the glass, cutting from exactly end to end without skips. If the cut is done correctly, it will create a gritty sound and leave a white line. Only one pass should be made, since the glass is stressed from the time the cutting wheel is placed down until it is removed. If the cut is clean, the sheet can be easily broken in one continuous crack, especially if it is in line with a straight edge for guidance.

Round and unusual shaped cuts can be made by first cutting the shape in a continuous cut and then applying additional overlaying lines bursting outward to the glass edge. The waste sections need to be carefully removed one at a time with pressure from the hands or tool, depending upon the size of the cuts. Old glass needs to be avoided. Glass becomes brittle with age and easily shatters. Newer glass has fewer imperfections and is more predictable in the direction of the break.

Tube and cane glass can be cut with a fine file, usually a diamond file. The tube or cane is literally etched or notched with one stroke partially encircling the surface.

A straight edge is used as a cutting guide on a glass mirror.

Placing the notch between the tubes while pulling down on both sides, the tube or cane will easily snap on the mark.

Glass is polished by wheels coated with powdered grits lubricated with water. Glass edges can be sanded and smoothed with the right equipment, including belt sanders. *See* ***Belt sander***.

Glass can be glued with silicon glue to ensure a watertight fitting leaving a slip of almost transparent seal.

Glass beads Glass particles in specific sizes used as an abrasive grit for sandblasting. *See* ***Sandblasting***.

Glass blowing Forming an art object by blowing air into molten glass through a blowpipe (tube).

Glass is broken along a cut on the glass. Notice the glass cutting tool.

Basic glass work involves melting glass in a furnace, gathering it on a preheated blowpipe or punty, working it by blowing a hollow shape or keeping it solid, shaping it by various methods, then removing it into an annealer to slowly cool. The process can become especially involved depending on size, shapes and number of workers needed. Skill gained through practice is invaluable. Because of all the heat involved, the working place is called a hot shop.

To accomplish glass blowing, the glass studio has these pieces of equipment:

1) A **glass melting furnace** that is constantly hot in order to keep the batch fluid. The temperatures are in excess of 2000°F (1093°C).
2) A **glory hole** (opening to furnace) to reheat glass as it is being worked on, making it possible for the glassblower to keep the work hot enough to remain plastic until the piece is finished.
3) A **pipe warmer** with the ends of **blowpipes** (hollow tubes) and **punties** (steel rods) inserted to keep them hot enough to gather the glass from the furnace.
4) A **marver**, which is a flat smooth steel table used to roll, shape and cool the glass.
5) A **gaffer's bench** constructed with a seat for the blower and side rails to prop up the blowpipe while it is being rolled to keep the work symmetrical or centered on the pipe. The bench also has a handy tray for the tools.
6) **Tools,** including jacks to neck the work and tweezers to further work on the molten glass.

GLASS BLOWING
by Alan Arns

Glory hole (left) and pipe warmer (right).

A gather is removed from the glory hole.

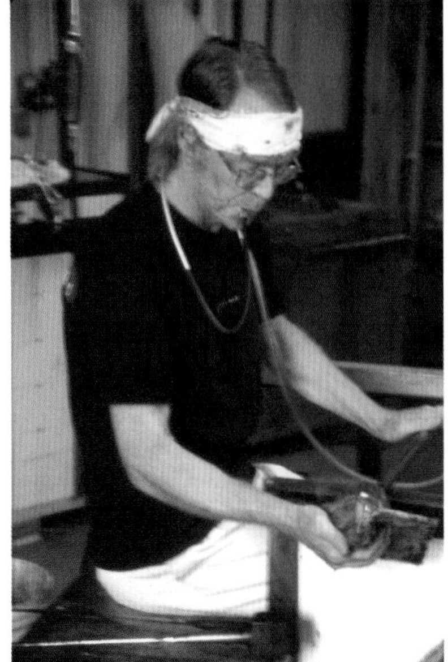

Air is blown into the glass to secure the shape.

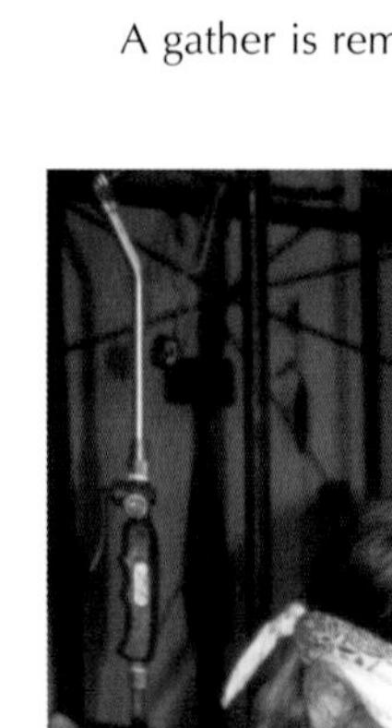

Alan Arns uses tweezers to perfect the shape of the glass as he works from his gaffer's bench

7) An **annealer** or box, which is an electrically heated container that retains temperatures of more than 900°F (482°C) as it is being loaded. It gradually cools with a computer control that makes certain the glass is not cooled too rapidly.

8) Possibly a **hand torch** and a gas supply for hand working the surface or neck of the piece. The commonly used fuel is propane.

9) Other **assorted items** include blocks to shape the gather, safety clothes, fire extinguisher and first aid kit.

Glass engraving is normally a low relief created by abrasion into glass. These three are the most used methods:

1) **Copperwheel engraving** produces a more silky cut than do the other methods. It is produced by a stabilized copper wheel mounted on a lathe-like machine. The wheel itself is encircled with a felt pad that is oil saturated and constantly coated with either silicon carbide or aluminum oxide to achieve the etching. The glass is handheld and forced into the wheel.

2) **Stonewheel engraving** is completed with a mounted, stable, extremely fine grit, stone cutting wheel that can be from over two feet (60.96cm) in diameter to smaller than a penny. Water is used to keep the cutting process cool. As with the copperwheel engraving, the glass is pressed into the wheel to achieve abrasion.

3) **Diamond burr engraving** is accomplished with a variable speed flexible shaft or air operated hand piece with a diamond burr engraving tip. This method allows fine engraving with minimal tool cost and is reasonably easy to learn. Though it can be polished, it is usually left with a frosty appearance. Tips are available in several shapes and sizes to achieve the desired result.

Christine Barney, *Smooth Ruby*. Furnace formed glass, wheel cut, hand polished, 14″x10″x6″ (35.6cm x 25.4cm x 15.2cm).

Boyd Graham, *Moonscape*. Crystal trapezoid, 5½″x3″ (14cm x 7.6cm).

Glass etching Creating a design in glass with hydrofluoric acid. *See* ***Etching*** *(glass);* ***Engraving; Glass engraving.***

Glass molding Casting glass using a mold. While there are many individual mold materials, wood is the most universally used. An experienced caster can use many kinds of wood, though cherry and other hard woods like oak are preferred. The mold is generally a one- or two-piece solid construction. If it is properly soaked and vented, it will work better and have a longer life.

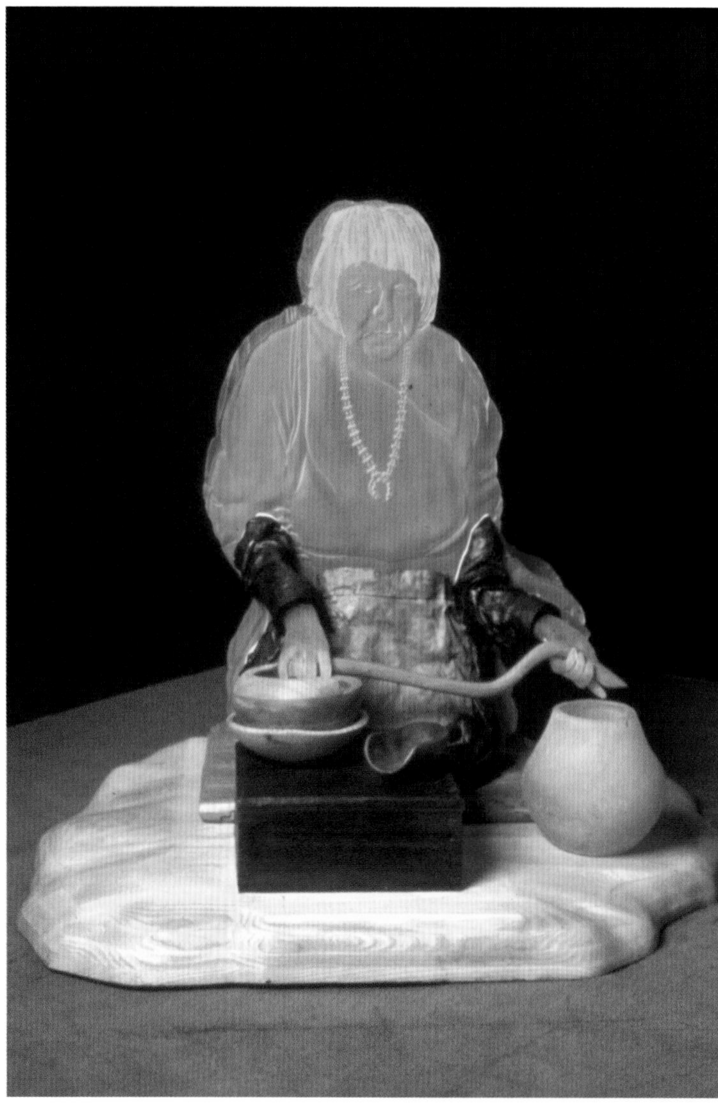

Steve Linn, *Maria.* Glass, bronze, wood, 112″x120″x130″ (285cm x 305cm x 330cm). Collection: Dan Greenberg and Susan Steinhauser.

Gary Bolt, *Icy Core.* Sand cast glass, cut and polished, 8½″x8½″x5½″ (21.6cm x 21.6cm x 14cm). Photographer: Vince Klassen.

GLASS MOLDING

by Kristin Gudjonsdottir

Previously bisked cone molds are used in an electric kiln.

The cones are at 1600°F (871°C).

After the cones have been ground, they are mounted on a prepared ceramic body.

Kristin Gudjonsdottir, *Seekers*. Clay cast glass and ceramic, 18″x18″x18″ (45.7cm x 45.7cm x 45.7cm).

GLASS MOLDING
by Gene Koss

Molding glass is an individual process. **Gene Koss** preheats a uniquely designed press mold to 900°F (482.2°C) for one of his glass castings. Later, he coats it with transmission oil and graphite in a continuous process to build up a skin on the steel to avoid adhesion.

Removed from the press mold, the glass is further worked. After that, it will be annealed for about a week.

Gene Koss, *Amish*. Cast glass, steel, 4½'x8'x15' (1.37m x 2.44m x 4.58m).

Gene Koss casts glass in a well-soaked oak mold. The mold is held together with wood clamps for the initial pour.

After opening the mold, **Gene Koss** continues to work with the glass.

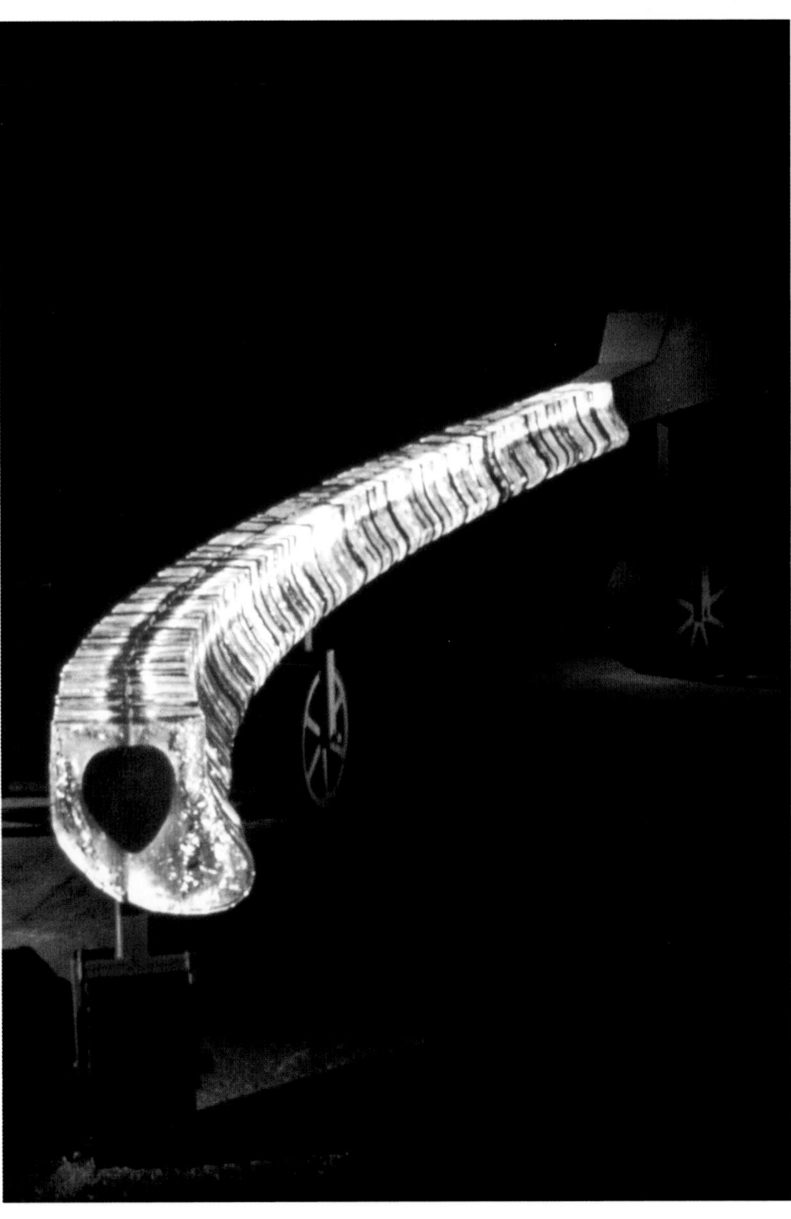

Gene Koss, *Night Harvester*. Cast glass, steel, neon, 9'x26'x3' (2.75m x 7.93m x 0.92m).

Glaze A permanently fused thin, glassy surface on top of a clay body as a result of a kiln firing. It is a compound of silicas, fluxes and stabilizers forming a glass-like, liquid, vitreous substance fused together over a clay body by a high heat (kiln firing). It seals the body (waterproof), enhances the appearance, and strengthens the clay. A glaze can be from a high gloss to a flat matt finish.

A glaze can be applied by dipping, pouring, brushing or spraying onto a pre-fired (bisque) clay body. Dipping is utilized for small works. Brushing is not frequently used, due to unevenness, although it does add good surface design. Spraying is more common for larger works because of the evenness and ease of application. Wearing appropriate clothing and using a respirator should be common practices.

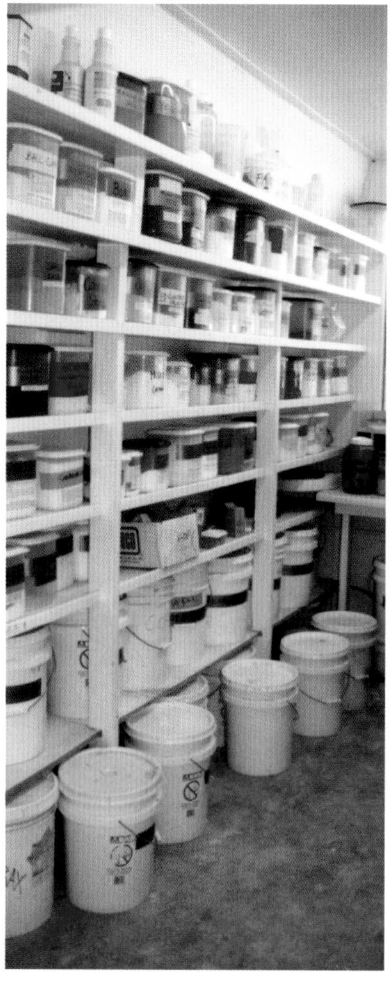

Stored glaze materials in marked containers at William Carey College on the Coast, Gulfport, Mississippi.

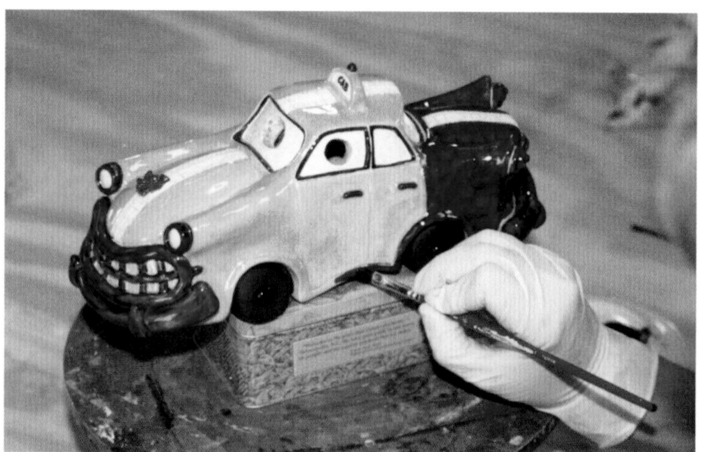

Patz Fowle glazes *Going. . . Hog Wild.*

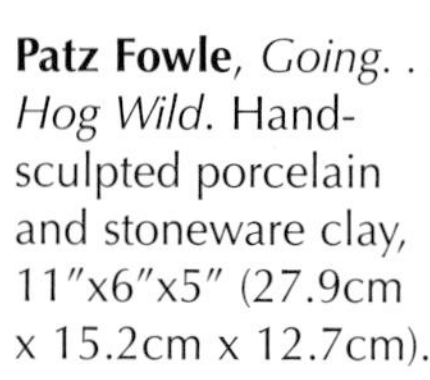

Patz Fowle, *Going. . . Hog Wild.* Hand-sculpted porcelain and stoneware clay, 11″x6″x5″ (27.9cm x 15.2cm x 12.7cm).

Glaze firing To fuse the glaze to the clay body by high heat. It is similar to the bisque firing in preparation and procedure, except it is ordinarily applied after the bisque firing. The kiln is fired at a higher temperature depending on the glaze and body structure. Glazes and bodies must match, or the glaze will craze (shrink into crack-like surface designs), crack and literally flake off, or not mature and remain flat or powdery. *See **Firing**; **Silica**; **Kiln**; **Glaze**.*

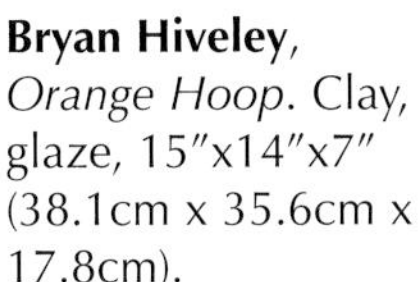

Bryan Hiveley, *Orange Hoop*. Clay, glaze, 15″x14″x7″ (38.1cm x 35.6cm x 17.8cm).

Jaymes Dudding, *Nuesta Señora*. Ceramic stoneware, clay slips, 3′1″x2′6″x1′ (94cm x 76.2cm x 2.5cm).

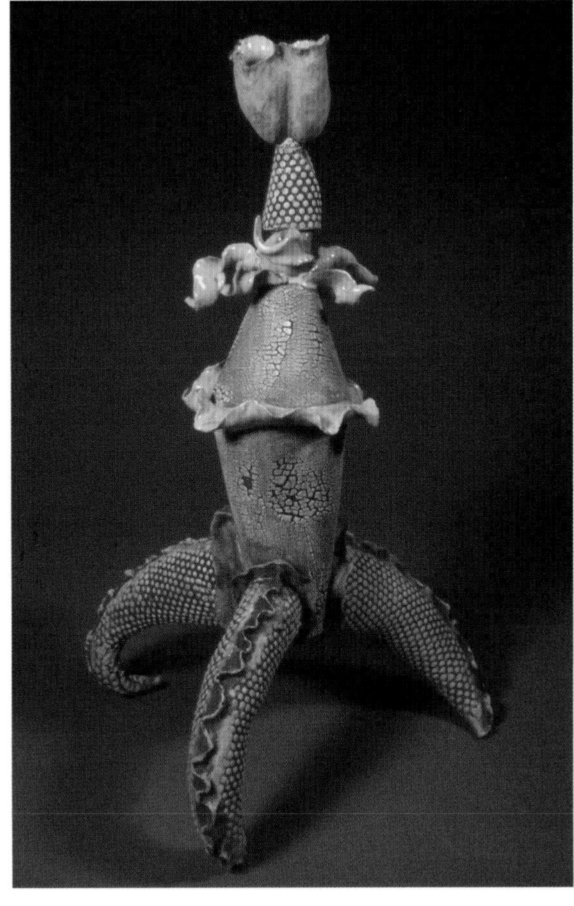

Melissa Parrott, *Squid Flower I*. Clay, glazes, 20″x12″x9″ (50.8cm x 30.5cm x 22.9cm).

Glory hole The space or hole that serves as an entrance from the outside to the inside of a furnace that is used for working glass. This space is created as the door, usually on a side track, is ajar in either a limited or complete opening. The furnace is horizontal with the glory hole on one end. The glory hole may simply be referred to as "glory." *See **Glass blowing.***

Gloves Protection for the hands during working conditions. There are several varieties available for specific work, including leather for welding, latex and rubber for chemical work, kevlor and insulated gloves for heat work, etc.

Gloves. Top: long sleeve sandblaster rubberized; top left: calfskin work, latex. Bottom left to right: heavy insulated heat reflective top, insulated leather, cloth and leather, suede, backed vinyl, cotton.

Glue An adhesive material used to attach or join two parts or materials. It can be epoxy, a paste, contact cement, etc. Each glue has its own chemical makeup and purpose. To glue something together is to adhere one part to another. *See **Adhesive** (chart).*

Goggles Eye protection, such as firm fitting eye visors or eyeglasses. The lenses are strong enough to protect the eyes from flying objects, wind or rays from bright lights or intensive welding brightness.

Gold The most ductile and malleable metal in its pure form. It is sometimes alloyed for strength or used for electroplating decoration.

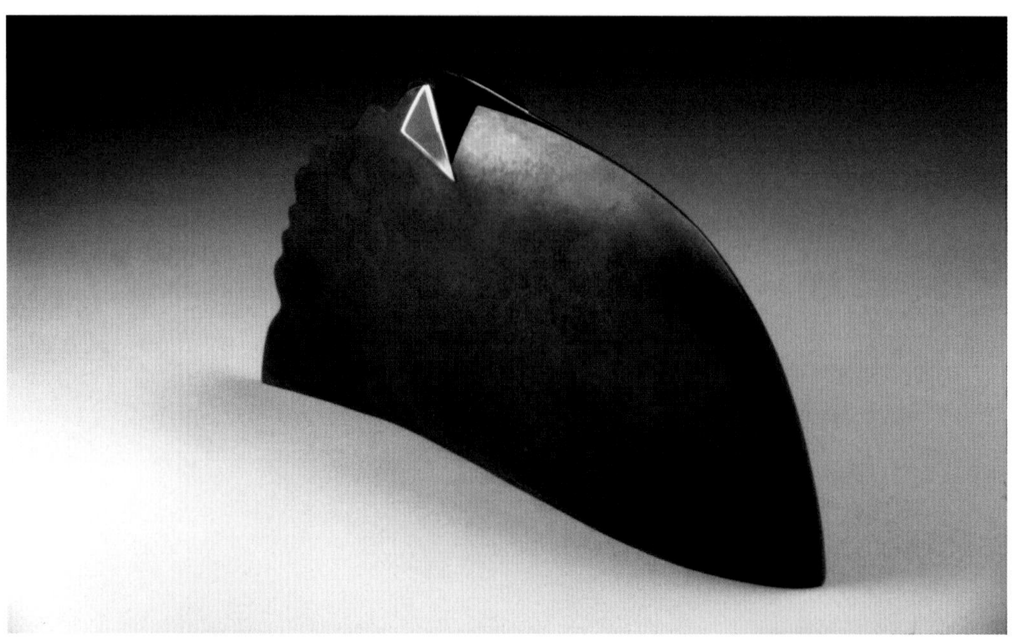

Gail Dial, *Madison Pocket*. 14k gold, bronze, 10″x2″x7″ (25.4cm x 5.1cm x 17.8cm). Photographer: Jim Turner.

Gold leaf Extremely thin layers or sheets of beaten gold used as a coating over sculptures because of its beauty and tarnish resistance. It can be purchased in small packs of leaf of about 1/300,000 inch (8.466×10^{-6}cm) in thickness in squares of about three inches (7.62cm). It takes 2000 leaves to equal an ounce (28g). *See **Gold size**.*

Gold plate Process of electroplating to deposit a thin layer of gold film onto another surface. *See **Electroplating**.*

A pad of gold leaf ready to use.

Gold powder Gold crushed into a powder with a binder added to make it usable. It can serve many enhancing purposes, including decorating fired, glazed ceramics. Properly prepared and applied ceramics may then be refired for permanence.

Gold size The adhesive used to retain the gold leaf when gilding. *See **Gold leaf**; **Gild**.*

Gouge A carving chisel with a curved scoop-like blade that can be obtained in various sizes and shapes. Usually used for wood, it is known as a "U" gouge. A "V" shaped gouge is also a carving tool known as a parting tool. Both are used for soft stone.

Gouger A tool that uses a carbon rod and electrical arc to cut or gouge metal. It is also called a carbon arc. *See **Carbon arc**; **Arcair** (torch).*

Grade The term used to describe the quality of wood, specifically lumber. No. 1 is better than no. 2, etc. *See **Lumber**.*

Grain Direction of cells in wood following the length of the trunk or branch. The term, "across the grain" means right angle to the grain. "Against the grain" refers to the opposite direction of the grain. "Along the grain" or "with the grain" is in the same direction of the grain. It can also be used as the term for the direction of stone strata layers.

Nancy Azara, *Circle with 7 Hands*. Carved and painted wood with gold leaf, 60″x40″ dia. (152.4cm x 101.6cm).

Granite An extremely hard igneous rock containing a large quantity of silica. Though hard and slow to carve, it retains the finish well. Granite is considered the major outdoor sculpture stone because of its durability. *See **Stone** (chart).*

Installing *Spirit Foundation* by **Jesús Moroles**.

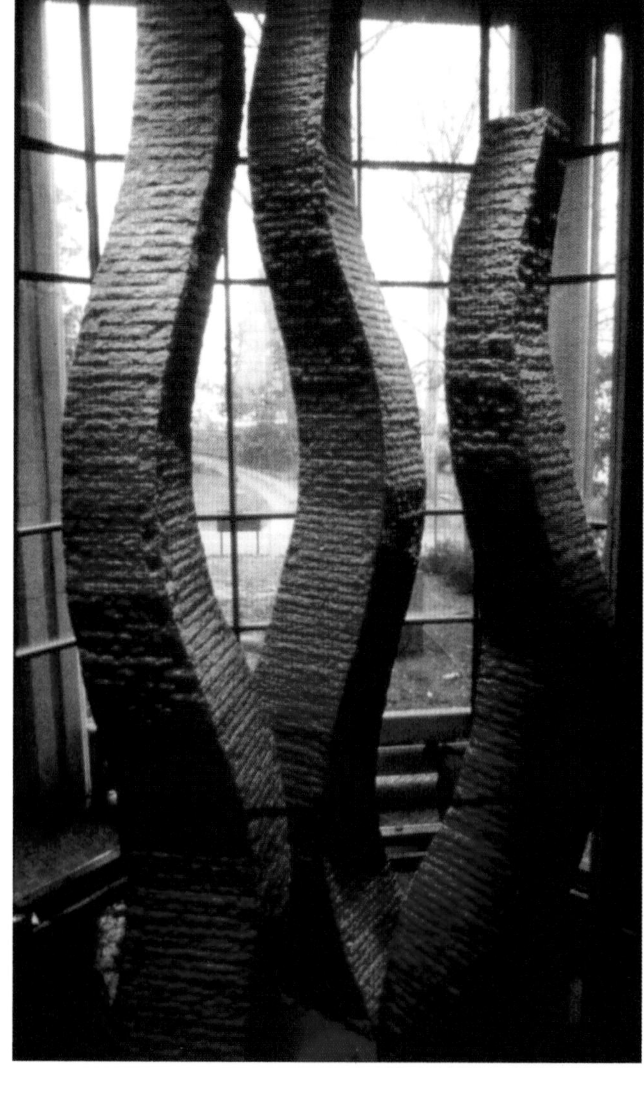

Jesús Moroles, *Spirit Foundation*. Fredericksburg granite, 30′x27′x24′ (9.15m x 8.27m x 7.32m).

Sue Nees, *Untitled*. Black granite, 17″x15″x8″ (43.2cm x 38.1cm x 20.3cm).

Elyn Zimmerman, *Morbihan*. Granite, 16′x4′x10½′ (4.9m x 1.2m x 3.2m).

CARVING GRANITE
by Enzo Torcoletti

A disk grinder with a diamond blade is used to score the granite.

A carbide tipped chisel and hammer continue.

Installation of **Enzo Torcoletti's** *Kami I*. The top piece is added.

Enzo Torcoletti, *Kami I*. Granite, 40′ (12.2m) from base.

Gravel Small stones or fragments used for various purposes, including cement and concrete work. Gravel may or may not be uniform in size, color or texture, depending on the requirements for the work. *See* ***Concrete; Aggregate*** *(chart)*.

Green Freshly cut wood or lumber product that has yet to be seasoned. The wood contains moisture beyond the desired level or has not aged long. Also, a green mold means not yet completely cured, or it is not ready for use. When referring to clay, it indicates a clay body that is still wet or not yet dry. *See* ***Greenware***.

Green soap (liquid) Soap used as a release agent and sometimes called caster's soap or mold soap. Tincture of green soap was once easily obtained as a favorite liquid hand soap for restrooms. However, today's biodegradable liquid soaps rapidly break down in use, rendering them of little or no value as a release agent. *See* ***Release agents*** *(chart);* ***Mold soap***.

Greenware Clay bodies formed and finished but not completely dry. They are not ready for kiln firing. This condition is observed by the darker (wet) clay color and the coolness of the clay body as the remaining moisture escapes. *See* ***Clay***.

Grinder A handheld air or electric powered tool with an easily replaceable bit or disk. The die grinder holds a burr or bit designed for cutting into wood, stone, metal, etc. The most common RPM is 20,000, though it may go over 60,000 rpm and under 8,000. The spinning bit, sanding wheel or other device effortlessly removes or shapes surfaces. It is also the term for a handheld motorized tool with cutting and grinding disks of various sizes, ranging from over nine inches (22.86cm) to less than four inches (10.16cm) in diameter in speeds around 5,000 rpm. *See* ***Sharpening***.

Arthur Williams uses a disk grinder on a steel sculpture.

Sarah Sweetwater with an electric die grinder works on stone.

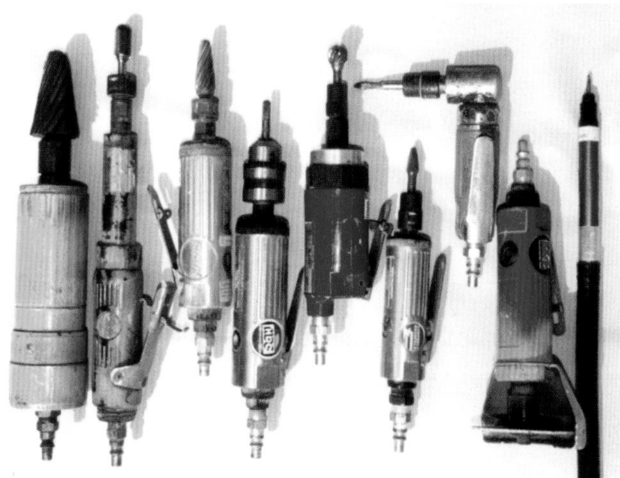

Air operated die grinders at various sizes including 3/8″ (0.953cm) collett, 1/4″ (0.635cm) collett and 1/8″ (0.318) collett.

Electric die grinders.

Die grinder bits of various sizes and shapes.

Assorted grinding stones for die grinders.

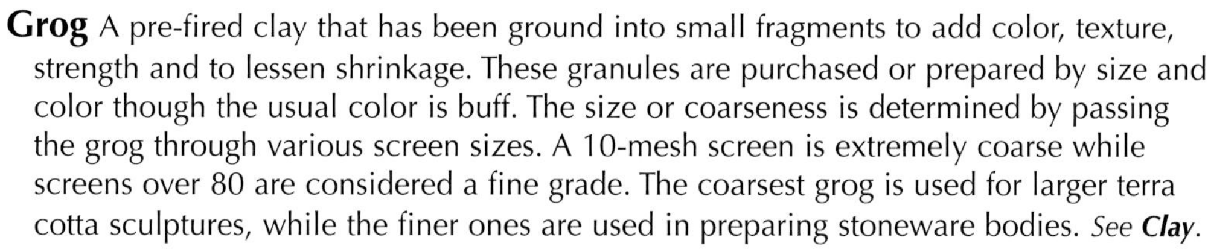

Die grinder sanding disks, pads and spiral winds.

Grog A pre-fired clay that has been ground into small fragments to add color, texture, strength and to lessen shrinkage. These granules are purchased or prepared by size and color though the usual color is buff. The size or coarseness is determined by passing the grog through various screen sizes. A 10-mesh screen is extremely coarse while screens over 80 are considered a fine grade. The coarsest grog is used for larger terra cotta sculptures, while the finer ones are used in preparing stoneware bodies. *See* ***Clay***.

Grooved weld A weld placed into a previously prepared groove. Sculptors use this type of weld to be ground flush. *See* ***Carbon arc***.

Ground connection The electrical connection from a welding machine to the earth for safety. Also a work piece clamp (ground clamp) that serves as a lead to the work. *See* ***Welding***.

Growth ring (growth layer, annual growth ring) A layer of wood, originally bark, that is visible when looking at a cross section of a tree trunk or end of lumber. Established around the stem from the center out, the layers can be counted to determine the age of a tree since a new layer (ring) is added each year in the temperate zone.

Gunite A building product made with concrete and sprayed into a mold or onto a surface. Used with steel reinforcement, gunite presents an extremely strong structure. Not only used for sculpture, it has been used for swimming pool walls, especially larger pools with unusual shapes.

Gypsum Hydrated calcium sulfate used in the production of plaster and plaster products. Fine grained gypsum is known as alabaster. *See* ***Plaster*** *(chart);* ***Plaster****;* ***Stone*** *(chart).*

Gypsum cement Hydrostone™, Hydrocal™, etc. is similar to plaster in makeup, but stronger. As an example, Hydrostone™ is about two and a half times stronger than plaster, takes less water and sets more quickly than concrete. *See* ***Cement****;* ***Plaster****;* ***Hydrostone™****;* ***Hydrocal™***.

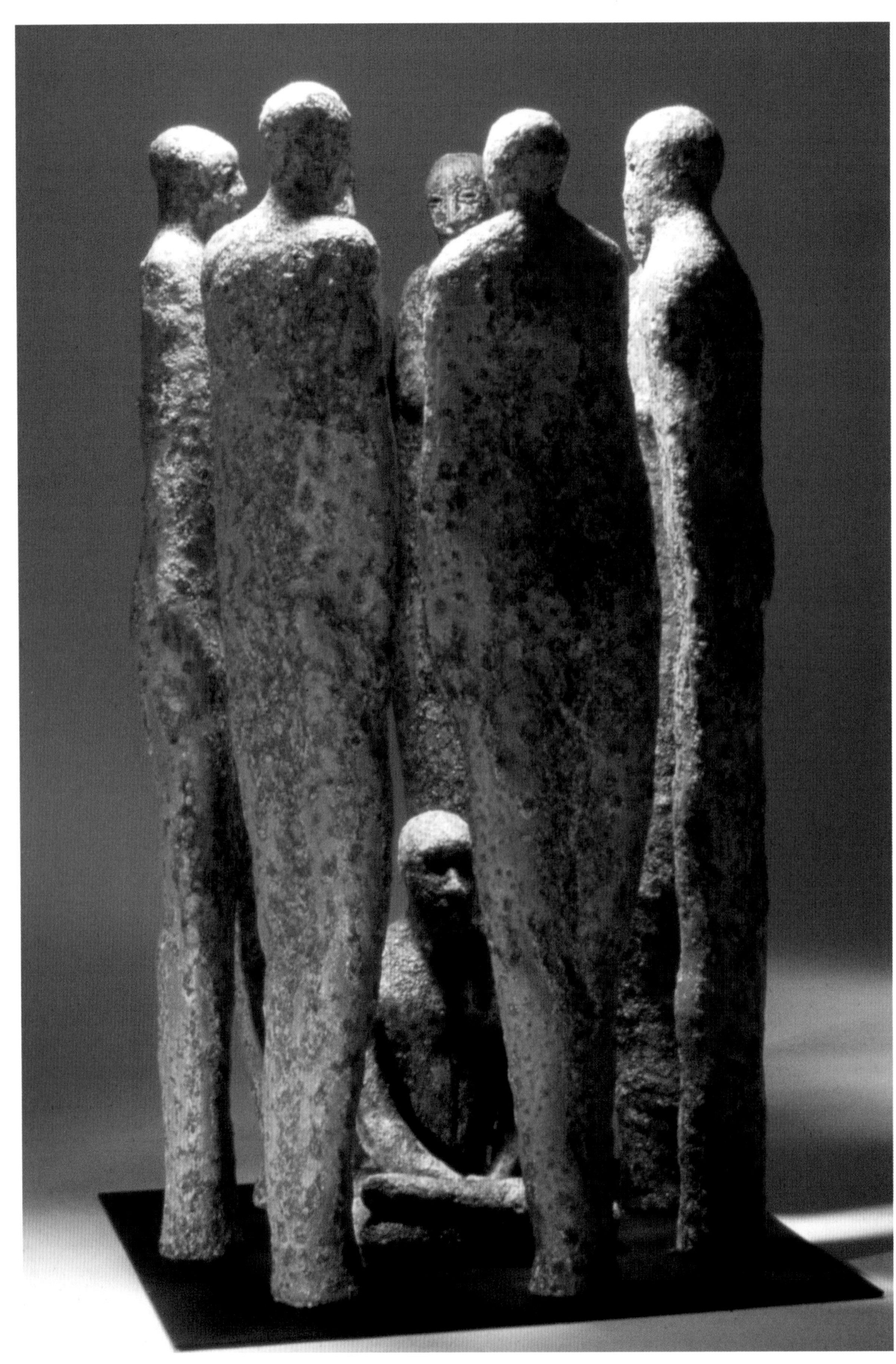

Mark D. Chatterly, *Surrounded by the Ancestors*. High fired clay, 4'x4'x7' (1.22m x 2.14m)

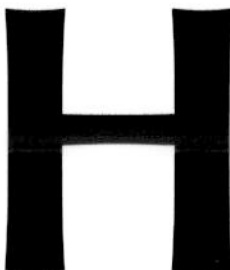

Hacksaw A small handheld saw with a narrow, replaceable, thin blade drawn tight between the handle and the opposite end. The blade is fine toothed and designed to cut metal, though it is also used for other materials, particularly PVC pipe.

Half relief The mid-point between low and high relief. *See **Relief**.*

Hallmark Traditionally, a mark that is stamped on gold or silver to indicate the quality and purity. Today, it is used on artwork to indicate the artist and/or other information about the artwork.

Hammer A handled tool with a head to strike blows. Various designs and shapes are used with sculpture for specific purposes. It is referred to as a mallet when designed for stone or wood. Single handheld hammers are intended to be less than four pounds (1.82kg). *See **Die-forming**; **Die cast**; **Power hammer**; **Forge**.*

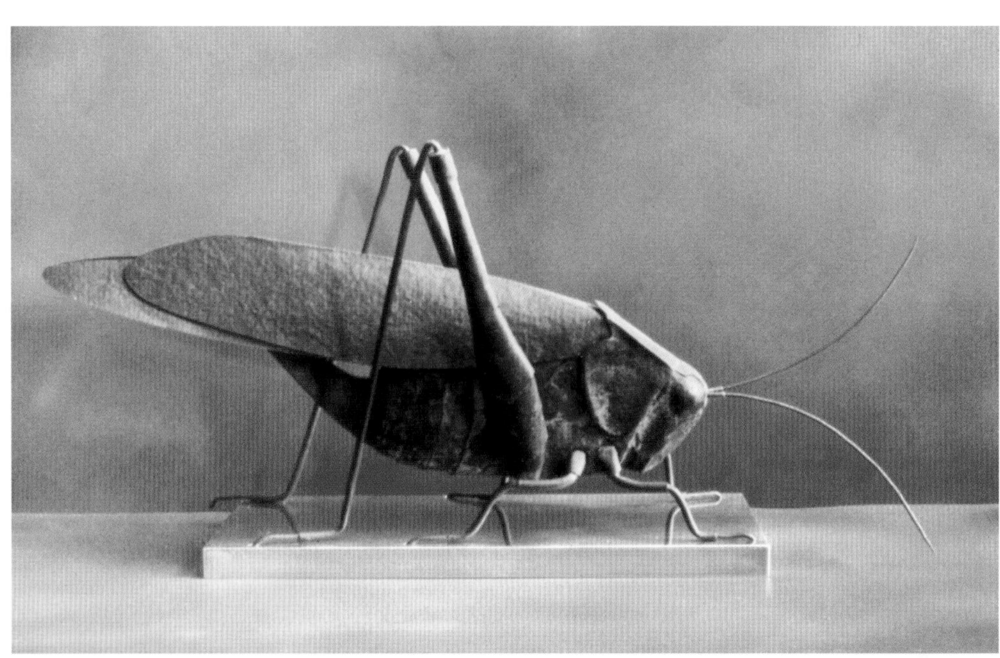

Mary Lewis, *Katydid*. Hammered copper over wood, brass base, 22′ (6.71m) long.

Wendel Broussard shapes heated metal.

Jeff Mohr (at anvil) and **Richard Dawdy** hammer steel.

William Baran-Mickle, *Along the Way* (detail). Brass, copper, nickel-silver, found objects, mounted on plywood.

Hand lay-up The process of placing a casting material into a mold or onto a surface by hand, as com pared to pouring, spraying or other mechanical methods. An example would be to take thin strips of ceramic clay and press (by hand) the pieces onto the mold wall to create a casting. Another example would be to coat the mold with resin and then to place fiberglass cloth into the resin. Perhaps the most common is hand lay-up (brush in) of wax into a mold to gain the surface detail. *See **Casting; Mold**.*

Handpiece A pneumatic hammer, which is a handheld tool that is used to carve stone and wood. The piece itself serves as a holder for inter changeable chisels that make con tact with the carving substance. It also refers to the handheld tool at the end of a flexible shaft or welder. *See **MIG; Flexible shaft**.*

Hand tool A tool held in the worker's hands and used without any other source of power unless it is designated as a power hand tool.

Hand trucks Used for moving heavy objects, it is a portable upright (vertical) frame that supports a small platform at the bottom with a wheel on either side. When tilted to the rear, the platform raises the load from the floor and allows the operator to balance the load on the frame as it is being moved. Different sizes of frames and wheels are designed for specific loads.

Hand vise A handle with an adjustable clamp (vise) on the opposite end. It is used for holding hot metals or metals as they are being ground or buffed.

Haptic The tactile sense of touch. The more haptic a person is, the more he/she enjoys various textures from the third dimension. *See **Tactile**.*

Hard edge The tempered cutting edge of a tool or blade. Uses determine this edge. It also describes works with readily defined shapes, especially simple geometric shapes.

Hard hat Lightweight helmet-like hat of a strong material worn by workers in situations where the head is in danger. Other than the hard surface, the interior head band keeps an air space between the hat and head for additional protection from hard blows, as well as supplying ventilation.

Hard solder Silver solder. (Soft solder is lead solder). *See **Solder**.*

Hand truck moves a stone.

Hardening The process of drawing out the hardness of metal using heat. The cutting end of the metal tool is heated to a cherry red color, then quenched in cold water or motor oil. This brings out the hardness, depending upon the initial quality of the metal. If it is heated beyond cherry red or into white heat, the metal may become useless. Afterwards, the tool is tempered to reduce brittleness. *See* ***Temper***.

HARDENING STEEL
by Greg Moran

Hardening steel begins with heating. A forge is used.

If the metal is to be shaped, it is done after reaching cherry red heat.

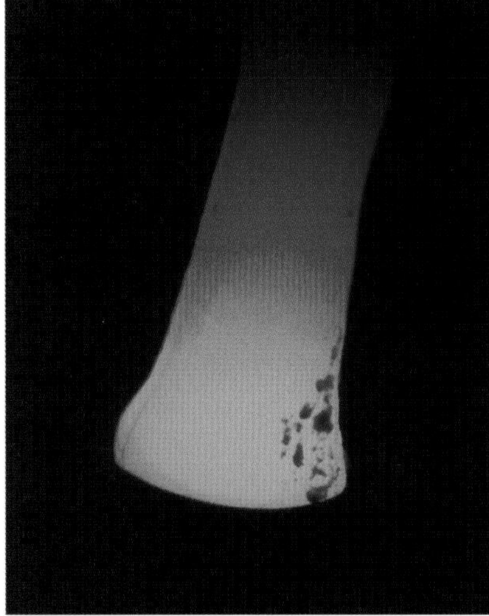

After shaping, the tool end should be once again brought to a uniform cherry red.

After reaching heat, it is immediately quenched (plunged) into water, or oil, to secure the hardness. It is held until it blackens.

The quenching crust is scraped off, then polished with a piece of emery cloth to allow the worker to see the metal. Afterwards, it is tempered to secure the temper color.

Hardwood Broad leafed, deciduous (broad leafed) tree wood that furnishes unusually hard wood, due to the high density or close grain. *See **Wood** (chart).*

Hardy A tool used for cutting hot metals. It is inserted into a square hole (hardy hole) on the anvil.

Head peg The upright vertical support column with a shape or construction attached to the top to hold molding material in place. It serves as the armature for a portrait bust. The entire construction is mounted on a flat baseboard to hold it erectly in place. *See **Bust peg**.*

Hearing protection Ear muffs and plugs designed to reduce noise to a level that will not injure the worker. Some muffs allow normal communication and moderate sounds. The sculptor needs to select protection for the level of noise involved, such as high or low frequency.

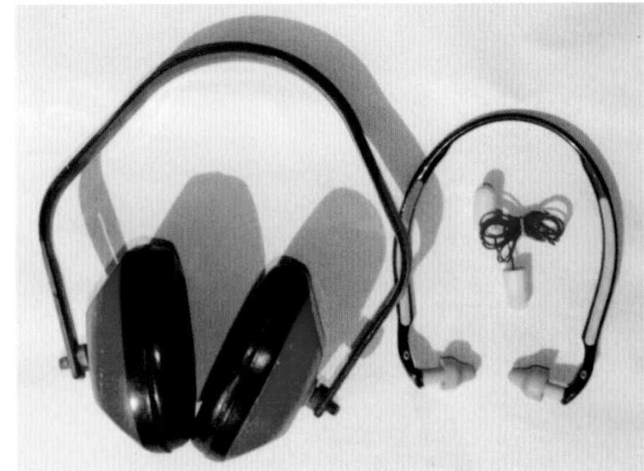

Hearing protection: ear muffs and plugs.

Heartwood The center, the strongest part of the tree. The heartwood is usually darker in color. It is the most preferred for woodwork.

Hearth A heat resistant surface and the lowest part of a furnace used to contain or support the hot fuel. The term is associated with a forge and is called an open hearth. *See **Forge**.*

Heat Designates how long a hot metal from the forge can maintain the temperature necessary to be forged.

Heat treating A process of tempering metal by heating and then cooling it in a liquid. The process is repeated until the desired hardness or temper is achieved. *See **Tempering**.*

Heliarc Common name given Gas Tungsten Arc Welding because of the use of helium. It is known as TIG (tungsten inert gas welding) in the United States and WIG ("wolfram," German for tungsten) in Europe. *See **TIG**.*

Hemp after dipping in plaster.

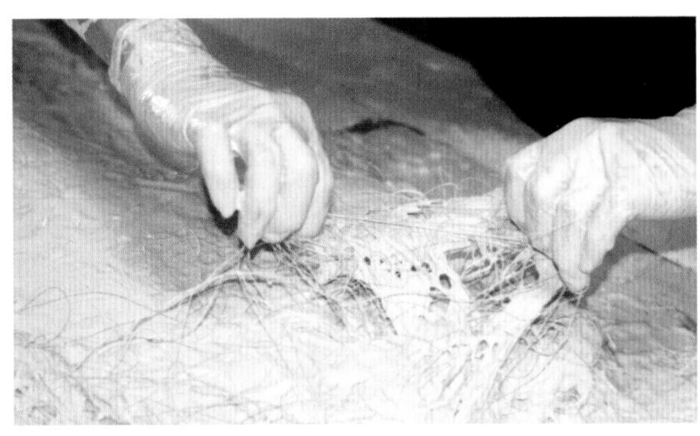

Hemp placed onto a plaster mother mold.

Hemp Fibers from hemp plants, such as cannabis. The stem fibers are used to make ropes, etc.; however, in sculpture, the hemp is used in a raw, non-braided state. Hemp soaked in plaster furnishes strong reinforcement in mold making. The fibers crisscross in various directions holding the plaster tightly together. *See **Mother mold**.*

Herm (herma) A portrait bust mounted on a square or rectangular tapering post. The term originally referred to an imagined likeness of the Greek god, Hermes, for boundary markers.

Hex head A six-sided object, usually a bolt head. *See* ***Fastener*** *(chart).*

High relief The three-dimensional part that extends one-half or more of the total form from the base or wall surface. *See* ***Relief***.

Hoist An apparatus mounted on a high support to lift heavy loads. By a series of contained gears using a chain ending with a hook for lifting, the hoist can raise from hundreds to thousands of pounds (kilograms), depending on the size and design. Smaller hoists are operated by a looping chain, while larger hoists are electrically powered and operated by extension controls. *See* ***Installation*** *(installing);* ***Lift***.

Enzo Torcoletti and **Joe Segal** install a stone sculpture using a portable tripod with chain hoist.

Enzo Torcoletti and **Joe Segal** use a chain hoist mounted on a trailer.

Arthur Williams prepares to use a permanently mounted I-beam chain hoist to lift a limestone.

Hollander paper beater A mechanical paper beater. It is used to make a delicate pulp from cloth and plants adaptable for paper, especially used by paper making artists. It is named Hollander, because it was invented in Holland. *See **Paper**.*

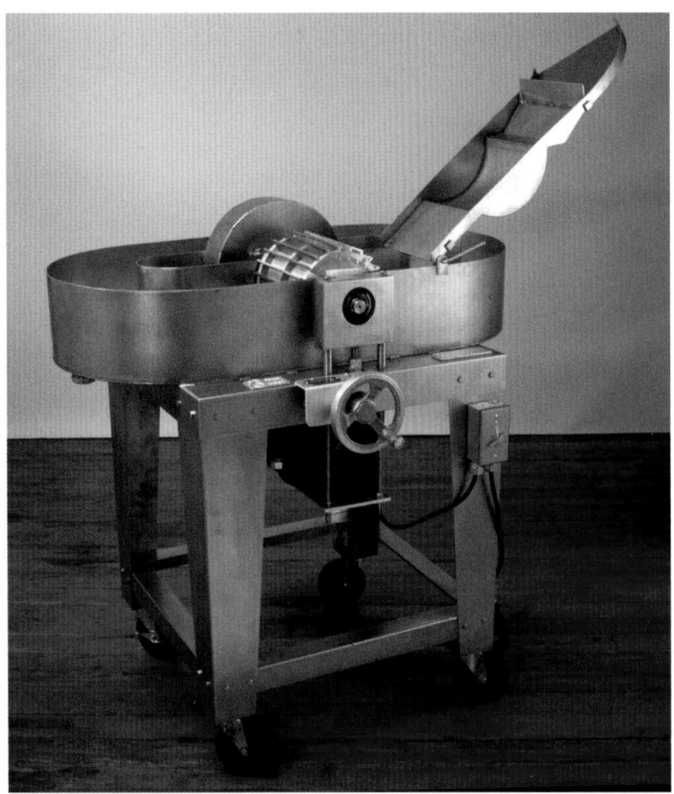

A stainless steel Reina Hollander Beater by David Reina Designs, Carriage House Paper.

Hold-down A clamp used to hold a material or shape in place while it is being worked on. The traditional hold-down is designed with a strong board on top of a work table with a rope attached about mid way but placed through the table top. A stirrup or loop on the lower end is where the worker's foot maintains enough pressure to hold the board down firmly on the wood and is easily released to change or remove the work.

Hollow casting Preparing for or creating a casting that is hollow as opposed to solid. Molds with thin hollow walls are desirable for casting. There are many ways to accomplish this depending upon the mold type and purpose. The most obvious methods are coating a mold interior by brushing a liquid into it, by packing clay into it, or by slushing to produce a hollow cast. *See **Slushing**.*

Hollow-ground A saw blade's cutting tooth with a concave edge.

Hollow out Removing inner material from a work in progress to achieve light weight or to enable the material to set or age properly. Wire ended tools are used. In ceramics, a hollowed out form is made from a solid lump of clay, usually terra cotta. While the work needs to be hollowed out as soon as possible, too soon can result in a slumping design and too late in a cracked surface or toughness in removing the interior mass.

Technique

Leather hard clay works can be moved and stored. They should never be placed into a kiln for firing until they are dried, devoid of all foreign material and hollowed out. Works can be placed on a cushion of foam rubber while the inside is scooped out. Depending upon the sculpture size, the hollowed out work could vary from one-eight inch (0.318cm) to upwards of two inches (5.08cm) in thickness. The major consideration is evenness of the wall thickness, ventilation and proper drying. If the wall cannot contract at the same rate because of drying on one side or quick drying from the outside, it will crack. If the inner part has not been correctly hollowed out, the work will crack.

However, inner clay braces and some exorbitant thickness can be tolerated if the work has been ventilated. This requires openings (holes) in the sculpture. Small solid works can be fired if air holes, even as modest as pin size are placed throughout the piece. If the work is to be hollowed out and it cannot be done from the bottom, then the work must be opened, or parted, for the sculptor to remove excess clay. If it is to be sectioned for hollowing out, a ceramic hand wire can be used. After the clay has been dug out, the parts are attached by scoring the joining edges, adding a heavy slip and uniting the works, removing any surplus slip. The slip is made from the same clay body except it has been mixed with water to form a thick paste.

Now ready to complete the drying process, the work needs to be covered or placed into a damp box for slow curing to allow all the joints to settle and merge, as well as keep the clay shrinkage at a controlled rate. Once completely dry, the clay temperature will not vary from the room temperature to the touch. It is now ready for firing. *See **Slab; Coil; Pinch; Kiln; Firing; Wire end tools; Slip: Damp box**.*

HOLLOW FORM
by Norman D. Holen

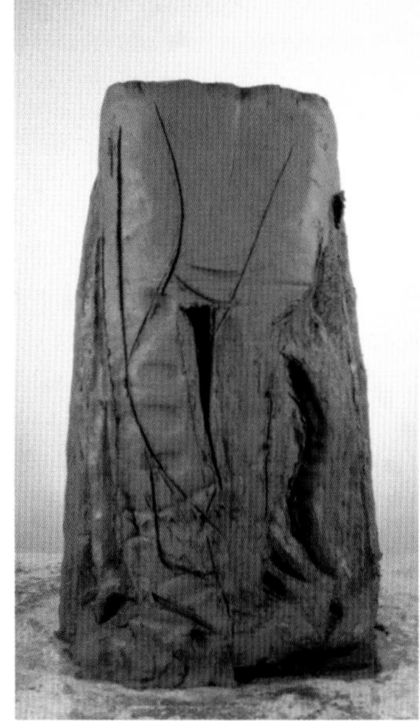

Terra cotta is used.

The front folds are determined.

The basic form, front with head added.

The rear folds are determined.

Rear view with the head added.

Norman D. Holen, *Dressmaker II*. Terra cotta, 9¾"x8¼"x18¼" (24.8cm x 21cm x 46.4cm).

Hologram Patterns of laser light recorded on a two-dimensional surface that produces a three-dimensional effect/depiction.

Holography The process of using a laser light and photographic plate to project and exhibit a three-dimensional shape in space.

Hone (honing) To fine sharpen a tool by using an extremely tight grained whetstone or leather strop. The tool is repeatedly passed over the surface at a close angle until the edge is achieved. *See* ***Benchstrop; Stropping***.

A wood gouge is honed across a leather and canvas strop.

Hood A metal cover that is placed above a tool or workspace to receive fumes or smoke. The hood may be either mounted by chains from the ceiling or on the wall from a kiln, spray booth, etc. The ventilation is normally unaided, being a natural updraft. However, it can be assisted with an electrically driven fan mounted in the system. The fan needs to be enclosed or other wise designed for any chemicals or heat involved. *See* ***Burnout furnace; Furnace; Forge***.

Horsepower (HP) A unit of power equal to a pulling horse or 33,000 foot-pounds per minute or 745.7 watts. It is a common measurement of power for a motor/engine driven tool.

Hot dipped metals Metals that are dipped into a tank of molten, liquid metal. The hot liquid metal adheres to the colder, solid metal to form a coating. This is the process used for zinc coating or galvanizing metal by applying a protective coating to avoid corrosion. Metals with lower melting points include lead, zinc and aluminum. While galvanized zinc and aluminum products are used for building purposes, the sculptor uses it in a similar fashion, but strictly for the aesthetics and sometimes with a patina applied. These coatings produce toxic fumes if welded. *See* ***Electroplating***.

Hot glue gun A handheld gun-shaped device that heats specially formulated small glue sticks and emits them in a ready-to-use thin paste. The glue sticks or adhesives are designed for a variety of materials including paper, fabric and wood. The process is sometimes called hot melt. *See* ***Hot melt***.

Hot melt The adhesive for the hot glue gun. *See* ***Hot glue gun***.

Hot tear A fracture or disruption of metal surface occurring during the cooling contraction of cast metal. It could be caused by an improperly designed thin/thick section or mishandling of an extremely hot metal before it has solidified. *See* ***Cold cracks***.

Humidity Airborne dampness, airborne moisture. Because moisture is absorbed into chemical compounds, humidity becomes a factor when working with resins, molding materials, finishing materials, etc. Humidity affects the increase or decrease of setting (drying). Chemical properties need to be checked for use in relation to humidity amounts.

Hump mold The mold used to press a sculpture material onto to create a three-dimensional shape. *See* ***Press mold***.

Hydrate A solid compound containing water (of crystallization). Clay and gypsum are hydrates.

Hydration Complete progression of adding water with dry ingredients to form a solid. Plaster and cement are good examples.

Hydraulic The pressure forced movement of a liquid, air or gas to lower, raise, or otherwise move an object. Hydraulic also means the ability to set in water, such as some cements and epoxies.

Hydrocal™ White gypsum cement. A product of USG known for its white color and working approaches resembling plaster uses. The manufacturer recommends mechanical mixing. It is good for slip casting with strength at two and a half times that of plaster. It is not for outdoor use. *See **Plaster** (chart).*

Robert Pulley, *Grandfather's Vision*. Sycamore, Hydrocal™, 54″x44″x39″ (137.2cm x 111.8cm x 99.1cm).

Carter Jones, *Angel for P.B.* Hydrocal™ and steel, 22″x24″x8″ (55.9cm x 61cm x 20.3cm).

Hydrochloric acid A colorless, highly active, poisonous solution of hydrogen chloride. This acid is sometimes used for cleaning metal. *See **Soldering**.*

Hydrostone™ (Product of USG) A cement that snap sets and is five times harder than plaster. The manufacturer recommends mechanical mixing only. *See **Waste mold**; **Plaster** (chart).*

Maria Alquilar, *Two Weeping Women and Tunnel of Love*. Cast iron, 10' (3.05m) tall. The sculptor is pictured with her work.

Ice sculpture A three-dimensional form carved from a solid block of ice. A variety of tools are used from ice picks to chainsaws.

Dawson List, *Louis Armstrong*. Carved ice in freezer, 28″ (71.1cm) tall. Photographer: Robert Horan.

Jimmie Jackson demonstrates his method for carving ice sculpture

ICE SCULPTURE
by Dawson List

Dawson List examines a 300 lb. (136.2kg) block of ice prior to beginning his carving.

The preplanned drawing is placed on the ice with a hot iron.

A chainsaw is the best tool for roughing out.

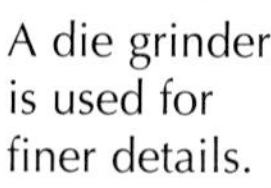

A die grinder is used for finer details.

The sculptor adds a top section to his work. Color has been added by freezing in colorful plastic strips.

Dawson List, Carved ice. Photographer: Robert Horan.

Igneous Stones formed by the heating and cooling of the molten earth into a solid mass. Though this includes the most recent lava, most of the stones are found beneath the earth's surface. The structure of the stone depends on the cooling rate and the depth below the earth's crust. he process results in extremely hard stones that require considerable time to carve. Igneous stones include basalt, dior ite, granite, lava and obsidian.

The most common carving stone is granite, which is primarily of a granular structure consisting of feldspar and quartz. Because of the durability and availability of granite, it can weather the out-of-doors. While granite takes a high polish, finishing it requires a great deal of time. Hand carving is difficult and protruding details or deep undercutting should be avoided without the best carbide tipped tools.

Thermal torches are used to carve granite. They use high heat applied by torch to the surface of the granite to spall small flakes of granite loose. These are washed away by a steady stream of surface water that not only keeps the surface clean but keeps the stone cool, resulting in a more predictable carving. *See* ***Stone; Stone*** *(chart);* ***Granite***.

Shawn Phillip Morin, *Empty*. Granite, 23″x13″x8″ (58.4cm x 33cm x 20.3cm).

Igniter A handheld tool used to create a spark to ignite gas. Sometimes called a sparker, it is used primarily for lighting oxyacetylene welding and cutting torches. *See* ***Oxyacetylene welding; Oxyacetylene cutting***.

Imitation stone A mixture of resins, cements or other binding substances with stone and/or pigments in an attempt to duplicate a solid, cohesive stone such as marble or alabaster. It is used in casting. The term may apply to surface decorations that match the look of stone or for some metal patinas. *See* ***Cast stone***.

Incandescent A light created by an electrically heated filament or a glowing heat (light) as a result of intense heat.

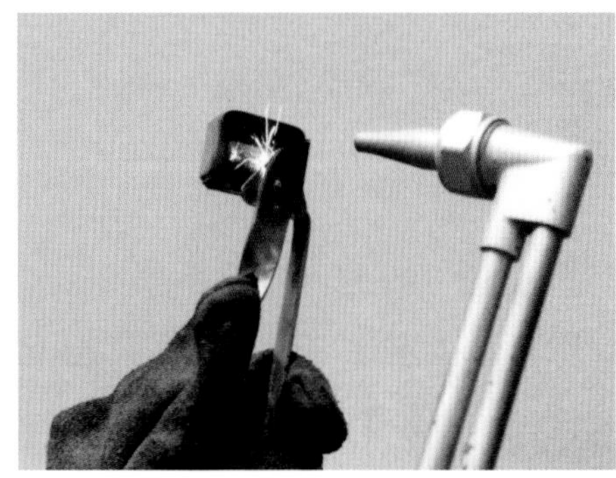

Igniter in use.

Inclusions Mold particles, crucible pieces or slag oxides that have fallen into molten liquid metal and remain in the casting. If not removed before pouring, gas problems on the surface or the patina may result. Inclusions can be caused by the careless joining techniques of the running system, resulting in small areas that allow the mold material to gather, then later to break off during the flow of metal. Dewaxing with the cup turned up instead of down allows trash to fall into the mold. Generally, loose mold particles can be expelled from the mold by gently turning the cup downward and shaking the particles out.

Arthur Williams, *Genesis*. Incralac coated cast bronze, 23″x23″x15″ (58.4cm x 58.4cm x 38.1cm).

Incralac™ A trademark name for a hard, clear coating that prevents corrosion and maintains the natural colors of metals, especially bronze. It is especially useful for high gloss finishes requiring protective surface barriers. Incralac™ is usually thinned and applied by spraying or dipping. It dries so quickly that the operator needs to experiment with sample bronze scraps prior to use. The exact lifespan of the coating is determined by the atmospheric conditions, specifically the weather, if placed out-of-doors. Though the manufacturer assigns a long life to the product, it must be periodically refinished, especially if vandals scratch or break the surface seal. *See* ***Patina***.

India gouge A long cone-shaped sharpening stone designed with an inner and outer curved surface. It is used for sharpening gouges.

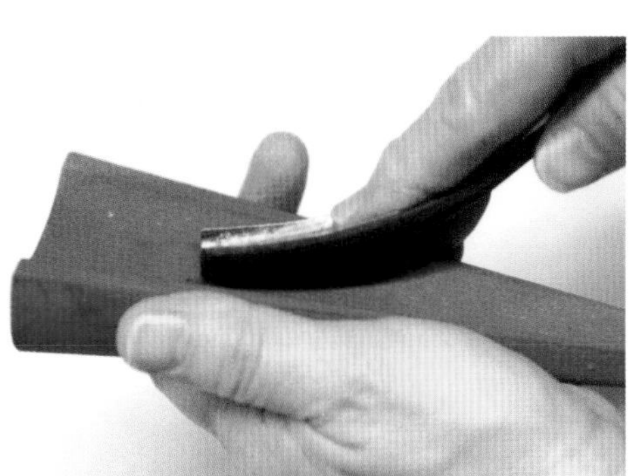

India gouge sharpening stone.

Matthew Weir, *Timepiece*. Indiana limestone, 27″x35″x16″ (68.6cm x 88.9cm x 40.6cm). Photographer: Brian Bohannon.

Indiana limestone An oolithic stone, limestone with a fine grain. It is an excellent, but hard carving stone. *See **Stone** (chart).*

Indirect carving The substance is carved with the use of enlarging or duplicating devices.

Induction furnace A metal casting furnace designed to liquefy metal with the heat produced by the charge (metal) itself. Using electricity as the fuel, it is without combustion gases and over 50% more energy efficient than other types of furnaces. However, the high cost of smaller units is absorbingly expensive as compared to other types of furnaces. *See **Furnaces**.*

Inert gas A gas that is non-reactive and does not combine chemically with welding filler or base metal. An example is argon gas used in TIG welding.

Infrared rays Invisible but highly penetrable rays created by the intense oxyacetylene flame and welding arc. They can burn and blind a worker if proper safety clothing is not worn. *See **Burns**.*

Ingot A precast brick/block of metal, such as bronze or aluminum, designed for future casting convenience and storage. Leftover liquid bronze and melted bronze scraps are often converted into ingots for future use. *See **Metal casting**.*

Bronze ingots with one cut in half.

Ingot mold A heat resistant mold designed to receive molten metal. The molds are made of iron or steel with a draft (taper) to allow easy removal after the metal cools and solidifies. The ingot mold is no longer than the interior length of the crucible nor is it larger than half as wide as the furnace lid opening. Sizes vary, but a common size is about ten inches (25.4cm) long by three to four inches (7.62cm to 10.16cm) wide and two inches deep, weighing approximately 20 pounds (9.08kg). *See* ***Ingot; Metal casting***.

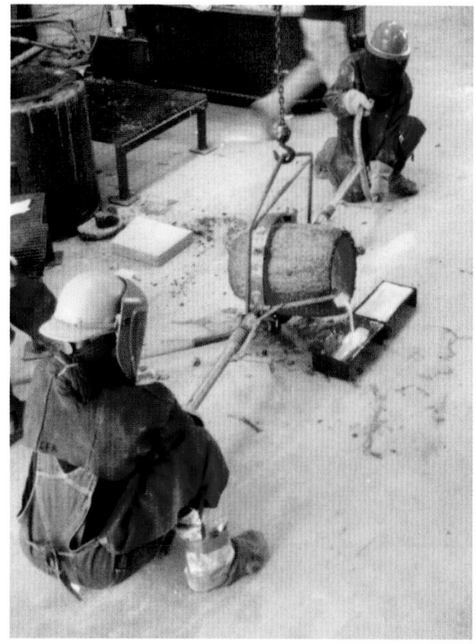

Inferno Foundry, Atlanta, Georgia, Workers remove the excess bronze into ingot molds.

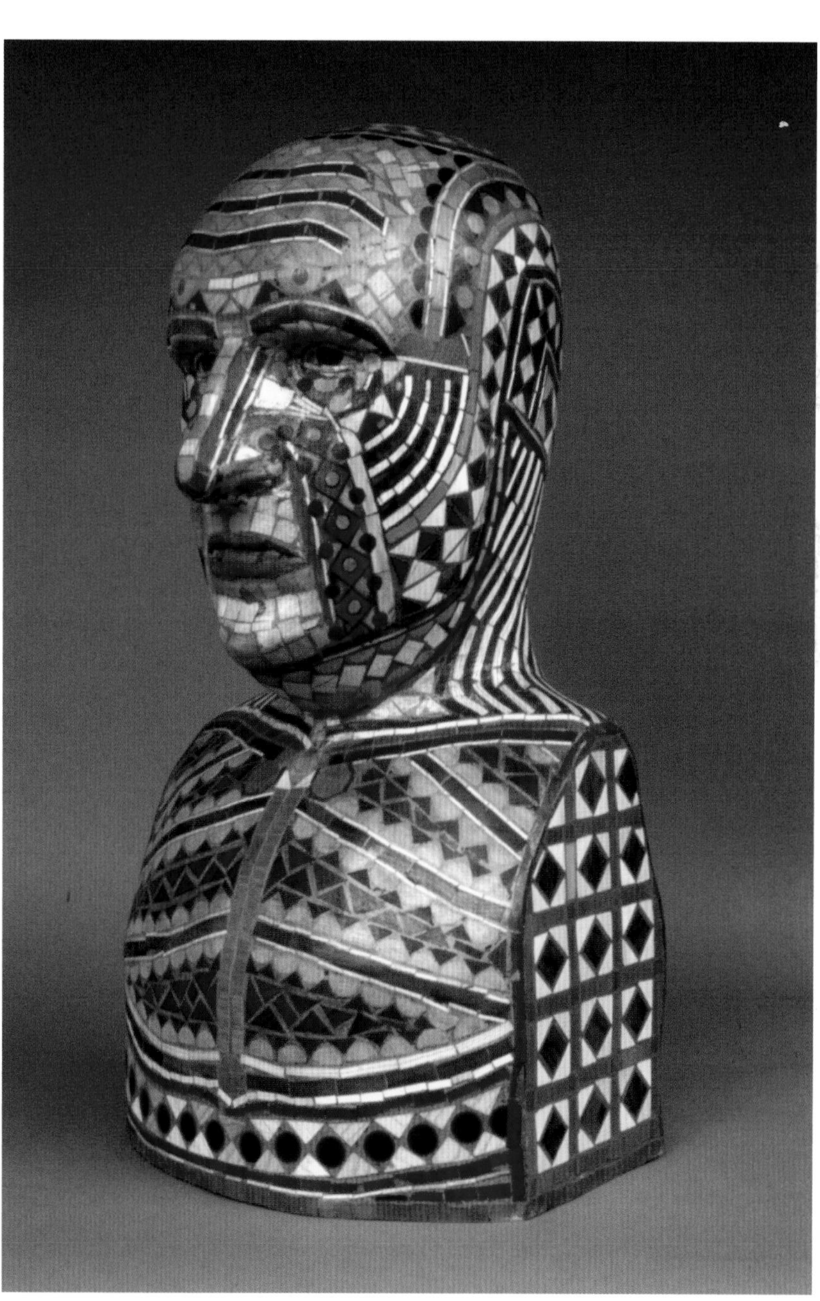

Inlay To set or insert thin strips or pieces of a material into a shallow groove for design. Thin pieces of substances, such as shell, wood, stone, ivory, etc., are used to create these designs. An example would be the ebony wood inlay in a violin's spruce body. Inlay is sometimes the term used for the final product.

In situ "On site" or original position. In situ sculpture is work that has been completed at the permanent location and is not to be moved. It is also a designation for the setting with all of the environmental considerations.

Michael Ferris, Jr., *Cliff*. Wood/inlaid wood, 26″x13″x9″ (66cm x 33cm x 22.9cm).

Installation (installing) The process of placing a sculpture, especially a large work, on a specific site. This involves hoists, trolleys, transportation, cranes, etc. Even the lighting is a part of the process. *See* ***Hoist; Lift; Lighting***.

INSTALLATION
by Arturo de la Riva

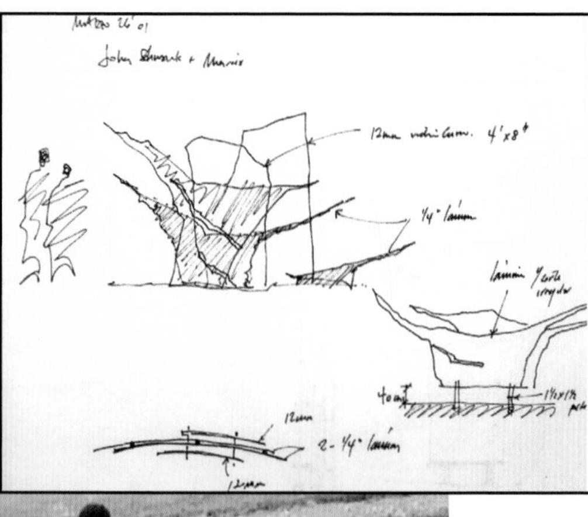

The original sketch with installation notes. Photographers: Luis Ponce and Lourdes Menendez.

The completed work in the sculptor's studio is taken to the site and laid out.

The work is in place, ready for a permanent mounting in a concrete form.

The fragile parts are added last.

Arturo de la Riva, *Welcome*. Bent glass ½″ (1.27cm), ¼″ (0.635cm) metal sheets.

Iron casting an open face bonded sand mold for *Suspended Landscape* by **Matthew C. Wicker**.

Matthew C. Wicker, *Suspended Landscape*. Cast iron, oak, steel, 10'x10'x15' (3.05m x 3.05m x 4.58m).

ron oxide Iron and oxygen compounds. Iron oxide is used for stains, especially red and black iron oxides.

vory The hard, creamy white substance comprised of elephant and other mammal's tusks. It has been used for carving for centuries. It gradually yellows, sometimes to a pale gray color. It is fine grained and carves to a high polish.

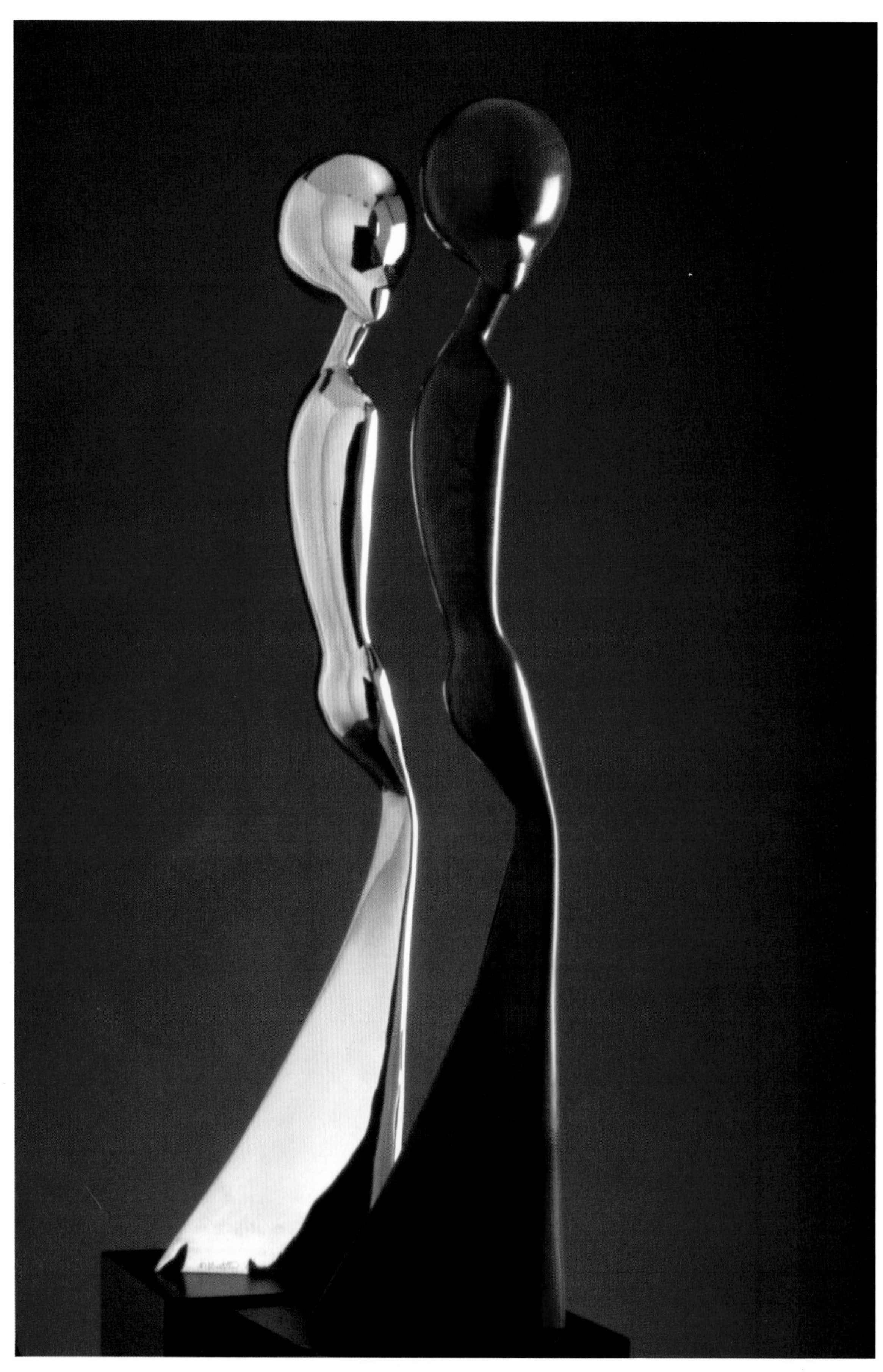

David Hostetler, *Elegant Women*. Wood carving and bronze casting, 5′8″ (172.72cm). The original is carved in walnut; the polished bronze was cast from the woodcarving.

J

ack hammer The name given for extra-large air or electric hammers used to break up concrete or pavement, as opposed to smaller carving hammers. *See* ***Air hammer***.

acks A glassblower's tool that resembles tongs. It is used to constrict (neck) and shape hot molten glass

ade An exceptionally hard mineral stone, either nephrite or jadeite. While difficult to carve, intricate designs and shapes can be created. The mineral is known as Jade green though the color can vary, even to white.

apan drier A quality drier used to accelerate the drying time of oil-based varnishes and paint products. Especially useful in cold weather, it is added to the paint or other thinners in a limited amount as part of the finish for furni ture and wood sculpture.

ig (jigger) An apparatus that is used as a guide for tools or a type of template for repeating the same shape, hole or design. It is custom made for a specific task. In ceramics, a jigger could be a plaster holder placed on a wheel head, creating an even rotating mold to hold clay pieces, while a stationary trimmer is held to the piece resulting in the desired shape.

ig saw A handheld or powered saw with a thin, flexible blade designed to cut short turn radiuses.

oint The intersection of two or more parts that have been attached (joined) with glue, welding, clamps, design or by other means.

ourneyman A worker who has complet-ed an apprenticeship but is not yet ready to work on his/her own. She/he is ready to work with someone having more experience.

unk art Sculpture created from discarded items. Sometimes used as a slang term for poor art or art in which the whole never transcends the parts. *See* ***Assemblage***.

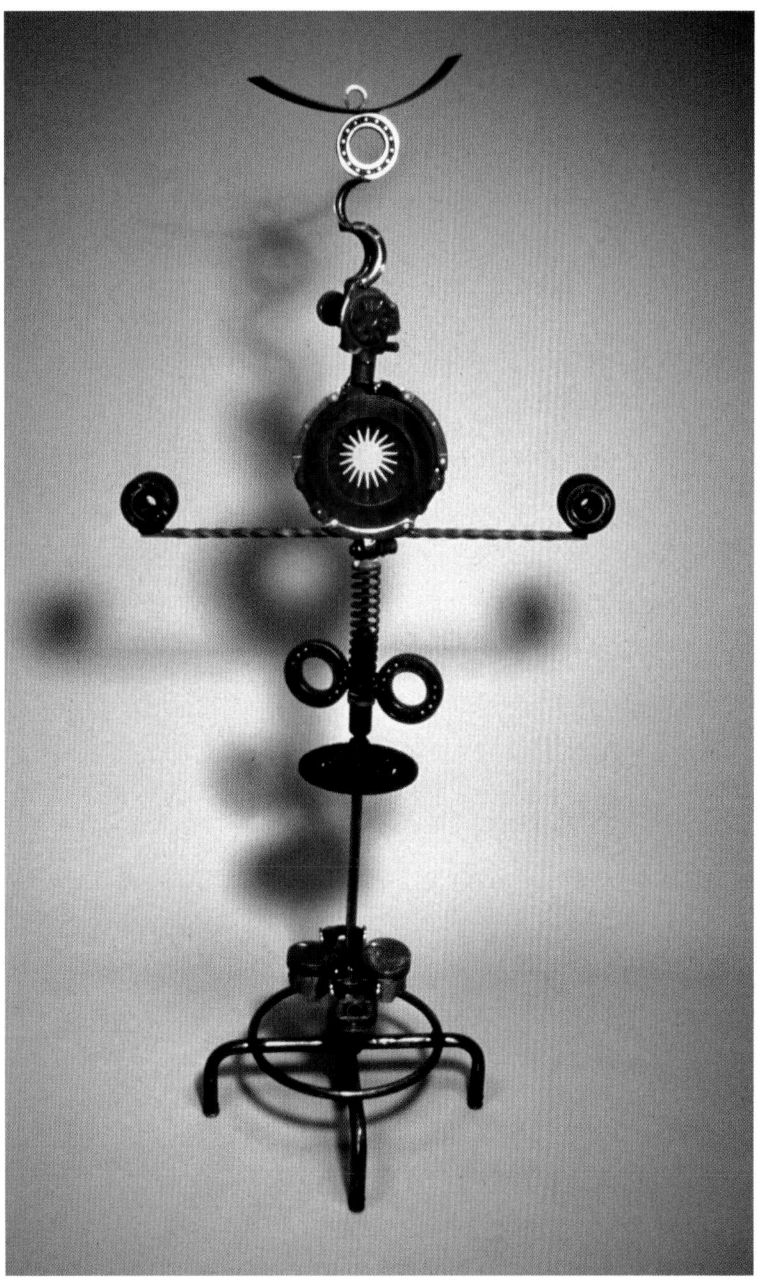

Milt Friedly, *Pressure Plate*. Steel, cast iron, clutch plate, pistons, bearings, welded steel, cast iron, 76″x33″x22″ (193cm x 83.8cm x 55.9cm).

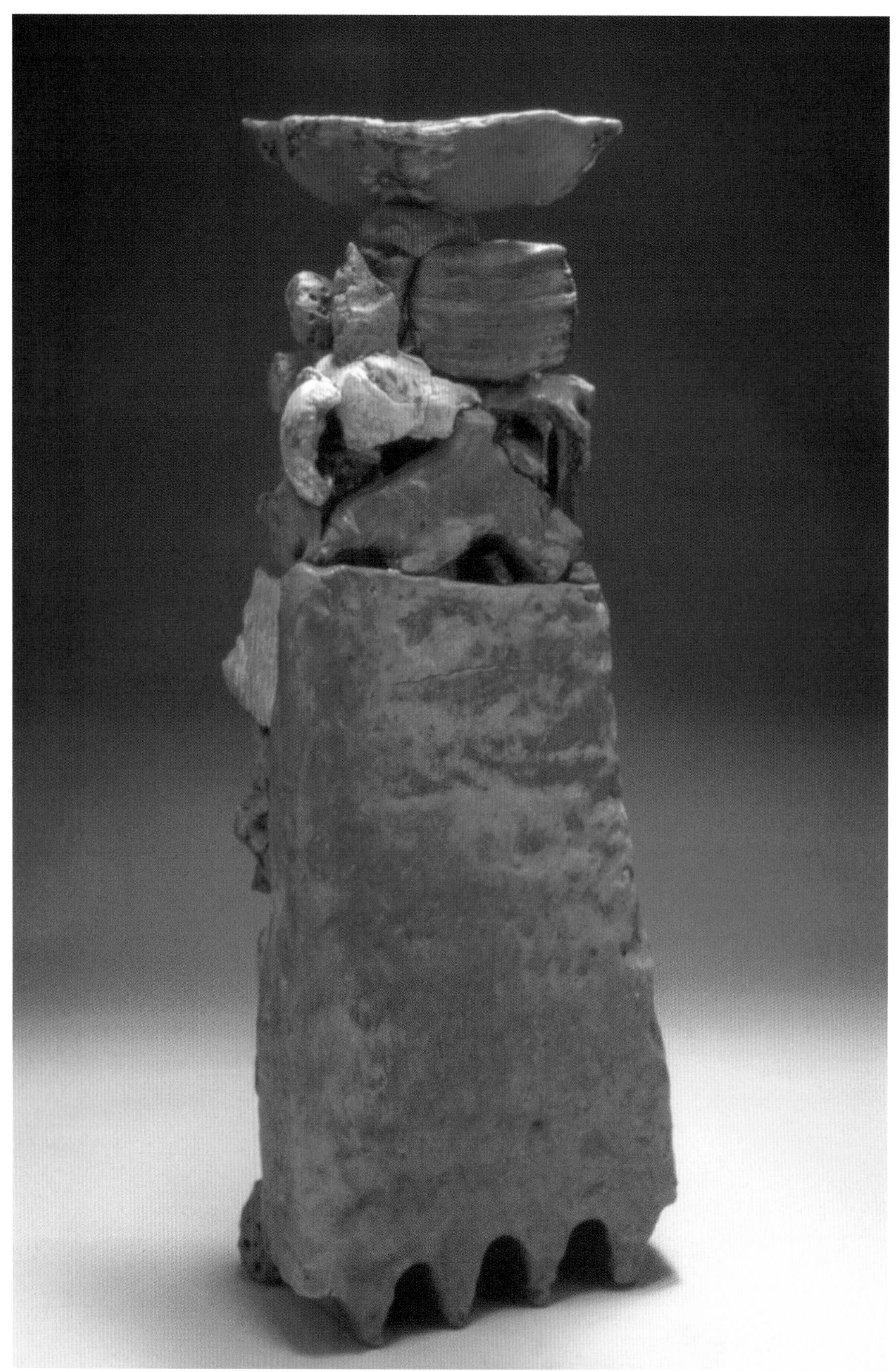

Keith Ekstam, *Toy Stack II*. Wood fired stoneware, 25″x10″x6″ (63.5cm x 25.4cm x 15.2cm).

K

Kaolin (China clay) A clay that is primarily used for its white color. The major clay in porcelain. Kaolin is a good refractory product melting at over 3218°F (1770°C); however, it is not very plastic. *See* ***Porcelain***.

Kerf Cut width or resulting empty space after a cut. It is the groove or cut made by an oxyacetylene cutting torch, plasma cutter, saw or punch.

Kerosene A clear, thin oil fuel or solvent distilled from shale oil or petroleum oil. It is referred to as coal oil and is used for lamps, as well as home heating. Because of its slow dry rate, it is a good solvent for removing wax residue but is not usable as a paint thinner.

Kevlar™ A strong, lightweight material made of aramid fiber that resembles fiberglass. It is a heat resistant material especially used for protective work clothes and gloves when encountering extreme heat, such as metal casting.

Key groove A recess designed for a corresponding registration key when mold making. The key and the groove should fit tightly together when properly designed. *See* ***Mold making***.

Keyhole saws A small stiff, narrow, taper-bladed, handheld saw used for tight radius cuts. The cut is not considered a smooth cut.

Kick wheel A machine designed for centering and making pottery. It has a flat, round head mounted to a shaft that is manually turned from a large flywheel that is powered by consecutively stroking (kicking) it for movement. The head allows the clay on it to be centered and worked. *See* ***Wheel***.

Killed plaster Water saturated plaster of little setting value; hence, little strength. *See* ***Neat cement; Plaster***.

Kiln An insulated structure designed to hold extremely high heat. A kiln consists of a closeable opening, heat chamber and source of heat. The common fuels used are electric or gas (which requires a flue). A kiln is primarily designed for ceramic (pottery) use, but can also be used for sculpture forms.

Patz Fowle, *Fowle-Play. . . The Big Adventure*. Porcelain, stoneware, 16″x11″x9″ (40.6cm x 27.9cm x 22.9cm).

The kiln needs to be a strong, rigid furnace (oven like) to fire (bake) clay to a permanent mature state and to fuse glazes to the new body. Kilns are designed for maximum control of high-reaching temperatures. They are well insulated with special bricks, castables and liners able to withstand and maintain high heat. The interior chambers can be less than 12 inches (30.48cm) in diameter to walk-in sizes. They have doors or openings to load the sculptures and a control system (dampers) to regulate the passage of heat and air through the system. The burners create intense heat directed into the furnace. There are many heating fuels with ranges of heat possible, including cow chips, wood, oil, etc., but the most popular high heat fuels are gas and electricity.

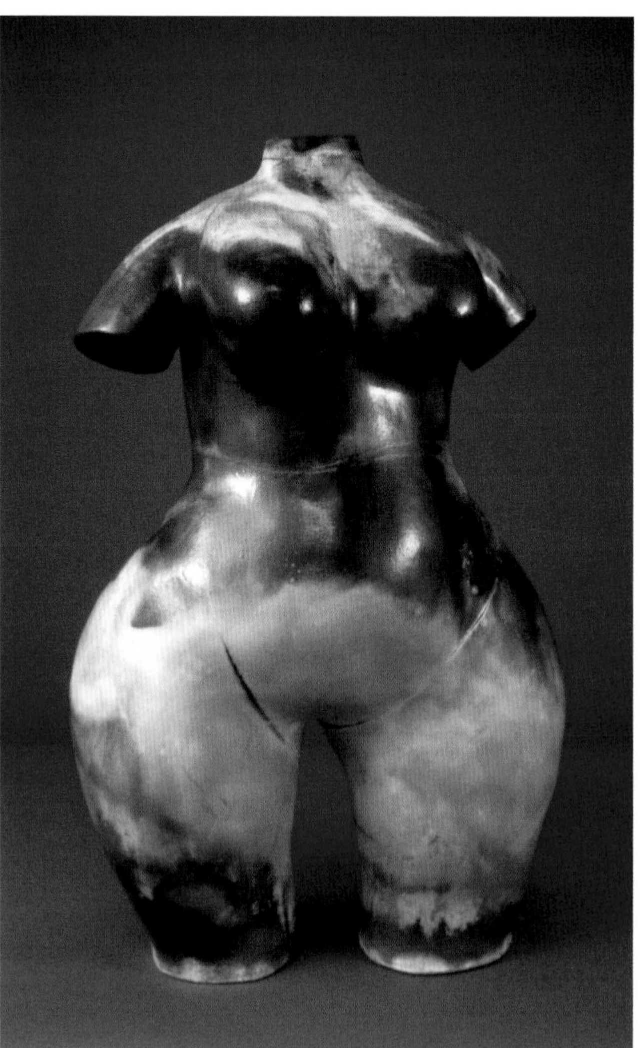

Gudrún Halldórsdóttir, *Saga*. Ceramic, 26″x16″x9″ (66cm x 41cm x 23cm). Photographer: Arni Sigurdsson.

Down-draft kiln.

The two basic gas kiln types are **up-draft** and **down-draft**. With **down-draft** kilns, the energy (flame) source is directed upward by a baffle (bag wall). The burners are usually a venturi type in which the gas and air are united in a mixing chamber (pipe), released and ignited and are controlled by gas valves as well as air vents located at the rear of the chamber.

With **updraft** kilns, the energy (flame) source is directed upwards, circulating toward the top stack (flue) and out. Dampers or baffles are located at the top to control the firing, and venturi burners are used.

Kilns are located in an open, but usually covered, area for ventilation, as well as weather protection. A metal hood is used to capture combustion gasses and direct them from the firing area. It also serves to protect the structure from the escaping heat and flames. The necessary gas supply must be

Up-draft kiln.

determined by the size and type of kiln burner. If the kiln is a professionally manufactured chamber, then the requirements should be observed. Careful planning with the available gas source is a priority. Bottled gas is available in remote locations, but the burners should be designed for the purpose, and a large tank needs to be used to assure a complete firing.

There are many designs for gas kilns from the cantilevered arch to a square walk-in kiln. Whether it is big or small, the sculptor's obvious question is, "How does it load?" Placing clay sculptures into a kiln is when most of the breakage occurs, so it is of paramount importance. The door and door placement have to be considered. Can the sculpture be placed in from the front or top?

Electric kilns are favored among sculptors because of their portability and less rigid fire codes. Electric is more expensive than gas except where gas is not widespread. Most electric kilns require 220 volts at about 50 amps. The heat is produced by radiation from coiled elements placed into the side wall indentations. They are either top loading or front loading. The top loading is preferred since side doors require more structural strength and involve additional design problems because of the coils in the door.

Nickel-nichrome wire can serve as a heating element up to 2000°F (1093°C) for low fire. Kanthal is the element that fires up to 2300°F (1260°C). Other elements are available that can operate with higher temperatures, but because of the makeup, they are very expensive. Automatic temperature controls are normal, and a kiln sitter (an automatic shut-off device) is included.

Since oxygen is not a factor in electrical firing, live flames are not present, and all heating is inside the kiln. The units are easy to locate in a studio. Without fuel lines or chimneys to contend with, they are portable. However, the sculptor must be certain that good ventilation is present, since some of the clay bodies and glaze materials can release toxic fumes during the firing. *See* ***Firing; Down-draft kiln; Up-draft kiln; Bisque firing; Glaze firing; Pyrometric cones; Venturi.***

Kiln dry (dried wood) Drying wood in a heated chamber with controlled humidity, as well as heat and air circulation. The naturally drying process takes much longer. Kiln dried wood will re-absorb some atmospheric moisture after completion; whereas, naturally seasoned (air dried) does not.

Electric Kilns.

Kiln furniture: shelves and shelf supports.

Kiln furniture High temperature refractory posts (shelf supports) shelves and other shapes used to separate and hold clay objects apart and in place during kiln firing. *See* ***Kiln***.

Kiln wash A protective covering of refractory substances brushed on the kiln interior walls and shelves to prevent clay and glazes from adhering during the firing process. Common materials used for this purpose are equal parts of kaolin and flint added to water to achieve a cream-like fluid. *See* ***Kiln***.

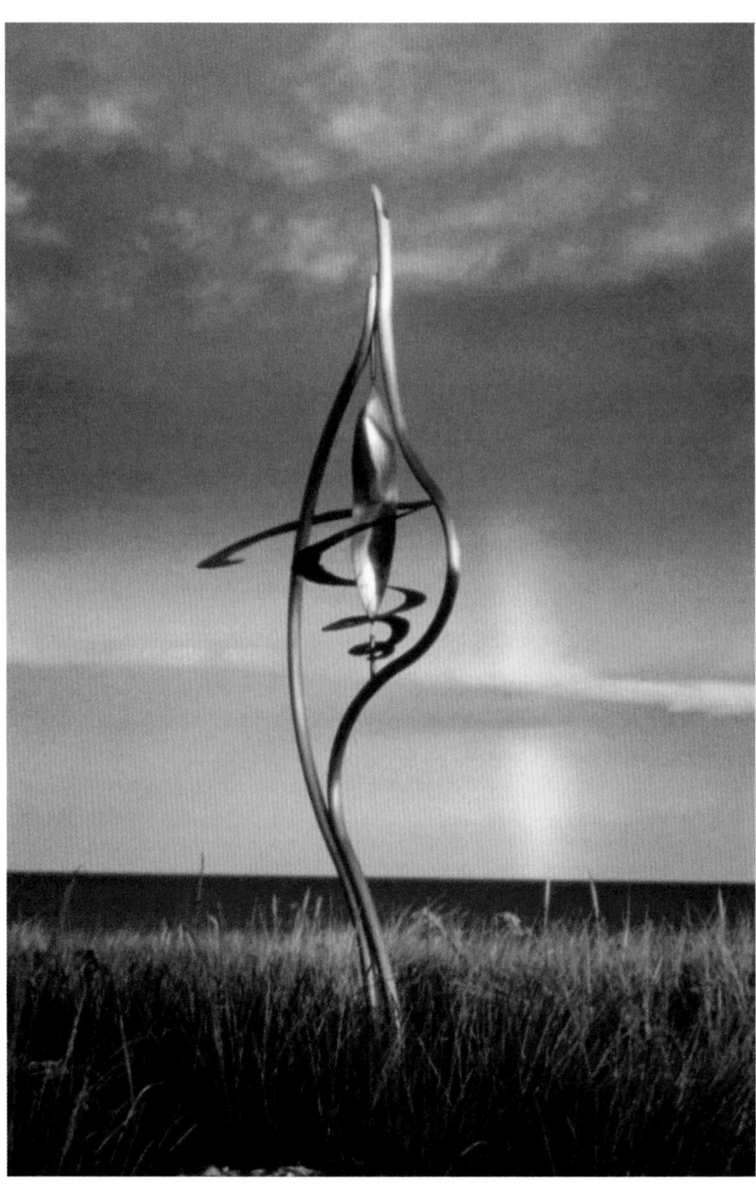

Meryl Taradash, *The Caged Bird Dances*. Kinetic, rotating aluminum within stainless steel, 10'10'x3'x3'1" (3.3m x 0.94m). Photographer: Sara Mendoza.

Kinetic (sculpture) Sculpture that moves or has moving parts as a result of forces of nature (wind and water, for example) or by mechanical means. Mobiles are kinetic sculptures.

Kneading (clay) Preparing ceramic clay for use, especially wheel throwing. It resemble the same process of kneading flour dough. The worker rolls the clay into itself, using both hands, and afterwards, picks it up and slams it onto a surface to eliminate air bubbles and create a more compact mass. As compared to wedging, it is used for smaller pieces of clay. *See* ***Wedging; Wedging table***.

Knife check Cyclical blade marks left on lumber by lathes, especially near knots or ends of boards.

Knock out Removing investment casting material from the artwork using hammers and sometimes chisels, but never striking the actual cast artwork. *See* ***Divesting***.

Knots The location in wood where branches intersect into the main body. The places are darker and can be considered as a mark of beauty or a distraction in an otherwise clear board.

Ceramic clay is kneaded to compress and remove air bubbles.

Lin Emery works with scale model for *Flower Dance*.

Lin Emery, *Flower Dance*. Kinetic, polished aluminum, stainless steel ball bearings, 36'x30'x30' (10.98m x 9.15m x 9.15m). Amhurst Park, Waukegan, Illinois.

Wayne Forbes, *Shadow Warrior*. Laminated wood, 28″x18″x14″ (71.1cm x 45.7cm x 35.6cm).

L

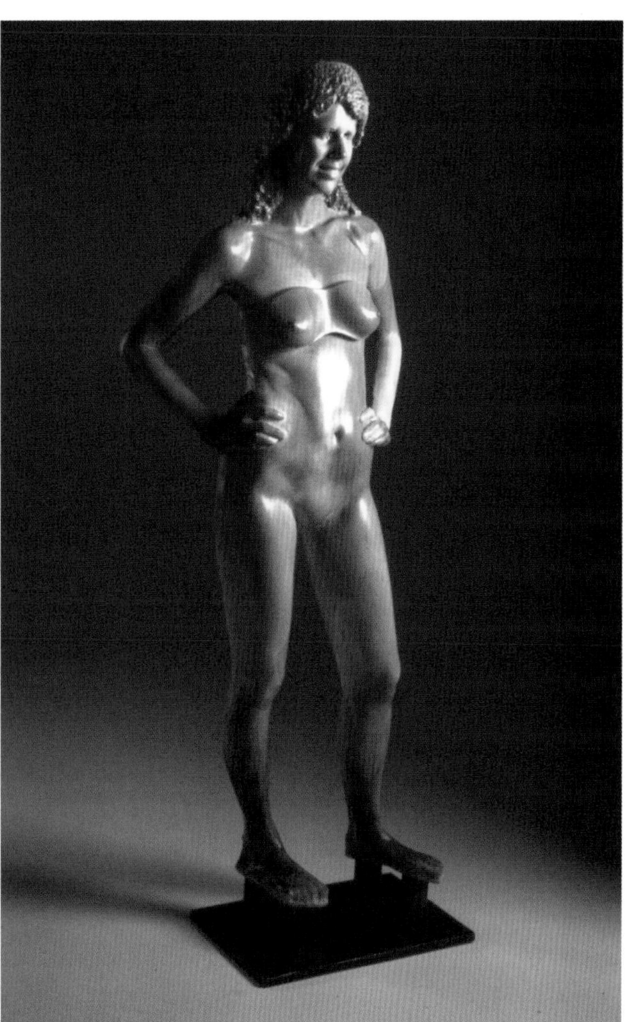

Michael J. Cooper, *Gayle*. Carved maple with lacquer over oil paint, 68"x29"x15" (172.7cm x 73.7cm x 38.1cm).

Lacquer A solvent known for its use with paint products having glossy surfaces. It is extremely active, capable of melting plastic products and removing old paint. However, its toxic fumes are capable of doing physical damage by osmosis. It was originally a popular auto paint because of its ability to dry rapidly and produce a beautifully thin layered glossy coat. Lacquers are very hard and wear well but ultraviolet rays affect them. *See* ***Paint***.

Lamination A layer of a substance held together by a bonding agent to achieve strength, size, beauty or a combination of these. The layers are usually thin, such as countertop or surface wood covering. Fiberglass can be laminated in layers to achieve strength. *See* ***Paper; Plywood; Fiberglass; Wood***.

Shawn Philip Morin, *Remnant*. Mixed granites, marble, limestone, bronze and nickel silver, 62"x48"x19" (157.5cm x 121.9cm x 48.3cm).

LAMINATION
by Walter Driesbach

Wood freshly laminated with the clamps removed, ready to carve.

Wood partially roughed out.

Walter Driesbach, *Citizen*. Walnut, 39.5" (100.3cm) tall.

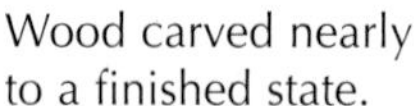

Wood carved nearly to a finished state.

LAMINATION
by Tim Kinard

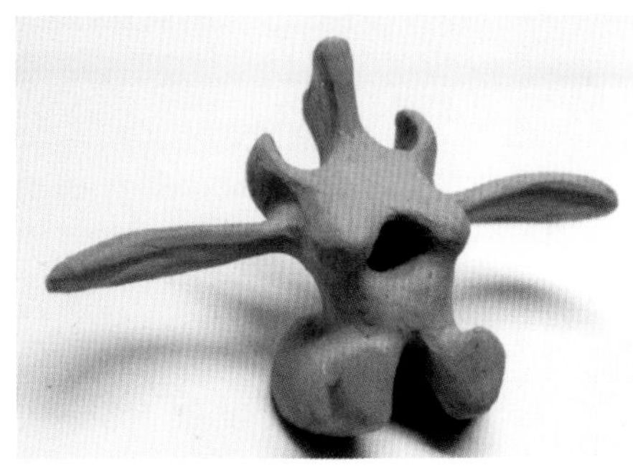

The modeling clay model is 4″ (10.2cm) tall.

The wood is glued and stacked with glue clamps applied.

The model was measured and sliced into scaled thicknesses. Proportionally enlarged, it was then cut a board at a time to match the model pieces.

Tim Kinard applies tung oil to the finished sculpture: *Of Flight through Evolution* in mahogany.

Lapidarist (lapidary) A worker of gemstones who can cut, polish and engrave them. Lapidary is the working of gemstones.

Latex (molds) An extract from rubber trees, milkweeds and other plants. Mixed and combined with other chemicals, latex produces a flexible molding material that is usually air cured and brushed on layer by layer as it dries. Latex also refers to a paint that contains similar compounds. Latex mold material can be applied immediately from the container. Since it is air curing, it does not need a catalyst. Because of the required number of coats when using it as a molding material, it has often been replaced by other flexible molding materials. There is no mixing involved for latex molds, though stirring is necessary. Latex molding material is ammonia or water-based. Both require extensive drying times between layers, though the ammonia base dries more quickly. However, the ammonia-based product requires more ventilation and precautions when handling.

Latex can be used for casting many materials, including resin, concrete, wax and plaster. To use latex, the form must be completely sealed with no moisture present. The separator is frequently wax. Though latex can be sprayed on, brushing is the most frequent application method. Complete drying has to occur between each coat. Small molds may take only five or six layers.

After all layers are dry, a mother mold is made to ensure the strength and rigidity of the material. Even small molds should be allowed to cure two or more days. A good test to ensure that the latex is completely cured is to tug on a small section to see how elastic it is. If it readily springs back to the original shape, it should be dry. Another indicator is that it tends to dry to a darker color. Small latex molds can sometimes be taken off sculptures, like removing a glove, in just one piece. Storing latex molds creates problems, since they tend to distort and shrink. *See* ***Molds; Flexible molds; Release agent*** *(chart)*.

Wood lathe in use. Photographer: Michael J. Cooper.

Lathe A turning tool of a mechanical nature used to shape/turn/round wood or metal as it is held in a rotating position between two holders. A cutting tool is pressed into the moving material to shave it into cylindrical shapes. The term is also used to describe the process of using a turning tool. *See* ***Woodturning; Metal turning lathe***.

Lava Igneous rock created from a flowing volcano. It is characterized by multi-sized air pockets (holes) throughout, created by volcanic gases. The result is a porous but glassy appearance.

Lay-up Process of applying a material to a surface. It is commonly applied by hand depending upon the substance. *See* ***Fiberglass; Concrete; Plastics***.

Lead (electrical) The flexible covered electrical line leading out of the welder to the work. One end is connected to the machine (welder), the other end has the ground clamp or a rod holding device. *See* ***Arc welding***.

Lead (metal) A soft, ductile, metallic element with a silver appearance that rapidly oxidizes to a dark gray color. It can be hammered because it is a malleable metal. As a casting metal, it pours at a low temperature, melting at 620°F (327°C). Because of its long-lasting poisonous qualities as a pigment, it is no longer used in paints and is cautioned against in low-fire ceramics. Lead can be cast in an ordinary cast iron skillet or pot because of the low melting temperature. The mold can be a simple mix of half sand and plaster that has been baked for at least 24 hours at 500° F (260°C) or higher. However, lead emits poisonous fumes and creates other health problems as it is being worked.

Leather hard The stage in clay drying where the clay is no longer malleable, is firm and can be trimmed. In the earliest stage, the clay can be hollowed. Moisture remains, but the shrinkage is nominal after this stage, though the clay color and appearance is still that of wet clay. While the clay is in this rigid state, it can be burnished with glass, wood, metal, etc. However, the work can be broken and is nearly impossible to repair. *See* ***Clay; Ceramics***.

Leggings placed on.

Leggings Lower leg protection worn by workers when around extreme heat such as metal casting. The leggings are made of a heat resistant material and held in place by straps, Velcro™ or special leg hugging clamps. *See* ***Safety clothing; Spat***.

Lens Any shield to protect the eyes but, specifically, the tinted glass or shades designed for welders and metal casters. They are designed to dispel spatters, sparks, etc. Concentrated acute bright heat will injure the eyes when the rays are viewed without protection. Welding lens are known by the shade number. As an example, a number 5 is standard for oxyacetylene welding, while a number 10 is typical for arc welding.

Life casting Creating a casting from a live person. *See* ***Body molding***.

Life mask A casting or impression of the face (sometimes the body) of a living person, as opposed to a death mask of someone deceased. The process of relying on plaster as the molding material is decreasing; alginate is more commonly used. *See* ***Body molding; Alginate; Moulage***.

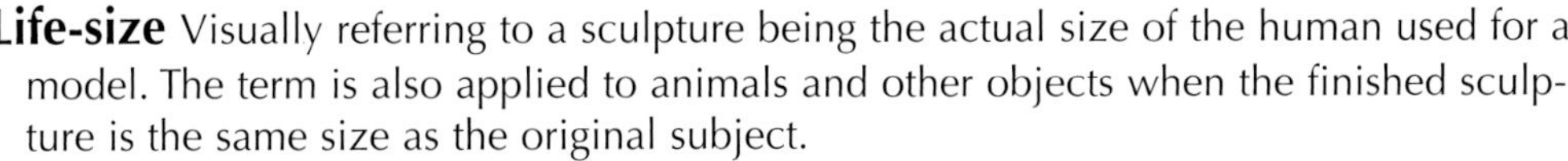

Life-size Visually referring to a sculpture being the actual size of the human used for a model. The term is also applied to animals and other objects when the finished sculpture is the same size as the original subject.

Lift To raise a sculpture. It may involve nylon straps, hoists, etc. *See* ***Installation*** *(installing)*; ***Hoist***.

Jack Ransom Arvin carves a marble form on a scissor lift portable cart. He uses this to change heights as he carves.

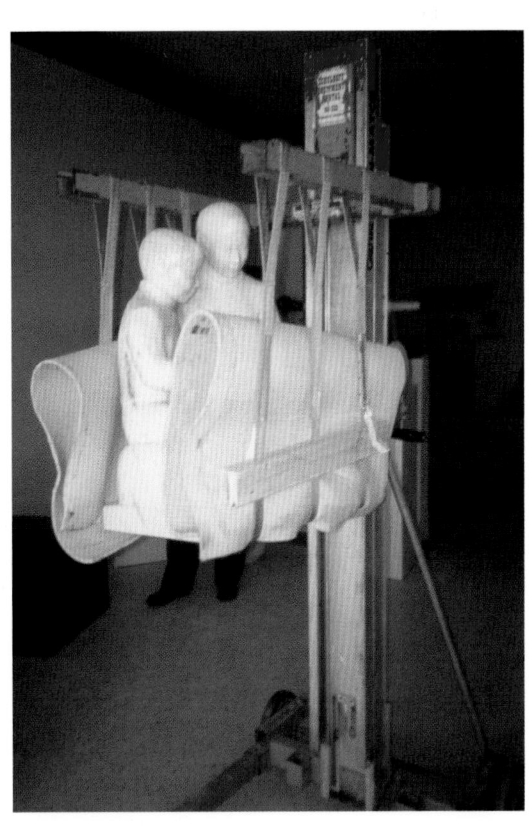

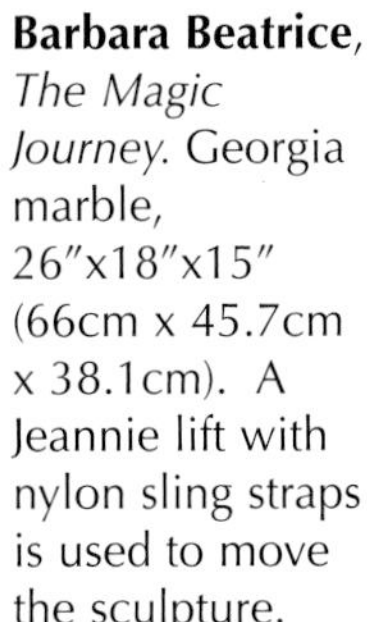

Barbara Beatrice, *The Magic Journey.* Georgia marble, 26″x18″x15″ (66cm x 45.7cm x 38.1cm). A Jeannie lift with nylon sling straps is used to move the sculpture.

Lifting tongs A tool used for removing a crucible from a metal casting furnace. For smaller crucibles under 20, they are usually a one-person device that is placed down in the furnace (with the lid open) and around the crucible. The handles are long and a distance from the hottest heat. As the handles are raised, the pull firms the grip on the crucible so that the pot can be safely lifted. Once out and placed on a pouring block, the pressure is released which in turn loosens the tongs from the crucible, allowing easy removal. Two person lifting tongs operate the same way, except the handles extend out to each side, and the grip is even stronger because of the longer leverage. *See* ***Blast furnace***.

Lighting (of sculpture) Correct lighting is essential for viewing three-dimensional forms while working, especially for relief sculpture. Display lighting will enhance all sculptural forms. Display lighting includes the concentration of light, electrical supply, fixtures and location. *See* ***Installation; Site specific***.

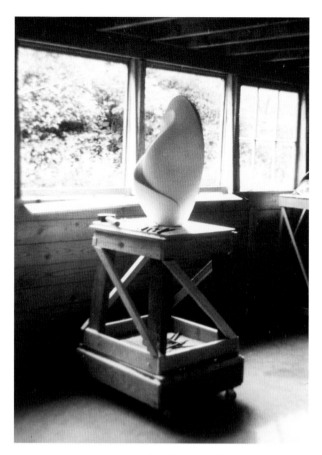

Ali Baudoin, *The Moon Came Down to Kiss the Mountains*. Stainless steel, mixed, 48″x30″x30″ (121.9cm x 76.2cm x 76.2cm).

Mary Lewis, *Skunk Cabbage*. Carrara marble, 28″x15″ (71.1cm x 38.1cm). Good lighting helps the sculptor to visualize the form and secure a finer finish while working.

G. David Burch, *Eurydice*. Bronze and granite, 53″x25″x32″ (134.6cm x 63.5cm x 81.3cm).

Annette Blocker, *Adapting to Man's Presence*. Limestone, bronze, patina, 18″x10″x8″ (45.7cm x 25.4cm x 20.3cm).

Lignum vitae An extremely hard wood with a fine grain. It is preferred for tools and handles of tools, such as full wooden mallets. It is rarely used for carving but can be carved. *See **Wood** (chart).*

Lime Calcium oxide. Calcium hydroxide is used in building products, such as mortar sand cements, while calcium oxide is used as a flux in ceramic glazes. Lime products will dry and chafe the skin. *See **Cement**; **Quicklime**.*

Limestone A sedimentary stone of calcium carbonate. Limestone is a builder's favorite due to its durability and cutting properties. While limestone is present in most locales, local limestone is not always preferred for carving because it may be too soft or too hard. The softer varieties are chalky and tend to crumble when carved. These are used for road construction. The hardest varieties are seldom used because the crystalline structure is treacherous to carve. These are used for lithography due to the tight grain.

The preferred limestone, oolithic, is of statuary grade. It is composed of small, rounded particles and can retain good details and undercuts with minimal difficulty. Examples of carveable limestone would be Indiana or Texas limestone. Though limestone can be found in many colors, the most common are buff (Texas) or gray (Indiana). *See: **Sedimentary**; **Stone**; **Stone** (chart).*

Limited edition A specific limited number of castings. After the number is reached, the mold is destroyed. Originally, the edition was of great concern because primitive molds would rapidly deteriorate resulting in later, poorer castings. Now, with better molding materials, edition numbers can be considerably larger. However, by limiting the edition number, the value of a work is increased by making it rare. The term can be used to describe a limited number of the same artwork in other media. *See **Edition**.*

Jack Ransom Arvin, *The Three Hundred*. Alabaster, 35″x22″x11″ (88.9cm x 55.9cm x 27.9cm). Photographer: Billy Stone.

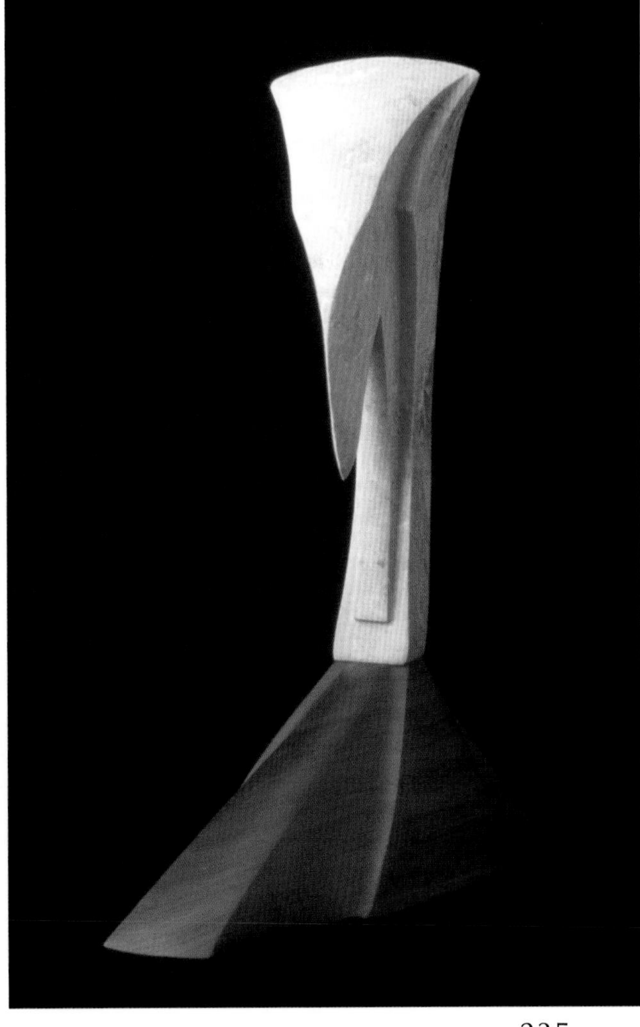

Jae, *Il Conduttore.* Cast bronze, 21"x14"x13" (53.3cm x 35.6cm x 33cm).

Linear A work with many sharp or straight edges, an extended form or a series of thin (linear) parts, etc. The term is normally associated with two-dimensional work.

Liver of sulfur Potassium sulfide; also known as potash sulfate. It is a common base chemical used for bronze patination to achieve various browns. *See **Potash sulfate**; **Patina**; **Patina** (chart).*

Lock key A small key or hump of mold material attached to a mold wall to hold the mold in place. It has a small undercut shape that can easily be removed from the mother mold. It is made in advance of the molding process from the same mold material, but pre-cast or cut into shape. A lock key literally results in a controlled undercut with enough strength and shape to stay in place and yet allow easy removal without tearing the flexible mold wall or resulting in a damaged casting. They are carefully placed to ensure even distribution where the mold needs additional support to keep from sagging, but designed to hold a flexible mold in position during the casting process. *See **Mold**.*

Long bent tools Wood carving tools with cutting edges at the end of a long, curved shaft.

Loop tools Tools with looped wire ends. They are used for removing clay or modeling clay from the main body and are commonly used for trimming in ceramics. *See **Modeling tools**.*

Lost pattern casting (vaporized casting) Metal casting wherein the artwork is consumed during the casting process. *See **Styrofoam**™; **Sand casting**; **Vaporized casting**.*

Lost wax (casting) A form of investment or cirè perdue casting. The wax artwork is set in a refractory mold and then melted out leaving a cavity. It is then filled with liquid hot metal to freeze into a hard metal casting. It is called lost wax because in past history the wax was lost (burned up), never to be used again. *See **Metal casting**; **Burnout**.*

Arthur Williams, *Prelude.* Lost wax cast bronze patinaed with liver of sulfur, 18"x29"x26" (45.7cm x 73.7cm x 66cm).

Low carbon steel Steel containing less than 0.2% carbon.

Low relief A low profile sculpture on a flat surface. It does not project far from the surface; hence, it does not have undercuts. *See* ***Bas relief; Relief sculpture***.

Lubricant Oil, grease, or other substances sprayed, brushed or rubbed on surfaces to lessen friction. The term is also used to designate release agents or mold releases. *See* ***Release agent***; ***Release agent*** *(chart)*.

Lumber Wood that has been cut, seasoned, dressed and usually graded for use. Wood products manufactured in easy-to-handle shapes and lengths for reuse by cutting, sawing, etc. Beyond the surface being planed, lumber is not considered a finished product. Lumber is not the designation ordinarily given to carving woods. Lumber specifies construction materials, such as boards, or even posts, used for functional purposes. Principal woods used for construction are pine and fir, although nearly all woods can be placed into interior furniture. Particle board, Masonite™, chipboard and plywood come under this heading.

Since lumber is commonly prepared in large thicknesses, the sculptor often takes advantage of the material for his/her use. Redwoods and pines are used as solid carving blocks, especially for beginners. Though the fibrous quality of the wood allows rapid waste removal, it also results in splinters and a softer finish. *See* ***Wood; Particle board***.

Luster Metallic sheen on a surface. It is especially noticed on ceramic glazes from a deposit of a particular metal, such as gold, silver or copper during the glaze firing.

Luto Crushed plaster investment that has been previously used in metal casting mold materials. Luto can be a recycled mold material if it is mixed with new plaster investment for new metal casting molds. *See* ***Investment***.

Lye Sodium hydroxide or potassium hydroxide in water. It is used for cleaning purposes.

Irene Poulton, *Maenad*. Raku, gold luster, 27.6″x15.4″ (70cm x 39cm). Photographer: Victor France.

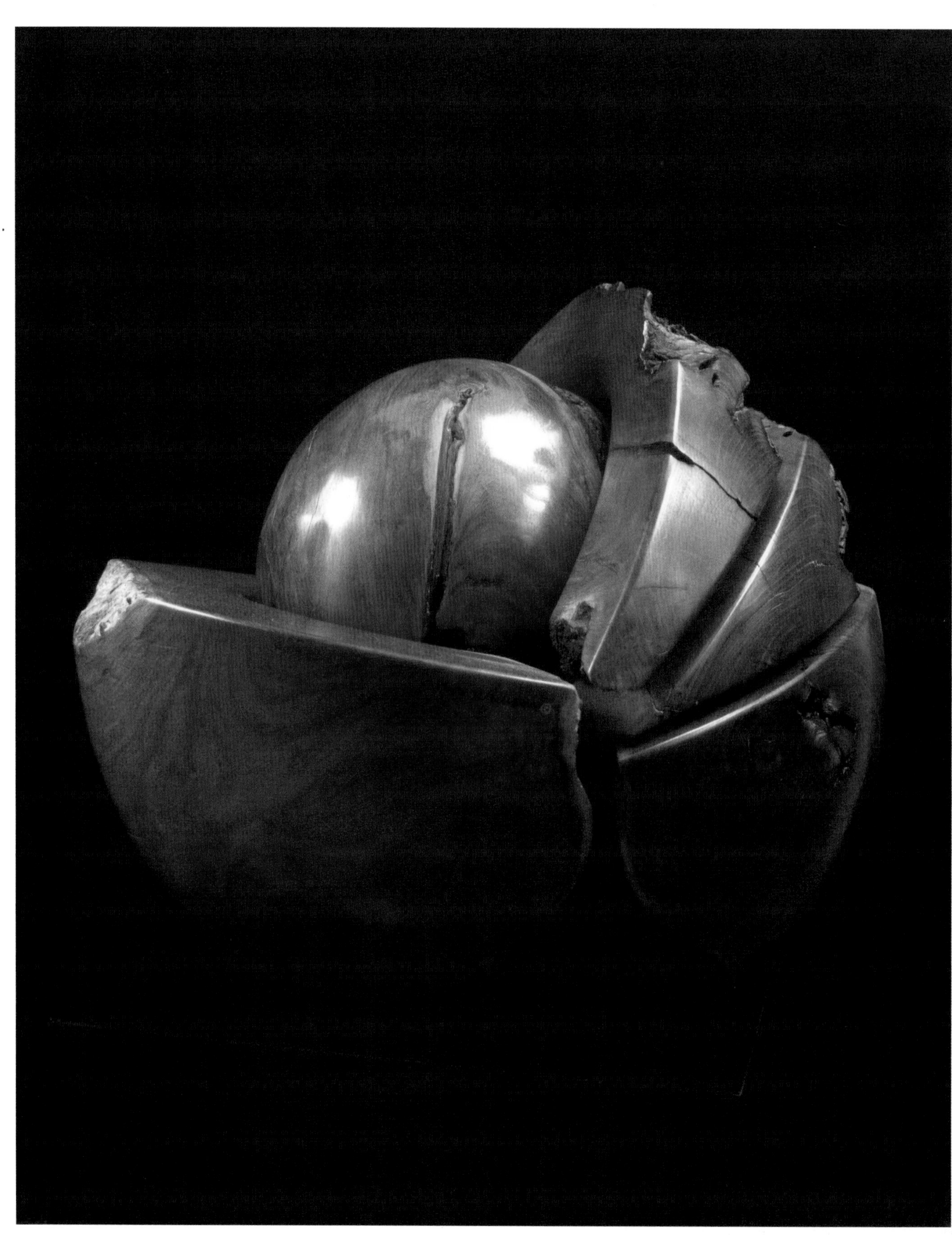

Arthur Williams, *Sliced Seed*. Mesquite,19″x24″x24″ (48.3cm x 61cm x 61cm). Photographer: Larry Sanders.

M

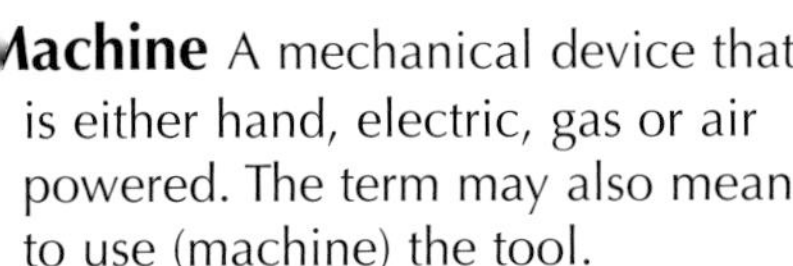

Machine A mechanical device that is either hand, electric, gas or air powered. The term may also mean to use (machine) the tool.

Mahogany A deep, reddish brown wood from light-grained hardwood trees. Although a hardwood, it is easily worked and possesses good strength. *See* ***Wood*** *(chart).*

Male A part or fitting of a tool that projects out or protrudes. It may also be called positive as opposed to negative, void or hole. It indicates a pattern for a positive (male) mold. Pneumatic air hoses end with a male fitting. *See* ***Female***.

Malleable The capacity to be formed without shattering, rupturing, cracking or breaking under the shaping force. Gold is very malleable and can be repeatedly beaten without breaking. A malleable sculpture object is one that can be maneuvered by hand or tool without breaking. *See* ***Plastic***.

Enrico Pinardi, *Fate*. Mahogany, 78″x58″x42″ (198.1cm x 147.3cm x 106.7cm).

Mallet Traditionally, a hardwood hammer with a cylindrical head and a wooden handle directly in the center extending down, often a one-piece tool. A mallet may be made by a lathe of one piece of lignum vitae. It is used for wood carving, though a smaller version with a zinc head is used for stone carving. The term also refers to iron head hammers used for stone carving, as well as plastic, rawhide and hard rubber head hammers. *See* ***Wood carving; Stone carving***.

Manganese Hard, light gray, metallic element used to strengthen steel and alloys. *See* ***Metal*** *(chart).*

Manipulate Moving, maneuvering, arranging or otherwise skillfully controlling a substance into another shape.

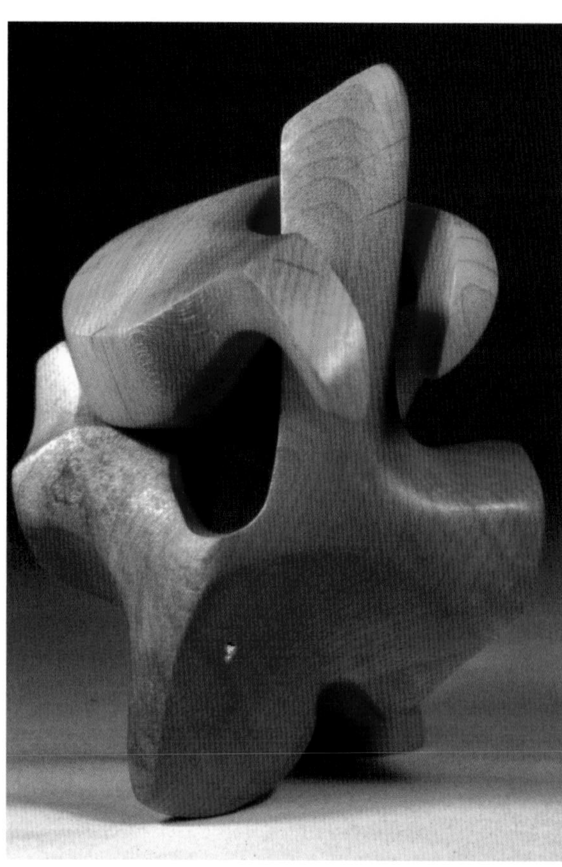

Bryan Grimes, *Masquerade*. Maple, 5″x4″x4″ (12.7cm x 10.2cm x 10.2cm).

Maple A predictably smooth carving wood with a yellow to light reddish brown color. It is a preferred furniture wood. *See **Wood** (chart).*

MAPP Methyl Acetylene Propadiene gas stabilized and used as a fuel instead of acetylene. Packaged in small disposable containers, MAPP is more stable than acetylene, since there is no limit on delivery pressure.

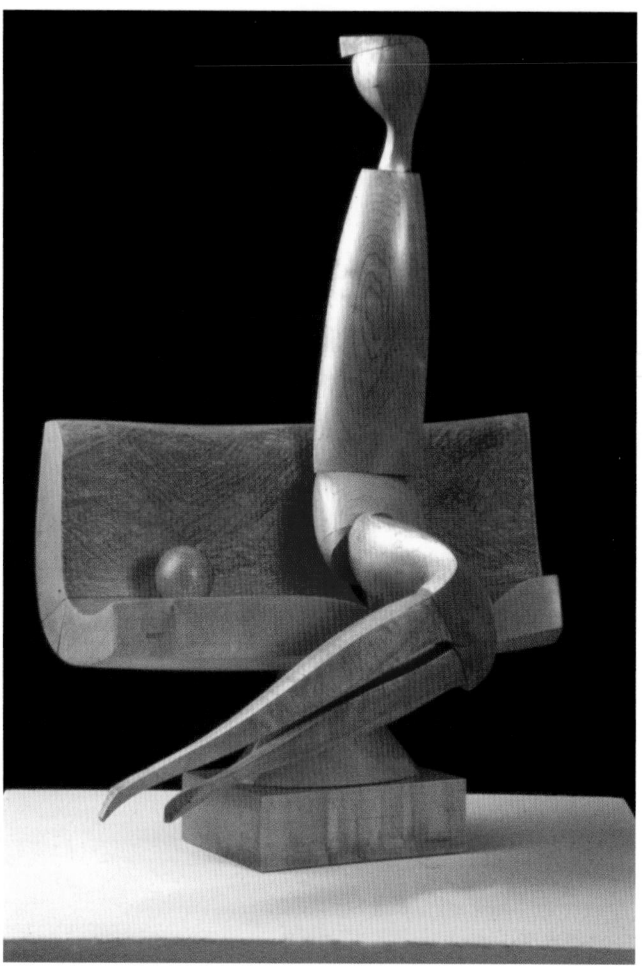

Philip John Evett, *Girl with Ball*. Maple with color, 23″x17″x9½″ (58.4cm x 43.2cm x 24.2cm).

Maquette French term for the initial "sketch" model. It is a small beginning model; the three-dimensiona thinking of the sculptor placed into a solid form. It i the working idea and not a finished presentable model, though it is sometimes presented to a patron for discussion. The common material is modeling clay, though it can be in any material conducive to the idea. *See **Model**.*

Marble A hard crystalline metamorphic form of lime stone desired for its fine-grained, dense texture that produces a predictable carving. It can be smoothed into a high gloss finish. It is not recommended for outdoor carvings, since it can be penetrated by atmospheric acids.

Varieties exist in almost any color, depending on which the location where it is quarried. Marble i the most widely known carving stone and the Carrara quarries of Italy have become the best known location for marble in the world. In the United States, the best known marble quarries are in Vermont, Tennessee, Alabama, Colorado and Georgia.

The color of marble is determined by its impurities. The most common impurities are iron oxides, pyrite, manganese oxide, silicas and clays. These result in pure color evenly dispersed throughout the stone or streaks, specks and splotches. Though these variations are often called blemishes, many sculptors enjoy working with a variety of multi-colored stones. *See **Metamorphic rock**; **Stone**; **Stone** (chart); **Alabaster**.*

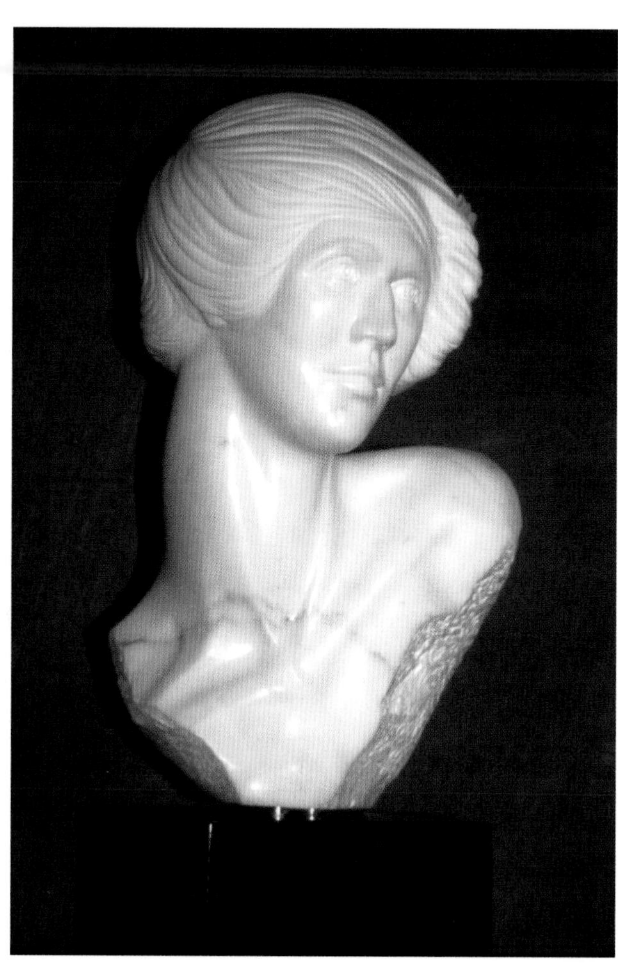

Sarah Sweetwater, *Maya*. Marble, 26″x14″x11″ (60cm x 35.6cm x 27.9cm).

John Greer, *Black Seeds* (detail: seed 4). Marble, 23.6″x23.6″x19.7″ (60cm x 60cm x 50cm).

MARBLE CARVING
by Charles L. Herndon

The Styrofoam™ model is painted black to simulate the final stone.

The stone is moved by a hoist.

A large wet saw does the preliminary roughing.

A dry cut blade is used for additional roughing.

The blade cuts are chiseled apart.

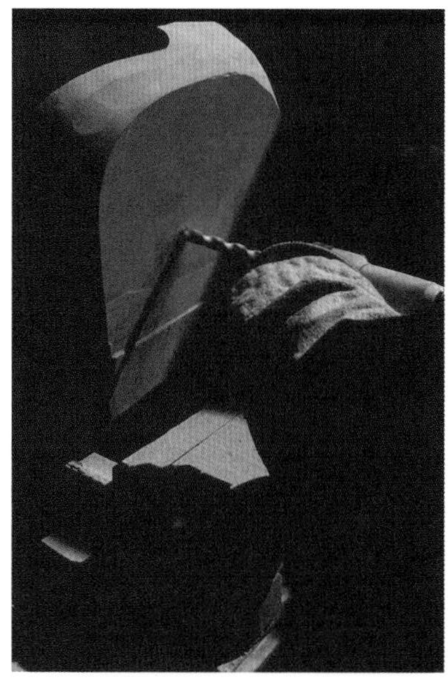

A drill begins a hole.

An air hammer carves the shape.

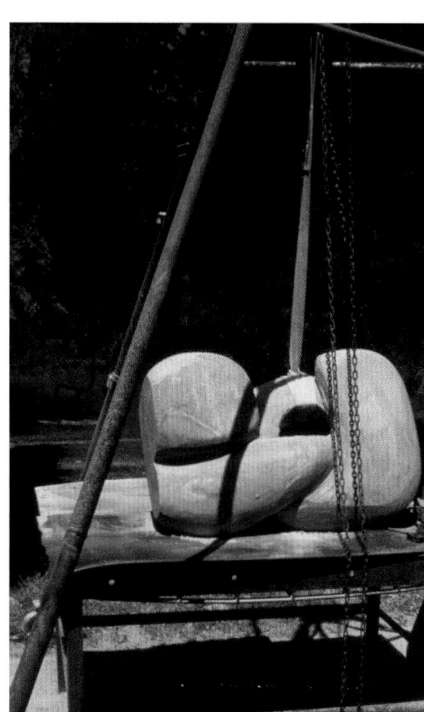

The stone is moved about as it is being carved.

Charles L. Herndon, *Spring's Promise*. Marble.

Marble Institute of America (MIA) The international association for the natural stone industry serves as a trusted resource on standards of natural stone workmanship and practice. It promotes the use of natural stone in commercial and residential settings on behalf of its members worldwide. *See* ***Stone*** *(chart).*

Marver A flat surface, originally a marble surface, to roll out, shape and cool molten glass. The term now means a steel surface in table form. *See* ***Glass***.

Mask An artificial covering often molded from and for the face. It is usually decorative. *See* ***Death mask***.

Masking tape A favorite pressure-sensitive brown tape used for temporary holding jobs. It is easily removed if not left in the sun or heat. It may be found in rolls of different widths and lengths with a textured surface for easier removal.

Mason Stoneworker.

Masonite™ A fiberboard of dense properties. Untempered Masonite™ is usually lighter brown and softer than the hard tempered Masonite™. One side is smooth; the other possesses a screen-wire pressed pattern. It will deteriorate if left to outdoor elements.

Mass The body, bulk or volume of a work. It is not necessarily a specific shape, though a mass will possess some unifying characteristics. It is also an arrangement of separate parts into a whole composition, a mass.

Master copy (cast) The foundry proof, finished with a patina to verify all castings after it. The original detailed model for stone carving. *See* ***Foundry proof***.

Master model The first or original casting. In extremely large castings, it is carefully cared for and saved so an additional mold may be made as the first mold begins to deteriorate or lose detail quality. This assures a large edition of reasonable quality.

Material Substance of which things are made. In sculpture, this can be permanent or impermanent, depending upon what the sculptor is trying to accomplish. The techniques of carving, molding, modeling, casting and construction can either dictate the material to use, or the material can dictate the technique. It all depends on the sculptor and his/her skills and knowledge of materials and techniques. *See* ***Technique***.

Matrix The inside of a casting (that is not seen).

Matting (tools) Hardened punches that are used for chasing (blending) metals. They are created by the foundry worker to resemble a specific texture to blend tool marks and surface defects into a quality or texture that matches the sculptor's intended surface. *See* ***Chasing***.

WEIGHTS OF SCULPTURE MATERIALS

	In Pounds per Cubic Foot	In Kilograms per Cubic Meter
Alabaster	170 lbs.	2550 kgs
Aluminum (cast)	160 lbs.	2400 kgs
Balsa wood	8+lbs.	120 kgs
Bronze (cast)	534 lbs.	8010 kgs
Clay	125+lbs.	1875 kgs
Iron (cast)	450 lbs.	6750 kgs
Limestone	160+lbs.	2400+kgs
Marble	162+lbs.	2430+kgs
Oak	48 lbs.	720 kgs
Sand (dry)	80+lbs.	1200+kgs
Steel	490 lbs.	7350 kgs
Yellow pine	28 lbs.	420 kgs

Measurements System or standard to determine size, volume, area, dimensions, quantity, weight or rate. *See* ***Measurement*** *(chart);* ***Weights*** *(chart).*

MEASUREMENTS

CONVERSIONS: METRIC/U.S.

LENGTH

U.S.	*Multiply by*	*For Metric*
Inch	25.4	Millimeter
Inch	2.54	Centimeter
Feet	30.48	Centimeter
Yards	0.91	Meters

Metric	*Multiply by*	*For U.S.*
Millimeter	0.04	Inch
Centimeter	0.39	Inch
Meter	1.09	Yard

VOLUME

U.S.	*Multiply by*	*For Metric*
Cubic Feet	0.028	Cubic Meter
Cubic Yard	0.76	Cubic Meter

Metric	*Multiply by*	*For U.S.*
Cubic Meter	35.31	Cubic Feet
Cubic Meter	1.35	Cubic Yard

AREA

U.S.	*Multiply by*	*For Metric*
Square Inch	6.45	Square Centimeter
Square Feet	0.09	Square Meter

Metric	*Multiply by*	*For U.S.*
Square Centimeter	0.155	Square Inch
Square Meter	1.20	Square Yard

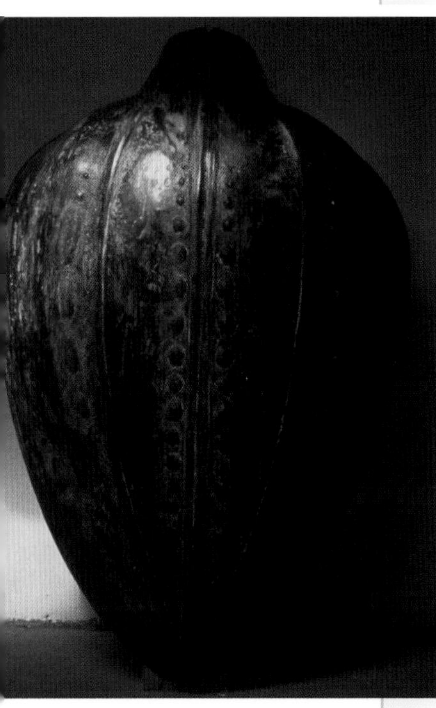

John Greer, *Beetle Wing Covers.* fiberglass and polyester resin.

LIQUID

U.S.	*Multiply by*	*For Metric*
Ounce	28.35	Gram
Pound	0.45	Kilogram

Metric	*Multiply by*	*For U.S.*
Gram	0.035	Ounce
Kilogram	2.20	Pound

MEASUREMENTS

EQUIVALENTLY CONVERTED U.S. TO METRIC

U.S.	Metric	
Inch	2.54	Centimeters
Foot (12 inches)	0.3048	Meter
Yard (36 inches)	0.9144	Meter
Gram	67.799	Milligrams
Dram (1/16 ounce)	1.7718	Gram
Ounce, dry (16 drams)	28.350	Grams
Pound (16 ounces)	453.6	Grams
Ton (2000 pounds)	907.18	Kilograms
Ounce, liquid (1/l6 to pint)	29.574	Milliliters
Pint, (liquid, 16 ounces)	0.4732	Liter
Quart, (liquid, 2 pints)	0.9463	Liter
Gallon (128 ounces)	3.7854	Liters
212° Fahrenheit (boiling)	100°	Celsius
32° Fahrenheit (freezing)	0°	Celsius

Medal A specific cut piece of metal of handheld size with a relief on it. The stamped design signifies an award. A portrait is common though not always present. Bronze is the common metal used. *See* ***Relief***.

Medallion A large metal disk with a relief sculpture upon it. It may be small enough to be worn about the neck by being attached to a chain (necklace). *See* ***Relief***.

For his Second Inauguration, President Ronald Reagan posed for the official inaugural medal by **Mico Kaufman**.

Mico Kaufman, *Official Inaugural Medal for Ronald Reagan*. Plaster model, 9″ (22.9cm).

Gary Eriksen, *Erasmus Hall High School Seal Medallion*. Bonded bronze, 3.5′ (1.07m) tall.

Megalith Enormous or of great dimension.

Memorial A three-dimensional work or space for public or private remembrance of an event or mourning of individuals. It can range from a simple plaque or sculpture to a building, garden, arch or elaborate installation.

Mesquite A hard wood found in dry climates from small trees with bean pods. They can become quite large if they are located in a watershed area. *See **Wood** (chart).*

Arthur Williams, *Mesquite Woman*. Mesquite, 26″ (66cm) tall.

Greg Moran, *Beam Reach*. Mesquite, mahogany, 30″x10″x14″ (76.2cm x 25.4cm x 35.6cm).

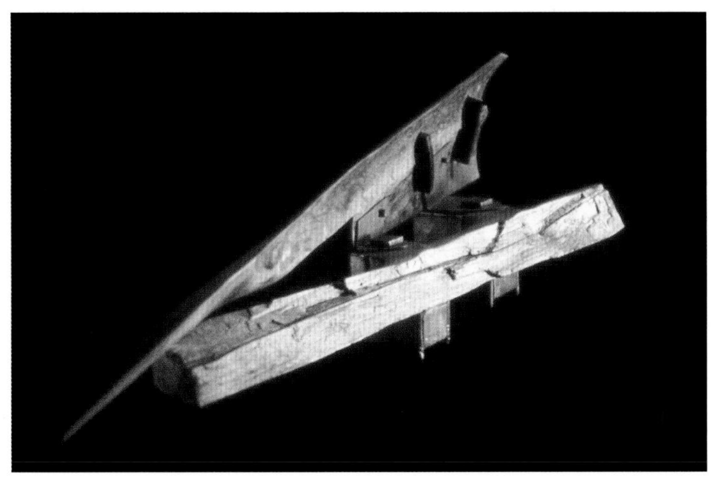

Storage of sheet metal showing various sizes.

Metal An elementary solid element of unusual strength that is ductile, malleable and frequently has a shining surface. Various metals combined with each other form alloys (mixtures). Ordinarily, metals are good conductors of electricity and retain cold and hot characteristics of the surroundings. Metals can be fused (welded), melted (cast) and are plastic (hammered). Metals are available from suppliers in various concentrations and dimensions of sheets: square, rectangular and round bars and tubes. Special sizes and thicknesses can be custom ordered from the manufacturer. Casting metals are separated by two groupings: ferrous, which are more prone to corrosion, in either iron or metals containing iron; and non-ferrous metals, which do not contain iron or, virtually, any other metals.

METAL MELTING POINTS

**Metal Melting Points*	*Fahrenheit*	*Centigrade*
Tin	450°	232°
Pewter	650°	343°
Lead	625°	329°
Zinc	790°	421°
Magnesium	1200°	648°
Aluminum	1225°	662°
Bronze	1300° – 1900°	704° – 1037°
Brass	1550° – 1875°	843° – 1023°
Silver	1750°	953°
Everdur™ Bronze	1790°	976°
Gold	1940°	1059°
Copper	1980°	1081°
Cast Iron	2100°	1148°
Hard Steel	2560°	1403°
Mild Steel	2725°	1495°
Stainless Steel	2800°	1536°
Pure Iron	2800°	1536°
Wrought Iron	2900°	1592°

**The melting points are not the casting temperatures. For example, Everdur™ bronze melts at 179°F (976°C) but pours best from 2000° to 2150°F (1092°C to 1175°C) for thin castings and from 1850°F to 1950°F (1009°C to 1064°C) for thicker castings.*

METAL HARDNESS

Common Metals: Listed from soft to hard

1. Lead ...... (least ductile)
2. Pewter
3. Aluminum
4. Gold ....(most malleable, most ductile)
5. Silver
6. Copper
7. Iron........ (least malleable)
8. Steel

Mac Hornecker,
Prairie Wind.
Steel, 15'x32'x12'
(4.58m x 3.66m).

Metal casting Placing metal into a heat resistant mold to create a new form. A simple process called the lost wax or cirè perdu has been used for centuries. Few changes have been made in this casting processes until the 20th Century, when new technology and materials allowed the same process to be practiced with more exactness within a rapid timeframe. The process still begins with a sculpture, usually in wax, covered with a heat resistant mold material, then melted out leaving a detailed surface to receive the hot, molten metal. After the metal cools and solidifies, the piece is extracted from the mold to complete and exhibit as sculpture. The original wax sculpture has accurately been displaced by metal, achieving the most exacting details. *See* ***Blast furnace*** *(operation);* ***Plaster investing****;* ***Slurry investing****;* ***Furnace****;* ***Metal pouring system****;* ***Sand casting****.*

METAL CASTING

From Armature to Finished Bronze

by Dawn Weimer

Metal casting begins with the artwork. The sculptor designs an armature to support the modeling clay used for her model.

The completed model.

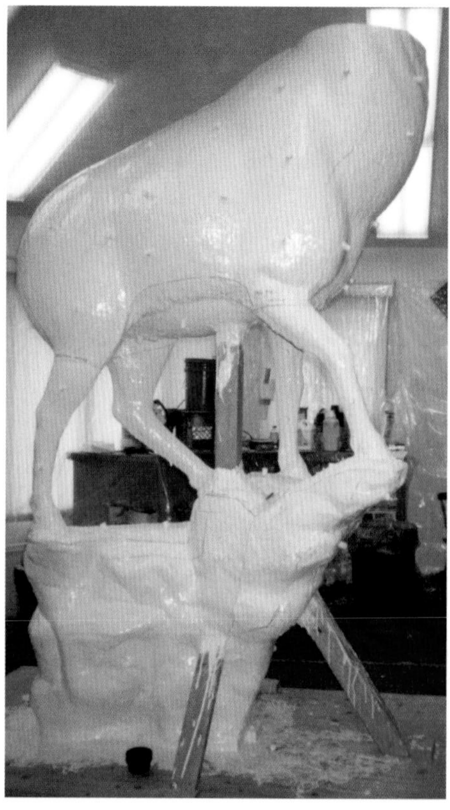

A flexible mold material is added and followed by a heavier supporting mother mold.

The mold is used to cast wax. The wax is then cut into castable size parts.

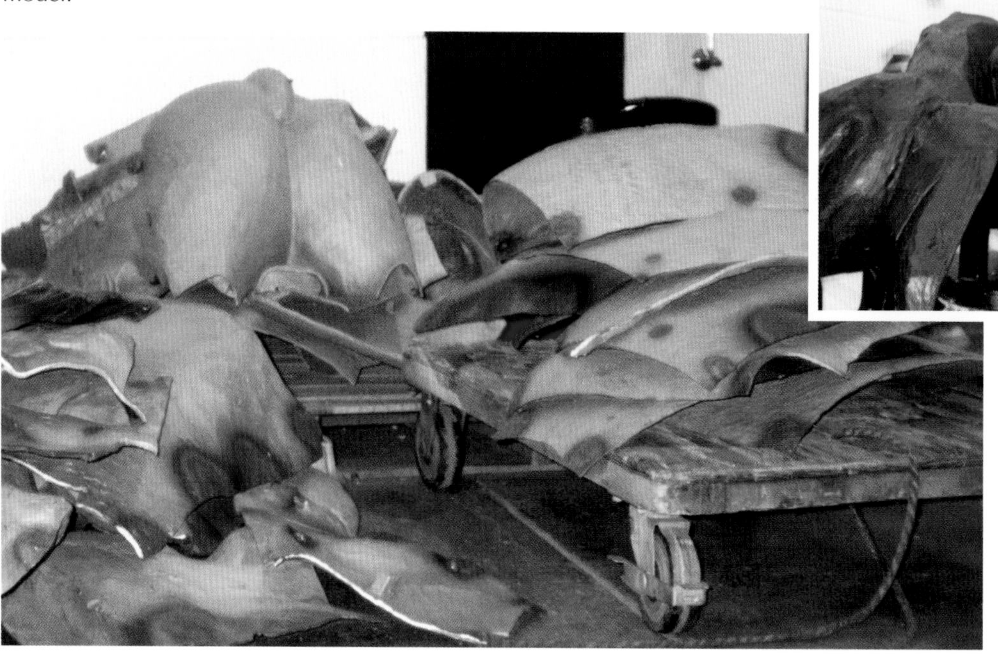

There are many parts to reassemble after the artwork has been cast.

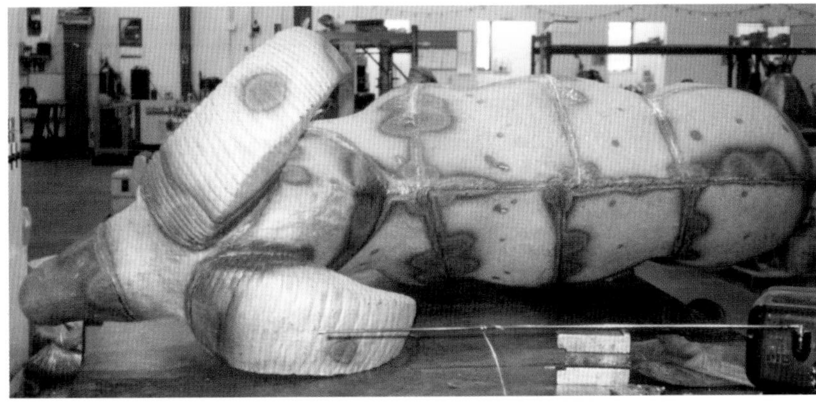

Art Castings of Loveland, Colorado, was the selected foundry. A TIG welder is used to weld the parts together.

A patina is added and hastened by heat.

Dawn Weimer, *Ram Proud*. Cast bronze, 12′ (3.7m) tall. Colorado State University, Fort Collins, Colorado.

Metal cladding The process of attaching or bonding different pieces of metal together to achieve more permanence or resistance to corrosion. Heat and pressure are applied to the metal to achieve the cladding. This metal can be purchased in sheets, strips or bars. Welding is a problem, since it is nearly impossible to find a good welding match for the cladding material. The most common materials placed over steel are copper, aluminum, nickel and stainless steel. *See **Electroplating***.

Metal fabrication A sculpture technique that has been practiced for several centuries by using riveting, forged works and other elementary fastening contrivances. However, in the 20th Century, metal fabrication became a significant method of producing sculpture due to fusion welding from the first half of the century and adhesives in the last half. Because of fusion welding, the use of metal in sculpture has become prominent with large scale metal works displayed throughout the world.

Metal fabricator A worker who constructs sculpture of metal by welding or otherwise fastening parts together. *See **Metal fabrication***.

METAL FABRICATION

Bruce Beasley fabricating *Vitality*

The welds are chased with disk grinders.

A heavy stainless steel interior structure is required.

As the work nears completion, it constantly has to be lifted and moved for the workers to continue.

'he bronze sheet
netal is patinaed.

Once completed, it is loaded for delivery.

The work is set in place by a crane on the chosen site. **Bruce Beasley**, *Vitality*. Fabricated bronze, 30'x11'x9' (9.15m x 3.36m x 2.75m). On location in Oakland, California.

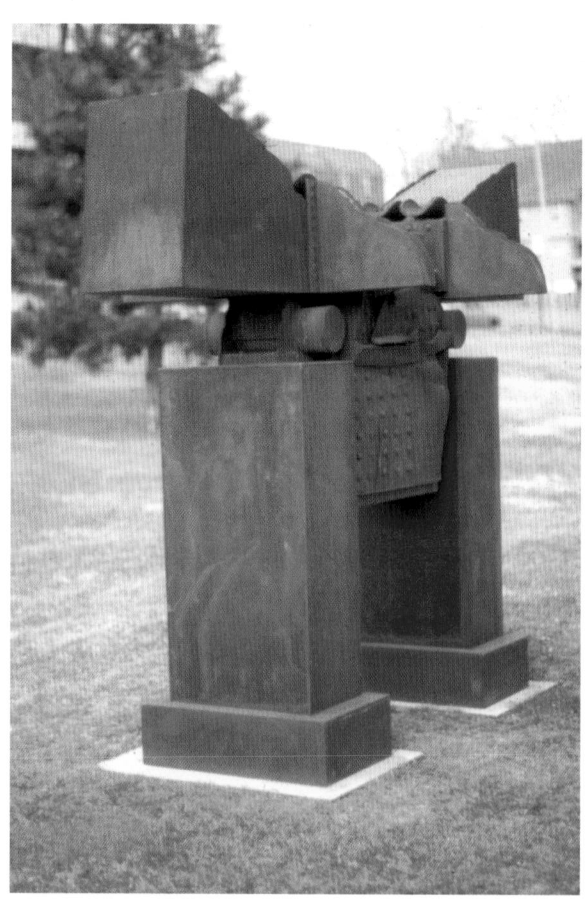

Sidney Buchanan, *Melissa*.Fabricated/ welded steel, 96″x108″x60″ (243.8cm x 274.3cm x 152.4cm). Omaha Public School Headquarters, Omaha, Nebraska.

Metal plating (electroplating) Coating metal with a thin deposit of metal by using an electrical current with chemicals. *See* ***Electroplating***.

Metal pouring cup The funnel or cup shape at the highest point of a mold. It is designed for casting liquids to enter a mold. For metal casting molds, the cup is attached to the sprue(s) designed to easily accept the molten metal.

A good pouring cup incorporates five things: 1) an adequate opening (target) for the crucible size used, 2) a sufficient reservoir for the metal needed in the pour, 3) a break-up of turbulence or stopping of the swirl of entering metal, 4) protected places to add vents (so that bronze will not enter the vents from the cup), 5) if it is for ceramic shell, a design to allow insertion into a burnout floor pan for dewaxing and wax recovery. *See* ***Metal pouring system; Burnout***.

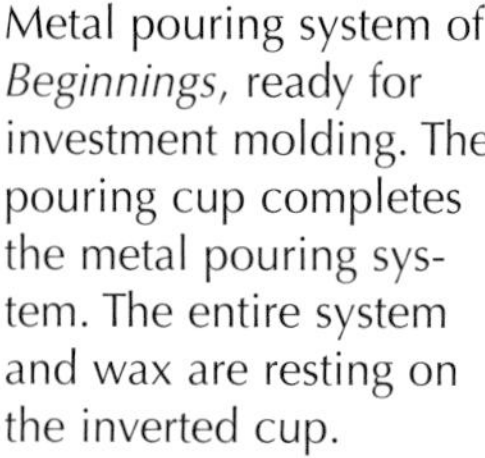

Metal pouring system of *Beginnings*, ready for investment molding. The pouring cup completes the metal pouring system. The entire system and wax are resting on the inverted cup.

Arthur Williams, *Beginnings*. Cast bronze, 12″x11″x7″ (30.5cm x 27.9cm x 17.8cm).

METAL POURING CUP
Using a Plaster Mold for Wax Cup

he wax pouring cup piece mold (made of laster) is placed together and soaked in water as a separator). Hot liquid wax is added. It is llowed to set until about ¼″ (0.635cm) has een deposited on the mold surface, before the emaining liquid wax is poured out.

The mold is inverted and the wax cup is removed.

The final cup after trimming. The top of the cup is designed to allow the slurry worker to firmly grip it as the mold is dipped. The mid-rim is for attaching air vents, placed out to avoid liquid metal from filling them during a pour. The bottom is a square design to help avoid metal swirl.

Metal pouring system A process to prepare the wax or other expendable material for the flow of hot, liquid metal. It consists of the artwork, a pouring cup, vents, gates and sprues.

The finished wax artwork is ready to encase in a heat resistant mold in preparation for casting. The artwork for lost wax metal casting can originate from any material, as long as it is translated or transferred into an exacting wax work with all the details desired for the final work. Though works can be one-of-a-kind made directly into the wax, they are usually reproduced from a pattern or master mold. This allows the wax work to be presented in a thin walled work, approximately three-sixteenths inch (0.476cm) to one-fourth inch (0.635cm) in thickness.

The work should be exactly as the sculptor desires, since every minute detail will be preserved in the final casting. After the wax is inspected and approved, the sculptor signs the work directly into the wax. This includes the name and edition number, date and © for copyright purposes. *See* ***Pattern mold; Fingerprint quality; Slushing; Edition number; Artist's proof; Foundry proof; Copyright.***

Technique

The metal pouring system includes adding a pouring cup, sprues, runners, vents and gates to the surface of the artwork. The wax artwork should be positioned for molding to avoid most undercuts. The handling of the mold during investing and filling is also significant in the design.

The pouring cup is placed at the top of the mold, usually centered, and large enough for the metal to fill the mold by gravity. The distance of the cup from the wax form can vary depending upon the piece. Normally, it should be at least an inch from the wax to allow more gravitational pull and to avoid excessive retention of heat on the sculpture's cooling bronze surface, which can result in a gas build up prior to solidification.

The cup is attached to a large single sprue (metal feeder) or sometimes two or more smaller sprues strategically placed. The sprues are joined to the wax by smaller ducts called gates. These are joined directly to the sculpture, enabling the liquefied metal to enter and fill the mold. As the metal rushes in, the metal gases and air are expelled through risers (air vents), allowing the incoming metal to replace the escaping gas/air. After the casting, the gating and venting will be removed and discarded.

A core may be desirable. It is a mixture of heat resistant material placed inside smaller wax sculptures to keep the walls separated in to ensure a uniform wall thickness and saving of metal. This means that the inside must be a separate solid mass so that the metal can flow around it to create a thin wall surface. The core needs to be held in place by strong metal pins to support the inside mass and that can be removed after the casting. The core material can be a mix of the mold material itself, or a special mix of refractories designed just for the core. The work is once again hollow by removing the core material after the casting. *See* ***Cup***; ***Metal pouring cup***.

Metal sprue bars are sometimes inserted into the pouring cup and down into a hollow sprue but left hanging out of the cup with a hook on the end. Properly attached to the wax artwork, the works can be dipped and then hung up by the hook to dry. Larger works can be elevated using this hook fastened to a hoist for easy lifting. Attaching sprues, vents and runners to each other and the wax form takes good technique, or the joint will not hold. A special wax, known as adhesion wax or sticky wax, facilitates the joint. Used sparingly and blended in, it can strengthen a wax joint or at least hold it in place while a better attachment is made. *See* ***Adhesion wax***.

Wax bars designed for sprues, gates and runners. The larger ones are hollow for faster wax melting and escape.

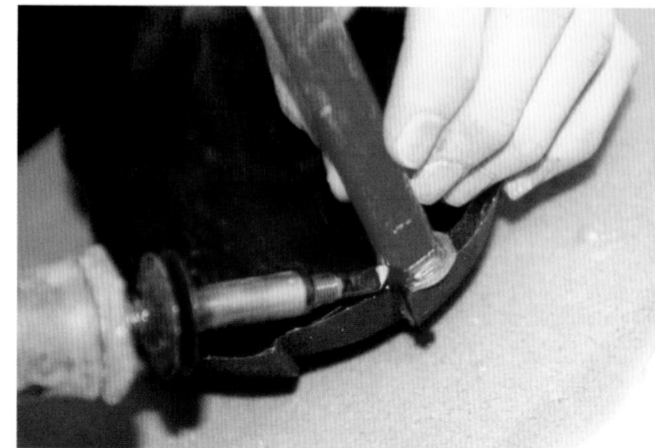

A burner heats the wax parts. Adhesion wax is used to secure a quick bond.

Gating systems

Top gating means that the entire sculpture acts as a canal for the liquid metal, since the major sprues are placed directly onto the upper (top) portion of the form. It is ideal for most solid castings. The advantages of this method are fewer gates, less complications and not as much chasing.

In **bottom gating**, the sprues are situated so the liquid bronze runs to the bottom of the mold and begins to fill from the bottom up. The advantages are that the gates cushion the heavy liquid bronze as it collides with the mold and the metal fills in a more even pattern.

Side gating is a variation of bottom gating. In sizeable castings, a large solid sprue system begins at the bottom and fills from the sides to ensure the bronze does not freeze up as the mold is filled. With proper step runners, the metal will continue to rise as the mold fills upward from runners/gates strategically placed on the sprues.

Interior gating is when the pouring system is placed inside the hollow wax form.

It is desirable if the work is large and the system can be removed. To sprue from the inside greatly decreases the surface clean up time and is especially useful if small surface details are abundant or difficult to add where the running system might otherwise have been placed.

Sprues (main feeds) need to downsize or taper at the end where they feed directly into the sculpture. This gating is sometimes referred to as a "choke" and serves three purposes: 1) to lower the possibility of gas build up at the connection due to the smaller concentration of metal, 2) to help eliminate undo shrinkage at the same point and 3) to cause the metal to enter with a greater pressure into the mold for stronger circulation.

The exact type of sprues, gates or risers varies. Commercially designed waxes for these parts can be obtained in solid rolls or in long, hollow and solid rods. The wax used is calculated to melt at a lower temperature to rapidly evacuate the pouring system, followed by the harder artwork wax. Runner wax over one-fourth inch (0.635cm) in diameter is usually hollow, allowing a better escape. The shape of the gates and sprues affects the castings. While round diameter sprues can handle more metal faster per size, square sprues and gates decrease the turbulence, churning or twirling of the metal as it enters the mold; as a result, less air is sucked into the mold, resulting in a less gassy metal.

Metal Pouring Systems

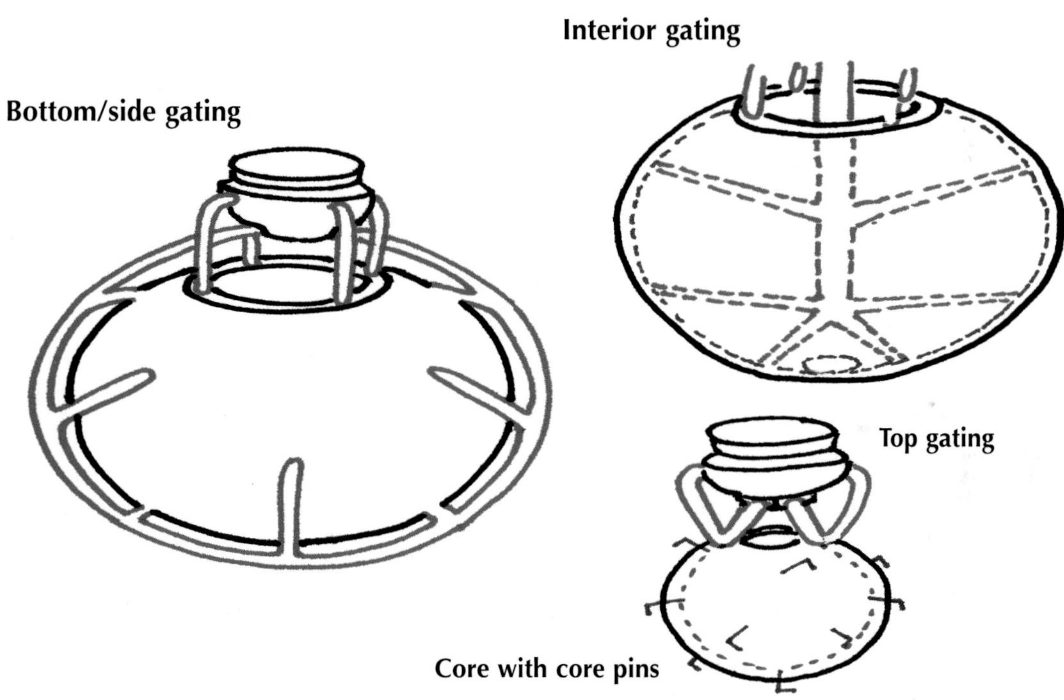

The **placement of the gates and vents** is critical. The system should allow a quick pouring with the least turbulence. In recent years, larger gates spaced further apart have become more popular. However, the danger is that too much distance in spacing will result in a miscast or area where the liquid metal does not lap or join; hence, a premature freezing of the metal, sometimes resulting in an area without metal at all. Though the runner normally has to allow a volume of liquid that is greater than the area it fills, a gassy surface spot may be the result of cooling metal being sucked back into the main sprue as the metal cools.

Enough air vents must be used to allow the gas to escape as quickly as the metal is poured. Also, they must be placed on every upper portion or appendage where the form ends in the mold or pouring undercut. Even though air vents should be used on all works, small forms, where the bronze is top-gated and the sprue is on the very top, do not necessarily require a separate vent, since the air will escape out of the sprue as it is being poured. Gurgling, or a slow pour, could result in a larger work with a si top sprue. Because ceramic shell is porous, there is some tolerance, but trapped ai gas should be avoided. Finer castings of small thinness require a more precise run system with the vents and gates placed at closer intervals, especially if the thinnes extends for any distance at all. When burning out the wax, the runner system allov the wax to escape the mold. If the system is not ade- quate, the mold may crack. For this reason, molds sc times have special holes placed into them prior to th wax burnout for rapid draining purposes. After burnc they are filled in.

Understanding the chasing process, gates an vents can be located so as to aid in the finishing pro For example locate vents and gates on areas that prc and are smooth or easy to resurface when removed. gate is located in a recessed area, it is difficult to rer and then complicated to duplicate the surface. *See* ***B furnace; Plaster investing; Slurry investing; Sand casting***.

A wax for *Self-Portrait* by **Tim Kinard** has been divided for molding. The metal pouring system has been added.

With this cup design, the wax is invert- ed to rest upon the cup as the wax is worked on and balanced for storage.

The mold pouring system with several slurry dips of ceramic shell.

Waxes with the metal pouring system ready for molding.

Metal turning lathe A mechanized machine designed to create round symmetrical shapes in metal. This is done by rapid rotation of a metal blank placed to allow the operator to systematically remove the excess. *See* ***Wood turning; Lathe***.

Metal turning lathe.

Metallizing (flame spraying) Spraying liquid metal onto a surface by a spray gun that combines air, roll wire, oxygen and acetylene. The wire is supplied through the gun as it is being liquefied by the hot oxyacetylene flame and blown onto the sculpture. The coating can vary but is often up to one-eighth inch (0.318cm) in thickness. The melted metal droplets do not actually weld into a mass; rather, they adhere to each other creating a less than solid matt surface. Even though the resulting surface can be polished, it does not fully provide corrosion resistance. The surface does not have to be as hard as steel, since the droplets are freezing in mid-air to take the immediate shape of the object's surface.

Metals used for this process include copper, aluminum, brass, stainless steel, lead, zinc and nickel. All surfaces must be clean and dry. The steel should be sandblasted. Zinc and aluminum can even be applied over a cloth. If all of the equipment is properly adjusted, an object can be covered with a cloth, metallized, and the object removed, undamaged. Sometimes, more delicate sculpture substances are first cooled with lower melting point metal followed by higher temperature melting metals for effect or additional protection. *See* ***Wire-arc; Electroplating***.

Metamorphic rock Stone that is brought about by severe forces of heat and pressure upon sedimentary or igneous rock. The reaction results in an altered stone not even resembling the original. The most commonly carved metamorphic stones are marble, alabaster and steatite. *See* ***Marble****;* ***Alabaster****;* ***Steatite****;* ***Stone****;* ***Stone*** *(chart).*

Gerald Balciar, *Canyon Princess*. Colorado Yule marble, 18′ (5.5m) tall. National Cowboy and Western Heritage Museum, Oklahoma City, Oklahoma.

Methylcellulos (CMC) An emulsifier and thickener used in adding stability to pulp for paper. *See* ***Paper***.

Metric A standard of measurement using the meter as a basis. *See* ***Measurements*** *(chart).*

Microcystalline wax A fine wax made up of petroleum products. Depending on the composition, the softness and melting point vary. It is a wax preferred by sculptors for lost wax casting purposes. *See* ***Waxes***.

Micro-wire welding Gas metal arc welding. *See* ***MIG***.

MIG Gas metal arc welding, flux-cored arc welding. Metal Inert Gas (MIG) or Gas Metal Arc Welding (MGAC) is similar to ordinary arc welding. Both use electrodes, but the MIG has a roll wire continuous feed electrode or wire welding that allows a lengthy unbroken weld. The wire generally does not have a flux coating, since the handpiece releases a steady flow of an inert gas around the tip into the welding area. This produces a gas shield that keeps the weld from oxidizing during the weld. The gas is usually carbon dioxide but can vary depending on the choice of wire. The welder operates on DC and is most often set to operate with reverse polarity. While the machine has many intricacies, it is easily managed if the manufacturer's settings and operational procedures are followed.

MIG welder with the handpiece and ground clamp displayed.

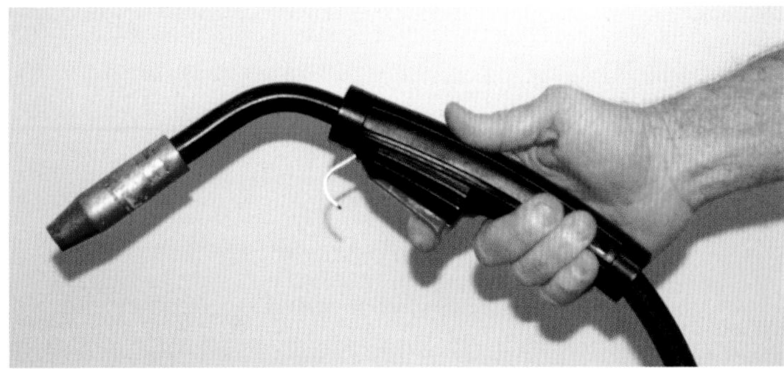

Typical MIG welder handpiece with the wire feed pushed from the welding machine.

Technique

Though the wire is automatically fed into the handpiece, it is generally on a separate motorized spool that must be adjusted manually at the source. The gas is adjusted the same as for the TIG, and the pressurized bottle is frequently mounted on the machine for portability. The amperage is selected at the machine, but trigger operated on the handpiece. Machines are available with low to high amperages.

When all the controls are correct, the welding is fast, easy and continuous, producing a beautiful, clean, penetrating weld. The method is an excellent choice for industrial purposes and large heavy sculpture. However, there are several details to consider, including the size and kind of wire. While shorter feed lines run without problems, longer lines can be obtained and produce good results if they are kept reasonably straight. The average size line is 20 feet (6.1m). (Some softer wires, like aluminum, create more feed problems due to a lack of strength and distance of push through the line.) If an extremely long feed is necessary, a handheld portable MIG

MIG handpiece with a self-contained motor for pulling the wire feed to the work.

wire feeding gun is available. Though the spool is considerably smaller, it works well except for the heavy operating weight involved. Also, handpieces are available with small enclosed motors to aid in pulling the wire to the work.

Once the adjustments are made, and the wire from the tip of the handpiece is about one-half inch (1.27cm) out, the process can begin. The wire is focused on the grounded metal as the trigger is held down to begin and continue the process. Seldom does the wire stick because the small sizes burn loose, but if it should happen, the trigger needs to be released, and the wire cut loose before continuing.

The handpiece is held much the same as the arc stinger. The arc is smooth and easy to sustain, and the operator does not need to move the handpiece about as the regular arc method requires. If the weld needs additional buildup for strength, the work can immediately be reworked, since there is generally no flux to chip off. All welds must be done in an environment without direct air flow (wind or fan) on the weld, since the gas would be blown away resulting in an ineffective, unsightly, troublesome weld. *See* ***TIG; Arc welding; Welding***.

Arthur Williams, *Birth II*. MIG welded steel, 192″x96″x92″ (487.7cm x 243.8cm x 233.7cm), Dallas, Texas.

Mild steel A low carbon steel. In large pieces, it is heated to increase the working ability. *See* ***Carbon steel***.

Mineral spirits A petroleum product refined for paint thinner uses. It is substituted for turpentine, especially since it is nearly odorless. The flash point is low, and it is not too powerful as a solvent.

Miniature A small scale (almost microscopic) version of a subject with all details intact. From one-sixteenths to one-twelfth scale and smaller, it holds up under scrutiny.

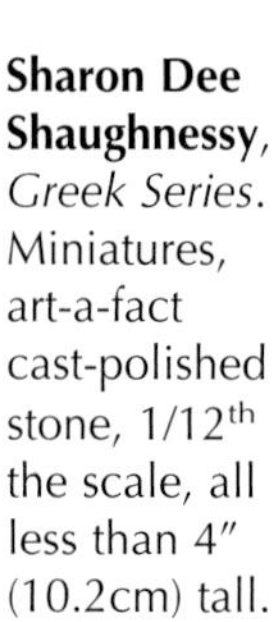

Sharon Dee Shaughnessy, *Greek Series*. Miniatures, art-a-fact cast-polished stone, 1/12th the scale, all less than 4″ (10.2cm) tall.

Miter saw A saw designed specifically for making miter (angle) cuts. It can be powered or of hand use. Some saws are designed to complete compound cuts with one motion.

Mixed media More than one material used to create a form. The materials can be anything from found discarded materials to well-known construction materials. *See **Assemblage**; **Found object**.*

Richard Newman, *Shrine for Prayers*. Mixed media, 2"x23"x7" (5.1cm x 58.4cm x 17.8cm).

Jon M. Stine, *Suspension*. Mixed media, 59"x12"x12" (149.9cm x 30.5cm x 30.5cm).

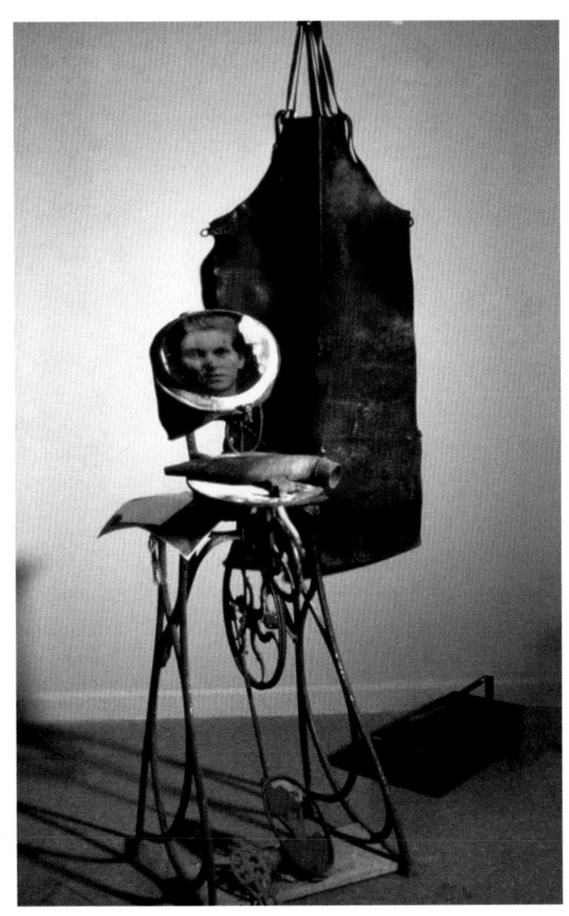

Carol Rosen, *To Ashes*. Mixed media, 73"x39"x33" (185.4cm x 99.1cm x 83.8cm).

Mixer The chamber in the oxyacetylene torch (blow torch) where oxygen and acetylene are blended together for ignition. Any machine or tool that blends (mixes) material or liquids together, especially by mechanical means, may be called a mixer. *See **Oxyacetylene torch**.*

Heavy duty upright mixer adapted for mixing clay bodies.

Electric upright mixer used for plaster or slip.

Mixing blades designed for hand tools.

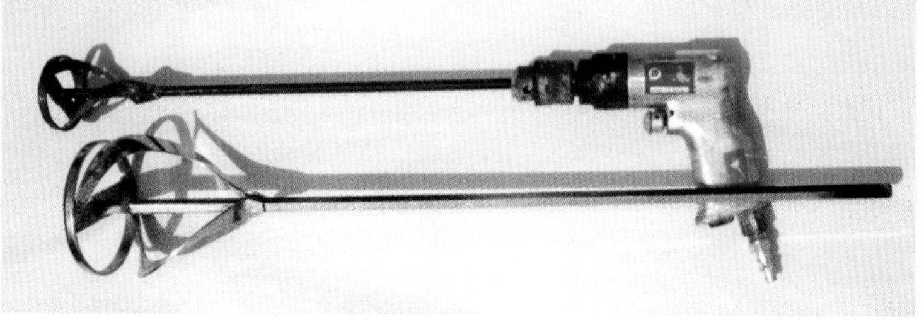

Mixing bowls Traditionally, a round, flexible rubber bowl used in sculpture for mixing plaster. Easily cleaned by flexing, the hard plastic does not adhere to the rubber. The term may be applied to any container used for sculptural mixing purposes. *See **Plaster**.*

A rubber mixing bowl.

Mobile Sculpture designed to be moved by air currents. A sculpture, usually hanging, composed of separate parts attached by wires, cables, steel, etc. To enable the parts to move freely with air currents, a mobile is balanced and anchored by one central point. Alexander Calder gave the name "mobile" to his sculptures of this type.

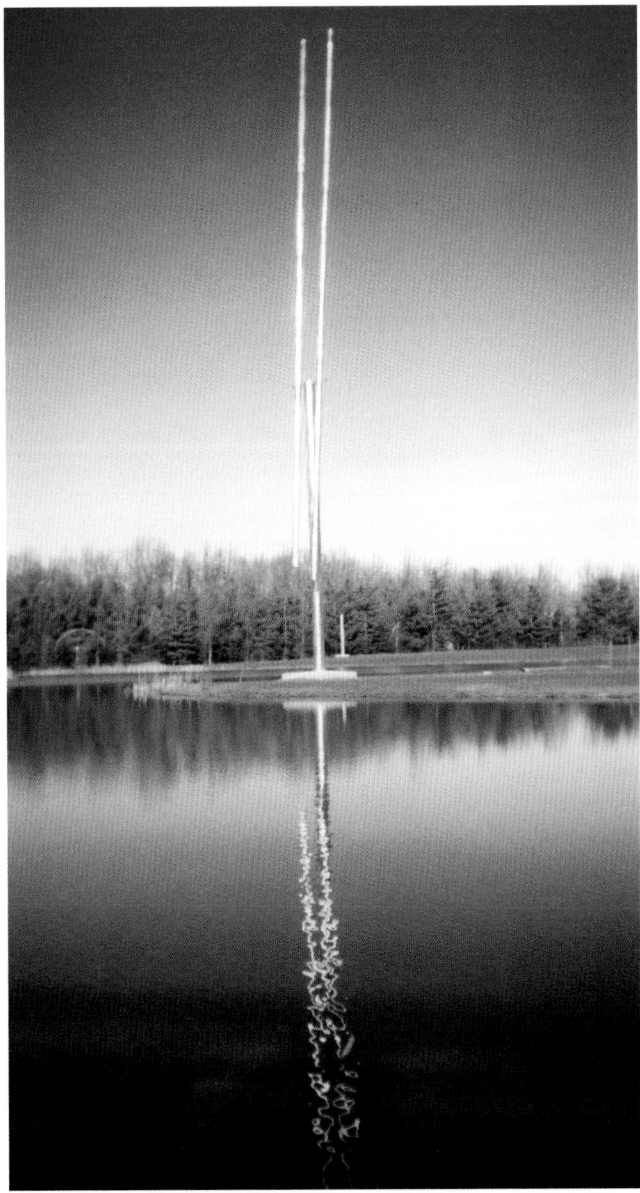

Rod Dowling, *Twin Towers*. Stainless steel mobile, 90′ (27.5m).

Finished clay model for *Mississippi 11th* by **William N. Beckwith**.

Mode Part of the gathered glass on the blowpipe (or punty) that remains after the usable gather has been removed. It is initially necessary to strengthen the molten glass hold on the blowpipe.

Model An original sculpture made to scale size, possibly from a sketch maquette, that is used for a facsimile, or an actual work to be formed into the same or other material. The term "model" may be applied for one certain work, or it may be the model for the casting; it also applies to the person (live model) or object used as a visual reference for a work of art. *See* ***Maquette***.

Model poses for sculptor **William N. Beckwith**.

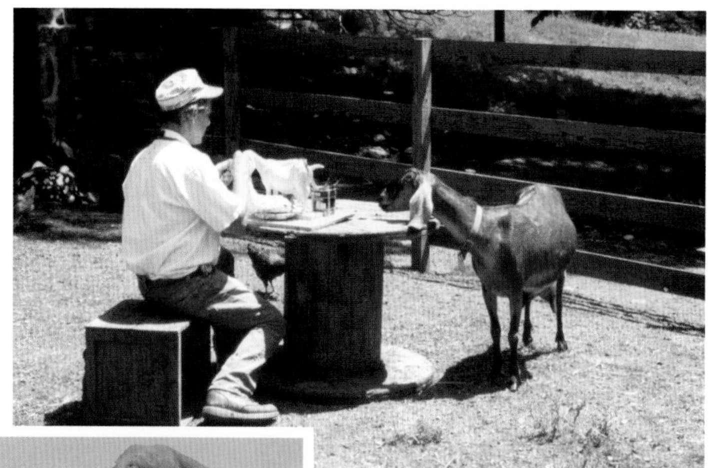

Andrè Harvey works on a clay model with his live Nubian goat model.

Modeling The technique of manipulating a plastic material into an artistic form. The sculptor's hands are the best shaping tools. Being on display for an artist's reference is another way of using the term. *See **Slab**; **Coil**; **Pinch**; **Hollow out**; **Clay** (oil-based); **Clay** (water-based).*

Andrè Harvey places finishing touches on *Chloe and Lucinda* in preparation for the final work to be cast into bronze.

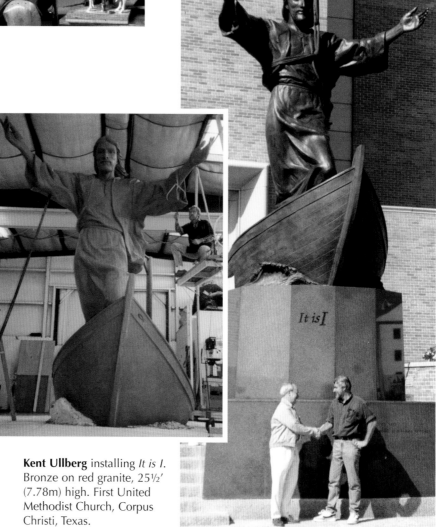

Kent Ullberg works on *It is I*. Monumental clay works often require scaffolding.

Kent Ullberg installing *It is I*. Bronze on red granite, 25½′ (7.78m) high. First United Methodist Church, Corpus Christi, Texas.

Modeling clay An oil-based substance primarily composed of earth clays but cooked and mixed with oils, waxes and greases. The clay is used for modeling a temporary art form that is molded for harder, more permanent substances, such as bronze. Many colors are available. *See **Modeling; Clay** (oil-based); **Enlargement**.*

Modeling stand A stand, usually with a turntable, that holds a plastic substance for creating sculpture. Depending on the stand, it can be raised or lowered, tilted, and can hold heavy materials.

Modeling tools Tools used for modeling purposes, such as modeling clay, ceramic clay and other substances that can be manipulated to create art forms. *See **Clay** (modeling); **Clay** (water-based); **Wire end tools**.*

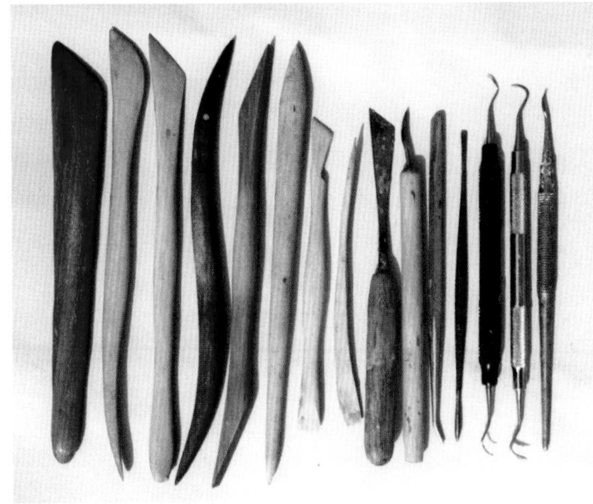

Modeling tools are used with modeling and water-based clays.

Modeling stand in **Arthur Williams'** studio.

Modello A scale model of a three-dimensional work. It may be presented to the potential buyer as a possible work. *See **Model; Maquette**.*

Moisture content Water weight in cell walls of wood, or other substances, designated by a percentage of the over-dry weight.

Moisture trap A device constructed to separate moisture from compressed air when mounted into an air line. Some traps drain moisture automatically; others require occasional manual draining. *See **Air line system**.*

Mold A container or hollow vessel used to transfer a desired shape from a model or pattern into a selected material. The mold is often called the negative, while the casting is called the positive. It is used to create duplicates or is part of the working process to arrive at a unique work of art.

The mold can be made of several substances, such as clay, fiberglass, rubber, silicone, metal, etc., but generally plaster is used by the artist, either as the actual mold material or as a support for the surface. The form to be molded can be plaster, modeling clay, ceramic clay, natural and manmade objects and even the human figure in whole or parts. A mold may be designed to take a shape from a liquid, spray or pliable pressed substance. Castable materials include plaster, resins, metals, wax, concrete, paper, clay, etc. The mold can also be a surface or shape, not necessarily negative, that a substance can be pressed upon to secure a desired form or part of a form. An example is a hump mold made from plaster to press clay on for a particular shape. The culminating form from the mold is the "cast."

There are three major types of molds used for sculpture: waste, piece and flexible. Generally, waste and piece molds are made from hard or firm materials; whereas, flexible molds are made from soft materials to be reusable. Waste molds are broken into pieces or destroyed as they are removed; hence, the term "waste," meaning waste or becoming useless. *See* ***Waste mold***.

The choice of mold material or kind depends on the use of the mold, the object being molded, the cost factor versus time, and if the casting material is accessible. Use involve the final material to be molded (resin requires a different mold than does hot metal), the edition size (flexible mold materials will hold up better than plaster materials), the desired details (some materials, such as silicone, ensure a more detailed surface than plaster). Objects to be molded involve the following considerations: 1) the surface *(Is it hard, soft, coarse or smooth?)*; 2) the separators that can be used on the object *(Will there be a reaction to the molding material?*); 3) the model object *(Will it be destroyed or must the object be saved?*); and 4) the size of the object *(Will there be handling problems?)*.

Mold Design

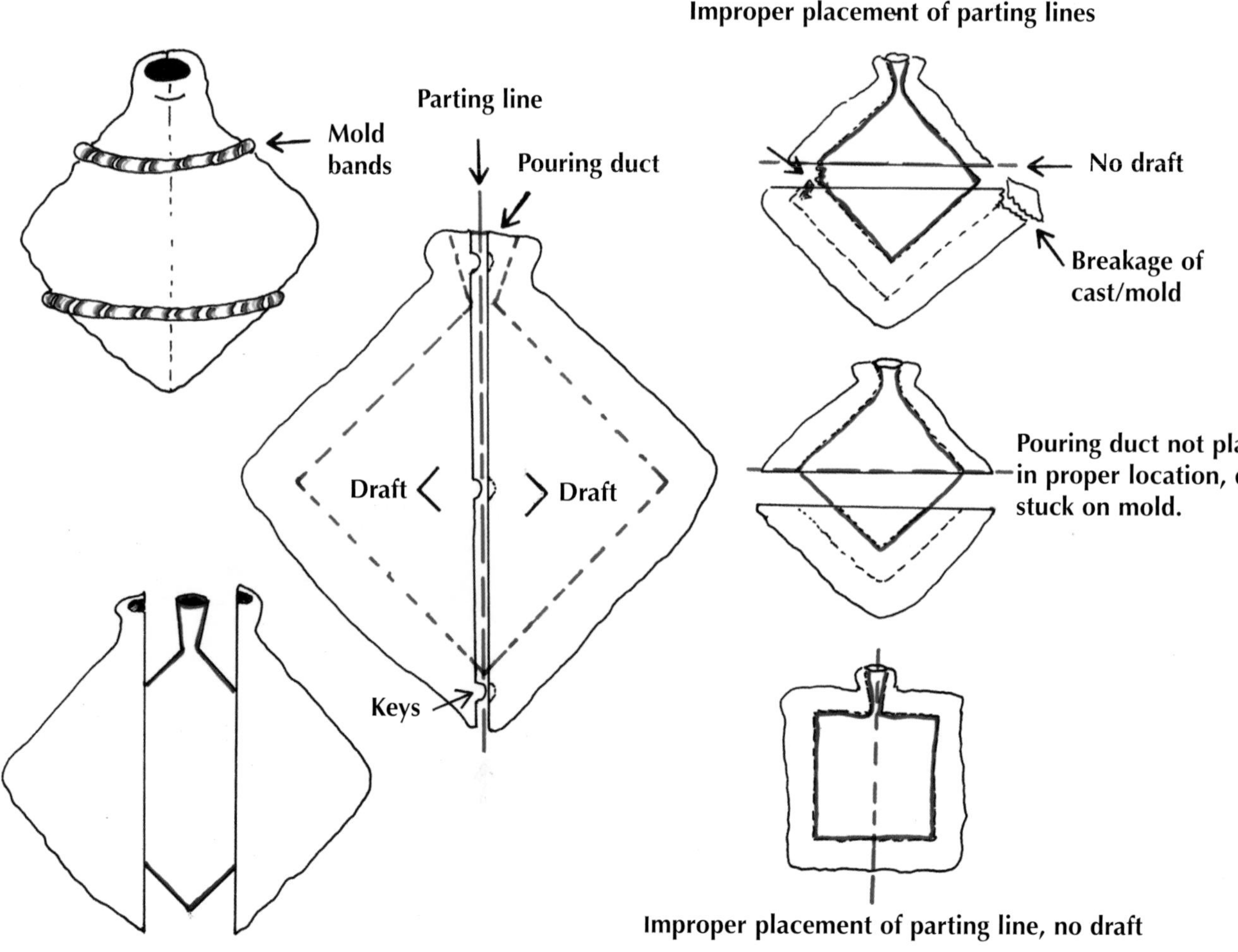

Good parting line

Mold design

The type of mold and material used are crucial. However, almost every mold has several things in common. These include the draft, undercuts, parting line, shim or dividing wall, key and lock keys, pouring duct, mold binding, withdrawal angle and release agent.

The **draft** is the shape or taper of the artwork that permits the mold to be released and removed. The resulting mold has walls that angle or slope outward. Correct draft enables the mold to be dislodged without damaging the mold or artwork. Flexible molds can be extracted by stretching or bending for taper, but hard mold materials, such as plaster, must be designed to ensure taper. Taper is less noticed with some casting materials, such as a liquid resin, as compared to plaster. This is because resin shrinks as it sets while plaster expands. Thus, resin can be used when taper is non-existent, while plaster needs an obvious amount of taper.

The **withdrawal angle** is the angle or alignment that the mold has in relationship to the artwork. As the mold is removed, it is important that it is unsheathed without catching or breaking any of the molded substance. Improper withdrawal can result in creating an undercut. Artwork with a simple draft aids the withdrawal angle.

An **undercut** is a protrusion or indentation that inhibits draft. The protrusion may be in a unique shape or simply be beyond the artwork surface that does not allow the mold to typically encase the artwork. An alcove or indentation may trap and keep the mold inside an area or on the artwork. The undercut(s) can be resolved by designing the mold to eliminate them and allow draft. Sometimes, it is merely repositioning the mold line; sometimes, it requires more pieces. A vacuum may be created as the mold is removed. If properly drafted, the vacuum will be little and can be dealt with easily. Compressed air directed into a mold seam will serve as a vacuum separator.

Edward J. Fraughton, *The Spirit of Wyoming*. Cast bronze, 14' (4.27m) high, Cheyenne, Wyoming.

The **parting line** is where the mold is divided to open it. The best mold design results in fewer final pieces. Correctly placed, parting lines eliminate undercuts with the fewest mold pieces. An experienced mold maker can determine the parting line(s) by examining the artwork visually in every direction. In most cases, a simple front-back view of the artwork will determine the best location. The silhouette (outer edge) becomes the parting line, much like cutting an orange in the direct center to determine two halves. Divided on the line, the parts can be easily removed.

Shims are traditionally thin brass strips that are pressed into the artwork (such as modeling clay or ceramic clay) to part the mold into separate pieces. They are placed on the parting line to avoid undercuts, which allows the mold to be systematically removed from the artwork. The shims can be thin metal of sufficient width to allow insertion and the desired mold thickness. Cut-up thin cola containers and aluminum baking pans work.

When shims (usually metal) cannot be injected into the original artwork because of a hard surface (such as plaster, wood or stone), a softer, more pliable material must be used as the fence. It may be a thin strip of modeling clay placed to one side of the parting line. After the opposite side has been molded, the fence is removed, leaving a mold wall instead of a shim that serves as a separation from the new half of the mold. Soft fences are not only used for hard surfaces, but also when an exact mold tolerance is needed (no shim space remaining).

Keys, called register keys, are corresponding concave and convex shapes in the mold, shim or fence designed to locate and hold the mold parts together. They are termed keys because they need to be a perfect match to the other part to properly open or close the mold much like a key and lock. They help to line up the pieces to ensure a tight fit. Usually in the seam of small works, they are located throughout the walls of larger works. Keys can be designed several ways: as less than a half round ball shape to match the same shape or as a V groove to match a V shape protrusion. They are added during the molding process.

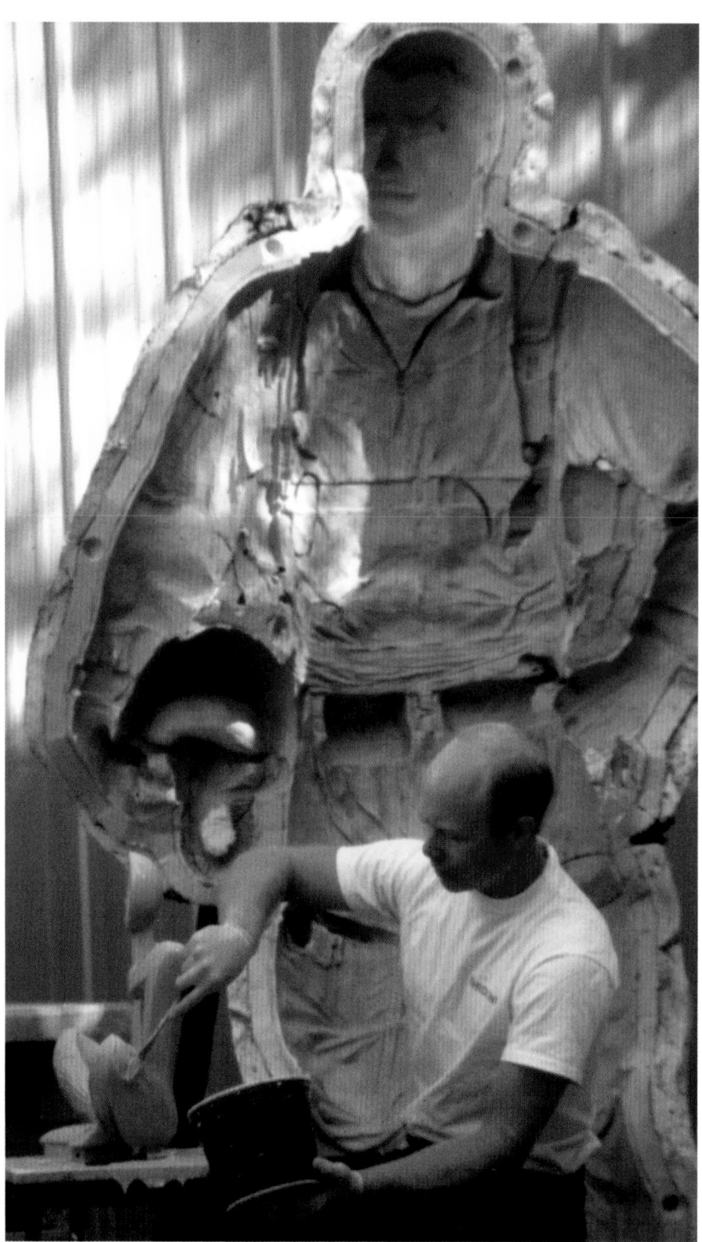

Mold-making involves working with various sizes of molds. **Shidoni Foundry**, Tesùque, New Mexico

A **lock key** pops into place, or once pressed into a supporting mold (mother mold) remains intact until some pressure is exerted to dislodge it. It is used only on flexible molds. It is formed in a wall section, since the primary purpose is to hold the mold onto the supporting mold as the contents are added.

A side benefit of lock keys is that they keep the mold in place during long periods of storage. This helps eliminate distortion from molds collapsing. Lock keys are pre-cast with matching flexible materials and pressed into the top brush-on coat. They can also be carved into the supporting mold shape of a pour-on mold about to be cast. *See **Lock key**.*

The **pouring duct** is the entrance hole or opening where liquid passes into the mold. It is the natural opening of the flat bottom of an upside-down mold. When this is not possible, it is a specially designed funnel shaped duct placed at the top of the artwork. Ideally, it is placed on a part where few surface details will be lost. A good pouring duct design will be split by the parting line, so the mold can be smoothly removed.

Mold bands, ties, fasteners, rubber bands, metal clamps, and soft wire are used to hold the mold together. A simple spring metal clamp can be used if the seams are of uniform thickness. Smaller molds are bound with bungee straps or cords. When automobile inner tubes are available, large rubber bands can be cut for use. The mold design should include indentations or slots for straps. Soft wire is sometimes used, but tends to damage the mold. Bolts with wing nuts are also used on larger, heavier shim walls.

The **release agent,** separator, parting agent or parting compound is a substance that is applied to the artwork to keep the mold material from bonding or sticking to it during the molding process. It facilitates the removal of artwork from the mold. Applied by means of spray, brush or rag, it must be thin or fine enough so as not to create a new detail or affect the existing details. The same terms are used for a substance that is applied to the finished mold surface to keep the new casting material from adhering to the mold. *See **Release agent** (chart).*

A **mold cradle** is used to support exceptionally large molds from the outside, but is anchored to the molding material. It is in place for strength, ease of handling and keeps the mold from warping. The cradle can be designed with parts for handholds or even chain hoist holds for larger molds. Also, the cradle may be designed for simply holding the mold upright or in place while working with the mold.

Mold reinforcement is added for additional strength. It may be necessary because of size, shape or material. To keep it intact, strong, lightweight and usable, mold reinforcement materials include hemp, scrim, canvas, jute, wire mesh and rebar. After the first coat, a reinforcement, such as hemp, is applied into the second or third coat for strength.

Hemp is obtained in bales that are easily pulled apart into smaller lots. It does not take much to significantly strengthen a mold. A small amount can be loosely dipped into liquid plaster. The sculptor will immediately notice how it appears to form a fabric-like sheet ready to drape over the plaster mold surface. Afterwards, additional plaster is added to maintain the strength and shape.

Gerald Balciar, *Above All*, Bronze, 6"x15"x12" (15.2 cm x 38.1cm x 30.5cm).

Jute or scrim, a strong, loose, coarse fabric are also good reinforcement additions for plaster molds, especially smaller ones. Strong cloth fabrics may be used on small molds. Burlap, a cotton fabric, denim, a bluejean fabric, or canvas will work. The closer woven fabrics may need to be soaked in water prior to use. Once soaked, the fabric is rinsed out (twisted) to remove excess moisture before adding the plaster. If the fabric has excess moisture, it will weaken the plaster mix. If dry cloth is used, it may suck the moisture from the plaster, resulting in a mold casting material that dries too quickly.

Metal is the ultimate reinforcement, though weight can be a problem. Wire mesh can be used in larger molds, as well as lightweight aluminum conduit pipe (electrical wire container) or even stronger, but heavier rebar (concrete reinforcing steel). While conduit pipe is regularly added for rigidity or for handles, it is not necessary on small molds. Rebar is seldom used except with molds that will contain extremely heavy substances or substances in volume, such as concrete. For molds that must be stored for long periods of time, a coat of shellac on the rebar will keep rust from forming.

Wood strips are not normally a good support, since the wood tends to swell and fracture the plaster, which also expands about the wood. Molds that contain wood reinforcement are seldom designed for multi-use.

Plaster mold storage must allow it to dry and be kept in a ventilated area to avoid mold. It must be stored intact to avoid distortion or warpage. Ideally, it should be upright with the opening down or covered to keep dust and studio trash from entering it.

Repairs to broken sections can easily be made by saturating the area so that the plaster will not pull moisture from the fresh plaster. The new plaster should be a neat mix. *See **Neat cement**.*

Fiberglass is sometimes used for additional rigidity, strength, lightweightness or compactness. Fiberglass requires respirators, special ventilation and is flammable. It is quick to set, resulting in some heat buildup. Since it is strong and durable, it does not have a mother mold reinforcement. Basically, the surface coat is brushed or sprayed on and allowed to set. The next coat is then applied with limp cut sheet or fiber particles added for strength. Depending on the size of the mold, other layers are added for strength. Fiberglass is considered rigid, but if it is used in larger scale, it is somewhat flexible. While there may be an advantage to this in demolding, it can also create warped or misaligned castings. For this reason, reinforcement, such as aluminum conduit pipe, is used about the mold, leaving most of the pipe exposed for handling purposes. *See **Casting**; **Mold making**; **Pattern mold** (for metal casting); **Piece mold**; **Flexible mold**; **Latex**; **Body molding**.*

Sculptor **John Houser** and assistant, **Miguel Cardenas**, prepare molds for casting the 35′ (10.7m) tall *Don Juan de Oñate Monument*. The work is carefully drawn into one of over 250 mold sections. Each section receives a flexible mold and is then covered with fiberglass protective backing for additional support.

Mold blowing Using a blowpipe to force air into a hollow glass that has been placed in a mold to secure a molded form. *See* ***Glass blowing***.

Molding A way to indirectly create sculpture by substituting one material for another one. The new material is typically harder, more durable or stable than the original. By using a softer, more pliable substance, such as modeling clay for the original, the sculptor's idea is quicker and easier to shape. Once molded, the new substance is tougher and more durable, such as metal or concrete. *See* ***Molds***.

Mold soap A liquid potassium soap used as a separator for molds, especially plaster molds. The mold should be coated with the soap just prior to use, or it will dry and saturate, resulting in a diluted or ineffective release agent. After applying within a short time span, the soap coat should be brushed to clear any residue or excess that could cause casting damage. To determine if the separator is working for casting plaster, drop some water on the surface. If it saturates, the separator is not adequate. *See* ***Release agents*** *(chart);* ***Waste mold****;* ***Green soap****;* ***Soft soap***.

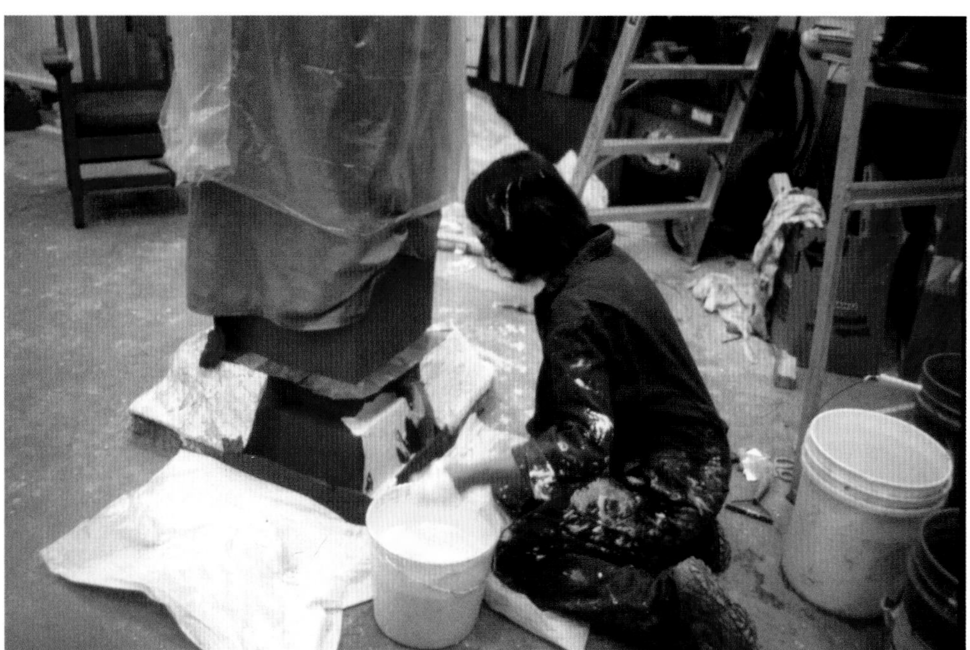

Linda Einfalt molds a large clay sculpture from the bottom up.

Monochrome A single color as opposed to multi-color. A sculpture material's natural color may be referred to as monochrome. *See* ***Polychrome***.

Monolithic Extremely large mass. A very large sculpture could be called monolithic. *See* ***Scale****;* ***Monumental***.

Monument A sculpture designed and erected as a memorial. *See* ***Statue****;* ***Enlargement***.

Monumental Exceedingly large; a larger than life-size sculpture. It may apply to an idea for a grand sculpture or monument (memorial). *See* ***Monolithic****;* ***Enlargement***.

Mortar Mixed binder of cement, sand and water. It is placed between building material, such as brick or stone to permanently bond it into place after the mortar hardens. Normal mortar mix is about one part cement to three parts sand. Mortar is also the term for the vessel used in crushing small substances. *See* ***Cement****;* ***Mortar and pestle***.

Mortar and pestle A crushing tool (pestle) and a bowl-shaped vessel (mortar) that holds the substances being pulverized. The mortar and pestle are made of porcelain or ceramic materials.

Mortise A square or rectangular cavity in one material that is designed to receive an end piece (tendon) to fill the cavity (joint).

Ernest Kotkov and **Nikolai Bartossik**, *Meteorite*. Mosaic over concrete, 49.2′x23′x9.8′ (15m x 7m x 3m). Dnipropetrovsk, Ukraine.

Mosaic A design created with colored pieces of tile, stone, glass or other material set into a surface, such as cement.

Mother mold Termed a jacket, case or containing mold, it is designed to enclose a smaller, weaker, usually flexible mold to provide support ensuring the original artwork's shape without distortion. It is commonly made of plaster with an additive, such as hemp, for added strength and to decrease the size and working weight. Because of its protective enwrapping nature, it is called a mother mold. *See* ***Pattern mold; Mold; Flexible mold; Piece mold; Latex***.

Carole A. Feuerman, *Sunburn.* Oil painted resin, 38"x17"x13" (97cm x 43.2cm x 33cm), Photographer: David Finn.

Moulage A reusable, heat activated, mold material that can be used for body casting. The small chunks of moulage are placed into a double boiler and heated until all is melted together. Water can be added. Mold release is not necessary except on the most porous of objects. When using on human skin, it is allowed to cool to about 100°F (37.7°C). It is brushed onto a depth of one-fourth to one-half inch (0.635cm to 1.27cm). A gauze cloth is added into the hot moulage for strength and more moulage is added to the warm surface with a spatula. Careful removal is needed as even small undercuts tend to tear the substance. Defects can be corrected with additional hot moulage. *See* ***Body molding; Molds***.

Movement The suggestion of motion or the flow of form as seen in sculpture. *See* ***Principles of order***.

MSDS Material Safety Data Sheet compiled by a material supplier. The sheet is a listing of hazards and safety precautions when using a specific material.

Muller A large machine that mixes sand and the binder together for sand casting. *See* ***Sand casting***.

Museum A building or location for displaying, studying and preserving artwork (as well as historical objects or artifacts). *See* ***Gallery***.

Mushroom The head of a chisel with severe wear, especially a stone carving chisel. The head appears as a mushroom top. It can easily be removed by grinding it off.

Mylar™ A stout, thin sheeting of polyester. Used as a separating material, an example would be the various widths commercially sold in rolls that are placed between pipes for plumbing purposes. It not only separates but tightly seals. Balloons may be made of Mylar™.

Mushroom on metal carving chisel.

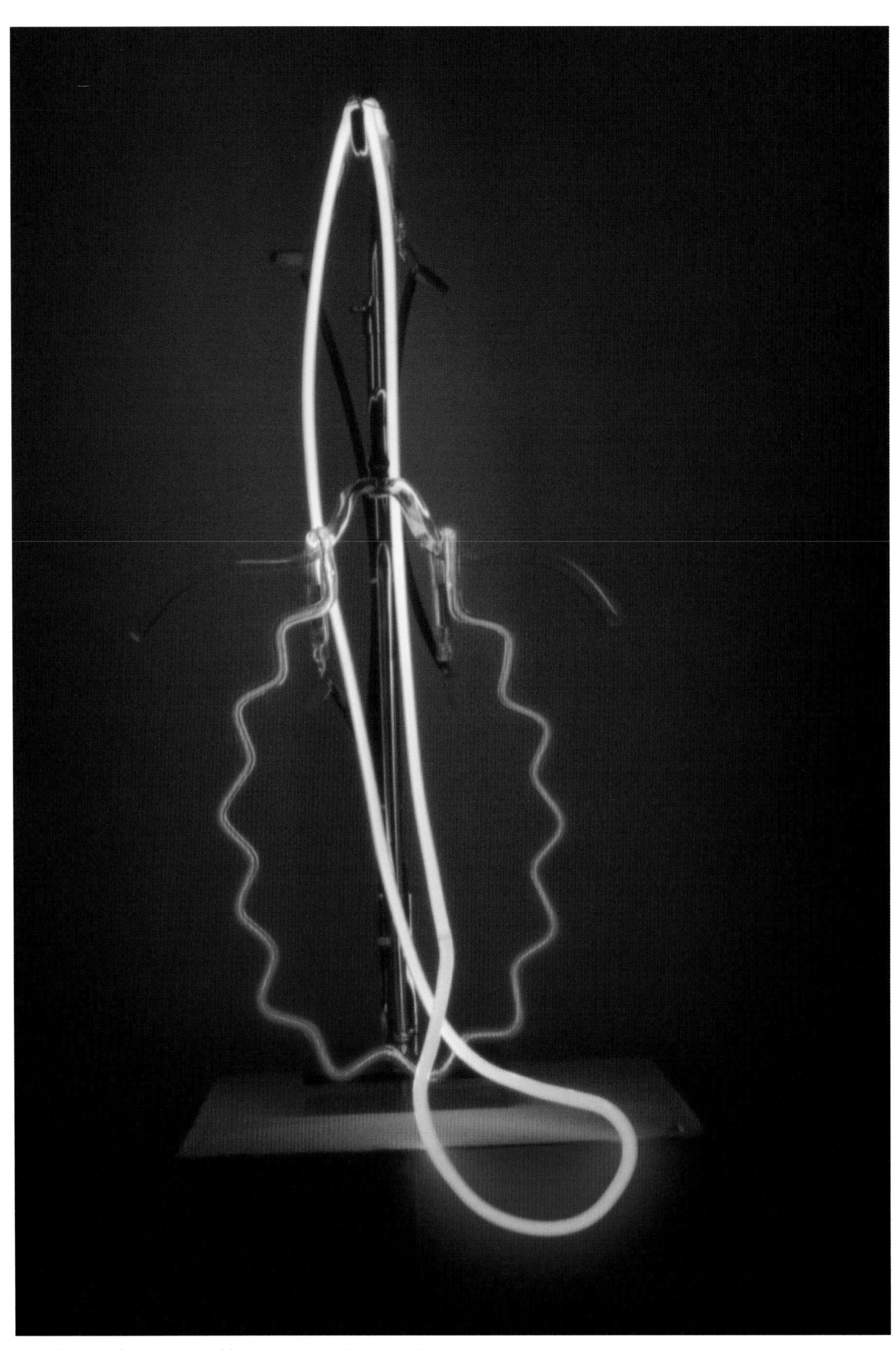

Daniel E. Mader, *Two Necklaces*. Neon, 30″x12″x12″ (76.2cm x 30.5cm x 30.5cm).

N

Nails Metal fastener with a narrow pointed shaft that is capped on the opposite end. It is driven into wood using a hard metal hammer or mechanical device until the cap (usually flat) is on or in the surface. The cap holds the nail firmly in place. Box nails and common nails have a flat head. However, box nails have a thin body that allows them to be driven into wood with less splitting, while the heavier, common nails are used for stronger construction. Finish nails, with small heads, can easily be countersunk into the wood to be hidden from view. Concrete nails are hard-tempered to withstand the rigid concrete that they are driven into without bending.

National Society of Sculptors (NSS) An organization of sculptors and friends of sculpture to promote figurative sculpture. The Society publishes a quality magazine entitled ***SCULPTURE REVIEW***.

Naturalism Reproducing exacting details and qualities of an object "as nature left it," as opposed to artwork possessing a realistic but similar (not exact) shape.

Neat cement A mixture of cement and water without sand or other aggregate. Because it is so fine, it is used for detail or minute filler where a casting is flawed. A plaster mix for touch-up may be made by taking a small bowl or paper cup and adding a minimal amount of water followed by carefully sifting plaster over the surface. The addition of plaster is halted when it will no longer sink into the water and continually float. After settling for a few minutes, the plaster is removed, unstirred and placed into the defects. Neat cement tends to retain moisture better than other mixes and is sometimes called paste. *See* ***Cement***.

Neck (necking) Drawing in a ceramic shape by squeezing hard about the form. It is also the process of constricting a hot glass form by squeezing a jack around the form.

Negative (shape, space) The penetrating space; holes that are part of a sculpture design are negative shapes. It is not a preferred term, since this space can be seen as a very positive attribute to the work. It can include all the space or air flow that is contained in dips in and about sculpture. Negative is sometimes used to refer to a mold (negative interior). *See* ***Female***.

Herb Parker, *Containing the Beast*. Rammed earth, 8′x6′x6′ (2.44m x 1.83m x 1.83m).

Jane Haskell, *Double Helix*. Neon, 4'x14'x4' (1.22m x 1.22m x 1.22m). Photographer: Lockwood Hoehl.

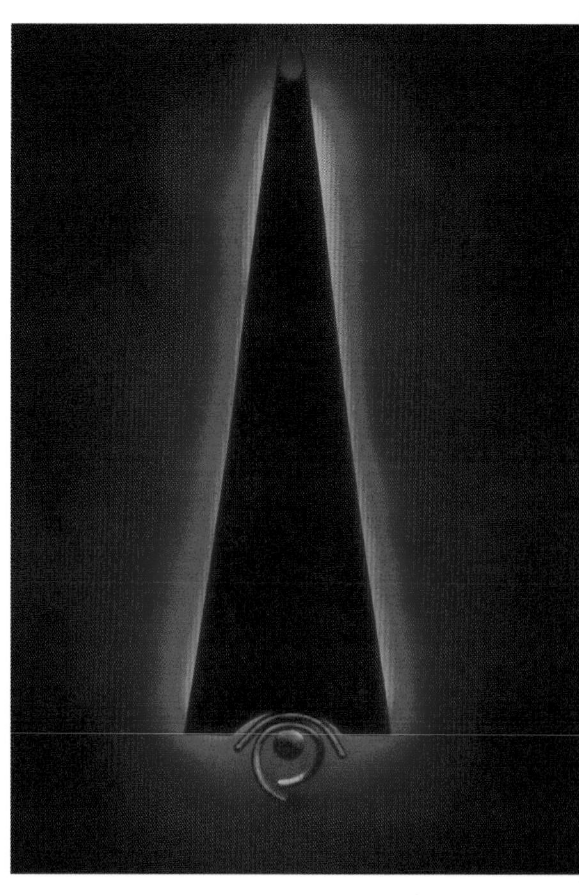

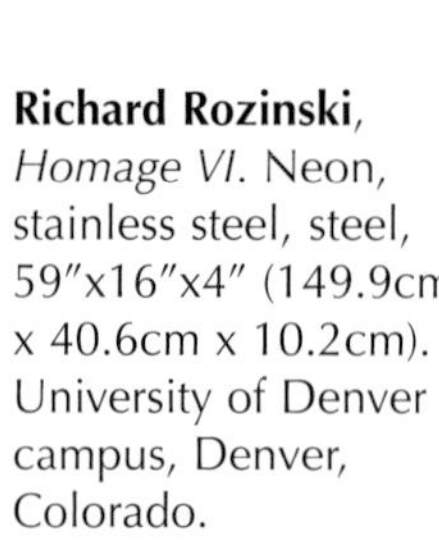

Richard Rozinski, *Homage VI*. Neon, stainless steel, steel, 59"x16"x4" (149.9cm x 40.6cm x 10.2cm). University of Denver campus, Denver, Colorado. Photographer, Nona Stewart.

Richard Rozinski, *. . .Not to be Taken Litely*. Neon, mixed media, 18"x16"x8" (45.7cm x 40.6cm x 20.3cm). Photographer: Red Earth Photo.

Neon An inert, gaseous element contained in glass tubing that glows when connected to electricity. Capturing and using neon gas is called "neon lighting." The total fixture is also called neon.

NEON
by William Volkersz

William Volkersz works on the *Newlyweds* in his studio. Photographer: Tom Ferris.

He adjusts the neon on his *Newlyweds*.

William Volkersz, *The Newlyweds*. Neon, chalk, wood, paint, found objects, 87″x93″x11″ (221cm x 236.2cm x 27.9cm). Photographer: Tom Ferris.

James L. Lawton, *The Specter of America: The Wagon*. Wood, steel, moss, fungi, neon; viewer movement activated.

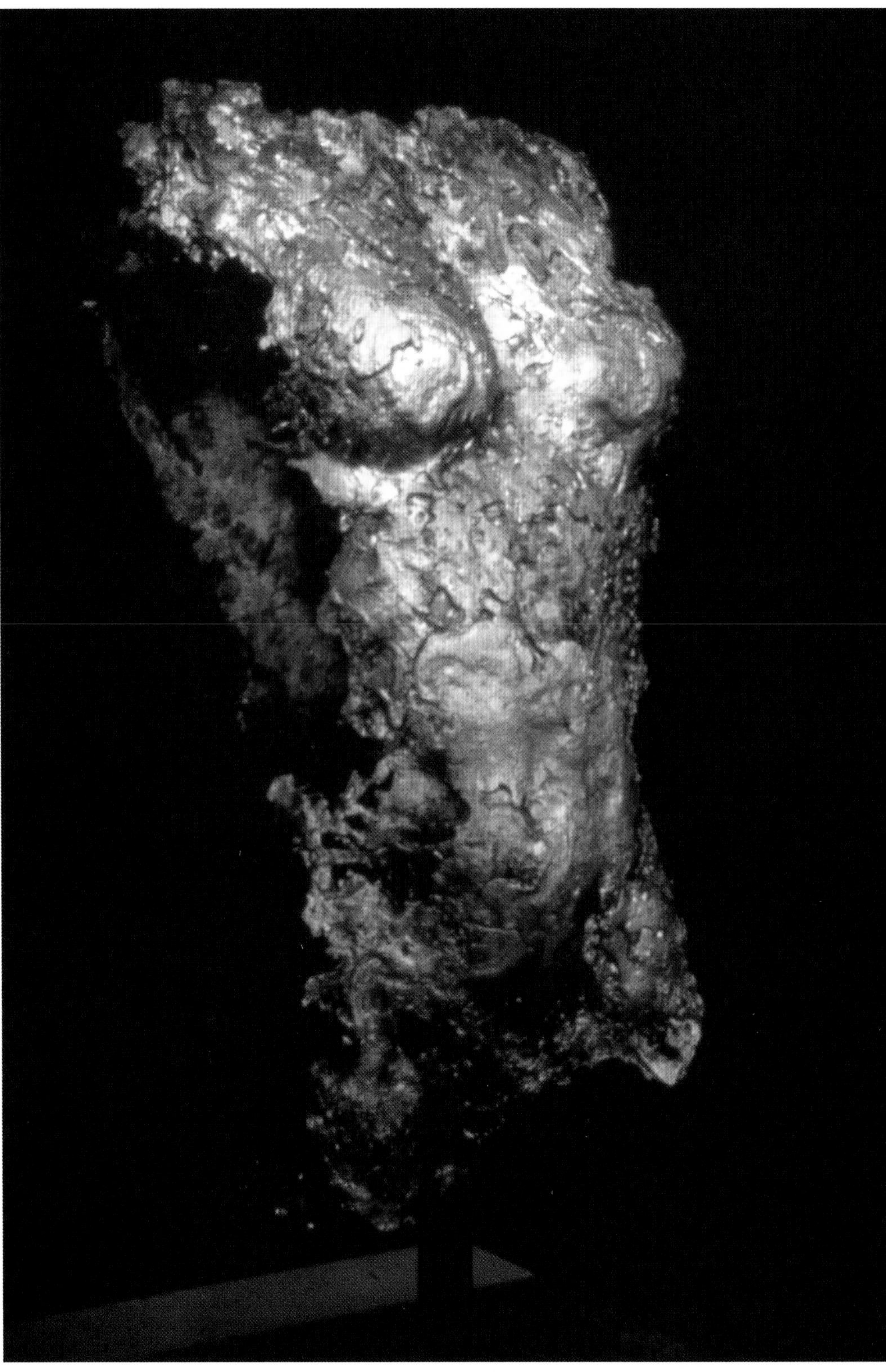

Carole A. Feuerman, *Aphrodite*. Aluminum and bronze, 29"x17"x13" (73.7cm x 43.2cm x 33cm).

Neutral flame The flame created by a blending of oxygen and acetylene (or other gas). This is the preferred flame for welding and cutting. *See* ***Oxyacetylene flame*** *(chart).*

Nichrome A metal capable of sustaining extremely high heats. It is used for kiln heating elements. Wires of nichrome are used for small ceramic objects, such as beads, when firing in a kiln. Styrofoam™ cutters may be made of nichrome wire to endure the heat generated onto the wire used to cut (melt) through the Styrofoam™. *See* ***Electric kiln; Styrofoam™***.

Nickel A hard, silvery, metallic element combined with other substances in alloys to prevent corrosion.

Niello Black metal surface design and decoration regularly applied to gold or silver. A niello consists of a composite of metals, including silver and copper, that are heat fused into an incised or engraved space.

Nigged The process of using a pick instead of a chisel to finish a stone. The term is also used for the marks created.

Noncorrosive flux A flux used when soldering. It does not leave corrosive residue or cause chemical injury to the work. The flux is made of resin or resin substances. *See* ***Flux***.

Nonferrous Metals that are not iron or do not contain iron. Bronze and aluminum are nonferrous metals.

Nonobjective (art) Art without recognizable subject matter. No-object or nonobjective artwork will possess titles that are non-subject oriented, as opposed to abstract art that will give a title to steer the viewer into the thought pattern or subject matter of the artist. *See **Non-representational** (art).*

Nonrepresentational (art) Artwork that is the opposite of representational or figurative. The term may be used to describe abstract work. *See **Nonobjective** (art); **Abstraction**.*

Normalize To permit a material, such as a steel, to completely cool without quenching after it has been heated. This is not equivalent to annealing. *See **Anneal**.*

Jack Zajac, *Small Skull after Orvietto, III*. Bronze, 12.75″x16″x 8″ (32.4cm x 40.6cm x 20.3cm).

Noxious Fumes that are harmful, often poisonous, or damaging to living things. The odor may cause permanent damage depending on the substance or condition.

Nude Naked, featuring the body without clothing. Sculptors prefer to do nude works due to the body's natural beauty and timelessness. To use clothing blocks the form and dates the work.

Numbered A system of designating the number of works involved in a series of artworks. A specific number is assigned to each piece. Numbered does not have to mean a limited number, but it does keep record. (The number can be unending.) *See **Edition**.*

Nuts A small metal block in a hexagon shape with a threaded hole centered in it. The threads match a bolt's shaft. The nut is twisted onto the bolt's end and tightened as a fastening device.

Nylon A strong synthetic polymer frequently configured in straps for lifting or wrapping (tying) strength.

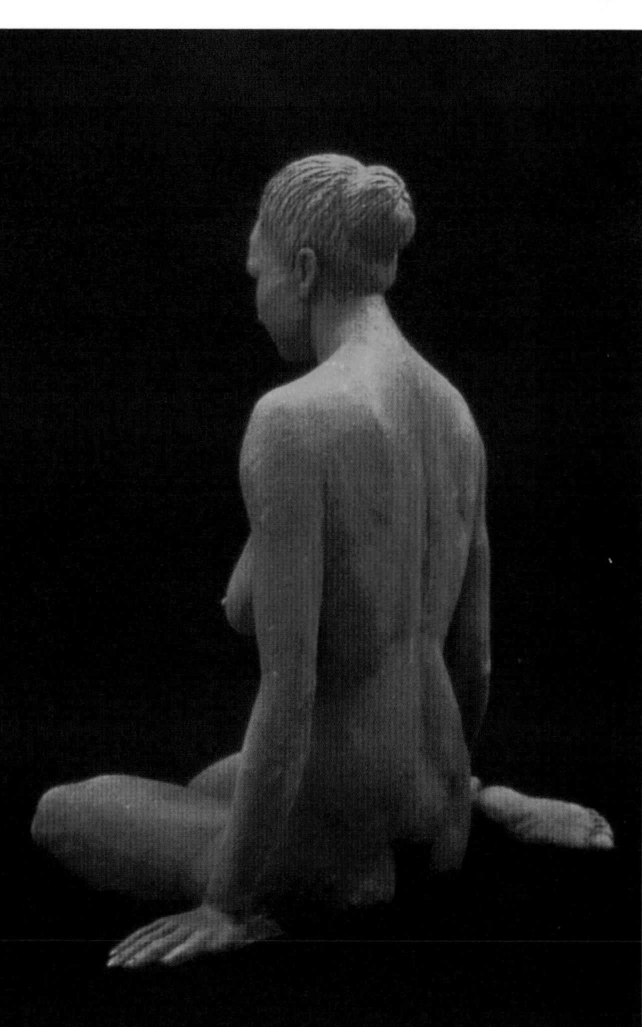

Lampo Leong, *Nude Study*. Clay (sculpture mix), 9″x5″x5″ (22.9cm x 12.7cm x 12.7cm).

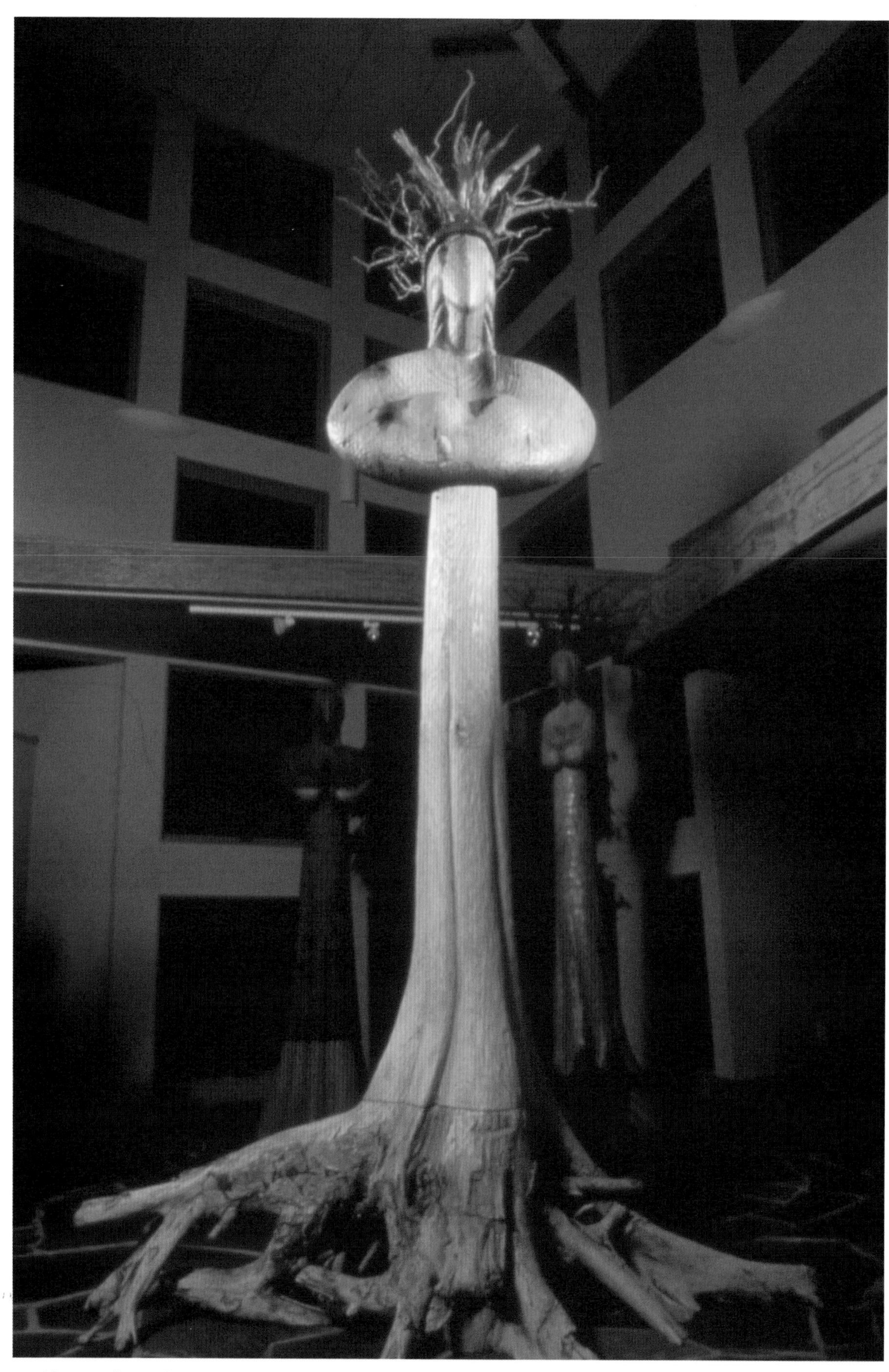

David Hostetler, *Ashera Tree Root Goddess*. Catalpa, oak, ash, 13′ (3.97m) tall. Photographer: Brian Blauser.

Dawn Stubitsch, *Time Currents.* Oak, 12″x17″ (30.5cm x 43.2cm).

Oak Blond to reddish in color, oak is a durable hardwood with a distinctive grain. It is preferred for furniture and tool handles because of its strength and ability to take a variety of stains. *See **Wood** (chart).*

Obelisk A four-sided stone column that tapers to a pyramidal peak. The shape is specifically used for monuments.

Object d'art Artwork with materials of personal significance that are worth more than the aesthetic value of the piece. It refers to small works of gold and silver or personal items not necessarily designated originally as an art object.

Objective art Representational art or art with recognizable objects as opposed to non-objective (no object in mind) art. *See* ***Nonobjective***.

Object trove Found object art or art that is exhibited in common form with few or no alterations. The artist serves only to select and display the object. *See* ***Assemblage***.

Obsidian An extremely hard, dark (black) volcanic-glass stone.

Oil clay Oil-based modeling clay. *See **Clay** (oil-based).*

Oilstone A sharpening stone using a small amount of oil for lubrication in the sharpening process. The oil also helps to wash away ground particles from the abrasive surface. *See* ***Arkansas stone***.

One-piece mold An open face mold that has only one piece. If reusable, it is either firm and without undercuts or flexible with undercuts. If it is firm with undercuts then it is usually a waste mold. *See* ***Molds***.

Onyx A gemstone from the mineral chalcedony. It is a tight-grained hard stone that is frequently in multi-layers of colors. Used for cameos, onyx is difficult to carve. *See* ***Stone*** *(chart).*

Oolithic rock Limestone formed with small spherical granules. *See* ***Stone*** *(chart).*

Open face A mold of little depth in which the entire inside is open and visible to the viewer. It is a relief mold without undercuts. These can easily be worked, since all parts of the surface are visually and physically apparent. Not only can these molds be filled with liquids, but they are used to press materials into. *See* ***Open mold; Mold.***

Opening The beginning of an art exhibit. The opening may be during the night or day. It is sometimes a private viewing for only those who are invited.

Open mold A mold that is open, usually from the bottom, and is turned bottom-side up and filled from this opening. Though the inner wall may be partially visible, it is not necessarily accessible. If they are piece molds and accessible, pressing materials may be used for casting. *See* ***Open Face; Mold.***

Organic form A shape that represents living matter (animal or vegetable).

Joseph Rotella, *Mother and Child.* Onyx, 35″x12″ (88.9cm x 30.5cm).

Organic peroxide A chemical used primarily as a catalyst for casting resins. It can cause blindness if it comes into contact with the eyes. *See* ***Resin.***

Orifice End opening for gas, air or liquid to flow out within a controlled hole size.

Original The first work or art that has not been done before. The prototype of a certain style of art may be referred to as being original. Original in casting is the artist's own artwork during his/her lifetime with his/her control and direction. The originals are either unique (one-of-a-kind) or a limited numbered edition. *See* ***Reproduction; Replicas; Artist's proof; Edition.***

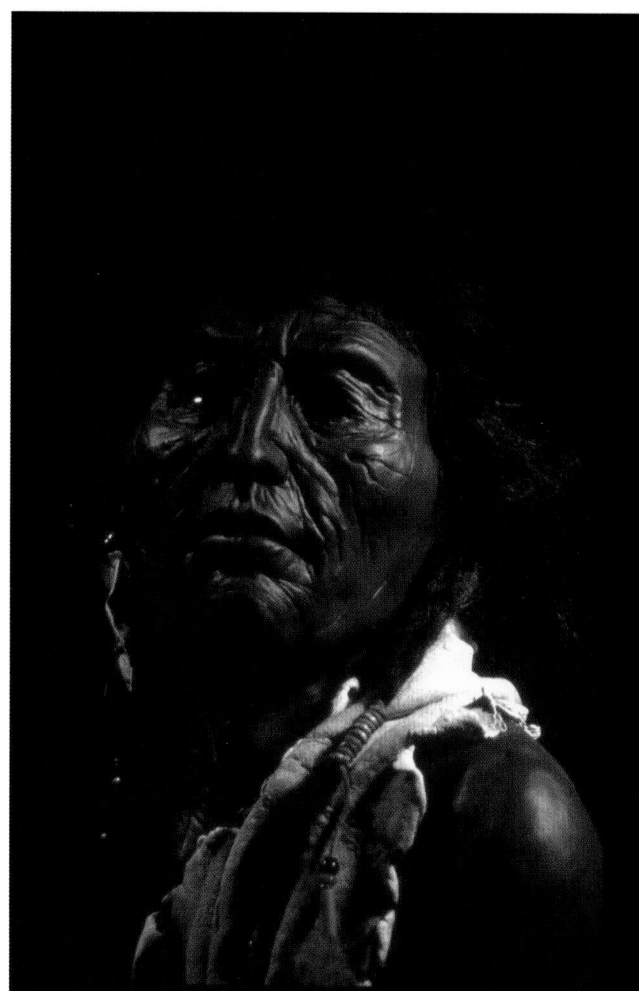

Sharon Dee Shaughnessy, *Dakota*. Mixed media, clay, stone, 18″ (45.7cm) tall, one-of-a-kind original.

Origami The technique of folding paper into three-dimensional shapes, especially flowers and birds. Paper can vary from plain white to intricate patterns on colored paper.

ORIGAMI
by Kathreen Chrisman

Paper in progression of folds.

All work is hand folded.

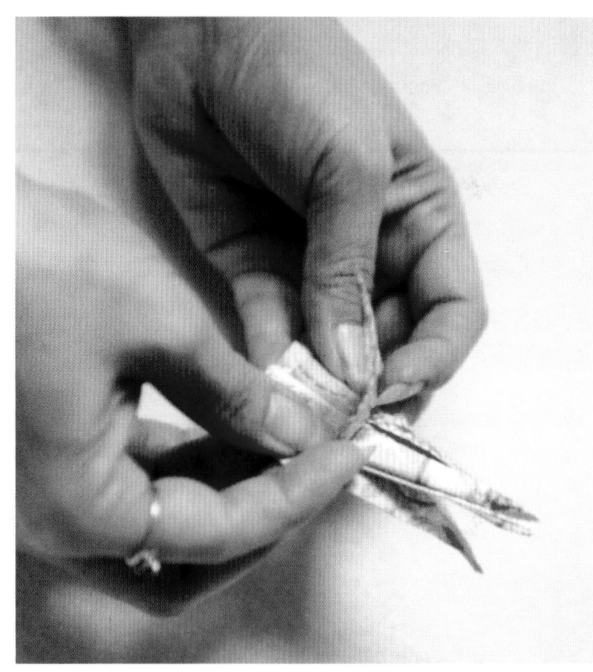

As it progresses, the form begins to emerge.

Kathreen Chrisman, *Origami Tsura*. Origami paper, 4″x5″x3″ (10.2cm x 12.7cm x 7.6cm).

Thomas H. Sayre, *Origami Bird*. Wood truss, cloth, lacquer, 24′x12′x8′ (7.32m x 3.66m x 2.44m).

Christopher Vicini, *Stele*. Porcelain, oxides, 32″x13″x13″ (81.3cm x 33cm x 33cm). Photographer: Mark Johnston.

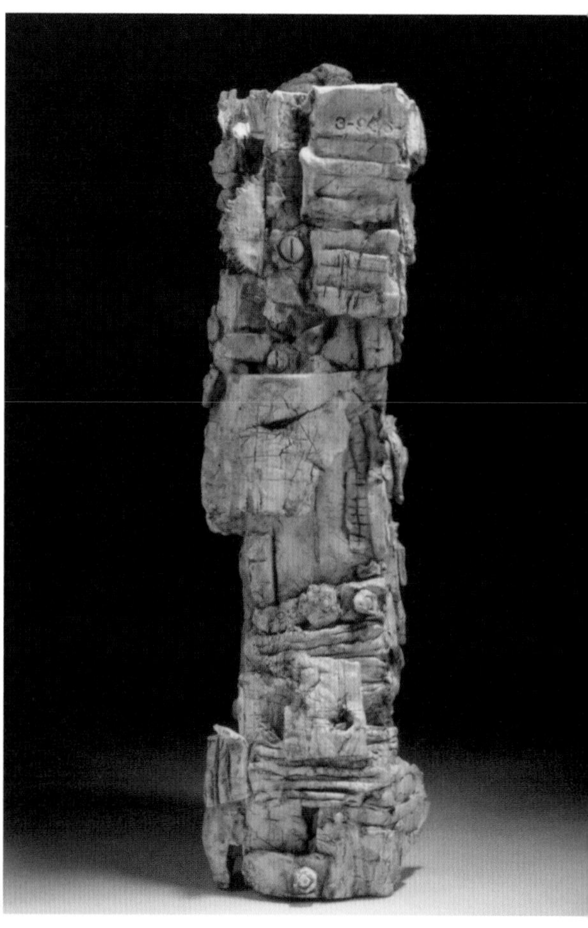

Osmosis Absorption of a fluid through a membrane, or the tendency of liquids to disperse this way. The process is gradual. It can prove to be very dangerous on one's skin when using several sculpture products, especially patinas. *See **Patina**.*

Oven-dry (wood) Wood that is dried in an oven at constant temperatures of 210°F to 221°F (98.9°C to 105°C). *See **Kiln dried**.*

Oxidation The combination of oxygen with another substance. The resulting oxidation of steel, for example, is rust.

Oxidation firing Typical kiln firing using electricity or gas that includes a substantial oxygen supply within the chamber during the process. *See **Kiln.***

Oxide A compound including oxygen. Oxide occurs in combustion with metal. Afterwards, the metal is said to have oxidized. As used with ceramic clay, an oxide lends color to a fired work.

Oxidizing flame The flame that results from excessive amounts of oxygen being mixed with gas in the chamber of the oxyacetylene torch. *See **Oxyacetylene welding, cutting**.*

Oxyacetylene A combination of oxygen and acetylene, especially with an oxyacetylene torch in welding and cutting metal.

Oxyacetylene cutting Using oxygen and acetylene gas in combination to melt metal and afterwards pressure the liquid metal away. Safety clothes, flame adjustment, equipment, and operational procedures are similar to oxyacetylene welding with the exception of the torch. *See* ***Oxyacetylene welding***.

Technique

Using oxyacetylene cutting for ferrous metals is simple with the specially designed torch (cutting head). The torch is easily screwed into the existing fittings attached to the hoses. After properly setting the torch valves, the torch is lit and the flame is used to heat the metal. The metal becomes bright cherry red. A full strong surge of controlled oxygen from the center of the torch aims directly into the path or kerf to be cut. The oxygen causes the steel to burn or oxidize as it is applied, exerting enough force to blow the molten metal out of the cut. Compared to mechanical cutting methods, oxyacetylene cutting is considerably quicker, less expensive and less laborious. Many sculptors prefer the jagged edges that the cut produces.

Correctly adjusting the pressure valves is essential. The oxygen tank valves should be almost wide open. A good supply of oxygen is essential; the regulator to the torch is opened over 20 psi (138kPa) and sometimes in excess of 40 psi (275.7kPa), depending on the torch tip size. This results in about two times more oxygen being used in proportion to acetylene gas. The gas tank valve is turned only once and the regulator to the torch is seldom operated beyond a pressure setting of 10 psi (69kPa). The operation of hose controls, etc., is much the same as for gas cutting.

Oxyacetylene rig, including cutting/welding regulators, hoses, torch, oxygen and acetylene cylinders secured on portable cart.

Oxygen regulator and gauges with operator's hand on regulator control.

Acetylene regulator mounted in cylinder with operator's hand on cylinder valve.

Oxyacetylene cutting

The torch is specialized with a long neck for versatility and to allow the welder to be a greater distance from the cut. It has a second valve control, closer to the tip end, to control the force of the pure air stream that is required. The cutting tip has one large center hole encircled by smaller holes (usually five or six). The center hole allows a large stream of oxygen to surge out into the middle of the preheated area to oxidize and move the metal.

The smaller holes produce the oxyacetylene preheating flame. The center oxygen hole is controlled by a large lever valve (handle) mounted on the mixer handle of the torch towards the tip. After the metal is properly preheated, the valve should be held wide open (down) as long as the cut is in process. The two valves (knobs) at the base of

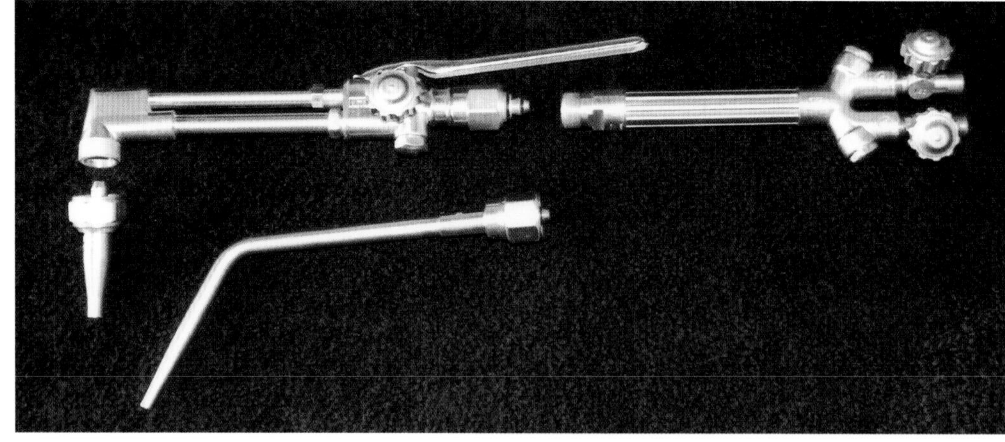

Oxyacetylene torch, handle, head, cutting and welding tip.

Oxyacetylene cutting torch in use.

A machine-mounted torch for precise straight cutting.

the mixer handle control the oxygen and gas mixture the same as for oxyacetylene welding.

The environment should be as fireproof as possible. Avoid wood buildings, wood floors or flammable materials in the vicinity of the equipment. The same applies to gas welding, except that it is desirable for the operator cutting metal to wear boots covered by pant legs to keep searing, glowing hot sparks from becoming encased within the footwear. Since the hot metal slag (waste) is removed by a powerful force of air, it can travel through the air a great distance while glowing hot. Cutting off from the edge of a welding table can result in sparks on the feet or legs or worse, falling on the supply hoses. While the rubber hoses resist burns, they will burn through if the hot spark lingers on them. Sometimes a sand bed is placed beneath the cutting surface to slow and catch the hot slag.

The torch tip size is of paramount importance. The larger cut requires a considerable oxygen supply. If the tip is too large, then the finished cut will neither be clean nor sharp. While it is possible to cut extremely thick metal, most sculptors will seldom encounter cuts larger than two inches (5.08cm) with the tips available at welding suppliers. It is best, and economical, to use the smallest tip for the cut.

OXYACETYLENE CUTTING FLAMES

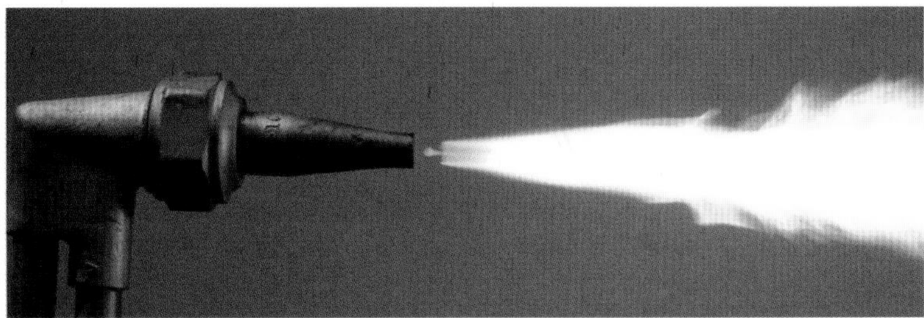

Too much gas, not enough oxygen.

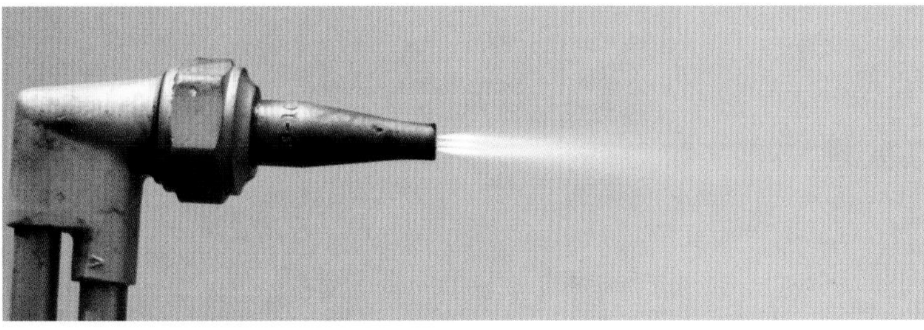

Too much oxygen for gas mix.

A good cutting flame.

Cutting oxygen is released in the center of the flames.

With the oxygen valve open and the acetylene valve at a half turn, the regulators are adjusted. To match a 0 tip, the oxygen should be set at least 25 psi (172kPa) and acetylene between 3 and 5 psi (34.5kPa to 55kPa). The main torch valve should have access to a full flow of oxygen when it is needed. With proper gloves and eye protection (colored face mask or goggles) in place, the torch is ready for a flame. To start, turn the gas valve (knob) about one-eighth turn and ignite it with a friction lighter. After it is lit, the gas can be increased until the smoke ceases; then add oxygen to produce a neutral flame.

A good way to check the flame is to completely depress the air lever. If the flame flutters then more acetylene may need to be added. If the flame increases, then the gas may need to be turned down or turned up.

Holding the torch vertically to the metal (with the tip off the metal but at the point of contact), it should be heated to a cherry red. Compress the air lever immediately If everything is correct, the cut will begin. With the flame in place, proceed by preheatin the path as the flow of the oxygen is unbroken along the kerf. If the movement is too rapid, the cut is partial and will cease, ending in flashbacks. If the movement is too slow or the tip too far from the metal, the metal will merge in an unspent slag that is difficult, if not impossible, to remove and the tip may gather waste or overheat. If this occurs, the tip needs to be cleaned with tip cleaners.

OXYACETYLENE CUTTING Tip/Metal/Settings

Tip Size	Metal Thickness	Acetylene Set	Oxygen Set
000	1/8 -1/4	3 - 5	20 - 30
00	1/8 - 3-5	3 - 5	25 - 35
0	3/8 - 1/2	3 - 5	25 - 35
1	1/2 - 3/4	3 - 5	30 - 35
2	3/4 - 1	4 - 6	35 - 40
3	2	4 - 6	40 - 45
4	4	7 - 8	65

Oxyacetylene welding

The process of mixing an extremely combustible gas, acetylene, with oxygen to achieve a flame hot enough to melt and fuse metal together. The heat can exceed 6000°F (3316°C).

Acetylene is formulated by uniting calcium carbide and water under pressure. Acetylene burned in the atmosphere without pressurized oxygen is not fully consumed, resulting in a lingering black carbon smoke residue. While oxygen is noncombustible and has no odor, raw acetylene has a sweet distinctive odor.

There are three basic flames: 1) The **neutral flame** has a white inner cone with a blue to orange outer flame. This flame is primarily used for steel.
2) The **oxidizing flame**

Rochelle Ford, *Silver Streak*. Metal, 38″x24″x8″ (96.5cm x 61cm x 20.3cm).

also has a white inner core but has an almost colorless outer flame because of a mixture slightly more air to less gas. It is used for brass and bronze welding. 3) The **carbonizing** or reducing flame with its inner core of white has an orange colored outer flame due to the mixture of more gas to less air. This is the flame best suited for cast iron.

The equipment includes an acetylene cylinder (tank), one oxygen cylinder (tank), a cart for storing and moving the tanks, oxygen and acetylene regulators with gauges, a combination fitting wrench, hoses with fittings, the welding torch, welding tip cleaners, striker (spark starter), dark tinted face mask or goggles, heavy gloves, appropriate clothing (dark heavy canvas or leather outer wear, maybe an apron), and a safe working table or space that can withstand heat and sparks without combustion.

OXYACETYLENE WELDING FLAMES

Excessive gas.

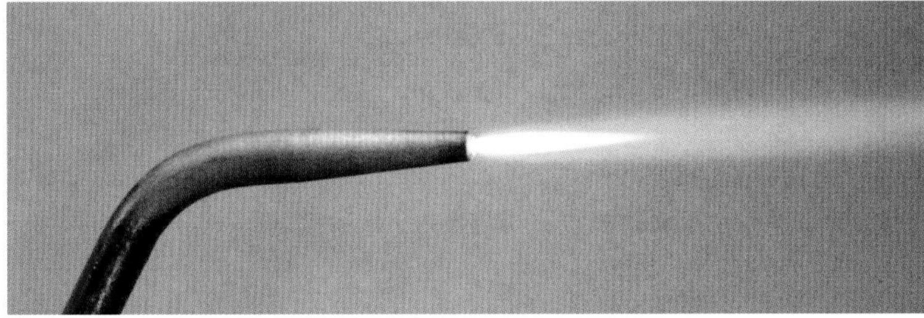

Carbonizing flame.

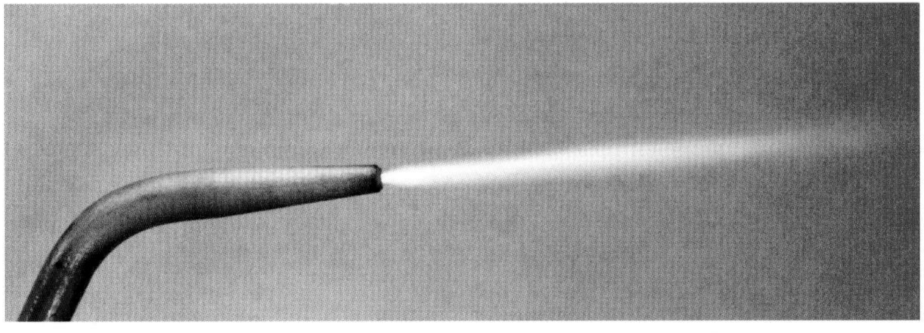

Neutral flame.

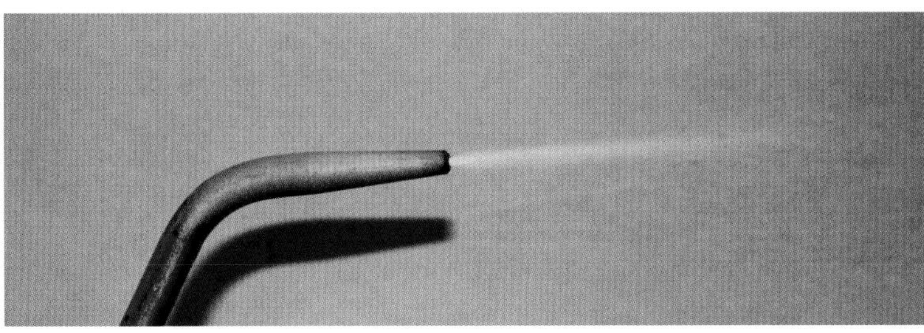

Oxidizing flame.

While regulators can be single or double stage, double stage regulators are more common. They are larger and control the pressures better, especially when sizeable works are involved. Single stage regulators are used for small portable lightweight rigs. The high pressure tanks vary in size, but since more oxygen is used, the oxygen tank is about 50% larger. Ideally, the oxygen tank is green, and the acetylene tank is red, though this is not always the case. All tanks should be stored upright, either fastened to a cart or to a stable horizontal fixture or wall. If the tanks are moved without attached regulators, the screw-on cap (lid) must be in place. Bottles should never be placed in extreme heat or where they could be struck or damaged, since they could become volatile and even airborne. Hoses that are too long can become a safety hazard as well as wasting their contents if they are excessively long.

Technique

Begin by mounting the regulators onto the tank. After the cap is twisted off, the tank valve is cracked, or allowed a brief quarter turn to blow any dust from the valve, and then quickly closed. Using the fitting wrench, the regulators are placed on the tanks, remembering that gas (acetylene) fittings are in reverse of the normal (counter-clockwise threads). Avoid excessive force and never use grease or oil on the brass fittings. Brass is used to eliminate any potential sparks when lighting, and oil or grease cannot be used near oxygen, since spontaneous combustion will result. After the hoses are attached and the torch is mounted, the working pressures can be determined. Leaks can be discovered by applying soapy water to the joints and looking for the resulting bubbles.

TIP	METAL	ACETYLENE SET	OXYGEN SET
000 - 00 - 0	1/32 - 1/16	3 - 5	3 - 5
1 - 2	1/16 - 1/8	3 - 5	3 - 5
3	1/8 - 3/16	4 - 8	4 - 8
4	3/16 - 1/4	5 - 10	5 - 10

OXYACETYLENE WELDING
Tip/Metal/Settings

The regulators need to be adjusted according to the metal to be worked. Heavier metals require more released pressure. The oxygen tank valve is turned several turns. The gauge itself reads to 4000 psi (27600kPa). However, the tank pressure will read at approximately 2200 pounds (999kg) when the cylinder is full. The acetylene tank valve is only opened to one half turn. A full tank will register approximately 320 pounds (145.3kg), though it reads all the way to 600 (272.4 kg). As the working pressure is set, the operator needs to remember that the regular valves are closed when they are out or loose. As they are tightened, they force an inner diaphragm open, allowing pressure to escape. Over-tightening can burst the diaphragm and too loose can cause the turning handle to literally fall off.

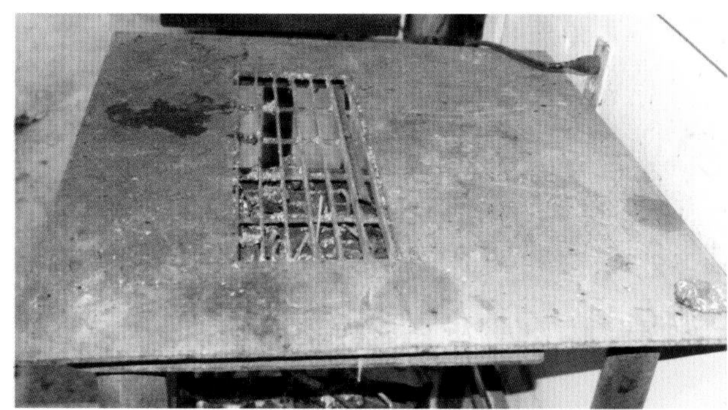

A cutting/welding table that allows hot sparks to pass down.

The oxygen supply valve is first opened from 3 to 10 pounds (1.36kg to 4.54kg), depending on the tip size and heat desired. (Oxygen can be opened all the way to 40 [18.l6kg] for cutting purposes.) The acetylene supply valves are best set for three to ten pounds (1.36kg to 4.54kg), averaging five (2.27kg), but never more than 15 (6.81kg). (At 15 pounds [6.81kg], the gas becomes unstable and can spontaneously ignite.) After 15 (6.81kg), the gauge reads on a red background providing a further safety warning.

After placing the face shield on, the acetylene is slightly turned on the torch head and the striker ignites the gas. Air is slowly added. The fuels are mixed to achieve the desired flame. To cease operation, the acetylene torch is first turned off, then the oxygen, followed by turning off the acetylene and oxygen tanks' valves. The system is then bled by opening the oxygen at the torch head, draining the air hose and then closing it. The acetylene is done the same way. If this step is properly completed, the regulator valves should show a zero torch pressure for both the oxygen and acetylene on the supply gauges.

In torch welding, the torch consists of two major parts: the interchangeable torch tip and the handle or mixer. The tip can easily be removed by a wrench. The handle has two knobs (valves) to control the gas/air mixture. Pointing the flame at the metal, at about a 45° angle, with the inner cone nearly touching the metal, a puddle of melted metal is formed. The tip should be constantly moving, applying the heat evenly, or the metal will burn through.

The welding rod is usually composed of an identical metal to that of the metal being welded. After the puddle has started and while the flame is still being applied, the rod is placed slightly ahead of the flame, also at a 45° angle. It should flow uniformly into the puddle as it melts. Continue moving along the joint until the work is completed. If the torch tip becomes contaminated, hissing and popping noises will occur. The tip needs to be cleaned by inserting and withdrawing a tip cleaning wire into each of the tip openings. (The tip cleaner steel wires are bound together to provide a variety of measured sizes to fit a variety of flame holes.) *See* ***Oxyacetylene cutting***.

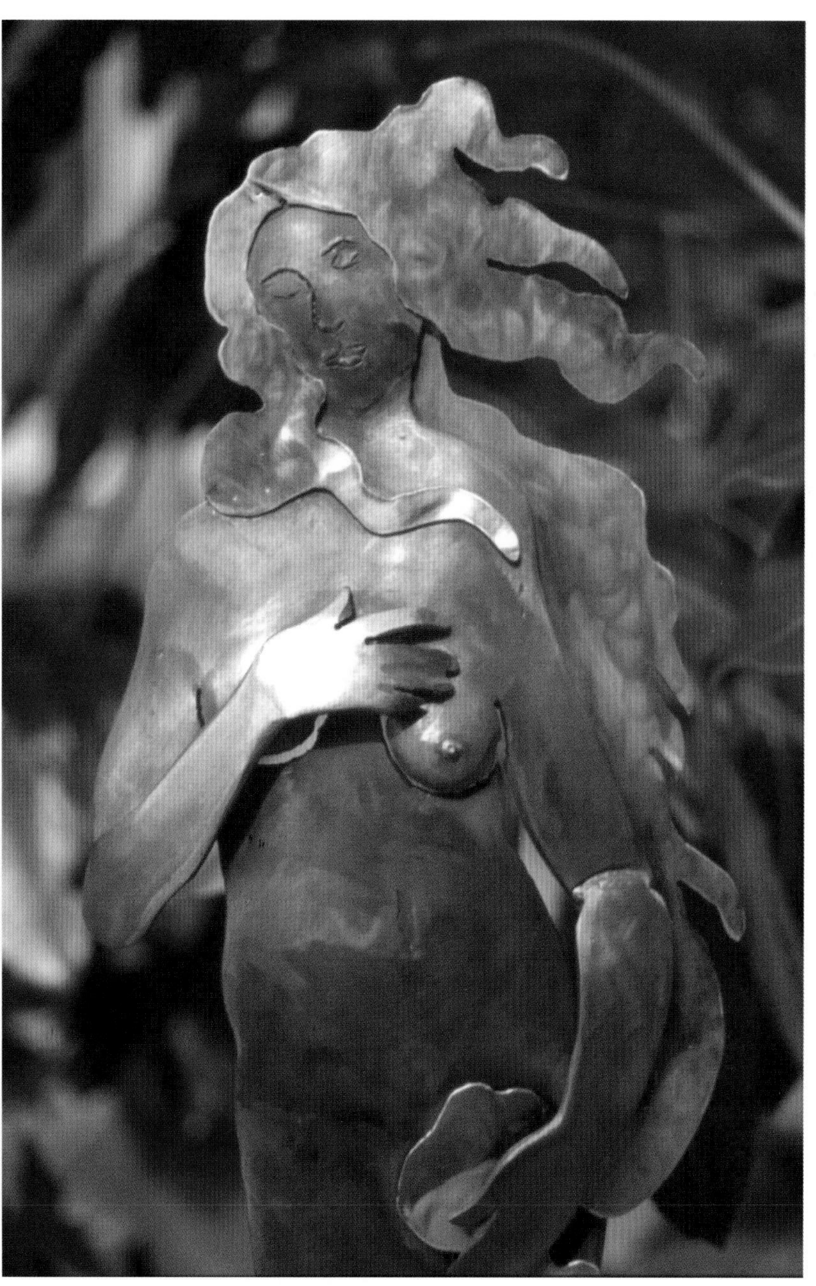

Marvin Tadlock, *Ode to Botticelli.* Cut and hammered steel, 30″x10″x9″ (76.2cm x 25.4cm x 22.9cm).

GAS WELDING
by Norman D. Holen

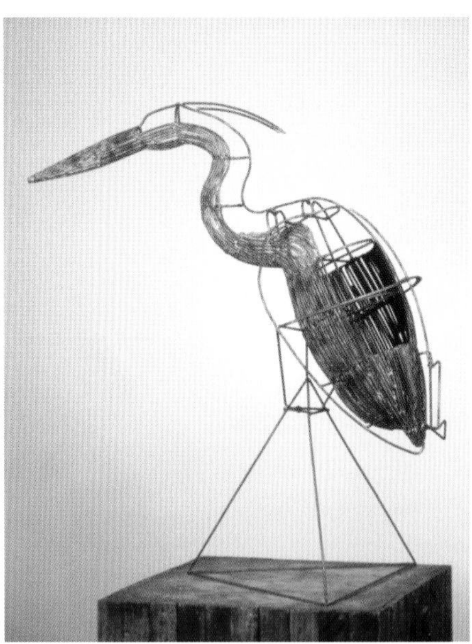

Metal is added in a uniform pattern.

The armature is strengthened to accommodate the new weight.

He begins his gas welding with a carefully designed steel armature.

Norman D. Holen, *Great Blue Heron*. Welded steel, 20¾″x11¾ ″x30½ ″ (52.7cm x 29.8cm x 77cm). Photographer: Peter Lee.

Oxygen A gas that forms 21% of the atmosphere. It is used to support combustion, especially in oxyacetylene welding and cutting. *See* ***Welding; Cutting; Oxyacetylene***.

Oxygen regulator A valve that automatically reduces oxygen tank pressure and keeps it in constant flow to the torch for oxyacetylene welding and cutting. *See* ***Welding; Cutting; Oxyacetylene***.

Ozark stone A sharpening stone of extremely dense mass. It is found in the southern part of the United States.

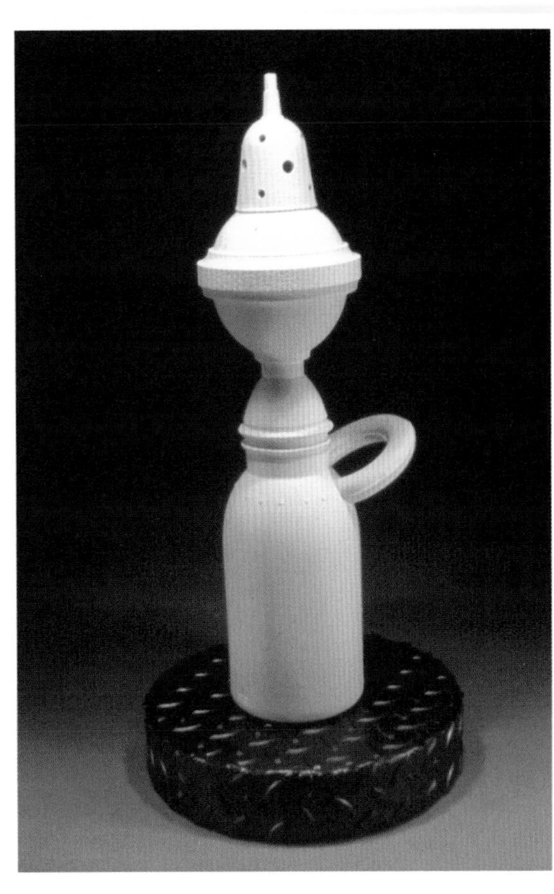

Von Venhuizen
Got Milk?
Ceramic, metal, 10"x10"x10" (25.4cm x 25.4cm x 25.4cm).

Floyd Shaman, *Our Lady of the Bunnies.* Polychromed laminated wood, 4'9" (1.45m) tall.

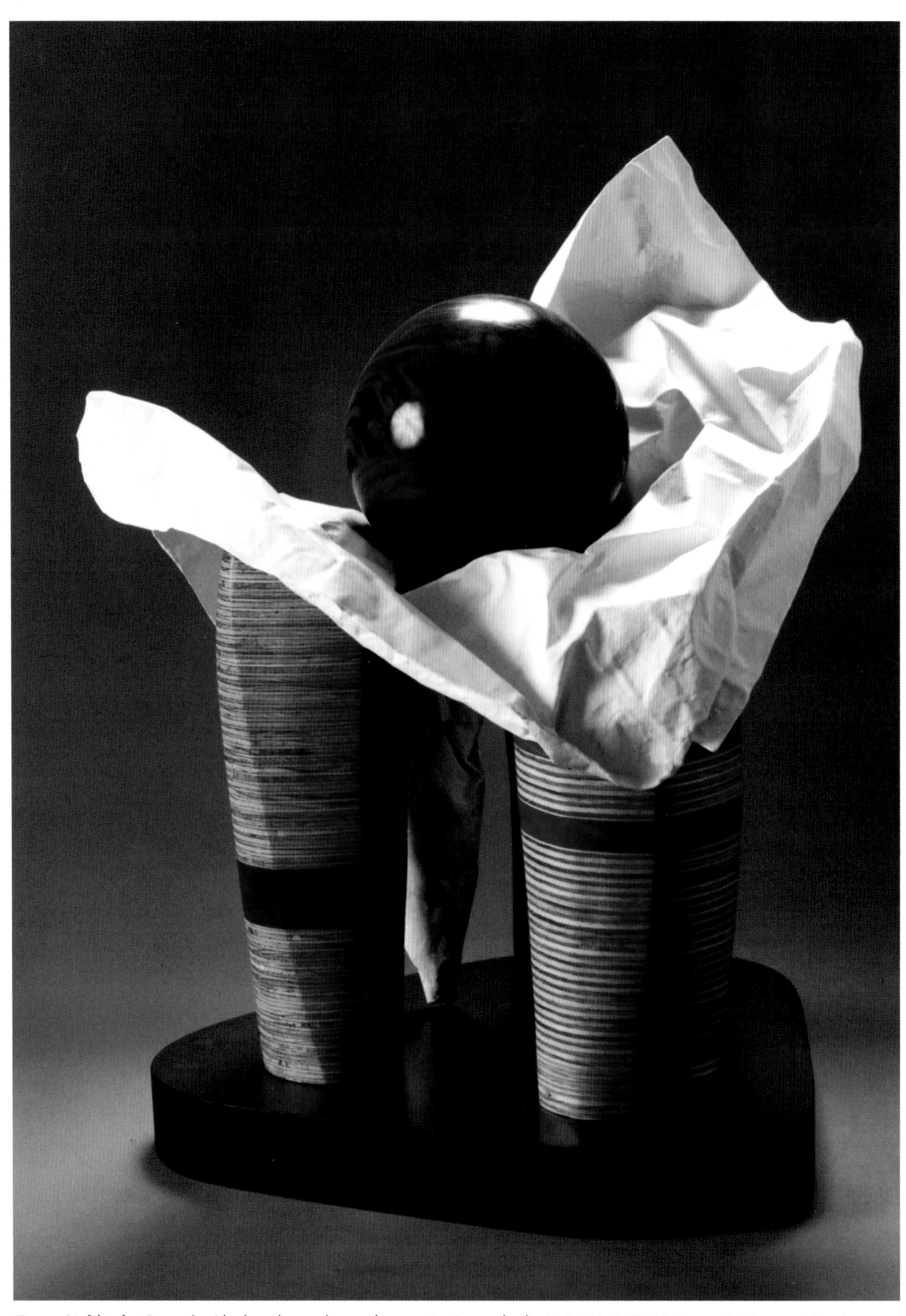

Dawn Stubitsch, *Cascade*. Black walnut, plywood, paper/resin, padouk, 20″x20″x26″ (50.8cm x 50.8cm x 66cm).

P

Packing Improving high-carbon steel by compressing it. This is accomplished by bringing the steel to a cherry red heat and then striking it with substantial hammer blows.

Padak (padouk) Asian tree with reddish brown wood and darker striped layers or grain. *See* ***Wood*** *(chart)*.

Paddle A wood slab with a handle to pat or paddle clay into shape. Used with a ceramic anvil (round stone or wood, for example), the paddle forces pressure on the clay wall that may have a ceramic anvil (interior round stone or wood, for example) pressed against it to form the desired shape. It is also a term for a flat block of wood with a handle used to shape (flatten) molten glass.

Paint A finely ground pigment (color) blended with a liquid medium for easy distribution and adhesion to a surface. It is designed for decoration and/or surface protection.

Pantograph A tool that assists in enlarging or reducing sculpture. The best known pantograph is a point or pointing machine. *See* ***Pointer***.

Paper A material made from the pulp of plants. In sculpture, it is usually pressed into a mold cavity to achieve a casting, though sometimes it is formed into sheets. Paper is lightweight, easy to handle, and if properly sealed can hold over a long period of time. The materials are easily acquired, and the process is not difficult. While molding is not difficult, placing paper over armatures requires more complex or intricate designs, especially if the armature is to be a large one. Paper can support little of its own weight without molding or an armature. In the wet working stage, it is very pliable and yields to almost any shape. However, when dry, the paper may be bendable but not truly flexible. Once a bend causes a crease, the paper will no longer be self-supporting. *See* ***Papier machè; Paper casting; Paper lamination***.

Paper casting Press molding with paper pulp as the casting material. Various pulps are used, including cotton for strength and natural found plant fiber for texture. Pulp is the substance evolved from heating (pulverizing) cloth or plant fibers. It is cellulose matter (sometimes paper, wood or cloth) ground into a state useful for paper manufacture.

Yasue Sakoaka, *Installation NCB*. Paper, wood, fiber, 35'x50'x12' (10.68m x 15.25m x 3.66m). Photographer: Allan Zak.

Technique

The pulp process requires the paper to be torn or fragmented into small pieces, soaked in water to form a mash, paste or pulpy mass. If a small mixer, such as a food blender, is used, the paper should be torn into small pieces and soaked for at least 24 hours before use. For larger amounts, a commercially made Hollander paper beater, or a clay or dough mixer, can be used with coarser papers, such as machine shredded office paper. (Even a washing machine can be used, but paper can get trapped and clo the machine.)

Still, the paper needs a good soaking period, even up to a week. As the soaked paper is added to the mixer, a binder is added, such as wheat paste. If the work is to b small, white carpenter's glue can be added for additional strength. Bleach can be added to avoid fermentation as the mix dries. Mixes in large machines may have the binder added prior to the mix for easier and better blending. *See* ***Hollander paper beater***.

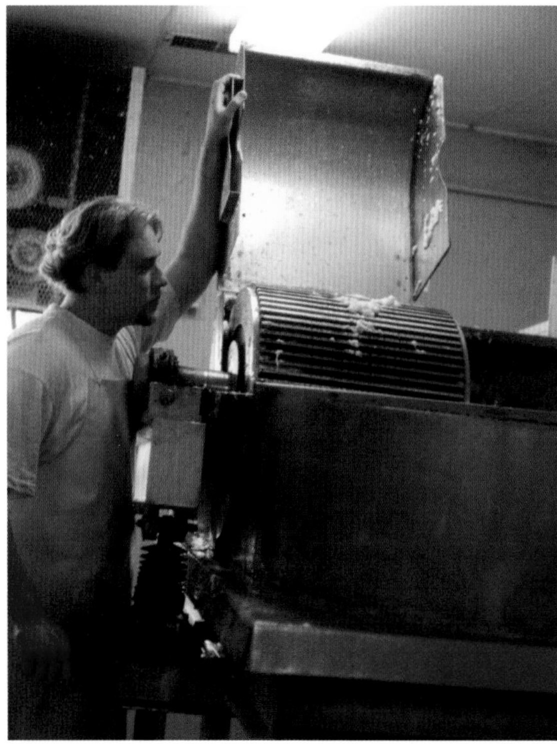

PAPER MAKING

at Twinrocker, Brookston, Indiana

Travis Becker prepares the Hollander paper beater for pulp.

Kathryn Clark dips the screen mold into a vat of prepared pulp to form a sheet.

The deckle is removed.

The pulp clings to the screen as it is raised and drained.

The paper is couched onto felt.

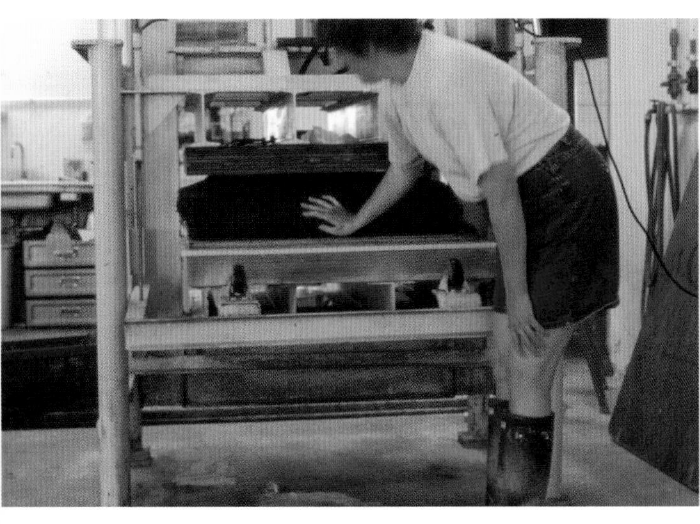

A hydraulic press is used to squeeze out the water.

The paper is removed from the press.

The paper is hung on a special rack at **Twinrocker** to complete the drying.

Kathryn Clark, *Cube Visiting Double Page Spread*, Diptych. Unique hand-made paper, color lamination and collage, 48″x72″ (121.9cm x 182.9cm).

The type of mold is almost unlimited from a found object to a hard rubber mold. It can be made up of virtually any article that can be held firmly enough to place the paper on, including wood, glass, plastic, steel, firm latex, modeling clay and, the most obvious, plaster. Epoxy or hard rubber furnish a good surface, especially if an edition or repeated number of castings are made. Whatever is used, the mold must be sealed without a porous surface and not effected by water. Two coats of a shellac will suffice for most objects. Though silicone molds do not need a release agent, other materials need one that will not react with the paper. Wax is preferred. Plaster must be dry, coated and waxed. The paper pulp completely dries in or on the mold to form the shape. It can be added piecemeal by hand or carefully screened and added in sheets for the finest surface.

Methylcellulos (CMC) is a **binder** combined with paper tears or pulp. It is commonly found in wallpaper pastes. Liquid pulp obtained commercially already has CMC blended into it. Since the manufacturer tightly packs it for shipping, water must be added to form a usable substance. The mixing, or blending, needs to be thorough enough to form a smooth liquid without any unevenness or pulp lumps.

A **screen mold** is a frame encasing a fine screen. When the paper pulp is gathered on top of the screen, the water empties through the mesh leaving a layer or sheet of pulp. The screen is made of fiberglass, brass or other material that does not readily react with water. The frame is generally made of wood. On the flat side, a deckle or open frame (usually wood) sits in place near the outer edges to keep the pulp from flowing out. It canals the pulp and then is removed, leaving a layer or sheet of pulp.

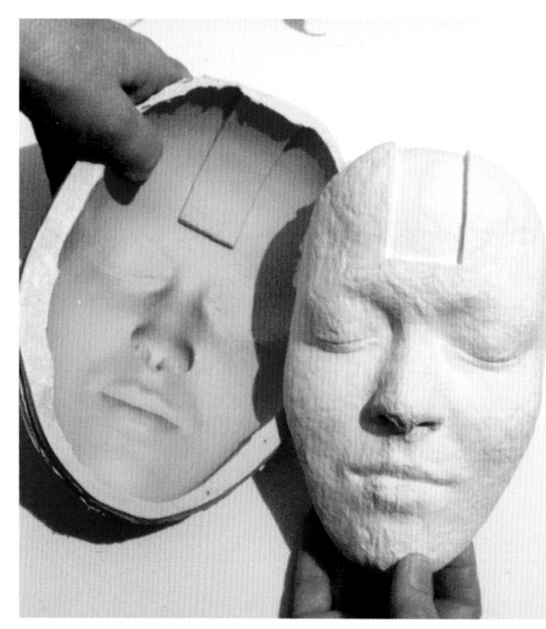

A pressed pulp mask from a flexible silicone mold by **Elisha Gold**.

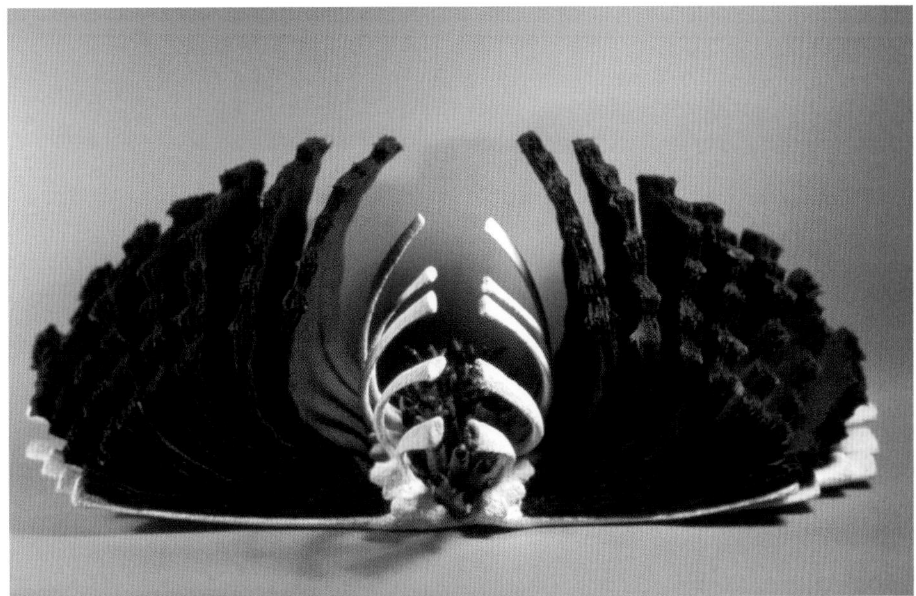

Dianne L. Reeves, *Seizing Penumbra*. Handmade dyed abaca paper, cow rib bones, mixed bones, 12½"x30"x15" (31.8cm x 76.2cm x 38.1cm).

Couching describes removing the pulp sheet and placing it onto a surface of absorbent fabric to eliminate more moisture. The pulp can be couched and immediately laid into the mold, or it can be set into the mold by hand, a piece at a time. The couched sheet provides an even layer of pulp that is especially useful for relief or shallow areas without undercut problems. This sheet is applied in either one large layer to cover an entire relief or in torn parts that overlap to achieve the shape.

Couching helps the paper fibers to line up forming a stronger sculpture than the addition of pulp by hand. Depending on the size of the sculpture, several layers may be needed, each overlapping previous joints. After the paper has been inserted into the mold, it must be pressed into place. This can be done with the fingers, though a strong, stiff, motor parts brush, sponge or other device can help. Sometimes the sculptor places wads of pulp onto the surface and presses them into the desired shape with sponges or absorbent papers. They are overlapped to achieve the shape.

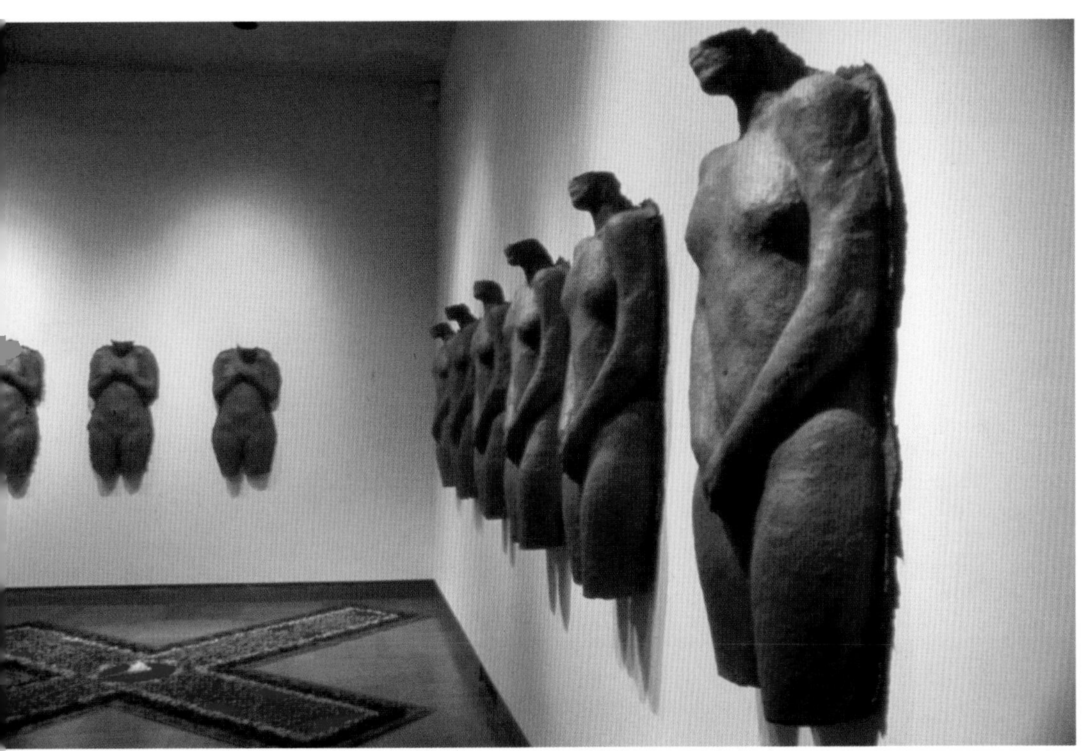

Virginia Maksymowicz, *Lily of the Mohawks* (detail). Paper, clay, acrylic, Tyvek, silk flower and petals, perfume, 20'x20'x20' (6.1m x 6.1m x 6.1m). Mitchell Museum, Mt. Vernon, Illinois.

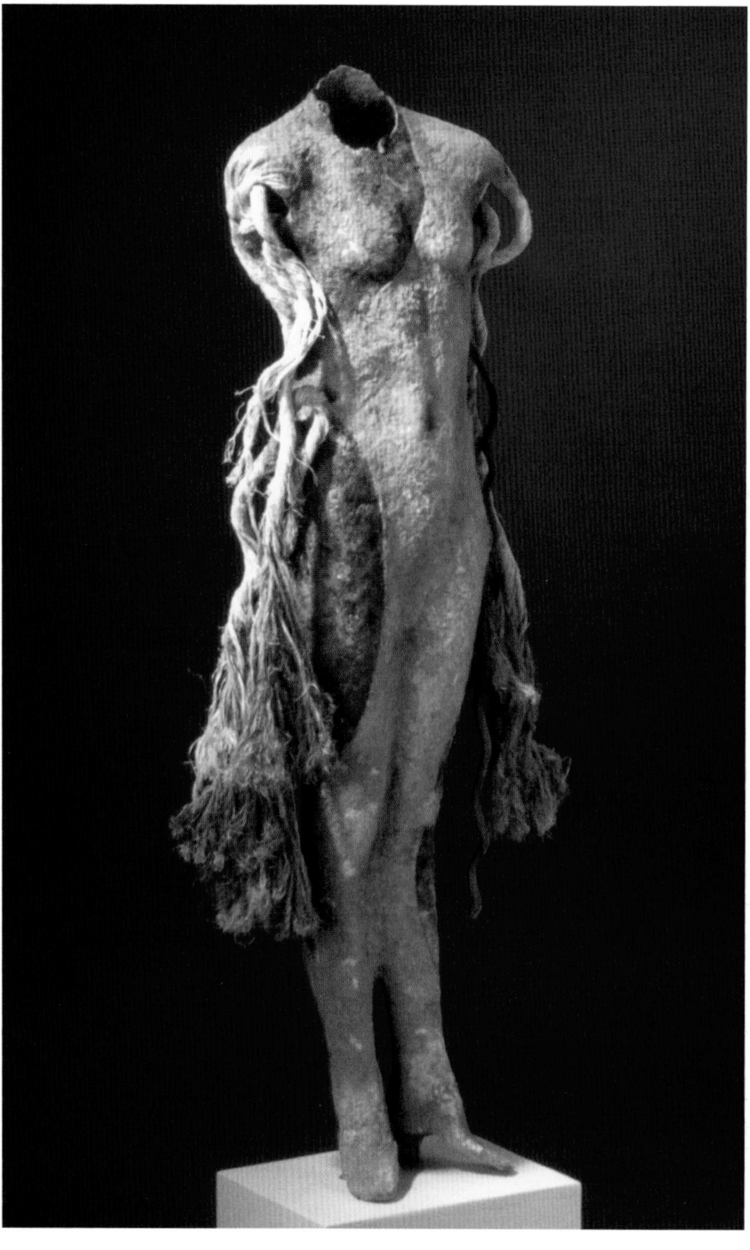

Kathleen Girdler Engler, *Kore II*. Scorched pulp, rope, vine, gesso, pigment, 79″x18″x14″ (200.66cm x 45.72cm x 35.56cm).

To avoid warps, some type of hold-ing device must be used to ensure the paper will retain its shape until it is dry.Air must circulate to the paper for it to thoroughly dry and to prevent mildew. A bed of rust resistant nails freely hanging through a screen mesh down onto the paper can be used to help hold the paper in place. Even small rust resistant chains can be placed over the paper to hold it in place and yet allow air to circulate. *See* ***Papier machè***; ***Paper lamination***; ***Paper***.

Paper lamination Applying paper in laminations over an armature or mold to form a sculpture. Traditional method of lamination, sometimes called the strip method, is the most common method of papier machè. Tears of paper, usually newspaper, are submerged into a container of binder, drained or wiped of excess liquid between the fingers, then applied in lamination, one on top of the other, crisscrossing in even layers to form a gradual buildup for strength, though the irregular edges actually provide strength. Placed on an armature or in a mold, this process affords good strength but must completely dry before moving.

Paper can be torn in different directions, though newspaper comes from a large roll. The grain, or direction of the fiber, is with the long direction of the roll. This means that the paper will tear more predictably and evenly with the direction of the grain, or up and down the pages, not across.

Sylvia Wald, *East Village, New York*. Japanese paper, cord, paint. Photographer: D. James Dee.

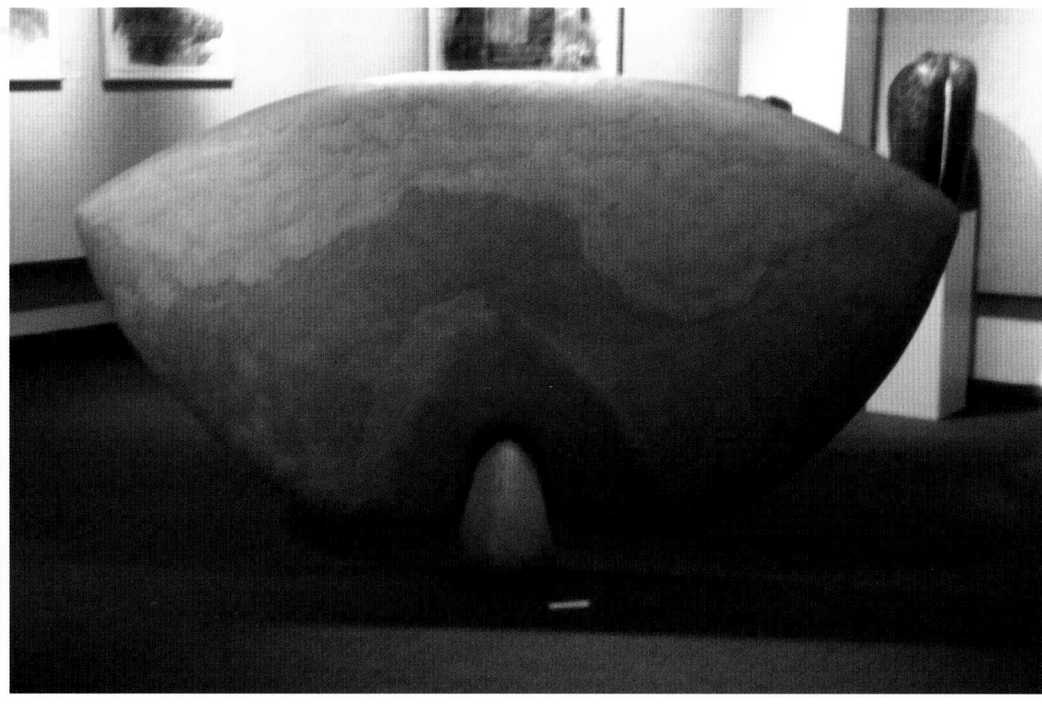

Chryl L. Savoy, *Cuerpo y Alma*. Polystyrene and paper compound, 60″x96″x12″ (152.4cm x 243.8cm x 30.5cm).

Technique

Lamination can be completed with water soluble soaking binders or contact cements. However, the first layer of paper should be freshly soaked in water without a binder. This will create a stronger surface that will resist adhering to the mold surface. Any trapped air bubbles between the layers should be wiped over to eliminate them. The number of layers depends on the size and use. If it is going to be thicker, then it is good to use several layers. It should be allowed to dry out as additional layers are added. This helps with drying warpage, thus controlling the form.

Contact machè lamination is paper that has an adhesive applied to hold the strips or tears of paper in place as layers are applied. The contact cement, when dry, will immediately bond upon contact with another strip or tear of the same coating. This approach of laminating has a more immediate effect, since the work does not need a total drying time to finalize. Contact glues dry in 20 to 30 minutes and require the sculptor to use them within a short timeframe, or the contact properties will not work. Though some are flammable, many are non-flammable and use water for thinning.

Armatures for paper lamination are designed for the specific size and application. They can range from a balloon to a huge wooden and chicken wire construction. Many sculptors use Styrofoam™, crushed paper, cardboard or even lightweight found objects. The armature may be a construction of many of these materials on one piece. A larger armature may be built out of chicken wire but have parts with Styrofoam™ or even smaller parts made from a smaller, mesh screen wire for finer detail in certain areas. There are no rules except for strength and weight. Once the papier machè is in place and dry, the armature may not be necessary and can be removed. To use paper as an armature material itself, quickly build up a solid lightweight shape to obtain volume for other materials. *See **Paper molding**; **Papier machè**; **Paper**.*

Various **binders** can be used to keep the form together. Sifted flour is easily mixed with water to form a simple paste, though it cannot be stored without becoming rancid. It is mixed into water to form a creamy-like paste. Wheat paste is also mixed into water until it forms a thickened cream. It is smoother than flour, and a mixture can be kept in use for a longer period of time without spoiling. Methylcellulose is mixed into water to form an easy-to-use, wheat paste gelatin-like mix. It only takes an ounce per gallon of water. It does not leave a noticeable coating and is the easiest to use. Carpenter's white glue blended with water also works especially well for strength and toughness. The mix can vary, but a one-to-one (1:1) ratio works well. However, it is expensive.

Papier machè (paper machè) It appears to have come from a French term for chewed paper, though it may also have evolved from an English verb meaning to mash. Papier machè is accomplished by one of two processes: lamination or pulp. Layers less than one-eighth inch (0.318cm) are easily achieved by lamination, but the pulp method is usually around one-fourth inch (0.635cm). If the thickness is over one-fourth inch (0.635cm), drying and molding become a problem. After these new forms are dry, they are frequently painted. Bright colors are a favorite. Finished forms are used for Mardi Grás and carnival masks, decorations, the piñatas found in Mexico, small Oriental boxes, jewelry and sculpture. Almost any kind of sculptural shape can be made with papier machè.

Patricia L. Verani, *Skateboarder*. Paper sculpture, 45″x14″x17″ (114.3cm x 35.6cm x 43.2cm).

Papier machè requires binders. The soaking binder process uses different papers, such as newspaper, magazines, computer printout paper, tissue or a heavier brown paper, such as brown paper bags. The binders are common materials such as flour, white glue, wheat paste, methylcellulose or readily mixed wallpaper paste. Each ingredient, though similar, works slightly differently. Though new binders are available that resist moisture and mildew, many artists, especially in schools, still prefer to use wheat binders because of the availability and freedom from toxic problems associated with the quicker binders. However, insects become a problem because of the food attraction of some binders.

If the sculptor desires to use tissue (toilet) paper or paper towels, it is not necessary to blend the paper, but a binder does need to be added. Tissue papers are easily formed but notoriously weak. If they are used, they are placed over a heavier paper or a stronger paper is used over them.

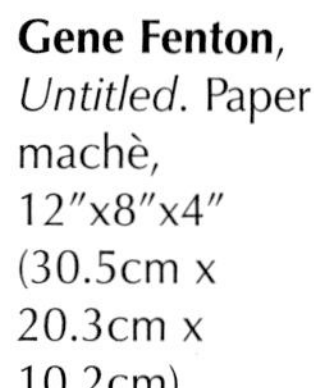

Gene Fenton, *Untitled*. Paper machè, 12″x8″x4″ (30.5cm x 20.3cm x 10.2cm)

When the mix is completed, the sculptor may choose to squeeze out some of the moisture and place the pulp directly on the armature. Some sculptors form sheets and then apply them to a mold. The pulp needs to be thin enough to dry without fermentation and within a reasonable working time. Some mild heat can be used with a hair dryer or increased room temperature. *See* ***Paper; Paper casting; Paper lamination***.

Particle board is placed in layers to create **Jerry Monteith's** *Quatrefoil.*

Jerry Monteith, *Quatrefoil.* Particle board, 6′8″x11′4″x11′x 4″ (2m x 3.5m x 3.5m).

Paraffin wax A semitransparent or white refined inert waxy product of petroleum that is often used for candles. In sculpture, microcrystalline waxes are preferred. *See* ***Microcrystalline wax***.

Parent Metal The major metal that is being worked. *See* ***Base metal***.

Particle board Pressed wood and chipboard are hard, flat sheet products formed under pressure from wood chips, sawdust or particles. They are in four by eight foot (1.22m x 2.44m) construction sizes with varying thicknesses. These products seldom hold up under wet moisture conditions. Very absorbent, the pressed wood swells and remains swollen when it comes in contact with water. *See* ***Masonite™; Wood***.

Floyd D. Shaman, *Gabriel.* Wood, wood products, found objects, 4′10″ (1.5m) tall.

Parting agent A substance (release agent) applied to material that is to be molded or cast to allow the mold or casting to be easily removed. The term can be applied to a variety of agents from silicone spray to talc powder. *See **Release agent**; **Release agent** (chart).*

Parting line The seam, ridge or indentation remaining in the location where mold pieces were separated. *See **Mold making**.*

Parting tool A "V" tool with a wooden handle that is mallet driven to cut grooves or deep ridges into wood sculpture. It may be used on soft stone as well. *See **Wood carving tool** (chart).*

Pass One continuous weld, such as the first "pass." The word is also used to refer to the metal deposit left as a result of this one continuous weld. *See **Welding**.*

Paste A glue that is soft and in thick, syrupy form. *See **Glue** (chart).*

Patching wax A soft, pliable wax with a texture of thick petroleum jelly. It is used to repair small indentations on waxes prior to investment. *See **Wax**; **Disclosing wax**.*

Patina The visible color or skin of coloring that forms on a surface as a result of handling, weathering, heat, chemical placement or superficially adding dyes or pigments. A good patina is utilized to preserve, add color, create texture and depth, while highlighting key areas of the form, and sometimes unifying the sculpture's surface. The actual environment, sea level, altitude, rain frequency, dryness, and manmade pollution greatly affect patina patterns or change patinas in time. The term is commonly used to deal with the surface color of all metals; however, patina is almost synonymous with bronze. The high copper content of bronze leads to a multitude of surface colors. *See **Patina** (chart).*

Glenna Goodacre, *The Irish Memorial*. Cast bronze, 11½′x35′ (3.5m x 10.7m). Photographer: Marcia Ward.

COLORFUL PATINAS
by Joseph Rotella

Joseph Rotella, *The Dreamer*. Cast bronze, patina, 25"x5" (635cm x 12.7cm).

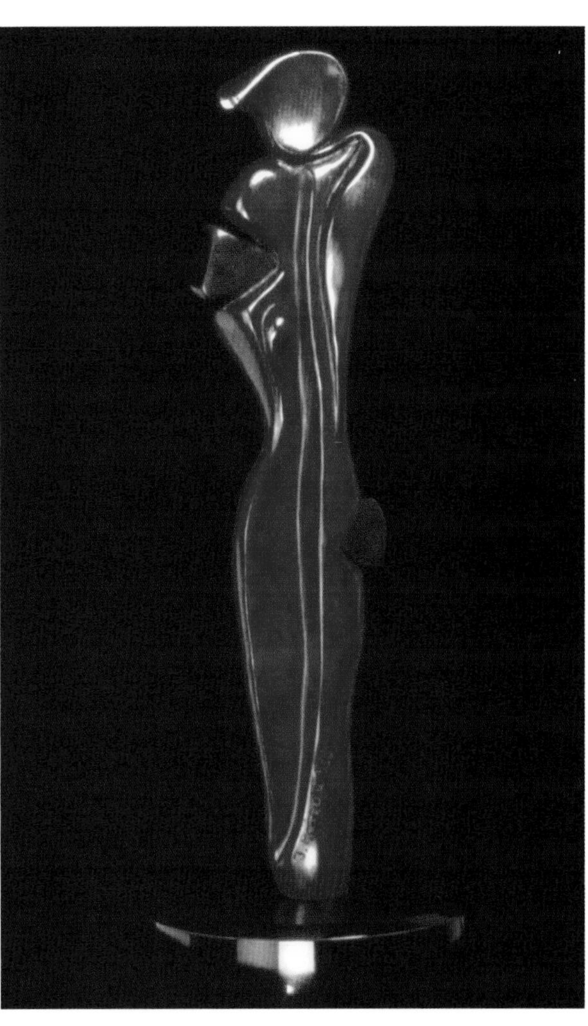

Joseph Rotella, *The Lady*. Cast bronze, patina, 19″x4″ (48.3cm x 10.2cm).

Joseph Rotella, *Venus Rising*. Cast bronze, patina, 36″x12″ (91.4cm x 30.5cm).

Patination (process) The manner in which the patina is formed. It can be brought about naturally over a period of time as the object weathers, or it can be manmade by controlling the chemical and atmospheric conditions to hasten the process and determine the color. Other than specific chemicals, heat is the primary method used to hasten the process. Improperly done, a patina can disrupt and ruin the sculpture's appearance.

The patination of bronze is determined by several things, but the metal elements have primary importance. These include copper, tin, zinc, nickel and sometimes silicon in various proportions. Older bronzes have more zinc, tin and lead in them and though they readily take patinas, they are not favored because of the lead content. When using a published patina formula, it is necessary that it be formulated for silicon bronze, or the user may need to be prepared for unexpected results.

Patina processes are affected by five components:

1) The **metal** itself. A greater volume of copper in the metal results in a greater variety of colors that tend to adhere better. More copper content means that chemicals will predictably react without difficulty. Adding a larger amount of tin, zinc or silicon can greatly alter the color.

Thomas D. Gipe, *Up North with Loon and Fish*. Silicon bronze, welded steel, cast bronze, 3″x5″x11″ (7.6cm x 12.7cm x 27.9cm).

2) The **temperature**. Heat hastens the chemical process. Some chemicals will not properly respond without heat. Heat binds the patinas better, and the colors are obtained faster. However, too much heat can cause a drastic change in color and texture.

3) The **application methods and tools**. The sculpture can be left untouched for natural forces to work, but it is slow. The sculpture can be placed into a fuming container to receive the patina strictly from fumes. Smaller sculptures can be placed into a chemical bath. However, most sculptures are now either brushed or sprayed with a patina. Small sculptures are sprayed with a handheld spray bottle while large works may be sprayed with a paint sprayer. Sponges and brushes are also used.

4) **Preparing the metal**. If the metal is not clean, especially free of oil or wax, the patina will not adhere or will be spotty in adhesion and color. Even a fingerprint can disrupt an otherwise clean surface. All brushes need to be clean as well. If the bronze surface is exceedingly smooth, beyond 400 grit, the patina may flake off, resulting in an uneven surface color. Clean surfaces with more open pores result in a stronger grip of the patinas, as well as a better variety of colors.

5) The **chemicals** or ingredients used to induce the color. Some are true and some are false. True chemicals react with the bronze to create a new color and become part of the metal itself. False substances are added to the surface to build up a color or pigment.

Technique: Completing a Patina

Preparing the surface

A sandblasted surface will result in better adhesion since the metal pores need to be open to receive patinas. However, heavily blasted surfaces or surfaces blasted with large grits cause problems. Glass beads that are 180 grit serve as sandblast for a good number of cleaning jobs prior to patina application. Air pressure of 90 psi (620kPa) or below will result in less damage to the surface. Most surfaces are cleaned in a sandblaster cabinet designed to capture and reuse the blast particles.

The sandblaster gun should be in constant movement, never held too closely to the surface, or the surface will become pitted or different in one area. Too hard a blast or too directed a flow will uncover a flaw or gas pocket not otherwise detectable. The air supply needs to be clean and free of oil or water. The grit itself needs constant screening to remove mold particles, as well as blasted surface particles. A work can be re-patinaed by taking it back to the original surface. Simply sandblast the work and start over again.

The two best cleaning solvents prior to patina are: 1) xylol (xylene), which should be carefully handled because of strong toxic vapors and the volatile liquid itself, 2) denatured alcohol, which is safer to use than xylene, but still has many safety precautions. A weaker alcohol, isopropyl alcohol, is readily found in hardware or grocery stores. It requires several rinses to clean and also to ensure all film or residue is completely removed.

Nicole Fall, *Headlong to the Edge*. Cast bronze, patina, 30″x24″x15″ (76.2cm x 61cm x 36.1cm).

Tri-sodium phosphate is sometimes sprayed onto surfaces with a lot of texture and rinsed off. It will clean the surface without destroying the finer textures. A surface that has had an acid bath or "pickling" for cleansing could still have some acid remaining in a gas pocket. Sculptures containing permanent cores should never be placed into an acid bath, since the core material absorbs the acid, only later to slowly release it, destroying a patinaed surface.

Steel wool can be used to highlight a work, but if it is beyond a #1 medium, it may scratch. A grade below #O will have little effect or actually create an artificial sheen. Using steel wool always runs the risk of bits left, causing rust spots and reactions to the surface. *See* ***Steel wool; Scotch Brite***™.

While sandpaper grits of 220 will leave small marks on the sculpture, anything coarser will tend to scratch rather than surface the work. The finest details can be blurred or even destroyed. Grits over 400 will smooth the surface to a point where patinas do not adhere. Buffing compounds should not be used, unless they are water based. They must be carefully cleaned off afterwards. Hard erasures, especially those with a gritty makeup, are good to pick out accents. Wire brushing using a slow RPM wire wheel preferably less than 2500 rpm can help blend the surface, but it may destroy intricate textures on others.

Ingredients (chemicals)

Chemicals obviously determine the outcome. But within the chemical, grades and qualities become important. All types are available from full strength uncontaminated chemicals through the U.S.P. (pharmaceutical) grades to the technical grades, which are the least pure but also the least expensive. To achieve patina consistency from batch to batch, the best grades should be used.

Storage of the chemicals, freshness of mixes and the purity of the water are all factors in achieving a predictable color. Only distilled water can ensure consistent results, especially if the patinas are mixed in different geographical locations. It is best to use small, fresh mixes of chemicals than to mix larger volumes that may weaken prior to use. Small sculptures need less than a cup of mix; however, to keep consistency in mixes the same size, batch container and chemical amounts need to be used.

Sarah Sweetwater oven warms bronzes for patination.

Sarah Sweetwater, *Sea Goddess*. Patinaed bronze, 23″x27″x13″ (58.4cm x 68.6cm x 33cm).

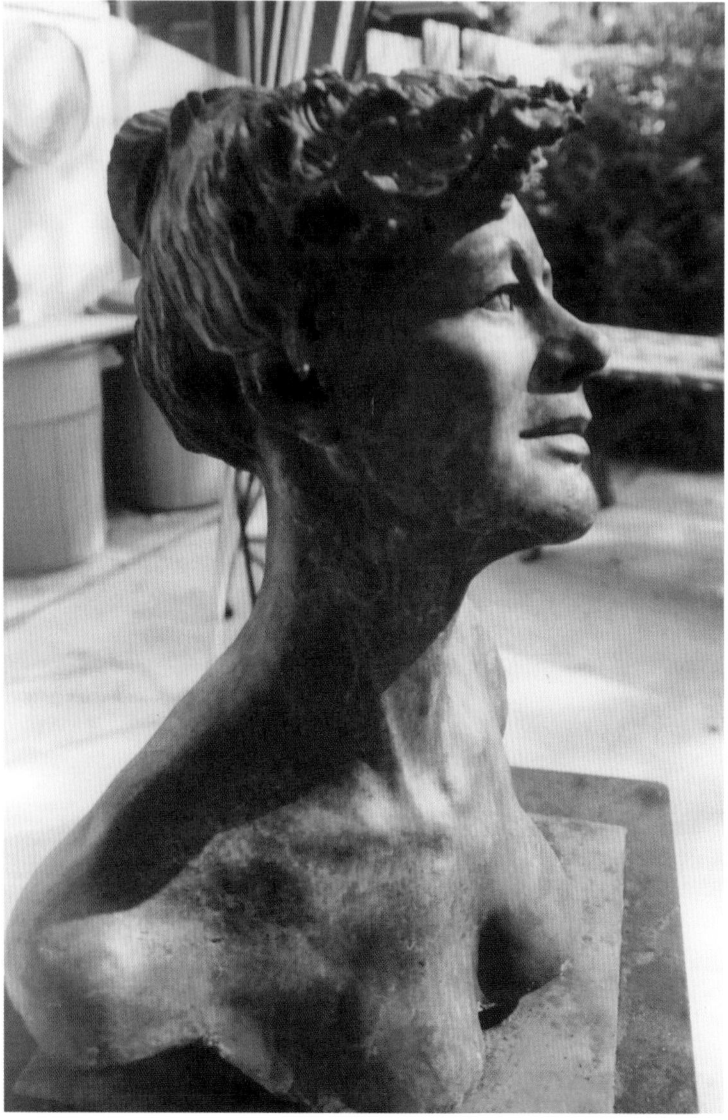

Chemicals come in solids as well as liquids. Plastic measuring spoons are good measuring devices, as well as plastic or glass measuring cups. Though mixing and applying patinas can be approached from a scientific viewpoint, exact results are difficult to duplicate. Experience and experimentation will serve the patinaer best.

Application

Handheld sprayers, such as plastic spray bottles, are desirable, since they can hold small amounts of mix. If larger quantities are needed, stainless steel handheld paint sprayers with a low pressure of not more than 20 psi (138kPa) will work. Small air brush sprayers can be used for fine details, delicate surfaces or extremely small works. However, some patinas cause corrosion damage to metal sprayers.

Brush applications should be completed with natural bristle brushes. Synthetic or nylon brushes will melt if caught in flame or heat, resulting in a coarse texture or even adhesion to the metal surface. Any size of brush can be used, depending upon the sculpture. It is best to keep brushes for each chemical separate and always cleaned to avoid contaminating the chemical or surface.

The base coat or undercoat is the first patina chemical used to achieve a depth to the color. Highlighting is better, and adhesion of later chemicals is improved.

Usually in brown or black tones, the undercoat can be rubbed down, buffed or removed to create a highlight or add additional modeling to the sculpture. Untouched and left in crevices, these areas can add greater depth to the sculpture. However, a base coat may not be used if the natural bronze color is desired.

Base coats must be receptive for future coats of chemicals. Transparent patinas result when a transparent chemical is used in layers over a base coat. It is similar to a glazed painting in that the top, more translucent or transparent coat allows the base coat to enhance or add depth to the additional coats. This layering of patina allows light to penetrate more deeply and disperse in glimmering light. Thin layers are best if several layers are to be used.

The chemicals react differently to heat, surface and mixing. Not all penetrate the surface. Methods of application vary, depending on the chemical. Some are more frail, toxic, opaque or transparent. The student patinaer should experiment but with an understanding of the individual chemicals. It is better to apply patinas in weaker solutions for more control over the values.

Multi-colored sculptures are possible if the individual chemicals are carefully applied, usually by brush. Heat can be localized or cold patinas can be applied. Multicolored bronzes depend strictly on the sculptor's idea of a finish; however, hues and tints seem preferable to full, bright colors on the same work.

Heat application

Depending on the chemical and desired color, the surface to be patinaed can be preheated. The hot surface should hiss, sizzle or steam but not ricochet off in balls (too hot). If it is too cold, it will drip or run off with little reaction. The best color of heat for most applications is a straw color on the metal surface.

When applying heat, it should be done as evenly as possible beginning with larger or potentially thicker sections but spreading the heat throughout the bronze, avoiding too much heat on thin or isolated small sections. Slowly heating the bronze will allow a more even heat. The normal heating of bronze first achieves a gold color that turns into a straw yellow hue. If too much heat is applied, an orange color begins that results in a deep maroon with blue-black to follow. After the entire work is heated, re-warm the lower base. *See* ***Patina*** *(chart).*

Heat sources vary, but butane and natural gas are readily available. Perhaps the most important aspect to heating the bronze is the torch tip. It needs to be designed for the heat source involved, as well as the purpose of patination. The heat should spread the flame in a large pattern to cover more surface. A rosebud torch tip with a wider, bushier flame spread is preferred. A kiln or oven can be used for exacting temperatures of smaller works, but handling becomes a problem.

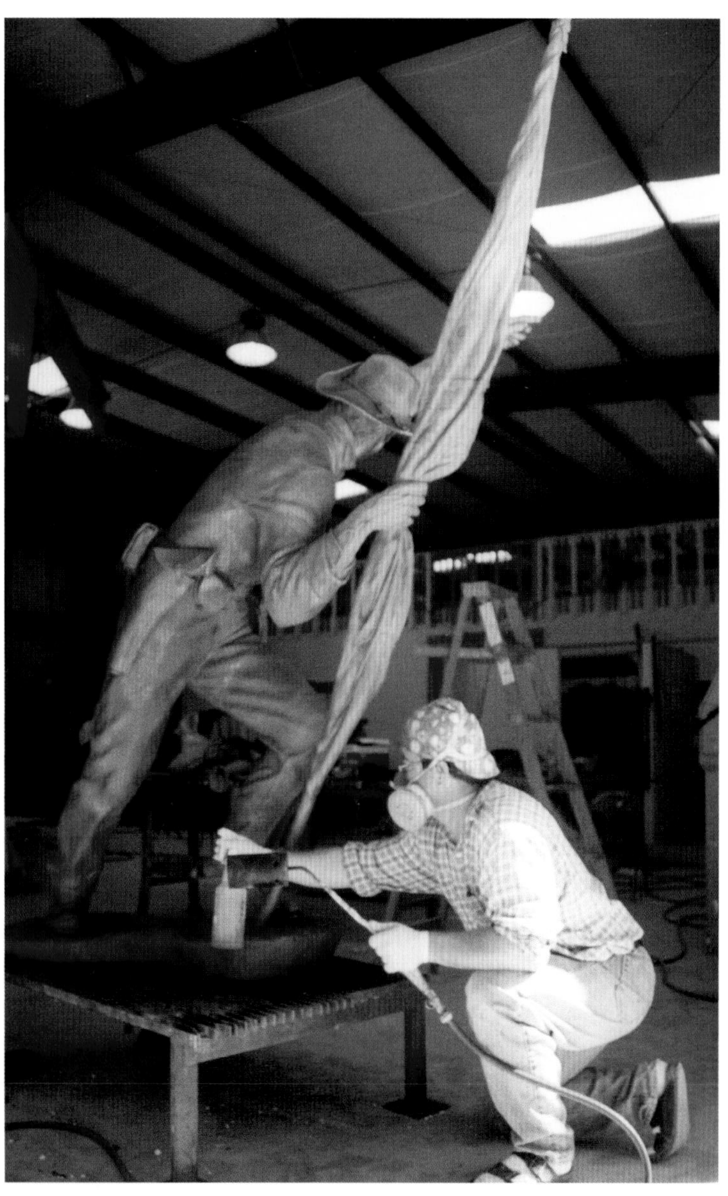

A foundry worker uses a spray bottle to apply patina on **William N. Beckwith's** *Mississippi 11th Monument* at the **Inferno Foundry**, Atlanta, Georgia.

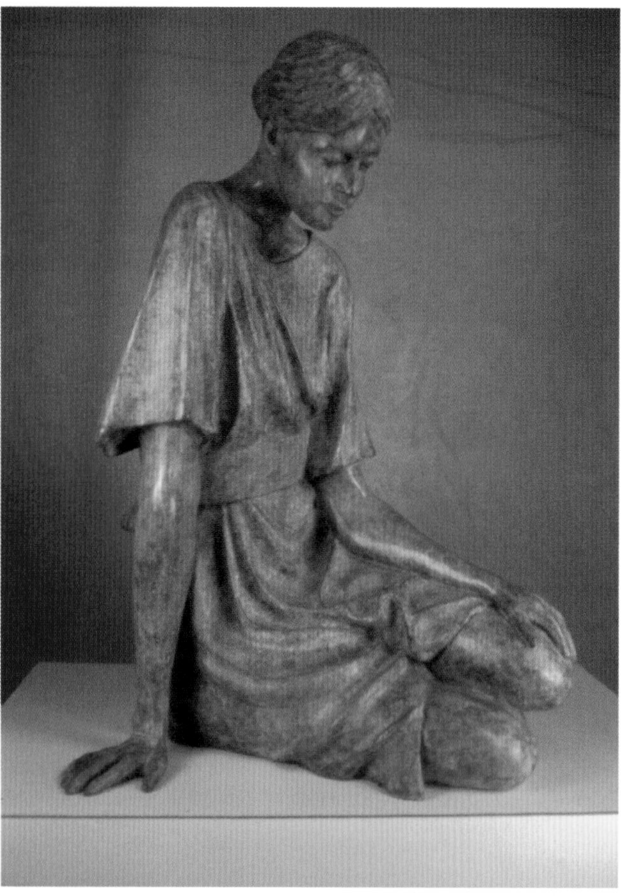

B. P. Barwick, *Musing*. Patinaed bronze, 12″x14″x21″ (30.5cm x 35.6cm x 53.3cm).

A metal turntable is required to achieve an even treatment of heat. The top of the turntable needs to be cleaned or replaced (metal or brick) between each sculpture. Where to begin actual patina application is an individual matter, but it is recommended to start from the base upwards since heat rises.

Basic Chemicals

Liver of sulfur (potash sulfate) is one of the most used base coats available. Known by its pungent sulfur odor, it is secured in small to moderate size yellow chunks and must be kept in an airtight container to avoid dissipation. Liver of sulfur mixes need to be fresh to have maximum effect and predictability. A small chunk about the size of a coin is needed for a quart or liter of water. Since it is difficult to determine the exact strength of a piece of potash, the color of the mixture or reaction on the metal is important until the correct mix is achieved. A yellow mix is usually best for cold surfaces. A lighter color from a more diluted mix is better for heated metals.

Liver of sulfur (brown, gray, black) used on cold bronze covers well. Using a spray bottle, sponge or brush, the surface should receive an even coat and be allowed to set for a few minutes. If it is not dark enough, repeat the process. Afterwards, the coating needs to be neutralized by rinsing it with water. A Scotch Brite™ or steel wool pad can be used to accent or highlight the surface. Liver of sulfur can be applied to a warm or low heated surface, though it darkens quickly. The mix should not be too strong; it is best to use less chemical and more water at the beginning. Do not rub liver of sulfur patina while it is hot or a dark leaded surface will result. While it may be desirable, it is extremely difficult to remove.

Birchwood Casey™ (dark grayish brown to black) is a premixed solution manufactured primarily for antiquing works and as a gun-bluing agent for steel. However, it is common in foundries, since it works exceedingly well on bronze. It is customarily applied cold and results in a metallic black color that adheres even better than liver of sulfur. It must be thoroughly rinsed to neutralize, since it is corrosive and will continue to bite. It is mixed 50/50 with water. After rinsing, it needs to be brushed or rubbed down to eliminate flaking. Brass or nylon brushes can be used on the cold metal. It is difficult to highlight because of its bonding ability.

Andrè Harvey applies patina to *Helen,* a sitting bronze pig.

Cupric nitrate (blue-green) produces better greens when used with hot water. With cold water, better blue-greens are achieved. It should be applied with low heat, or it will turn black. With low heat it is more transparent as high heat causes it to become opaque.

Ferric nitrate (yellow to a reddish or burgundy brown) produces redder browns with stronger solutions. As more heat is applied, it produces a darker red. It is a good transparent patina. It does not adhere well with low heat; it can flake off.

Sodium thiosulfate is a binder. One tablespoon (15mL) in a pint (0.47L) of hot water and one tablespoon (15mL) of ferric nitrate applied to a hot surface will produce a strong dark color, near black, on Everdur™ bronze. In hot water alone, sodium thiosulfate will achieve a warm, but thin, brown. It causes metals to have a sheen or metallic look.

Ferric oxide is blood red but does not adhere well and tends to flake. It should be used in moderation.

Safety is always a concern. While some chemicals can be intermixed, they should be carefully mixed for two reasons: 1) Some are not compatible, resulting in mixtures not holding together and settling out, or 2) together, they may produce toxic, even lethal gases. The sculptor should always consult a chemist prior to intermixing chemicals.

Even seemingly harmless chemicals can cause eye and lung irritation. Avoid ammonias and hard acids. Good ventilation is a necessity, as well as rubber aprons, proper respirators, eye and, sometimes, face protection. However, contact lens wearers could still have problems. Some compounds demand sealed eye protection. The sculptor needs to be familiar with the compounds being used.

A **Shidoni Foundry** worker applying a patina with a pneumatic spray gun. Tesúque, New Mexico.

Since chemicals can enter by osmosis (through the skin), watertight rubber gloves should always be worn when applying wet chemicals. If patinas are regularly applied, an application booth should be used that has a hood vent, rapid fan exhaust and drain system to catch excess chemical spray or clean up fluids. (It is important to keep patination areas clean to avoid contamination from one application to another.)

Fire safety is an obvious necessity. All gas bottles need to be a clear distance away from the work and tightly anchored. Strong fire resistant gloves need to be provided to move warm patinaed works. Clothes should not be synthetic which could melt and stick to the skin if they are overheated. Wool lined gloves provide excellent heat control.

Patina preservation

Incralac™is a lacquer formulated to serve as a final, hard, clear coating for metals, especially polished ones. It can be used as a spray, pour-on or a dip. It tends to dry too fast for a brush-on.

Wax maintains the patina color and provides a sheen if it is buffed, but it also causes it to appear darker. When possible, the sculpture should be warmed to allow greater wax penetration. However, wax mixed with naphtha or other paint thinners can be applied in a thinner state to cool bronzes. Natural brittle brushes should be used. Do not apply to damp or wet surfaces, as well as unusually cold surfaces. Though beeswax thinned with benzene has been used to coat patinas, carnauba wax produced from palm leaves is the easiest to apply and produces long term results. Trewax™, Renaissance™, and Constantine™ waxes are preferred. If necessary, wax can be removed by cleaning with xylol. *See **Silicon bronze**; **Sandblasting**; **Incralac**™; **Patina** (chart); **Wax**.*

PATINA SAMPLES using a Silicon Bronze

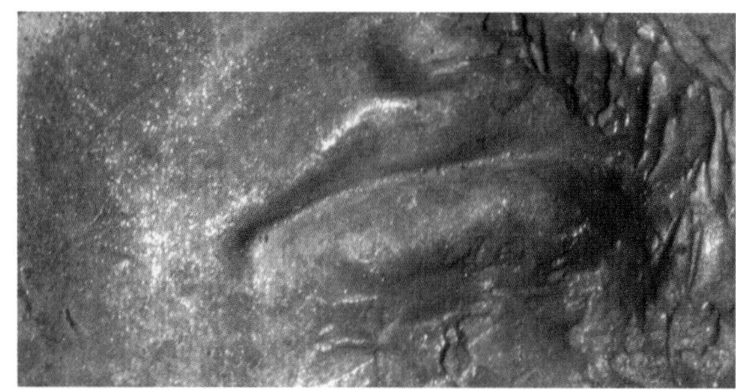

Bronze directly from the mold ready to work.

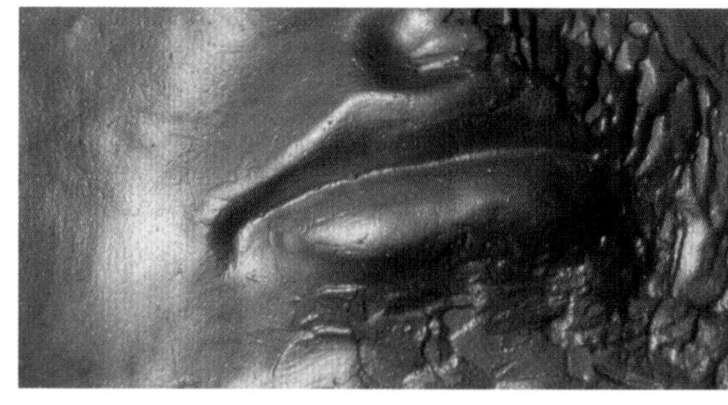

Sandblasted bronze using glass beads.

Wire brushed with a grinder.

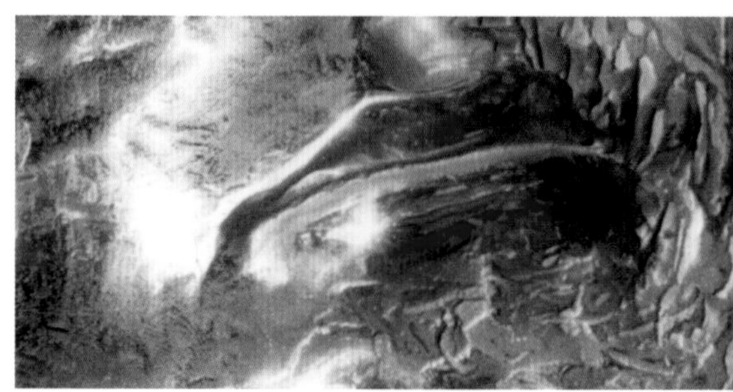

Polished bronze with rubbing compound.

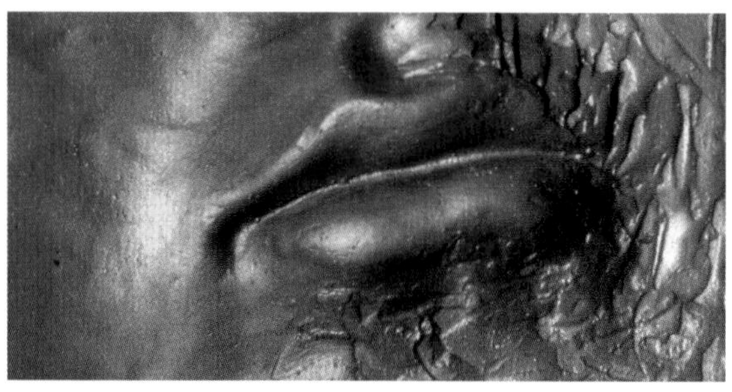

Heating/overheating bronze for patina. The left side is a straw color that is best for patina.

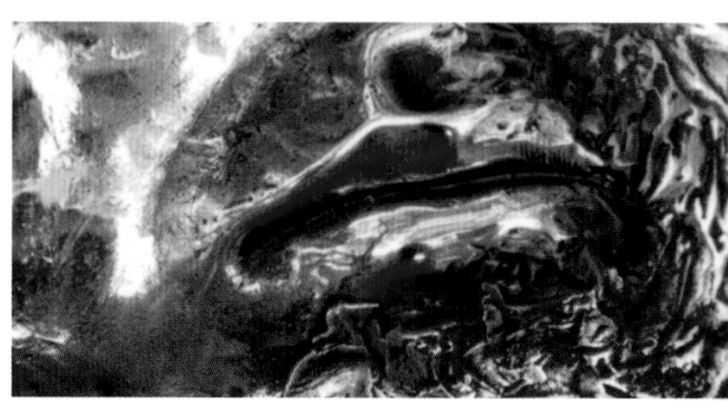

Surface buffed, then Birchwood Casey™ applied to cold bronze, then re-buffed.

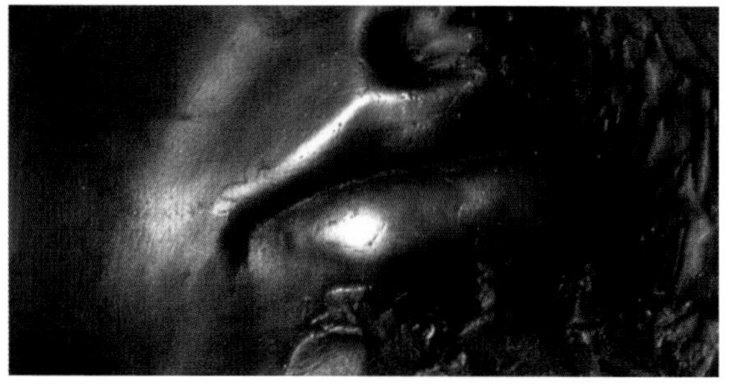

Liver of sulfur applied on cold bronze.

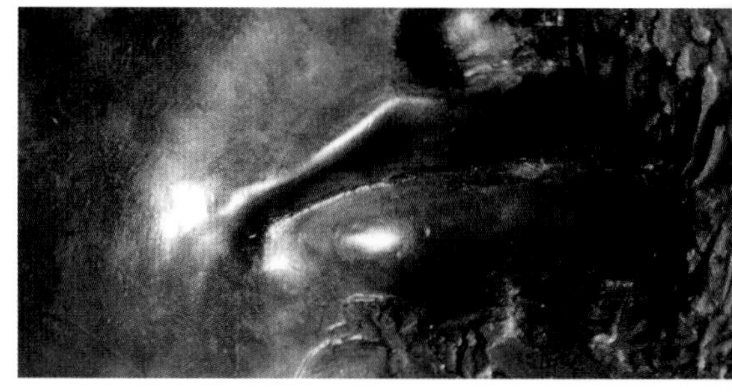

Birchwood Casey™ applied to cold bronze.

All patinas are applied onto hot bronze with a hand sprayer unless otherwise described. All are highlighted with #000 steel wool or ScotchBrite™ unless otherwise noted.

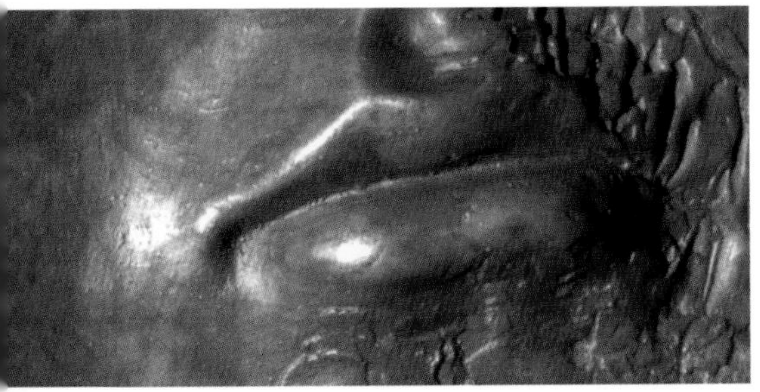

Veak solution of ferric nitrate applied with a brush.

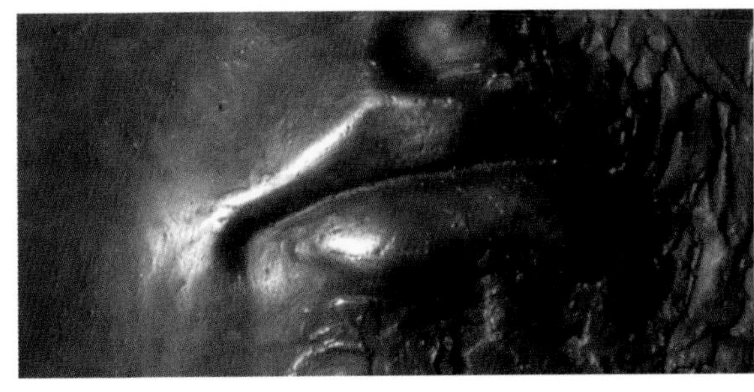

Regular solution of ferric nitrate applied.

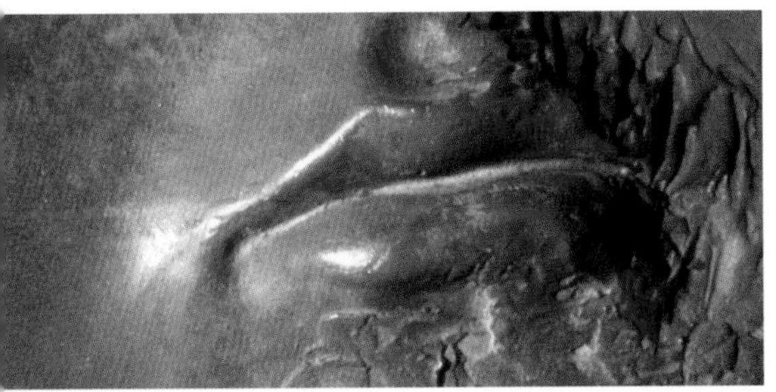

Cupric nitrate applied.

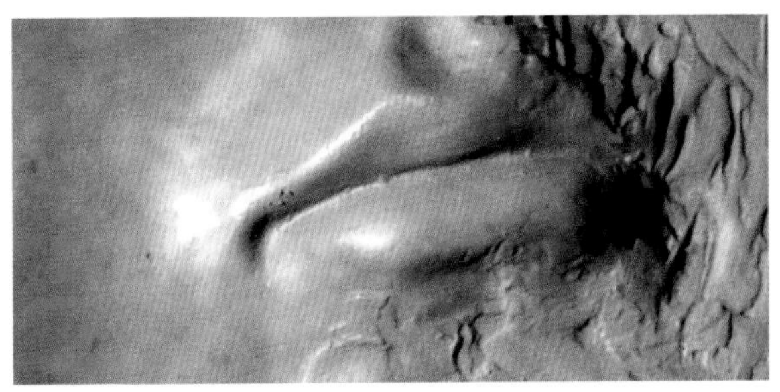

Bismuth nitrate applied with a brush.

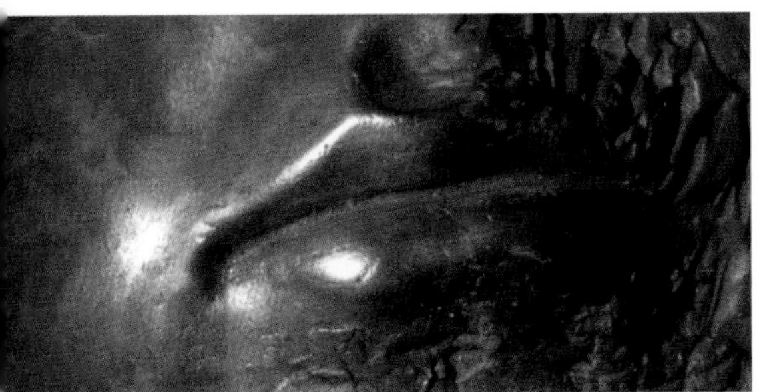

Silver nitrate applied.

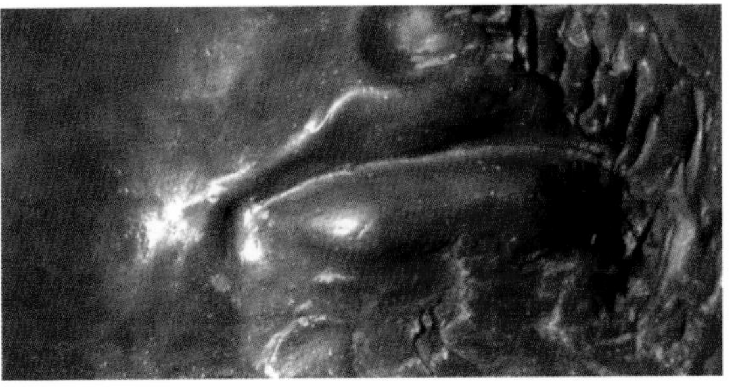

Ferric nitrate applied with a small amount of ferric oxide in the mix.

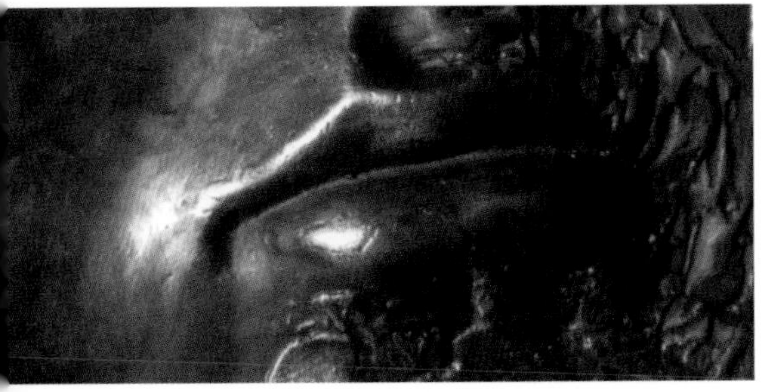

Liver of sulfur applied to a cold bronze, then a top coating of cupric nitrate to a hot surface.

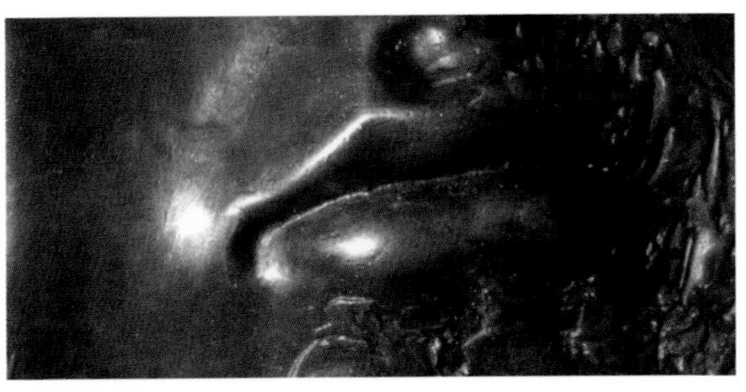

Liver of sulfur applied to a cold bronze, then ferric nitrate applied to a hot surface.

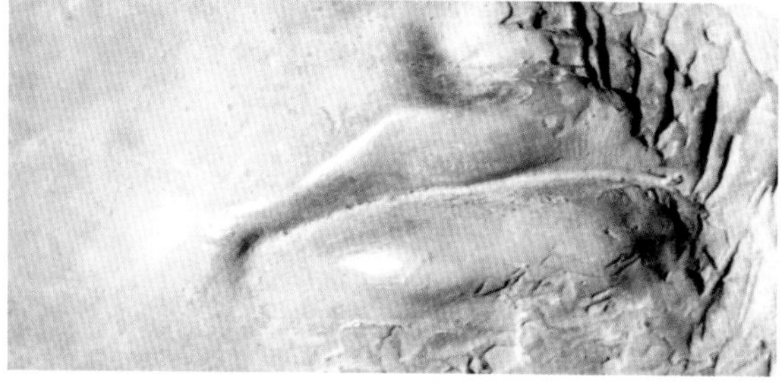

Liver of sulfur applied to a cold bronze, then bismuth nitrate applied to a hot surface.

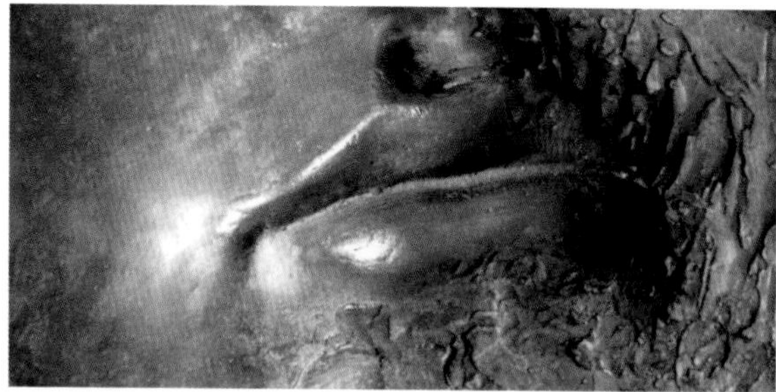

Birchwood Casey™ applied to a cold bronze, then cupric nitrate applied to a hot surface.

Birchwood Casey™ applied to a cold bronze, then cupric nitrate applied to a hot surface followed by another coat of Birchwood Casey™.

Karl Reichley, patineur, works on **Leitha L. Thrall's** *Pyramid Pyre.*

Patron One who supports the arts; specifically, the buyer of artwork.

Pattern The original or model used as a positive for mold making. *See* ***Model; Original; Sand casting***.

Pattern mold The main mold in metal casting designed for numerous uses with casting wax. Depending on the size and shape of the artwork, the mold could be a single piece or multiple pieces. Though plaster can be used for mold material, flexible urethanes, polysulfides and silicones are in more common use. They easily yield, allowing accessibility and undercuts. The wax surface for the artwork is nearly perfect as it is removed from the mold. These mold materials can be poured on the artwork, brushed on or even sprayed on depending on the shape, size and details involved. A supporting and a reinforcing mother mold is used with flexible molds to keep the mold's shape after it is removed from the artwork. *See* ***Mother mold; Flexible molds; Release agents*** *(chart);* ***Mold***.

Pedestal Stand, sometimes referred to as a support, for a sculpture, especially a figurative work (statue). *See* ***Stand***.

Peening Repeated hard blows to metal to secure a shape. It can be done by hand or by machine.

Penetration weld The depth from the base metal surface to the start of fusing a weld. *See* ***Welding***.

Performance art An art drama in which movement by the artist (performer) and sometimes the audience takes place. It can resemble a ritual with elaborate props. There are no set rules; it is often very absurd and sculptural forms may not be involved. Sometimes a sculpture technique, such as an installation or iron casting, is designed to evolve into a performance.

HOOP

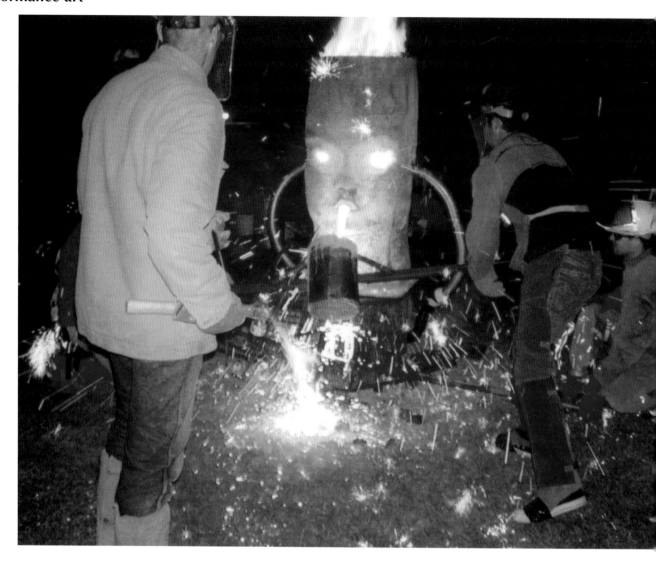

A two-hour performance casting at the 2002 International Conference for cast iron art. This was a ceramic castable cement refractory with stainless steel pins in the mix. The air enters the ears, slag comes out of the nose and iron is tapped from the mouth. Furnace by **Gene Koss**. Photographer: Rick Batten.

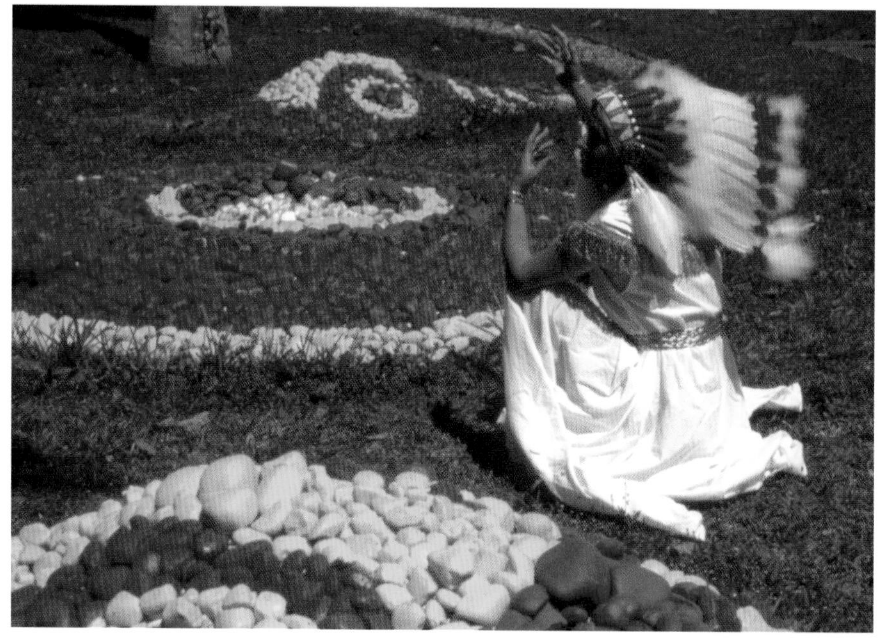

Kyra Belán, *Performance Art: Nature Goddess Sekhme*. Artist performing.

Ira D. Sherman, *Pavlovian Trainer*. Steel, brass, plastic, 36″x12″x18″ (91.4cm x 30.5cm x 45.7cm).

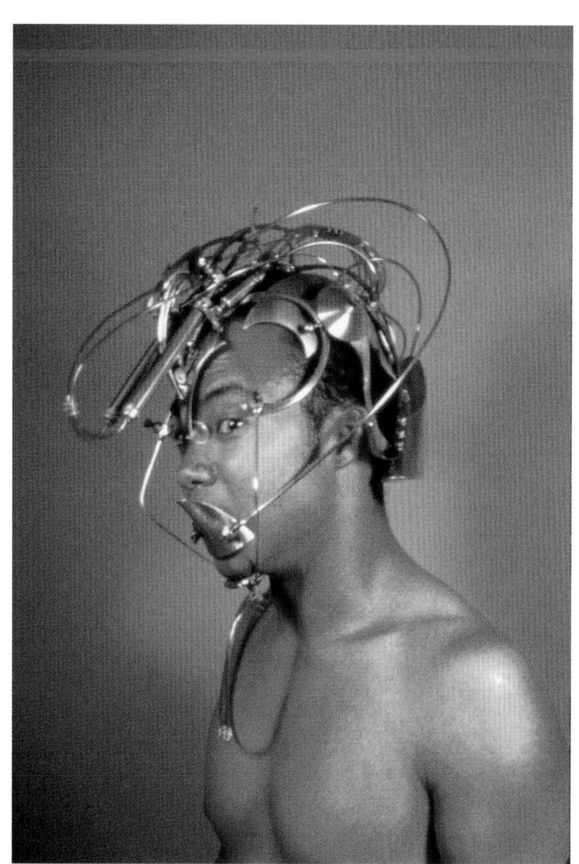

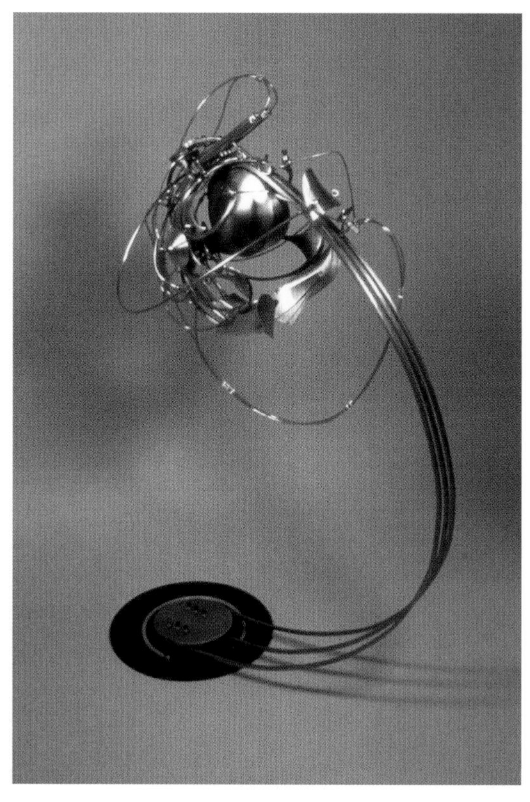

Pavlovian Trainer placed on a model.

J. Jaia Chen, *Red Tide*. Installation performance, 1,000 pieces of dough, fabric and string, 35′x48′ (10.7m x 14.6m).

Permeable The condition that exists when moisture or gases pass (permeate) through a substance.

Petcocks Tank drain valves. Drain cocks are located at the lower part of air compressor tanks to allow the condensation moisture to drain out.

Petroleum jelly A nearly colorless, petroleum based byproduct used as a release agent by sculptors. It readily adheres, and yet is easily removed because it does not penetrate. For this reason, it stays in place, but if too thick, swirls or even fingerprints in the paste are cast as part of the surface design. It is a lubricant. *See **Release agents** (chart).*

Pewter An alloy consisting of tin and other metals. It is silver in color and possesses a low melting temperature. It has a tendency to be brittle, although it can be alloyed to be of limited malleability. Pewter can easily be cast in cast iron pots. *See **Metal** (chart).*

Ph A symbol for the measure of alkalinity or acidity in a liquid. 0 is the most acid state, while 14 is the most alkaline.

Sharon Dee Shaughnessy, *Dream Catcher*. Pewter, patina, 14″x5″x6″ (35.6cm x 12.7cm x 15.2cm).

Phenolic resin Extremely hard thermosetting resin. It is used in several products, including Bakelite™ and Formica™.

Pick A handheld stone carving tool resembling a two-headed hammer except with a sharp point on each end of the head. Long handled for more power, the tool is not particularly heavy. It is used for rapid stone removal.

Pickle A chemical bath used to clean metal surfaces. The bath is customarily an acid solution. *See **Acid**.*

Pickup tongs Metal tools fashioned like large, long-handled pliers that are used to pick up metal and add it to the heated metal casting furnace. *See **Tongs**.*

Piece mold Piece molds consist of two or more portions that when placed together form a complete mold. The pieces are designed so that all undercuts are molded in separate parts to be easily removed from the casting without damage to it. Afterward, the pieces can be reassembled into the original mold shape for additional use. Smaller pieces or several pieces may be held together by a mother mold, ensuring that they are in a correct placement, as well as lending strength to the mold. This type of mold can be used on almost any substance, hard or soft. The mother mold material is generally plaster. *See **Mold**; **Mother mold**; **Plaster**; **Waste mold**.*

Piece mold technique

To make a piece mold, determine where the undercuts are, as well as the draft and the location of the pouring spout. Draw the dividing lines where necessary. If the original does not already have a release agent, then one should be added after placing shims or a fence on the form. If a clay fence is used, it should be on one side of the dividing line and held in place by clay wedges. If metal shims are used, they should be inserted about one-fourth inch

((0.635cm) into the parting line. Be sure to have keys.

Apply the mold material. If plaster, finalize it with a reinforcement material, such as hemp, then smooth the top and trim the shim or fence top coat so that it is easy to handle and is less likely to flake off into the mold. If different sections of the mold are completed separately, so are the mother mold parts. When the fence is removed or if shims are removed as the mold is being completed, then each seam edge section is also coated with a separator. If the sculptor is not confident about the mold division, then it is better to make extra divisions to avoid removal problems.

If several smaller sections are needed, then a mother mold, or encasing mold, is placed over all the smallest pieces to hold them in place as the casting material is added. Each smaller piece needs a string or wire added by the center as it is completed. The ends stick out like rings or loops and clay is placed on them prior to the mother mold. This wire is then placed directly into or through the mother mold and held in place by wedges or ties to the outside. The mother mold, in effect, serves as a wall and support much like a two-piece mold. The smaller pieces should allow register keys for the mother mold.

The piece mold should disassemble without breakage or marring the artwork. It should be cleaned and stored as an assembled mold to avoid warpage or damage. The mold must be completely dry if clay or resin is the casting material.

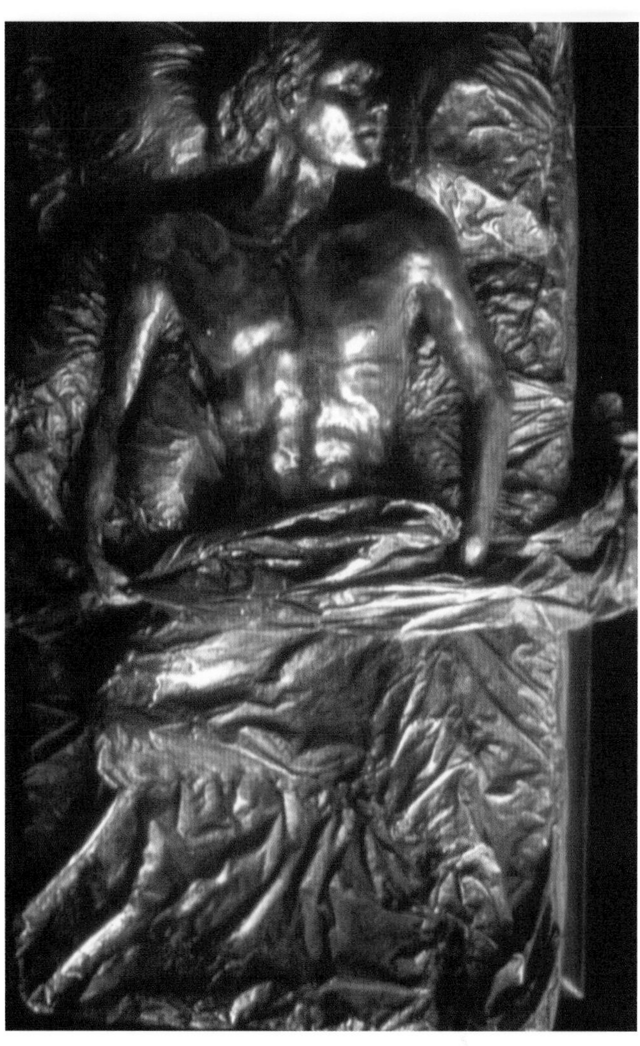

Aaron Royal Mosley, *Egyptian Sleep*. Cast pewter, 7″x18″x24″ (17.8cm x 45.7cm x 61cm).

While reassembling the mold, a separator should be applied to each piece and then fit together and anchored with bungee straps, large rubber bands or other devices that hold tightly, but do not damage the mold. On the largest molds, the seam walls are regularly anchored with bolts, washers and wing nuts. They are placed through holes that have been drilled through the seam walls at spaced points throughout the piece. Sometimes plaster impregnated burlap tightly wound over the seam serves as a temporary binder and guards against leaks.

The mold can be charged with the selected material. If plaster, then a creamy mix, enough to fill about one fourth of the mold or less, is added and the mold is gyrated or turned in all directions to ensure an even coating on all parts. As this thickens, the mix can be partially drained or more added to secure the desired thickness. This should be allowed to set, at least overnight, prior to removal.

If a stronger plaster casting is desired, an armature (reinforcement structure) can be plunged into a liquid mix that would completely fill the mold. However, the steel may touch the surface and damage the appearance of the artwork. The best way to add an armature is to place the armature into the mold prior to assemblage to calculate the exact location and best placement. It can be held in place by small amounts of plaster, being careful not to later block access to the flow of the liquid plaster as the actual casting is completed.

Once set and the casting removed, the mold should be cleaned for storage. The artwork is cleaned and retouched immediately to provide better adhesion and match of plaster to the casting.

PIECE MOLD for a Clay Pressing by Norman D. Holen

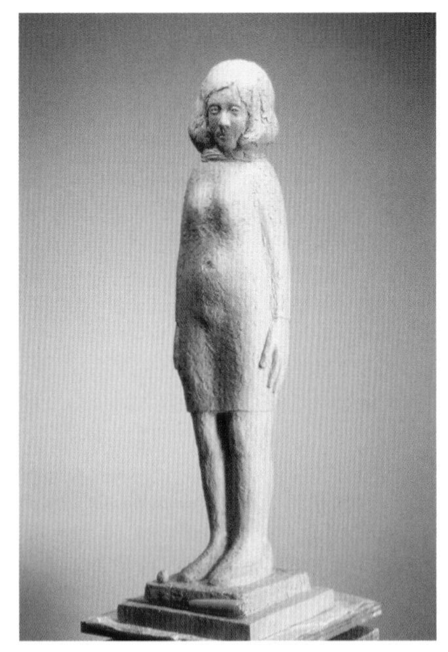

The finished model.

A solid clay wall shim is placed on the model.

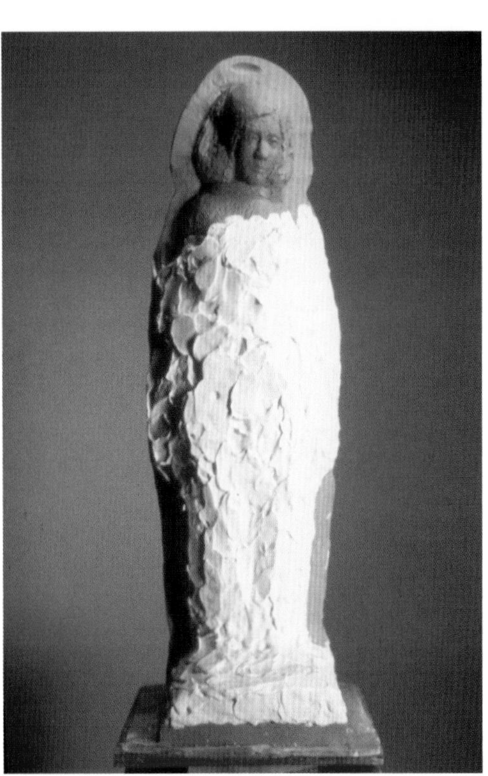

The plaster is applied from the bottom up.

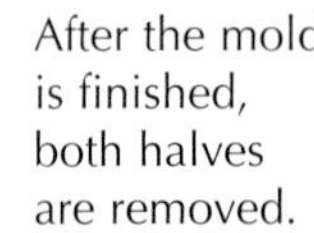

After the mold is finished, both halves are removed.

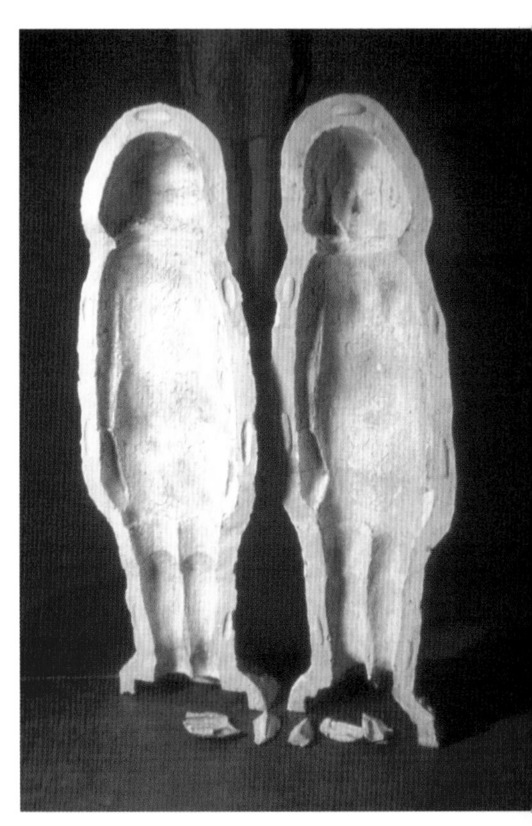

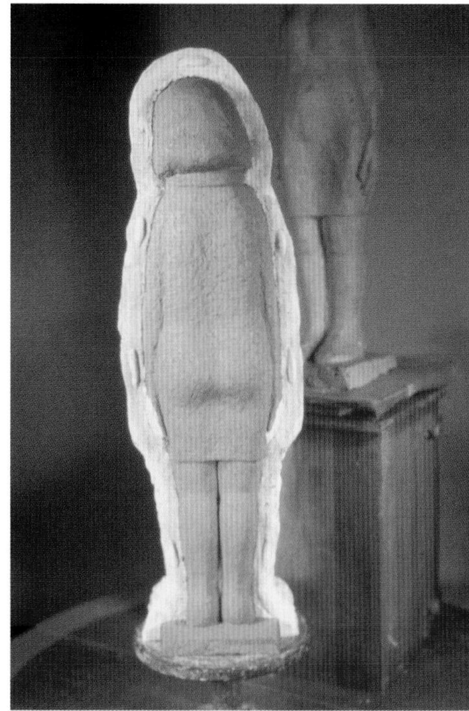

Clay is pressed into each half of the mold.

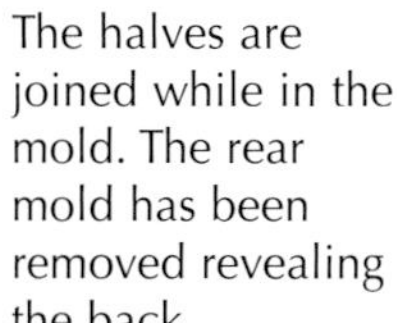

The halves are joined while in the mold. The rear mold has been removed revealing the back.

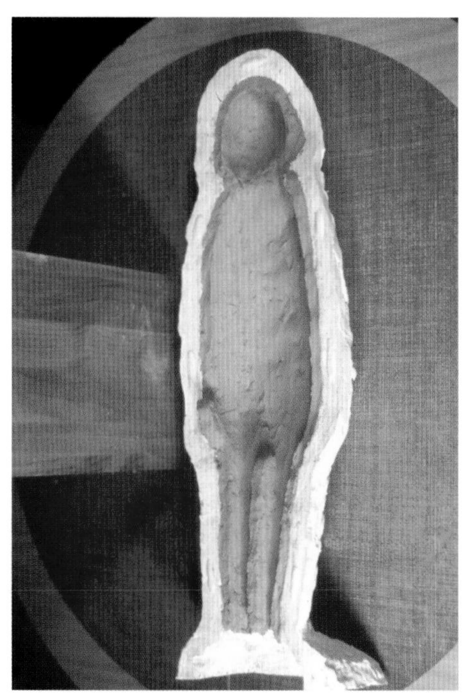

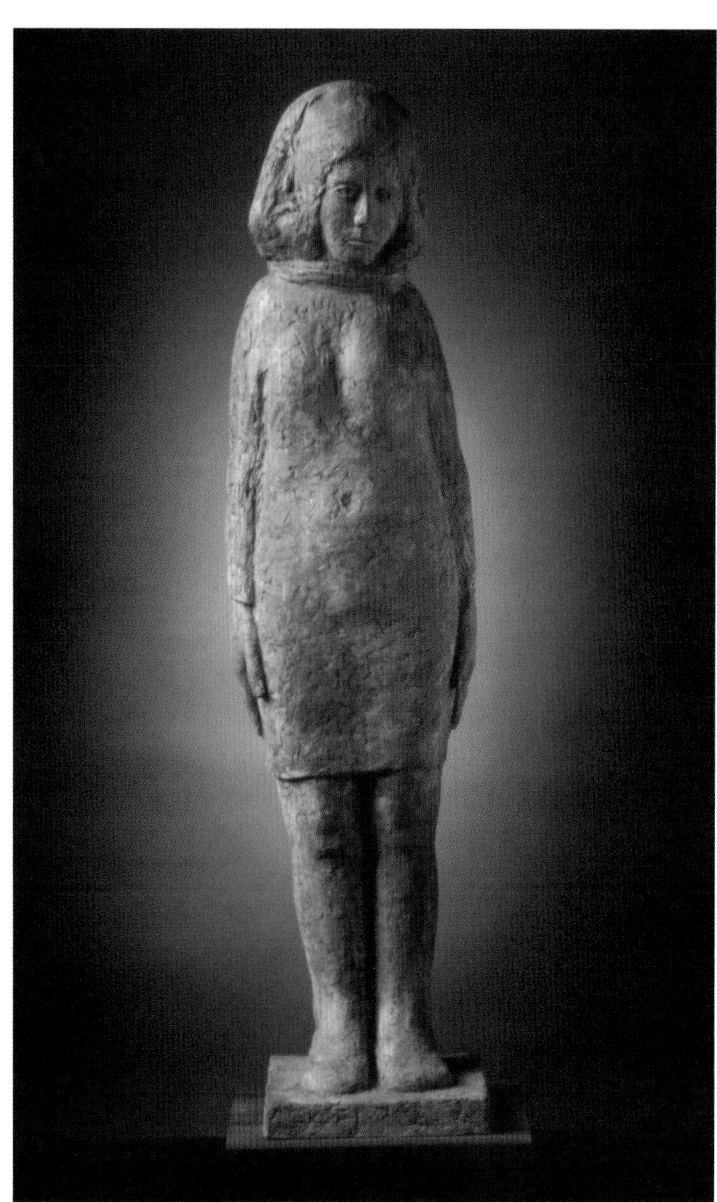

Norman D. Holen, *Woman in the Wind II*. Stoneware, oxides 8″x 8½″x 27¾″ (20cm x 21.3cm x 70.5cm). Photographer: Peter Lee.

PIECE MOLD
by Sheryl McRoberts

The clay model with shims applied for the first casting to the front lower part. A release agent is applied.

The finished clay model.

With the front plaster applied, the shim on the side is removed. A release agent is applied to the plaster before completing the rear section.

The lower part is completed, then a shim and release agent are applied to the head.

Sheryl McRoberts' completed mold, setting up in preparation for de-molding

Thread or wire piece molds

Plaster molds that divide along the parting line by a wire or thread are a unique form of piece mold. Dental floss or a strong nylon fish line are desirable threads to use because of their strength. After deciding where the dividing line on the form is and adding a release agent, a thread or wire is placed on the line with both ends out several inches beyond where the normal plaster wall will end. The plaster mold material is applied with only one mix and no reinforcement material. As the plaster starts to set, reaching the rigid stage, the wire is held on one end and pulled out by the other. In effect, this cuts the mold into two (or more) parts that are allowed to finish the set stage for strength and then are easily removed.

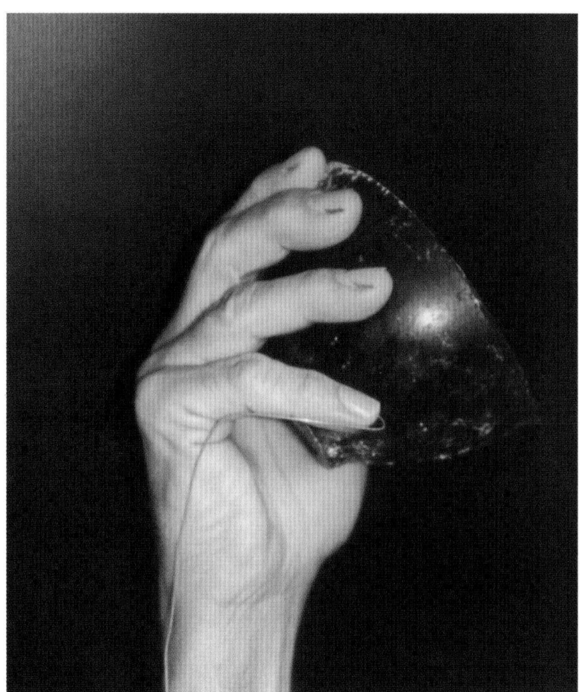

A hand is prepared for the piece mold. Wire is placed next to skin.

Plaster casting from the wire mold. When the wire was removed, it left an impression on the plaster.

This is an easy way to make a quick mold on modeling clay over the hand or on other parts of the human body. However, there are two cautions: 1) If the wire is removed too soon, the soft limp plaster will merge back into one piece after the pull; thus, the mold will not be divided and be difficult, if not impossible, to remove. 2) If the wire is pulled too late, it either cannot be taken out because of the hardness of the plaster, or it will break, leaving the form encased in the mold. If parts of the human anatomy are used, after applying a liberal amount of parting agent (petroleum jelly), the thin wire or string is set in place. Two more cautions: 1) Do not use a wire so sharp that it can cut. 2) Be very alert and cautious. Timing is everything, or the model can be trapped inside a plaster mold.

Plaster piece molds are still the primary type of molds used for clay slip casting and clay press molds. Though plaster is very good for casting waxes, flexible molds result in less leakage and better detail. Plaster piece molding was the most exacting method of mold making prior to flexible molding materials. Now more complex forms are almost encased in flexible molds. *See* ***Molds***.

Pietà A sculpture (or painting) depicting Mary embracing the lifeless body of Christ.

Pig An unfinished or rough bar or block of metal that has been poured from a smelting furnace. It is intended to be reshaped into a more refined use. Called an iron bar or pig iron, it can include several metals other than iron.

Pinching Creating a shape by squeezing the clay between the thumb and finger. Starting with a small round mass of clay, the material is pressed outward from the center into the perforation or shape desired. This is a process used in making clay pottery and some small sculptures. *See* ***Clay***.

Pine An evergreen tree producing a yellowish colored wood valued for its commercial construction properties. The wood is carveable but rather soft. *See* ***Wood*** *(chart)*.

Pipe warmer A small kiln-like, heated chamber used to accept the gather ends of blowpipes and punties prior to use. *See* ***Glass***.

Pitcher A large, flat-ended chisel that is first used to remove large sections of stone in preparation for more refined carving.

Plank A supporting or structural piece of lumber due to its horizontal width. It is used as a support for heavier objects.

Plasma arc Gas Tungsten Arc Welding. Welding with an arc created by a tungsten electrode surrounded by a protective inert gas. *See* ***TIG***.

Plasma cutter An electric machine similar to a welder with a torch to produce an arc that also directs a flow of high pressured air to blow the melted metal (slag) away from the kerf. The torch tips are replaceable, and the cut is so quick and intense that chrome can be cut with minimal burn-back. It produces an exceptionally clean cut in either ferrous or non-ferrous metals with little sign of slag. It is especially valuable for cutting bronze, brass, aluminum, and stainless steel from flat sheets. The small machine is easy to operate but requires a strong air compressor. The compressed air must be continuous enough to sustain the entire cut and powerful enough to be effective in the selected depth of cut. The air must reach the torch without moisture.

The machine is operated with a ground lead connected to the work, and the torch head connected to the additional lead and air line. The torch trigger ignites the arc as the tip is held close (within three-sixteenths inch [0.476cm]) to the metal.

John M. Weidman, *Friendship Succor*. Red pine, 10′x5′x2′ (3.05m x 1.53m x 0.61m). Photographer: Reimann.

Plasma cutter torch.

Automatically, the air follows to remove the slag. If the arc or air fails, the torch automatically shuts down. The cuts are so immediate and fast that the base metal receives comparatively little heat. Even chrome can be cut with minimal burn beyond the cut. Precut wooden jigs can be used as guides for the torch without igniting. Stainless steel and bronze can be cut with ease.

The restrictions and disadvantages are few, but they have to be considered. Metal thickness is limited to the power of the machine and it works best in thinner metals (one-half inch to one-sixteenths inch [1.27cm to 0.159cm]). The metal needs to be flat (but not necessarily level), without protrusions or awkward bends. The torch head is temperamental and requires constant care and replacement parts that are quite expensive. If the torch is too closely held to the metal, the tip can be damaged and become inoperable. If the compressed air gathers moisture, the torch will not work and the tip becomes pitted, requiring replacement. *See* ***Cutting****;* ***Carbon arc****.*

Plasma cutter, torch and ground clamp.

Plasteline (plastilina) A common name for oil-based modeling clay. *See* ***Clay*** *(oil-based).*

Plaster Calcined, hydrated calcium sulfate, a milled white gypsum powder that solidifies into a hard shape when mixed with water. The substance is commonly used for mold making and castings from molds. Plaster is manufactured by heating pulverized ground gypsum to expel part of the water of crystallization contained in the rock/gypsum. This is called calcining. It results in an endless appetite for water by the plaster. It is screened for size becoming the dry, white powder that is ready to use. In using plaster, water is added and mixed, resulting in a recrystallized rock (hard state).

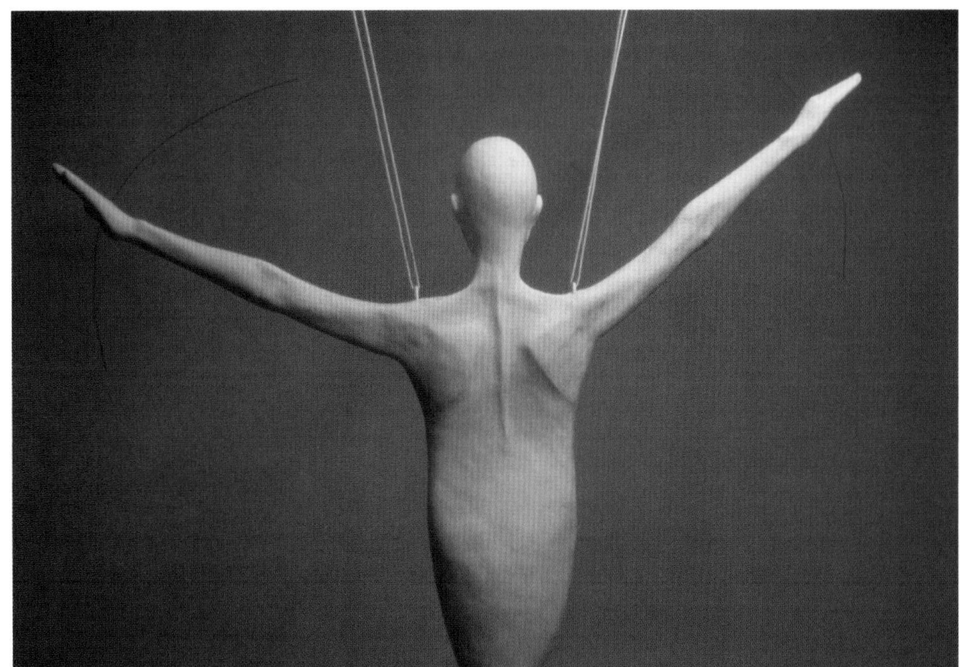

Ellen Lowenstein, *Of Gravity and Grace*. Plaster, steel, 88″x60″x7″ (223.5cm x 152.4cm x 17.8cm).

Plaster is one of the least expensive sculpture materials in common use. It is normally available in 100 pound (45.4kg) paper bags. Other than the common plaster used by sculptors, there are two other major types of plaster. Gypsum plaster is utilized for wall plaster and sheet rock, while lime plaster is used for decorative and fresco work. Plaster is not toxic (except for dry, flying dust particles) and nonallergenic, making it one of the safest sculpture materials to use. *See* ***Plaster of Paris****;* ***Plaster*** *(chart).*

Arthur Williams, *Searching the Scriptures*. Plaster model for enlargement (commission proposal), 16″x16″x7″ (40.6cm x 40.6cm x 17.8cm).

Plaster is exceptionally functional, since it can be the model, molded and then used for the final product with a good surface treatment (stains, powders or paints) to resemble brass, gold, copper or bronze. Hardened plaster is homogenous when it is correctly mixed with water. It has an identical consistency throughout without grain. Because of this, it is an ideal substance to cut and shape, because it is very workable. The disadvantage is its lack of permanency, especially with exposure to out-of-door conditions.

Locations with high humidity cause stored plaster to lose some of its strength creating clods of plaster. U.S. Gypsum states that 90 days is the proper storage time. However, in warm, dry climates, one year seems to have little effect; whereas, just a few days in a humid climate can take a toll on the stored plaster. One way to eliminate the problem is to encase the unused, unopened plaster in an airtight container. This drastically improves the shelf life.

Less water when mixing results in harder plaster, while softer, weaker plaster will be the result of additional water. Too much water keeps the plaster grains apart, causing the plaster to become more porous, while too little water causes the mix to be uneven. Even though the manufacturer suggests exact water amounts, the sculptor creates the plaster mix visually or by touch in small proportions. Perhaps the best gauge of such a mix is to create a thick cream so opaque that when a hand is dipped into the mix, no hint of skin color can be seen.

Never add water to plaster; add plaster to water. Otherwise, the mix will be weak. The ratio of water to plaster averages two to three (2:3). This means that for every 100 pounds (45.4kg) of plaster, approximately 66 and two-thirds pounds (30.27kg) of water would be added. This is approximately nine gallons (34L) of water.

The setting time and drying time are not the same. The setting time is required for the plaster to go through recrystallization to become a hard solid mass. Though it is stable, it expands slightly. The swelling rate is constant and predictable. A vast amount of heat is shed with larger volumes of plaster noticeably emitting much more heat than smaller, thinner mixes.

The drying time is the period after the setting has finished, and the plaster is no longer warm or hot. Setting causes the plaster to sweat and be damp. As this moisture and dampness leaves, it is drying. Setting takes only a fraction of time, usually within an hour or two, as compared to the drying time, which can take days and even weeks to complete.

The three most significant variables are: 1) the storage location (humidity), 2) the thickness of the work, and 3) the amount of water used. Actually, the setting time is hastened by larger batches, because the heat created multiplies faster, is retained within the volume, and reaches a higher point. However, the drying time is slowed if the work is poured thickly.

Because the plaster hardens chemically, care must be taken in disposing it. Plaster is soluble in water at a rate of .25% which will allow for some excess remaining afloat in water but not much. Plumbing furnishings for plaster work require a plaster trap. If spilled in a sink and down the drain, it will set. However, without a built-in plaster trap, the sculptor can wash with water stored in a flexible garbage can. The excess plaster will settle to the bottom, the sludge can be removed, and hands and tools can later be rinsed with a regular water supply. *See* ***Plaster trap***.

Spent plaster can be reused if reprocessed. This involves grinding and reheating the used plaster to a temperature up to 350°F (176.7°C) where two-thirds of the chemical water is driven off. The actual process begins at 225°F (107.2°C) and should never exceed 350°F (176.7°C). To heat beyond 350°F (176.7°C) or to heat too long at this temperature results in a useless, inert powder.

The traditional **tools** designed for plaster include spatulas, scrapers, plaster knives, rasps, files and flexible bowls or buckets. Other adapted tools include Surform™ rasps, woodcarving wire brushes, gouges and chisels, saws, screen wire and sandpaper. All steel tools must be kept clean or the plaster can cake up, making it difficult to remove and resulting in rust.

Plaster can be moved and modeled with the spatulas in the early stage of work. The scrapers, knifes, plaster rasps and Surform™ rasps work in the in-between stages. The harder files and tools are used in the last stages. Round, bottom flexible rubber bowls have been replaced with flexible plastic buckets and bowls. Sandpaper can be used on dry plaster, while the screen wire allows sanding in wetter stages.

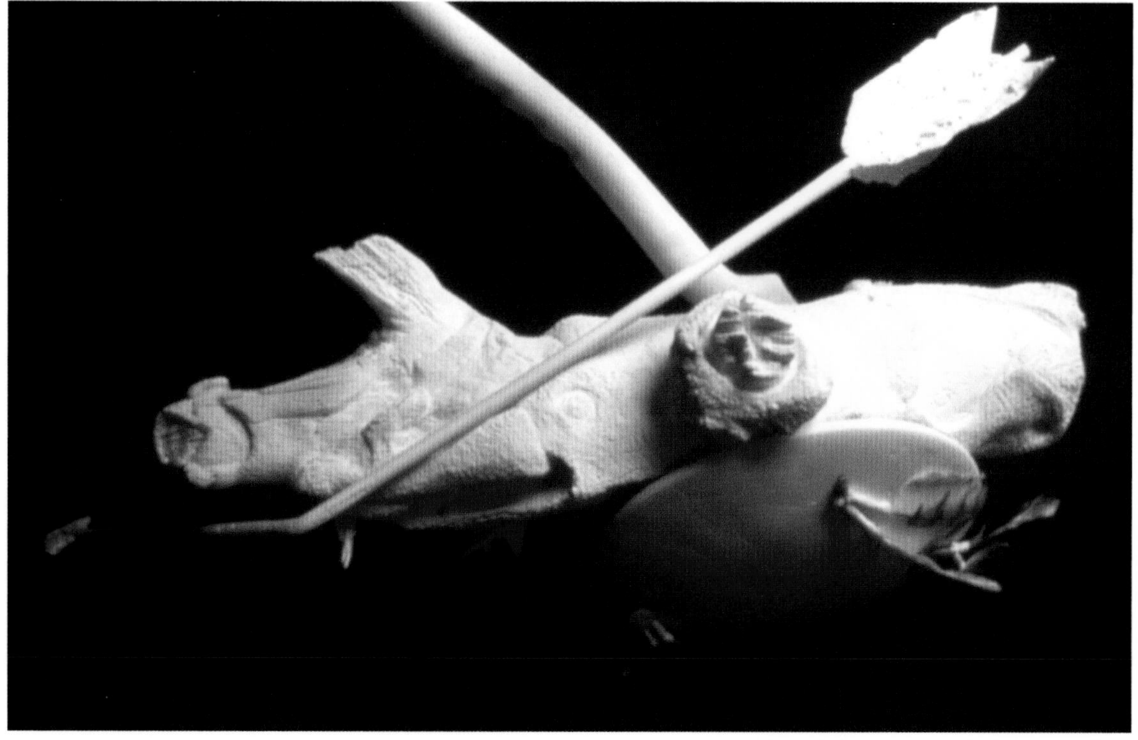

Andrès Hill, *After the Battle*. Plaster, 18″x10″x11″ (45.7cm x 25.4cm x 27.9cm).

Hand powered **mixers** include air and electric drills with homemade and manufactured blades and adaptable food and paint mixers. The mixing speed must be at a low RPM (revolution per minute) or an excessive amount of air will be captured while mixing, creating a weak, porous mass.

Heavy-duty power mixers, made for the purpose, are used for mixing large plaster batches. They have stainless steel blades mounted on a stainless steel shaft to avoid corrosion or pollution in the mix. Pneumatic mixers are best. They have a complete range of variable speeds and will continue to function without damage to the machine even if the thickened mix clings to the blades causing them to slow down or cease operating. It is always easier to clean the shaft and blades as soon as possible to avoid a difficult task at a later time. Also, power mixed plaster sets quickly. Depending on the conditions, it can literally begin solidifying as soon as the blades stop turning. A good way to solve this problem is to avoid unnecessary mixing time and to try for a thinner mix to slow the setting time.

Additives are used to manipulate the setting time or alter the product. While temperature is not considered an additive, it definitely affects the setting time, especially with the water. The safest way to increase the setting time is to use colder water. However, water that is too cold, below 50°F (10°C), can inhibit good adhesion among the plaster particles and can also be unpleasant to place hands into while working. Conversely, hot water is the best way to decrease the setting time. However, the optimum solubility is at 100°F (37.8°C). Water beyond this point causes the setting time to slightly expand until 135°F (57.2°C) is reached. This temperature affects the plaster setting the same as 75°F (23.9°C) water. The best test for maximum hot temperature is to never use water that would hurt the hands when mixing.

Retarders and **accelerators** are best avoided, since the final strength of the mix is affected. However, they can be helpful. A retarder will cause the mix to set slowly. An accelerator will cause a chemical reaction that speeds up the setting time. Commonly found additives are table salt (sodium chloride), unused plaster powder, alum and lime to accelerate the mix, while lemon juice, citric acid, carpenter's glue, vinegar, alcohol, sugar and urine will decrease the setting time.

The mixing process itself will modify the setting time. Extra time or extreme agitation while mixing will result in a rapid setting time. Larger batches, properly mixed and allowed to stay as a liquid in the container, will hasten the chemical heating process to cause quick setting.

Additives, such as marble dust or pebbles, are added for visual effect. Sand can be added to increase the refractory ability, while Vermiculite eases the carveability. Fiberglass, steel, hemp and canvas are added to strengthen the mix. The sculptor must be cautious with what is added. Too much mix will cause the plaster to be so thinly coated that it becomes weak. Some objects such as burlap will absorb the moisture causing the mix to dry up or set more quickly. Fiberglass can be added for strength but can cut the sculptor's hands if it is mixed or handled with bare hands.

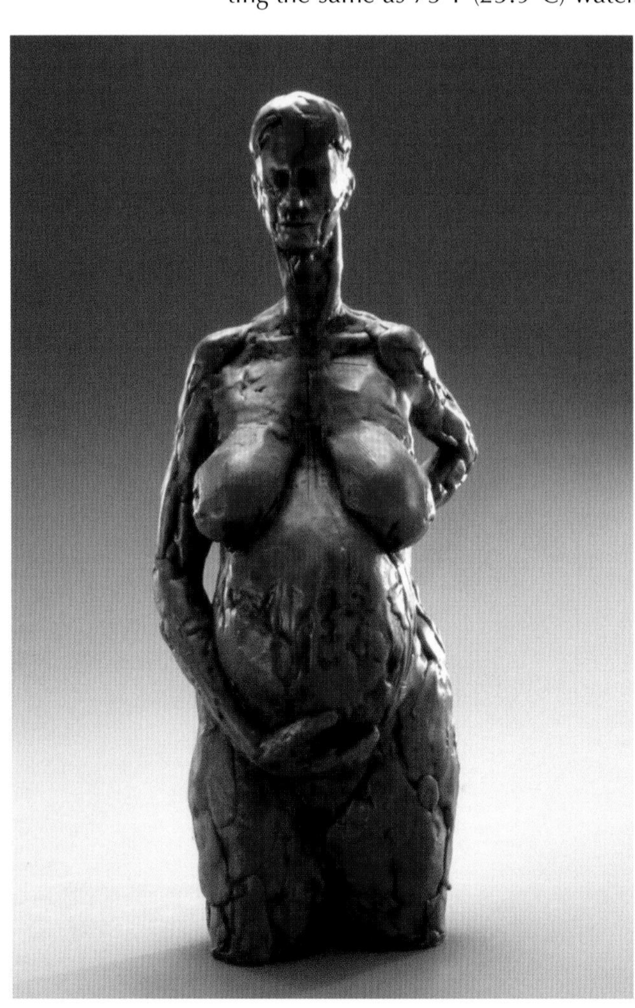

Diane van der Zanden, *Laurie IV*. Plaster, 11½″x5″x5″ (29.2cm x 12.7cm x 12.7cm).

William N. Beckwith, *Midnight*. Plaster, 17″x9″x6″ (43.2cm x 22.9cm x 15.2cm).

PLASTER CHARACTERISTICS

U.S. Gypsum Plasters/Gypsum Cements

Material	Setting Time	Wet Strength	Dry Strength
White Art (pure white)	30 min.	1000 psi (6893 kPa)	2000 psi (13786 kPa)
Molding (most porous)	30 min.	1000 psi (6893 kPa)	2000 psi (13786 kPa)
Casting (hard surface)	30 min.	1200 psi (8272 kPa)	2400 psi (16543 kPa)
Hydrocal™ (most expansion)	30 min.	2500 psi (17233 kPa)	5000 psi (34465 kPa)
Fast Cast™ (requires aggregate)	30 min.	2500 psi (17233 kPa)	8000 psi (55144 kPa)
Hydrostone™ (snap sets)	18 min.	4000 psi (27572 kPa)	10,000 psi (68930 kPa)

MIXING PLASTER

1. Select a flexible container. Pour one-third or less water in, depending on the amount of mixture needed.

2. Sprinkle the plaster into the water by sifting it through the fingers

3. After the plaster begins to float on the surface, momentarily stop adding it. As it begins to sink in, resume by slowly sifting additional plaster into the water. When the water can no longer absorb plaster, the remaining plaster floats. Suspend the operation.

4. Allow the composite to rest for two to three minutes as the plaster becomes part of the solution. Begin stirring the mix. Check for thickness by coating the hands and lifting them out. If the skin color can no longer be detected, it is thick enough.

5. Compress any lumps between the fingers. It is ready to use.

Mixing plaster is a simple process: Water is poured into the mixing container, plaster is added. The two are stirred together, and the final product is used for various purposes. However, to achieve the best results or to obtain a specific type of mix, there are several details to consider.

The strength of the mix is partially determined by the time spent mixing it . The most commonly used plaster, molding plaster, can endure 1300 psi (8961kPa) pressure (stress), if it is mixed for only one minute. However, it can sustain 2000 psi (13786kPa), if it is mixed eight minutes longer. Extending the mix beyond nine minutes will result in less strength as the compound quickly freezes. Merging in the ingredients should not ordinarily extend beyond the necessity of blending the water and plaster into a smooth, thick cream. Longer mixing results in a brief, less effective working time.

Sometimes plaster needs an inner structure or armature. A plaster armature is a skeletal structure designed to hold the outer portions in place as the surface is formed and worked to achieve the desired design. Almost any material can be used in these armatures. It all depends on whether the sculptor needs fast volume, less weight or strength of form.

Some of the common armature materials are: 1) wire wrapped with plaster impregnated cloth; 2) Styrofoam™ in large shaped pieces covered with plaster; 3) shaped chicken wire or wire screen with plaster saturated cloth; 4) plaster soaked foam rubber; 5) coated (shellacked) welded rebar for especially large or strong armatures, and 6) any material at hand: such as coated wood, fiberglass, found objects, spent plaster, PVC pipe or almost anything that can temporarily hold its shape while the plaster hardens on the surface. If unsealed wood is used as an armature, it will gather moisture and swell, ultimately causing the mix to fracture. If steel is used, it needs to be coated to avoid rust. If colored burlap is used, the color will bleed throughout the final mass as the plaster cures. *See **Plaster** (chart).*

PATINAED PLASTER RELIEF

by Gary Ericksen

Drawing for *Tempus Fugit C – Opportunity*.

Plaster relief from drawing.

Gary Eriksen, *Tempus Fugit C – Opportunity*. Patinaed plaster, 17″x24″x1″ (43.2cm x 61cm x 2.5cm).

SIX STAGES OF PLASTER

1. **The Liquid Stage** This is the runny, liquid substanc that can be poured, dipped, thrown or brushed.

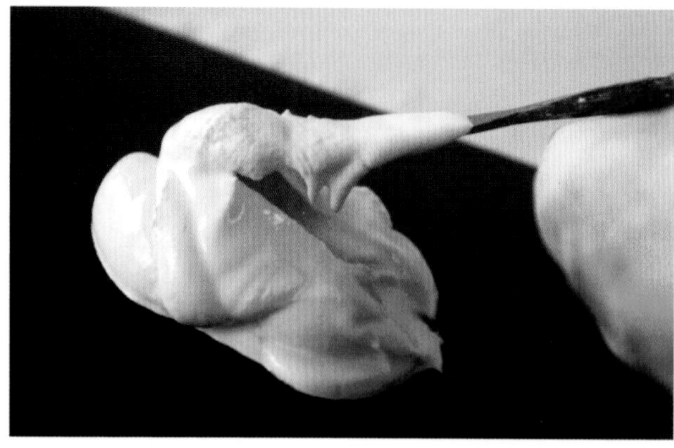

2. **The Putty Stage** The plaster is an extremely thick paste, though it will sump and remain on a spatula for spreading onto a form. The plaster is beginning to set, so the stage does not last long.

3. **The Rigid Stage** The plaster becomes a soft mass that can be cut and trimmed with tools. It is frail and will shatter. With care, large sections of plaster can be removed during this brief stage.

4. **The Set Stage** The plaster becomes quite warm, even hot, depending on the volume of plaster. It can be worked with a plaster rasp or knife, but it quickly becomes difficult to do so. At the end of this stage, approximately 18.6% of the water will remain.

5. **The Cure Stage** The plaster slowly loses its moisture. It can be manipulated with Surform™ rasps and wire screen, since the still damp plaster can pass through these porous tools.

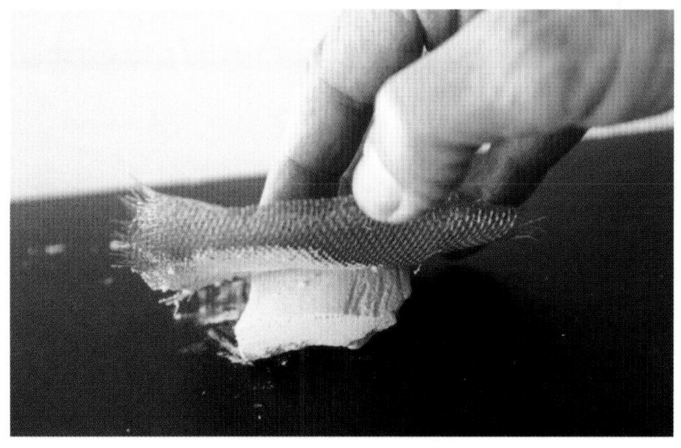

6. **The Dry Stage** The moisture has evaporated, the plaster is lighter and no longer feels cold to the touch. The cycle is complete. The surface is refined with dry sandpaper. In this stage, it can be used as a slip casting mold.

Plaster gauze (cloth bandage) A commercially packaged gauze (cloth) that is impregnated with a dry adhesive plaster mix often used for body molding. When the bandage is placed into water, the plaster immediately activates and, depending upon the warmth of the water, will set in three to five minutes. This is the product used to set broken bones in hospitals. It yields a tough but lightweight thin cast. It does not achieve the exacting detail that a pure plaster casting does.

Using plaster gauze for body molding is easier that regular plaster. It is best to precut lengths and place two or more layers together prior to dipping in water, since the gauze is thin. However, it does not take many layers to accomplish a strong mold. As with other plaster, petroleum jelly is the best release agent. Common widths of commercial plaster bandages are from two to six inches (5.08cm to 15.24cm) in width rolled in various lengths. It is possible to submerge an entire roll and roll it over the form. Even though the set time is quick, the model needs to hold still for seven more minutes to prevent the mold from tearing or damage. Afterwards, the cast can be cut off by inserting round nose scissors beneath the bandage around the skin.

Body castings have all the same precautions as facial castings: Use plenty of release agent (petroleum jelly), cover all major hair areas, do not cover any parts of the body without providing escape means. 1) Since the molding process takes a great deal of time, the model needs support during the entire period to remain rigid, avoiding a cracked or weak detailed surface. Ideally, the model is placed against a pre-designed, rigid support to avoid movement. 2) Divide the body into casting sections. An erasable magic marker can be used to draw sections throughout the body. Larger sections are preferred. Ideally, one single layer section should be completed to serve as the framework for all the other pieces to fit. A solid back casting is good. *See* ***Body molding; Press mold; Alginate.***

PLASTER GAUZE BODY MOLDING

by Jack Thompson

The sculptor cuts the plaster gauze into workable strip sizes and places them into stacks for use.

The model and helper cover the body with a petroleum jelly release agent.

With assistance, the sculptor begins to add the plaster gauze that has been quickly dipped into warm water. The body is covered one section at a time. The release agent is applied to each adjoining gauze surface.

The model's body is encased with gauze wrap, taking care to place the sections correctly to allow a trouble free removal.

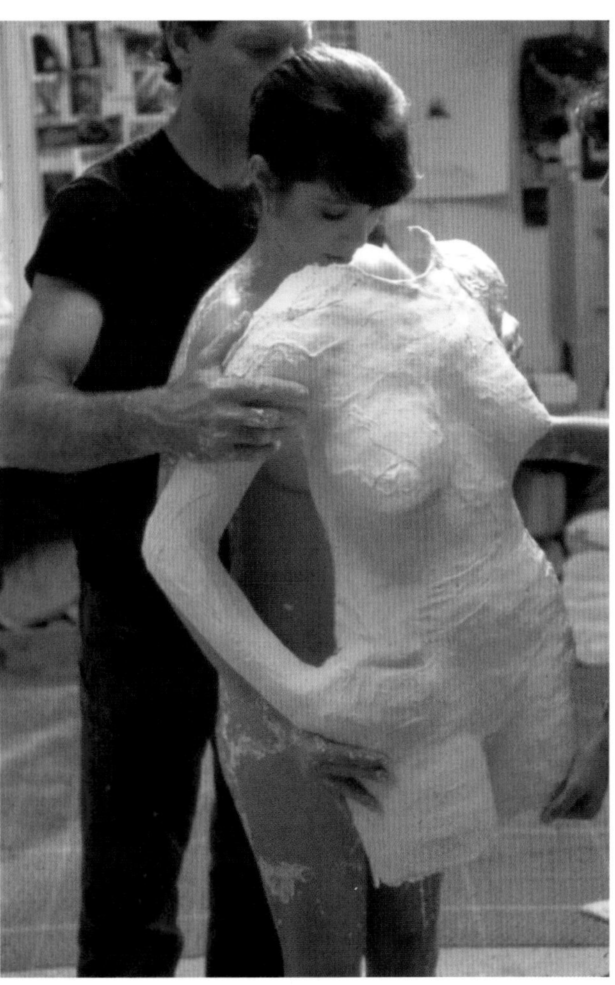

Jack Thompson works one section at a time until the model is freed.

Plaster investment (investing) Encasing a wax form with a heat resistant material in preparation for pouring a hot liquid metal that results in a casting. Investment, as used in sculpture, usually indicates the refractory mix used as a molding material that coats the wax form in preparation for metal casting. Investment casting is traditionally equated with lost wax casting, referring to a plaster mix, though it can also refer to ceramic shell material or sand. *See **Slurry investing**.*

The plaster investment must be heat resistant enough to withstand extremely high heats of liquid metals (over 2000ºF [1093ºC]), retain fine surface details and stay undamaged under pressure long enough for the metal to harden. The material needs to have enough porosity to help the metal gas escape without shattering or cracking the mold. Plaster alone cannot endure the temperature or temperature fluctuations without an additional refractory.

Plaster investment consists of water, a binder (plaster), a refractory (sand, silica, grog, fireclay or luto), oftentimes a mica (Vermiculite) to allow porosity and a strong reinforcement (chicken wire or wire mesh). The face coat or surface investment applied to the wax should not contain mica, since it would result in a porous uneven surface. Commercial mixes are readily available for jewelry and dental use that are adaptable for sculptural forms, though expensive in large quantities. U.S. Gypsum has a special mix that is used specifically for investment.

Plaster investment

Technique

There are many **formulas** and variations of formulas for sculptors to use. The following are suggestions for investment materials using plaster:

1. Face coat, investment for fine detail.
   - 1 part powdered silica (100-200 mesh)
   - 1 part masonry sand
   - 1 part molding plaster
2. Regular investment (backup coat for all additional coats)
   - 1 part ordinary sand
   - 1 part mica
   - 1 part molding plaster

It is possible to use one part plaster to two parts of ordinary sand for all coats, but it lacks the detail quality of the fine silica on the first coat and the porosity of the later vermiculite coating that avoids mold fractures. Ceramic grog can be substituted for sand but at a greater expense.

The mold method that is used, **hand lay-up** or the **basket** (container), will determine the thickness, weight and strength. The **hand lay-up** entails adding coats by hand until about one and one-half inch (3.81cm) thick and encasing the mold with chicken wire (or wire mesh) and adding a layer of at least one to two inches (2.54cm to 5.08cm) of thickness.

The metal pouring system has been completed with two wax face masks by **Elisha Gold**. A Styrofoam™ pouring cup is used.

A metal lathe basket has been made to fit the wax artwork.

Larger molds will require more thickness for strength. Though the final mold will not resemble the detailed form's exact shape, it produces a lighter weight and is easier to burn out. The mold can actually be better, since the reinforcement wire is closer to the form, and it requires less time in the furnace. Being smaller and easier to handle, larger shapes are lighter and maneuver with less difficulty, thus allowing more molds to be placed into the burnout furnace at one time.

The **basket** system involves using a container to enclose the wax with the pouring system suspended in the investment mix. It is a quick method for completing an investment mold. The container can be a garbage can, rolled metal taped together or simply rol roofing felt temporarily tied together. Whatever the container, it needs to be lined with metal lathe on all sides and the bottom (chicken wire will work, but is not as strong), preferably about an inch (2.54cm) from the outer wall.

After the pouring system has been added, a thin layer of **surface coat** is added to the wax for details. At least one-fourth inch (0.635cm) but seldom more than one-half inch (1.27cm) of the finer mix is brushed or flicked on. The best procedure is a combination of both methods with a small stream of compressed air applied to eject air bubbles within the crevices. The finer coat contains more plaster or finer silica allowing a more refined coverage of miniscule details. This coat does not have to cover the pouring system.

Three possible containers for plaster investment casting: Black roofing felt rolled and tied together, a cardboard concrete pouring tube, a roll of roofing metal tied together with wire. Metal lathe baskets are fitted for each.

The artwork has the face coat of investment brushed on.

The **face coat** is mixed by first adding plaster then sand and silica to the water until the mix opaques or covers the hand without revealing the skin color. The formula can vary slightly as long as the binder is adequate, and the mix is not too thin, resulting in a weak mold that will fracture and sometimes crumble as it is heated. All coats must be applied in succession without any coat drying out.

Though there is no set thickness, the basket wall needs to be at least two inches (5.08cm) from the wax in every direction except for the top, where it will be flush with the vents and pouring cup. It does not have to be round and it can be beneficial if it resembles the overall shape of the form. Using an exaggerated or enormous container for a small wax accomplishes nothing but an excessive weight, taking up unnecessary space in a furnace that will require hours longer of burnout time. Also, if the reinforcement wire is too far away from the wax, any inner surface cracks tend to widen, causing flashing. The wax may still need a face coat to be applied by brush and/or throwing to maintain detail. The container needs a layer of about two

Once the face coat adheres, the artwork is placed into the container. The investment top coat is poured around the artwork.

inches (5.08cm) of regular investment added to the lower part of the cage to seal the bottom for additional mixes. As the mix hardens, the top surface needs to be roughed up, allowing parts to readily submerge and interlock with successive coats.

When the bottom is firm, wax (with or without a face coat) needs to be added with the open vents slightly protruding from the container's top wall. It can be held in place or rested on the bottom, being careful to center it and watching for the possibility of floatation or displacement in the mold. The investment is added to bring the mix to the top of the container where the vents and cup are displayed. The outer cage material can ordinarily be removed to expose the investment mold ready to be dewaxed.

The **core** is the investment placed into the interior of a hollow wax form serving as an inert solid that separates and keeps the wax walls at an even thickness. In effect, it ensures a hollow wax, though the wax form has been filled with a substance (core investment). A core of plaster investment is essentially the same mix as the final coat, which includes a mica product.

In a hand lay-up, if a hollow wax form needs a core mix, add it after the mold thickness has been reached; however, it could be added first before any investment to small waxes and allowed to cool before proceeding. (This becomes difficult to handle and may require a wax touch-up). Using the cage method, the core investment (if needed) can be added to the wax either as the container is filled or after the wax has been anchored to the lower interior investment.

Since the wax will be melted out of the plaster investment leaving a cavity with a core, **core pins** are used to hold the core material in place as the liquid metal is poured about it. The core pins should be made from metal with melting temperatures greater than the metal being poured. (They will melt in the burnout or pouring.) Stainless steel is exceptionally strong. Regular steel should not be used because of possible electrolysis. The pins need to be placed from the outside and into the mold deep enough to lock into the core. They are located in such a way as to ensure that the core cannot shift out of place. The part hanging outside should have a bend for additional support. After the casting, these pins can be removed.

Some waxes are easy to core, such as an open core form of a portrait bust with a large neck opening. Waxes like this can have heavy core rods, perhaps one-fourth inch (0.635cm) or larger in diameter that are placed into the interior with parts hanging out. The rods need to be bent at various angles to better support the core without slippage or shifting the core. They are used to fasten the

After the investment has hardened, the cup, runners and edges are smoothed and cleared of any loose investment.

inner core to the outer investment. When possible, an additional core wire should be added to the cavity for reinforcement to ensure the core does not break or fracture during the burnout or metal pouring.

Once completed and trimmed, the molds must remain wet prior to dewaxing. If the molds cannot be dewaxed in a matter of days, then they need to be kept in airtight plastic bags or covering. The water content in the molds resist the wax soaking in. Also, as the heat builds up while dewaxing, it becomes steam that helps the wax to loosen and melt out at a better pace. This avoids saturation of the wax into the mold.

Burnout furnaces must withstand temperatures in excess of 1500ºF (816ºC) as the wax is removed in preparation for metal insertion. It is best to load the molds with the cup and vents down so that the wax can quickly escape. The liquid wax can be captured in a metal container that is partially filled with water to avoid fires. The actual process takes in excess of 48 hours. *See* ***Burnout furnace***.

The finished plaster investment mold is ready to be burned out. *See* ***Burnout furnace***.

Plaster of Paris Plaster that was first mined and used commercially in Paris, France, late in the 17th Century. As a result, plaster is still referred to as plaster of Paris. *See* ***Plaster***.

Plaster rasps A handled rasp with sharp open teeth to allow the wet plaster to be grated through. Surform™ rasps are a good substitute for plaster rasps when they are not available. *See* ***Surform™ rasp***.

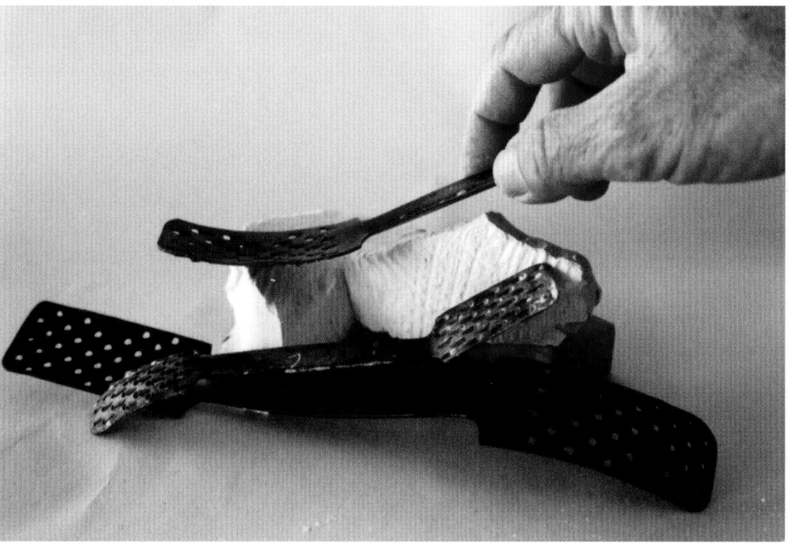

Various sizes of plaster rasps.

Plaster trap A container as part of the drain system used as a reservoir for plaster that escapes with drain water. The fluid (water and plaster) drains into the trap with the heavier particles of plaster sinking to the bottom. The water proceeds to move through a series of baffles as the heavier, surplus plaster continues to fall to the bottom. Finally, the water exits through a pipe on the opposite high end of the trap. The trap is designed to be opened and cleaned. If the plaster sludge is not removed periodically, it will coat the trap walls and produce noxious odors, eventually rendering the trap useless.

Plastic The quality of a material to be shaped; the more plastic, the more malleable. Plastic art is three-dimensional (sculpture) as opposed to two-dimensional (painting, for example). Very plastic is extremely easy to manipulate. Plastic sculpture materials include earth and oil based modeling clays, because they freely yield or submit to the sculptor's touch. Also, plastic may be organic compounds made by polymerization. *See **Plastics; Plasticity**.*

Plasticine (plastelina) Modeling clay made from oil, wax, clay and grease. It is a generic name. *See **Clay** (modeling).*

Plasticity The quality of molding or modeling. Clay, either oil- or water-based, possesses plasticity. The trait of certain solid substances to be manipulated, modeled or molded and yet maintain a final form. More plasticity means that it is easier to model. For the wheel-throwing of clay, a small amount of bentonite can be added to increase the plasticity or flexibility and slipperiness. Larger grain clays are less plastic than smaller grain clays. *See **Plastic**.*

Hilda Appel Volkin, *Nine Muses on the Moon*. Plexiglass, wood, 3'x5' (0.92m x 1.53m). Photographer: Pat Verrett.

Plastics (resin/acrylic) Organic compounds that can be cast into shapes, extruded, molded, made into filaments, etc. The material itself is a result of polymerization or monomers (molecules) linking to other monomers to create polymers. This product is made hard and strong by a catalyst or by using heat.

Plastics have a high degree of thermal expansion that is not as strong, rigid or stable as metal. However, there are so many kinds of plastics that they cannot be identified in a few terms. They can be rigid, soft, hard, dense, porous, flexible, clear or opaque. They can be manufactured into sheets, solid blocks, liquids, films, fibers, rods, adhesives, etc., for many different uses.

Mark Oxman, *Untitled*. Plastic.

The two major categories that plastics fall into are **thermoplastics** and **thermosetting plastics**. Within these categories there are numerous kinds of plastics for all sorts of uses. Plastics may be known by their commercial names, such as Lucite™ or Plexiglass™, other than the universal or generic name of acrylic. **Thermoplastic** is heated to secure the shape. When heated, it loses its hardness, becoming pliable and easily molded. Plexiglass™ is an example. It can be reheated and shaped numerous times. **Thermosetting plastic** begins as a liquid and with the help of a catalyst, heats up as it hardens into a solid permanent form. Epoxy and polyester resins are examples. They can be cast into only one usable shape and cannot be reshaped by heating.

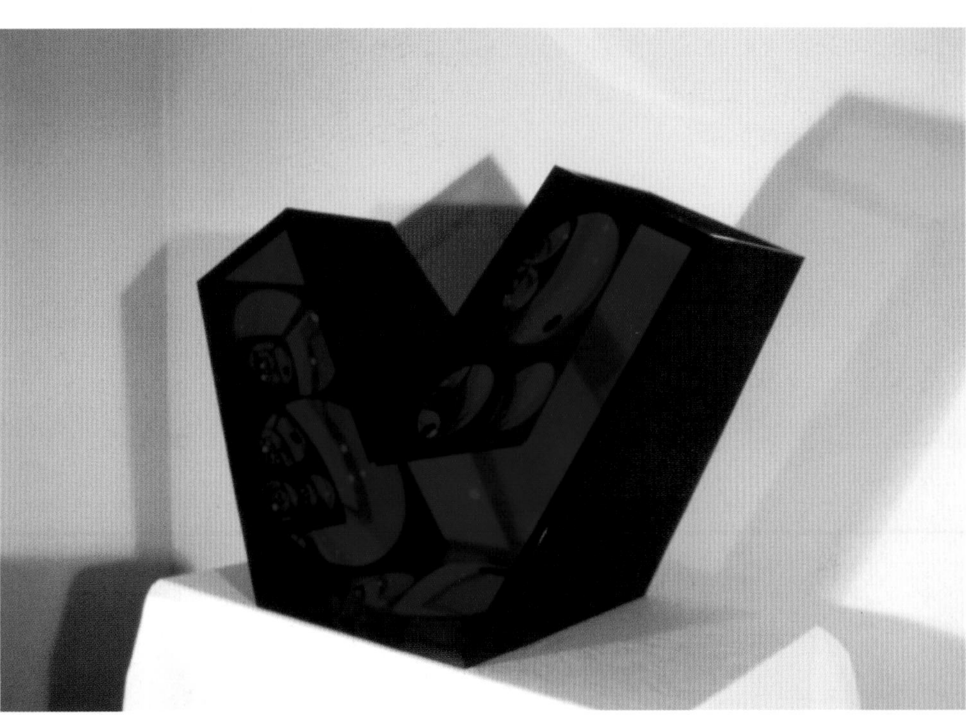

Roger Shipley, *P.O.*#*26*. Plexiglass, mirror, wood, 9″x36″x21″ (22.9cm x 91.4cm x 53.3cm).

Technique

Molding is often used for sculpture. The plastic liquid, with all additives, colorants and catalyst is poured into a mold to harden. There are four types:

1) **Injection molding**; forcing a plastic (thermoplastic) in a mold to cool into a new shape.

2) **Rotational molding**; rotating the plastic from a heating container to a cooling mold so as to freeze it into the new form.

3) **Blow molding**; feeding the plastic into a two- sided mold with a hard stream of air added to force the plastic onto the cold mold walls.

4) **Vacuum-forming** sheets of plastic (thermoplastics) are made limp by heating and placing them over a mold with a vacuum pulling the air from between the form and plastic so as to tightly set it over the form and cool it to a new shape (Thermoforming plastic is molding heated plastic by using air pressure or vacuum with or without molds or other tools to achieve the desired shape.)

Hand lay-up plastics are applied with reinforcements, such as fiberglass, by brushing, spraying or spreading with spatulas. Sometimes several layers are required for strength.

Built-up fillers like those used for autobody work, such as Bondo™, can be used as sculpture materials, especially coatings. The main considerations are the armature and the thickness. The armature must be able to support the putty-like mix and not be dissolved (such as uncoated Styrofoam™). The armature can be uncoated steel since the filler is so adhesive. Even cardboard can be used. For a thick work, several thinner layers of mix should be used, one on top of the other after the previous coat has hardened. Each layer needs to be roughed up to help with adhesion grip for the next layer. Layers can be up to three-sixteenths inch (0.476cm) without crazing or cracking (depending on the manufacturer's suggestions).

Heat and humidity affect the setting times, especially heat. Working time can be reduced to a few minutes (even seconds) when mixed in hot weather. The mix includes the body material with a paste hardener that is proportionally a small amount. The mixing does not have to be exact, although poor percentages affect the hardness and setting times. It is applied with a flexible, flat, handheld mixing spreader.

Finishing is relatively simple if the sculptor works the material immediately after hardening. The mix tends to get considerably harder in a brief time. It can be machine ground, sanded and finished to over 600 grit for a reflective coat of surface paint. (It is the same process used for autobody finishing.) *See* ***Fiberglass; Resins; Acrylic*** *(sheet);* ***Molds***.

Plywood A flat lumber product made by laminating several layers of thin sheets of wood in a crosshatch fashion to add strength to the finished product. Formed into four feet by eight feet (1.22m x 2.44m) sheets, plywood is made from many woods, but pine or fir are preferred. The finishes on these products vary from a coarse C or D grade to a cabinet grade of "A" (clear). Marine plywood is bonded with glue that is waterproof and does not have inner repair plugs that could later cause disintegration. *See* ***Lumber*** *(chart)*.

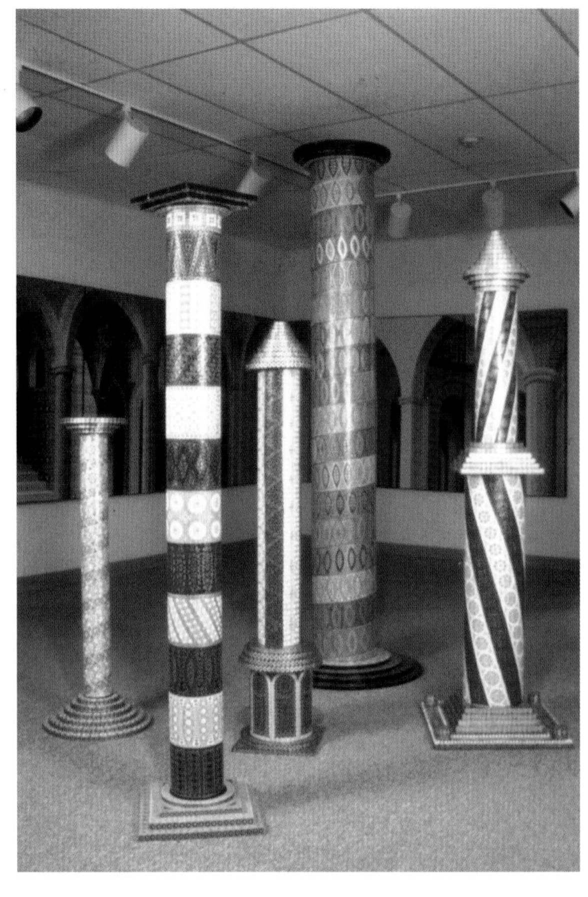

Liz Whitney Quisgard, *5 Columns*. Plywood, composition board, acrylic, 4 1/8′ (1.26m) to 8 1/2′ (2.59m) high.

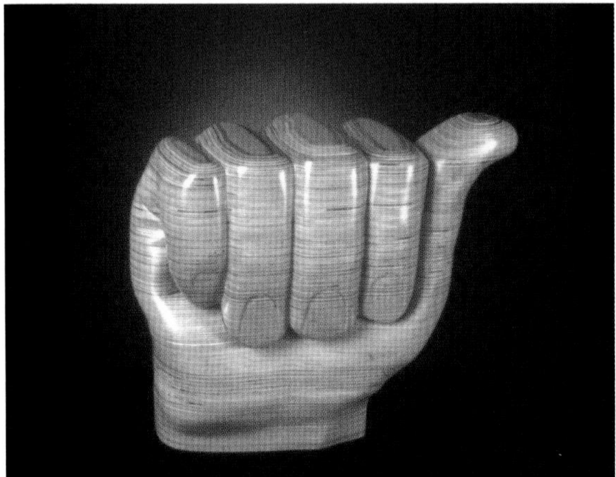

Barbara Smith, *Something in my Hand*. 40 layers of Baltic birth plywood, 2″x24″x11″ (5.2cm x 61cm x 27.9cm). Photographer: Barbara DeMoulin.

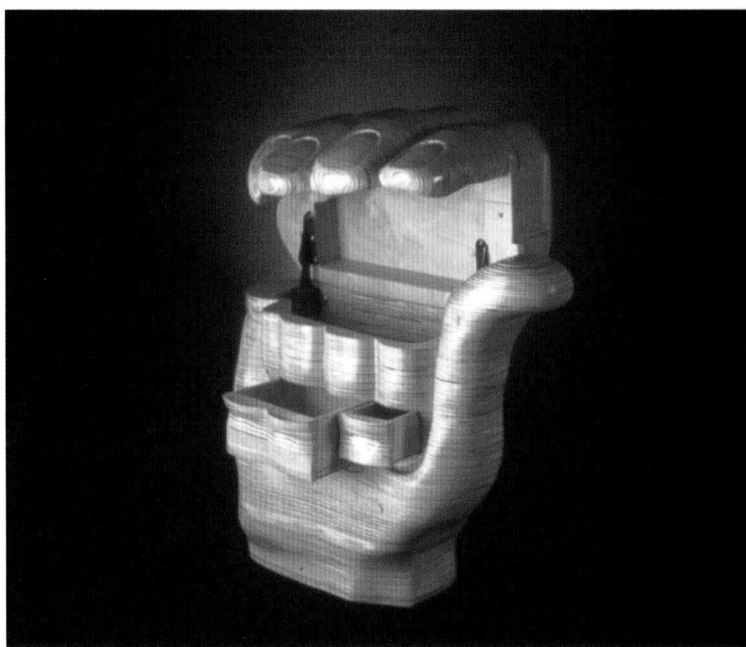

Something in My Hand, open view.

Pneumatic Operated by using compressed air for power. Air drills, air hammers and air grinders are common pneumatic tools. Most air tools are compact and lightweight since they do not have the heavy mechanical structure that electrical and gas tools require. *See **Air tools**; **Air compressor**; **Air hammer**.*

Pneumoconiosis A lung disease caused by long-term breathing of metal or mineral particles. *See **Silicosis**.*

Point A handheld metal shaft (chisel) with a pointed end that is hammer driven into the stone to remove chips of the stone. Points are basic tools for rouging out in stone carving. A punch is the bulky point used for granite and other hard stones.

Pointing machine (pointer) A device that uses points on the model and a corresponding point on the work designed to copy, enlarge or reduce a sculpture from an original with accuracy. The process involves three stable fixed points on both the model and sculpture material. A fourth point can then be measured from the model and easily transferred to the material. The points are drilled to depth (in stone or clay, for example) and then the encircled material is removed until the correct proportion is achieved. *See **Enlarging**.*

A stone carver in a Pietrasanta studio makes measurements with a pointer. Photographer: Enzo Torcoletti.

Carving stone based on the pointer measurements. The pointer is placed over the model. Photographer: Enzo Torcoletti.

Polish Rubbing a surface to achieve a smooth, slick and sometimes reflective finish. *See **Buffing compound**.*

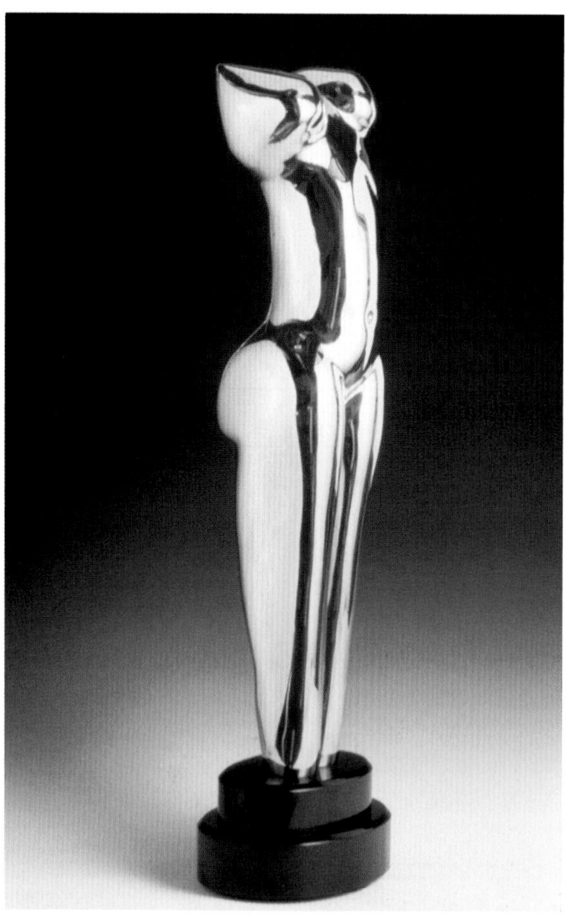

Joseph Rotella, *Torso*. Polished bronze, 36″x9″ (91.4cm x 22.9cm).

Assistants **Shannon Boles** and **Kenyon Williams** prepare a bronze surface to polish a section of *Genesis* by **Arthur Williams**.

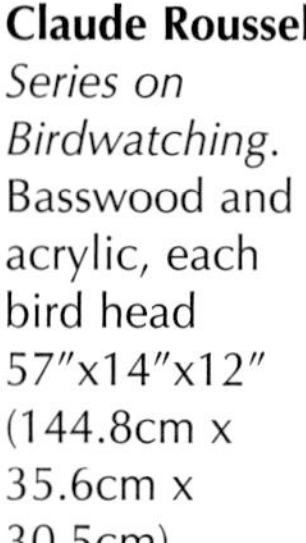

Claude Roussel, *Series on Birdwatching*. Basswood and acrylic, each bird head 57″x14″x12″ (144.8cm x 35.6cm x 30.5cm).

Polychrome Referring to multicolor or full color. The opposite of monochrome. To polychrome a sculpture is to cover the surface with a color (of paint) to decorate and/or preserve the material. *See* ***Monochrome***.

Polyester resin Synthetic thermosetting transparent resin. Additives, filler or opaque colors can be mixed into liquid resin for specific effect and color when catalyzed into a hard mass. *See* ***Resin***.

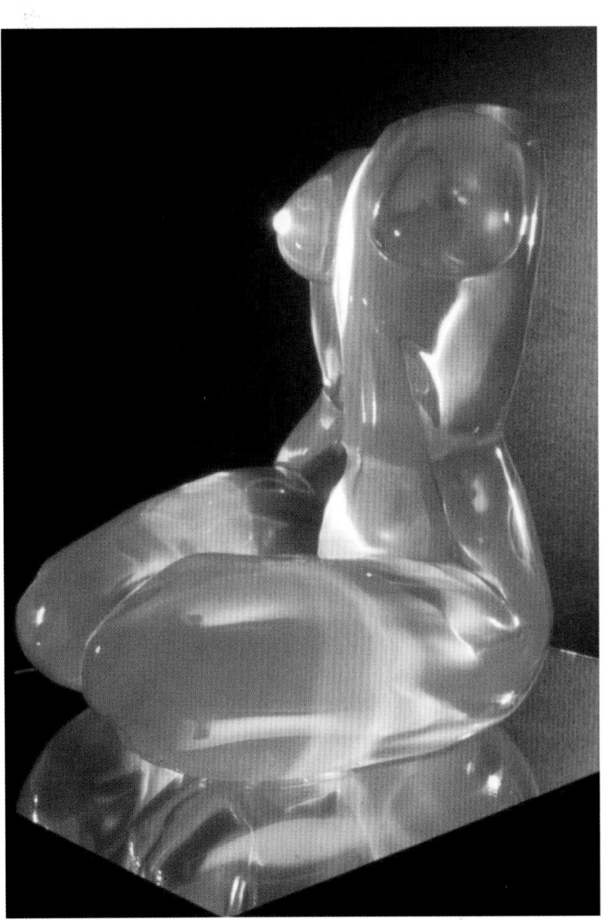

Arthur Williams, *Seated Split Figure*. Polyester resin, 18″x17″x12″ (45.7cm x 34.2cm x 30.5cm).

Norman D. Holen, *Woman at the Well II*. Polyester, 12″x10¼″x33¾″ (30.8cm x 26cm x 85.7cm). Photographer: Peter Lee.

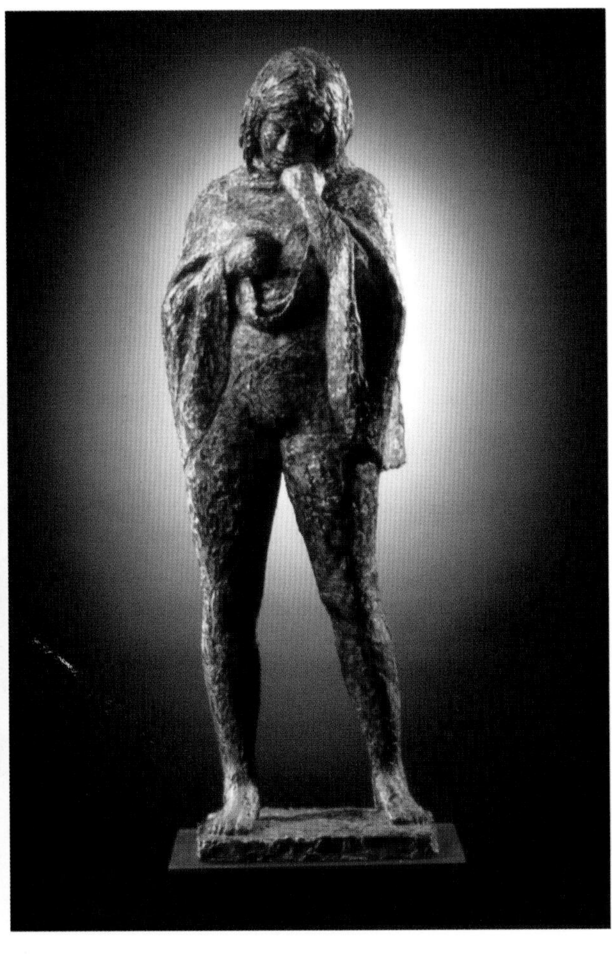

Polymer (paint) Pigment placed in an acrylic polymer resin solution. It is designed in convenient packaging for artists as a fast drying water-based artist's paint. It has excellent adhesion and cannot be removed with water when dry. *See* ***Acrylic*** *(paint)*.

Chryl L. Savoy and **Dee Cornell**, *Digillactus*. Polystyrene and paper compound, 4½'x4'x7'8" (1.4m x 1.2m x 2.3m). Children's Education Gallery, Alexandria Museum of Art, Alexandria, Louisiana.

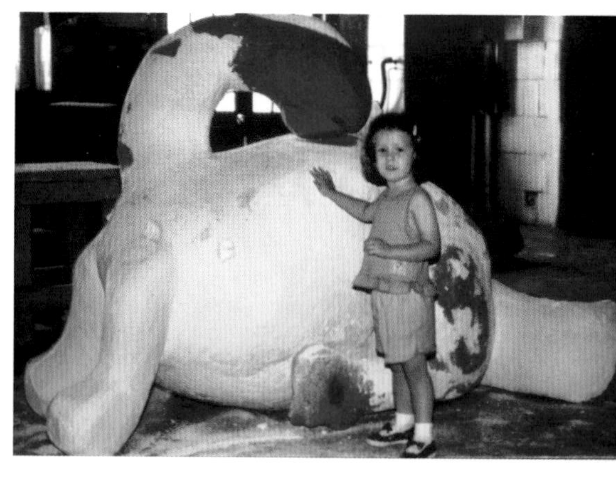

Chryl L. Savoy in collaboration with **Dee Cornell**: shaping a sculpture made of polystyrene and paper compound.

Jane Kelsey-Mapel, *Growing Him for the World.* Porcelain, underglaze, 21"x9"x8" (53.3cm x 22.9cm x20.3cm).

Polystyrene A lightweight rigid form of styrene often used as expanded polystyrene for armature materials in sculpture. *See* ***Expanded polystyrene; Styrofoam***™.

Polyurethane Thermoplastic polymers used in resins to create chemical-resistant coatings, foams and adhesives known for toughness.

Poly Vinyl Acetate (PVA) A vinyl resin that can be sprayed or painted on a mold surface as a release agent for polyester resin. *See* ***Resin***.

Porcelain A white clay and a near-translucent clay body fired in excess of 3272°F (1800°C). It is best known for slip casting and as a pure white body for multi-color glazes. Made primarily from kaolin (china clay), the result is low in shrinkage but minimum strength when dry. It has poor plasticity and slumps easily during modeling. Unless a fine grog is added for strength, it cannot be modeled to much height. In pottery, it is usually wheel thrown. *See* ***Clay*** *(water-based)*.

Jeff Schmuki, *Horse and Rider*. Porcelain assemblage, stains, decals, multi-fired, 14″x13″x5″ (35.6cm x 33cm x 12.7cm).

Porosity The ability of a substance to absorb a liquid.

Porous Full of holes.

Portfolio A representative sample of an artist's work. A sculptor's work is typically retained in slides. The artwork is selected and shown with the intention of securing exhibitions, commissions or other desirable positions. It is proof or validation of the artist's ability. The portfolio may also include a written resumè. Sometimes the portfolio contains actual works when practical (drawings, in particular).

Portland cement The most commonly used building cement for sculpture. It received its name from its resemblance to an English construction stone of a dull, light, pale gray color. Portland white cement is a medium used by sculptors, especially if a colorful aggregate is added which gives the aggregate a brighter look. *See* ***Cement; Sand casting***.

PORTLAND WHITE CEMENT

by Shane Snider

Armature by sculptor in preparation for the cement.

Portland white cement (1 part sand to 10 parts cement) with saturated coarse steel wool is wrapped around the armature. When the shape has been obtained, it is allowed to dry for 24 hours with loosely wrapped plastic to prevent drying out so quickly and cracking.

A final layer of Portland white cement can be added with or without a fine grade of steel wool. It is again covered and allowed to dry. **Shane Snider**, *In Balance*. Portland white cement, 22″x10″ (55.9cm x 25.4cm). Photographer: Roman Sapecki.

Shane Snider, *Melete*. Portland white cement and steel, 24″ (61cm) tall. Photographer: Roman Sapecki.

Portrait (head) A sculpture of the head, especially the facial area. A portrait sculpture is ordinarily a representative likeness of the model. *See **Bust; Armature; Clay** (modeling).*

Carter Jones, *Adolescence*. Terra cotta porcelain, 18″x16″x17″ (45.7cm x 40.6cm x 43.2cm).

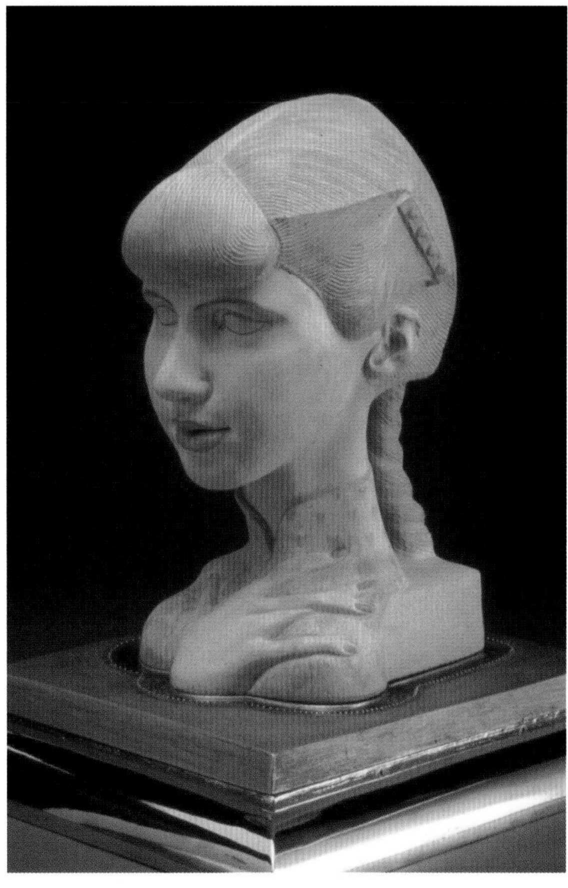

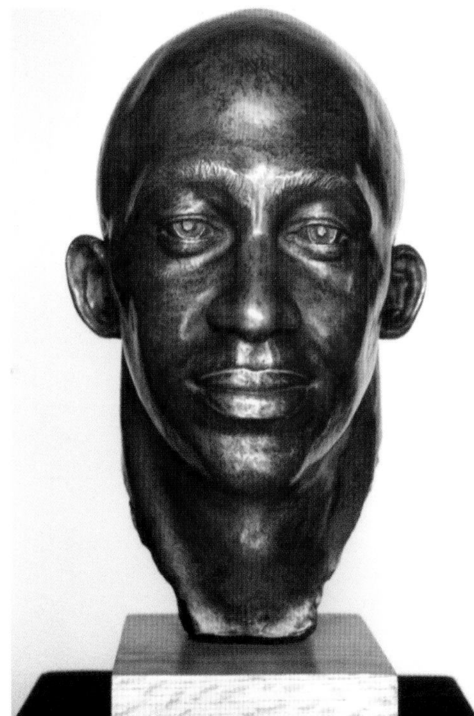

William N. Beckwith, *Chucky Mullins*. Bronze, life-size portrait bust.

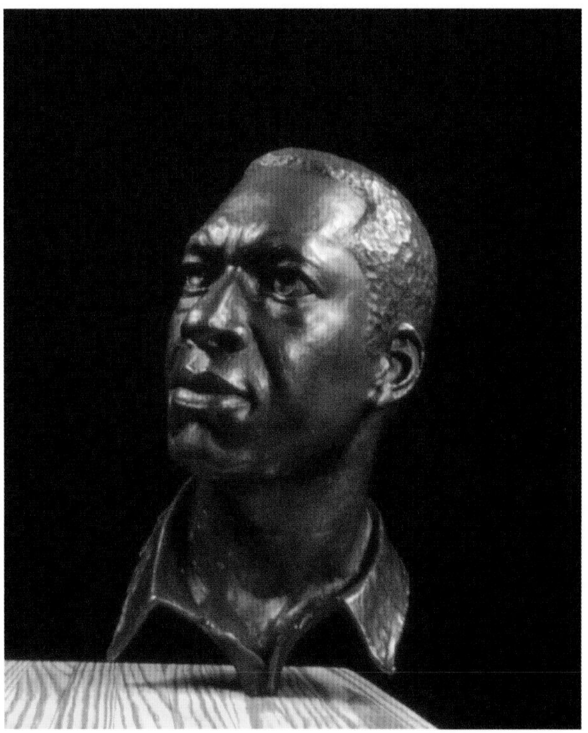

Ron Ott, *John Coltrane*. Bronze portrait bust, 19″x16″x13″ (48.3cm x 40.6cm x 33cm).

PORTRAIT
by William N. Beckwith

The sculptor begins with an armature for the portrait bust of his son, Clay Beckwith.

The armature with some modeling clay added.

The shape is roughed in.

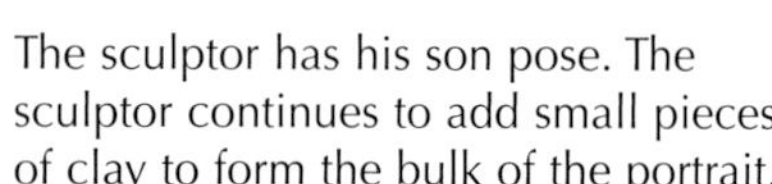

The sculptor has his son pose. The sculptor continues to add small pieces of clay to form the bulk of the portrait.

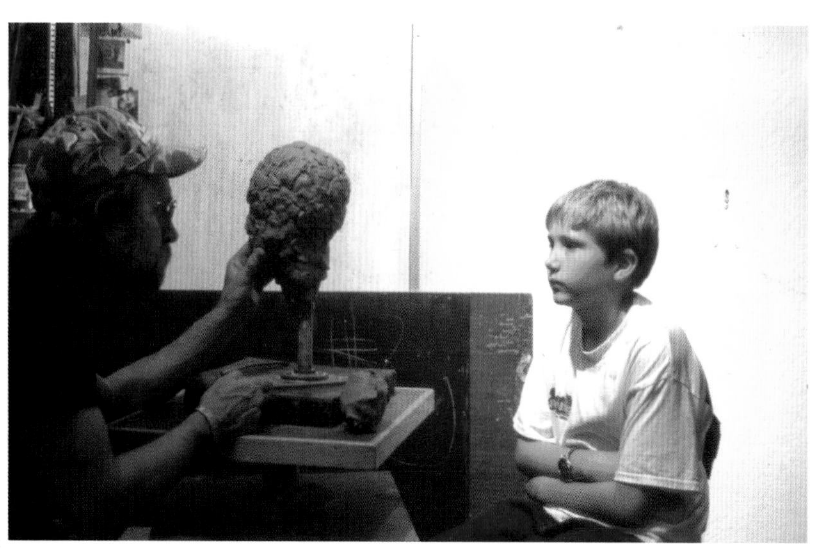

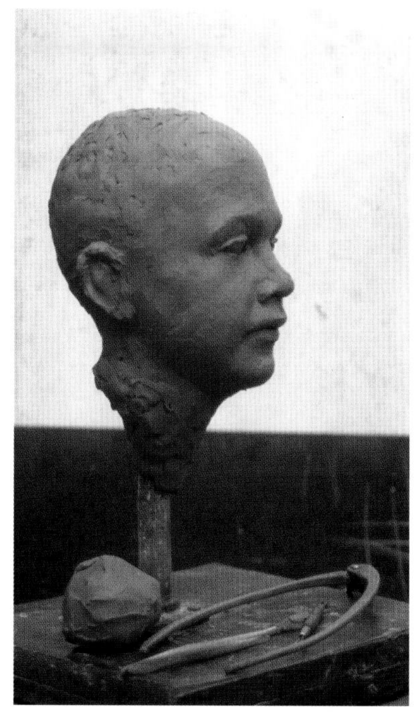

The surface has more detail added.

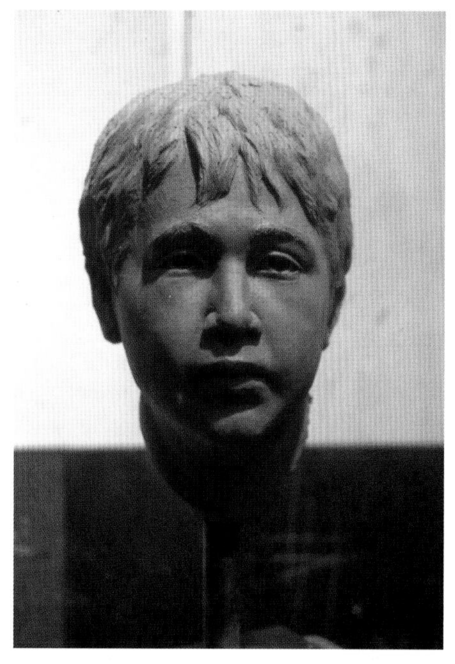

The sculptor continues to add details.

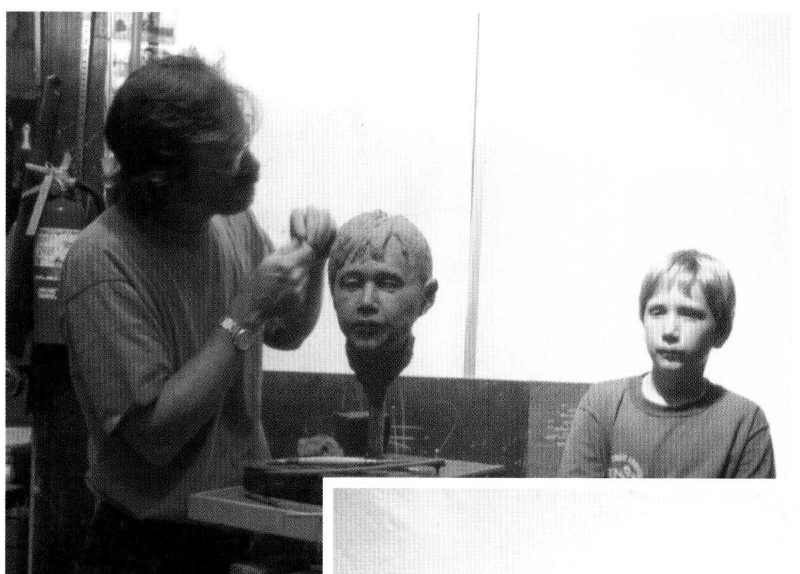

Final corrections with the model.

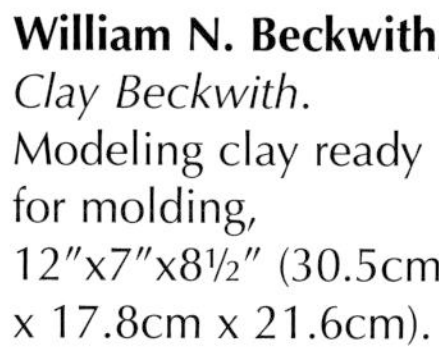

William N. Beckwith, *Clay Beckwith*. Modeling clay ready for molding, 12″x7″x8½″ (30.5cm x 17.8cm x 21.6cm).

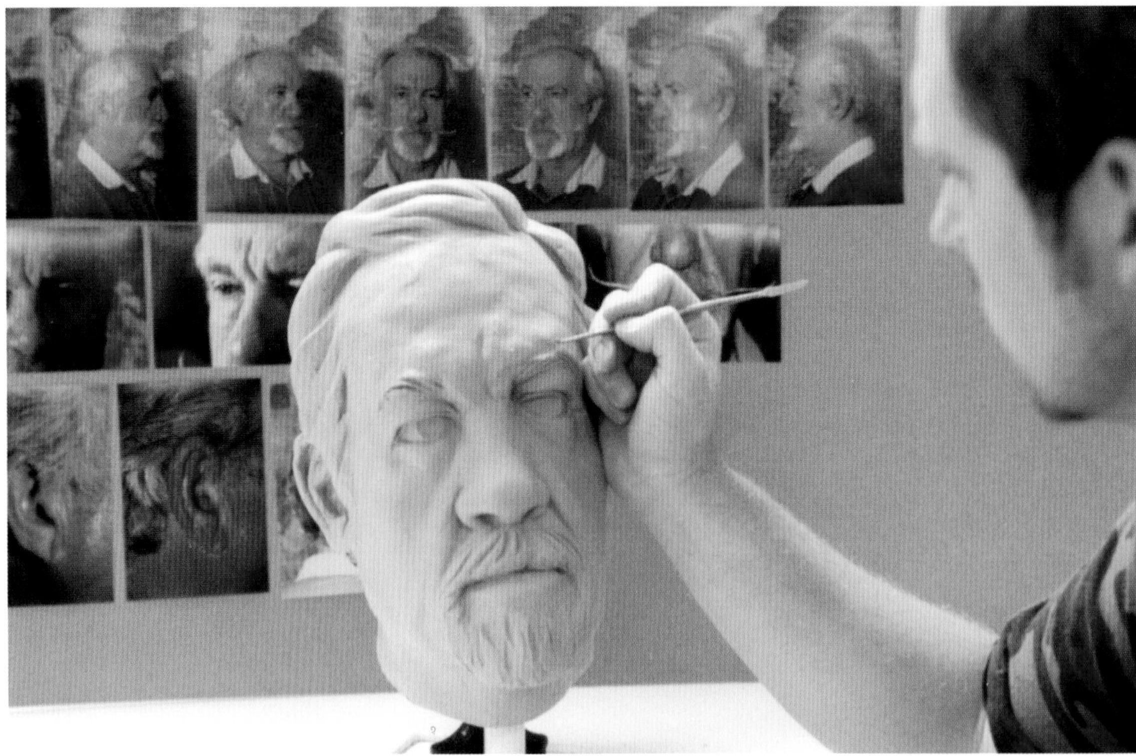

Tim Kinard models a portrait bust of John Kinard. Several photographs are on the wall near the portrait for reference as the sculptor works.

Potash sulfate (liver of sulfur) The name used for potassium sulfide. It is one of the most common base chemicals used for patination. In a weak solution on bronze, it creates a walnut brown appearance. In a strong solution, it can create a black surface color even without heat. It has the obvious sulfur odor and dissipates if not stored in a sealed container. *See* ***Liver of sulfur; Patina; Patina*** *(chart).*

Potter's wheel A complete machine for making clay into pottery-like forms. Also, the top of a spinning device designed to hold moist, centered clay to create round, thrown shapes. The wheel is operated by kick or crank, or it may be mechanically controlled by a motor. *See* ***Wheel***.

Pottery (potter) A more common form of ceramic ware, especially functional forms. A potter is one who makes the pottery. *See* ***Ceramics***.

Pouring gate Part of the metal casting pouring system nearest the wax artwork in the mold. *See* ***Metal pouring system***.

Pouring shank Designed to hold the crucible in preparation for pouring the liquid metal. The pouring shank can be a one-man, two-man or overhead hoist type, depending on the size of the crucible. A one-man shank has a pouring ring or yoke with a long shaft attached ending with a handle to maintain control and balance. The crucible fits snugly and securely into the yoke and is held firmly into place with a safety clamp.

The two-man pouring shank has a long shaft to each side of the yoke. One shaft end is straight while the other is split into two handles for control. The overhead hoist shank is of the same design but has two holders, one on each side of the yoke that extends upward to the hoist chain. Both the two-man and overhead shank have one or two safety clamps attached with a strong spring to the sides of the crucible to prevent it from falling from the pouring yoke. The crucible must always be centered into the shank with the pouring spout to the middle front to maintain a straight pour. *See* ***Blast furnace***.

Pour-on A molding process that involves a liquid molding material being poured over an encased model to form the mold. *See* ***Molding; Mold; Flexible mold***.

Power hammer An upright, foot operated, mechanical hammering device capable of delivering hard blows to metal. Used in forging, it can be electrical, air or foot powered. *See* ***Forging; Hammer***.

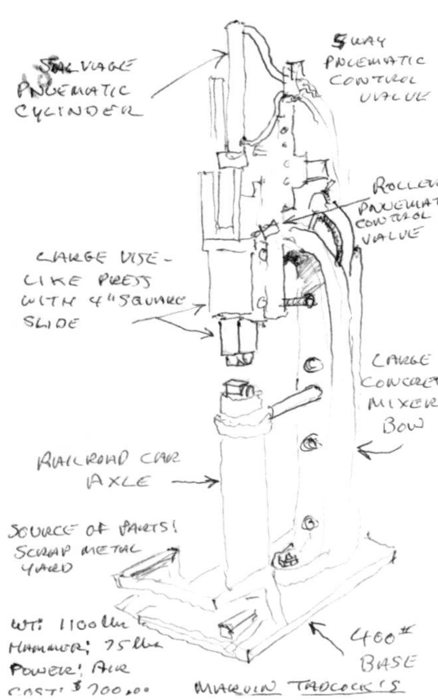

Drawing for *Power Hammer* by **Marvin Tadlock**.

Marvin Tadlock, *Tad Jaw III*. Handbuilt power hammer.

Greg Moran uses a power hammer.

Close-up of power hammer jaws in action.

Pre-cast panels Reinforced, cast and cured concrete sheets (panels) used for construction. *See **Concrete**.*

Preheating Heat that is applied to the base metal immediately prior to soldering, brazing, cutting or welding. A refractory mold is preheated prior to filling with hot metal as well. *See **Welding; Preheating furnace**.*

Preheating furnace A furnace designed to heat molds to a desirable high temperature prior to filling with hot metal. When metal casting, the refractory molds need to be prewarmed to keep the metal from freezing too fast on a cold surface, thereby clogging the runners.

Preheating assures the sculptor that all moisture is out of the mold. Otherwise, the bronze could hit a cold or damp surface and explode outward. When firing clay, preheating it expels much of the moisture, allowing the rest of the firing to proceed with less steam that would cause the clay body to burst or explode. *See **Metal casting**.*

Preheating furnace designed by **Arthur Williams**. The top is raised by a power lift. The ceramic shell molds are temporarily wired together for support. No other anchoring device is necessary.

Pre-warmed molds accept the hot, liquid bronze in the preheater.

Preheater used by the **Inferno Foundry**, Atlanta, Georgia.

Shannon Calhoun, *Pain of Childhood*. White stoneware clay, rutile stain, 22"x9"x1" (55.9cm x23cm x 2.54cm). Photographer: Sheldon Ganstrom.

Von Venhuizen, *The Optimist*. Ceramic/wood, press molded, wood fired stoneware, 14″x14″x12″ (35.6cm 2 x 35.6cm x 30.5cm).

Press mold The mold used in wet- or oil-based clay to secure a shape. If water-based clay is used, the mold, usually plaster, needs to be completely dry to absorb moisture from the clay. This causes clay shrinkage allowing the mold to release the casting. When not using a plaster mold, the surface of the mold still needs to be dry but additionally coated with a sheet of release material, such as polyurethane, canvas, etc. After taking out or off the mold, the material can be removed to display the surface.

Oil-based clay ordinarily does not need a separator, depending on the mold surface, though a thin layer of transparent food wrap can prevent adhesion problems. Because of the open nature of a relief mold, this is frequently the technique used to cast it. If several sections of a mold are needed, then each section is pressed and fitted together. If the casting material is pliable, the seam is completed as a squeeze joint. *See* ***Hump mold; Molds; Piece mold***.

PRESS MOLD
by Jack Thompson

The sculptor uses a body cast plaster press mold. The clay is pressed onto the surface of each side.

The sculptor places the two molds with clay together.

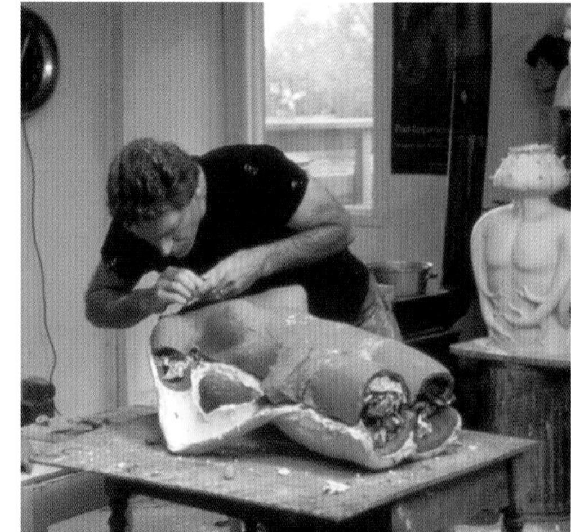

Wadded newspaper is stuffed in the center for support, and the top section is removed to better join and correct the surface.

With the clay out of the mold, **Jack Thompson** continues to work on the surface and adds other press molded parts for his sculpture.

Prewarmer A furnace used for preheating molds in anticipation of pouring a hot liquid metal into them. *See **Preheating furnace**.*

Primer An initial surface coating designed to adhere to the substance serving as a covering for the next layer (of paint).

Principles of order The use of design elements for sculpture. These include proportion, unity, balance, variety, movement and repetition. *See **Elements of design**.*

Proof (artist, foundry) A first or early casting primarily cast to check the mold's quality, use of patina, or sometimes, simply an unnumbered casting for the artist or foundry. The sculptor keeps a proof copy for his own records. *See **Edition**.*

Proportion The relationship of one part of the sculpture to the other or the relationship to the environment around the sculpture. Traditionally, the human body is seven and a half heads tall as a proportional measurement.

Proportional calipers Calipers that have a large jaw on one end and a small jaw on the other. They are used to reduce and enlarge an art work or model. A sliding wing nut set screw allows easy adjustment, so that the measurement can be several times proportionally larger or smaller. If the work is to be enlarged, the model is placed in the small jaws for the work to correspond to the scale in the large jaws. Reversing the model to the large jaws also reverses the proportion to decrease. *See **Enlarger**; **Pointing machine**; **Calipers**.*

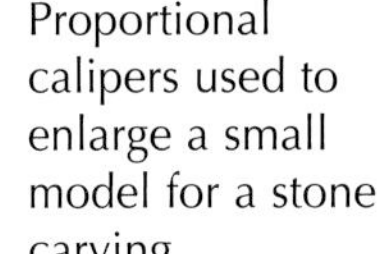

Proportional calipers used to enlarge a small model for a stone carving.

Prototype The original work, not a copy. *See **Original**; **Model**.*

PSI Pounds-per-square-inch, a measurement of air pressure associated with air compressors. *See **Measurements** (chart); **Air compressor**; **Air tools**.*

Pug To mix clay in a pug mill for immediate use by the ceramist. It is also a term used to describe the mixing of clay with water. *See **Pug mill**.*

Pug mill A machine used to mix and refine clay materials into one cohesive tight body. Through a series of powerful, but slowly turning blades and compression, the clay is mixed with water or refined into a near airtight consistency. It is then forced through an opening from within the strong metal machine. A pug mill with a vacuum, de-airing hopper prepares the clay body without air pockets so perfectly as to be ready for immediate use out of the machine. *See **Wedging**; **Ceramics**.*

Pugmill used for mixing clay.

Pulp A combination of cellulose materials cut and ground to make paper. The materials can come from previously made paper, wood, plants, rags, etc. *See* ***Paper; Paper casting; Papier machè***.

Pumice stone A volcanic stone used for its abrasive qualities to smooth surfaces.

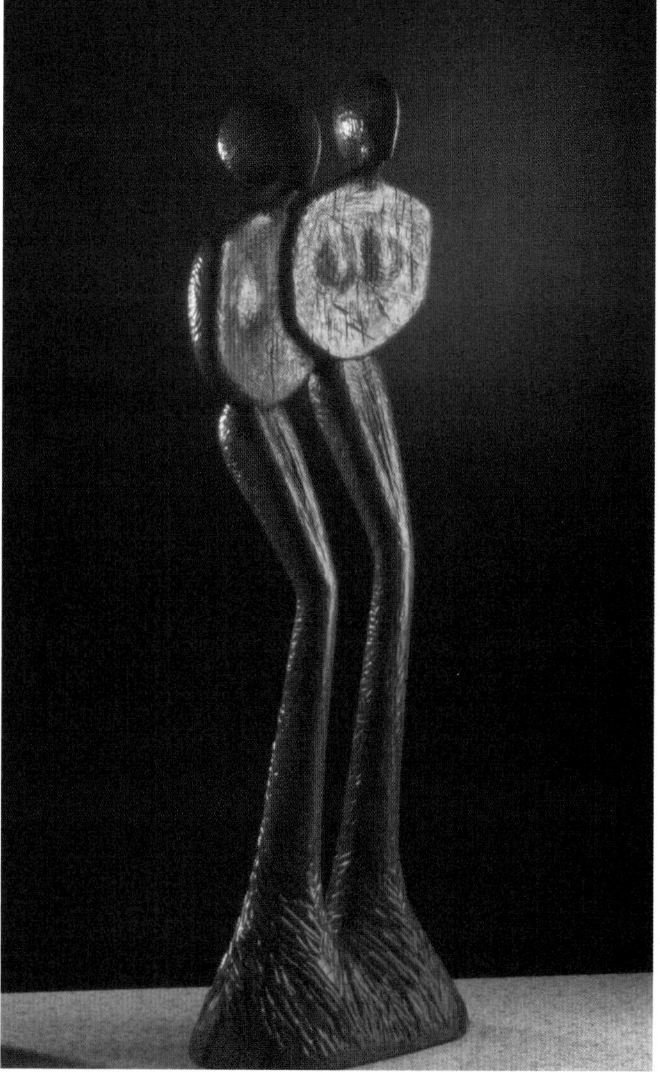

David Hostetler, *Duo*. Purple heartwood, 41″ (104cm) tall. Photographer: Terry Eiler.

Punch tool A handheld shaft with a tempered tip designed for a single purpose, such as stone carving, metal work, etc. The tempering enables the tool to be used over a long time without sharpening.

Punty A metal shaft (rod) used to accept hot glass from a blowpipe or another punty. The punty is also used to gather molten glass from the furnace. *See* ***Glass blowing***.

Purist An artist who holds fast to older traditional materials and processes. This results in works that are quite time-consuming, especially without modern power tools, but often more satisfying to the artist.

Purpleheart A wood that is known by its bright purple color. *See* ***Wood*** *(chart)*.

PVA Symbol for Poly Vinyl Acetate, a vinyl resin. *See* ***Poly Vinyl Acetate; Resin***.

PVC Poly vinyl Chloride, a thermoplastic resin, commonly the designation for a hard pipe and fittings. This is used for armatures or functional lines, such as air lines, because it is so easy and rapid to use. *See* ***Air compressors*** *(stationary air lines)*.

Pyrite Iron pyrite, otherwise known as fool's gold because of the yellow crystals resembling gold.

Michael David Fox, *The Squirm*. PVC pipe, multi-position, 12′ (3.7m) wide.

Pyrometer A device for measuring extremely high temperatures. It can be handheld to insert into a kiln or metal casting crucible. It may be mounted on a kiln wall with leads to the inside. It may be an optical device that focuses on the heat, etc. Most electric kilns have built-in pyrometers; whereas, metal casting is best served by handheld units.

Stationary pyrometer alongside a pre-warmer.

Handheld pyrometer being placed directly into the furnace.

Pyrometric cone These are small, specially formulated clay bodies in pyramid-shaped cones placed into a kiln to be watched through a peep hole during the firing. They soften and bend at precise temperatures and begin to melt. Since the cone base is broader, the tip will begin the melting process and continue to bend down. Each cone has a number stamped into the body for easy reading. The lowest cone is 022 at 1085°F (585°C), and the highest is cone 42 at 3659°F (2015°C). *See **Kiln**; **Firing**.*

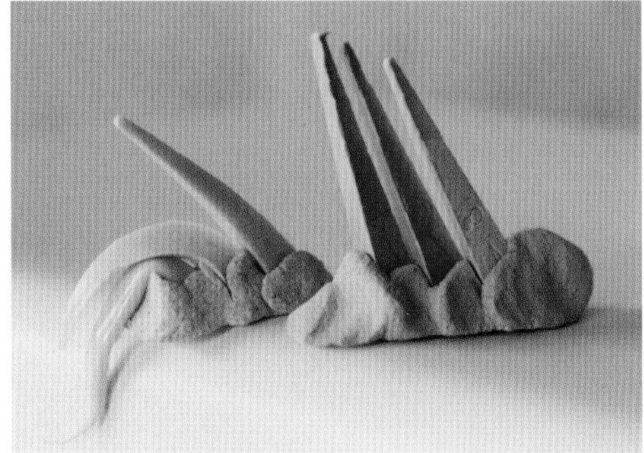

Pyrometric cones are grouped into sets of three different temperatures. The lowest temperature cone is the first one to slump followed by the desirable temperature cone. The final one, a guard cone, should not slump unless the kiln is overfired. The unused cones (on the right) are colored to represent different firing temperatures on sight. Once used, they turn white. (Cones furnished by **Jim Francis** of Mississippi Mud Works, Ocean Springs, Mississippi.)

Patz Fowle, *Pyrometric Primate*. Clay, 3"x3"x6" (7.6cm x 7.6cm x 15.2cm)

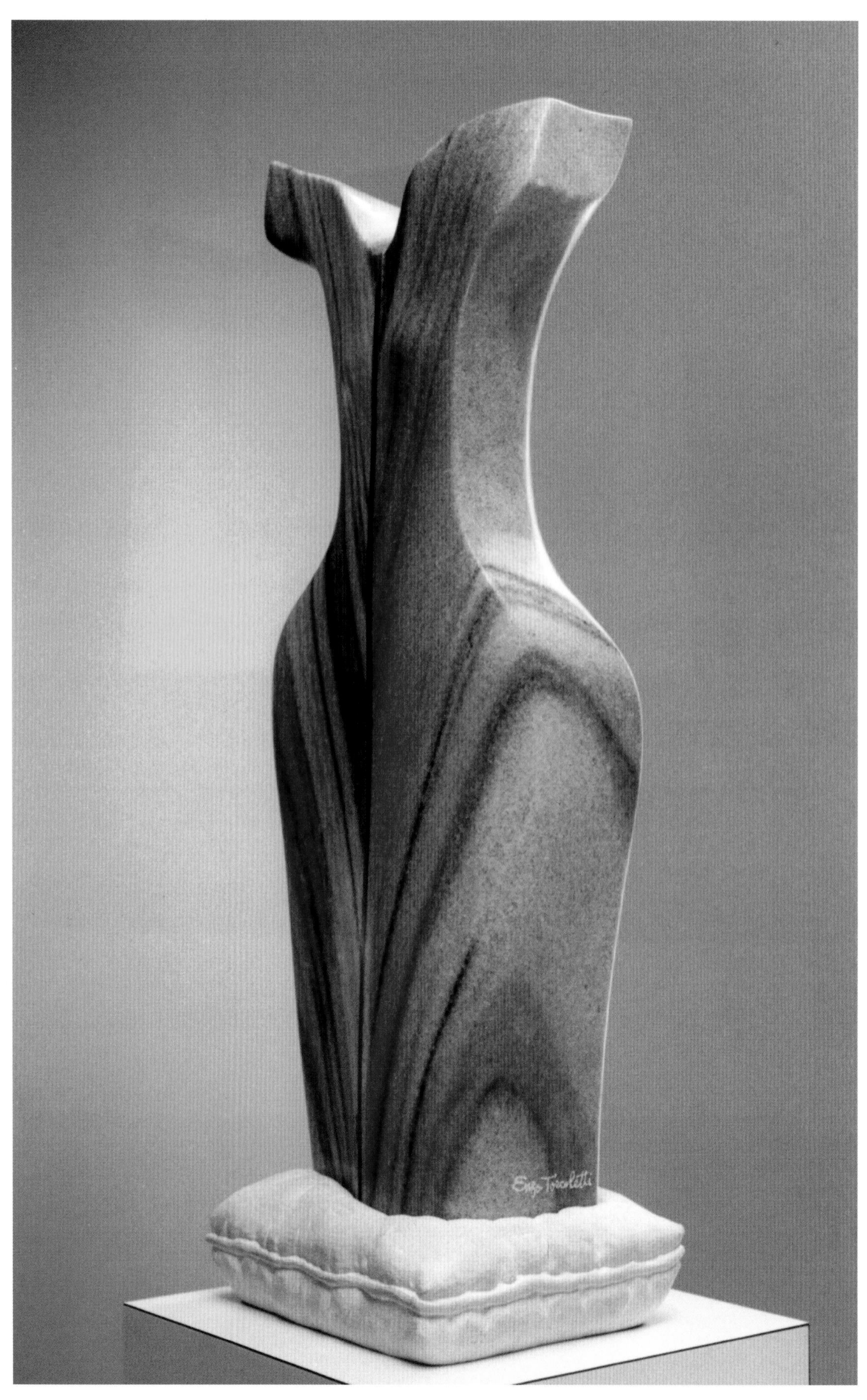

Enzo Torcoletti, *Victory at Rest*. Pink Georgia marble, Texas and Portuguese limestone, 29″ (73.7cm) tall. Photographer: Walter Coker/*Folio Weekly*.

Q

Quarry A site where specific stone is located and yielded for artistic or building purposes. The stone is removed by blasting, cutting, etc. Depending on the quarry, stone can be harvested for several years by going deeper or further into the hillside. Carrara in Italy is the best known marble quarry because of its use by sculptors, especially Michelangelo.

Marble quarry in Carrara, Italy. Photographer: Enzo Torcoletti.

Marble quarry in Marble, Colorado, USA. Photographer: Jim Boyd.

Limestone quarry in Alabama, USA.

Quarry water The moisture content that is temporarily retained in stone after it is newly quarried. As the moisture evaporates the stone becomes harder and more brittle.

Quartz A hard, crystalline mineral of silica that is transparent and found in almost all kinds of rocks. Layers of it are undesirable in carving stones, though some varieties are considered gemstones. In ceramic use, quartz is pulverized into a fine powder and used as silica for glazes and clay bodies.

Quartz inversion The conversion from a dried clay product to a hardened glass-like body. The changes in the crystalline structure are brought about by extremely high temperatures in the firing process. *See* ***Firing***.

Quench Thrusting a heated piece of metal into a container of liquid, usually water or oil, to temper or cool it. Quenching is used to harden metal but may result in brittle metal if not properly done. *See* ***Temper***.

Quick connect couplings placed together.

Quick connect couplings removed. Left to right: female coupler, male quick connect plug.

Quick connect couplings Fittings used with compressed air. The (female part) air line automatically keeps the air supply cut off until the quick connect plug (male) from the tool source is inserted. It readily clamps and stays in place until the sculptor chooses to disconnect it. The connect plug is easily held in one hand, while the connector is held in the other as the tool is inserted or released.

The couplers are either: 1) A longer sleeve type that requires the worker to pull the outer sleeve back to insert the plug or to remove it, or 2) The push type connector that is slightly easier to operate, since the plug is easily inserted without having to pull an outer sleeve back. A temporary rush of compressed air escapes as the connection is completed. Typically, the couplers are made of brass and the plugs of steel with a zinc dichromate finish.

There are several different sizes, shapes and manufacturers of plugs and connectors. The sculptor is advised to purchase matching sets that can be easily obtained near his/her studio. Some of the size fittings may be available from one manufacturer to another. *See* ***Air compressor; Air tools***.

Quicklime Calcium hydroxide that has been recently calcined. *See* ***Limestone***.

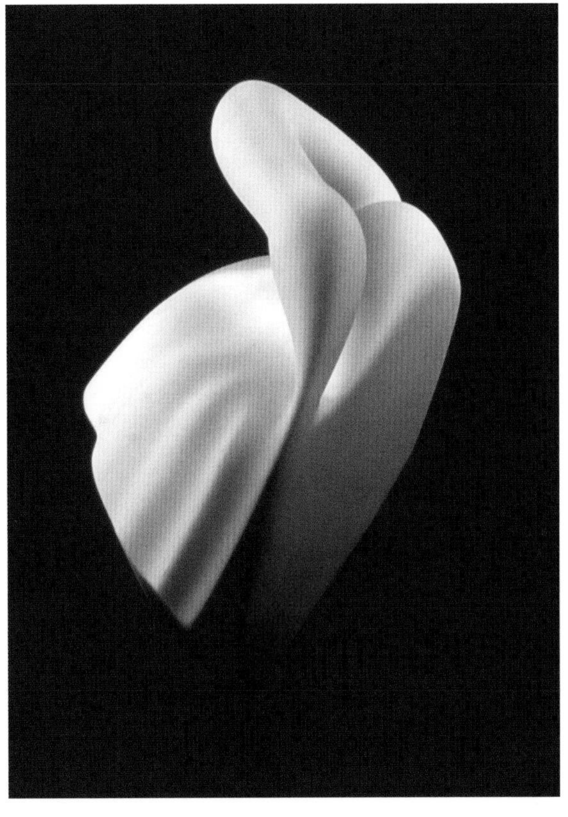

Dahrl Thomson, *Meditation on White*. Marble, 19″x38″x28″ (48.3cm x 96.5cm x 71.1cm).

Gerald Balciar, *Mountain Princess*. Colorado Yule marble, 25″x48″x18″ (63.5cm x 121.9cm x 45.7cm).

Arthur Williams, *Rachel*. Cast resin, Life-size.

R

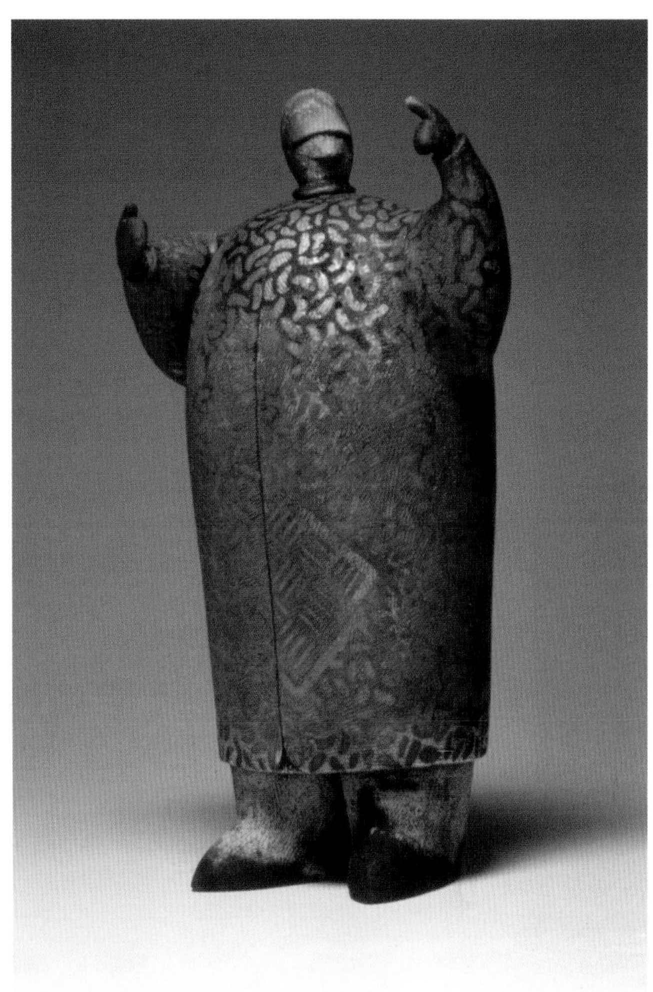

Radial (balance) All sides of a form are in equal balance with a middle or center point of reference. A sphere best represents a radial form. *See* ***Symmetrical***.

Raised grain Cells of wood that reach above the surface after planing, or cells that stand above the surface by a light, deliberate addition of moisture prior to the final sanding. *See* ***Wood***.

Raku Placing ceramic work that has been bisqued (with or without glaze) into a hot kiln structure, arriving at the desired temperature, and then rapidly removing it. It involves a clay body that can withstand a rapid heat buildup and heat loss without fracture. Though the body can be one of several lower firing clays, it usually contains a large amount of grog to aid in the sudden temperature changes. To achieve reduction, the work may be placed into black oil or a covered container of sawdust, newspaper, etc., to create an unspent fuel creating a dark or black clay body. *See* ***Clay***.

Fred Yokel, *It Was Like This*. Raku, 19" (48.3cm) tall. Photographer: Roger Dunn.

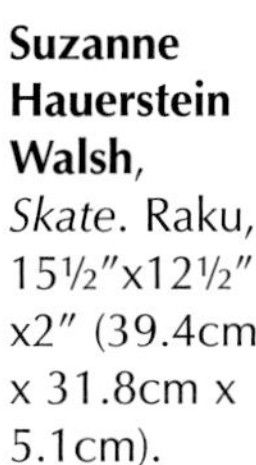

Suzanne Hauerstein Walsh, *Skate*. Raku, 15½"x12½" x2" (39.4cm x 31.8cm x 5.1cm).

Rasp A sharp, coarse-toothed handheld tool in a file configuration. The raised sharp pointed teeth replace the linear ridges found on files. Rasps are used for rough shaping of stone and wood, plaster, etc. Riffler rasps have different rasp shapes and configurations on each end. Also, a rasp is any sharp toothed tool used for rapid material removal, such as a rotary rasp. *See* ***Riffler***.

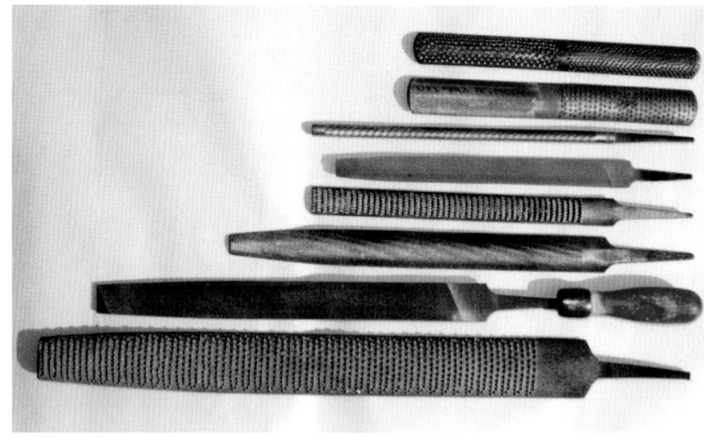

Rasps and files.

Rattail file A file with a long, narrow tapered handle (tail). The tail may be inserted in a handle designed to hold it securely.

Ready-made A mass produced manmade article that is taken from functional use and designated for sculpture display. The original object may be without artistic intent but recognized as an object of art or part of an object of art with little or no change in structure. *See* ***Found object; Assemblage***.

Realism A work of art that represents a readily recognizable human form or object. Realism is the opposite of abstraction. The term "representational" may be applied. *See* ***Abstraction***.

Rebar Ribbed steel designed for use with concrete. The ribs allow the concrete to grip the bar for added strength and tension. It is rather soft and easy to bend and cut into special shapes. It is used in sculpture armatures for support. *See* ***Concrete; Armature***.

Red heat Bright or cherry red heat at 1292°F to 1382°F (700°C to 750°C). Red heat is the temperature where plaster investment molds are held for burnout. *See* ***Tempering***.

Reducing (agent) A paint thinner or other liquid that thins or weakens the paint or another liquid substance.

Reducing flame An oxygen-gas flame with an excessive amount of gas resulting in dark smoke, even soot. *See* ***Oxyacetylene flame***.

Stored Rebar.

Rebar: close up.

eduction (in kiln firing) Depriving oxygen from metal oxides in a glaze firing by closing the openings to a kiln during the latter part of the firing. Even though reduction begins once the moisture has escaped, it can be controlled by reducing the oxygen. This drives the unspent carbon into the clay body to combine with the metallic oxides. The oxides (primarily iron) adds new color to the body or alters the glaze. The resulting body is considerably darker if the clay contains much iron oxide. Over reduction accomplishes nothing and may even result in body blisters or dull glaze colors. *See* ***Firing; Kiln***.

efractory Resisting heat. Refractory materials can withstand high temperatures. They are used for metal casting furnaces, burnout furnaces and ceramic kilns. The refractory materials may include clay bodies, cast bricks or a fiber insulation. *See* ***Furnace; Kiln***.

efractory cements Specially designed high aluminum cements. They can go as high as 2800°F (1538°C), and magnesite cements can go even higher at 4000°F (2204°C). Some are designed to be higher/lighter in weight for insulation only, while others are much stronger for surface use. *See* ***Furnace; Kiln***.

efractory washes A protective covering of refractory substances brushed on a furnace or kiln interior prior to use. *See* ***Kiln wash***.

egulator A device to control the flow of air, gas or liquid. In sculpture, a regulator is used to control the air supply for pneumatic equipment or the controls on oxyacetylene cutting/welding equipment. Regulators are installed on gas bottles used for welding, and cutting as well. *See* ***Oxyacetylene welding; Oxyacetylene cutting; TIG; MIG***.

elease agent A substance added to the surface of a model or mold to prevent adhesion by additional mold parts. The substance may be used to prevent a casting substance from adhering to the mold container. A good release agent does not distort or mix with the casting and is easily applied. A release agent is also called a separator. *See* ***Release agent*** *(chart)*.

Sharon Dee Shaughnessy, *Paradise Found*. Art-a-fact cast polished stone, 36″x39″x5″ (91.4cm x 99.1cm x 12.7cm).

RELEASE AGENTS
Notes

Most **liquid dish detergents** are no longer acceptable for molding release agents unless carefully tested to prove that they have desirable separator qualities. *See* ***Mold soap***.

Paste waxes can be excellent separators, but sometimes several coats may be required to ensure the porous nature of the object being molded is completely sealed.

Silicone sprays are in common use, since they can easily be applied from a spray can in a fine mist that ordinarily does not interfere with the artwork or mold surface. All warnings on the spray cans should be observed. However, since they are a thin separator, they furnish little depth or saturation on the positive. Care must be taken not to use a silicone spray or to use it sparingly on modeling clays. Once coated, the modeling clay may not be able to re-adhere to itself for further use.

Water is a natural separator for a plaster mold when casting with wax. A well-soaked mold will easily resist the hot liquid wax. Cold water applied after the slush or brushed surface will accelerate the hardening time of the wax and aid in the slight shrinkage making the removal even easier.

Oils are characteristically good separators, especially **petroleum jellies** such as Vaseline. How™ever, if the petroleum jelly is thickly applied, it will show application (brush) marks or fill intricate details of the mold or artwork. Sometimes, it is best to apply the jelly with a rag that is only partially saturated or to dilute the jelly with a paint thinner. Motor oils can be applied directly out of the can. Non-fibered bearing grease can also be used, though it may need thinning with kerosene or a paint thinner. Care must be taken in using oils on artwork for plaster molds that will later be used as clay slip molds. If oil residue remains in the plaster, the properties of the mold will not be useful for slip casting. Also, oil surfaces can cause liquid waxes (used for metal casting) to adhere to the mold, rather than resist it.

RELEASE AGENTS*

Mold Material	Cast Material	Release Agent
Alginate	Plaster	Petroleum jelly
Plaster *Cautions:* ***Avoid damp surfaces*** ***Avoid porous surfaces*** ***Avoid undercuts***	Plaster/Hydrocal™ Slip clay Wax Casting Resin Concrete Cast Stone Paper Pulp	Petroleum jelly Total dryness/Talc Water Wax/PVA Clay wash, Motor oil, Lard Clay wash, Shellac and Wax Vegetable oil, Wax and PVA Wax
Polyurethane Rubber *Cautions:* ***Avoid damp surfaces*** ***Choose best mold hardness***	Plaster/Hydrocal™ Wax Casting Resin Paper pulp	Silicone spray Petroleum jelly No agent Light silicone spray PVA Wax
Silicone Rubber *Cautions:* ***Avoid sulfur products***	Plaster/Hydrocal™ Casting Resin Ceramic Clay Paper Pulp Wax	No agent, Petroleum jelly Manufacturer's spray PVA No agent Wax, No agent No agent, Manufacturer's spray
Latex *Cautions:* ***Avoid cold casting compounds of non-ferrous nature***	Plaster/Hydrocal™ Wax Resin	Petroleum jelly Wax and PVA Silicone spray Wax and PVA
Hard Resin/Epoxy	Plaster Casting Resin Resin/Glass Fiber Paper Concrete	Wax Wax and PVA Wax and PVA Wax Oil, Lard
Metal	Plaster Concrete	Oil, Petroleum jelly Oil, Lard
Gelatin	Skin, Plaster	No agent
Polyester Resin/Fiberglass	Plaster Wax Concrete/Cast Stone Paper	Petroleum jelly, Silicone spray Silicone spray Petroleum jelly Wax
Hot Melt Vinyl *Cautions:* ***High heat, Avoid low melting temperature casting products***	Manufacturer's recommendations Materials that can withstand high heat up to 250°F (121°C)	Manufacturer's recommendations
Wood	Plaster Concrete	Sealed/Petroleum jelly Motor oil

****Release Agents*** *vary with the application, substance, surface, temperature, humidity, technique, moisture, etc. See* ***Release Agents Notes***.

Relief The projection of figures or objects from a flat background surface creating the illusion of full display. Good relief displays effective light and dark shadows instead of two-dimensional lines. Low relief (bas relief) has only partial projection with no undercuts such as coins. Bas relief allows greater protrusion but without undercuts. Mezzo relief occurs when figures partially protrude but with acute undercuts. High relief is approximately half to a full figure standing out but an intricate part of the flat or shallower relief background. It is still anchored to the flat surface. Concave relief, hollow relief or relief in reverse is accomplished by carving a depression with an illusion to raised relief. Relief sculpture is the opposite of sculpture-in-the-round.

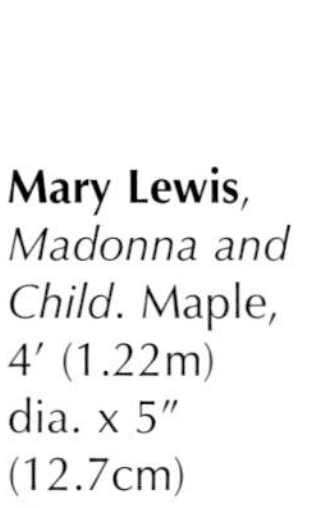

Mary Lewis, *Madonna and Child*. Maple, 4′ (1.22m) dia. x 5″ (12.7cm) deep.

Pencil sketch for *Madonna and Child* by **Mary Lewis**, 5½″ (14cm) diameter.

Glenna Goodacre, *Sacajawea Dollar* ©. U.S. Mint, 1999.

Glenna Goodacre in her studio at work on the relief for the *Sacajawea Dollar* with model Randy 'L Teton. Photographer: Doug Merriam.

Sheryl McRoberts, *Still Life with Frogs/Crustaceans*. Clay, underglazes, oil paint, 36″x24″x6″ (91.4cm x 61cm x 15.2cm).

Replica A copy of a work by the original artist, though completed in a different scale or material. The sculptor may choose to make smaller replicas of larger scale sculptures, for example. The term also refers to a mold taken from a previously cast sculpture though the practice is not regarded with favor. The replica may be cast in another substance (not the original casting material) intended to serve as instruction, especially for younger artists.

Repoussè (metal) A technique of hammering metal (usually the back side) into different shapes. A wooden mold is used for soft metals like copper. Some metals are heated to be more flexible and used for tempering purposes. There are many shapes of hammers used for this purpose. *See* ***Die-forming***.

Tools used by **Wendel Broussard** for metal shaping.

Reproductions Works made from the mold of the original sculpture but not always with approval from the sculptor or under his/her oversight and, generally, not during his/her lifetime.

Mary K. VanGieson, *A Short History of Education*. 36 gauge tooling foil, bolts, 9¼″x7½″x3″ (23.5cm x 19.1cm x 7.6cm). Photographer: Paul D. VanGieson.

Resin (polyester resin) A common liquid form of plastic used for clear castings by sculptors. Resin, being a thermosetting plastic, depends on a catalyst to activate it into a solid form. Temperature, humidity, mold shape and catalyst are significant considerations for casting resins.

Temperature greatly affects the setting time of resin. If the temperature is below 65°F (13.3°C), it is not advisable to begin the casting process, since the liquid may not harden properly. Temperatures around 70°F (21.1°C) are best. After the temperature increases beyond this point, resin begins to set faster and the catalyst needs to be adjusted to accommodate this. Extremely high temperatures result in a nearly uncontrollable, quickening rate of setting. This is especially true with greater thicknesses. Thick castings need a slower setting time to avoid cracks or rising air bubbles.

Humidity can determine the clarity, setting time and amount of catalyst in the mold. High humidity causes the setting time to slow. Extremely high humidity can also cause a cloudy appearance in the casting. While additional catalyst may be added, it is not advisable for the best and most predictable castings.

Technique

Molds for liquid resins are of several types; however, not all work the same. Any container that does not leak is a potential mold. The sculptor needs to be certain that a good sealer on porous molds is used, as well as a separator to prevent adhesion to the mold. If plaster is used, it must be dry and coated with enough shellac or lacquer to seal the pores. (Two coats of shellac will usually suffice.) The unrivaled separator is wax, and the best way to use it is to coat the mold, then buff it and re-coat it. Place a top coat of PVA (polyvinyl alcohol) on the wax to complete the best possible release.

Carole A. Feuerman, *Lady Neptune*. Oil painted resin, 46″x27″x38″ (116.8cm x 68.6cm x 96.5cm). Photograph: David Finn.

Use flexible mold materials that are designed for the purpose. While most will tolerate some heat buildup during the setting period, not all do well with the extreme heat generated by large thick castings. One of the most predictable mold materials is silicone. Not only can it be placed next to a damp plaster surface, it seldom needs a parting agent. It is durable and retains a good, even density for a uniform distribution of heat.

Whatever the mold material, undercuts need to be small and few since resin shrinks from 3% to 6% depending upon the thickness of the casting. Thicker works tend to show greater shrinkage. If a large undercut is necessary, the sculptor should consider a flexible insert into the molding material, such as a sponge slightly soaked with the molding material in place. If possible, the undercut should be cast in a solid part to be ground down later, as resins are easily worked using sharp, high RPM grinding bits.

Extreme or multi-thicknesses within the artwork cause setting problems. Thick areas will set more quickly and with less catalyst, while thin areas need more catalyst to cast at the same rate. If these two areas are joined, the catalyst needs to be selected for the thicker areas to avoid rapid setting and cracking. If there are thinner areas, the work should be left in the mold longer for more setting time and then cured longer once out of the mold to reach full hardness. Care must be taken to avoid damaging the soft areas still going through the hardening process.

Irene Mendonis, *Eleph-ant*. Cast resin, 12″x7″x6″ (30.5cm x 17.8cm x 15.2cm). Photographer: Diana Pearson.

The mold must be completely sealed. A large seam-lip on the mold helps to keep a tight seal, especially if it is a flexible mold. Mother molds are required on flexible materials. All molds need to be tightly bound and leveled prior to pouring. An additional measure to ensure a liquid proof seal is to cover all seams with plaster impregnated canvas or denim fabric before the pour.

Liquid resin demands excellent ventilation. The operator needs a respirator designed for the purpose, latex or rubber gloves and eye protection.

Mixing containers need to be spotless and large enough to allow a strong but moderate stirring action. Smaller mixes, less than three gallons, can be mixed by hand with a mixing paddle. Larger ones should be mixed with power mixers at a moderate speed to avoid whipping air bubbles into the plastic.

Colorant is mixed first. Avoid using too much. One drop in a thick form is many times more potent or darker than one drop in a thin form. (An accurate way to envision transparent colors in a mix is to use a clear glass container about the same thickness as the sculpture. Fill it with water and then slowly add one drop of color at a time while mixing it with a non-absorbent paddle. The resulting color and transparency is almost identical to the same thickness and color amount used in resin.) With resin, the color is stirred until the mix is even, perhaps five minutes. Afterwards, the mix should set for several minutes to allow some of the stirred-in air bubbles to surface. (If uniform fillers are to be added to the mix, this is generally the best time to do so.)

The **catalyst,** organic peroxide, is hazardous if touching the skin and can cause blindness if entering the eye. Measurements are crucial. Thick works with several gallons (liters) of resins need only a small amount, even ten times less than a thin, light relief size would. The amounts are either measured in grams (milligrams) or drops per ounce (grams). If a large amount is to be used, it needs to be pre-measured and then slowly poured into the resin as it is being stirred. Additional catalyst is needed if much colorant or fillers are used. There is no substitute for experimentation. Records should be kept that include room temperature, humidity, drops or grams per ounce (milligrams per gram), amount of resin, type and thickness of mold. Different brands of resins react differently to catalyst formulas. There are resins that are available for thin castings as well as larger castings.

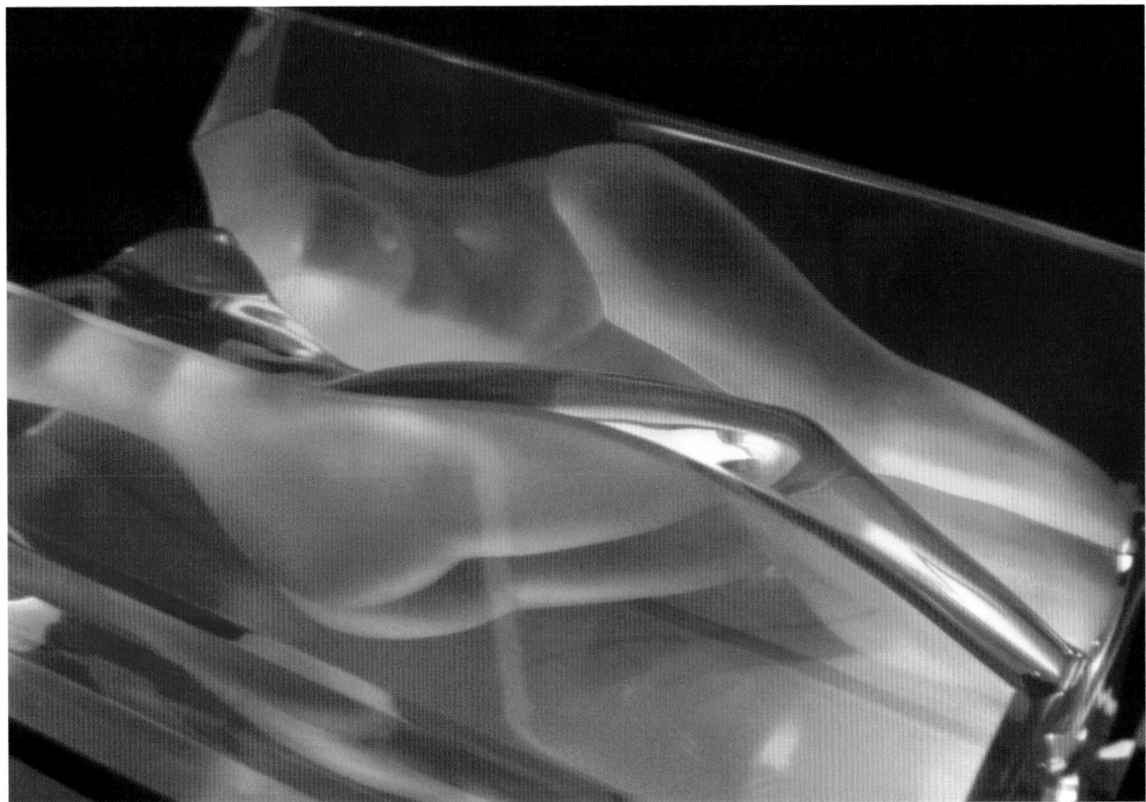

Arthur Williams, *Reclining Figure*. Resin with transparent dye, approximately 52″x32″x13″ (132cm x 81cm x 33cm).

The catalyst is mixed from five to ten minutes, depending on the mixer and speed. After letting it settle for a few minutes to allow air to surface, it can be poured. Avoid using a large container of mix that requires a large percentage of catalyst for smaller works. It will harden too quickly, even before it is poured out. Pour the resin through a fine filter to eliminate any trash that has entered during mixing and to help eliminate air bubbles.

Wearing a respirator, the mix should not be left alone until the operator is sure the resin has settled and there are no leaks. This could take an hour or longer depending on the mold quality and the air surfacing from the resin. Some extra resin from the original mix is needed to accommodate air escaping, mold settling, and possible mold leaks. Small mold leaks can be temporarily patched with modeling clay. Larger molds may need a plaster overlay.

Depending on the thickness of the casting, it usually goes into a thermosetting heat cycle and cools within a 24-hour period. However, thin pieces with more catalyst will harden faster, while thick pieces need to harden slowly to avoid heat fractures. This could take days. Too little catalyst will result in a gelatin-like floppy mass that will harden in time but is probably not worth the effort, while too much catalyst results in a fractured casting. An extreme amount of catalyst can actually burn the resin, causing it to yellow or brown.

Once hardened enough to take from the mold, if it is firm all over, it can immediately be worked on, but it is not advisable because of the sticky or tacky surface. It is better to let it cure a few more days. The molds can also be temporarily opened to the sunlight to harden thin resins, making it easier to remove. While placing a resin work into direct sunlight to help the annealing process is good, more than one day can cause it to yellow or affect the coloration as if yellow had been added.

Lylian Klimek, *Cold Flower*. Resin, foam rod, glass beads, 26″x48″ (66cm x 121.9cm).

If the surface is primarily a large, broad area, then air and power tools can be used to aid in the finishing. Since the surface is rather rough, especially on larger works, the rough, softer, outer layer must be removed to get to the hardened inner work. Orbital sanders, even disk sanders, can help in moderation. The sanding supplies, whether hand, power or air, will readily clog up with the soft resin surface.

Once the surface has been cleaned, a good sanding paper is used. Wet-or-dry papers are ideal because of the strength, ability to clean out and re-use, and the care with which the different grit sizes are measured. Eighty grit is a good beginning size paper to eliminate all scratches from the surface cleaning and to get the entire work back to an even surface. The work is taken through several grits all the way up to 1000. (With wet-or-dry papers the resin can be water sanded. This is advisable to keep down the airborne resin, especially after 220 grit when the particles become so small.)

Buffers, rubbing compound, polishing compound and slower RPM buffing machines secure the best finish. If the RPM exceeds over 2000, then the resin begins to melt, causing a surface disruption. After the work has been thoroughly sanded, a rubbing compound is used to blend all the sanding grit marks, followed by a polishing compound. Transparent works can appear as crystal clear as glass.

Resin castings should never be allowed to sit in direct sunlight, regardless of the manufacturer's chemical makeup. All tend to yellow; some do it faster than others. Indirect sunlight tends to bring out the best qualities of the resin.

Resins collect dust. An ostrich feather duster is the best way to remove surface dust. Warm water or alcohol and soft paper towels are good cleaning tools to remove fingerprints and built-up dust. Professional glass cleaner solutions should not be used, because they contain abrasives and chemicals causing surface damage. Denatured alcohol is used for cleaning, as well as commercial, waterless soap.

Acetone is the chemical used for cleanup and for cleaning tools, but not for the human body. Once used, straining screens, stirring paddles, etc., should be discarded. Mixing containers cannot be used again for casting resin. They pose the possibility of inadvertently adding trash to the casting. Resin molds should be cleaned and stored after the casting. Compressed air cleaning is best. Soap and water are used for skin cleaning. *See **Plastics; Acrylics; Flexible mold**.*

Resin bonded Products that are held together with resin, such as resin-bonded molding sand and resin-bonded abrasives *See **Sand casting; Sandpapers**.*

Resin glue A strong glue in two parts: resin and hardener. *See **Adhesive** (chart).*

Resist A temporary material used to mask (block) part of the surface to decorate or finish the surrounding area. For example, masking tape is used to keep paint off surfaces; wax is applied to ceramic bisqueware to keep glaze off the foot or design areas.

Respirator A breathing device that separates dust and gaseous vapors from the air being inhaled. It is worn over the nose and mouth and sometimes over the entire head or body. It may add oxygen to the air being breathed. Different respirators and filters are designed for specific purposes. Some masks are designed for floating dust particles only or specifically for toxic vapors. *See **Safety dress**.*

Respirators. Top right to left: respirator with dust/chemical filter system, dust respirator. Bottom right to left: dust cartridge, chemical cartridges, one-time use paper filter.

Restore To repair sculpture or refinish it back to its original state.

Retaining wall The flat barrier separating sections of molds to allow easy removal and assemblage of the mold. It may be made of clay, metal strips, etc. *See **Molds**.*

Retarder A substance or chemical used to slow the setting time of sculptural materials, such as plaster or concrete. *See **Plaster; Concrete**.*

Re-tempering To harden metal again. When metal tools have been overheated, especially while sharpening, they lose the ability to hold a sharp edge (the temper). As a result, they need a new temper. *See **Temper**.*

Reversed polarity DC welding, the result of electrons flowing from the base metal to the electrode. *See **Welders**.*

Rheostat A control to regulate electrical current. A resistor that is variable with a fixed terminal and moveable contact to control the flow to power a tool or machine. Primarily used to regulate the rate of speed for electrical motors. It is easily controlled by switch, knob or foot pedal.

Rib A tool used in ceramics to shape clay while in a wet state. The rib is made of a flexible material, such as rubber or a thin metal. It resembles an ear shape with a flat side.

Riffler A handheld rasp or file of unique shapes designed for various areas within a sculpture. It may be a fine toothed file or a coarse rasp. The sizes vary, but are quite small for intricate work, especially for wood and stone carving.

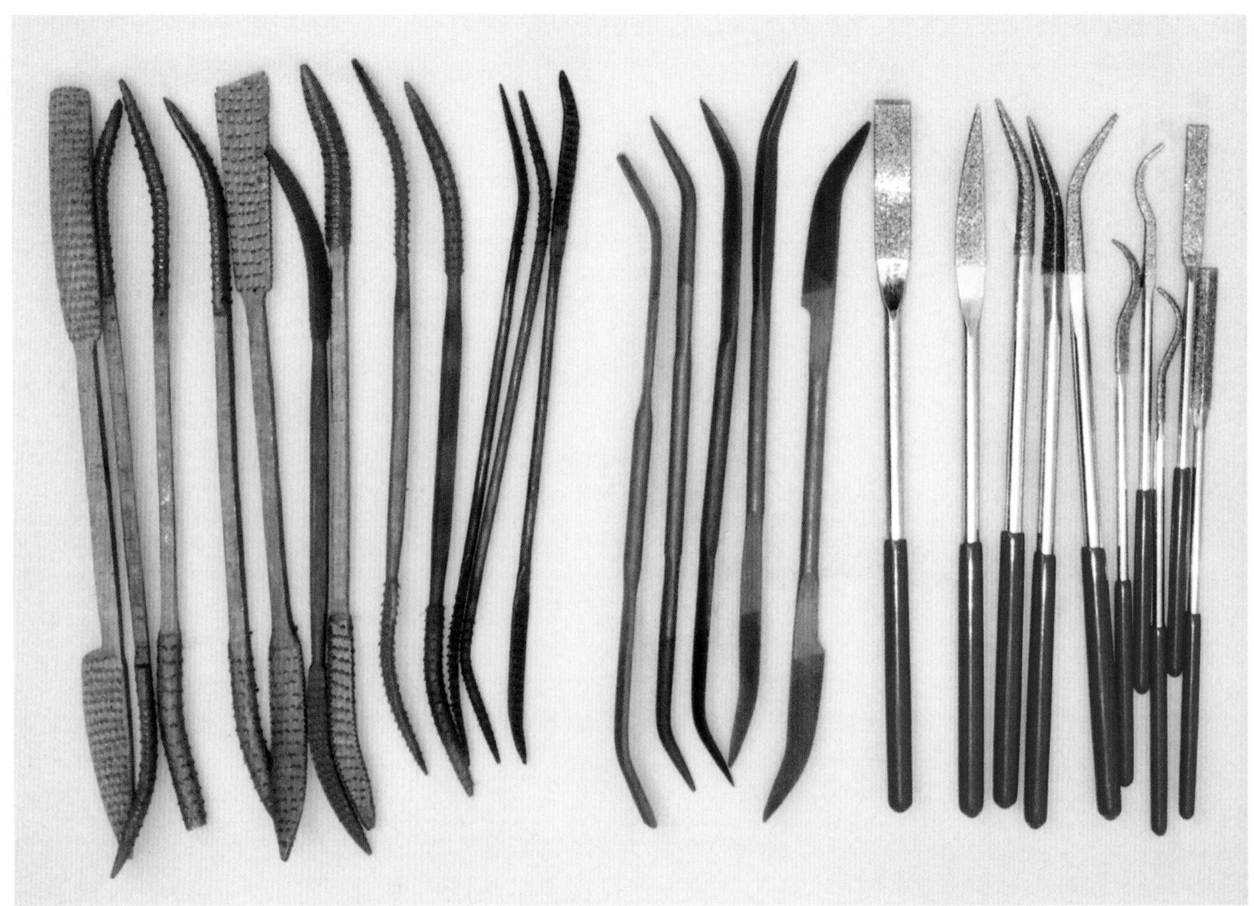

Rifflers. Left to right: steel riffler rasps, steel riffler files, diamond coated files.

Rigid mold A mold made of plaster or other hard materials. A rigid mold is the opposite of a flexible mold. Plaster, metal or fiberglass molds are firm and do not flex. *See* ***Molding***.

Risers Part of the metal pouring system, a vent that allows air and gases to escape. *See* ***Metal pouring system***.

Rivet (ing) A short, metal fastener stem with a head used for building construction. When the stem is placed through holes into two materials (usually metal), it is hammered or flattened to form a second head, thus holding the materials together. Rivets come in a variety of sizes.

In riveting, the materials are sandwiched together and then clamped. A hole slightly larger than the rivet is drilled. The rivet is inserted by hand or by a gun. If by hand, the rivet must be hammered to spread flat; if with a gun, the gun automatically pulls the rivet tight into a flattened end.

RIVETS

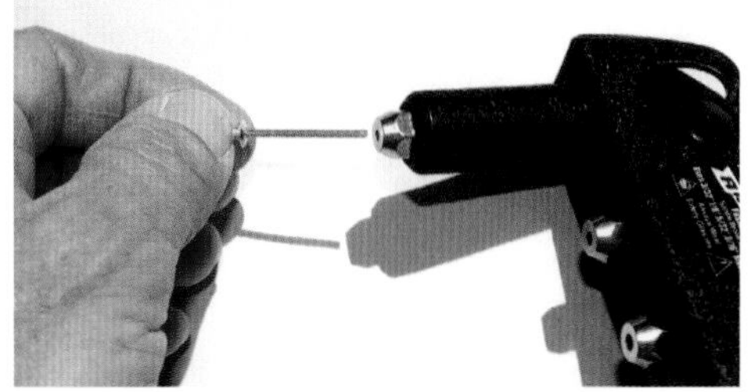

Rivet fastener being loaded with rivet.

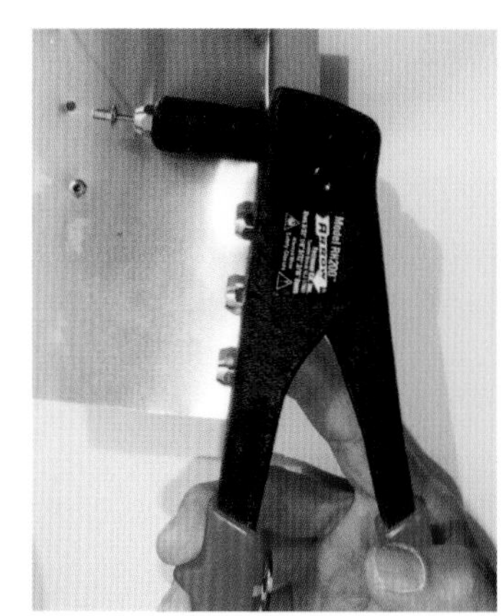

Rivet fastener in use.

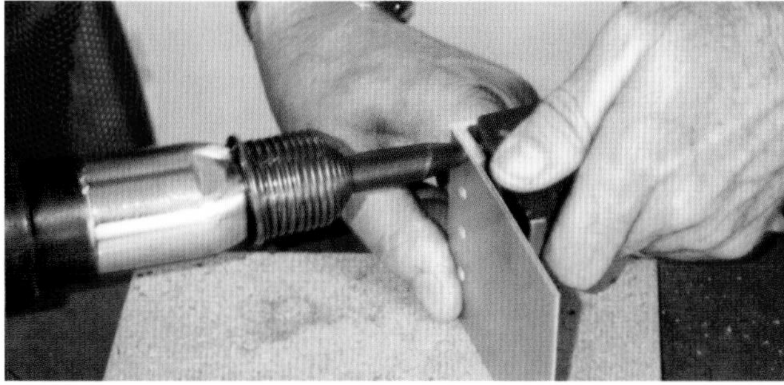

Air operated rivet hammer.

Michael L. Aurbach, *The Administrator*. Galvanized sheet metal, wood found objects, 8′x18′x12′ (2.44m x 5.49m x 3.66m).

Gene Koss, *Sculpture on the Ridge*. Cast glass, steel, stone, 3½'x5'x1' (1.1m x 1.5m x 0.3m).

Rock Separate stones found in fields, streams and river beds. Larger masses of rock are called boulders. They contain the same elements in differing proportions as stone. However, as long as they are uncut and unattached, the term "rock" is applied. *See **Stone**; **Igneous**; **Sedimentary**; **Metamorphic**.*

Rod A narrow shaft of metal, especially formulated and sometimes coated for specific welding filler. The metal rod is activated by arc or gas heat. *See **Electrode**.*

Roman joint A joint that allows sculpture parts to be assembled or disassembled from each other. It is used for protruding parts, such as arms. It may be found on plaster works. Store mannequins make good use of the joints for storage and transportation.

Rosebud A widespread torch tip with several holes around the oxygen center used for heating large sections of metal. *See **Welding torch**; **Patina**.*

Rosewood A wood favored for its beautiful dark rose color and toughness. It can be seen on musical instruments and ornamental handles and knobs. *See **Wood** (chart)*

David Hostetler, *Susan 1* (detail). Rosewood, 42" (106.7cm). Photographer: Lynthia Eiler.

Rot Decay or decomposition, especially in wood that is not properly sealed.

Rotary casting Accomplished by machinery that rotates the mold. The mold contains the casting substance and slushes it onto the surface until it hardens enough to remove the mold, leaving a hollow casting. *See **Mold; Slushing; Centrifugal casting**.*

Roughing out Taking an unshaped stone, clay, log or other raw material and beginning the sculptural form. Once the basic form has been achieved, it is said to have been roughed out.

Roundel A sharpening stone. *See **Sharpening**.*

Router A high speed, hand power tool that is air or electric driven. It contains a collet that holds various types and sizes of bits to cut laminate, grooves, molding, etc.

RPM Revolutions per minute. The number of times a shaft completes a turn within a minute.

RTV Room Temperature Vulcanizing. Rubber, especially mold material, that does not require heat to vulcanize (cure). *See **Mold making; Flexible mold**.*

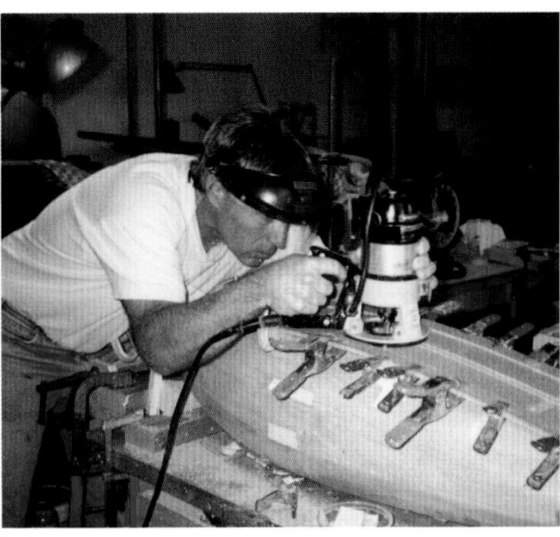

Michael J. Cooper using a router between guide templates.

Rubbing compound A mixture of chemicals and abrasive particles designed to remove scratches when applied to a surface with a cloth or buffing wheel. *See **Buffing compound**.*

Runners Part of the metal pouring system. They are the channels that carry the liquid metal from the sprue to the pouring gate and into the casting wax ducts, or feeds, from the larger sprue to the form. Sometimes referred to as secondary sprues, they are located throughout the form as they feed the liquid metal to the sculpture. The entire network is called the runner system. *See **Metal pouring system**.*

Rust Hydrated iron oxide, reddish-brown in color. Rust is a coating of iron oxide from moisture on ferrous metal. Rust is porous, and flakes fall off or mixes with water (rain) and runs off. As rust forms, it weakens the base metal. Cor-Ten™ steel is designed to form a protective coat of rust that adheres to the base metal, actually protecting it (but it does eventually come off and rusts from both sides). *See **Cor-Ten™**.*

Deborah Butterfield, *Rondo*. Found steel, 94″x79″x31″ (239cm x 201cm x 79cm).

Pamela Phillips, *Faith*. Porcelain, cloth, leather, mixed media, 27″ (68.6cm) tall.

S

Safety Good working conditions. Safety involves all precautions to prevent injury, harm or damage to the health or work of a sculptor, as well as the correct use and upkeep of all the equipment and supplies involved.

Safety dress Protective wear required for a particular task. Examples are resins, which require respirators for chemical protection, while working with wood requires dust respirators. Almost all working conditions require safety eye wear, while welding lens are designed for protection from ultraviolet rays. The sculptor must be familiar with the technique to maintain proper safety dress.

Some processes require an extensive combination of safety dress. An example is metal casting. A face shield or clear welding mask is part of the head covering. The gloves need to be high heat resistant. A heat resistant coat or jacket and apron must also be worn. Heat resistant leg guards with boot or foot coverings and strong boots, such as steel-toed boots, are needed. The radiant heat can cause severe burn to unprotected skin. While a respirator is not a normal piece of equipment for bronze casting, it could be necessary for toxic alloy mixes, especially fumes associated with iron. *See* ***Spat; Eyewear; Gloves; Welding safety dress***.

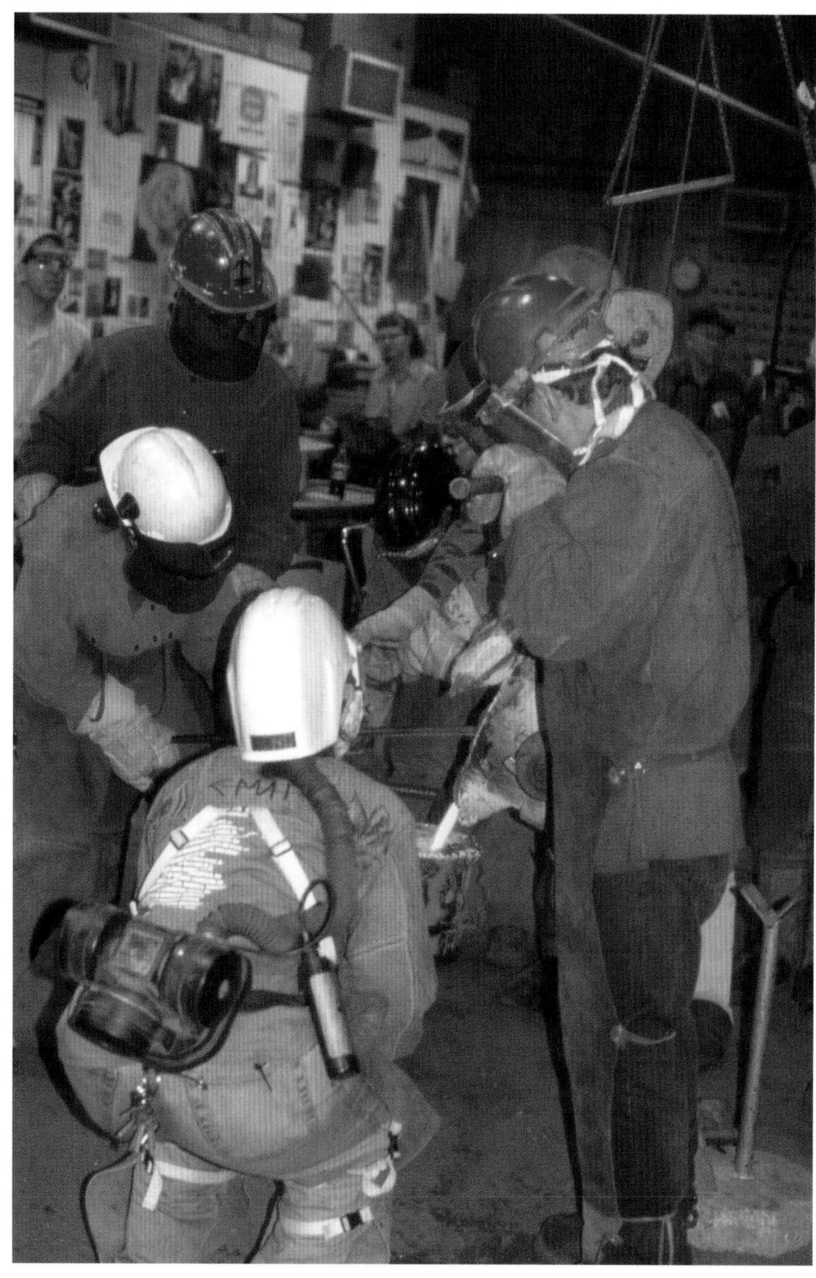

Safety dress for iron casting sometimes includes a portable air filtration system. Iron Casting Conference at the University of Minnesota, Minneapolis, Minnesota.

Saggor A high heat refractory container that encases clay works during kiln firings to achieve specific body colors. It prevents flames from making direct contact with the work. *See* ***Kiln***.

Sairset™ Trademark name for a high heat refractory mortar used in building furnaces and repairing metal casting molds.

Salt Sodium chloride. It is used for salt glazes, though it can be used as a catalyst to speed up the setting time of plasters and concretes, etc. It is seldom utilized as a sculptural material.

Salt glaze Glaze created by introducing wet salt into the kiln during glaze firing. It is thrown or blown in through special vents. The salt volatilizes as sodium oxide combines with silica and aluminum oxide in the clay body to conceive the glaze. The glaze is recognized as a distinctive, consistent spatter-like raised pattern on the surface. *See* ***Glaze***; ***Firing***; ***Kiln***.

Sand Small fragments of sedimentary material found in abundance in deserts and beaches. It can be added to clay bodies instead of grog. It serves the same purpose as grog but offers a new color or texture to the clay. Sand is also a key ingredient in plaster investment mixtures. *See* ***Sand sculpture***; ***Grog***; ***Concrete***; ***Cement***; ***Sandblast particles***; ***Plaster investment***.

Elizabeth Kronfield, *Through*. Rope, steel, salt, 138″x68″x46″ (351cm x 173cm x 117cm). Photographer: Tony Walsh.

Linda Einfalt, *Cleansing*. Cast bronze, sand, 55″x13″x32″ (139.7cm x 33cm x 81.3cm).

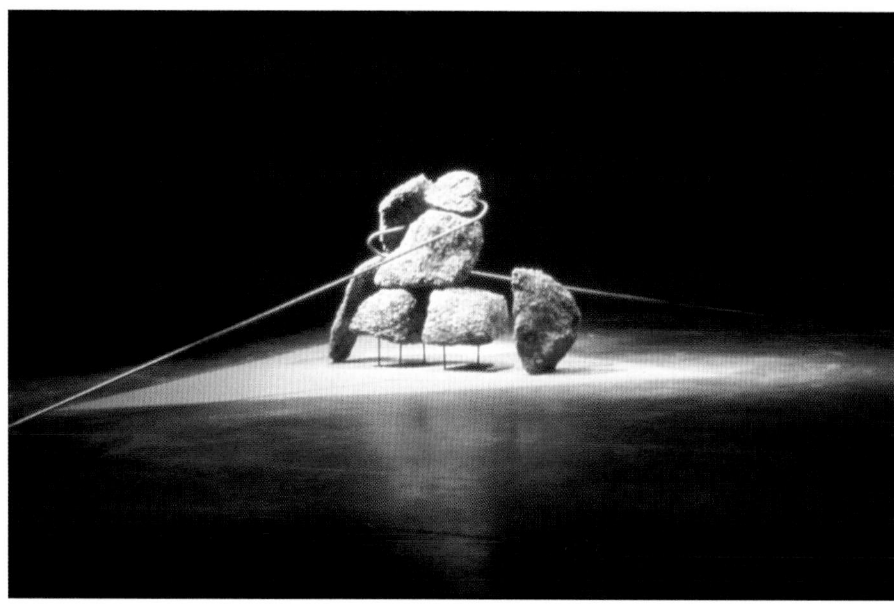

Milt Friedly, *Passing Through*. Stone, steel, sand, 16′x9′x3′ (4.88m x2.75m x 0.92m).

and bag A strong cloth container loosely filled with sand and then placed under stone or wood for support while carving. The bag may be made of canvas or denim. Being loosely filled allows the bag to conform to the sculpture medium. The weight serves as a solid base for stability. *See* ***Stone carving***.

Sandbag used to support stone for carving.

andblast(ing) Directing sand or other abrasive particles by means of compressed air to force abrasion action on a surface. The best way to clean a metal casting is by sandblasting, if the particles are not so large as to damage the surface texture. *See* ***Patina; Patina*** *(chart).*

andblast (particles) Abrasive particles available in a variety of sizes and materials from ordinary sand to glass, coal slag nutshells, metal grits or shot, and even baking soda. The most common abrasives are sand and glass. Sand is readily available and inexpensive, and is used in portable blasters where recovery is not possible. Sand comes in grits rated by number with no. 4 fine being a more common one for use on steel works, while a no. 2 medium might be considered for a coarser job.

Aluminum oxide is available in a range of grits. For example, a 16 grit is very large and heavy while a 220 grit is much finer. Glass beads are also graded by sieve size (size that can go through a particular screen). While sizes of 25-40 are available, so are extra fine sizes of 170-325. Depending on the finish, foundries may use two sizes, coarser for initial cleaning with a finer one for finishing.

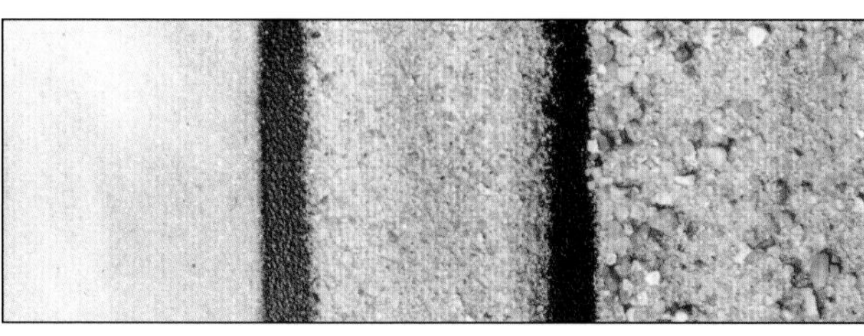

Sandblast particles. Left to right: 60-120 sieve glass, #4 sand, #2 sand.

Sometimes a coarse, angular or sharp cutting abrasive is needed such as sand or aluminum oxide. At other times, a more delicate spherical shape, such as glass beads, is best on soft metals like bronze for less surface destruction. Ground glass particles with sharp edges in larger sizes are ideal for rapid cleaning that allows a rough surface. For fine, delicately detailed surfaces, ground up walnut shells can be used, especially on precious metals (such as gold or silver) where loss of metal needs to be held at a minimum. If too coarse or sharp of an abrasive is used, the surface detail can be eliminated, becoming an uneven, coarse texture.

andblast cabinet An airtight steel cabinet designed for abrasive blasting that is calculated to retain the recycled blasting materials. The abrasive blast cabinet/unit must be large enough to accommodate castings completed in the foundry. The entrance is an airtight access door or by lifting off the top of the unit as the work is placed inside.

All units have a replaceable sight window/covering placed at a height and angle so that the operator can easily see the work in progress. All have interior lighting, usually hard spot lights or protected fluorescent light. With strong fiber backed rubber gloves protruding from the outside of the wall into the machine, the operator is well protected and does not even get his/her hands dirty.

A good sandblast cabinet will include a vacuum collection system to remove the finer dust particles that inhibit a clear view of the work. The built-in handheld carbide or ceramic nozzle

Dennis St. Pierre operates a sandblast cabinet.

inside the machine is aimed directly at the work as the blast materials are siphoned or pressured through the nozzle of compressed air. The cabinet drains abrasive particles for reuse into a hose connected to the bottom. The activator switch is usually operated by a foot pedal that controls the compressor air flow. A compressor delivering at least 12 cfm at 90 psi (0.36m^3/min at 620kPa) is recommended. The ultimate unit is a walk-in room with fully recoverable blasting particles. *See **Sandblaster; Air compressor; Sandblast particles**.*

Sandblaster Can be anything from a small, portable, handheld container with a nozzle gun siphon system to a large diesel operated pressure unit designed to forcefully spray abrasive materials onto a surface for cleaning purposes. All units are combined with compressed air. All can use glass beads and aluminum oxide while some units can apply larger blast materials, depending on the compressor and manufacturer's design.

Portable siphon-type sandblasters are used for small jobs, especially those that require mobility. However, these units seldom afford much power and to remain portable, they are limited in the amount of blast material they can hold. Since the blast material is shot into the open, it is lost (without a heavy plastic curtain backdrop) and articles around the work need to be protected. The gun's nozzle is either ceramic or carbide, attached by a short hose to the lower part of the blast container activated by a trigger on the gun itself.

Pressure sandblasters afford the most rapid removal of surface materials. The machines consist of a heavy pressurized tank mounted on wheels for portability with a heavy long hose leading from the bottom of the tank to a strong end nozzle that is either ceramic or carbide. The size of the air compressor is determined by the size of the unit. Large units can be portable by using a gasoline or diesel fueled air compressor. The unit manufacturer places specific requirements on each machine to be followed for best operation.

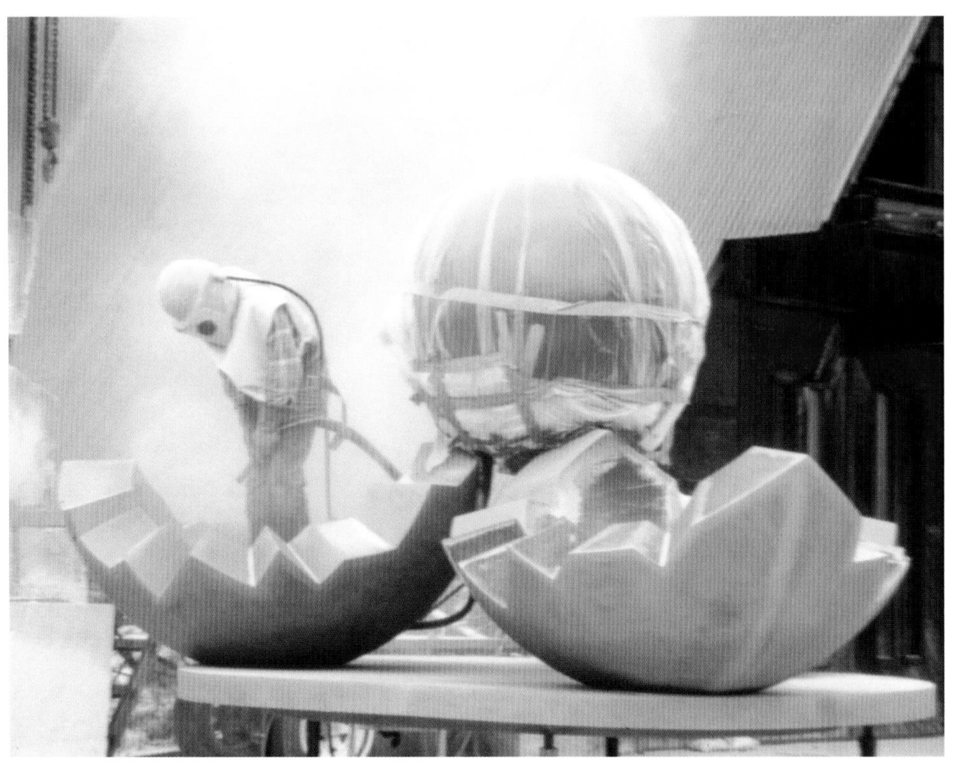

Arthur Williams pressure sandblasts the steel *Genesis* with a pressure blaster.

Pressure blasters are of great value for large scale works or surfaces, such as buildings that require heavy sand blast particles. If blasters are used out in the open, the operator must be protected with a hood respirator, heavy rubber gloves, plus heavier clothes and possibly a fresh air breathing system, depending on the work and machine. Because of the tremendous pressure involved, the nozzle has a deadman control that stops the blast flow when it is released.

Sandblast nozzles can be ceramic, mild steel or carbide. Mild steel does not last long as the abrasive particles immediately begin to wear away the steel. They are very impractical and need constant replacement. Ceramic nozzles are common and will last three times longer. Available with the greatest range of sizes from under three thirty-seconds inch (0.238cm) to over one-fourth inch (0.635cm), the larger the nozzle, the larger the blast particle can be, but more air pressure is needed for propulsion. Tungsten carbide nozzles last the longest, up to 20 times longer than ordinary steel, but the cost is high.

Steve Linn, *Jackson Pollock #29*. Sandblasted glass, bronze, 206″x217″x90″ (523cm x 551cm x 229cm).

and box (carving) A container with sand for holding carving stones in place. The box is usually wood construction, large enough to contain the stone, and an appropriate carving height.

and box (casting) Directly casting into a box filled with moist sand. This is especially useful for large castings on site. However, the final surface is very rough. *See **Sand waste mold**.*

anders Powered machines, hand or upright, that incorporate some form of replaceable abrasive material to remove surface irregularities or secure a better finish. *See **Sandpaper**.*

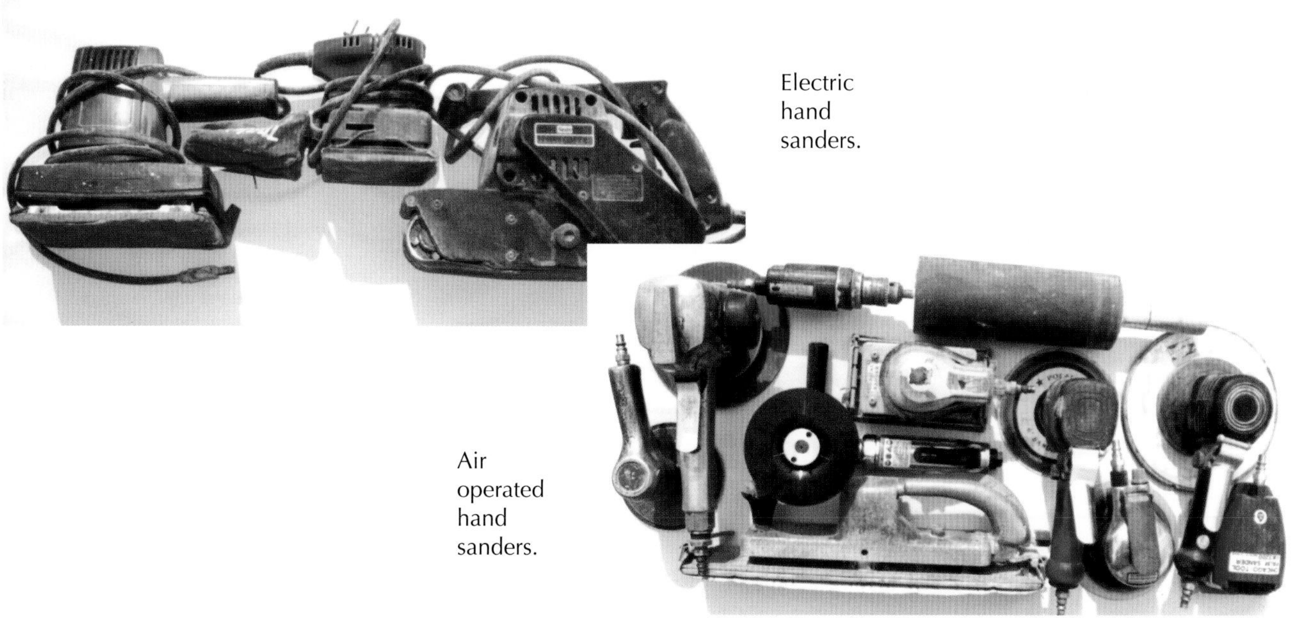

Electric hand sanders.

Air operated hand sanders.

Sanding Using abrasives to finish a work either by hand or mechanical means. *See **Sandpaper**.*

Tim Kinard operates an air disk sander to rapidly remove wood surfaces.

Michael Cooper cleans wood joints with an electric sanding disk grinder.

Sand molding A method of casting metal sculpture using sand as a key refractory mold material. Sand readily withstands the high heat of liquid metal during the process. There are several sand casting mold materials, but all involve some method of using tightly packed sand to remain in place after the original artwork has been removed or vaporized by the hot metal. Styrofoam™, for example, is used as the artwork substance when vaporization is used. The sand has a binder to hold the sand in solid form. The binder can be natural clays and other substances of a chemical nature.

Sand molding is not quite as surface refined as other metal casting methods because of the very nature of the granular structure of sand. Though finer sands produce finer molds, there is still a more textured surface compared to traditional lost wax techniques.

Technique

The supporting frame around the sand is called a flask. A pouring cup or opening at the top helps the gravity fed hot liquid metal to enter and fill the mold. Though the mold has air vents, there are only a few, since the sand is porous enough for the gases to escape and yet the sand is solid enough to contain the metal. Once the casting is allowed to cool, it is removed and finished using the same methods as all the other metal castings. Because of the high heat refractory, not only is this process used for metals, such as aluminum or bronze; it is a preferred molding process for iron.

Sand molded surface demonstrating a rough texture. **Brimmer Casting Inc.**, Gulfport, Mississippi.

Different sands are used for different purposes. Finer sand is best for aluminum and brass, while coarser sand will suffice for bronze and iron. The sizes and shapes are important. Sizes are determined by grains per linear inch (100 per inch equal one hundred sand particles lined up in a row of one inch length [about 40 per linear centimeter]). Sharp or angular particle shapes are used for stronger molds that are less porous. Round grains produce more porosity with a mold. A mixture of grain sizes removes most of the spaces between particles to be filled, resulting in a dense and less porous mold material.

Green sand is sand bonded with clays consisting of fireclay, kaolinite or bentonite. Fireclay is added for endurance and to help the sand be more cohesive during the shrinkage of the metal as it cools. The sand is strengthened by the addition of bentonite. Sand that is correctly mixed with the right amount of moisture can be held and squeezed in the sculptor's fist. If it holds the shape within the hand without crumbling and can then be cleanly broken into two pieces without fragmenting, it is ready for use.

Baked sand molds usually contain oil, or sometimes clay, for a binder. These molds are heated until they are completely dry at temperatures of about 300°F to 450°F (148.9°C to 232.2°C) for a period of up to 12 hours.

Resin bonded (no bake) sand molds require a catalyst resin binder. The manufacturer specifications need to be studied and closely followed. Most require about two pounds (0.09kg) of resin to be mixed into 100 mesh sand. After a thorough mix, the catalyst is added. Depending upon the product and mix, the working time can vary from 15 minutes to over an hour prior to solidifying. The actual hardening or complete curing takes longer, but it is cured at room temperature. Iron oxide is added to increase the heat resistance (from 1% to 5%). The resulting molds can be used for iron casting because of their superior strength.

With all binder-catalyst mixtures, the binder must first be mixed with the sand, and then the catalyst added. To directly mix a binder with a catalyst can cause an intense and possibly explosive reaction. Rubber gloves should always be worn to protect the hands from burns.

Terms/tools used with sand casting

Flasks are reusable containers, usually steel frames, used to hold the sand. The top frame is the **cope**; the bottom frame is the **drag**. Flasks are rectangular in shape, though they can be designed in other shapes for specific works. Lightweight aluminum flasks are the easiest to handle.

Mechanical reclaimer for reconstituting bonded sand.

A **pouring basin** (pouring box or pouring cup) is a separate box shape added to the top of the mold over the sprue to ensure a sufficient amount of metal will be entering the mold. It can be preheated and designed to impede dross from entering the mold.

The **sprue** is the major pouring duct where the metal will enter or begin the metal pouring system. It must be large enough to allow the mold to be completely filled without freezing up.

Runners are the smaller ducts that direct the liquid metal into the mold.

Vents are part of the metal pouring system that rise up and out of the mold, strategically placed to allow casting gases and air to escape as the metal enters the mold.

Feeders in sand casting are larger sections on a runner that store extra metal to feed the mold as the metal contracts drawing from it into the casting. They are also useful to catch dross that may have entered the runner.

Risers are placed in the pouring system to repress metal shrinkage by housing extra metal to keep the mold filled until it completely hardens.

The **bottom board** is a strong plank or flat surface that the mold is constructed upon.

Aligning pins are the metal pegs align the flasks and hold them in place.

The **sump** is the lowest part of the main sprue, a large dip or retaining area, slightly lower than the runners. It helps control the turbulence, as well as serving as a dross trap.

Cores are bound porous materials placed inside the mold to maintain an even wall thickness or to avoid a solid metal casting. They are held in place by **core pins** anchored in both the core and the mold wall. Smaller cores are not always vented, though it is good to design a hollow escape for the gases.

Flask bars are metal bars placed horizontally across the **cope** that assist in supporting the metal.

Gaggers are angle iron bars to assist the flask bars in supporting the mold material.

The **facing** is the coating of fine sand on the mold surface necessary to secure fine casting details.

Backing or backup sand is a coarse sand used as a filler or backing away from the mold surface.

The **unit mold or unit sand** is a mold composed of the same substance. It ensures a strong, unified mold without separation in the casting process.

Dross or trash is unwanted substances found in the liquid metal from flux and other substances, even loose particles of the mold.

Parting lines are the exact place on the artwork that divides it into a section to avoid an undercut.

A **parting compound** or release agent is fine silica or talc so fine that it is contained in a small cloth bag. It is porous enough to allow a fine sprinkling on the mold face to avoid mold sections from adhering to each other.

Refractory washes are sprayed or brushed onto the sand mold surface to ensure better surface quality and easier removal of mold materials after the casting. Zircon flours or graphite materials are often used.

A **muller** is a large mixing machine that blends sand and the binder together.

Speed riddles or power riddles are motorized riddles that mix as well as aerate and screen molding sand. The sand can be a petroleum or water sand.

Hand riddles are handheld framed screens used to sift (riddle) the sand, creating a smooth even layer, especially for the face or prime coat on the pattern.

SAND MOLDING
by Matthew C. Wicker

He begins a bonded sand mold with a plasticene positive inside that will later be removed. It is readied for the core to be rammed on top of the pattern for *Inertia*.

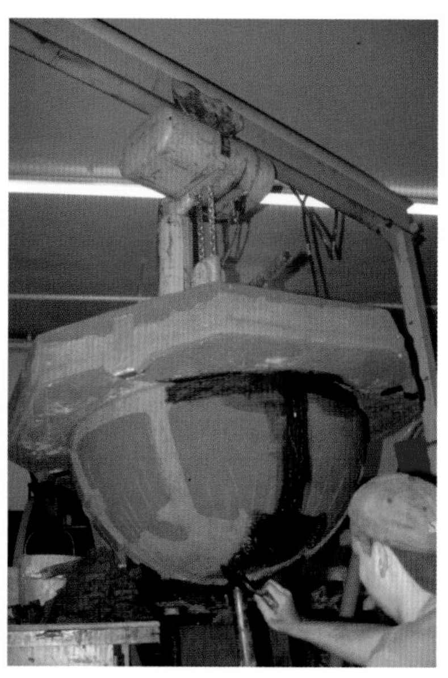

Matthew C. Wicker paints a mold wash of graphite and alcohol on the bonded sand core.

After the plasticene has been removed, the two molds, one for each half of the sculpture, are bolted and clamped together. They are leveled to prepare for the casting.

The molds are poured using a 700 pound ladle.

Matthew C. Wicker, *Inertia*. Cast iron, steel, pine, 6′x7′x25′ (1.83m x 2.14m x 7.63m).

SAND MOLDING
using a Flask at Brimmer Casting Inc.,
Gulfport, Mississippi

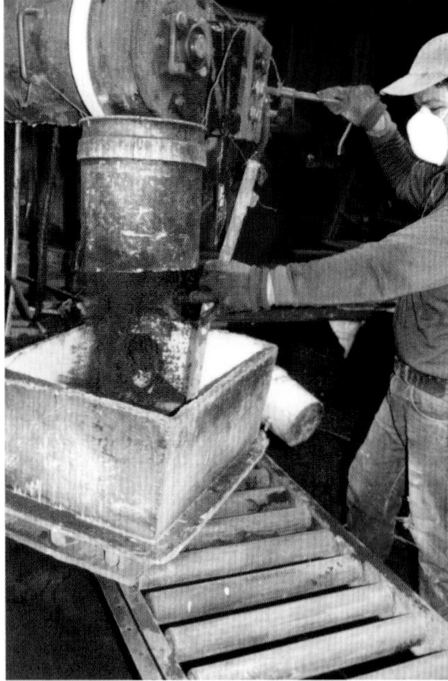

Chemically bonded sand mixed with a high speed mixer, then dropped onto a model in a flask.

The mold is rammed.

The top is scraped flush.

Prepared metal flasks with the model removed.

The flasks are aligned.

The flasks are placed together.

The casting is removed.

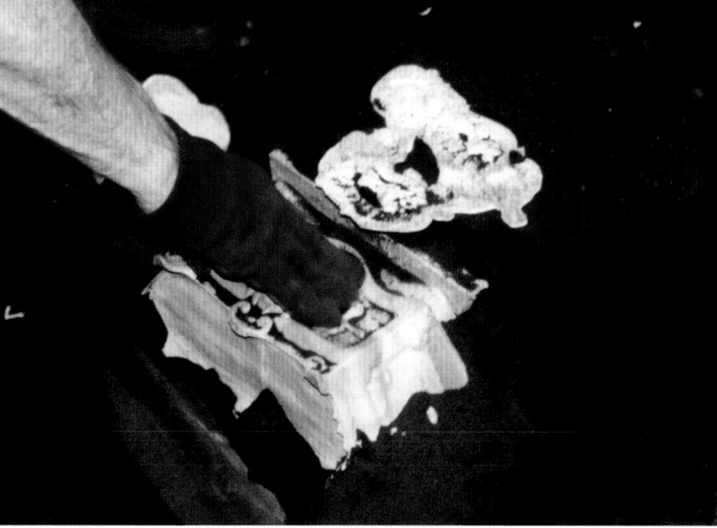

The bonded sand is loosened after the metal pour.

Sand molding process

A hard master pattern (original positive artwork) is used to form the negative molds. The pattern must be studied for exact dividing to avoid mold undercuts. It must be non-porous with a surface that can readily separate from the sand.

The flask is placed on the bottom board (a flat palette) and the prepared sand is sifted inside to a thickness strong enough to support the heat and weight of the liquid metal. The pattern is then laid on top of the sand foundation and forcefully depressed to form a solid, rigid backing beneath.

The sand is tamped down with a rammer (a tool that resembles a wood carving mallet, often with a wood chisel shape on one end for tighter tamping). Once the sand is rammed tightly up to the parting line, a parting agent, such as talc, fine silica dust or french chalk is dusted on the surface of the pattern, as well as the packed sand surface. This sand has already been trimmed about the surface at the top of the flask, making ready for the next flask. Each flask can be equated to separate pieces of a mold and should be placed as such.

Another flask is placed on top. If three flasks are needed, the middle flasks, called cheeks are placed on the lower or drag flask. The top or third flask is called a cope. The new flask is sifted with a layer of very fine sand to capture minute details. Later, layers may be coarser for more strength and less cost. The sand is carefully rammed into place about the pattern and over it. Each flask is aligned with the other by an aligning pin and clamped in place. The cope is removed leaving the exposed top of the master, pattern or original. The master is removed leaving two hollow spaces, one in each of the flasks.

If a core is needed, it is added and held in place by core pins or metal rods called spigots, which have been anchored to the core and overhang on the ledge of the mold.

A sprue cutter, a rod of sufficient thickness, is vertically placed on the top of the drag. It will later be taken out to leave the sprue channel. The metal pouring system is now completed, while the two sections of the flasks are separate. The sprue is cut to the runners, risers and vents in preparation for the liquid metal. A pouring cup, funnel shaped, is cut for metal entry. Any loose sand should be removed in preparation for closing. A light coat of graphite is added to the mold surface to provide a smoother surface for a more rapid filling.

A one inch (2.54cm) layer of sand is riddled over the top of the drag through the cope. Additional sand can be shoveled on top of the layer up to one-half of the flask, then all of the sand is rammed into a compact solid. More sand is added and rammed until the cope is filled. The sprue cutter is taken out and the cope is raised straight up. The model is removed.

Metal banding of resin molds is common, because it is quick, easy, strong and a secure way to hold the mold parts together.

Reinhard Skoracki, *Searching for a Better World.* Bronze, steel, 11.8"x11"x6.7" (30cm x 17cm).

Styrofoam™ pattern for a sandcast figure by **Barry Bailey**.

Vaporized sand casting utilizes an immediate approach to sand casting. Since expanded polystyrene foam vaporizes instantly upon contact with hot metal, artwork created in polystyrene does not have to be removed. This simplifies the casting process for some works. Low density foam products, such as Styrofoam™, can be easily placed into a bed of sand, packed, and then cast by pouring hot metal into the mold as the material instantaneously vaporizes and is replaced with liquid metal.

The original artwork has the metal pouring system already attached. The sprue and runners are of the foam material itself. While it is possible to design a core for foam, the real value of this molding type is in the quickness and spontaneity of the process and artwork. *See* ***Iron casting; Vaporized casting; Expanded polystyrene foam***.

Rough casting from a sand mold by **Barry Bailey** just prior to chasing and welding.

Sandpaper A strong paper coated with abrasives of various grit sizes used in the sanding process. The lower numbers represent coarser grits while higher numbers are for finer abrasion. *See* ***Abrasives***.

Sandpapers are known by their grit sizes or the particles that can be screened and placed in one linear inch (2.54cm). Common grits of 80 or 220 would mean than 80 particles can be placed in a row one inch long (2.54cm), while 220 grits could be placed in the same size. These grits are bonded onto a backing made of fiber, cloth or paper or a combination of these.

The most common handheld abrasive backing is paper; the most universal machine sanding belt backing is cloth, while machine sanding disks are usually fiber. The bonding agent can be glue, resin and waterproof, or a combination of these. The most effective heat resistant coating is resin; waterproof is the most water resistant; glue is very flexible but not very durable.

Sandpaper. Left: closed coat; right: open coat. Open coat allows from 30% to 50% open space between the grits to keep the paper from loading.

The coating can be open (space between the grits) or closed (grits that touch each other). Open coats are less likely to clog up and are generally used on softer substances. Closed coat is best for hard materials, such as steel or stone.

Sandpaper backing materials have specific designations. Cloth backing uses J for flexible thin cloth; X for middle weight, but flexible cloth; Y for thick, stiff backing cloth. Paper backings use A for good flexibility; C for moderate flexibility; D for moderately rigid; E for rigid but still flexible; F for very rigid.

Pressure sensitive adhesive backing is designated as PSA. It is adhesive, but does not form a permanent bond; it can be removed and replaced. They are used for orbital sander pads and tools with similar sanding pads.

Common sandpapers used for sculpture. Left to right: emery cloth, garnet, flint, aluminum oxide, wet-or-dry, drywall screen.

SANDPAPERS

	Hardness	Ex.Coarse	Coarse	Medium	Fine	Ex. Fine
FLINT	6.9	36	50	80	120-220	
GARNET	7.5-8.5	16-36	40-50	60-100	120-220	280
EMERY	8.5-9.0	30	40	60	120	
SILICON CARBIDE & ALUMINUM CARBIDE	9.0+	16-36	40-50	60-100	120-180	220-1200

Wet-or-dry sandpaper is used with water as a lubricant and cleaner while sanding. It also eliminates dust. Abrasives, such as garnet, flint and emery are designated as Extra Fine (220), Fine (120), Medium (60-100), Coarse (40-50), and Extra Coarse (16-36). Harder abrasives, such as silicone carbide, are designated by sizes such as 16, 24, 50, 80, 100, 220, 320, 400, 600, etc.

SANDPAPER GRITS IN DIAMETERS*

Ex. Coarse	Coarse	Medium	Fine	Ex. Fine
16 0.051	**40** 0.017	**60** 0.010	**120** 0.0025	**220** 0.0025
24 0.028	**50** 0.014	**80** 0.007	**180** 0.003	**320** 0.0014
36 0.021		**100** 0.005		**400** 0.0009
				600 0.0006

**Approximate diameters*

ABRASIVES HARDNESS *The following are listed from the most rugged to the least:*

Diamond - *black* industrial, can be natural or synthetic.
Silicone carbide (carborundum) synthetic - usually *dark (black)* but can be *white*.
Aluminum oxide – *dark brown* or *white*, synthetic.
Emery – *black* or *red*, aluminum and iron oxide.
Garnet – *tan*, iron and aluminum silicate.
Flint – *tan* quartz.

Sand quartz A stone found in natural deposits of small granules. It is used for silica when preparing plaster investment castings. It is also used as a grog additive in clay bodies for strength or effect.

Sandstone Sedimentary rock used more for construction than sculpture. Sandstone is difficult to carve. Care should be exercised when using mounted abrasives, such as diamonds or carbide. The heat generated when carving can cause the adhesive holding these particles to loosen, destroying the tool's cutting edge. Sandstone is not a preferred carving stone due to the excessive wear on tools, health concerns and finishing surface.

But as with other stones, sandstone comes in many varieties from those that can be broken apart like clumps of earth to those that are nearly impossible to carve due to the large amount of quartz. Quartz is the primary binding agent that holds the silica (sand) together to produce the sandstone. The tightest grain stones are used to sharpen tools. The best carving sandstone is called freestone that consists of fine granules of sand. Colors vary but can be red, brown, gray, black, blue, green, yellow, buff and white. Arenaceous stone is another name for stones made up of sand (sandstone). *See **Sedimentary**; **Stone**; **Stone** (chart).*

CARVING SANDSTONE
by Enzo Torcoletti

The sculptor began *Constructed Victory* by stacking several sandstone pieces to obtain the size and shape.

The individual stones were carved and then placed back together.

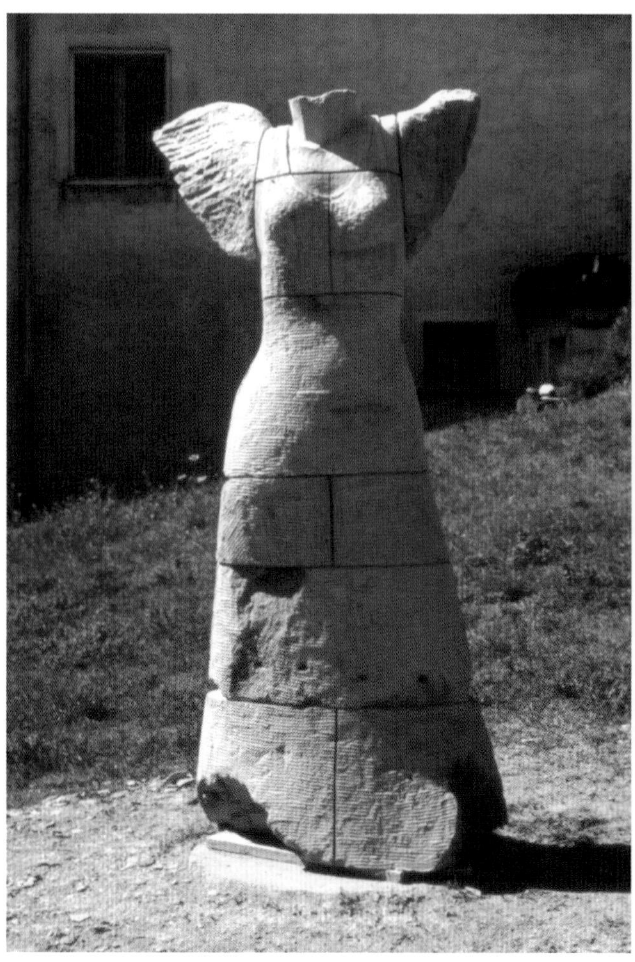

Enzo Torcoletti, *Constructed Victory*. Sandstone, 78″ (198cm) tall.

and sculpture Sculpture composed of sand. Traditionally, sand is modeled into three-dimensional forms at or near a beach. However, with greater compaction, additives and surface binders, the sculpture can be created indoors or at a distance from the seashore. While ocean sand tends to powder and crumble as it dries out, silty sand found in rivers away from the ocean will hold solidity for a longer period of time.
*See **Sand**.*

Ted Siebert and **Charlie Beailieu** (The Sand Sculpture Co.), *Rapunzel*. Sand, 100 tons, Peddler's Village, Lahaska, Pennsylvania. This sand sculpture is created with only water and sand that has been compacted in wood forms. The sand is then removed and carved. These sculptors prefer silty river bank sand that dries hard and stays intact after it dries out. Armatures are not used.

Sand waste mold A mold made directly into sand by removing unwanted sand, thereby, leaving a negative shape. It is then filled with the casting material, likely plaster or concrete. The molding material is cheap, since the casting can be made directly on the beach using sand at the site or in the sculptor's studio in a box filled with sand. The forms are fairly simple and sometimes large. However, they can be quite involved by digging out shapes or cavities and joining them.

The mold is easily removed by lifting the solid piece out of the sand or digging the sand from around it. If the sculptor desires imbedded sand, the cast can be made directly onto the sand. If a smooth finish is sought, a thin sheet of plastic can be placed over the sand prior to adding the casting material. Even casting made in dry earth or mud will work.

If salt water sand is used, some retardation of the surface will be noticed. As for an additive, unwashed salt water sand should never be used, because it will weaken the casting causing it to sometimes become powdery. The sea water also should not be used. Not only does it slow the casting process, but it causes efflorescence white salt crystals to develop on the sculpture from the evaporated salt-laden water. Salt water sand also causes efflorescence. *See* ***Waste mold****;* ***Concrete****;* ***Plaster****;* ***Efflorescence***.

Matthew C. Wicker, *Number 10*. Cast iron, 14"x14'x4" (35.6cm x 35.6cm x 10.2cm).

Andrè Harvey, *Helen*. Cast bronze, Life-size, 63"x23"x32" (160cm x 58.4cm x 81.3cm).

Sapwood The growth layers of a tree encircling the heartwood. In live trees, it contains the sap as it flows from the roots to the leaves. It is more yielding than the heartwood.

Saw A tool with a thin-toothed blade designed for cutting wood and other materials, even metal, depending upon the teeth size, shape, tempering, etc. It can be in a large, mechanically operated machine or in a handheld configuration used manually or designed to operate through power.

Electric saws. Left to right: circular saw, saber saw (top), disk grinder mounted with chain blade (bottom), battery operated saber saw (right).

Scab A paper-thin piece of metal not completely attached to a metal casting. It is the result of an irregular metal pour, or one in which the mold wall has been splashed by hot liquid metal and then poured over, resulting in two layers of metal.

Scagliola Plaster with pigment and fine particles of various stones (marble, granite, etc.) mixed together and placed on surfaces as an imitation of manmade marble.

Scale A ratio used to determine an exact proportion of one size object to another. An example is to compare a small scale model to a large, finished work that may be five times larger. The scale would be 1:5. *See* ***Monolithic; Enlarging; Miniature.***

Scale model Actual model proportions designed for a larger work.

Scales Devices used for weighing substances. *See* ***Measurements*** *(chart). See* ***Triple beam balance.***

Scotch Brite™ A strong, manmade fibrous pad designed for sanding. Similar fiber sanding pads are made by other brands. *See* ***Fiber sanding pads; Patination.***

Screen mold A frame made of wood and faced with fiberglass or other non-rusting screen. It is used to drain water through while making paper. *See* ***Paper; Deckle.***

Fiber sanding pads from coarse to fine.

Screw A fasting device in the form of a tapered round rod with sharp spiral threads leading to a point on one end and a slotted cap on the other. The cap, or head, is ordinarily designed to be turned by a tool (screwdriver) to sink (drive) the screw downward into the material.

Scrim (plaster's scrim) A strong, pliable, loosely woven cotton or linen cloth that is easily penetrated and used as a reinforcement in mold making. Plaster readily saturates the cloth, such as burlap or jute, as it is applied to the plaster mold material after an earlier coat of plaster for a face coat. *See* ***Mold; Hemp***.

Sculpt To manipulate a form or to make sculpture. The term is also used to mean to carve or to model a form. It is sometimes used as an abbreviation for sculpture. *See* ***Sculpture***.

Sculptor An artist who works with three-dimensional forms (shapes) of aesthetic value. The artist designs and produces sculpture. *See* ***Sculpture***.

Sculptress An older term for a female artist who creates sculpture. *See* ***Sculptor***.

Sculpture A physical three-dimensional form created, assembled or displayed by a man/woman for the purpose of aesthetic value. *See* ***Sculptor***.

Sculpture Garden Location for sculpture exhibited in the out-of-doors in a specially designed landscape environment arranged for the best display. *See* ***Courtyard***.

Edward J. Fraughton, *Bitter Strength*. Cast bronze, 25½"x21"x15" (64.8cm x 53.3cm x 38.1cm).

Barry Gunderson *Coventry Arch*. Welded aluminum, 14'x14'x5' (4.27m x 4.27m x 1.53m). Cleveland Heights, Ohio.

Sculpture-in-the-round Fully three-dimensional sculpture viewable from any point of view. It is a freestanding sculpture, as opposed to relief sculpture.

Sealer A liquid substance used to saturate an object, thereby eliminating its porous nature. Afterwards, the object takes fewer protective or decorative coat ings, and the coatings are easier to apply. *See* ***Stone carving***.

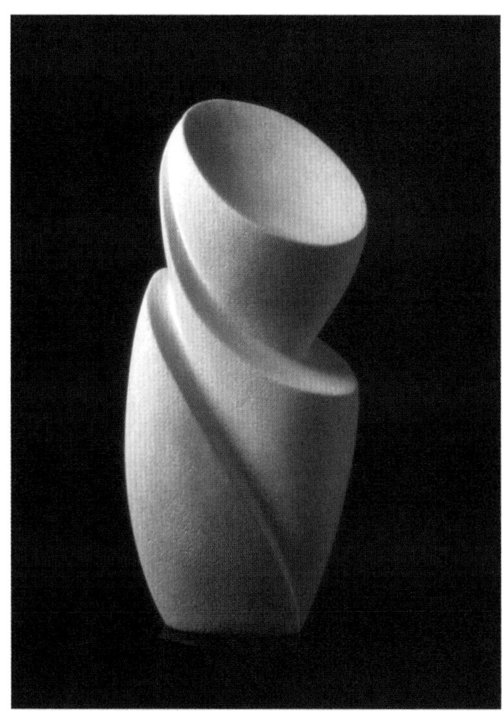

Eva Garrett, *Spiral Dance*. Limestone, 15″x7″x5″ (38.1cm x 17.8cm x 12.7cm).

Seam line The line, seam material, residue or flashing left where pieces of a mold are parted. When mold pieces are placed together, they sometimes do not quite close or line up properly resulting in an obvious seam. When this happens, the seam line is removed by abrasion, cutting or polishing so that the seam (line) no longer exists or is not noticeable. *See* ***Mold***.

Sedimentary Stone formed by erosion. The sediment is brought about as a rock and other surface particles weather in the rain and sun, slowly cracking in freezing temperatures into small, even minuscule fragments over centuries. It combines with small sea creatures, shells and other plant and animal remains that are washed away by surging water into a strata or layered sediment into oceans, lakes or river beds. As time progresses, the water recedes, resulting in sedimentary stone. Because of the process, the strata vary greatly in thickness. The stone is often porous. The common stones that the sculptor uses are limestone and sandstone. *See* ***Sandstone****;* ***Limestone****;* ***Stone*** *(chart)*.

Select wood A lumber designation by appearance. It identifies lumber graded as best quality without blemishes. *See* ***Lumber***.

Self-hardening clay A plastic clay that achieves complete cure and hardening by a single exposure to the atmosphere or by a mild amount of kitchen oven heat. The results depend on the manufacturer as to how strong it is or how to achieve the hardness.

Separator Often called a release agent, it is a substance placed onto one surface to prevent linking or bonding with another surface. *See* ***Release agent****;* ***Release agents*** *(chart)*.

Serpentine A hard green stone of hydrous magnesium. It greatly varies in color, value and veining, sometimes resembling the textures of a serpent. Caution should be taken when carving because of the airborne asbestos particles in this stone. *See* ***Stone*** *(chart)*.

Arthur Williams, *Serpentine Figure*. Serpentine, 28″ (71.1cm) tall.

Setting time The actual time that a substance, such as plaster, needs to convert into a solid or usable state. It does not mean that it is completely cured, which could take weeks. *See* ***Plaster; Cement***.

Sgraffito Scratches or texture in clay surfaces (often slip) to reveal another color, creating a design beneath the outer face.

Shank The piece of equipment that encloses and securely holds a heated crucible in place for metal casting. *See* ***Metal casting***.

Shank with a crucible filled for casting. Photographer: Leitha L. Thrall.

Sharpening Improving an edge for cutting purposes. For sculpture, the edge could be on a multitude of tools, including razor sharp wood carving tools to less precise stone carving tools. *See* ***Hone***.

Sharpening stones. Top left: coarse, fine (with gouge), hard Arkansas and India gouge (lower left).

Motorized grinder wheel with water bath. It is used for quickly shaping cutting tools.

Shear The force in effect as a material is rapidly displaced. A manufacturer may say to "shear" a material meaning to shake or stir forcefully. The term also describes a machine used to cut large sheets of metal.

Sheet metal Metal less than one-eighths inch (0.318cm) thick, designated in gauges for sizes. The larger gauge actually designates thinner metals; for example, 24 gauge weighs one half as much as 18 gauge for the same length and width of metal. *See* ***Rivet; Metal fabrication***.

Shellac A unique, thin varnish that mixes with alcohol. It originates from the resinous secretion of a lac insect left on trees. In its original state, it is orange or yellow, but it is often bleached white. It is ideal as a plaster mold sealant, drying to a hard glossy, near-clean finish.

Shellspin™ A ceramic slurry held in suspension so it does not require continual mixing. *See* ***Slurry; Ceramic shell***.

Shielded Metal Arc Welding (SMAW) An arc welding process that fuses metals with heat from a covered (shielded) metal electrode and the base metal. The melting electrode coating produces the shielding, as well as the filler metal. *See* ***Welding***.

Shim The material used as a sectioning device to separate mold parts from each other for easy removal and reassembly. The shim is usually thin brass or tin strips pressed into soft forms. It is also the term for a thin tapered strip of hardwood inserted into mold seams to force open the mold. An additional usage is as a leveling or gap filler. *See* ***Mold; Waste mold***.

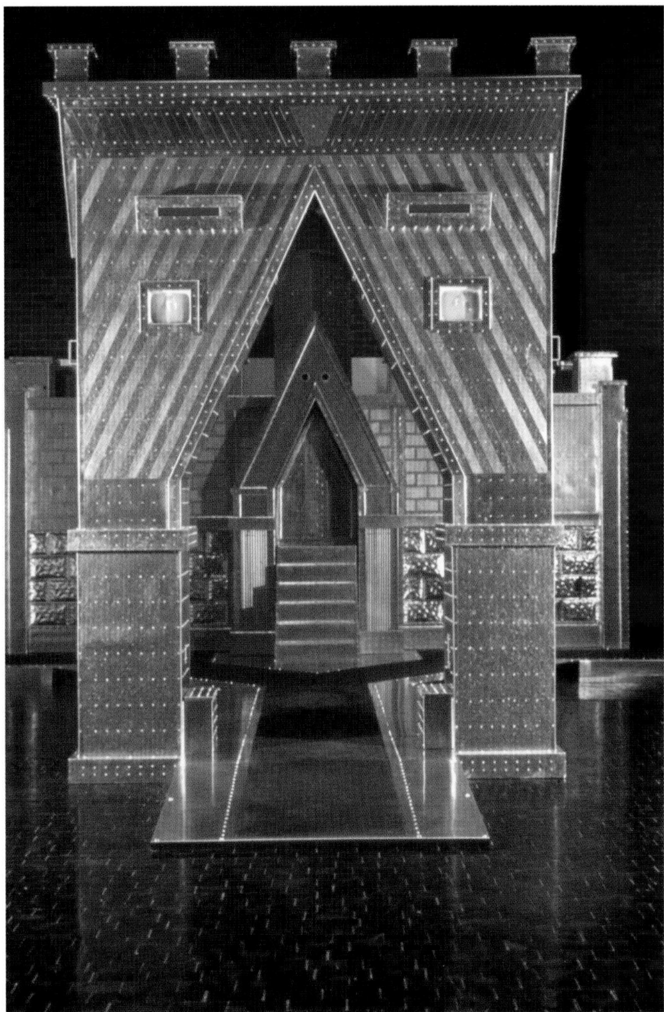

Michael Aurbach, *The Institution*. Galvanized sheet metal, wood, found objects, electronic devices, 10½'x20'x28' (3.2m x 6.1m x 8.54m).

Shore hardness The hardness of rubber. Shore can also be practically designated as "shear" or tear strength. The highest number designates the hardest material. An example of this would be a truck tire at shore 55, a hard rubber hammer at shore 70, or a battery case at shore 100. Soft mold materials would be a low shore number with 30 about a useful average to a hard shore of 50 or above. Soft shores show less shear strength but are more flexible without disrupting intricate casting as they are being removed.

Short clay Water-based clay that is not very plastic or workable for the purpose. The clay can sometimes collapse on its own weight; it is not very strong. When wheel throwing, a plastic clay such as ball clay needs to be added to the clay body to improve the throwing quality.

Shrinkage Decreasing mass size. In ceramics, this is caused by drying clay bodies or kiln firing the water-based clay. Adding grog to a clay body can decrease shrinkage. Shrinkage (warpage) in metal casting is from excessively thick areas being attached to a thin area; the thick area will contract and draw metal from the thinner section as it cools. A better designed runner system to disperse the metal more evenly can help, as well as avoiding thick walls and pouring the metal at a colder temperature. In resins, it is the natural process of thermosetting. *See* ***Grog***.

Sieve A screen supported by a frame used to sift and separate particle sizes, or to locate unwanted debris that is discarded.

Silica Silicon dioxide. Sand, flint or quartz rock that liquifies into a transparent, glassy state at 3110°F (1710°C). However, this is too high to use on clay bodies, so a flux is used to reduce the melting point. Lead oxides and alkaline compounds are used. Adding a refractory, alumina, creates a hard, tough surface. All of these ingredients in various formulas with other chemicals for colors and effects create the glaze. It is also used as a refractory material for metal castings, especially ceramic shell castings. *See* ***Glazes****;* ***Slurry****;* ***Ceramic shell****.*

Silicon A non-metallic chemical agent derived from silica and silicates. It is found in the earth and is of a crystalline structure. Silicon is used with other materials for glass, concrete, bricks, refractories and ceramics. *See* ***Metals*** *(chart);* ***Bronze*** *(casting);* ***Patina****;* ***Everdur***™*;* ***Silicone*** *(bronze).*

Silicon (bronze) An alloy containing silicon that produces good castings with higher tensile strength. Matching silicon bronze welding rods are readily available and ease of welding makes it a bronze of choice for sculptors. Silicon bronze does not take a patina as easily as more traditional bronzes. It inhibits corrosion, but also resists coloration by chemicals. Everdur™ is a popular brand of casting silicon bronze. *See* ***Bronze****;* ***Everdur***™*.*

Silicone A flexible mold material that is characterized by water repellency and excellent lubricity. Silicone is a preferred mold material because a release agent is not normally required. This allows it to be placed directly on moist plaster, wax or clay without any surface damage. *See* ***Flexible molds****.*

Silicosis A lung disease caused by prolonged inhalation of silica dust. Quarry workers, stone carvers and ceramicists are prone to silicosis if they do not wear proper respiratory protection. The inhaled silica lodges in the lung lining blocking the air supply. The results are shortness of breath and progressive fibrosis. *See* ***Pneumoconiosis****.*

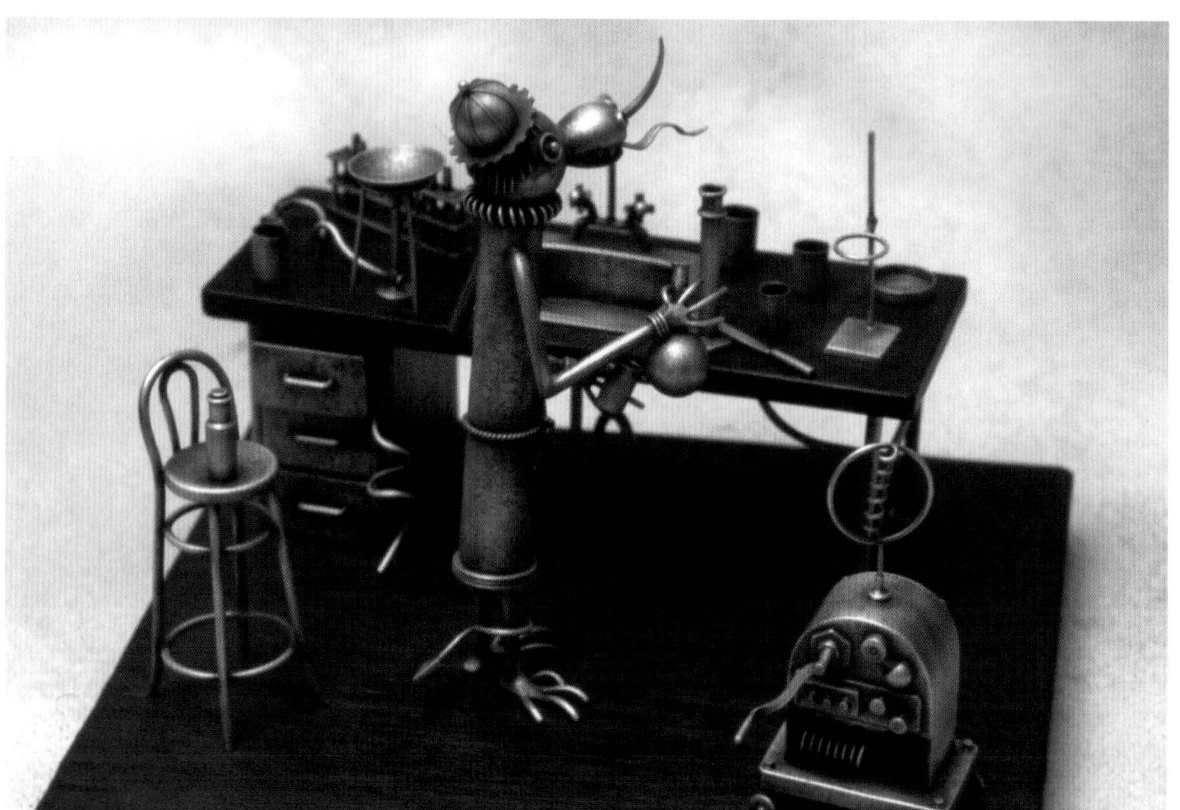

Earl Krentzin, *Scientist*. Fabricated sterling silv mahogany, 6″ (15.2cm tall.

ilver A malleable, ductile, metallic element of a bright white (silver) color. Since it is easily manipulated, it is valued for small sculptures or decorative jewelry.

ilver nitrate A colorless, crystalline compound used as a patina that induces a silver surface color. *See **Patina; Patina** (chart).*

ilver solder A silver based, filler metal used for brazing (soldering). Silver solders come in these categories: 1) hard solder that flows at 1460°F (793.3°C), 2) medium solder at 1360° (737.8°C), 3) easy melting solder at 1300°F (704°C). Hard silver solder creates the strongest weld. *See **Silver soldering**.*

Max S. DeMoss, *Platter #70*. Bronze and silver, 4′7″ (1.4m). Photographer: Jim Watters.

ilver soldering (silver brazing) Soldering that uses a rod of copper-nickel-silver applied over a flux coated pre-heated surface. The rod is never heated as the hot base metal melts the rod into a thin liquid. The rod cannot be flux coated or the flux could become a coating of insulation prohibiting the solder from liquifying before the base metal melts. A small oxyacetylene torch or gas torch is usually used with silver solder. Silver brazing is ideal for jewelry and fine electronics, since the thinner liquid alloy can seep into areas where other rods cannot penetrate. *See **Silver solder; Soldering**.*

inking The forming of sheet metal by placing it over a specific indentation or sunken shape and hammering it into the new depressed shape.

inter The natural binding of silica or lime found in oolitic rocks. In ceramics, the term designates an interactive bonding without fusion.

ite specific A sculpture designed and installed for a particular (specific) location (site). It may require special materials, colors, sizes, lights, etc. Sometimes performance work or sculpture of a temporary nature for a specific audience is site specific.

arbara rygutis, *anding eaves, Falling ght*. Steel, ght, 7′x4′x2′ .18m x .22m x .61m) each nit. Seattle, Vashington. hotographer: pike Mafford.

Lea Vivot, *Endless Bench*. Bronze, 14′ dia. x 6′4″ (4.27m dia. x 1.93m). Hospital for Sick Children, Toronto, Ontario, Canada.

Sizing A glutinous substance added to porous materials, such as cloth or paper, as a filler or glaze to enhance the working ability or stability. *See* ***Paper***.

Skew chisels A wood carving chisel with a flat blade that has an angled cutting edge. Various sizes are available.

Slab Working with sheets of clay. The clay may be flattened, becoming sheets to cut and join together creating in a form. It is ideal for larger geometric or flat shapes. Since the slab used is already prepared in the correct thickness, there is no need to remove clay from the interior. The work is completed by combining slabs of even thicknesses to create the form. Great care must be taken in merging the individual slabs to avoid separation either during the forming or firing process. The benefit of this process is that extremely large works can be completed even with interior supports of clay (of the same moisture content). Large identical or molded sections can be finished at a rapid rate. A uniform slab can be obtained by using a slab roller or a rolling pin. *See* ***Coil***; ***Pinch***; ***Hollow out***; ***Kiln***; ***Firing***; ***Clay*** *(oil based)*; ***Ceramics***; ***Slab roller***.

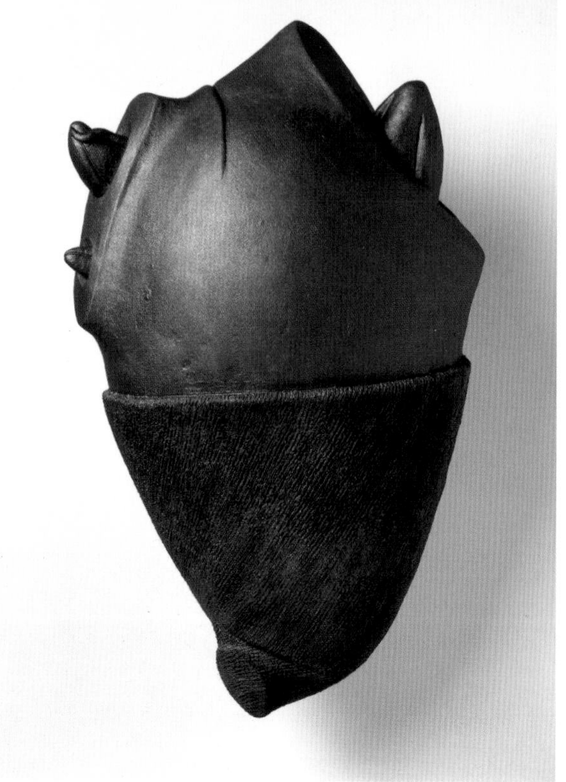

Juan Granados, *Spring and Seed*. Earthenware, metallic oxide, 29″x18″x11″ (73.7cm x 45.7cm x 27.9cm). Photographer: Andrew Martin.

SLAB CONSTRUCTION
by Juan Granados

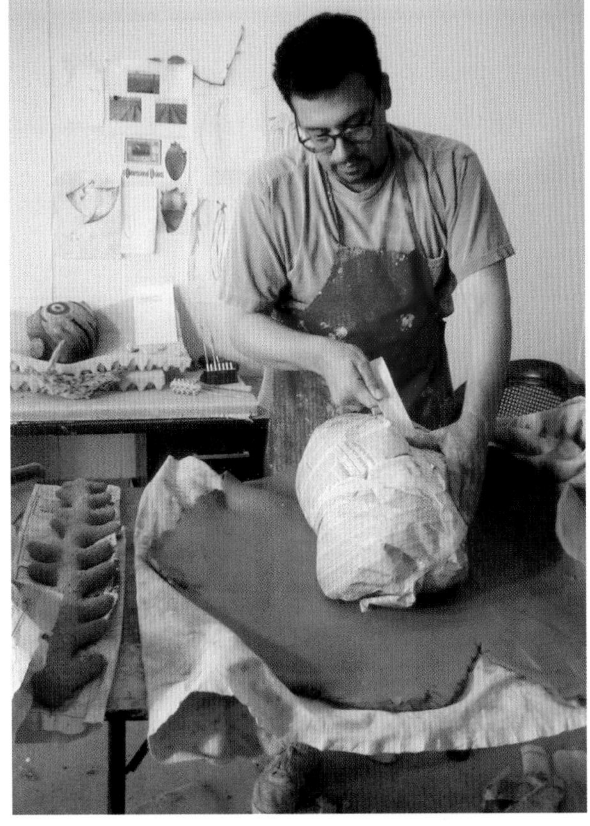

Beginning a slab construction, a wadded paper form is placed on a large slab of low fire clay. Juan calls it his "piñata form method."

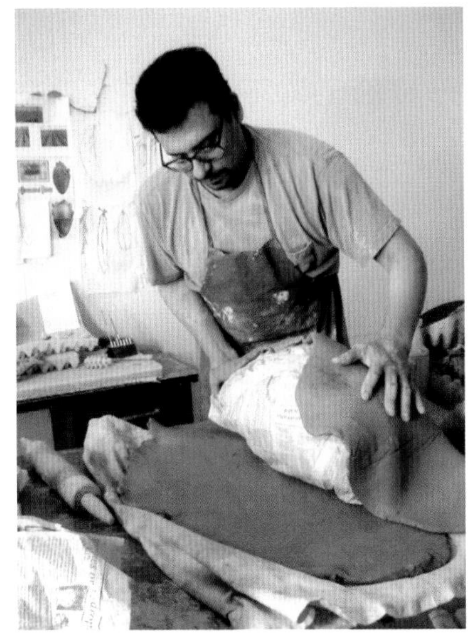

The clay covers the paper support.

The form is refined.

Slab roller A system of geared rollers controlled by a large hand-operated wheel. Clay is pressed through to create a uniform sheet at a given thickness. It is mounted onto a long bed that allows a long and wide clay sheet to be formed. It is especially useful for slab construction.

Slag Debris (dross) or refuse from non-combustible trash or impurities floating on top of a hot, molten, metal-casting liquid. It is cleared off prior to pouring the liquid. *See **Metal casting***.

Slake Adding plaster to water begins a process of disintegration, a slaking process. If the plaster is then mixed and used, the process stops. To continue to soak unmixed plaster in water (slaking) will result in dead plaster or plaster that has no setting ability. In ceramics, to slake clay is to immerse it into water until it falls apart.

Slate A dark blue or black metamorphic stone with a composition of thin layers. It is extremely fine-grained. *See **Stone** (chart)*.

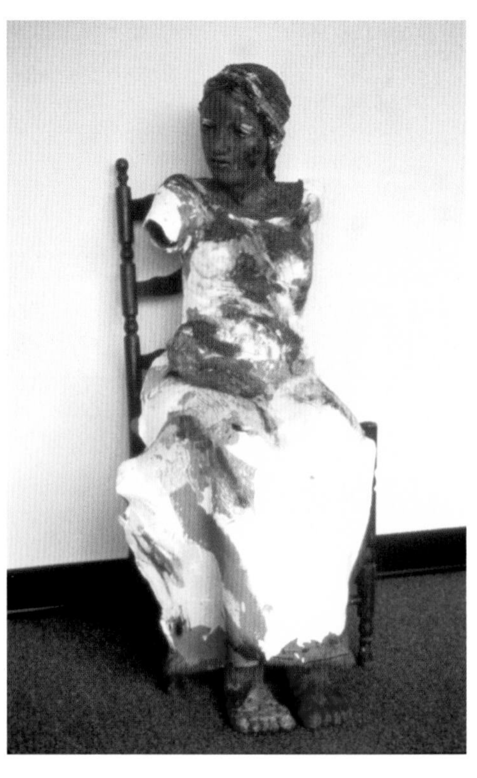

Marcia Polenberg, *Isis*. Slips, glazes, terra cotta, mixed, 52″ (132.1cm) tall.

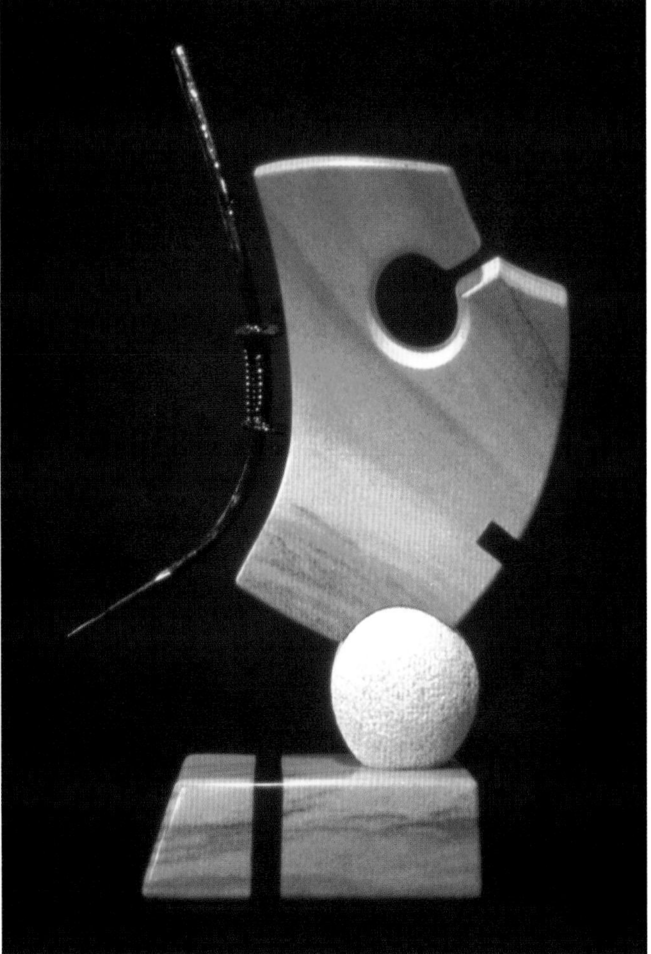

Slip A thick, fine-grained clay and water liquid mixture. It is used as a saturating and blending adhesive for placing sections of wet clay together. It can be utilized for decoration and color on clay surfaces. The term is also used for an extremely hard sharpening stone, such as Arkansas stone. *See **Slip stone**; **Slip casting**; **Sharpening stones**; **Arkansas stone***.

Shawn Phillip Morin, *Taming the Simple*. Marble, slate, steel, 34″x8″x11″ (86.4cm x 20.3cm x 27.9cm).

John Chalke, *Blue-Grey Expose*. Ceramic, slip, 17.3″ (44cm) tall. Photographer: Barbara Tipton.

SLIP MOLDING by Jack Thompson

A slip mold is used to cast a hand.

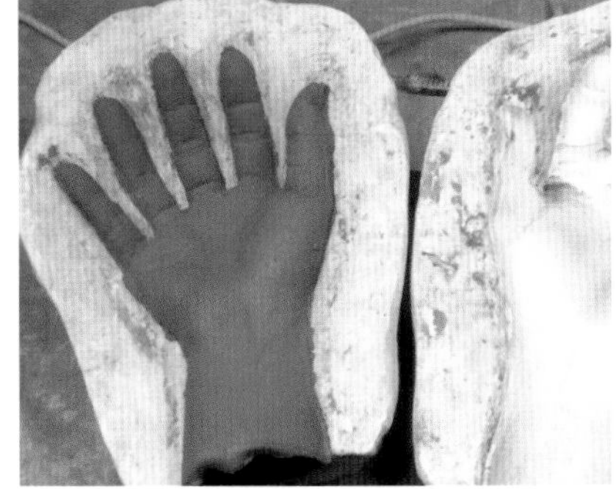

The mold is opened.

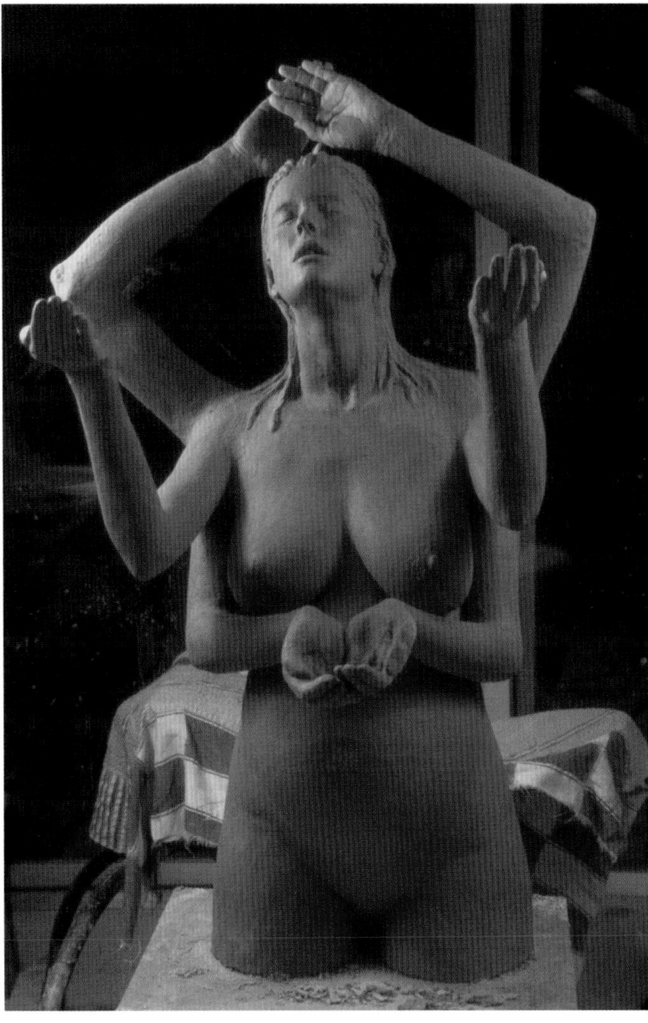

Jack Thompson's slip cast hands mounted onto a slip form.

Slip casting Pouring a slip clay into a porous (dry plaster) mold to absorb moisture from the liquid nearest the surface. After a slight thickness has formed, the remaining volume is poured out, leaving a clay wall. The clay shrinks from the mold wall as moisture evaporates, allowing the form to be easily removed for final drying, trimming and firing. Moisture is sucked out into the dry plaster mold's wall, leaving clay in a more firm state touching the wall. The longer it sits, the more moisture is removed, leaving a thicker surface.

Slip casting is used primarily for smaller works or works in multiple. The liquid clay body does not have grog and is smooth. Generally, the bodies are thin, averaging between three-sixteenths inch (0.476cm) and one-fourth inch (0.635cm). After the desired thickness is obtained, the excess clay is poured back into a container for reuse. Once the shrunken slip is leather hard, it is easily removed from the mold.

Slip casting molds are simple and must be designed so that there are enough pieces to eliminate all undercuts. Depending on the care and storage, they can have a good life expectancy, but eventually break down in surface composition. They must be clean without any surface oil to properly work.

SLIP CASTING
by Pamela Phillips

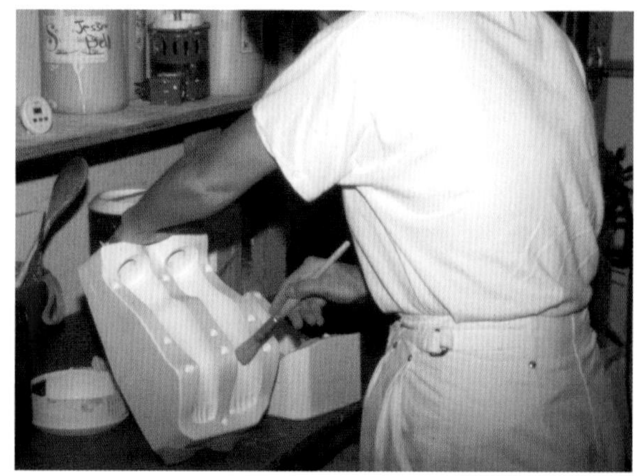

A dry plaster mold is dusted for slip casting porcelain.

Slip is poured into the bound mold.

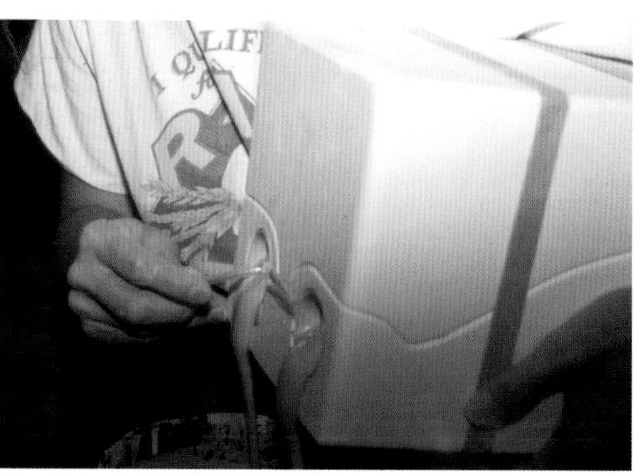

After the thickness is reached, the excess is poured out.

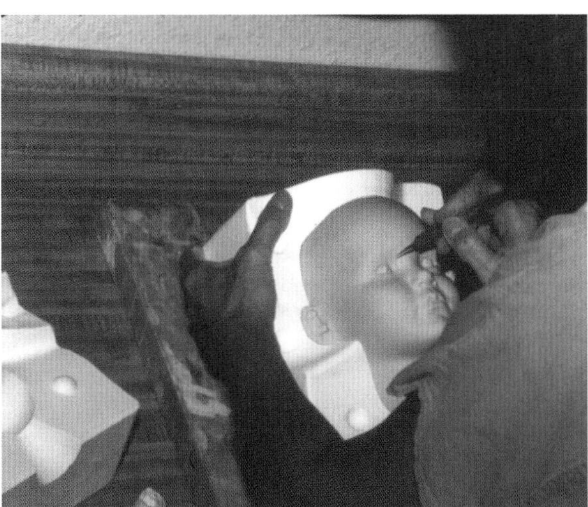

Trimming/chasing the work even before it is removed from the mold.

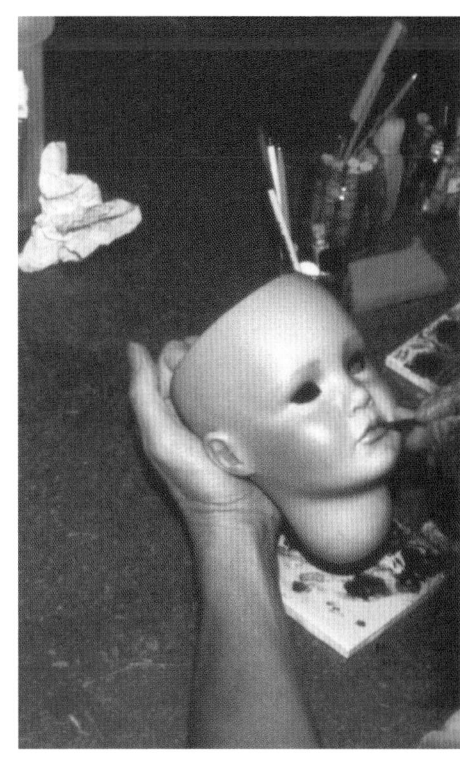

After kiln firing, the porcelain is hand painted.

Pamela Phillips, *Angelique*. Porcelain, mixed media, 27″ (68.6cm) tall.

Technique

The process can include a simple clay casting formula, without grog, mixed into a creamy mixture. It is allowed to sit for several days and then sifted through screens (from 40 to 80 mesh) to rid the composition of uneven particles or lumps. When it is added into the mold, it takes from ten minutes to an hour to complete. The final casting is trimmed in the leather hard stage and then allowed to dry before firing. A blunger (powered mixer) is used for combining clay and water into a smooth flowing slip mix. A larger tank, or ark, is used to keep greater quantities in preparation for the blunger.

Ideally, the water contained in slip needs to be as little as possible. This keeps the mold from having to absorb as much, resulting in a better, faster casting with less shrinkage and a longer life for the mold. By adding modest amounts of electrolyte, the slip's fluidity can be changed. Using a mixture of the electrolytes, sodium carbonate and sodium silicate, the amount of necessary water can be decreased by as much as 50%.

Determining how many electrolytes to use is obtained by trial and error. Beginning with small amounts of less than one-fourth of 1%, the electrolytes to the total mix, more can be added up to about 1%. They should be added to the water prior to mixing. Too much will cause the slip to jellify. Practice and preference will determine how thick the slip needs to be. If the slip appears too watery over a period of time, it may be because of the alkaline content in the water. A small amount of vinegar (an acid) can be used to impede or neutralize the alkali resulting in a smooth useful, flocculated slip. *See **Blunger***.

Slugging Adding small pieces of metal to a welding joint to either strengthen, fill or add to a design. This can be accomplished during welding or before the welding begins.

Slurry A fluid mixture of liquid colloidal silica and binders to create a refractory material used as mold material for metal castings. The wax form is encased with slurry, then melted out leaving a strong heat resistant mold that can withstand the high temperatures of the liquid metals that are poured into it. Slurry is the term used for the liquid mix, as compared to the same mix after it has been dried or fired into ceramic shell. *See **Ceramic shell***.

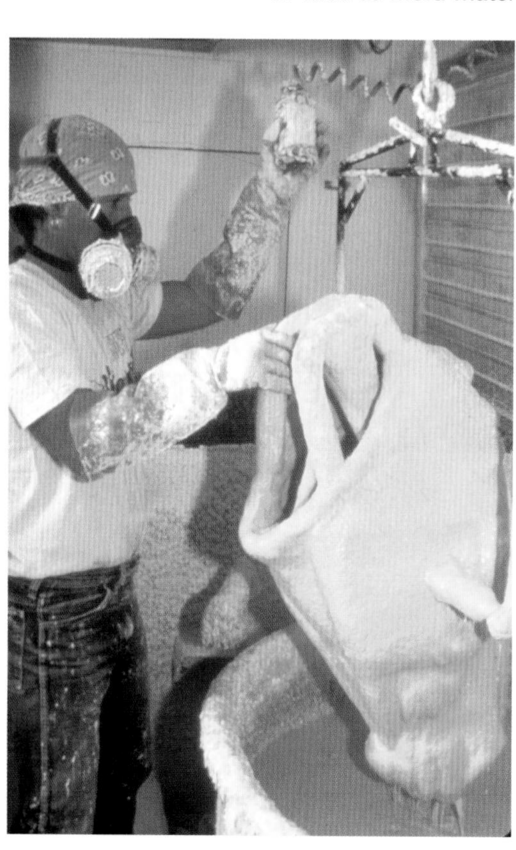

A wax dipped in slurry. An overhead hoist is used to support the very large work. **Shidoni Foundry**, Tesúque, New Mexico.

The base mix is usually prepared by a commercial manufacturer with a tested formula. It contains other materials that aid in casting. One ingredient is a wetting agent. Without it, the slurry will not adhere to the wax unless the wax has been dipped or sprayed with a thin shellac or varnish (resulting in a minor loss of the finest details). Another is an anti-foaming agent known as a debubbleizer. It aids in reducing and removing the air bubbles that rise to the surface as the slurry is being agitated or mixed and keeps all of the materials in suspension.

Some manufacturers place a colorant into the solution that changes color as the slurry dries, making it easier to know when to continue the dipping. However, all of these ingredients can be purchased separately and added as needed to amplify or create the same results. The colloidal silica manufacturer should be consulted in formulating a slurry.

There are two major types of premixed ceramic shell slurry: **colloidal silica** and **ethyl silicate**. The primary difference is the base: colloidal is water, ethyl is alcohol. Colloidal base is more common, since it poses fewer personal and environmental problems, creating a safer product that produces a tougher shell and has a considerably longer use and storage life. It is readily available and is not as expensive as ethyl silicate. However, it does require considerably more time to dry, thus prolonging the molding process.

Ethyl silicate's advantage is that it can complete a refractory mold in a rapid timeframe. This obviously allows an accelerated production schedule and less drying storage problems. However, the exact mixture of materials is more crucial and because of rapid alcohol evaporation, alcohol must constantly be added to maintain the slurry formula and to keep the liquid from drying up. All electrical mixers and switches must be spark proof because of the vapors that could result in fire or explosion. *See **Slurry investing**.*

Slurry investing Encasing wax artwork into a slurry mix in preparation for metal casting. Slurry is generally thought of as using colloidal silica. To create a mold using slurry is simple, having only three key ingredients: the binder of colloidal silica (commercially manufactured), the silica powder that is added to the binder in the mixing tank to create the slurry (liquid mix) and the stucco or the larger refractory particles that are added to the wet slurry surface to build up the strength of the mold.

The work is completely submerged in the mix.

Technique

A silica refractory powder is mixed with the colloidal silica until it has been saturated and absorbed into an even consistency. The powder comes in various grits depending upon the user's requirements. If the user is going to have two mixing tanks, one for a surface coating, and one for rapid build-up coatings, then the surface coating can be finer and the build-up coating can be considerably coarser.

All manufacturers have their recommendations, and they should be observed for best results. The initial powders (flour) vary from 200 to 400 grit, with the backup ranging from 200 to 100. Zircon flour is added for additional strength. It is an extremely high heat refractory especially used for iron or stainless steel. Because of its fine grit and strength, it aids with stronger, fine surface details. One tank slurry mix uses a middle range powder (200) with the addition of milled zircon (325) for intricate details.

The work is pulled out of the mix and allowed to drain.

The final mixes are usually checked for viscosity by using a zahn cup (a small cup with a critically measured hole in the center for draining the liquid out). The silica powders should first be added slowly to the liquid colloidal silica and mixed until the proper proportion has been obtained. After some mixing, if a wetting agent or anti-foaming agent is needed, then they are added. It is best to wait 24 hours after the initial mix before use. However, more mix may be periodically added with shorter mixing times. *See **Zahn cup**; **Wetting agent**; **Anti-foaming agent**; **Zirconium**.*

The work is dipped into the fluidizing bed.

Once the slurry has been added to the wax surface, usually by dipping, the temperature needs to remain as constant as possible to avoid wax expansion from heat or contraction from the cold. Such movement of the wax could result in a fractured mold. The best temperature for slurry application is approximately 70°F (21.1°C) depending on the humidity, etc. Even with the possibility of wax shrinkage or expansion, the temperature can vary as much as 10°F (12.2°C) in either direction of the original dip, providing it does not exceed this limit.

Slurry mixers are designed to keep the liquid in suspension to avoid a settling out, set or frozen slurry. The mixers generally have timers to allow the mix to be used and to avoid overheating the mix from constant motion. There is a slurry mix available that does not have to be in constant suspension called Shellspin™. *See **Slurry mixers; Shellspin**™ (ceramic slurry).*

A mixer should not be used while the dipping is in progress. Other than the obvious safety problem, the mix itself may contain air bubbles gathered or trapped by the mixing mechanism. A foot pedal that shuts off the machine while the operator is standing over it is desirable.

Stuccoing

The slurry needs a coat of refractory material between dips to gain strength and shorten the drying time and number of dips needed. These materials are referred to as stucco or dry additives and are applied to the form after it has been dipped into the drained slurry. It is silica or another refractory particle, called sand, due to the larger size used. Two or more sizes are required as the dipping progresses. The first one is a finer size, such as #100, to be used for the first few coats (perhaps three coats). A heavier particle (#50 or so) is used for coats afterwards for a stronger and faster build-up volume. The stucco readily adheres with any excess falling off. Air drying is a factor since the slurry must be completely dry between coats. Larger works are difficult to handle without specially designed hoisting equipment.

Stuccoing can be accomplished by several methods, but the two most common ones are either to sift the stucco on the wet surface or to dip the work into a fluidizing bed. The sifting method is easy, especially for very small works. The wax is placed in a

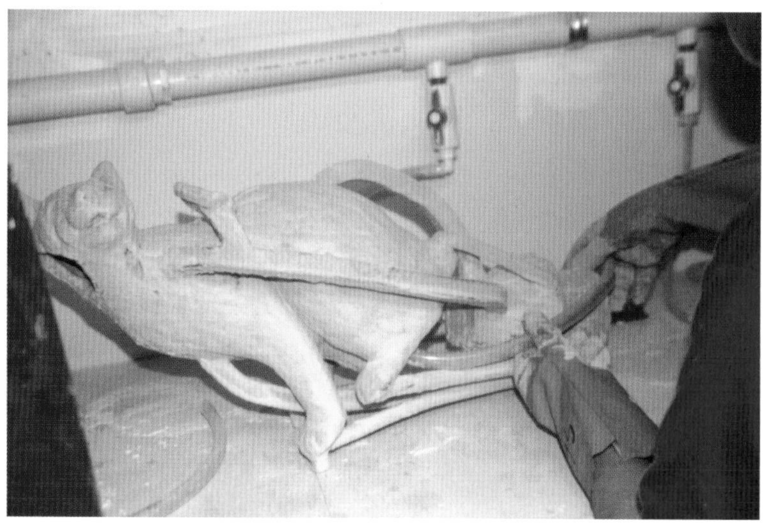

The work is placed in a drying area with fans, and, in this case, air hoses delivering blown air into the hollow part of the form for drying.

bed of stucco as the sculptor simply throws, sprinkles or drops the stucco onto the wetted surface. All interior spaces should be filled with stucco and drained.

A fluidizing bed is a container with compressed air evenly forced through the lower stucco, causing it to rise, float and become a dry fluid. In the suspended state, a work can be easily dipped and immediately coated inside and out with minimal effort. It is the preferred method of adding stucco. The only downside is that the largest particles of refractory available cannot be fluidized. As a result, a smaller particle is used, requiring additional dips of the smaller particles to gain enough refractory strength. *See* ***Fluidizing bed***.

After the desired thickness has been achieved (one-fourth to one-half inch [0.635cm to 1.27cm]) depending on the size of the wax), the work is top coated with a simple dip of slurry without any stucco. This leaves a smoother surface for handling and makes it easier to spot hairline cracks that could appear after the burnout

Circulating air is essential for the process to be completed within a reasonable timeframe. Using portable fans or a permanently installed system is preferred. However, too much fast circulating air, as the wax is dipped, can cause a premature slurry dry up. The stucco will not firmly bond. Measuring the drying time is tricky, especially if the wax is hollow or has interior areas to coat and dry. One way to ensure even dryness is to attach flexible air lines to an air source with the open end placed into the wax cavity to dispense a slow supply of air within the form as the coatings dry. A color changing chemical indicator added to the slurry mix displays different wet and dry colors. Noting the color changes is the best method to be certain of adequate dryness.

Once the mold is ready for burnout, the cup must be opened or cleared of obstruction. Normally, in coating the mold, slurry has also coated the top of the cup. The easiest way to remove the mold cover is to cut it off with a grinder with a thin abrasive cutting wheel. The cutting wheel does not have to be large, but it does need to be able to cut through the excess shell and wax, leaving an open cup to de-wax and then pour metal into. A good inexpensive tool to use is a small air operated disk grinder with a built-in protective shield. A safety face shield and respirator are also mandatory. *See* ***Plaster investing***.

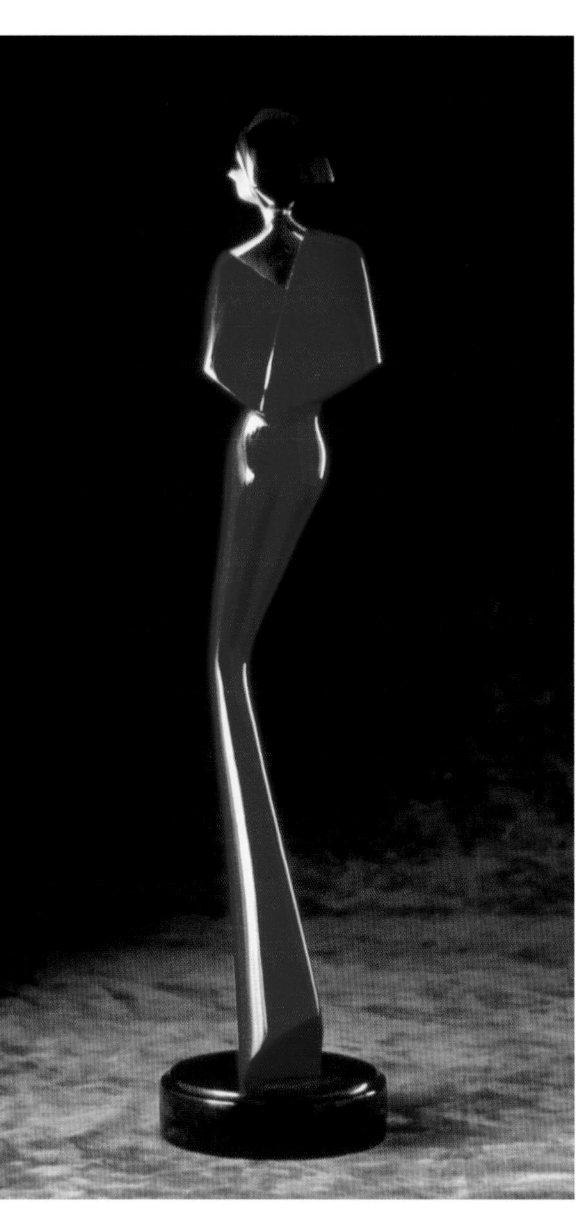

David Hostetler, *Red Cape Lady*. Bronze with glazurite paint, 42″ (106.7cm) tall.

Slurry mixer A machine with a stainless steel shaft and blades used for mixing ceramic shell investment coating. The basic slurry mixer operation includes a container for the mix, a motorized mixing device, and a timer to control the mixing cycle. If the slurry is to stay in suspension over a period of days, the mixing motor needs to be on a timer, such as on ten minutes, off ten minutes. This depends on the tank, mixing blade, mix and power. A foot pedal that will stop the mixer while in use is also good. The tanks need to be stainless steel or resistant to bending or surface corrosion. Fiberglass tanks or tanks coated with fiberglass are common. All have to be kept covered to avoid evaporation.

Types of slurry mixers

The **rotating tumbler** is sealed and then placed on a ceramic ball machine or on two rollers for constant rotation. One of the rollers is motorized causing the solution to stay in suspension as it rotates. This type of mixer is desirable only for very small mixes It is limited in size and requires constantly lifting the container off the rollers into an upright position for usage.

The **turntable mixer** spins around a stationary blade. The blade, close to the wall prevents the solution from building up on the wall (but it does significantly build up on the blade). While a flat bottom tank can easily be mounted on a motorized turntable, it takes some blade and lid engineering to accommodate the constant spinning. As long as the mixer quits spinning for use, the machine is easy to use.

Stationary tanks are chosen because of cost, sizes available and ease of arrangement. A commercial self-contained mixer of lower RPM (300 or so) with a stainless steel shaft and blade is preferred. Since the blade is usually down very low into the container, the mixer does not have to be moved for most of the works to be dipped. Some have a design that allows the mixer or blade shaft to be elevated out of the wax for extremely large forms. As the mix hits the blade, the blade becomes increasingly sharper, whether it is rotating or not. If the blade is brushed against, it can damage the wax or the operator.

Stationary tank slurry mixers.

A mixer can be easily designed with a strong (high torque) motor. The motor is mounted with a gear or pulley reducer to achieve a lower RPM (300 or so). The motor itself should be of low RPM (1750), enclosed, grounded, and moisture proof to avoid burnout and deadly electrical shocks. The shaft and blades should be stainless steel to avoid rust. It is possible to avoid the high priced manufactured stainless steel blades by welding a carefully balanced stainless steel blade to a collar that can be attached to the shaft. Care needs to be taken to avoid a poor balance that is harmful to the motor, too fast of a mix, causing excessive bubbles or too slow of a mix resulting in caking on the walls and blade.

Timers are needed to stop the blade while applying slurry to the artwork and also to avoid overheating the mix from constant friction. The timer should have a complete one hour cycle for better control. Different mixes, sizes of mix and blade speeds require different settings from three off and 15 on to five off and five on. The mix must be repeatedly homogenized and yet rest long enough to avoid a "hot" solution that could cause the wax to expand or the mix to swell with air. *See* ***Slurry; Ceramic shell; Burnout furnace***.

Slush(ing) (slush or rotational molding) Placing liquid molding material into a mold to create a thin walled casting. It involves pouring the casting material into the mold until it is partially or fully filled. It is then a process of rotating, moving, gyrating or agitating the mold to cover all the interior surfaces in a systematic way. A coating of the casting substance temporarily adheres to the mold's wall. Afterwards, the surplus material is poured out, leaving a layered deposit on the mold. This may be repeated until the correct thickness is gained.

One slushing method is to completely fill the mold with liquid and let it stand until the desired thickness solidifies on the wall. Then the excess liquid is poured out. This is much like forming an ice cube but removing the water prior to a complete solid freezing.

Most slushing is done by hand for small molds, but larger molds are rotated by specially designed machines. Large molds are held together with removable bolts while bungee cords or rubber straps are used to hold small molds together. *See* ***Casting; Molds; Slip casting***.

SLUSHING
by Remo Williams

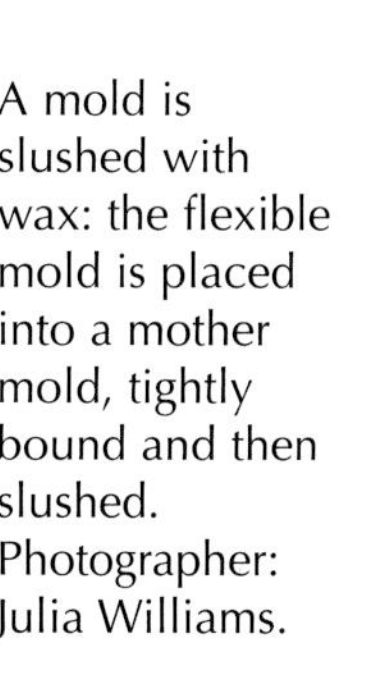

A mold is slushed with wax: the flexible mold is placed into a mother mold, tightly bound and then slushed. Photographer: Julia Williams.

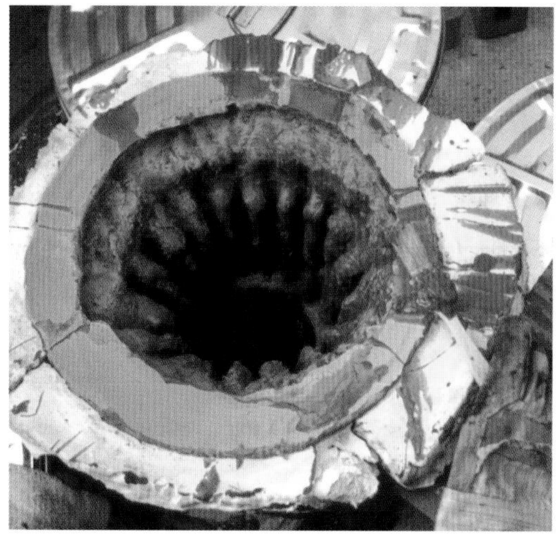

The completed wax pattern.

The wax is cut into two parts to demonstrate the different layers of wax applied during the slush. In the center is the completed *Saguaro Papoose*, 22″x8″ (55.9cm x 20.3cm) by **Remo Williams**. Photographer: Julia Williams.

Smelting furnace A metal melting furnace. *See* ***Furnace; Blast furnace***.

Smooth-On™ Flexible molding products. *See* ***Flexible molds***.

Soak The time allowed for temperatures to be evenly sustained during the firing cycle of clays, glazes or metal casting molds. High temperatures allow the glaze to mature and to flatten bubbles before cooling. With metal casting molds, soaking allows the mold to be completely de-waxed. *See* ***Firing***.

Soap A cleanser or release agent for sculpture purposes. *See* ***Soft soap; Release agent*** *(chart);* ***Green soap***.

Soapstone Also named steatite, a metamorphic stone called soapstone because of the slippery or soapy talc content. It is a soft, easy-to-carve stone possessing a multitude of colors. *See* ***Steatite; Stone*** *(chart)*.

Dahrl Thomson, *Avian Interlude*. Soapstone, 13½"x11"x5" (34.3cm x 27.9cm x 12.7cm).

Sodium chloride Rock salt or table salt used to accelerate plaster setting time. In ceramics, it is used for salt glazing. *See* ***Salt glazing***.

Sodium silicate (water glass) A water-soluble silicate compound used as a deflocculant for casting slips and as a fire resistant binder for concretes, etc. *See* ***Sand casting***.

Sodium thiosulfate A crystalline compound used as a binder with other chemicals to secure specific patina results, especially on bronze. *See* ***Patina; Patina*** *(chart)*.

Soft sculpture Three-dimensional work that visibly exhibits a soft quality generally associated with fabric. Sometimes called soft art, it is created from soft, bendable, pliable materials such as cloth, vinyl, cotton, etc. The end product retains the characteristics of these materials. *See* ***Fabric***.

Soft soap A liquid potassium soap product that is used as a separator for molds. *See* ***Mold Soap; Release Agent*** *(chart);* ***Green soap***.

Soft steel Sometimes the designation for mild steel. *See* ***Mild steel***.

Soft wood Wood from trees with narrow, needlelike leaves. Generally, it is easier to carve because of the open grain. *See* ***Woods*** *(chart)*.

Solder(ing) A fusing alloy used to join two metallic pieces. Tin and lead are commonly used. The process of joining two metals is known as soldering or to solder. Soldering requires low heat between 400°F (204.4°C) and 600°F (315.6°C) and using an electric soldering iron, gun or a self-contained propane bottle/torch as the heating source. Since solder is comprised of 40% to 60% tin to lead, the solder itself is not very strong and relies primarily on good close joints and capillary action. Some lead solders contain acid or rosin to complete the cleaning procedure and require no further flux. Being inexpensive and easy to use, soldering is used for electrical work. The soldering gun is best for smaller jobs, especially finer fittings for electrical work. The larger soldering copper (long copper tip with insulated handle) is better for larger works where control is an issue. Since the propane torch is portable, it is for situations requiring

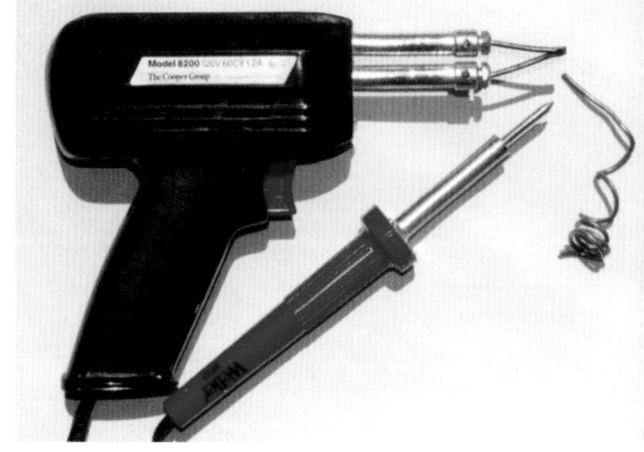

Soldering gun, iron and coiled solder.

less finesse or where a flame could better enter to complete the work. *See* ***Capillary action***.

Technique

The process is not difficult. The base metal must be cleaned with a wire brush, steel wool, sandpaper, emery cloth or sometimes hydrochloric acid. The work must be close fitting with a butt joint or preferably, overlapping or lock joint. While working, it is best that the joints are held down tightly by clamps whenever possible. The area is heated to a temperature that will allow the solder to instantaneously melt and flow thin onto the base metal. If the solder slags or balls, then continue heating the area needs to continue before applying more.

The term "sweating" is used when applying solder to metal joints or pipes because of the ease with which it runs into and between the joints. Too much solder may be a sign of a poor joint.

All welding procedures present some dangers. Ventilation is a necessity, especially when brazing or soldering with poisonous cadmium as part of the bonding alloy (found in silver solders). Fumes from lead solders are also toxic. Acid based lead solders possess obvious handling problems. Gloves and goggles should always be worn. The welding surface must be fireproof. Corrosive soldered flux surfaces ordinarily need to be rinsed in water. *See* ***Brazing****;* ***Silver soldering***.

Solvent A substance (chemical) capable of dissolving another substance. Acetone is a multipurpose solvent, for example.

Sound wood Wood without decay (rot).

Spacer A material placed between the artwork and mother mold to allow a correct thickness of flexible mold material to be added between the two. This is sometimes used when completing a pour-on mold. The spacers are the same thickness as the desired mold. They are made from pre-cast molding compound of the same material as will be used for the pour-on molding material.

The small pieces are usually square and placed into soft artwork with a thin straight pin (in the center of the spacer). On hard artwork, they need a temporary glue, such as rubber cement. They can also be applied by brushing a thin liquid mold coating on the model and pressing the spacers into it as it begins to set. Once the mother mold is replaced, the spacer will keep it away from the original artwork while the pour-on compound is added. Since a pour-on liquid readily adheres to its own pre-cast materials, the spacers hold fast and become a permanent part of the pour-on mold. *See* ***Flexible mold*** *(pour-on)*.

Michael David Fox, *Louisa, the Tasmanian Terrorist*. Mixed media including wig, wood chips and fiberglass, over life-size.

Spall A small chip with a sharp edge discharged from a larger mass, usually stone. Temperature fluctuation is the cause. The surface (chip) is unable to adapt to the more constant mass temperature. The contraction, or expansion, between the two results in surface fractures. One should avoid applying sudden heat to concrete (as with an oxyacetylene torch or welder), or the concrete will spall off at a damaging velocity. *See* ***Thermal torch***.

Sparker Spark igniter or flint lighting tool designed to ignite gas operated tools. *See* ***Igniter****;* ***Oxyacetylene welding***.

Spat A protective cover of leather or fire retardant material placed over the upper shoe and ankle that is fastened with a strap under the shoe. *See* ***Safety dress****;* ***Legging***.

Spatial presence The total presence/existence of a sculpture in space/area including the actual, as well as implied dimensions.

Spatter Flying metal particles. As the heat or arc is placed to the metal to weld, the hot metal rod and base metal shower (spatter) away from the weld. The spatter is not part of the weld and may deface the surface. *See **Arc welding; Oxyacetylene welding**.*

Spatula A tool with a handle with one or two flat ends of different sizes. It is used to manipulate modeling materials such as modeling clay, ceramic clay and wet plaster. *See **Modeling**.*

Speed riddle (power riddle) Motorized screens that mix and aerate molding sand in preparation for metal casting sand molds. *See **Sand casting**.*

Spiral rolls Wound rolls of abrasive materials used as finishing supplies.

Spit A wall piece from the interior of a pre-warmer or kiln breaking off and falling into a de-waxed mold or onto a sculpture resulting in an imperfection. It can be loose kiln wash.

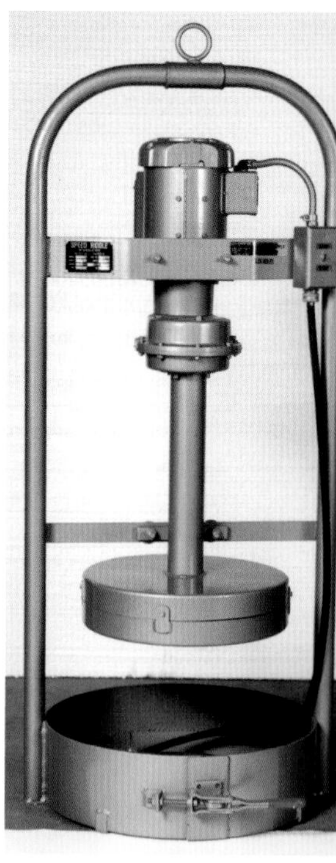

Speed riddle by McEnglevan Manufacturing Company.

Sponge An extremely absorbent marine invertebrate. Processed and dried, it is used for ceramic clay work and other absorbent uses. Other synthetic materials designed for the same purpose may also be called sponge(s).

Spot weld A small weld in sheet metal intended to hold two pieces together. It is a temporary weld placed in advance of final welding. *See **Welding; Spot welder**.*

Spot welder Quickly welding overlapping thin metal joints together. The electrical units can either be 110 or 220 volt depending on the machine. Two pencil size or larger electrodes form the end of jaws that clamp over the overlapping metal sheets to complete the weld. A sudden strong arc of electricity is released that creates a fusion of the metal. Since the small weld area is singularly focused by the electrodes, the tiny weld is hardly noticed as the small round spot that it becomes.

Spot welders can be stationary or portable units. The smaller handheld units can be easily moved in sculpture to complete the welds, but they lack the larger extension arms that upright units have. The larger stationary units have foot levers to make them more accessible as the operator holds the metal. *See **Welding**.*

Willie Ray Parish coats the surface of *Prayer Wheel* with a spray gun.

Spray booth An air filtering booth for operating a spray gun. It can be for several types of fluids, from ceramic glaze sprays to lacquers for metal.

Sprayer A tool that releases a fine mist of liquid substance into the air directed at a mass to coat its surface. Most sprayers consist of a handheld spray gun attached to a one quart (0.9463 liter) container that is powered by an air compressor. However, the sizes and types vary from a small atomizer that is mouth operated to those designed for continuous uses with several gallons (liters) of paint drawn into long hoses with a gun at the end. *See* ***Airless spray gun***.

Spray gun A device in a configuration similar to a gun, usually handheld, that directs a spray liquid toward the work.

Spray molding Creating a mold by spraying the mold material onto the artwork. The same term is used when spraying a liquid or mist of casting material onto the wall of an open mold. For example, a worker could spray resin into an open boat hull mold. *See* ***Casting; Molds***.

Sprue On the metal pouring system, sprues are the main metal feeders to the wax. They are a vertical duct or shaft attached directly to the pouring cup and then downward either directly into the wax form or to the bottom and attached by a system of wax runners and gates. The entire arrangement of sprues, including runners and gates, is called the spruing system or metal pouring system. *See* ***Metal pouring system; Sand casting***.

Spruing up Installing the metal pouring system. *See* ***Metal pouring system***.

Squeeze joint The juncture or location where two separate sections of a mold touch and come together to form a mold. The casting substance is placed or packed in tightly or compressed by the two sections to compact or force (squeeze) the casting material together into one piece. *See* ***Casting; Mold***.

Stain The tinting or coloring of an object by allowing the initial surface to keep some of its characteristics but in an altered state. To stain wood is to enhance the wood grain and color. Oil stain on wood does not affect the surface quality, but water stain results in some surface wood grain being raised. With metal, stains (oxides) may be used as a patina on the surface. With ceramics, oxides or dyes can be added into the body or onto the body, by slips or glazes to acquire coloration.

Stained glass Arranging glass pieces, shaped or broken, into a design traditionally held together by lead strips. There are now new construction methods that use many other products for the binder. Ideally, the artwork is displayed to demonstrate its translucent and transparent use of color.

Lorraine Jablon, *One World*. Stained glass, mixed media, 9½″ (24.1cm) diameter. Photographer: Lisa Hermanson.

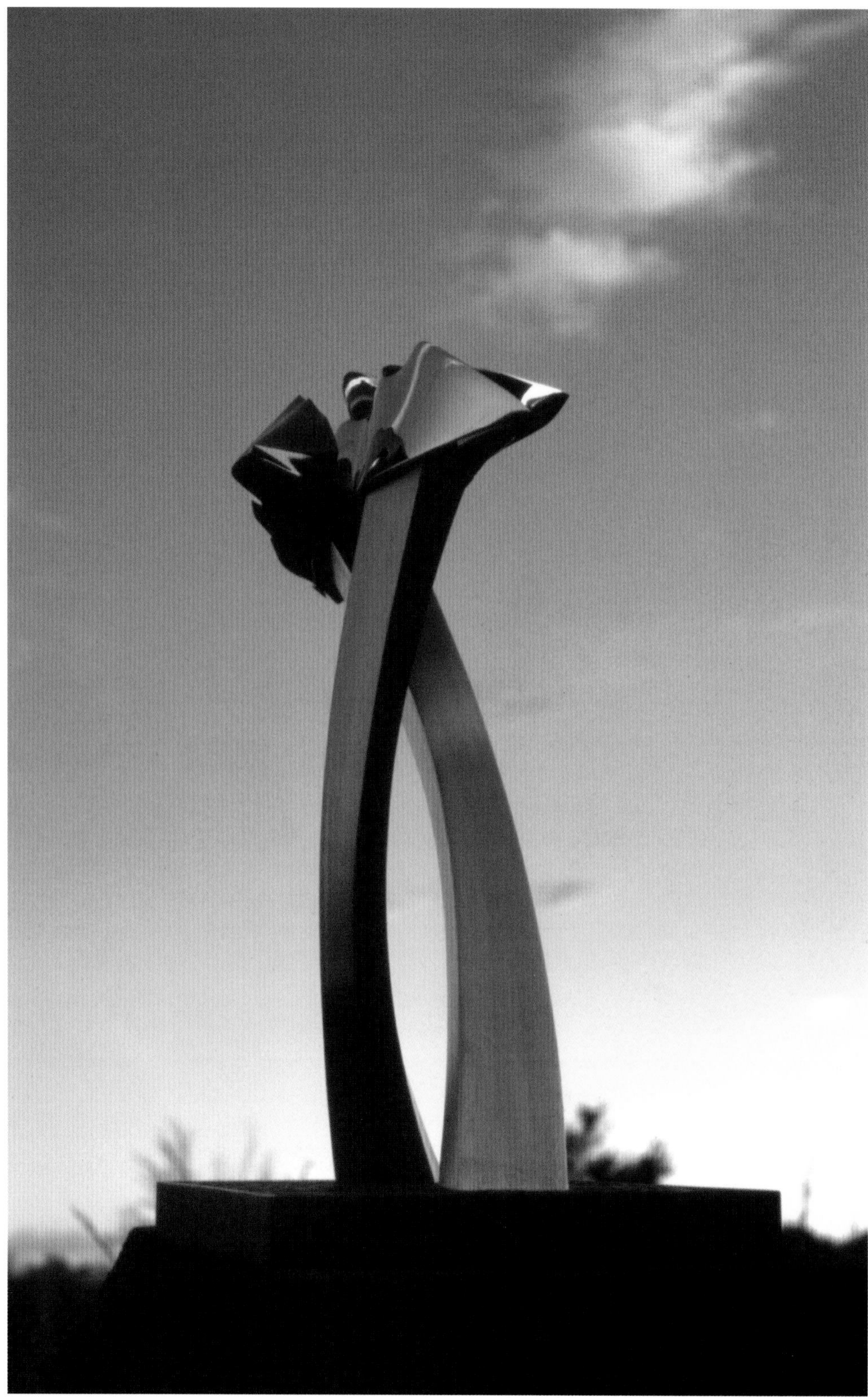

Ali Baudoin, *Earth Cooler*. Stainless steel, 48″x34″x15″ (121.9cm x 86.4cm x 38.1cm).

Stainless steel A hard, heat resistant steel alloyed with a minimum of 10% chromium. It resists rust when subjected to water. *See* ***Metals*** *(chart).*

Stand Upright self-contained base designed for artwork. A stand can be any size, design or material to enhance and display sculpture. It is frequently called a pedestal. The incorrect term, base, refers to the lower part of a sculpture or a smaller supporting platform. *See* ***Base; Pedestal; Plinth; Modeling stand***.

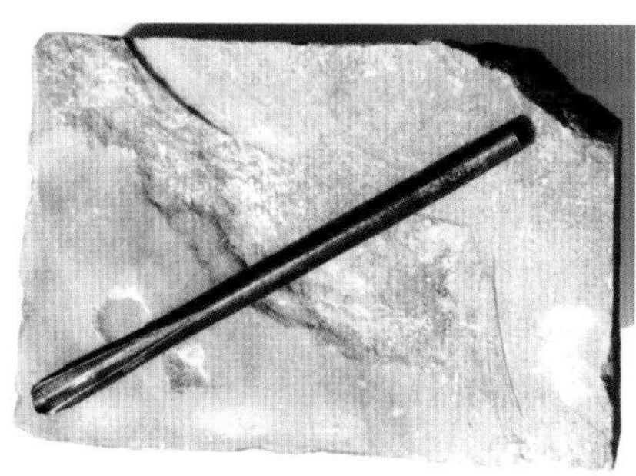

Star drill with initial drill hole (star shaped) and round hole as the hole progresses.

Star drill A chisel used for creating or drilling holes into hard substances, such as concrete or stone. The larger, striking tip has a star shape for cutting as it is struck on the opposite end by a heavy hammer or mechanically operated tool. Rotating it between the hits keeps it from sticking and aids in the cutting.

Statuary marble Marble of a fine texture that is typically white. It is used for sculptural purposes. *See **Stone** (chart).*

Statue A free standing sculpture generally of a human, though the subject matter may vary. The term is generally designated for larger works of realistic standing figures.

Statuette A freestanding sculpture, usually a figure, that is less than half life-size. It is known for details. The term is not used to define a larger statue or a smaller figurine.

Steam cleaner A machine that heats water to extremely high temperatures and then propels it in a directed flow of steam. A steam cleaner is an essential tool for cleaning fuel and gas vapors from enclosed tanks or metal surfaces prior to welding.

Steatite A soft, easily carved, metamorphic stone, also known as soapstone, found in a multitude of colors. It possesses an extremely high content of talc. The surface has a soapy feeling, and there is a lot of carving dust when sculpted. *See **Soapstone**.*

Arthur Williams, *Steatite Woman*. Steatite, 23″ (58.4cm) tall.

Steel A sturdy metal alloy made up of iron and carbon. Various other elements are added in small amounts to produce specific composition for different uses. *See* ***Welding***.

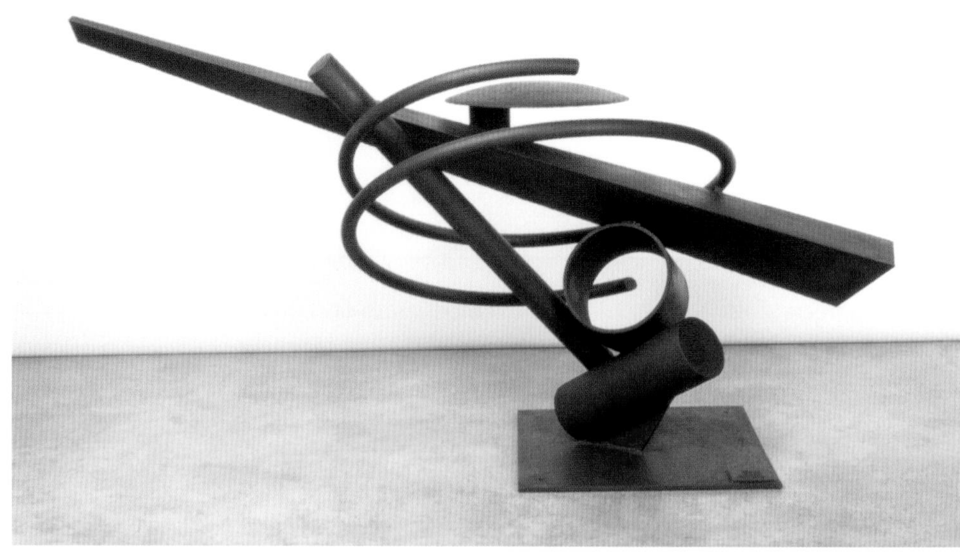

Jon Seeman, *Spiral Synergy*. Steel, patina, 43″x80″x33″ (109.2cm x 203.2cm x 83.8cm).

Steel reinforcement. A metal added to other materials, either internal or external, to strengthen the overall mass. *See* ***Concrete; Waste mold; Rebar***.

Steel wool Thin strands of steel lightly compressed into small masses (pads) to be used for abrasive purposes. Various sizes (grades) are available from 0000 (finest) for use with wax or oil on fine finishes; 000, 00, 0, 1, 2, 3 (coarse) for the removing of paint and varnish, highlighting bronze patinas, etc. *See* ***Patina***.

Steel wool from coarse to superfine: #4, #3, #2, #1, #0, #00, #000, #0000.

Sterin Animal fat or tallow used as a release agent for molding. It is mixed with a thinner, such as kerosene, often warmed up and then brushed on. *See* ***Release agent***.

Stick welding Shielded arc welding using a rod (stick) as an arcing filler device, better known as an electrode. *See* ***Arc welding; Electrode***.

Sticky wax The adhesion wax used to attach wax pieces together. *See* ***Adhesion wax; Metal pouring system***.

Stilts Small supports of hard-fired clay with prongs or points for sculptures to be set upon for firing, especially during glazing. *See* ***Kiln furniture***.

Stippling Placing chemicals (patinas) onto a surface by using short brush strokes to achieve random texture designs. *See* ***Patina***.

Carving stones stored at William Carey College on the Coast, Gulfport, Mississippi.

Stone A cut rock that is useful for building or carving. However, the sculptor classifies any rock as stone if it is functional for sculpture, whether it is cut or not. In the strictest, commercial use, marble has a separate classification from stone. The colors and unions of colors are almost endless. Yet, except for pure blacks and whites, each stone has its own uniqueness in color, especially when the stones are multi-layered with each layer producing a variation or new color.

Stone lasts through the centuries. There is no shortage of stone. The question is: *Is it carveable?* The answer is, *Maybe... depending on the form, tools and skill of the carver.* While the obvious choices for carving are marble, alabaster, soapstone and granite, some not-so-traditional stones furnish distinctive sizes and shapes for forms. Even field stones can be carved if the sculptor has the right tools, experience and knowledge.

There are three major classifications of stone: sedimentary, metamorphic and igneous. Sedimentary is the result of sediment, or layers, of the earth as the stone is formed over time. Limestone and sandstone are the best known examples.Metamorphic stones are sedimentary stones but formed under tremendous heat with pressure. Marble, steatite and alabaster are the most commonly used stones. Igneous stone is brought about by volcanic action. Granite is the stone that best represents this classification for sculptural purposes. *See* ***Metamorphic; Sedimentary; Igneous; Marble; Alabaster***.

Stone offers many possibilities to the sculptor. Subject matter varies greatly from full figure to thin nonobjective forms, from large to small and from indoors to out-of-doors. Depending on the sculptor's intent, work can be completed in a brief time using a soft stone such as steatite or much longer working with a hard stone like granite. Tools can range from an inexpensive pocket knife for soapstone to carbide tipped chisels for basalt to thermal torches for granite. *See* ***Stone carving; Stone*** *(chart)*.

STONE SAMPLES

These stones are only a few selections from among the hundreds available. The color names vary with the distributor/supplier. Many of the stone samples have been selected from *Dimension Stones of the World,* Volumes I and II, published by The Marble Institute of America, Cleveland, Ohio. All rights reserved. Images designated with an asterisk (*) are the property of the Marble Institute of America. *See* ***Marble Institute of America***.

ALABASTER

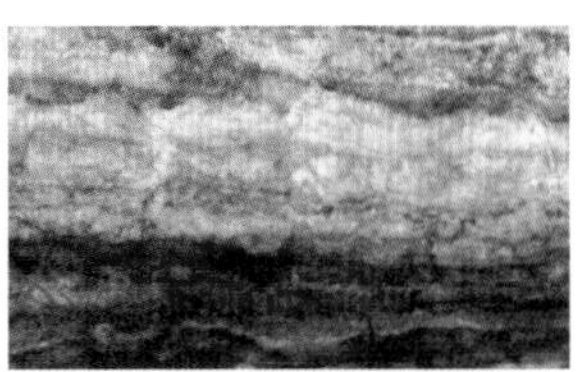

Aztec Gold, Utah.

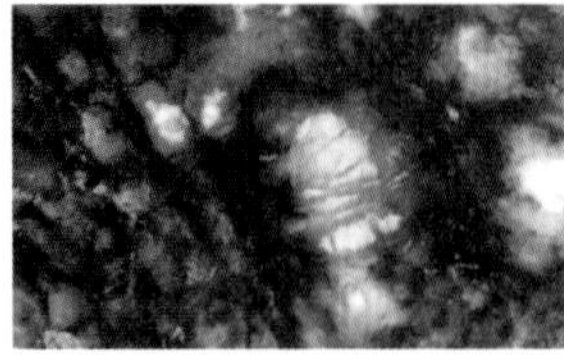

Black-White, Israel

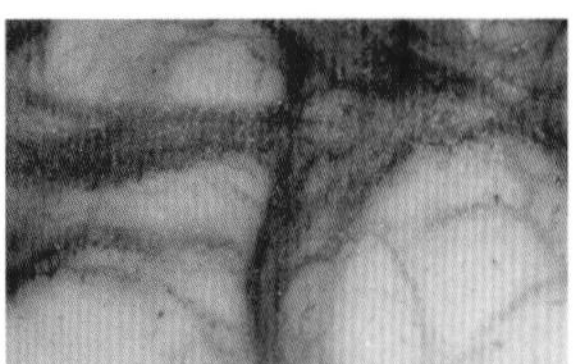

Coral Pink, Utah.

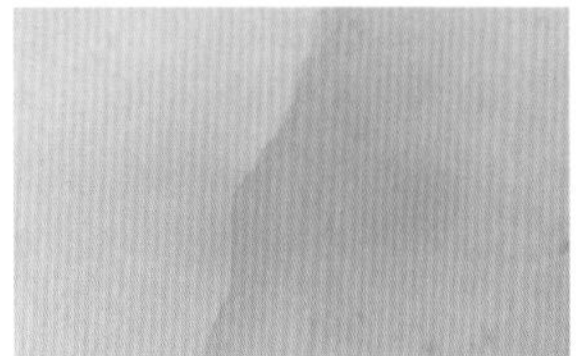

Italian Crystal, Italy.

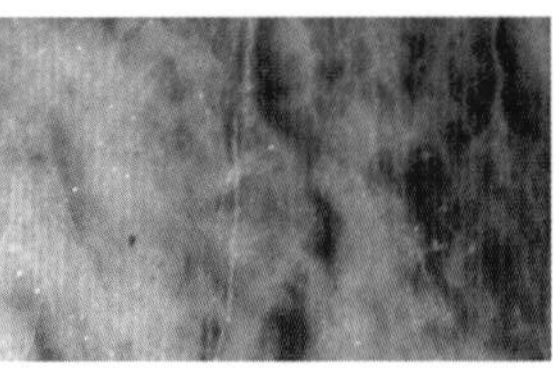

New Mexico Gray.

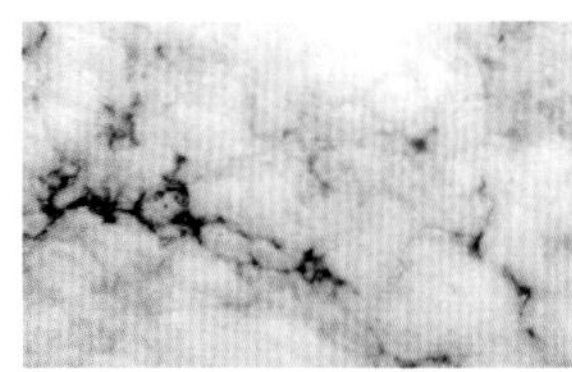

Oyster, Utah.

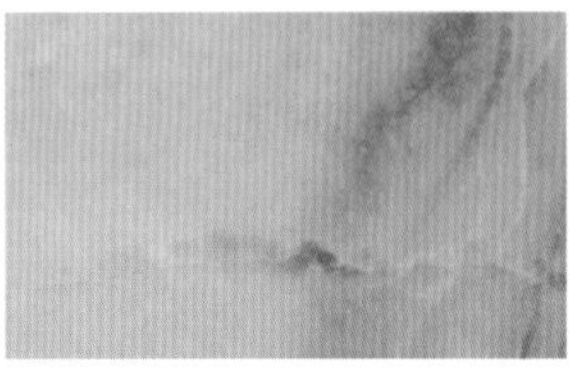

Palo Rosa Pink,Texas.

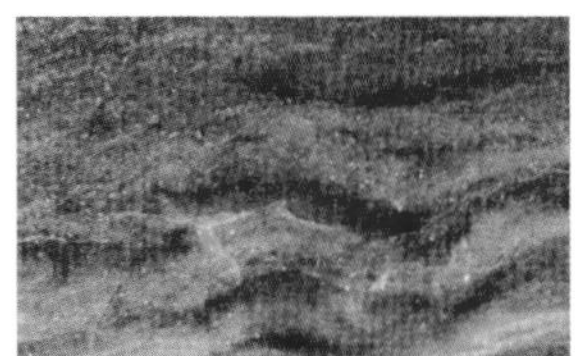

Raspberry, Utah.

Red Patterns, Utah.

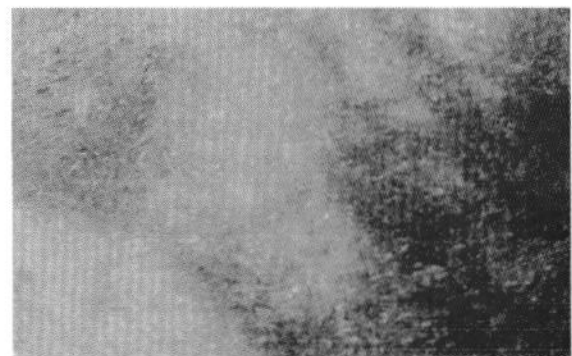

Translucent Orange, Italy

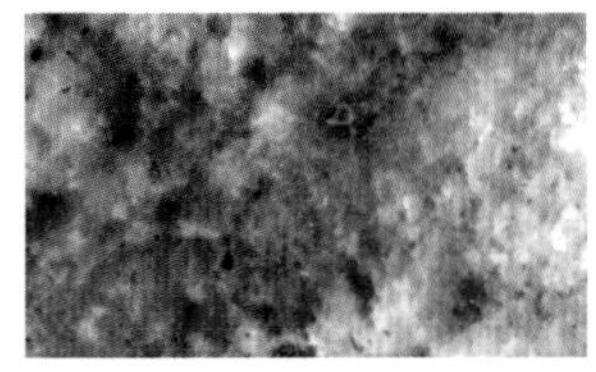

Utah Green.

GRANITE

*Balaban Green, Turkey.

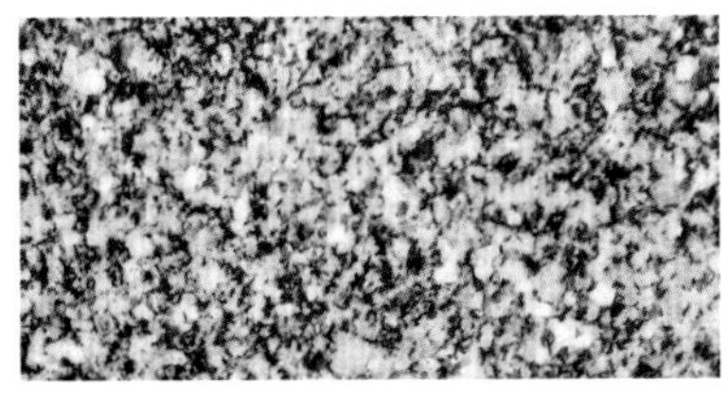

*Barry Gray, Vermont.

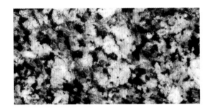

*Blue Crystal, Australia.

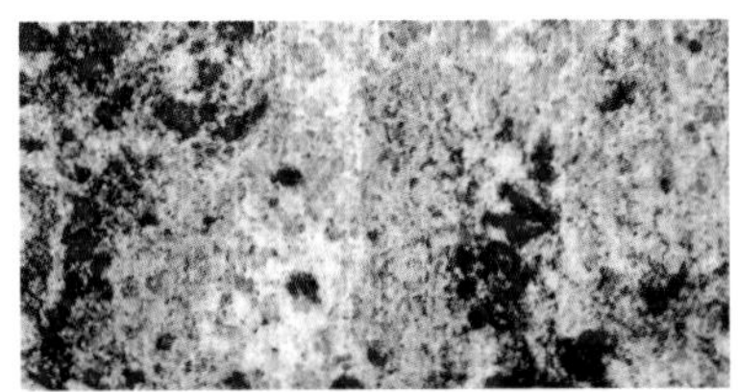

*Blue Garnet, Sri Lanka.

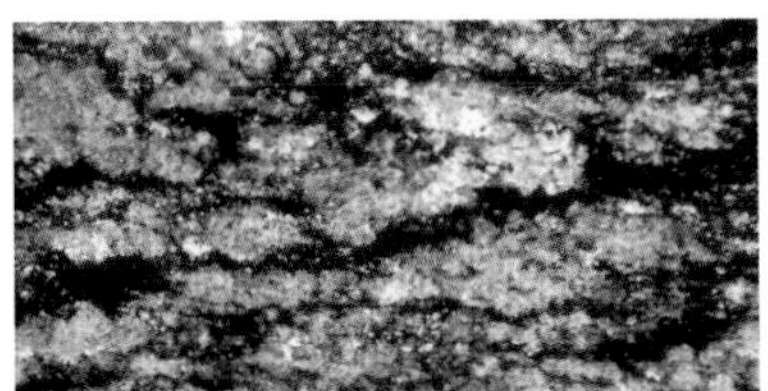

*Coral Missi, Brazil.

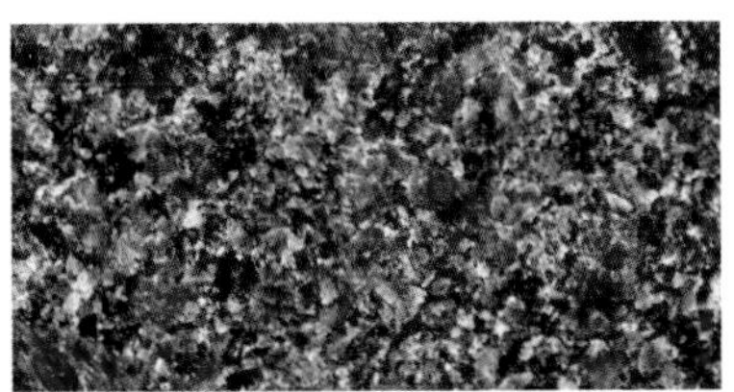

*Dakota Mahogany, South Dakota.

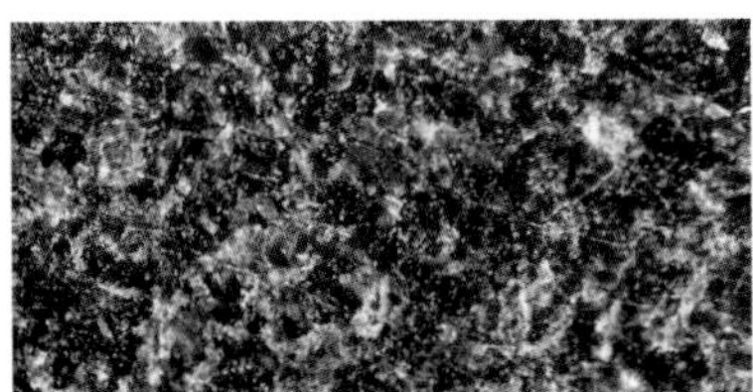

*Dark Steel, Canada.

*Lac du Bonne, Canada.

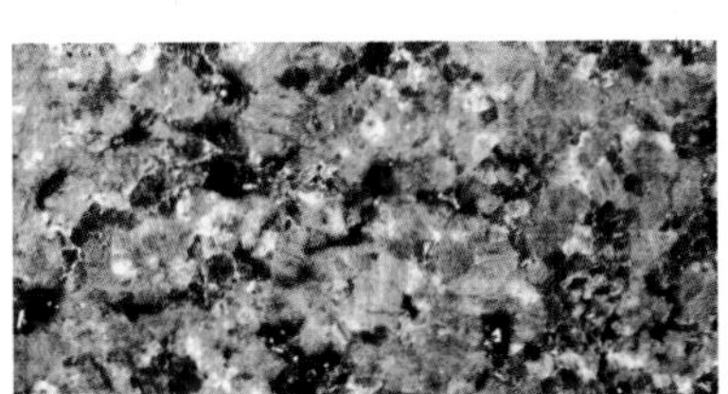

*Rose de la Glarte, France.

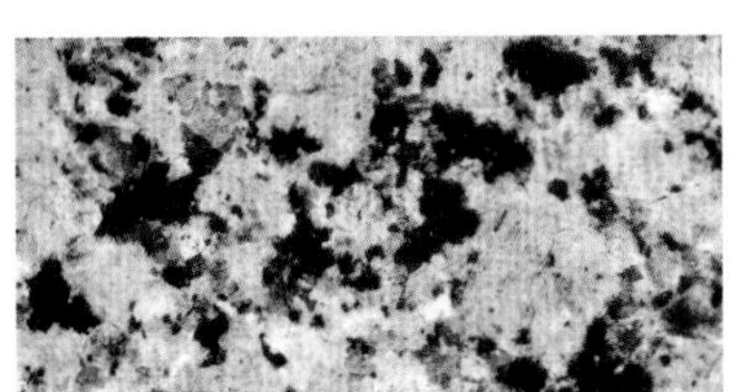

*Texas Pearl, Georgia.

LIMESTONE

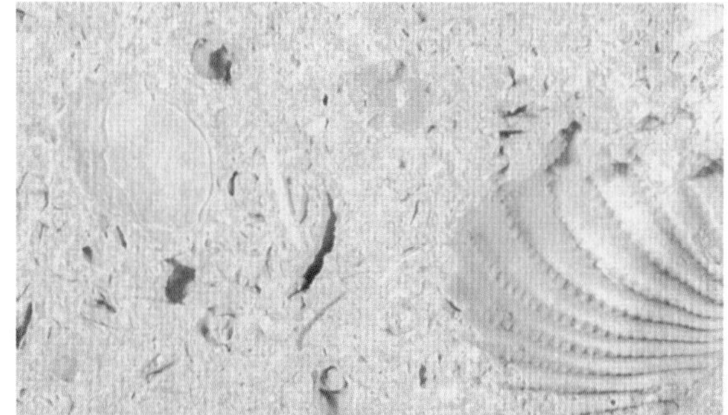

*Austin Shell, Texas.

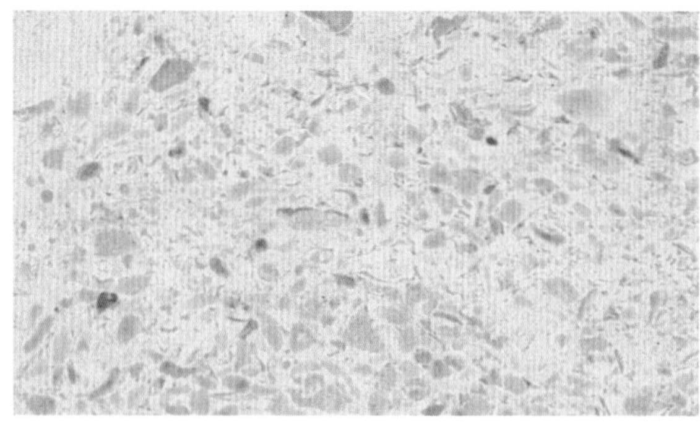

*Beaulieu Beach 3, France.

Permian Sea Coral, Texas.

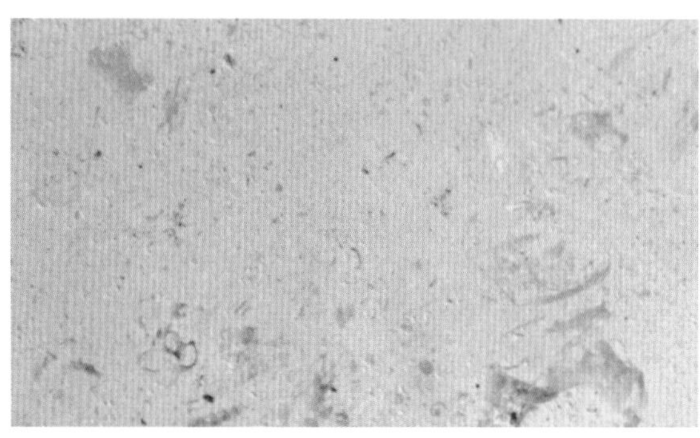

Texastone Pink, Texas.

*Yukon Silver-Vein Cut, Indiana.

MARBLE

*Alabama White Statuary

*Bianco Carrara, Italy.

*Colorado Yule, Colorado.

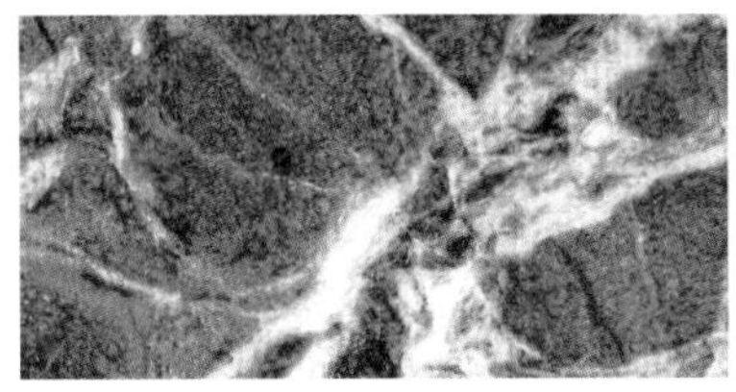

*Crystal Green, Canada.

*Highland Danby, Vermont.

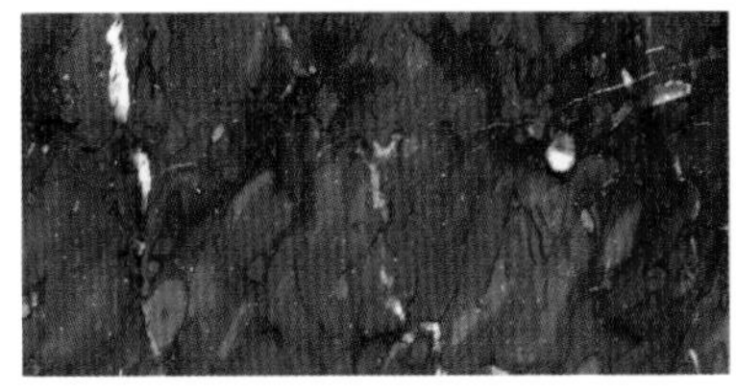

*Marbre du Roi, France.

*Pentelicon White, Greece.

*Pearl Gray, Georgia.

*Rosa Aurora, Portugal.

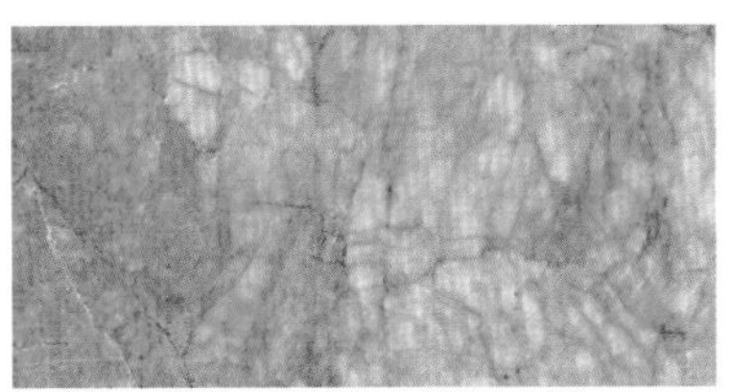

*Rosa, Mexico.

ONYX

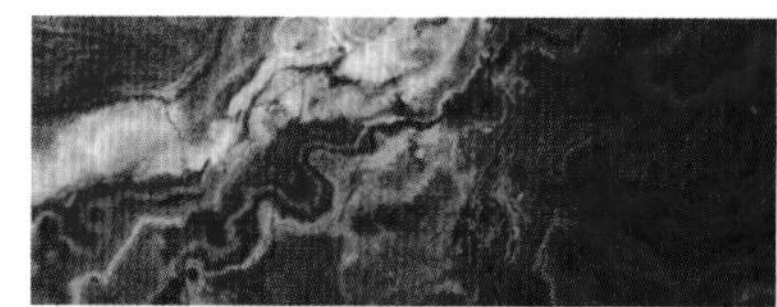

*Multi-color, Pakistan.

*Light Green, Pakistan.

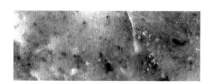

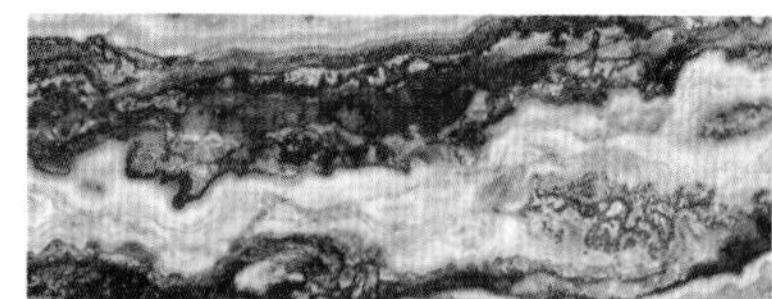

*Vista Grande, New Mexico.

SLATE

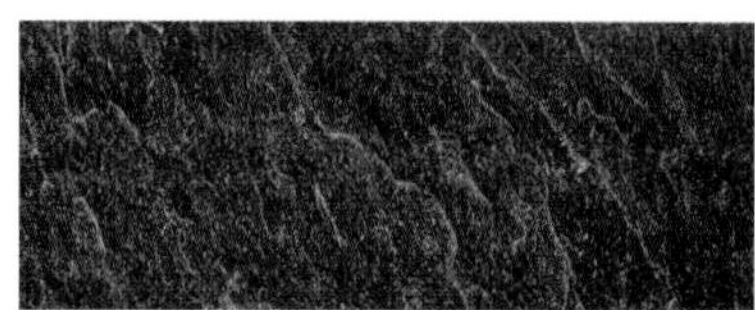

*Buckingham Virginia, Virginia

SERPENTINE

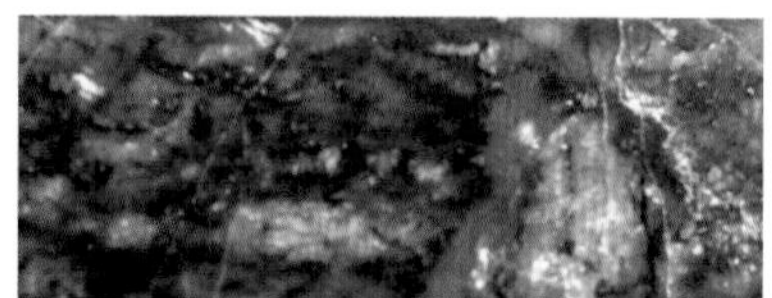

Texas Green, Texas.

STEATITE

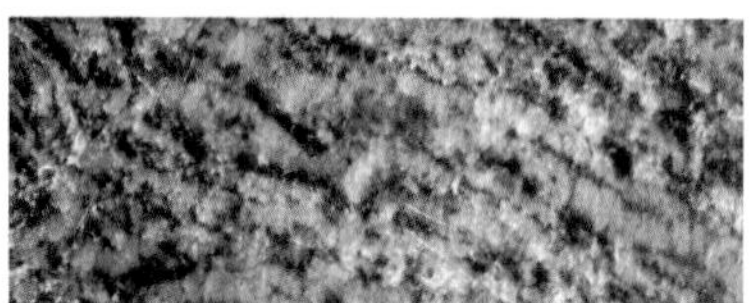

Mottled Gray, Italy.

Jade Green, Italy

TRAVERTINE

*Caesar, Italy.

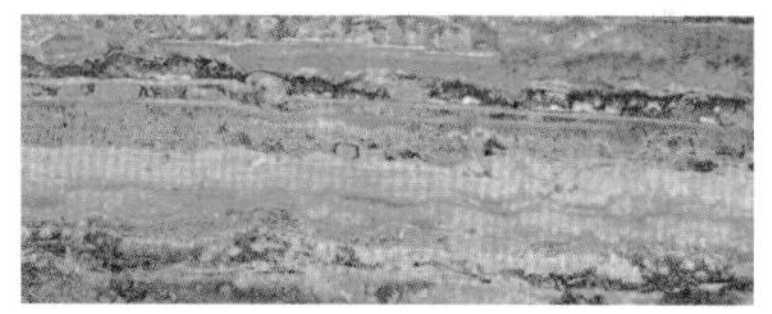

*Desert Gold Vein, New Mexico.

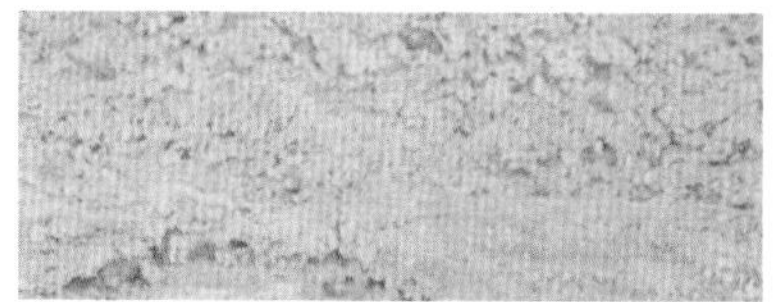

*Travertine Light, Mexico.

Stone carving The process and technique of shaping stone. Carving with hand tools requires hammers, chisels, rasps, files and sandpapers. Different types of stone involve different tools. The harder stones, like granite, require carbide-tipped tools, while softer stones, like steatite or alabaster, do not.

The process begins with a point to define the shape and progresses through tooth chisels ending with flat chisels. The chisels are held at about a 45° angle as they are struck with the carving hammer. Rasps and then files are used to refine the surface. Wet-or-dry sandpapers begin with grits of 60 or 80 depending on the stone's hardness. Water serves as a lubricant while the sculptor continues with higher grits of sandpaper, 600 to 1000, until the desired finish is achieved. The finished carving can be sealed with tile sealer and then waxed to maintain the finish.

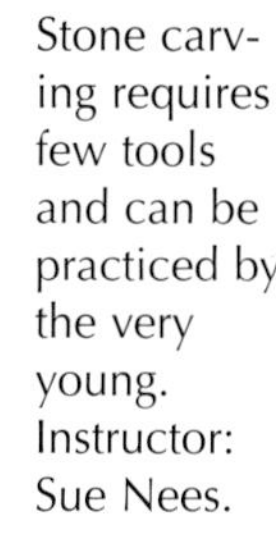

Stone carving requires few tools and can be practiced by the very young. Instructor: Sue Nees.

Carving with power tools, especially air tools, allows the sculptor to move at a rapid pace. Assortments of tools are used. Diamond saw blades in hand grinders make initial cuts. Air hammers then facilitate the roughing in much the same progression as hand tools except that the starting chisel is most often a large tooth chisel. Die grinders with stone, carbide and diamond abrasives refine the details. Among the sanders used, the orbital and disk are common. Though some large works may not require hand sanding, most carvings do, especially those with fine detail. See specific stone categories for carvings unique to them. *See* ***Mallet; Chisel; Marble; Alabaster; Granite; Sandstone***.

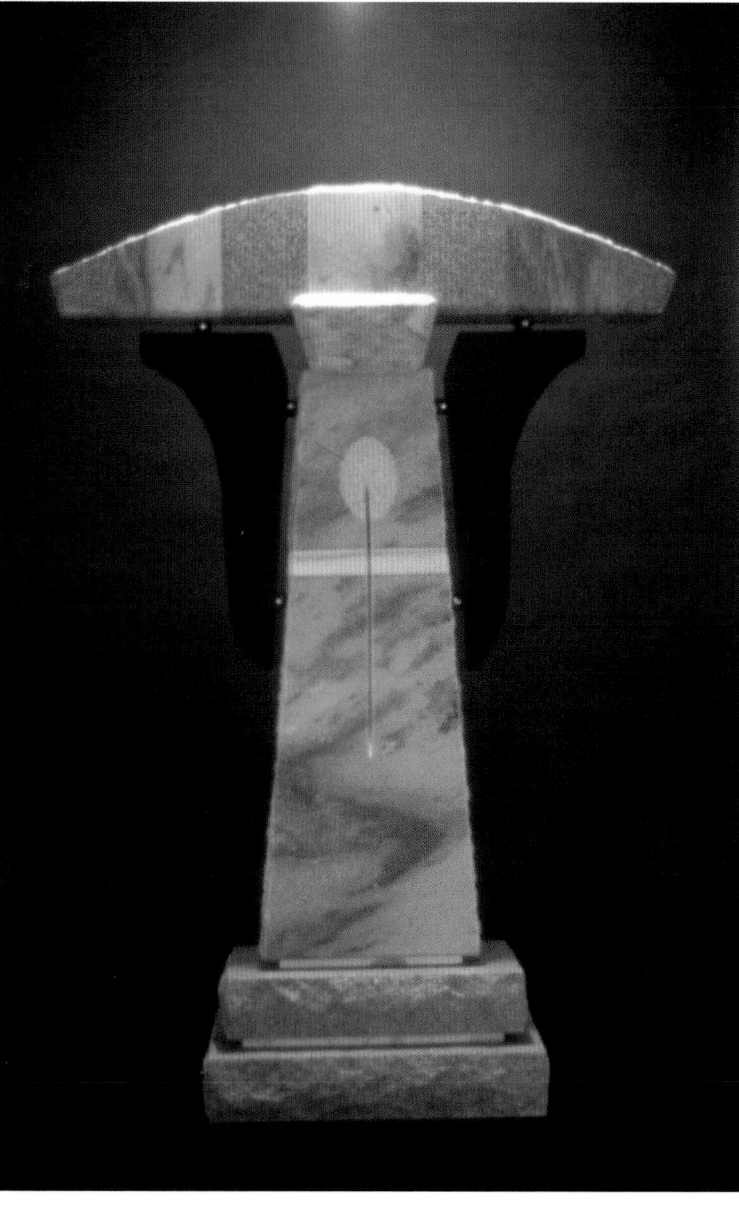

Shawn Phillip Morin, *Reoccurring Daydream*. Granite, marble, glass, 42″x30″x11″ (106.7cm x 76.2cm x 27.9cm).

Hammers used in stone carving from ¾ lb. (0.34kg) to 3½ lb. (1.59kg).

STONE CARVING TOOLS

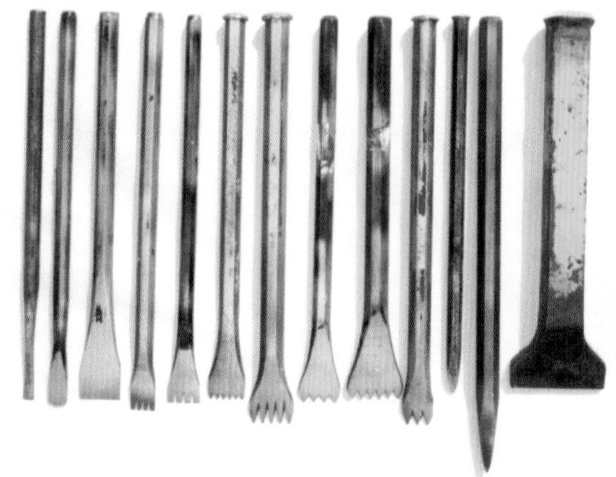

Hand chisels for stone carving with the pitching tool (bull set) to the right.

Air chisels for stone carving with air hammers.

Enzo Torcoletti uses a special cap that fits on his air chisels. The cap enables him to use a larger range of chisels (air) while keeping the end from mushrooming.

STONE CARVING
Chisels/Marks

Large point.

Small point.

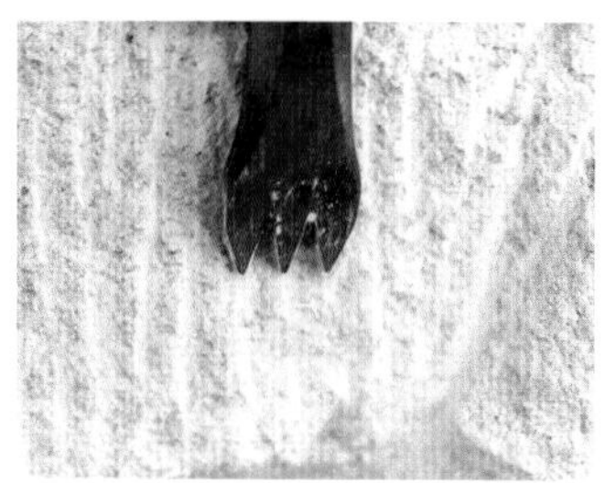

Three-point chisel.

Large six-point chisel.

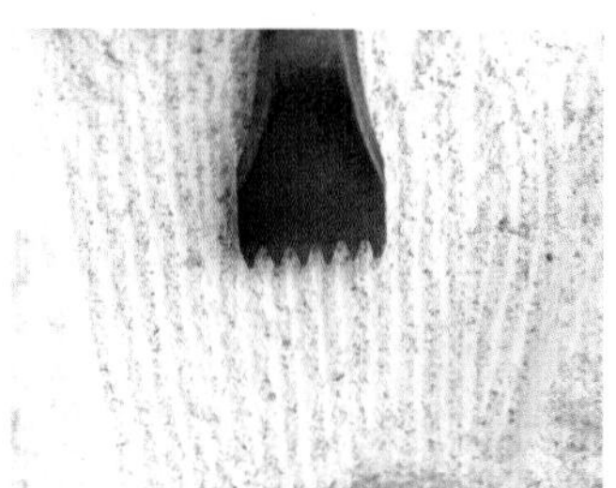

Small six-point chisel.

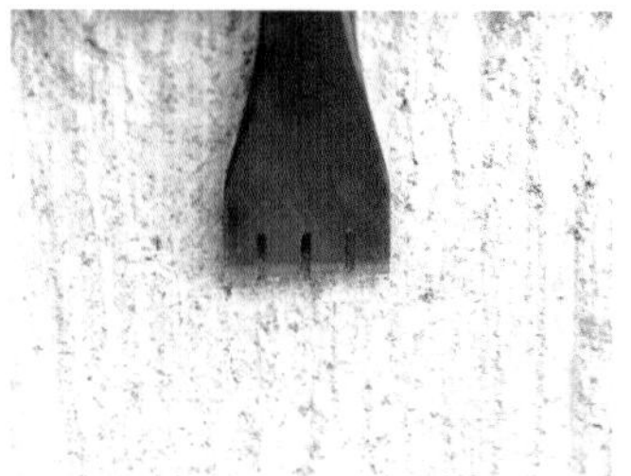

Large tooth flat chisel.

Small tooth flat chisel.

Shaping flat chisel

Flat chisel.

STONE CARVING
with Air Tools and Pointing System
by Lothar Nickel

The sculptor roughs out his marble using a pointing system to measure it to his original model.

A large diamond bladed grinder cuts the correct depth.

Wedges pry apart the cut pieces, removing them from the work.

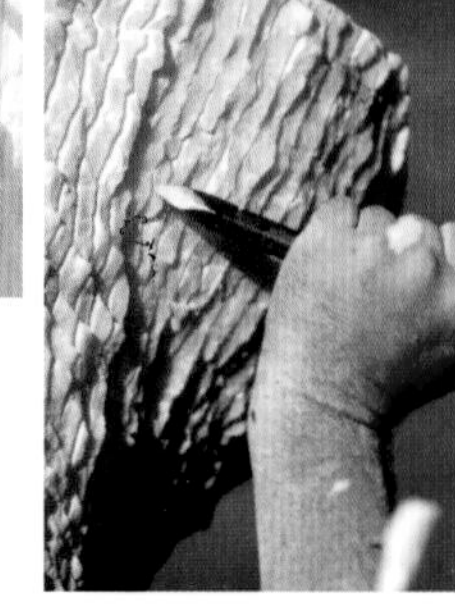

The new cuts are broken off with a point.

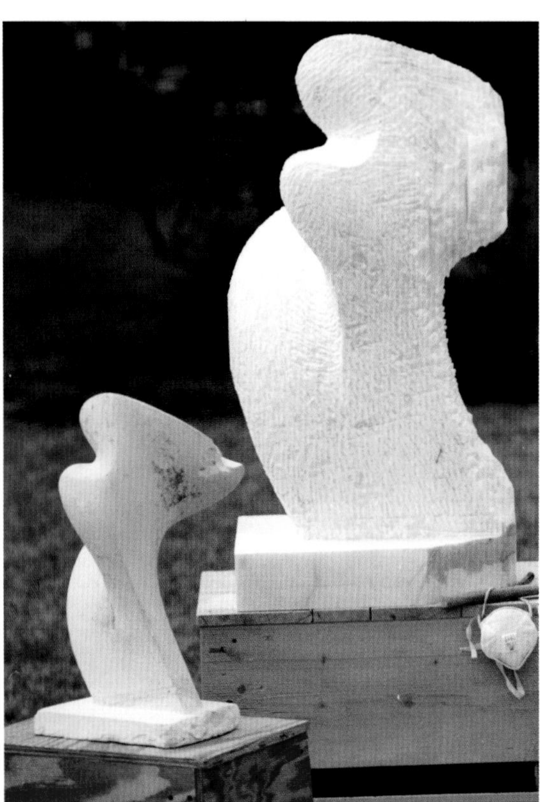

The sculpture is constantly being checked against the model.

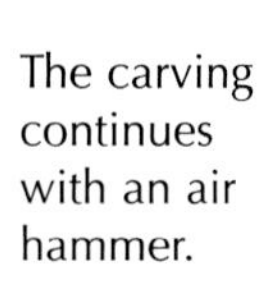

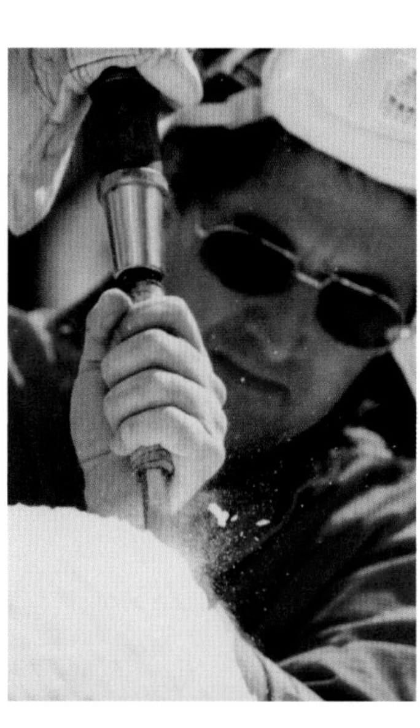

The carving continues with an air hammer.

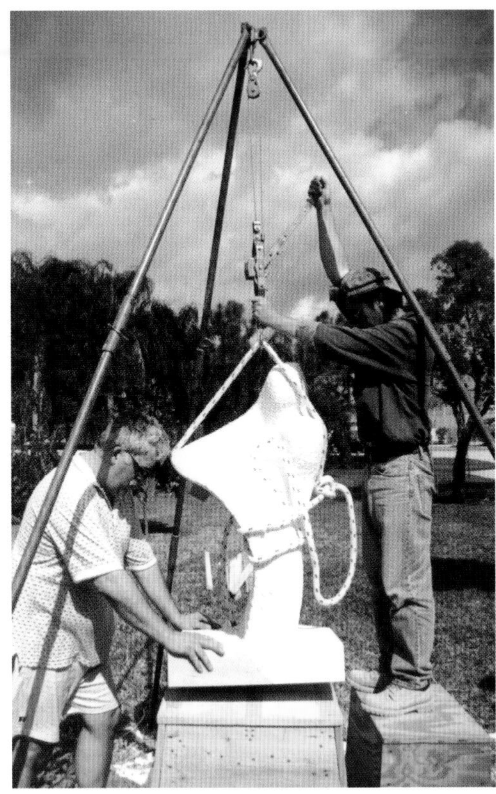

Because of the size and weight, a winch system is used to move the work around.

As the sculptor nears completion, he works with a smaller air hammer.

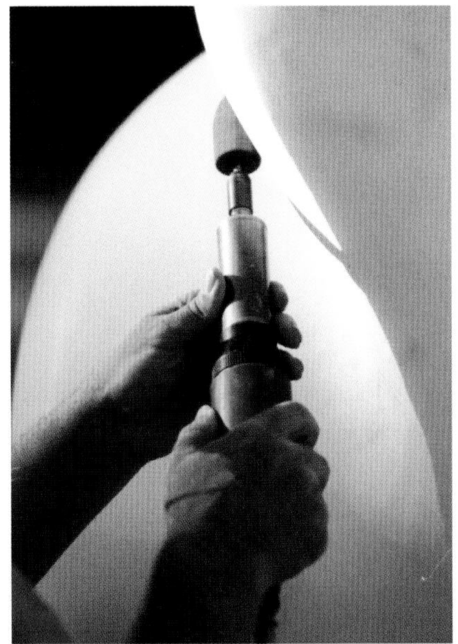

The shape is refined with a die grinder.

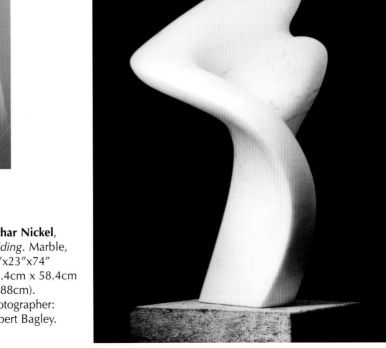

Lothar Nickel, *Striding*. Marble, 23″x23″x74″ (58.4cm x 58.4cm x 188cm). Photographer: Robert Bagley.

Stonecutter (stonemason) Skilled stone carvers who carve and complete stone forms. Stonecutting is generally associated with construction work. *See* ***Sculptor***.

Stoneware An opaque, vitrified, nonporous clay body fired above 2192° F (1200°C). Stoneware clays are designed to be more plastic and fire at higher temperatures than other clay bodies. They fire to a non-porous state that is easily glazed, and most bodies are used as a wheel throwing clay. The colors have a broad range, resulting from the clays and oxides combined to make the clay body. It is generally not used for handbuilt forms. The firing range i from cone 5 to cone 10. *See* ***Clay*** *(water-based)*.

Straight gouge A beveled hand chise used for woodcarving.

Strata Sediment from erosion that results in layers (strata). *See* ***Sedimentary; Stratification***.

Stratifications Layers found in sedimentary rocks. Also, a term for th rings formed in a casting by an inconsistent pouring technique or stratifications formed in wax castings due to rapid cooling. *See* ***Strata***.

Fred Yokel, *Oh Yeah? Watch This!* Stoneware, 15″ (38.1cm) tall. Photographer: Roger Dunn.

Stropping Systematically rubbing a metal tool blade against a leather or canvas strap tc achieve a razor sharp edge. Wood tools use this method for the final touch to sharpening. *See* ***Sharpening; Hone; Benchstrop***.

Stucco A mix of cement, lime and sand for a covering over stone used by Greeks in the Greek-Roman period. Today, it is still used for a wall covering. The term may refer to the silica that is deposited on the slurry coated wax in preparation for metal casting. *See* ***Ceramic shell***.

Studio The location or shop where an artist completes his/her artwork. Atelier is the French term for studio.

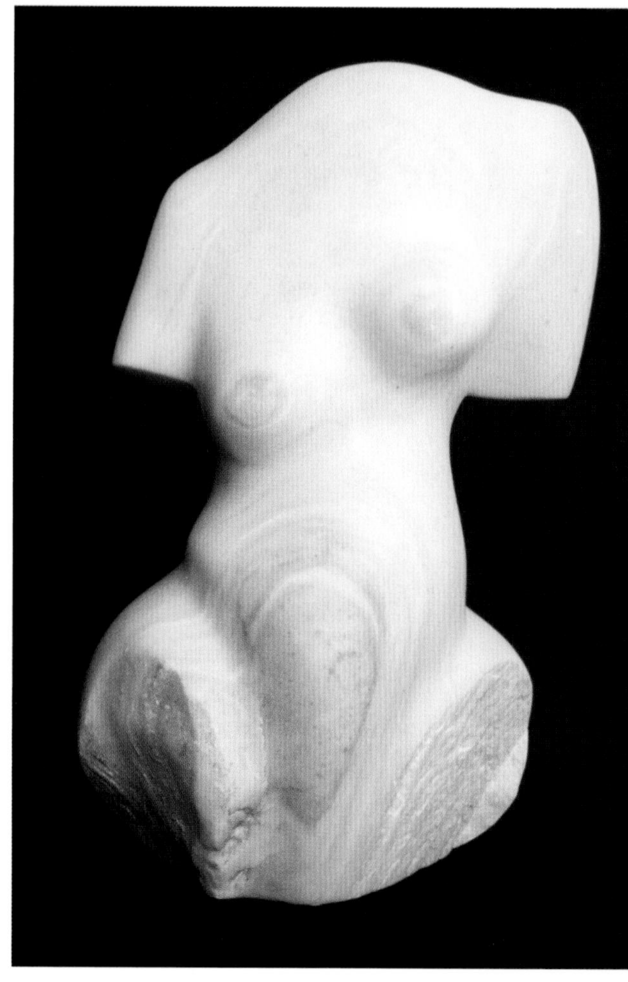

Susan Sasenick McCreary, *Womb.* Alabaster, 16"x10" (40.6cm x 25.4cm).

Studio of **David Hostetler**.

Stump The lower part of a tree that remains when the branches and trunk have been removed. Sometimes a compact tree trunk is referred to as the stump.

Styrofoam™ The common, lightweight, expanded polystyrene plastic used for molding and packing materials. *See* ***Expanded polystyrene; Sand molding; Waste mold; Papier machè; Armature; Urethane; Vaporized casting***.

Studio of **John Weaver**.

Tree trunk/stump to be carved by **William Harrington**.

William Harrington, *Pillar*. Butternut tree trunk/stump, 9' (2.75m) tall.

Elza Mayhew inspects her Styrofoam™ artwork for *Coast Spirit*. Photographer: Robin Clarke.

Elza Mayhew, *Coast Spirit*. 3,992 lbs. of cast bronze, 16'x30"x16" (4.9m x 76.2cm x 40.6cm). University of Victoria, Victoria, B.C., Canada. Photographer: Ken McAllister.

Elza Mayhew sawing Styrofoam™ for her sculpture. Photographer: Ken McAllister.

Elza Mayhew was a sculptor for a very large portion of her life. She received wide recognition for her work. As time went on, however, she suffered from dementia attributed to constant exposure of expanded polystyrene fumes while using a heating (melting) iron. See ***Vaporized casting; Expanded polystyrene****.*

Subtraction Removing material to arrive at a form. Carving wood and stone are common subtraction processes.

Super glue™ A quick-drying adhesive presented in thin liquid form that is especially useful for tight grained or smooth surfaced materials. It is an exceedingly rapid adhesive on human skin. See Adhesive (chart).

Super plasters Plasters beyond normal plaster strengths. *See **Plaster** (chart).*

Surface checks Cracks (checks) flowing with the grain, not large in nature but slightly penetrating the interior.

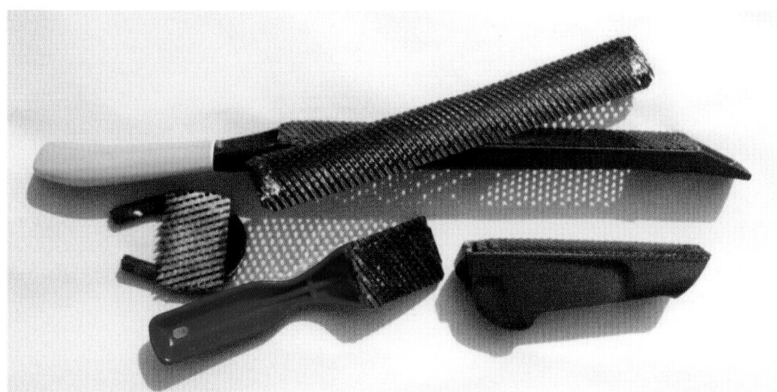

Surform™ rasps. All blades are replaceable.

Surform™ (rasp) Called a shaper tool, it is a rasp made from hard tempered sheet metal. The blades have open teeth, or teeth with holes above them to allow the rasped parts to pass on through without clogging the teeth. The handle allows the thin blades to be replaced. They are available in flat, round or convex shapes. These coarse-toothed rasps are used for many substances from wood to plaster. *See **Plaster rasp**.*

Sweat soldering Applying solder into metal pipe joints or pipes by capillary action. *See **Soldering; Capillary action**.*

Sweep The curved angle of a gouge or other cutting tool, nearly always designed for wood cutting. *See **Wood**.*

Symmetrical Having symmetry, an exactness of shape, such as roundness, as opposed to an odd shape.

Robert Pulley, *Seer.* Stoneware, 44"x30"x24" (111.8cm x 76.2cm x 61cm).

Mark W. Forman, *Solitude*. Terra cotta, 43"x13"x11' (109.2cm x 33cm x 27.9cm).

T

Tack weld A temporary weld to hold two pieces of metal (or other materials) together as the welding continues. It is commonly used for aligning pieces. *See* ***Welding***.

Lin Emery uses tack welds on aluminum to temporarily hold sculpture pieces together.

Tactile Touchable or perception by touch. The term alludes to three-dimensional texture or an object that visually begs to be touched. *See* ***Haptic***.

Taille directè French term for the direct carving of material, as opposed to pointing or machine measuring. *See* ***Stone carving***.

Talc Magnesium silicate, finely ground, used as a flux in clay bodies. It is also known to sculptors as French chalk. Steatite or soapstone is a variety of talc. *See* ***French chalk***.

Tank A pressurized cylinder (bottle) used for chemical storage while welding. *See* ***Cylinder***.

Tap and die A tool set that makes threads (tap) inside a drilled hole and the tool that fashions threads on the outside surface (die) of a slightly larger rod.

TAP AND DIE

After drilling a hole, a tap is inserted.

A die is applied to a matching size rod.

The metal has been threaded with the tap and die.

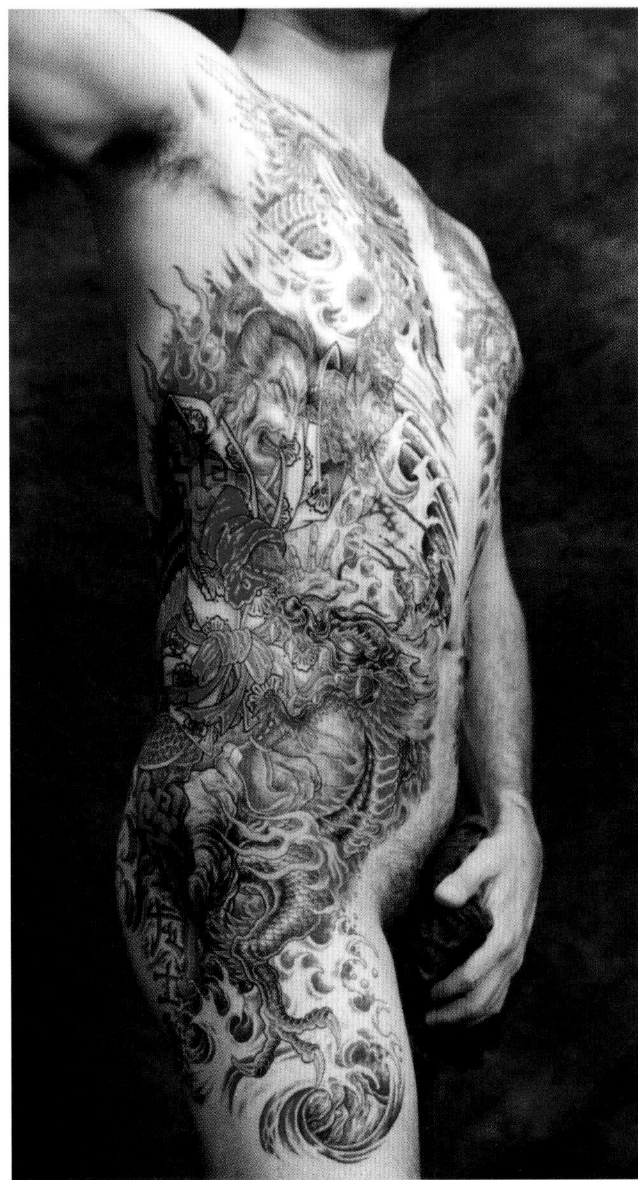

Paul Jeffries, *Body of Tom Donovan*. Tattoo.

Tare An empty container's weight.

Tattoo A form of body art made by pricking the skin and staining it with indelible dyes for design. The term is also used when surface scars are created for skin design. *See **Body art**.*

Tear The measure of a material's ability to withstand force against an imparting force. *See **Resistance**.*

Technique The skill of the artist as well as the process involved in working. It can be of an individual, personal or shared nature. The entire working process is to accomplish a task or artwork.

Teflon™ A substance with non-stick properties. Teflon™ is coated onto surfaces to obtain these properties. It is also designed in a thin tape form to wind on pipe threads prior to assembly to assure a tight, leakproof joint.

Telamon Roman term for the carving of a standing male used in building architecture. *See **Caryatid**.*

Temper (tempering) The degree of metal hardness; the act of hardening metal by applying measured heat and timed cooling.

Technique

To temper the metal, it must first be hardened by heating to cherry red and then cooled (quenched) at a specified interval. This makes the quenched metal extremely hard. Though it is now hard, it is probably too brittle for use.

After the hardening, the area is sanded or polished with emery cloth to remove any blackness and to show the color of the metal. The tool is reheated to secure the desired temper color. Tempering comes about quickly. Care should be taken not to overheat. It is quickly quenched to keep the desired hardness. Natural light is best to note the correct color. Properly tempered, a carving tool can be sharpened to hold the sharp edge longer.

To temper a tool, the worker must be familiar with the correct color brought about by ranges of heat as the metal's molecular configuration changes. As the heat increases, the hardness changes, including the brittleness of the metal. The worker must be able to recognize the color, how it travels and when to properly quench the tool. Colors follow a definite pattern: 1) pale straw, 2) dark straw, 3) bronze, 4) violet, 5) blue, and 6) dull red. The red range is too soft for a tool's edge, while a pale straw color is usually best for the tool's temper. Overheating the metal will eliminate the temper. The hard temper is usually confined to the cutting edge. Otherwise, the handle or end that receives a striking blow would be brittle and have a tendency to break. *See **Forging; Hardening**.*

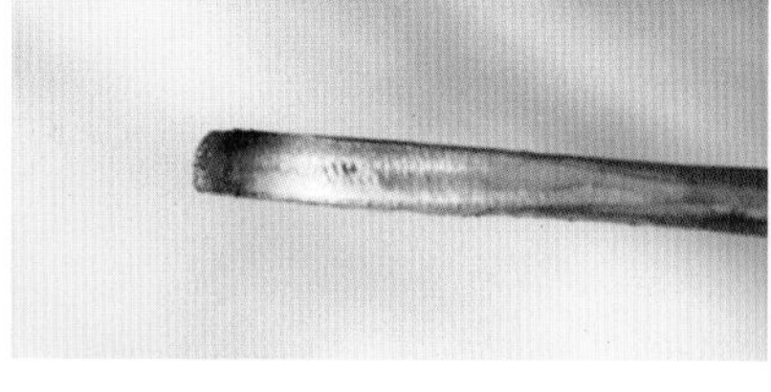

A demonstration of a good spectrum of heat colors. However, if it were allowed to cool as is, the tip would be too soft to be of value and the shaft would be too brittle.

A correctly tempered tip using a torch. The tip is the hardest while the shaft will be able to absorb the blows while hammering.

Preparation for tempering requires sharpening and hardening of the metal by heat. Good metal is a necessity.

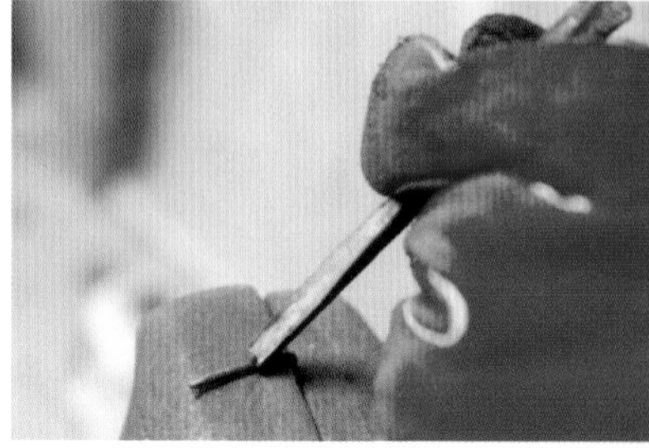

A properly hardened chisel can literally cut nails apart.

Tempering Colors *

Light blue	630° F	332° C
Dark blue	575° F	301° C
Violet	540° F	282° C
Purple	520° F	271° C
Bronze-brown	500° F	260° C
Dark straw	470° F	243° C
Straw	435° F	224° C
Light straw	400° F	204° C
No color	200° F	93° C

* *Exact tempering heats and colors are debated and vary from source to source.*

Hardened steel is best for tempering. Hardened steel throws sparks as it is ground.

Temperature A common measurement of heat or cold. Fahrenheit (F degrees) or Celsius (C degrees) are the scales universally accepted for this measurement. 0° is the freezing point for Celsius while 32° is the same freezing point for Fahrenheit. Thus 2000°C = 3632°F, for example. *See **Measurement** (chart); **Celsius**; **Fahrenheit**.*

Template A pattern or form used as a measuring guide. Models can be dissected into a series of templates for reproduction or enlargement. A cardboard template, cut to size, could be used as a pattern for holes and cuts made in steel sheet, for example. *See **Pattern**.*

TEMPLATE
by Jack Arvin

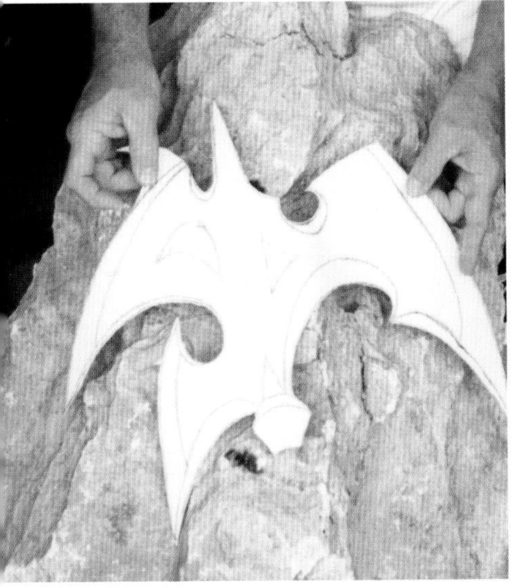

A template is placed over the chosen alabaster.

The template traced with caution lines drawn.

The silhouette remains after the initial carving.

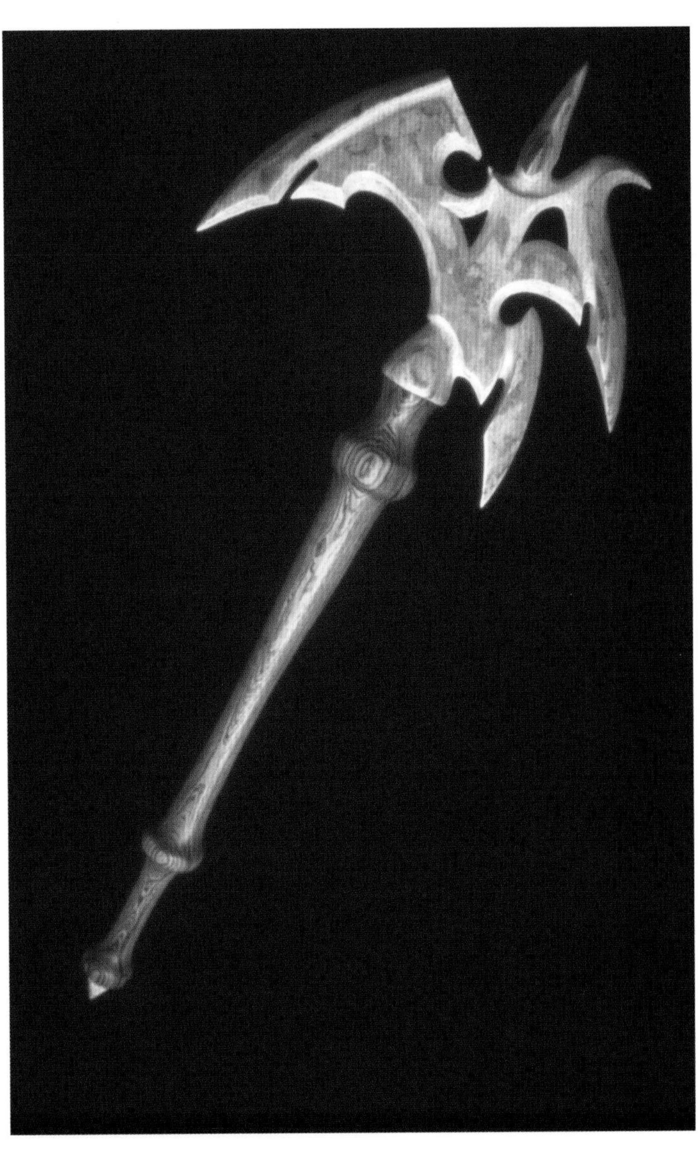

Jack Ransom Arvin, *Battle Ax*. Alabaster, Bocote. Photographer: Billy Stone.

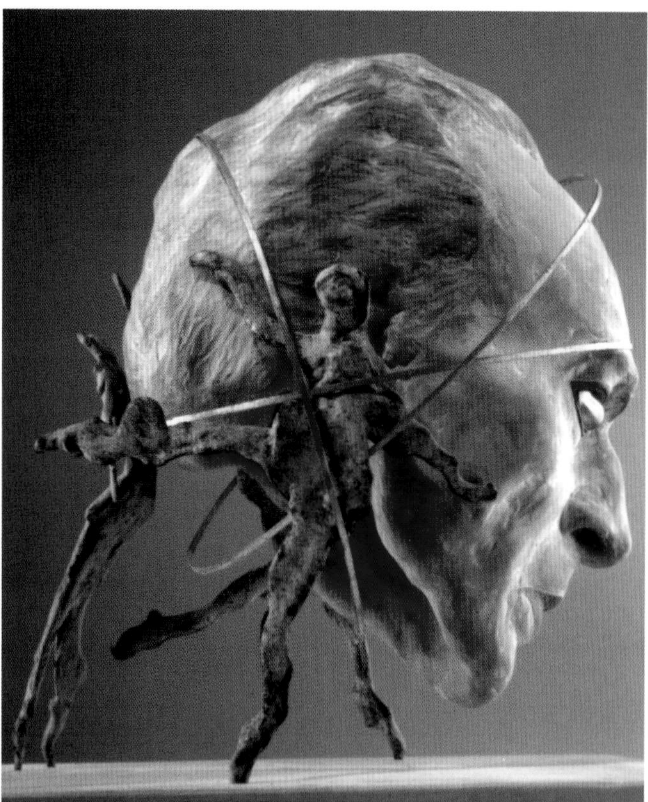

Tenon saws A strong, small, stiff saw designed to cut tenon joints.

Tensile Able to be stretched, considered ductile. *See* ***Tensile strength***.

Tensile strength The maximum strength that a material demonstrates when measured for its resistance as it is being torn or broken. It is measured at the maximum stress without breakage. *See* ***Tensile***.

Terra cotta A fire clay with larger particles of grog creating a roughly textured, porous body. As a result, clay sculptures, which are uneven in thickness, can undergo an even kiln firing. It is characteristically a red or brown color, from which it gets the name terra cotta or baked earth. In the traditional use, it is not intended for a glaze, but it is sometimes stained. A good terra cotta shrinks less than one inch (2.54cm) to a foot (30.48cm) in drying. The clay matures at low temperatures, seldom above cone 02. Earthenware is the most commonly used clay for terra cotta. *See* ***Clay*** *(water-based);* ***Earthenware***; ***Clay***.

Carter Jones, *George Balanchine*. Terra cotta, bronze, gilded copper, ivory, black pearls, 12″x10″x9″ (30.5cm x 25.4cm x 22.9cm).

Stephanie Adams, *These are the Pros and Cons. . .* Found wood, terra cotta, 41″x41″ (104.1cm x 104.1cm), 14″ (35.6cm) diameter.

errazzo Wall or floor mosaic made by placing marble or other stone fragments in a mortar and then grinding the surface to a smooth, polished finish.

exture The visual or tactile character of a material. It can range from reflective smooth to extremely coarse or rough. *See* ***Tactile.***

hermal shock Counteraction or stress caused by abrupt radical temperature shifts. Thermal shock is important to control when tempering metals or in kiln firing.

hermal torch A torch designed to carve granite (and other hard stones) by using heat to spall the surface from the stone body. *See* ***Spall.***

hermocouple An insulated probe inserted into the furnace or kiln to determine the temperature.

hermoforming Heating a material until it is pliable and then positioning it in a desired shape as it is cooled. Plastic shapes are regularly formed by this method. *See* ***Freehanding; Thermoplastic.***

hermoplastic Synthetic resins, such as acrylic, that become soft and somewhat pliable when heated. They are hardened into a new shape when cooled and can be reheated for new shapes. *See* ***Plastics; Thermoforming.***

hermosetting Synthetic resins, such as polyester resins, epoxies, etc., that become permanently hard when heated. A catalyst is used to hasten the reaction, generating heat to form a hard substance that cannot be reheated to a new shape. *See* ***Plastics; Resin.***

hixotrophy A gel that becomes fluid when shaken or stirred and then returns to its original state when left standing. *See* ***Thixotropic.***

hixotropic A liquid material that will not flow from a vertical surface. The material is like paste when still, but can sometimes move or flow when agitated (stirred). *See* ***Thixotrophy.***

Dahrl Thomson, *Core of Cores.* Stainless steel, sandstone, 18″x12″x6″ (45.7cm x 30.5cm x 15.2cm).

hree-dimensional Relating to the third dimension of having depth or being sculptural (depth as well as length, width and height). The term may be written as 3-D. *See* ***Sculpture.***

hree-phase (electricity) (3-phase) Electrical energy that produces 440 volts through an extra wire. The initial installation may require additional transformers from the electrical company, and the cost could be prohibitive. Also, power companies may refuse installation outside of industrial areas.

Throwing Creating a round, clay shape on a machine (wheel) designed for the purpose. The "throwing wheel" has a head or round flat surface that rotates at variable speeds controlled by electrical motor, hand or foot operation. A pliable clay ball shape is placed on the wheel head, and through force, is centered and opened by hand. Using both hands, one inside and one outside, a flexible clay wall is pulled up and out into the desired shape. *See* ***Wheel***.

TIG (Tungsten Inert Gas welding [plasma arc]). Welding with the arc created by a tungsten electrode surrounded by a protective inert gas. TIG welding produces the most predictable, cleanest weld with hard-to-use metals, especially nonferrous brass, bronze, nickel and stainless steel. It is so named because a gas, usually argon, shields or protects the weld. It has also been called heliarc or heliweld, because helium gas can be used for the same purpose, though helium is less available, and argon is easier to use. Regular arc welding can be done with an additional lead and an electrode holder.

The process uses a combination of welding techniques. It relies on an arc like the regular arc welder, but the tungsten electrode is noncombustible. It depends on a gas shield to protect the weld from the atmosphere like MIG welding, and it utilizes a hand held long rod like acetylene welding as the filler rod. Unlike the arc weld, TIG leaves a nice, flowing weld without any slag.

The machine itself has many adjustments that require several considerations: 1) correct current setting, such as DC straight polarity for stainless steel and bronze, 2) reverse polarity, AC for aluminum, 3) the correct gas flow adjusted to the size of the tip being used, and 4) the accessibility of the weld, the amperage, etc., depending upon the manufacturer's recommendations.

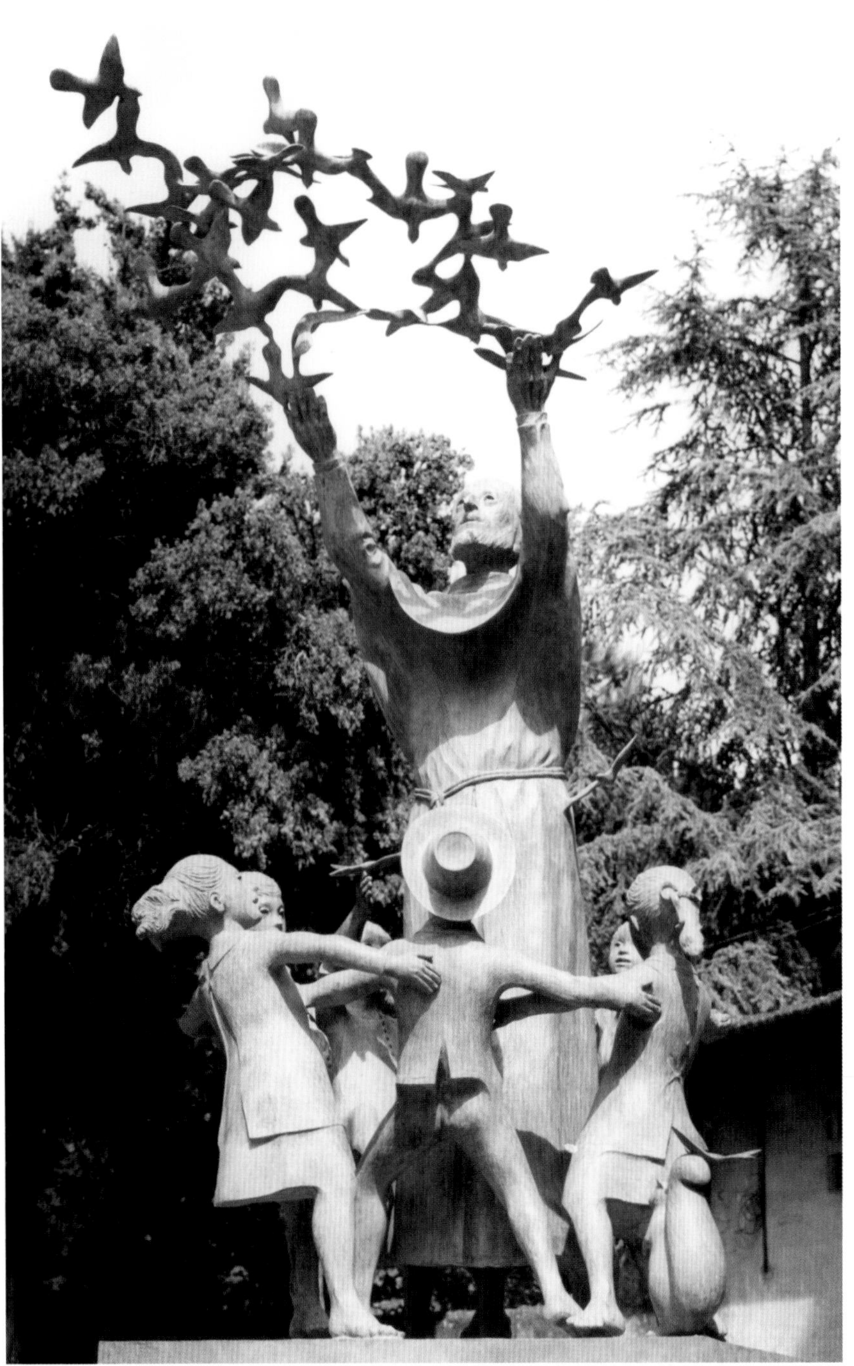

Harry Marinsky, *St. Francis*. Bronze, 9′ (2.75m) tall. City of Pietrasanta, Italy. Photographer: Stefano Sabella. Exact welding was required for strength and balance.

The **TIG torch** (handpiece) has several parts, including the rear end shank for a tungsten electrode can reside as it is being used. The shank can be long for storage or short for tight areas of welding. The handle is easy to grip and lightweight, especially if it is water cooled as most large machines are now made. (Antifreeze is used, not only to prevent freeze-ups but for a better cooling effect.) A trigger control may be mounted on the handle with variable control for amperages, or a spring loaded foot pedal may be used to control the amperage.

The inner copper collet on the handle, facing the tip, holds the tungsten electrode in place by simply tightening the shank. The collet needs to match the electrode in size. On the very end of the torch is a porcelain cup screwed in place around the electrode. The size of the cup also must match the electrode. It is for a heat resistant circulation of the inert gas to the tip.

TIG torch.

The tungsten electrode or tip is extended by one-eighth inch (0.318cm) or more, beyond the cup for most welding uses. The tip needs to be shaped according to the use. Ordinarily, a sharp pencil-like tip is needed that can be easily ground into shape with the finer wheel of an upright grinder. Depending on the welding task, the tungsten rod has several sizes available. Consistently used by sculptors, especially when working with bronze castings, are three thirty-seconds inch (0.476cm) and one-eighth inch (0.318cm), though other sizes are obtainable. Ordinarily the rod matches the electrode size and diversity.

TIG flow meter regulator.

The **argon** is kept in a pressurized bottle (like oxygen) and should be stored in a safe location securely fastened on a wall or the welding cart. The volume of gas is controlled by a regulator valve that adjusts the flow meter. The flow meter is a transparent, vertical tube gauge mounted in a brass framework with visual readings showing the amount of gas being released. If the operator is unfamiliar with its operation, the instruction manual should be consulted. However, most settings will work with the flow adjusted towards the middle of the gauge. (It is possible to extend the electrode tip out some distance from the torch for difficult hard-to-reach welds if the gas flow is strengthened.)

Operating a TIG

If the unit is water cooled, then the antifreeze needs to be checked to be certain there is enough and that it is flowing properly. TIG welding is not difficult and with practice can accomplish some unique, even contoured welds not possible with other machines. The rod does not have to be used, since the metal can butt and flow together (although a depression may occur). With bronze castings, clean runners can substitute for the rod when filling gaps or completing excessively heavy welding.

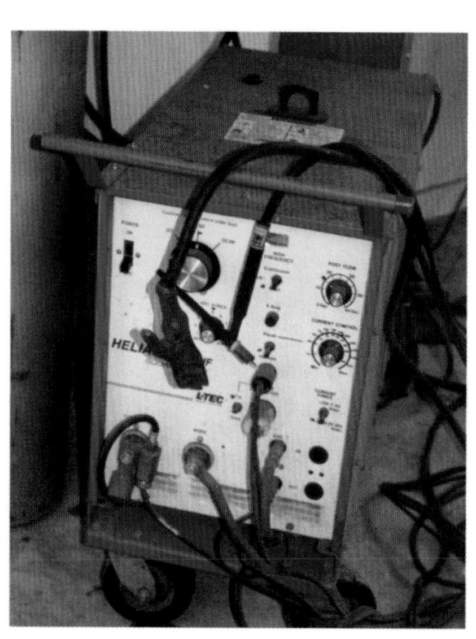

TIG welder with torch and ground clamp.

Start by turning on the amperage by hand or foot (depending on the controls) and then lowering the torch to the metal. It should not touch, since the welder is designed to arc between the gap without a torch. If it does touch and stick, the amperage should be discontinued and the tip removed. It may have to be reshaped. The work itself is all right, but if it is a metal (other than steel), the tungsten tip may need to be removed (dug out) from the work before continuing, since it will affect the finished appearance of the sculpture.

Because of the intense heat and brightness, the safety

apparel is the same as for arc welding except for the gloves. Soft, leather, suede gauntlet gloves are best, since an element of touch and control is necessary for rod usage in delicate areas of work.

The metal should be clean. If a bronze casting is sandblasted and clean, one welding pass should produce a superb joint that needs no re-touching. One caution: The last place that the tip heats may result in a pinhole puddle that will need a spot of touch-up filler rod. This can be avoided by slowly decreasing the amperage as the torch is removed. The weld should not be overheated, or a shrinkage crack can result.

Aluminum can be welded with the proper settings like all other metals; however a process called balling the electrode will produce very predictable welds. A flat-tipped electrode is placed into the torch. Using some precise maneuvers, turn the machine to DC reverse polarity and secure an arc against the copper or bronze. A ball will build on the flat tip. Then immediately turn off the current and re-configure the welder to AC The resulting ball produces a much easier welding tip than the normal sharpened tip. However, it does take practice to maintain the new configuration that may have to be repeated often.

Add-on TIG units are available for existing AC/DC welders. They have the same type of torch that the full TIG units do. Being small units, they work on thin metals only, usually less than one-fourth inch (0.635cm) in thickness. Their value is in the ability to complete small welding jobs on nonferrous metals within which a regular arc has problems. They are relatively inexpensive machines not intended for continuous use. *See* ***Arc welding***.

TIG WELDED SCULPTURE
by BaBa Scaturro

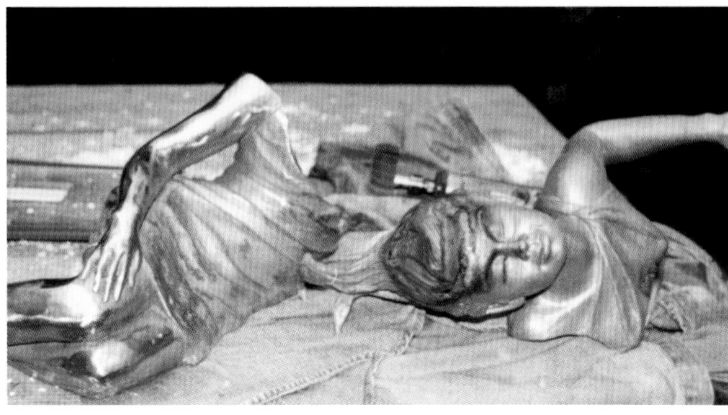

Cast in two sections; welding was required to unite the sculpture.

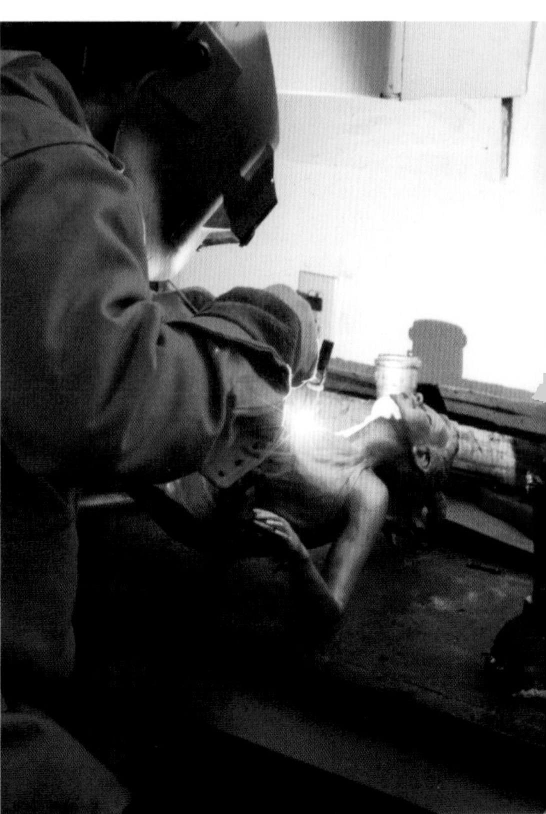

Welder with TIG torch making a weld. TIG welding requires that the artwork is welded in a horizontal position

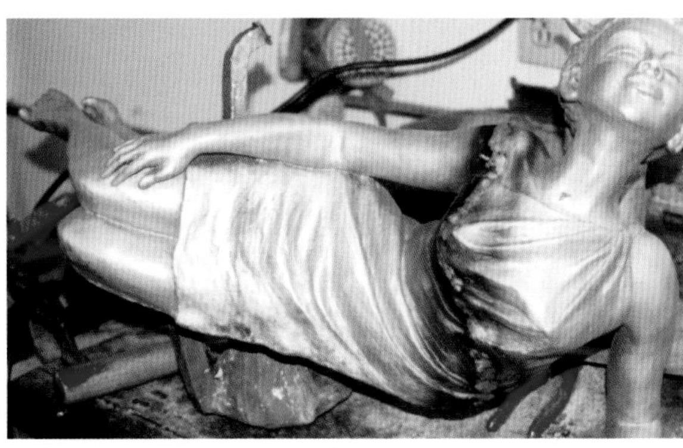

The completed weld.

BaBa Scaturro chases the work.

The sculpture is readied for patina after it has been welded, chased and sandblasted.

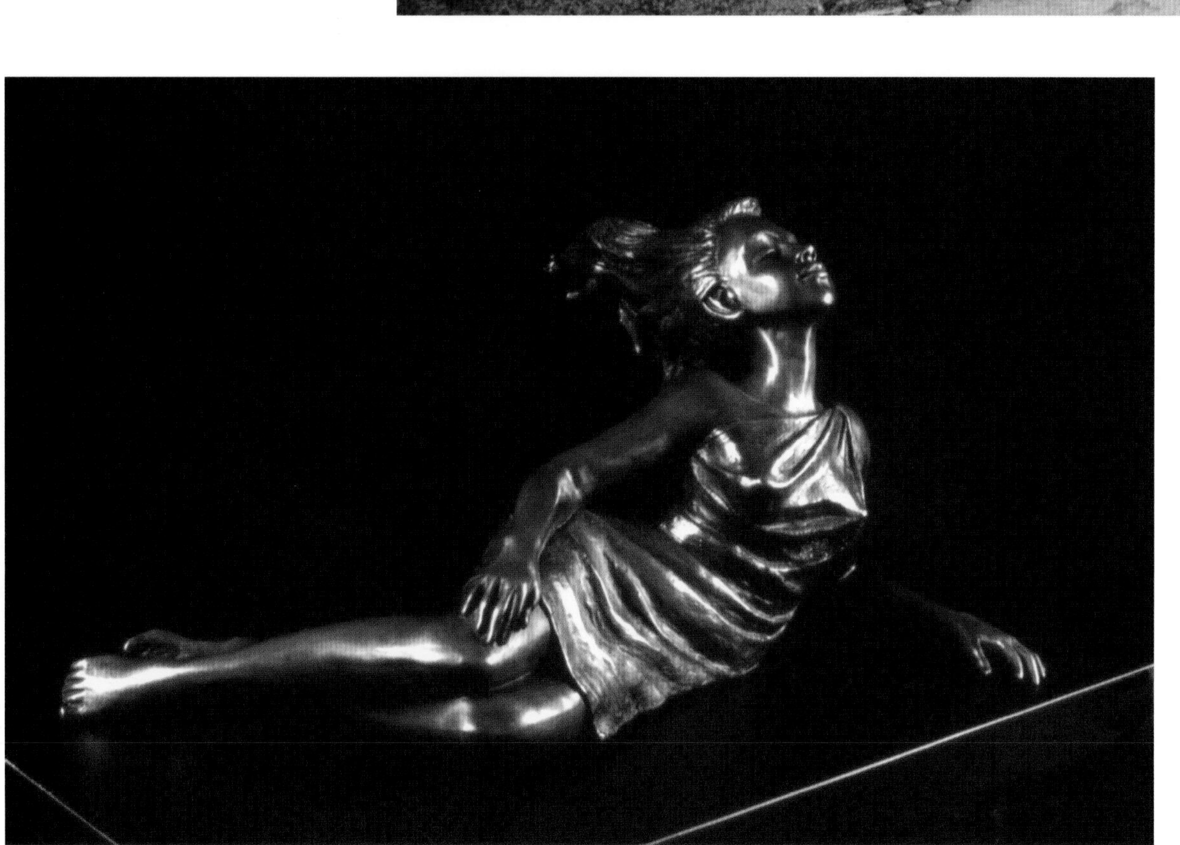

BaBa Scaturro, *A Place Called Serenity*. Cast bronze, 12″x27″x17″ (30.5cm x 68.6cm x 43.2cm).

Tile Flat or relief squares and shapes commonly used for wall decoration or flooring. Most tiles are ceramic and used where water resistance is needed, such as in bathrooms, kitchens and the out-of-doors. The tile alone, or in combination, may be artwork, separate and apart from other uses.

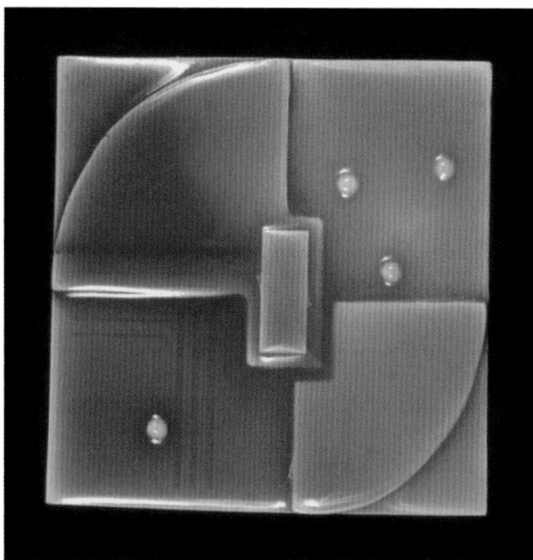

Lee Renninger, *The Moderns: #5*. Celadon on porcelain, 5¼"x5¼" (13.34cm x 13.34cm).

Timber Trees still standing that may be harvested for lumber. *See **Lumber**; **Woods** (chart).*

Tin A silver-colored, metallic element used as an alloy with bronze, pewter and other metals. Tin is also used as a metal coating to help prevent corrosion. *See **Metals** (chart).*

Tin oxide A polishing compound used for stone carving. Tin oxide may be used in glaze bodies for opacity (opacifier).

Tins The thin pieces of metal used for shims in mold making. The meta is usually brass, but is still called tins. *See **Mold**.*

Tin snips Metal cutting handheld shears resembling large scissors with strong but undersized blades.

Titanium oxide A chemical found in natural ore deposits, white titanium oxide is used to obtain white surface patinas on bronzes. It is also used as an opacifying oxide with ceramic glazes. The metal titanium is alloyed with other metals as well. *See **Patina**; **Patina** (chart).*

Tongs A clamping device to tightly hold substances. Tongs are used to hold raku as it is being fired, for example. Casting tongs lift the crucible out of a furnace. *See **Pickup tongs**.*

Torch A device that emits a flame, depending on the design. A torch can be used for detail work in wax or even in cutting metals. The fuel can be anything from alcohol to acetylene, depending on the purpose and device. *See **Oxyacetylene welding**; **Oxyacetylene cutting**.*

Torch brazing Using a gas for fuel as opposed to electrical heat when brazing. *See **Soldering**; **Braze welding**.*

Torso The human body of either a male or female; the trunk. In sculpture, it is almost always a nude.

Lampo Leong, *Nude study*. Wood-fired clay, 6"x5"x3" (15.2cm x 12.7cm x 7.6cm).

Arthur Williams, *Birth of Woman*, cast bronze, 28"x 17"x 34" (71cm x 43.2cm x 86.4cm).

Totem pole A tall wooden pole or post with carved and painted stylized designs of figures, plants, animals or emblems representing stories or memorials of a clan. It is indigenous to the carvers of the Pacific Northwest.

Touchmark The mark of an artist (blacksmith) in his/her finished work to create a permanent signature. The tool, a punch with a mark (logo), is hammered into the hot metal surface for an embossed look. The touchmark can be registered.

Toxic Poisonous, containing a toxin or poison, capable of causing serious health problems.

Translucent Allowing light to pass through; light diffusing through a substance but not with enough clarity to be transparent or to distinguish objects on the opposite side. Some varieties of alabaster are translucent.

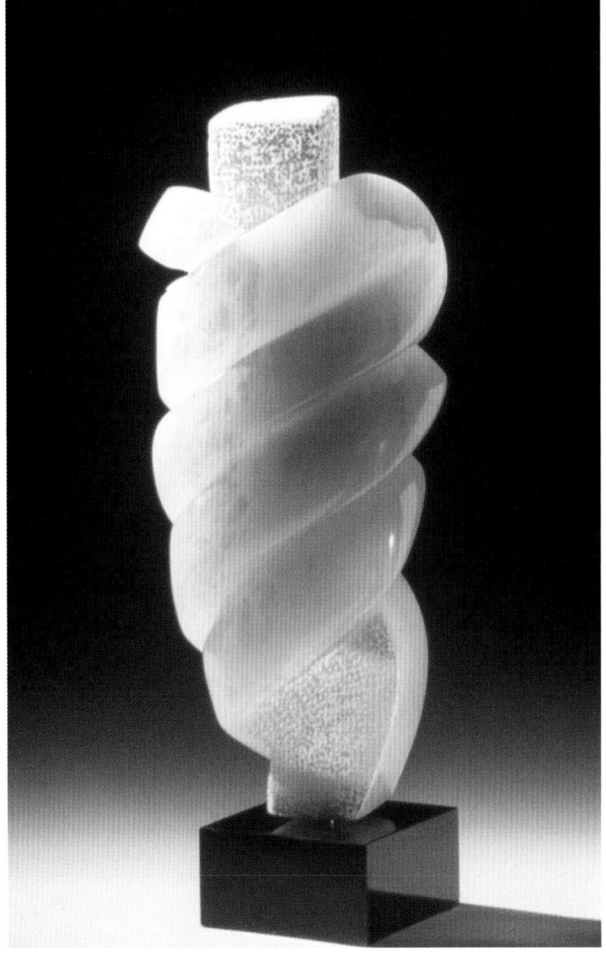

Joseph Rotella, *Infinity*. Alabaster, 28″x12″ (71.1cm x 30.5cm).

James L. Lawton, *Evolutionary Artifacts*. Screen printed images on acrylic, steel, photographs, Xerox™ copies, 112″x217″x94″ (284.5cm x 551.2cm x 238.8cm).

Transparent The capacity to transmit light without interruption, resulting in a clear view. The term is the opposite of "opaque." Many resins and acrylics are designed to make maximum use of this ability. *See **Resin**.*

Travertine A hard metamorphic stone known for its uneven texture and varied colors. It is carveable and polishes to a fine finish, but may demonstrate an open surface or holes that flow with the layers of the stone. *See **Stone** (chart).*

Treated lumber Wood soaked in insect repellent products and decay delaying chemicals to avoid rot in wet climates as well as wood eating insects such as termites. Creosote treated woods are used for telephone poles but are now out of favor in regions of wet environmental concerns. The sculptor should not carve creosote or treated woods without proper respirators. *See **Lumber**.*

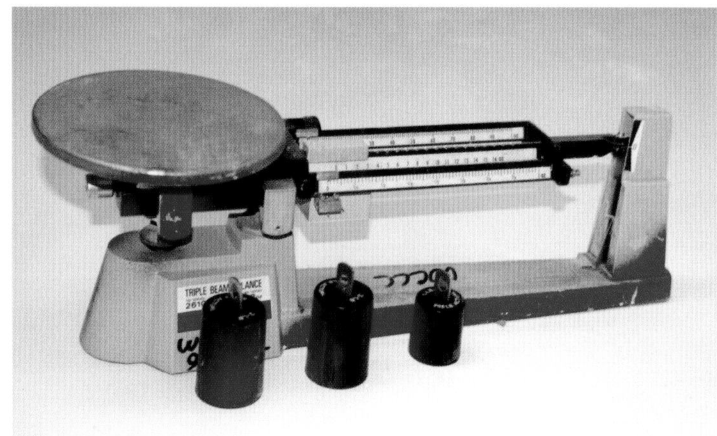

Triple beam scales.

Trichloroethylen A toxic liquid used as a metal degreaser or solvent for waxes.

Trimming Ridding clay of unwanted marks, shaping the foot of a pot or eliminating casting flashings. A term most closely associated with ceramic work.

Triple beam balance (scale) A weighing scale of high accuracy. The smaller versions are used for glaze formulation or small mold mixtures. *See* ***Flexible mold***.

Tripoli An abrasive metal polishing compound. It is pressed (loaded) into the surface of a spinning buffing wheel that is then pressed onto a surface to be smoothly buffed. *See* ***Polish***.

Tung oil seeds nearing harvest.

Trowel A handled tool with a flat, usually triangular, pointed surface used for working stucco and concrete. *See* ***Concrete***.

Tufa A porous limestone composed primarily of calcium carbonate. Deposits can be found near ground water or springs.

Tung oil (chinawood) A light, golden brown oil derived from tung tree seeds that is used for quality varnishes and furniture oil. It is found in China, South America and south Mississippi (Lumberton) U.S.A. For sculpture, it is used to preserve and bring out the natural color in wood. A high grade tung oil can be obtained in quantity from the American Tung Oil Company. *See* ***Lamination, Wood*** *(chart)*.

Tungsten Arc Welding (plasma arc) Arc welding with a tungsten electrode. *See* ***TIG***.

Tungsten carbide An exceptionally hard, metallic element with the highest heating point of all metals. It is used for long wearing tools, especially the cutting tips. *See* ***Drill bits; Sandblaster***.

Turning Using a lathe to shape wood or metal. Turnings are the resulting shavings, peelings or waste. Turning tools are the long handled lathe tools used for the process. The term is also used for a turning tool that shapes and trims clay on the ceramic wheel. *See* ***Woodturning; Metal lathe; Ceramics***.

Turntable.

Turntable A rotating surface permanently attached to a base for support and strength. It is used to hold work in progress or to display sculpture. It is universally called a "lazy Susan." *See* ***Modeling; Patina***.

Turpentine A colorless paint thinner, a mild solvent made of distillation by using extracts from trees (balsam). It is preferred when painting with artists' oil paints. Though volatile, it is not as flammable as most solvents. Mineral spirits (petroleum-based) occasionally replace turpentine for thinning purposes.

Tuyere The nozzle, pipe or opening where air is forced into a forge or furnace. The term is used when describing cast iron furnace air delivery systems. *See* ***Cast iron; Cupola; Cupolette; Forge***.

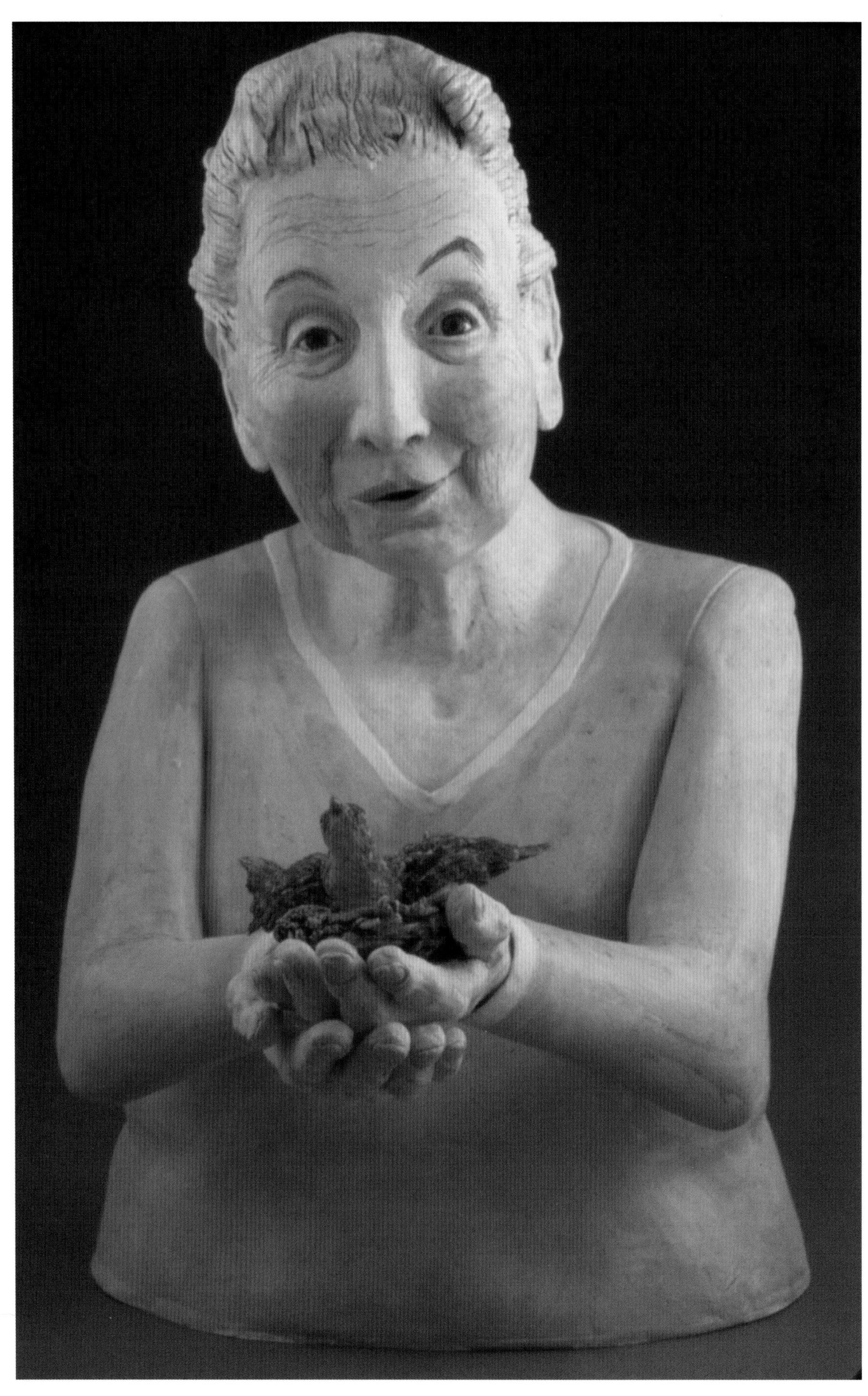

Jane Kelsey-Mapel, *Gift-Giver. Portrait of Lunette.* Stoneware, slips, underglazes and glazes, 26″x16″x21″ (66cm x 40.6cm x 53.3cm).

U

Ultraviolet rays (UV) Invisible radiation originating from the sun's rays; an arc or intense flame involved in welding. The radiation browns the skin and without proper clothing or eyewear, a brief exposure to welding arc radiation can cause severe burns or blindness.

Undercut A part of the sculpture that overhangs or protrudes in such a way as to make molding difficult. Without more than one piece or flexibility in the molding material, the mold cannot be removed. *See* ***Molds; Waste mold***.

Underglaze Applying a surface color prior to a transparent glaze application in ceramics.

Unity A theme (unity) of colors, shapes, etc., that causes the sculpture to appear complete or entire. *See* ***Principles of order***.

Up-draft (up-draught) (kiln) A kiln with a heat source located at the bottom that allows the heat to escape upwards while passing over the contents. It is the most straightforward type of kiln to build. With up-draft kilns, the energy (flame) source can be located from the rear, sides or front and from the floor. The heat circulates toward the top stack (flue) and out until the correct temperature is obtained. Dampers or baffles are located at the top to control the firing and will be closed after the heat is off to allow proper cooling. *See* ***Kiln***.

Christine Federighi, *Structure Low*. Ceramic, 71″x9″x6″ (180.3cm x 22.9cm x 15.2cm).

Upright Vertical, as opposed to being horizontal.

Urethane A type of surface coating used as a paint that has long lasting qualities. It is desired for a final, clear protection coat. In a more flexible, thickened form, it is a mold material used for various types of sculptural castings. Specially formulated urethane is used for puppetry primarily because of the plasticity and lightness.

It is an easily cut, tied, folded and glued foam that is a lightweight, soft, pliable, relatively thin-sheeted product commonly used for carpet padding. The thicknesses vary but can range from under one-fourth inch (0.635cm) to over one-half inch 1.27cm) in rolls six feet (1.83m) wide. As a sculptural medium, it is used for costumes and other quick, easy shapes. Using light but strong armatures of hollow framing, such as aluminum or PVC, large forms can be easily carried in parades.

Adhesives include hot melt glues, double-stick carpet tape and duct tape. As a finished product, it can be painted with spray paints (the best method of application) or air brushed for finer details. *See* ***Mold materials; Styrofoam™***.

Heide Fasnacht, *Demo 2000*. Urethane foam, metal screen with graphite coating, 112″x125″x120″ (284.5cm x 317.5cm x 304.8cm). Photographer: Liz Deshenes.

Megan Roberts and **Raymond Ghirardo**, *Hoodo*. Video, Ceramics, Sound, 30"x22"x12" (76.2cm x 55.9cm x 30.5cm).

V

Vacuum (pump) A machine that removes air by suction within a confined space. It is especially helpful in mold making by eliminating air bubbles from the material. The resulting material is stronger with fewer surface imperfections, allowing a longer useful life. The pump itself is not very large and usually involves gathering air by piston operation. It is commonly powered by an electrical motor, but can also be operated with a gasoline engine. An attached compressed air tank allows a quicker response. *See **Flexible mold**.*

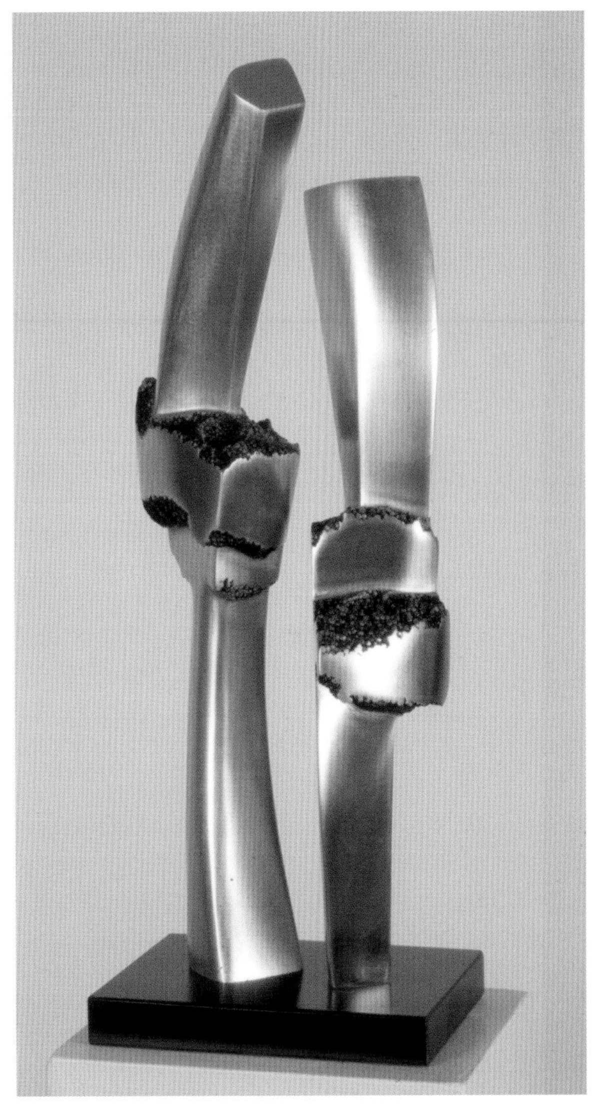

James Myford, *Emergence* (maquette). Cast aluminum, 24″x8″x6″ (61cm x 20.3cm x 15.2cm)

Vacuum forming Shaping a thermoplastic product like sheet plastic (acrylic) by placing it over a mold, heating it until it begins to collapse, then adding a vacuum to pull the plastic into the new shape. It will maintain the new form after cooling. The reverse of this is pressure formed plastic. *See **Plastics**.*

Vacuum metallizing Creating a thin metal coating using a vacuum chamber. It is coated over plastic to create a bright, silver-like finish. *See **Metallizing**.*

Value The light and dark areas of a sculpture. This is one of the most important elements, since sculpture is frequently of one continuous material and remains monochromatic. Value is the only way to see all of the form. Value is essential for relief sculpture.

Vapor blanket The cloudy steam, sometimes including gaseous content, that surrounds hot forge metal as it is submerged into oil or water for quenching. *See **Forging**.*

Vaporized casting (lost pattern casting) Metal casting using a model of expanded polystyrene (Styrofoam™) fully encased in a foundry mold of sand products. A pouring system is attached for the flowing metal. As the hot molten metal enters, the polystyrene burns out (vaporizes), leaving a solid metal in the new cavity. Styrofoam™ can be lightly coated with wax for surface details, though this can result in minor burnout and smoke problems.

Some expanded products with similar characteristics produce poisonous gases when burned. The sculptor needs to have a thorough knowledge of which product is being used for this type of casting. When burned, Styrofoam™ and other polystyrene materials give off toxic styrene gases that can cause visual difficulty, as well as memory loss. All manufactures' recommendations should be observed, including the use of respirators when using products for vapor casting. Urethanes should never be used since burning them yields toxic, even lethal gases.

Technique

Foams need to be as lightweight as possible. Large thicknesses of Styrofoam™ can be hollowed out with a prepared core of bonded sand. Carefully inserted chaplets

Janice Kluge, *Cargo of Consciousness*. Video with mixed media. 12′x8′ (3.66m x 2.44.

or core pins can keep the casting thickness even. The mold should allow the metal to move rapidly over any unspent original pattern material.

Though the mold can be fed from the top, it is best to be bottom fed to avoid the turbulence created by the incoming metal on the mold surface, which has not been rammed as hard as with conventional sand molds. Materials can include cardboard or balsa, but they should be used sparingly, since they do not always burn out cleanly and may block or solidify the flow of the liquid metal.

Flasks can be of several materials since there does not have to be a drag and cope to make the mold. They can even be sandpits. The most common flasks are large metal garbage cans and metal barrels, though wood boxes are sometimes used.

The **sand** can be almost any kind that does not react with the foam pattern. Reusable sands of petroleum bonding or green sand are used. *See* ***Styrofoam™; Sand casting; Iron casting; Expanded polystyrene***.

Variety The multiplicity or variation in the sculpture that adds to the interest of the viewer. It can be textural or shapes within the total form. Too much can cause chaos, while an absence causes boredom. *See* ***Principles of order***.

Varnish A hard, liquid coating that is brushed or sprayed onto a surface. It is usually clear and made of resins and solvents. Varnish is the last layer of protection applied because of its transparency or gloss.

Veining tool A gouge with a V-shaped cutting end used to cut sharp furrows (veins) in the wood.

Veneer A thin layer of wood mounted on top of other wood or wood products with glue to achieve a desired appearance. Veneer is composed of expensive or rare wood as compared to a cheaper underlying product. *See* ***Plywood***.

Vent (riser) Part of the metal casting system that allows air to escape from the mold. The term is also used for allowing air or gas to escape. The vents need to rise to the top of the cup for a complete fill of the mold. *See* ***Metal mold system; Ventilation***.

Ventilation A system to create air flow, especially to remove harmful fumes. It is essential to have good ventilation in sculpture; dust, noxious fumes and odors need to be removed. Good ventilation is necessary for the curing or drying of materials as well.

Venturi A constricted air passageway designed to generate a greater force of controlled air at the tip. The venturi effect helps to distribute the mixture of gas and air together, resulting in a more explosive mixture. *See* ***Burner; Kiln***.

Vermiculite A lightweight, hydrated, silicate mineral used as small particles to help in investment mold making or fillers for clay. *See* ***Plaster investment***.

Vibrator A mechanical device at the end of a strong, reinforced electrical cord that shakes or vibrates the mixture that it is placed onto or into. When placed into casting material, it vibrates the mix causing it to settle into all recesses of the form and to de-air it, such as when pouring concrete. The vibrator can also be attached to a flat surface used to support materials as they are being shaken/vibrated.

Victory (wax) A brown-colored microcystalline wax used for modeling and casting. It is used in the lost wax process in preparation for bronze casting. *See* ***Wax***.

Video Relating to television or recorded images. Sometimes a video tape or television image becomes part of a sculpture, especially with conceptual sculpture.

Viscosimeter (viscometer) An instrument that is used to measure a liquid's viscosity or thickness. *See* ***Zahn cup; Viscosity***.

Blacksmith vise.

Viscosity The ability of a liquid to move or flow. It is determined by the liquid's molecular structure or resistance to flow. Thick (viscous) liquids move slowly, while thin ones flow quickly. The hotter the bronze is, the thinner it becomes, creating a low viscosity. A colder bronze liquid has higher viscosity. The term can be applied to various things, including casting slurry, clay slips and ceramic glazes.

Woodworking vise used by **Michael J. Cooper**.

Vise A clamp with jaws used to tightly hold objects and materials as the sculptor works on them. It can be mounted on a workbench or on a stand by itself. Woodworking ones have protective coverings on the inner jaws, while metal working vises do not. Blacksmith vises are spring loaded and floor mounted.

Metal working vise.

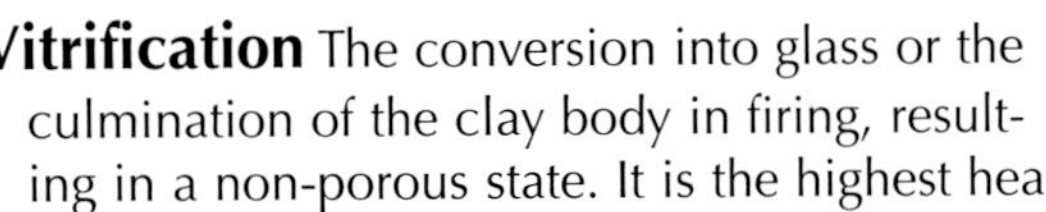

Vitrification The conversion into glass or the culmination of the clay body in firing, resulting in a non-porous state. It is the highest heat peak of the clay body during firing in which the body can remain stable without distortion. The clay particles literally flow and weld together, resulting in vitrification.

Volatile Unstable solution that rapidly evaporates or diffuses into the atmosphere in the form of a vapor. A flammable solution could easily result in an air explosion if a flame is near. In ceramics, some elements or combinations of elements release vapors that are volatile. Several commonly used solutions provide volatile vapors, such as acetone, gasoline, lacquer thinner, etc.

Volume The interior space of a container or form; the space used by a three-dimensional object (sculpture). The volume of a sculpture may be massive or small. *See* ***Measurements*** *(chart)*.

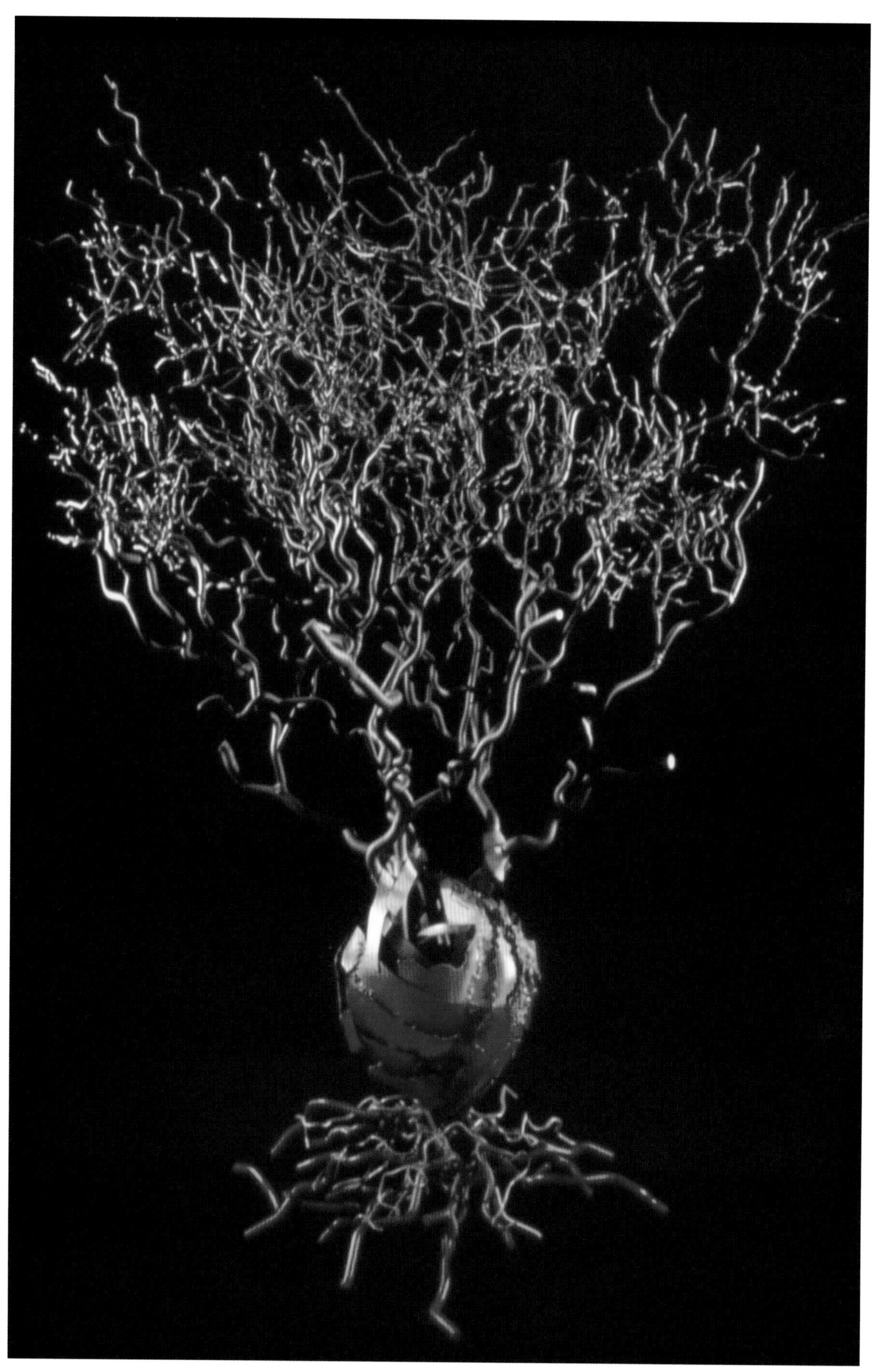

Nicole Fall, *Heart*. Welded steel, polychrome, 6′x3′x3′ (1.83m x 0.915m x 0.915m).

Walnut A dense dark wood desired for its beauty. Though hard, it possesses superior carving characteristics. *See **Wood** (chart).*

A walnut stump roughed out for *Dream Lovers* by **Jack Ransom Arvin**.

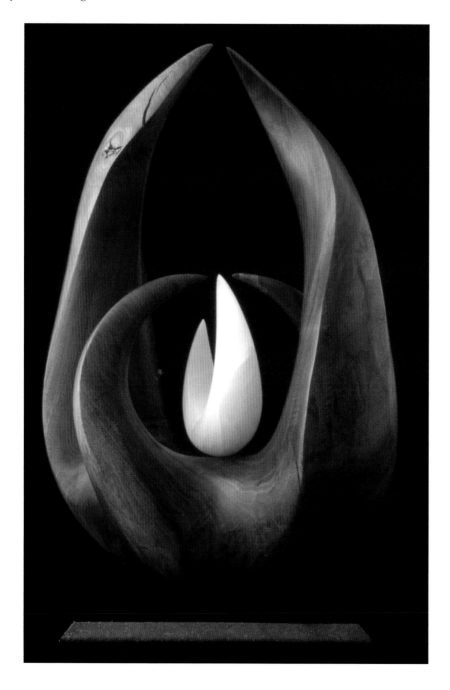

Jack Ransom Arvin, *Dream Lovers*. Walnut, alabaster, granite base, 10"x16"x25" (25.4cm x 40.6cm x 63.5cm)

Walnut shell Ground up walnut seed shells used for a sandblasting abrasive when blasting finer or more delicate materials. *See* ***Sandblasting***.

Elza Mayhew, *Moonpiece*. Unfinished Styrofoam™, 8' (2.44m) tall. *Zong* (bronze) and charcoal rubbings of *Spirit* on rice paper are in the background.

Warning coat A colored, face coat layer of plaster placed directly on the artwork in preparation for a waste mold. When the mold is finished and filled with casting material (as it is chipped off the artwork) the color of this coat warns the sculptor of the impending art work surface. Once this coat is seen, the mold removal should be more delicate to assure the new form will not be damaged as the mold is removed. This first layer has an added household laundry bluing agent or pigment that will not affect the setting of the plaster or the final casting. All other layers remain the natural plaster color. *See* ***Mold; Waste mold***.

Waste mold Used to make a single casting from a softer material (prototype) than the mold itself. Because of undercuts, or the time involved in molding, the mold is cast and then broken off, leaving the busted mold unusable or wasted after just one casting. It is discarded. It is probably the least complex of all molds, though it can handle complex shapes if the final casting is harder than the mold.

The waste mold is usually made with plaster, though other substances, such as sand or cardboard are used. The waste mold is used for hard filler substances, such as fiber glass, plastics, plaster, concrete, etc. Harder materials than plaster cast better in waste molds, because they are less likely to be damaged when removing the mold.

Though not considered traditional waste molds, casting molds, especially sand and ceramic shell molds are used once and then broken off in the same manner as plaster waste molds. *See* ***Ceramic shell; Sand molding***.

Designing a plaster waste mold

Normally, the original can be divided for shims or a clay fence. The shims/fence should be at an even height of up to one inch (0.64cm) in thickness, and the plaster needs to be applied to the full height but still leave the top exposed. These heights help the sculptor to ensure a correct, even thickness. Once these are in place, the artwork is coated with a colored warning layer of plaster.

This color coating will allow the sculptor to know how close he/she is to the artwork surface as the mold is being broken off. All layers after the first one remain white. *See* ***Warning coat***.

The plaster should be a normal mix, creamy in consistency. The form to be cast is initially coated by a spatter technique, placing the hand into the plaster and quickly flicking it off the fingers onto the surface. The spatters easily coat the form as the flicked

plaster enters even the smallest details with some force, spreading out and joining to form a uniform layer. However, sometimes the first coat is brushed on with a soft brush that will not disrupt the artwork's texture.

After the first coat of about one-fourth of an inch (1.91cm), the succeeding white coats are added either by flicking, putty knife or hand. These coats are of a thicker plaster mix, as a result of allowing the plaster to slightly thicken prior to application. The original artwork should be flicked from the bottom up to achieve an even coating without air pockets. Even though the plaster is setting up, the lower plaster will lend support without becoming a weight problem on upper areas. As the plaster is being cleared from the top of the shims, surplus plaster needs to be cleared from the base or platform top that the artwork is resting upon.

A rim or area of plaster should remain at the same thickness as the height of the shim walls. Undercuts should be flicked completely, as well as all recesses, and the entire surface (of one wall section) should be completed in one try. Ideally, the mold is completed in as few layers as possible or in a short timeframe to ensure adhesion of plaster from one moist coat to the other.

A reinforcement material is not ordinarily added to the plaster, since the mold will later be broken. However, a larger mold may need selectively placed reinforcement. Once the mold is completed, the original contents are removed with a mallet and hardwood wedges.

Making a casting

The mold is carefully cleaned in preparation for the final casting material. A separator is added and the mold is pieced back together with a holding device, such as bungee cords. Sometimes soft wire is used, or even burlap dipped into plaster and draped across the seams to ensure a liquid, light mold. Clamps can be used if they do not cause undo pressure on the mold. The mold needs to be slightly wet or soaked prior to use if plaster or concrete is the casting material to prevent a dry mold from absorbing the casting fluid's moisture, thus weakening the casting. *See* ***Bungee cord***.

Depending on how the casting is to be done, the mold could be slushed or poured solid. If the mold is filled solid, it is vibrated or shaken to make certain the contents have been evenly distributed and the bubbles have been removed. In slushing a life-sized portrait, the ideal thickness is from three-fourths inch to one inch (1.91cm to 2.54cm). A plaster soaked interior reinforcement (such as hemp, jute or burlap coating) can be added after the face coat has been firmly established.

Should leaks occur while casting, they can ordinarily be patched by plugging the holes with modeling or ceramic clay. A thorough hardening must occur, so the contents can withstand the blows or jolts required as the mold is being removed.

The mold is eliminated from the casting by steel chisels. It is struck with a chisel driven by a hammer until the outer layers are removed. Once the color coat is located, the mold removal is completed with more care. While some parts of a mold can be removed in larger pieces, detailed areas, especially those with undercuts, must be dislodged in smaller fragments.

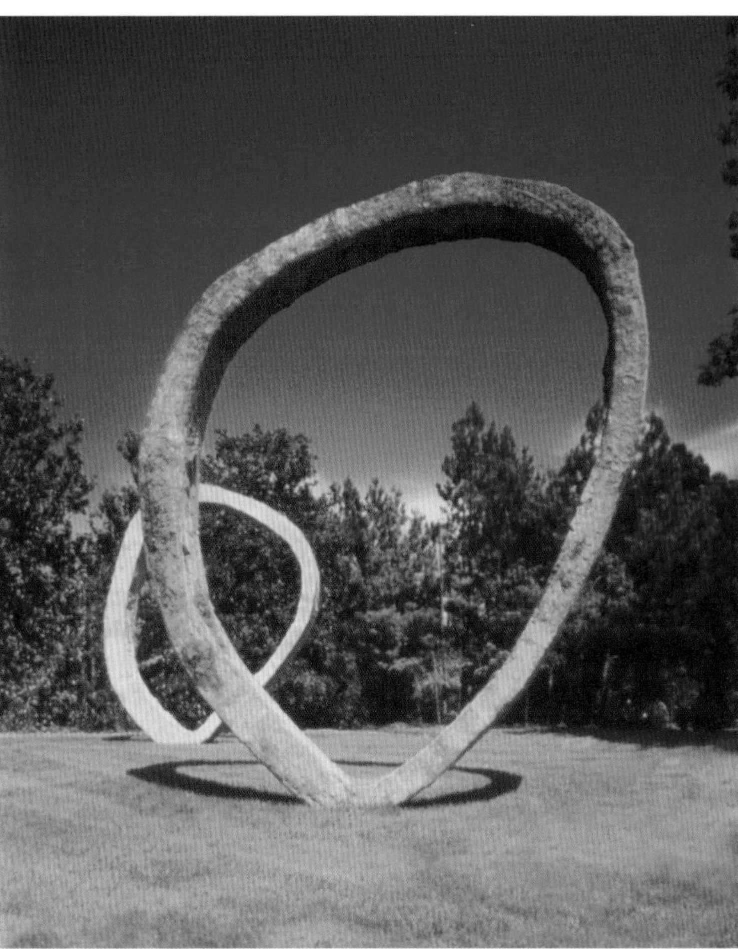

Thomas H. Sayre, *Grandifora*. Earth cast concrete, iron oxide, 25′x21′x60′ (7.63m x 6.41m x 18.3m). A sand waste mold is made directly into sand by eliminating unwanted sand to leave a negative (mold) shape. The casting substances are usually plaster or concrete. The mold is removed by digging the sand from around the casting. Earth is sometimes used instead of sand as a molding material. *See:* ***Earth cast concrete***.

WASTE MOLD
by Peter N. Cozzolino

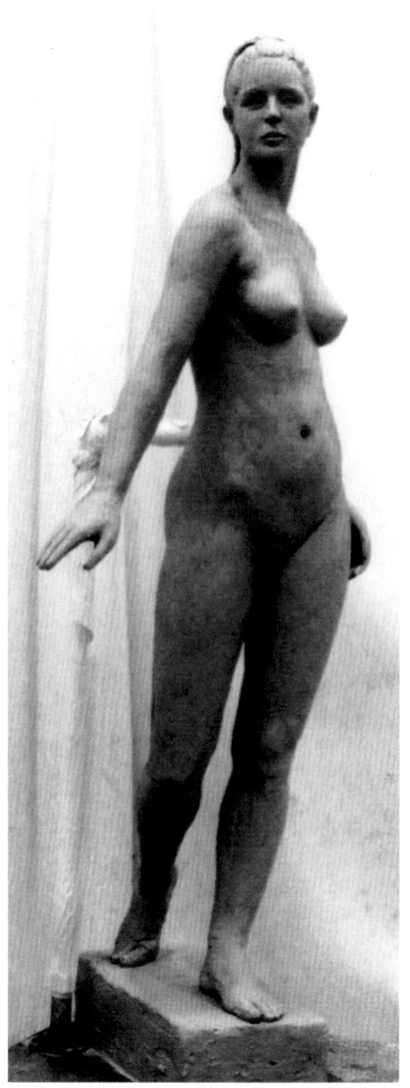

The figure, *Alice*, modeled with modeling clay in preparation for a plaster waste mold.

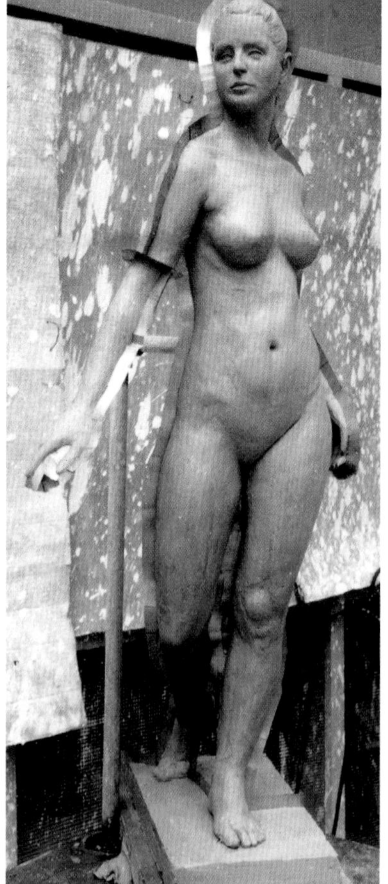

Clay with shims added, front view.

Clay with shims demonstrating various pieces, rear view.

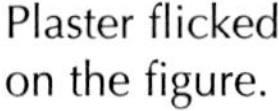

Plaster flicked on the figure.

The mold is taken from the clay and cleaned. A release agent and interior reinforcement will be added.

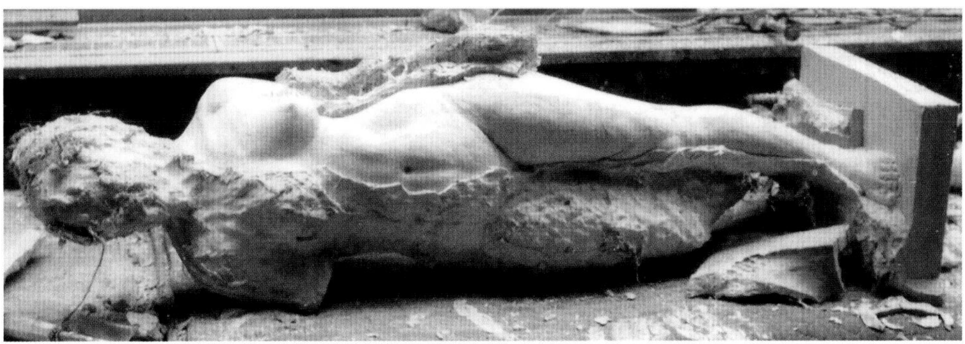

After the plaster casting, the work is laid on its side as the mold is broken off.

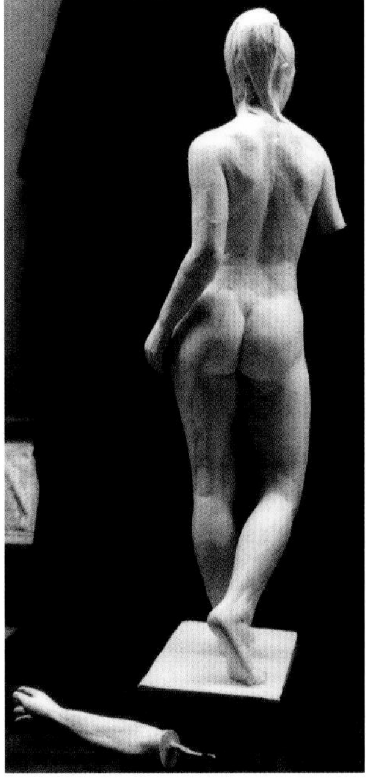

The arm that was cast separately is ready to be mounted.

Little of the waste mold remains to be removed.

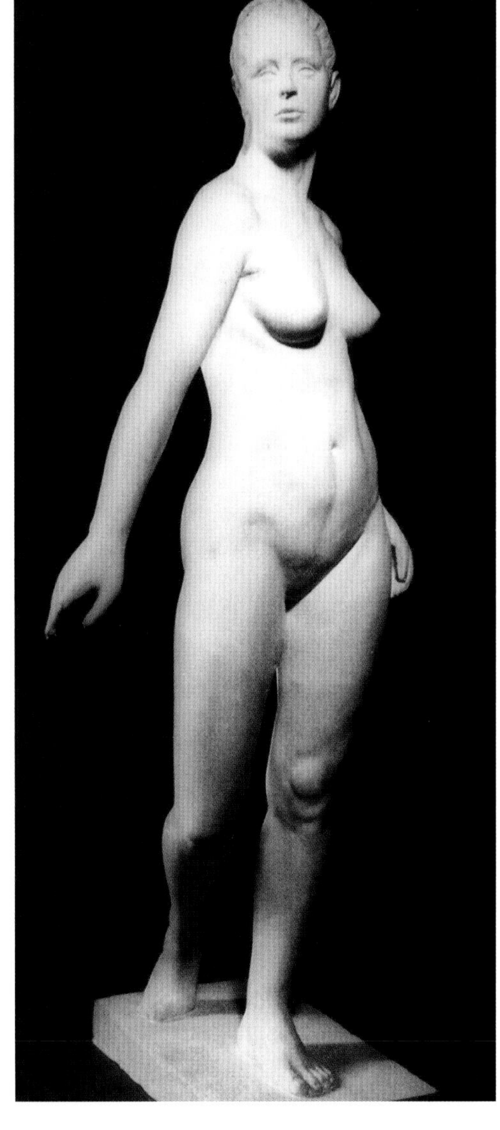

Peter N. Cozzolino, *Alice*. Plaster, 38" (96.5cm) tall.

Other waste mold materials

Oil-based clay waste molds are created by using modeling clay as a negative mold material and pouring the coating material directly into the temporary mold. This is helpful for small casts or partial castings for parts to repair larger castings. Modeling clay may also be pressed onto readymade or found shapes, creating an easily filled cavity. This is called pressed molding.

Carole A. Feuerman working on an open face "waste" mold at Tallix Foundry, Beacon, New York.

Cardboard molds can suffice for small shapes; however, the sculptor needs to waterproof the board or it will adhere to the liquid. If a larger casting is being made, the cardboard may not be strong enough without reinforcement. Care should be taken when using readymade or glued cardboard containers, since most container glues are not water resistant and can easily loosen, resulting in a split or broken mold with the contents running out. Small waterproof milk cartons can serve as molds.

Styrofoam™ can easily be carved into mold shapes. The liquid is directly poured into it or added after a thin plastic wrap is laid across the Styrofoam™ to keep the casting material from adhering to the foam. Depending on the process of mold removal, acetone or lacquer thinner (with proper gear and ventilation) can be used to dissolve the Styrofoam™, leaving the casting intact. If plaster is used directly on Styrofoam™, it will adhere unless it is coated with a release agent (such as petroleum jelly). Test all casting materials prior to use since many castable products will dissolve Styrofoam™.

Fabric waste molds can be created on the sewing machine using shaped containers in cloth, larger castings can be made using canvas. The shapes can be designed knowing how the liquid will fill the cloth vessel. It is not difficult to imagine how readymade clothing, gloves, purses, etc., could easily be used for molds to obtain obvious shapes. Plaster or cement are frequently used for casting materials. If the fabric does not have a release agent, it will tend to adhere. If it is not waterproofed, it can leak or be saturated with the moisture from the casting. *See* ***Sand waste mold; Casting*** *(molds);* ***Mold; Concrete; Earth cast concrete***.

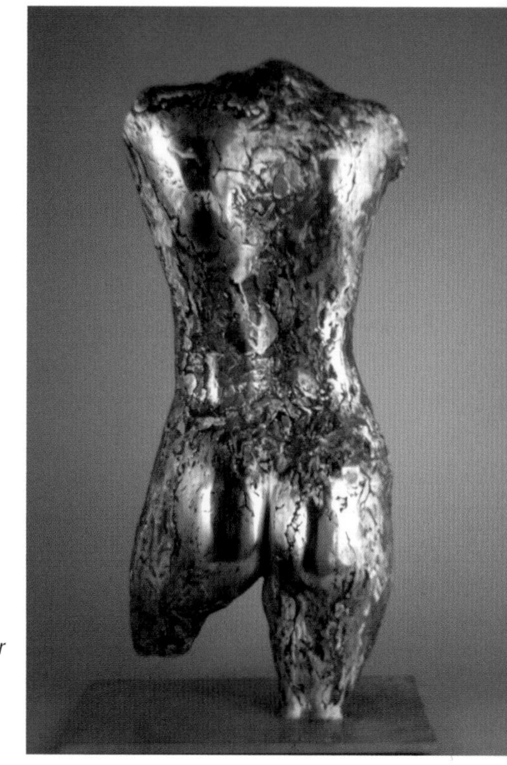

Carole A. Feuerman, *Silver Venis*. Cast aluminum, 34"x19"x12" (86.4cm x 48.3cm x 30.5cm).

Water (H_2O) A liquid that is clear, odorless, colorless and tasteless composed of two parts hydrogen and one part oxygen. It is the most used of all solvents, since it is harmless to the human touch. *See* ***Bound water***.

Waterproof The property of completely resisting water, as opposed to only being resistant to water.

Wax Beeswax, carnauba, microcrystalline, paraffin, etc., are all waxes prominent for sculptural purposes. Carnauba wax is known for its hardness as part of surface wax preparations. A petroleum-based microcystalline wax is used for casting or modeling, since it has smaller crystals in its structure as compared to beeswax. Wax can be heated in hot water to soften, and it can be heated and poured into sheet slabs.

Manufactured waxes are formulated according to use, such as the melting point and hardness. Carving wax designed to be carved with sculpture tools results in exceptionally defined details. Machinable wax is analogous to carving wax but is worked with lathes and similar power tools. Beeswax can also be used for modeling, but it is much more expensive by. There are many varieties, depending upon the purpose.

The term "wax" can also mean a completed model (in wax) that is ready to invest. Wax, as a pigmented finish material, is used for sculptures found in wax museums. Excellent realism can be achieved. Also, beeswax is used to lubricate hot jacks when necking glass works, and it is also used to lubricate the yoke. *See* ***Microcrystalline wax****;* ***Carnauba wax****;* ***Paraffin****;* ***Polishing wax****;* ***Patina****;* ***Stone****;* ***Wood***.

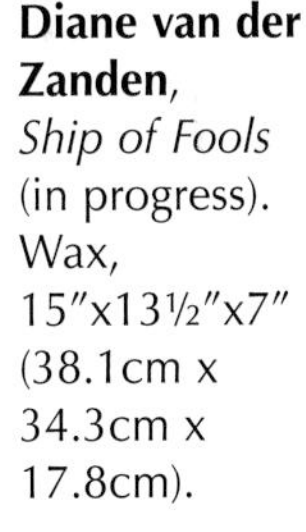

Diane van der Zanden, *Ship of Fools* (in progress). Wax, 15″x13½″x7″ (38.1cm x 34.3cm x 17.8cm).

Sharon Dee Shaughnessy, *Immortality*. Mixed, wax, 4″x5″x3″ (10.2cm x 12.7cm x 7.6cm). The hand is also sculpted.

Wax injection Inserting liquid casting wax into a mold by pressure. It is also termed pressure injection.

Wax melter A heated container designed for melting wax and maintaining a set, usable temperature. Since hot liquid wax is required for the lost wax casting method, a melter is necessary for foundry work.

WAX
Brushed into a Mold

The flexible mold is pre-heated.

Wax is brushed onto the mold.

The wax is finished and removed from the mold.

The wax injection pressure pot is ready to squirt hot wax into a mold with 5 to 15 pounds (2.3kg to 6.8kg) of pressure. The mold, clamp, mother mold plates and release agent are shown. **Andrè Harvey** is using the equipment to create a wax to cast into gold.

Large wax melter with automatic controls in the foreground. A 16 quart (0.9463 liter) electric roaster, used for wax melting, is in the background.

WD40™ A thin spray lubricant formulated to dissolve rust on metal. It is also used as a cleaner to remove wax from other materials.

Weathering Aging in the atmosphere.

WEDGING CLAY

Wedge (wedging) Preparing clay for use. Wedging eliminates air and blends the clay into a workable homogenous unit. It is used in preparation for wheel throwing. The hands work together to compress the clay on a surface; it is cut into two parts, and then the parts are slapped or wedged together, repeating the process until the clay reaches the desired consistency. This strengthens the clay and rids it of air, which can result in blistering or explosion during firing. As compared to kneading, it is more useful for larger pieces of clay. *See* ***Kneading; Pug mill; Wedging table***.

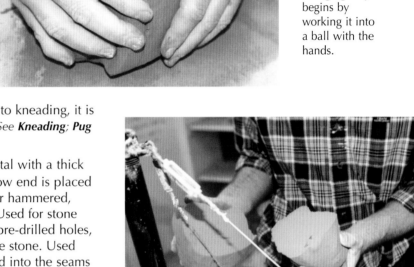

Wedging clay begins by working it into a ball with the hands.

Wedges (shims) Pieces of wood or metal with a thick end tapered into a thin end. The narrow end is placed into a crevice or seam to be tapped or hammered, using the taper to spread the pieces. Used for stone carving, carefully placed in a row of pre-drilled holes, metal wedges are used for splitting the stone. Used with molds, wood wedges are inserted into the seams to open the mold. They can also be used under works to level them, etc. *See* ***Waste mold; Feathers and wedges***.

The clay is cut into two parts, then more.

Wedging table A table with an absorbent body of dry cast plaster, canvas covered, and a strong thin wire mounted above it that is used for wedging. Slabs of clay are passed over the wire at an angle to cut it into wedging sections and then they are slammed together and kneaded on the table. *See* ***Wedge***.

Weights Measurements. *See* ***Measurements*** *(chart)*.

Weld(ing) To join metals by fusion using extreme localized heat (arc or flame) with or without filler metals or pressure. A weld is a completed place of fusion. *See* ***Welding***.

Welder The worker (operator) who welds. At times the term is often incorrectly made in reference to the welding machine; however, it is not the welding machine.

The clay is slapped together on the wedging table to become a compact shape.

Welder's eye Corneal damage as a result of ultraviolet light radiation from the welding arc upon the eye. It is caused by wearing inadequate eye protection during the welding process.

Welding Fusion welding, which includes arc welding and oxyacetylene welding. Arc is ordinarily used for larger works requiring heavier metals, while oxyacetylene is common in smaller sculptures with thinner metals. *See* ***Oxyacetylene welding; Braze welding; Silver soldering; Arc welding; TIG welding; MIG welding; Spot welder; Bead.***

Welding helmet with dark welding lens.

Welding lens Designed to protect the eyes from the harmful effects of the sudden and intense brightness of the welding flame and arc. **Lens shade plates** can vary in darkness, but the most common is a No.10. It meets the national standard and also easily replaced.

Auto-darkening welding lens will automatically go from a clear transparent lens to a No. 10 shade in times from 1/10,000 to 1/25,000 of a second. They can be battery operated or solar powered by the radiation produced from the welding light. The battery powdered lens require a special helmet and are heavier, while the solar powered lens fit within the same space as an ordinary lens.

The caution given for helmets is that they must cover all of the exposed areas without light leaks. If any light is reflected within the helmet, it either needs to be discarded or sanded for a non-reflective inner surface.

Jim Boyd, *Overtime*. Welded steel, 40″x20″x20″ (101.6cm x 50.8cm x 50.8cm).

Welding rod (electrode) A short, straight rod coated with a flux. It is used as an electrode to begin an arc and then serves as a filler metal. The broader definition includes any rod or wire of any length for arc or oxyacetylene welding. *See* ***Electrode; Electrode holder.***

Welding safety dress (clothing) The **apparel** worn while welding is of paramount importance. No part of the skin can be exposed to the **ultraviolet light radiation**, or severe and lasting damage can occur. The **gloves** need to be strong leather (except for TIG, wherein softer, more delicate leather gloves are better) with long ends (**gauntlet**) to cover all parts of the lower arm. A **welder's coat**, or **apron**, is necessary to keep out the rays, as well as for protection from the sparks. Either **denim pants** (heavy blue jeans without folds or cuffs) or **leather chaps** are needed. **Boots** are better than shoes, since they can be inside the pants, and the laces will not burn in two. A **welder's cap** is recommended if many vertical or over-the-head welds are to be made.

The **welding helmet** is a special piece of equipment. It is designed to fully cover the face, part of the top of the head and down the front for some neck protection from radiation. The helmet is made of a hard fiber material that is lightweight, heat resistant and molded for strength and heat resistance. It has an adjustable **headband** that allows the helmet to swing up over the head and remain up between welds. The helmet's **color lens** is always protected by a clear, transparent lens that will receive the welding spatter. It is designed to be easily removed and replaced. The actual lens is either a fixed protective shade or auto-darkening. *See* ***Welding lens***.

Welding tools Tools needed or helpful in welding. These include a chipping hammer for slag removal, wire brushes for pre-cleaning the welding surface, an igniter for gas welding and a welder's wrench that contains most of the wrench sizes for oxyacetylene welding and cutting torches, tanks and hoses. *See* ***Welding; Oxyacetylene welding; Oxyacetylene cutting***.

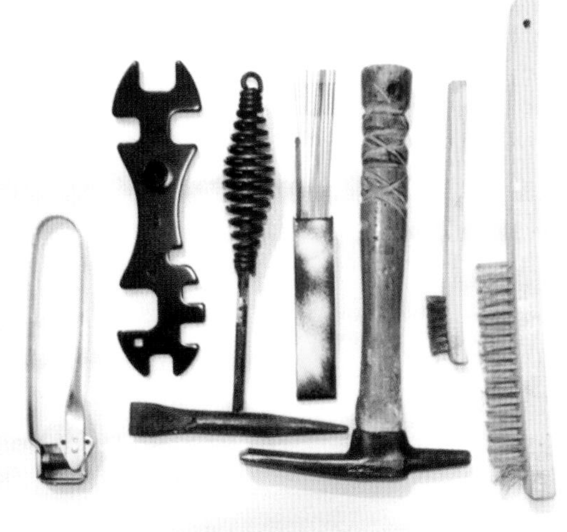

Welding tools. Left to right: striker, welder's head/tank tool, flux hammer, tip cleaners, flux hammer, brass brush, stainless steel brush.

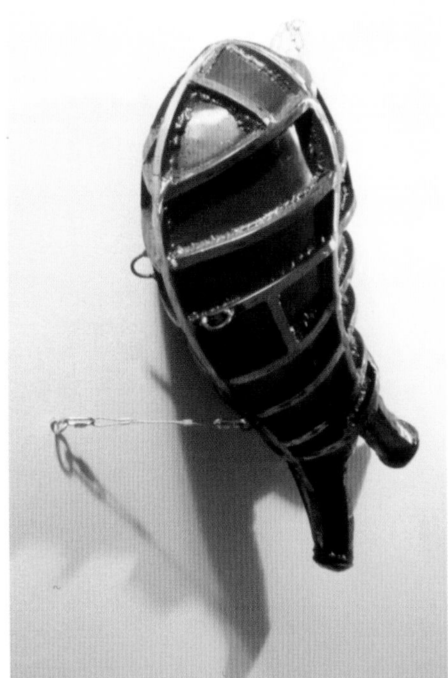

John Richardson, *Dura-membrane Series #4*. Welded steel, 23″x18″x8″ (58.4cm x 45.7cm x 20.3cm).

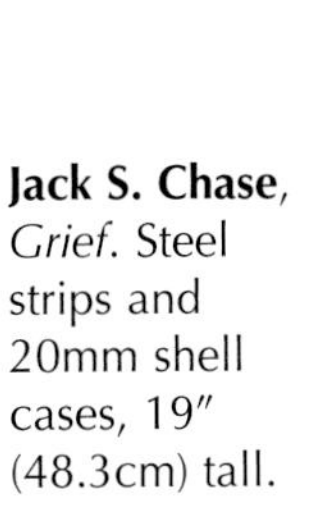

Jack S. Chase, *Grief*. Steel strips and 20mm shell cases, 19″ (48.3cm) tall.

Wet newspaper A handheld, folded, wet newspaper in which a gather on a blowpipe is inserted so that the glassblower can shape the hot molten glass without being burned. Steam from the moisture keeps the glass from sticking. *See* ***Glass blowing***.

Wet-or-dry sandpaper A carborundum, abrasive coated, water resistant sheet used for removing undesirable surfaces from a work. The sheets are consistently graded in sizes from larger than 60 grit to smaller than 1000 grit. They can be used dry or with water as a lubricant, to keep the dust down. The backing is flexible but water resistant. *See* ***Sandpaper; Sandpapers*** *(chart)*.

Wetting agent In sculpture uses, it is a liquid substance especially designed to ensure adhesion of wax and ceramic shell slurry. It is added in measured amounts to the liquid slurry during the initial mixture.

Wetting down Spraying or drenching water onto a stone to determine the suitability for carving or the best way to carve. Flaws and veins are easily discovered using this method. *See* ***Stone*** *(carving)*.

Wheat paste A binder used with paper to create papier machè. *See* ***Papier machè***.

Wheel A ceramic or potter's machine used to form round clay shapes. A rotating, flat round dish shape is controlled by electrical power or manually powered by hand or foot by using a flywheel. Soft workable clay is placed on the flat dish and formed by hand as it is forced into a rounded shape. *See* ***Wheel throwing***.

Wheel throwing Creating round, hollow clay works on a spinning potter's wheel. The resulting shape may be added to another process, such as slab, or used by itself. The shape is paddled or otherwise reshaped to

Dennis St. Pierre working on a ceramic throwing wheel.

Susan F. Molle[r] *Consider the Mundane*. Earthenware, 12″x24″x5″ (30.5cm x 61c[m] x 12.7cm). Photographer: Harrison Evans

create the form. Traditional terra cotta is seldom used on the potter's wheel, the clays used are more plastic and contain additional water and less grog. It is possible to unite several thrown and slab pieces to form a total. However, it is important that similar clay bodies are used throughout a work. Otherwise, different bodies will separate in the drying or firing process. *See* ***Ceramics***.

Whetstone A hard tool sharpening stone of a fine grain. The term is also applied to manmade combinations of abrasive materials for tool sharpening. *See* ***Sharpening stone***.

Whittler A carver who enjoys the process of carving wood more than the finished product. Works are small and handheld. The product is generally indicative of carving marks, especially of the pocket knife variety. The leavings are referred to as shavings. *See* ***Wood carving***.

Winches A tool used for raising or pulling a heavy weight by a chain or rope wrapped around a round, geared mechanism. *See* ***Lifting***.

Marlene Ferrell Parillo, *Waiting in a Jar*. Ceramic, 18″x9″x9″ (45.7cm x 22.9cm x 22.9cm).

Wire A continuous strand of metal. Soft wire can be easily bent or flattened into a design for use by the sculptor. Hard wire, such as MIG wire, serves as a specially designed electrode for arc welding.

Detail from *Vessels of Life* by **Connie Herring**.

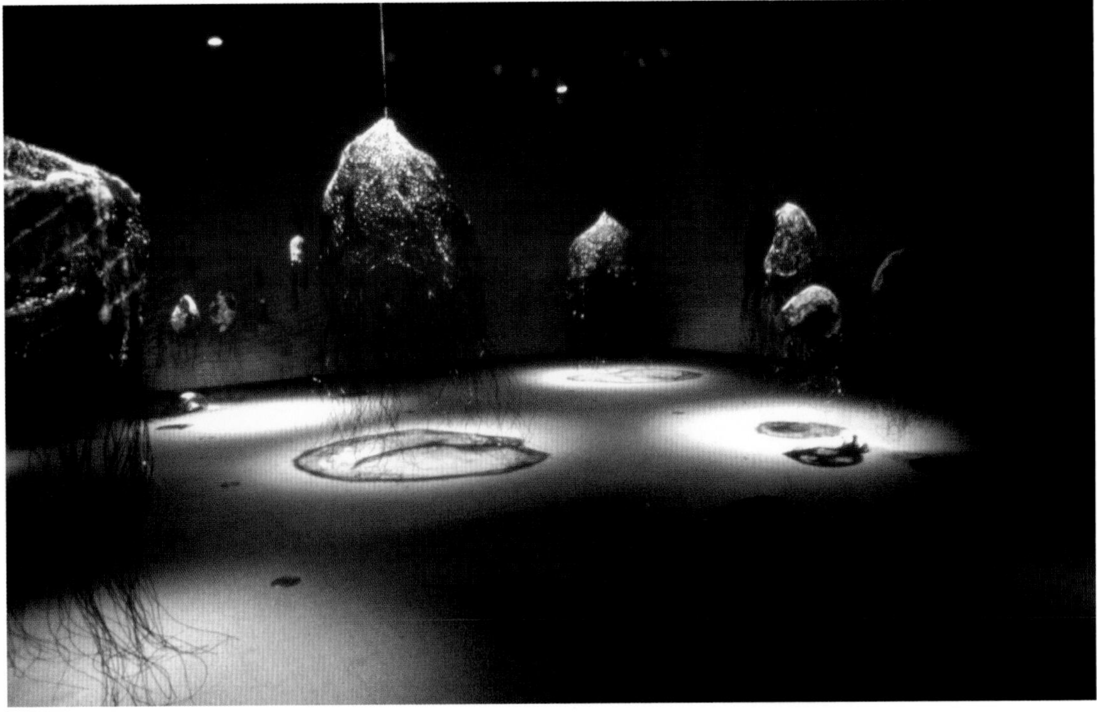

Connie Herring, *Vessels of Life*. Installation, copper wire, vessels from 24″ to 12′ (60.96cm to 3.66m) tall.

Lourdes de la Riva, *Relaciones Infinitas* (in progress). 1⁄4″ (0.64cm) Iron, 9.84′x13.11′ (3m x 4m). Photographer: Sergio Cabrera.

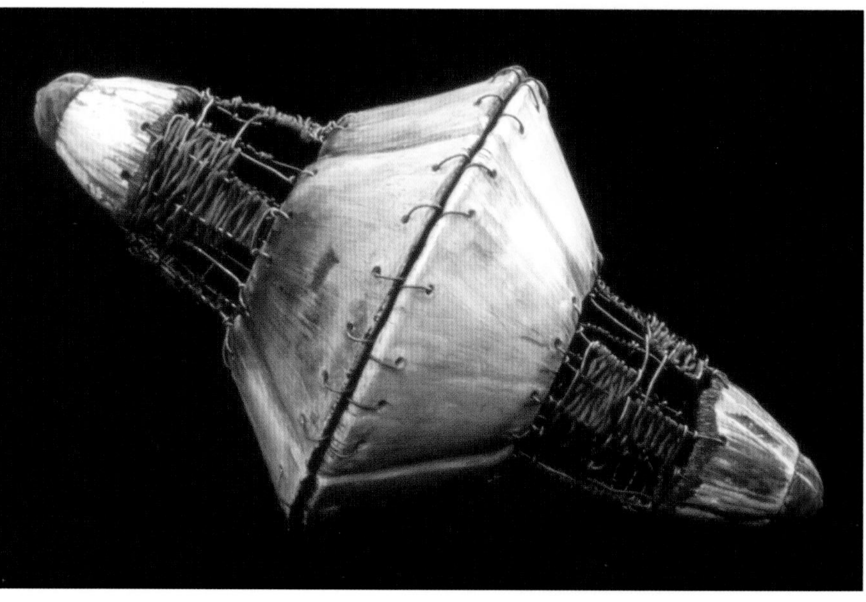

Kristin Gudjonsdottir, *Seed of Life III*. Ceramic clay, cast glass, copper, 30″x14″x14″ (76.2cm x 35.6cm x 35.6cm).

Wire-arc (electric arc spray) The use of two electrically charged wires to melt into a thermospray for surface coating sculpture. The wires are fed into the spray gun to reach an arc at the head. The high intensity heat results in a liquid metal that is atomized by a rush of pressurized gas onto the surface. The process allows a different coating to be selectively placed on a sculpture. *See **Metallizing**.*

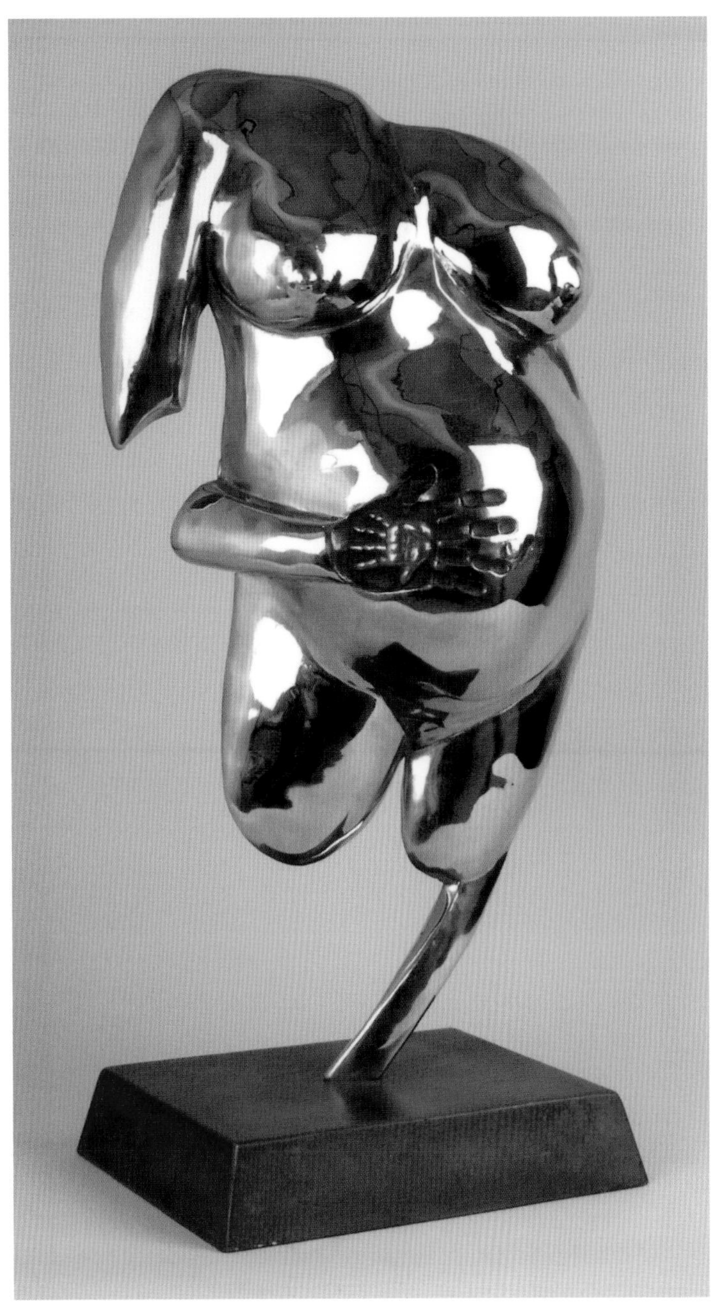

Thomas Jefferson Bollinger, *New Life*. Cast aluminum-silicon alloy, thermal spray coated with nickel and selectively with bronze. Photographer: Henry Bollinger.

Wire brush A handheld brush resembling a hair brush or a wheel consisting of cut wires that is mounted on a grinder. The wires can be stainless steel, brass, regular steel, etc., depending upon the working requirements. It is used to clean metal surfaces and highlight bronzes and patinas. A smaller version that resembles a tooth brush can easily highlight patinaed areas. Larger wire wheels on grinders can rapidly clean a surface, especially metals in preparation for a finer finish. *See* ***Brush***.

Assortment of wire brushes.

Shidoni Foundry worker chases with a wire brush, Tesúque, New Mexico.

Bench grinder with fine and coarse wire brushes.

Wire end tool
A handheld modeling tool with a stiff wire loop on the end. It is ideal for scooping out spaces in oil- and water-based clay bodies. *See* ***Modeling tools***.

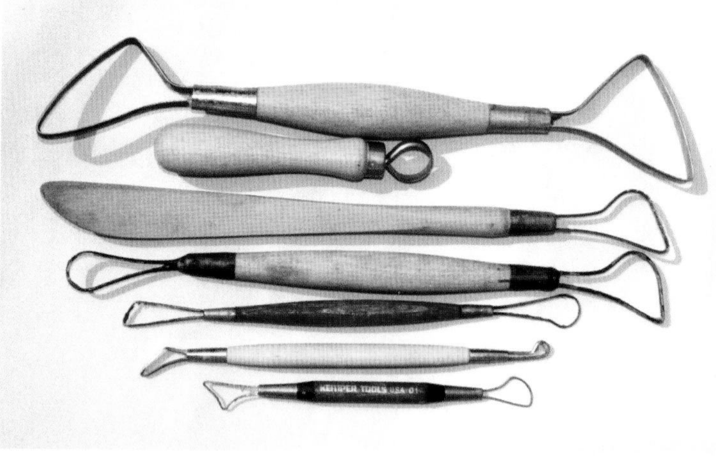

Wire end modeling tools.

Wire welding
The use of specially designed roll wire as the electrode when arc welding. *See* ***Gas Metal Arc Welding; Electrode***.

Wood The hard, fibrous substance found under a tree's outer covering of bark. Though used as a fuel, it is a major building material and possibly the most unique sculpture material available. It is easily obtained. Wood is an object of beauty and is the most copied visual texture used in plastics and laminates.

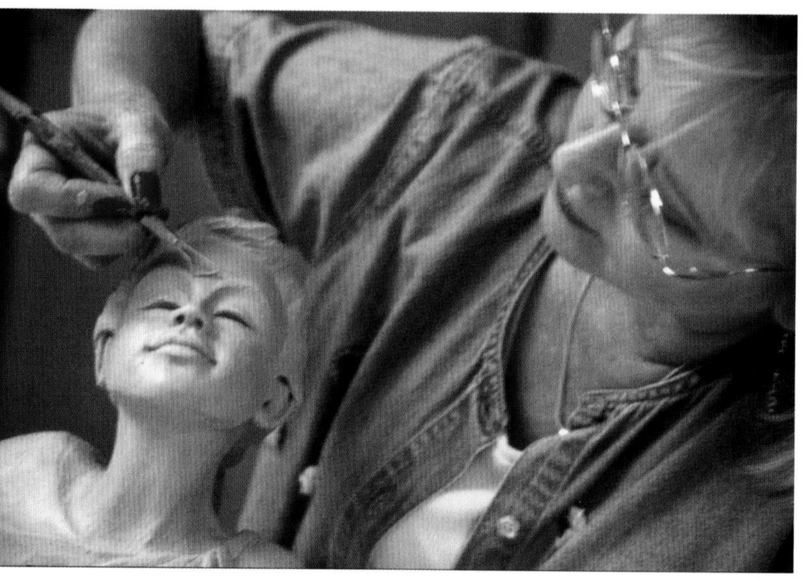

BaBa Scaturro uses a wire end tool to work on the clay model for *A Place Called Serenity.*

Not only does it come from what was once a living thing, but it retains the record of its life and endurance into its final beauty by growth rings. As the tree ages between seasons of the year, a new layer (ring) of growth is added. Growth rings display a tree's character. In some years, the tree has more water and the rings are wider, further apart, making the wood less hard. In a drought year, the rings will be narrower, darker and tough.

As the tree grows in altitude, the fibers follow the trunk direction. These fibers determine the grain or direction (height) of growth. Trees with soft wood grow faster than do hardwood trees. Consequently, the growth rings are usually less pronounced in harder woods; the resulting texture is more even. As a tree continues to grow, the middle of the trunk becomes darker as the sap migrates to the outer rings near the bark. This outer area is called sapwood, which is softer as compared to the darker center. The darker center is called the heartwood.

As branches grow and produce a new growth, a knot results. This is the beginning of new growth rings. Wood from trees without knots is called clear. While the construction worker prefers clear lumber, the sculptor enjoys the beauty of wood, however it is, especially with knots. *See* ***Treated lumber***.

Dry wood is preferred, since it is easier to carve and results in fewer splits. Sculptors who carve large tree trunks depend on their own drying methods. The most common way is to store trunks in a dry storage area, usually a well ventilated shed, with wax (melted paraffin) painted on all exposed cuts to avoid a rapid escape of moisture. Bark should be left on to avoid drying too quickly. Wood should not be stored in airtight containers or bags that may cause rot. Rather, they need air circulation for natural drying to occur. Also, all drying woods need pest control treatment for insects like powder post beetles and termites.

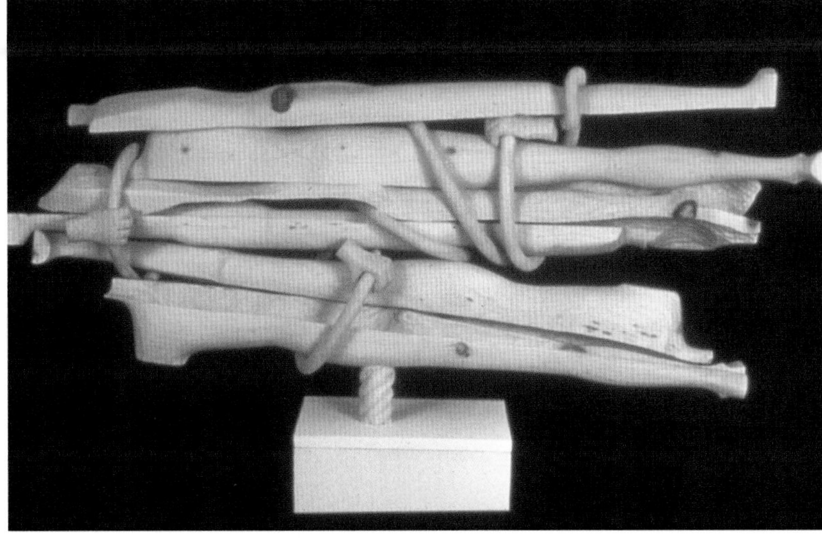

Lita Kelmenson, *Censored*. Wood, 21″x50″x8″ (53.3cm x 127cm x 20.3cm).

Drying time cannot be hastened and may last from two to ten years, even longer, depending on the thickness of the trunk. Commercially dried lumber is produced by placing it into a large kiln to maintain a constant drying rate. As a result, the moisture is driven out, and the lumber has minimal checking (cracks), if any, as it seasons. However, the thickness of kiln dried wood is limited; it is rarely more than ten inches (25.4cm) thick. Once kiln dried, it is carefully stored to avoid warping. *See **Kiln drying**; **Lumber**.*

Greenwood is also carved but with certain restrictions. Some commercial chemicals are available for smaller works (the sizes of gun stocks). The green wood is completely saturated for a period of time to soak up the chemical and avoid checking. Larger green works are carved on a day-to-day basis. After each day's carving, the work is either wrapped airtight or coated with floor sealants. Sometimes the sculptor coats the wood with linseed oil as he/she carves to retard checking. However, this can cause finishing problems. Another solution is to quickly hollow out the proposed form to decrease the possibility of checking. (This would obviously limit some shapes that would require interior carving).

David Hostetler carves wood in his studio.

Woods are traditionally divided into two groups, **hardwoods** and **softwoods**. This is based on the species of tree visible by the family of leaves in each category. Hardwoods have broad flat leaves, and the moisture circulatory system is on the outer part of the trunk. The oak tree with the large leaf is a good example. Softwoods have the more resinous, thin, narrow leaves. A good example would be the pine, with its readily recognizable needles.

Looking at hardwoods and softwoods, most classifications are obvious; however, some are unusual, such as balsa wood, which is classified as a hardwood, but is possibly the softest wood available. Yew is classified as a softwood, yet exceeds the hardness of many of the hardwoods. When choosing a carving wood, one needs to be aware of the true nature of the wood and how it will carve and take a finish.

Hardwoods, especially **fruitwoods**, take a beautiful oiled finish without staining or opaque substances to enhance the beauty though some sculptors prefer staining. The sculptor should carefully weigh the decision to stain wood in imitation of another. Opaque finishes such as paint add hard color to a wood but also hide the natural wood beauty. However, paint can also hide blemishes, glue joints and plywood layers if they are not desirable. *See **Stain**.*

WOOD SAMPLES

Sanded to 220 grit with the right half of each sample coated with tung oil.

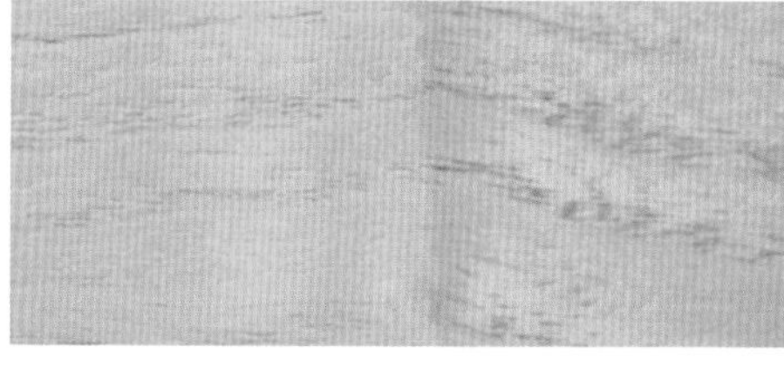

Ash.

Beech.

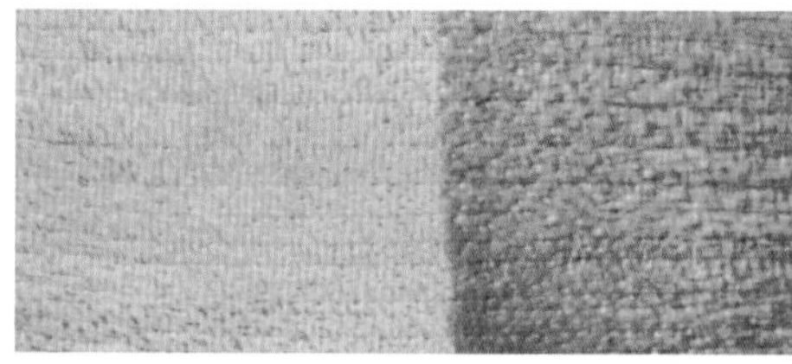

Birch.

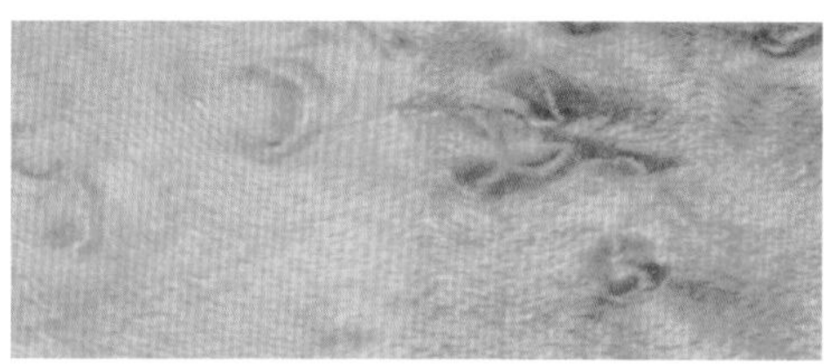

Bird's-Eye Maple.

Canarywood.

Cedar, America.

Cedar of Lebanon.

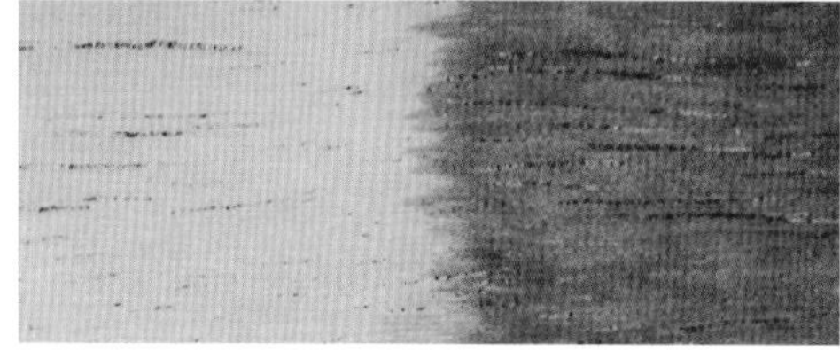

Cedar, Spain.

Cherry.

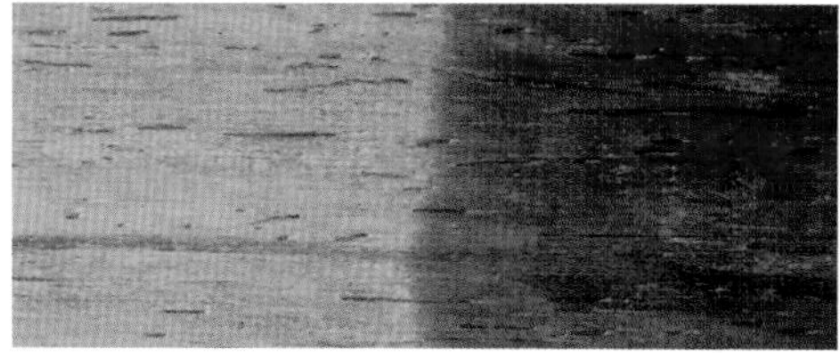

Cocobolo.

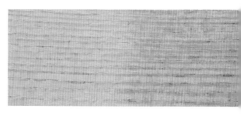

Douglas Fir.

Ebony.

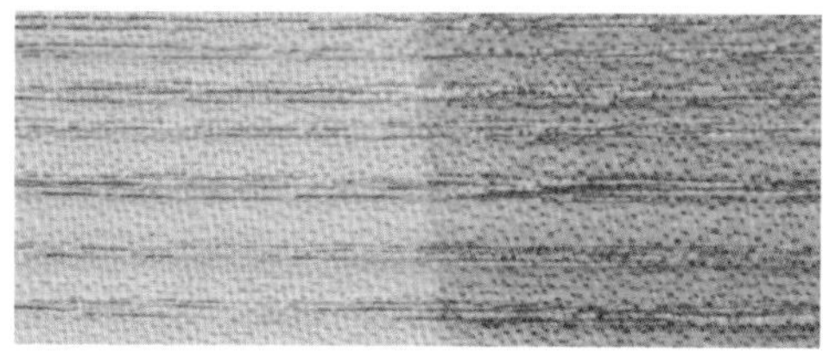

Elm.

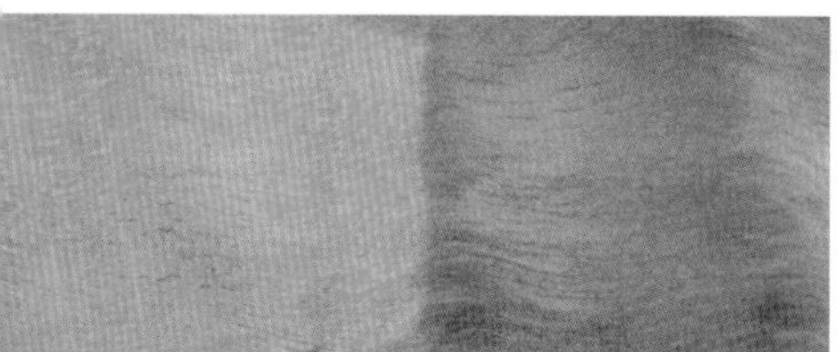

Eucalyptus.

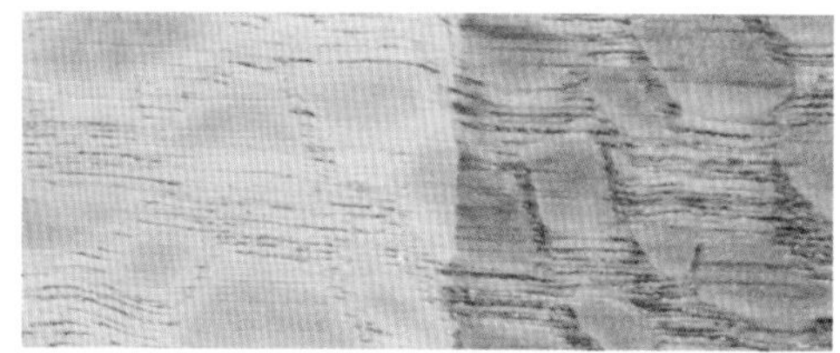

Lacewood.

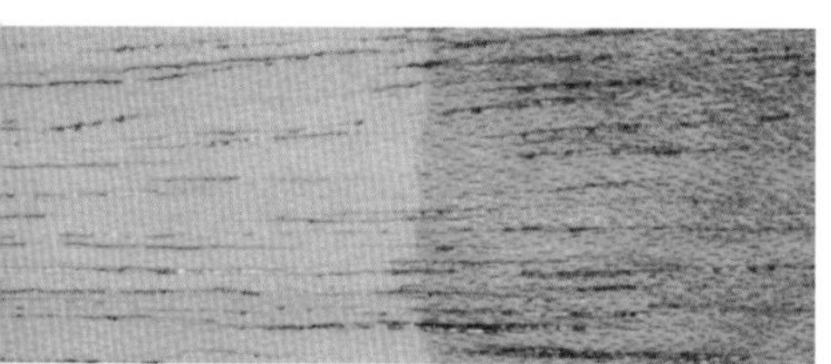

Mahogany, Africa.

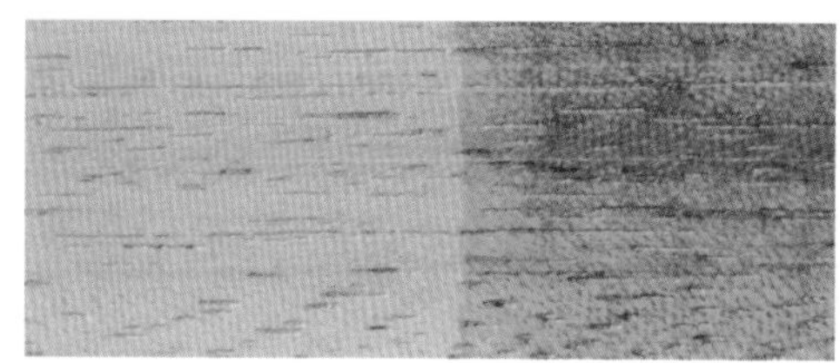

Mahogany, Honduras.

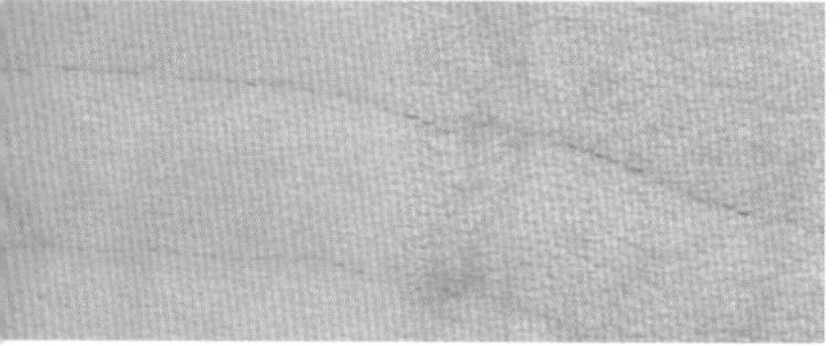

Maple.

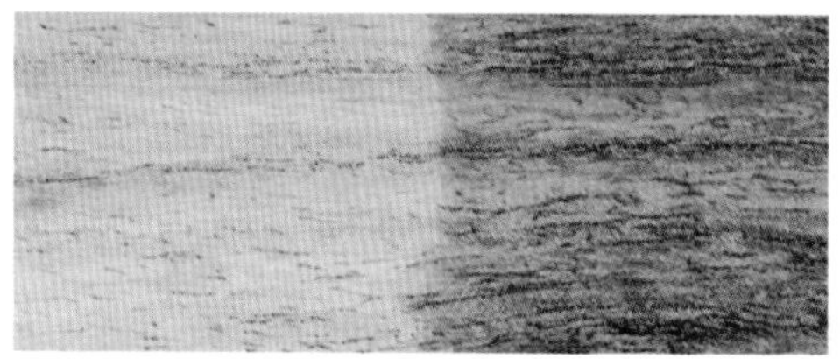

Mesquite.

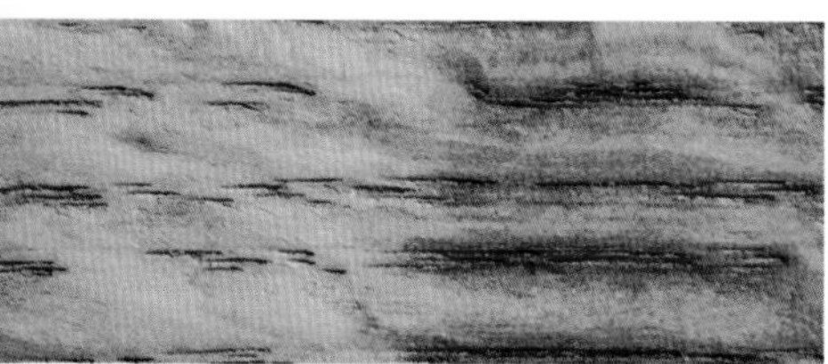

Oak, Brown.

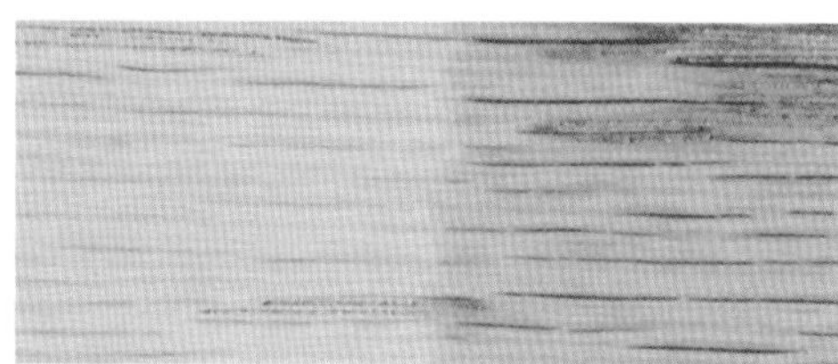

Oak, Red.

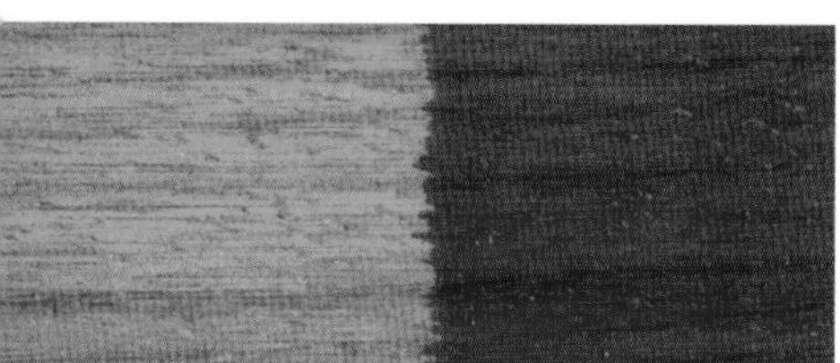

Padouk.

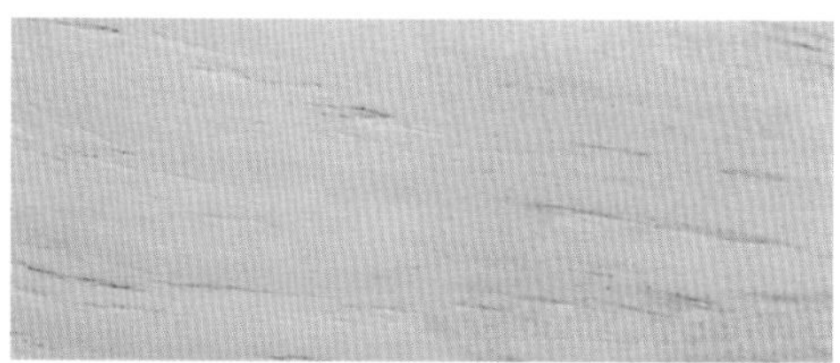

Pine, Ponderosa.

Primavera.

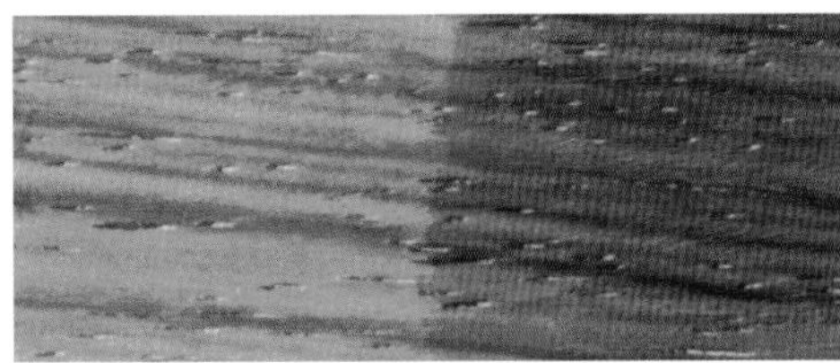

Rosewood.

Walnut, Australia.

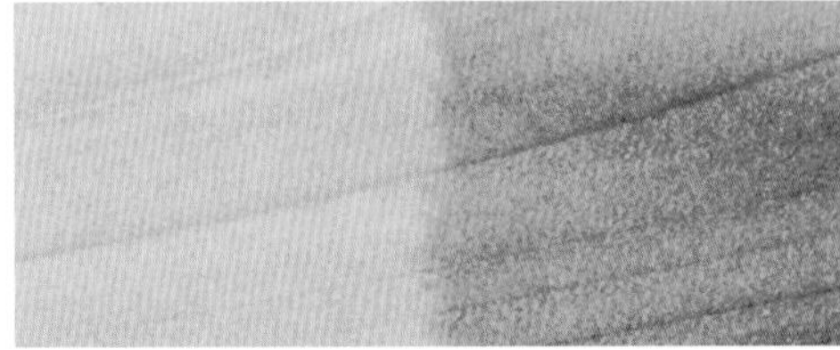

Willow.

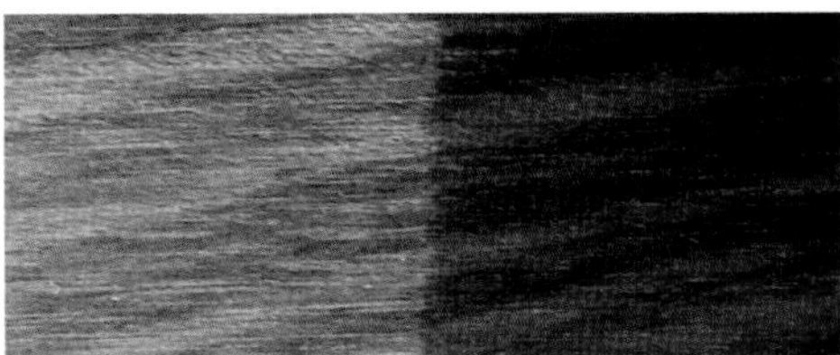

Ziricote.

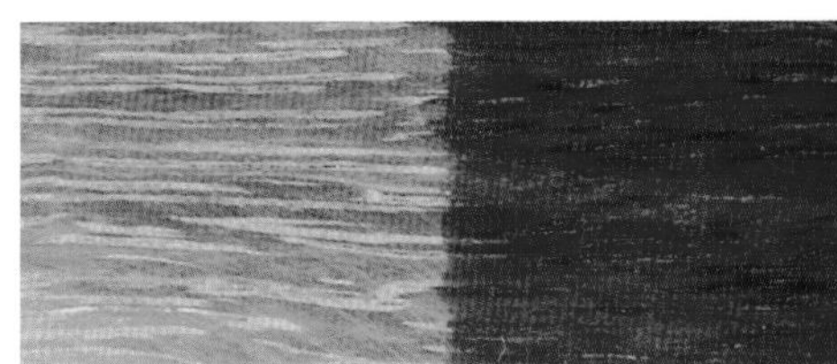

Purpleheart.

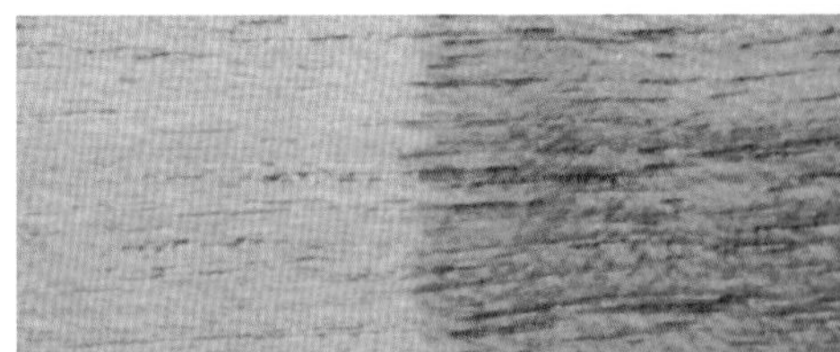

Teak.

Black Walnut, America.

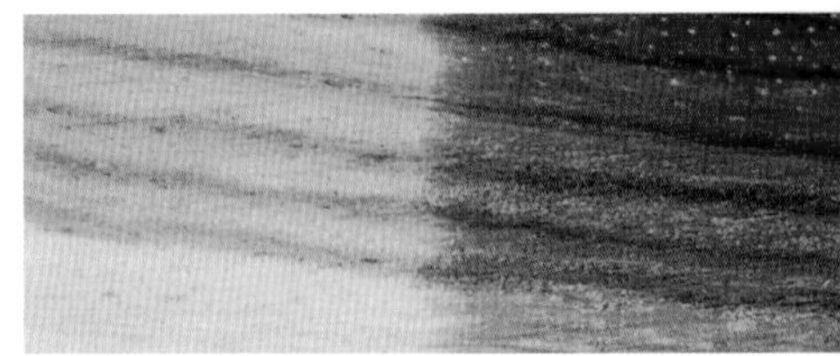

Zebrawood.

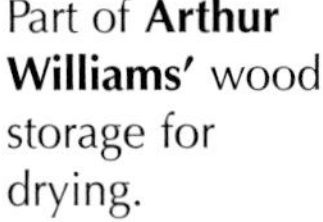

Part of **Arthur Williams'** wood storage for drying.

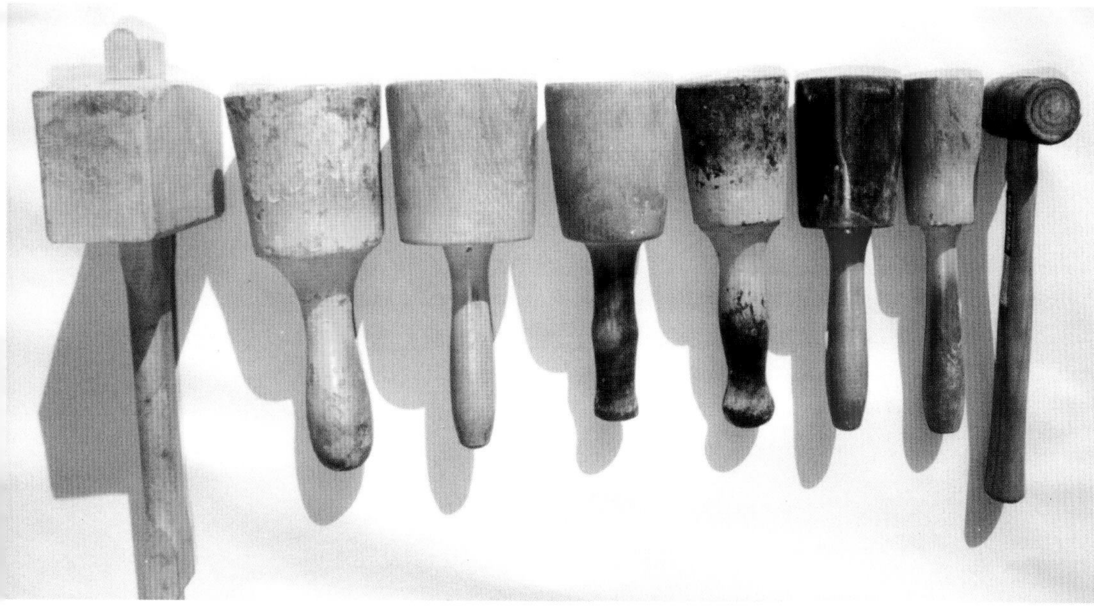

Wood carving mallets.

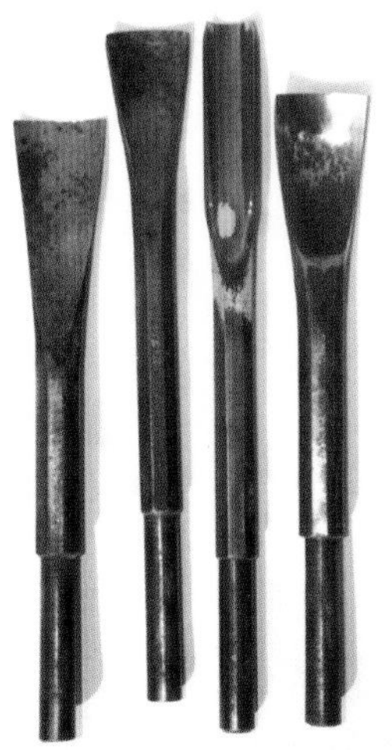

Wood carving gouges for air hammers.

Wood carving chisels.

Sweeps (curves) of wood carving gouges. The small top gouge has a very slight sweep, the middle gouge has a deep sweep, the large lower gouge has a mid-sweep. These sweep angles can be found in all tool sizes; the magnitude of the tool does not affect the sweep angle.

WOODCARVING WITH LOGS

by Walter Driesbach

The sculptor begins by placing logs together.

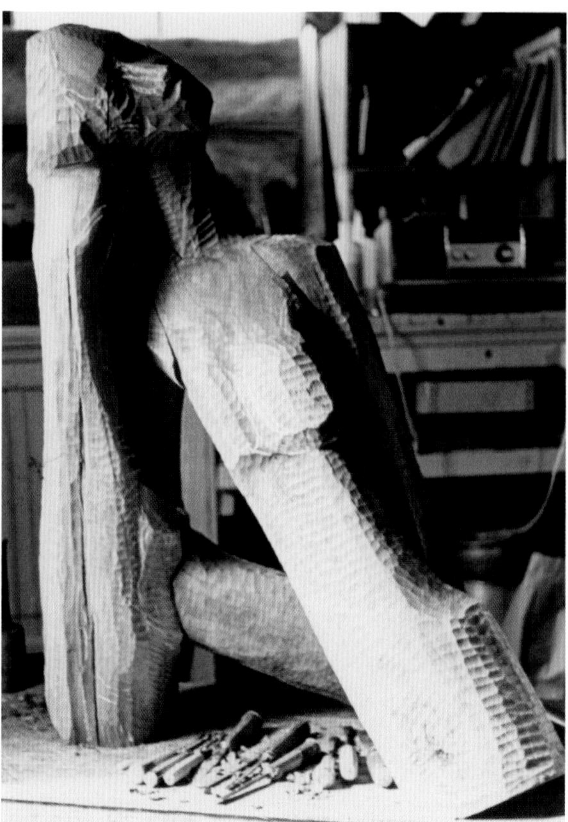

The form emerges as the sculptor roughs out the wood.

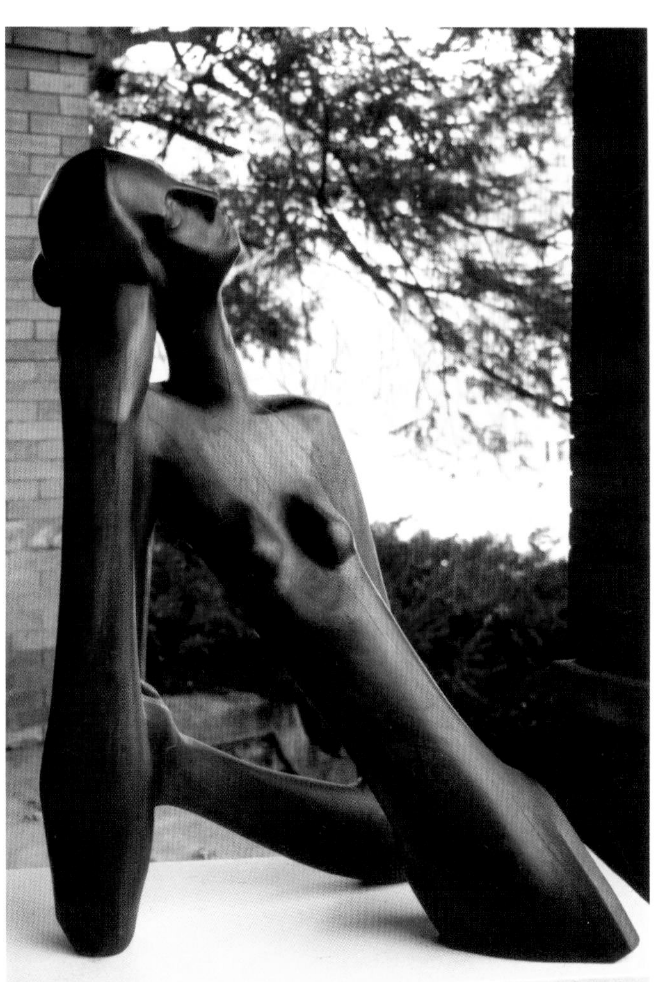

Walter Driesbach, *Muse*. Walnut, 40″ (102cm) tall. Photographer: Forest Atkins.

Laminating wood is used to achieve size, color or strength. Small blocks can be laminated into larger works. This is especially desirable with the thinner kiln dried wood. While woods can be mixed or cross grained for color or design, the sculptor should avoid woods that have density structures where moisture (humidity) could cause a different rate of expansion or contraction, resulting in checking or delaminating. Consider the form and finish sought when choosing a wood so that it will accomplish the design. If the wood is cut to sizes near the desired form, it will save lumber and carving time.

Supplies include the properly dried wood, wood clamps and an adhesive, which is commonly carpenter's glue for indoor works or waterproof glue for out-of-doors. The wood needs to be clean and surfaced on all sides that are to be laminated. Stack lamination can be achieved by placing one board on top of another with a generous supply of glue between layers. Clamps are evenly spaced and pressure is applied to ensure tight joints with the glue visibly squeezed from each layer. The work should be left undisturbed overnight, though the glue will usually firm up within six hours.

Philip John Evett, *Funny Girl.* Mahogany, 28″x22″x22″ (71.1cm x 55.9cm x 55.9cm).

The actual carving is with or across the **grain**. While carving with the grain is faster, it can result in unwanted splits if not carefully controlled. Carving across the grain is difficult and can best be accomplished with extremely sharp tools. Otherwise, the chisels will tend to bruise (compact) or damage the wood, sometimes to a good depth. Most woods have a readily recognizable grain direction while other denser woods have little. Some woods, such as lime, appear to have no gain and carve well in most directions, while others, such as pine, appear excessively grained and great care much be exercised in choosing the direction of carving.

Wood (polychromed) Wood that is coated with a surface paint or product as a decoration. Polychromed indicates many colors. *See* ***Polychrome***.

Woodcarver A woodworker who uses mallets and chisels, as opposed to the whittler who uses a knife only.

Woodcarving The process of working with wood. Carving with hand tools requires mallets, chisels, rasps, files and sandpapers. Even a wood adze is helpful for large works. Wood gouges are used in assorted sizes beginning with the largest deep sweep gouge that is practical and progressing to smaller shallow sweep gouges. Parting tools and flat chisels are used as needed. Tools must be constantly sharpened. Rasps are especially useful followed by files and then hand sanding. Sandpapers from 80 grit to 600 and higher are selected depending on the desired finish.

The finish can vary from being polychromed with paints to being hand rubbed with oil. For the latter, tung oil or a mixture of boiled linseed oil and mineral spirits are used. After the oil has been allowed to dry into the wood, it is followed by a hard paste wax such as Trewax™.

Carving with power tools is accomplished with a diversity of tools depending on the sculptor's personal taste and the size of the carving. Chain saws can rough out larger works followed by pneumatic air hammers and chisels. Smaller works may only require Dremels™ or die grinders. Rotary flap wheels and sanding disks are especially useful. Straight disk sanders with coarse grit disks and orbital sanders with finer grit disks can rapidly remove tool marks.

Whatever the tool used, it is almost always finished with hand sanding and oiling. *See* ***Adze***; ***Mallet***; ***Grinders***; ***Polychrome***.

WOODCARVING
by Brent Coffman

The sculptor begins a cypress carving by drawing on his proposed work.

Brent Coffman uses an air hammer with wood gouges.

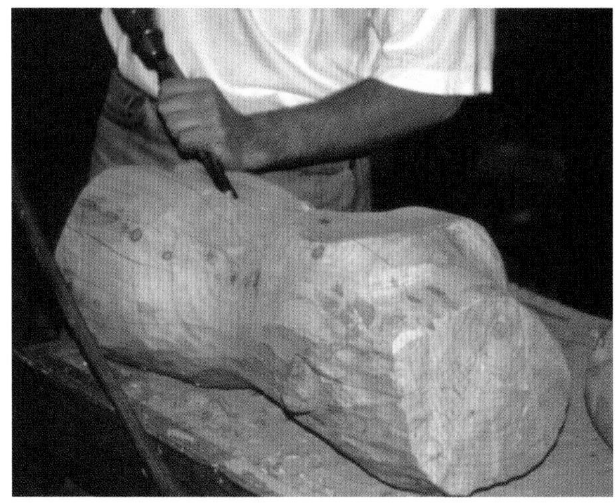

A disk sander is used to remove tool marks.

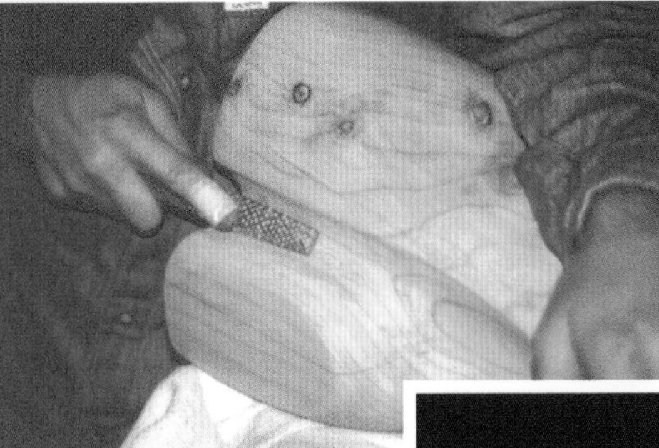

A rasp further refines the curves.

The finish is completed with hand sanding.

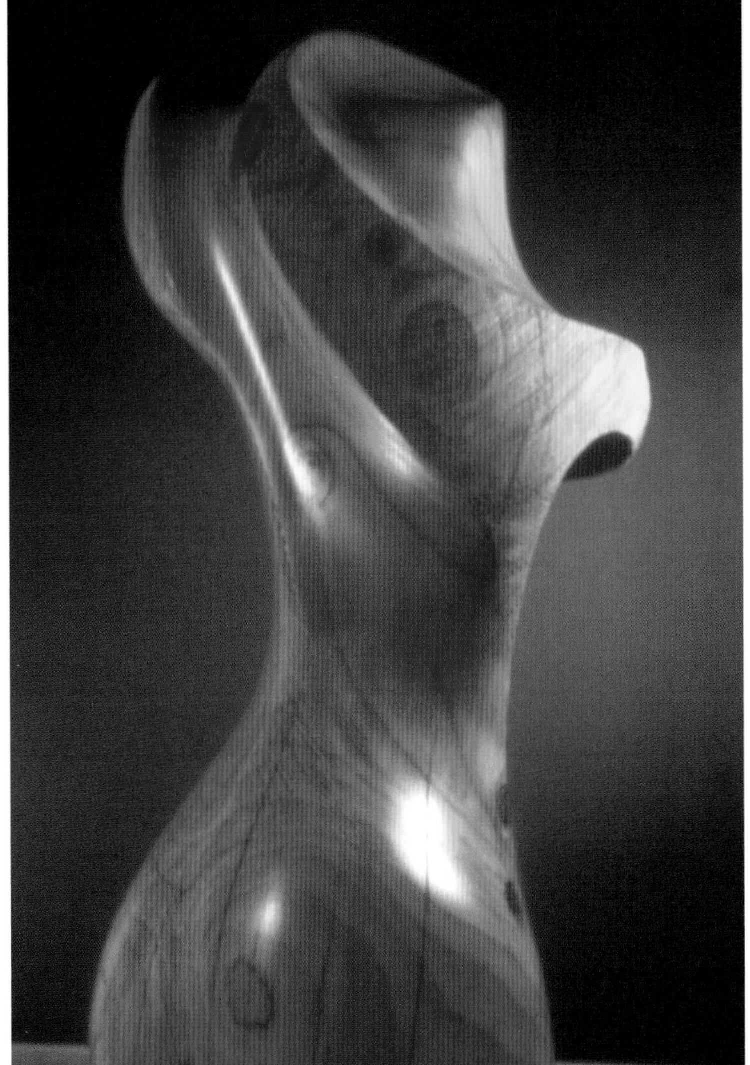

Brent Coffman, *Cypress Figure*. Cypress, 24" (61cm) tall.

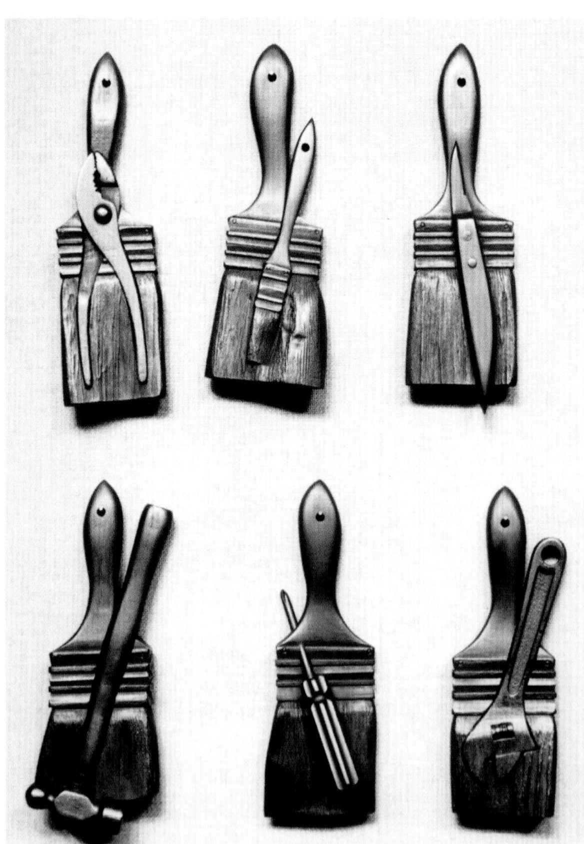

Ron Koehler, *Brushes with Embedded Objects – Set #7*. Carved wood, graphite,

Barry Gunderson, *Divergent Thinking*. Painted wood, welded aluminum, polyurethane, 25″x13″x4″ (63.5cm x 33cm x 10.2cm).

Woodcarving knife A sharp handheld knife designed for carving. It is different than a wood chisel in that it is not designed to be struck by a mallet.

Woodcut A printmaking method of carving a flat wood board just deep enough for the remainder (surface not carved) to accept ink by roller. Paper is then pressed onto it to form a print, called a woodcut. The surface of a flat block of wood that has been carved with woodcut tools leaving a relief impression is also termed woodcut.

Woodcut tools Small versions of woodcarving tools with similar cutting ends but with handles designed for a palm grip.

Voodturning Using a lathe to create forms in wood. The significant difference between this process and normal carving is that the material (wood) is moving while the tool is held stationary. *See **Metal turning lathe**.*

The process is reasonably simple. A single piece of wood, either laminated or solid, is prepared for the lathe. It needs to be in a cylindrical shape, or as close as possible to a cylinder shape, with the exact center designated on both ends. It is placed into the lathe and rotated by hand to ensure it is centered. This is accomplished by placing the tool rest near the wood and slowly hand turning it to find any points out of center. It can be readjusted to a more perfect center if necessary.

Care should be taken that the tool rest is not impeding the turning, and then checked to ascertain all fittings are tight. Beginning at a slow speed will ensure that all is sound. The wood will be slightly out-of-balance, because it is not yet round. If there is an aggressive vibration or the wood appears off balance, the wood must be taken out and trimmed more and re-centered.

Once the worker is satisfied with the balance, the turning begins to show results. Use the large gouge first by placing it firmly on the tool rest and make shallow cuts from one end of the wood to the other. These shearing cuts are to true up the wood and bring it into balance. Continue until a cylinder is visually obvious. Switch to smaller gouges until the form is reasonably smooth and ready for the actual shaping. Other tools are used as needed.

Michael J. Cooper, *Gunshy.* 48 varieties of laminated hardwoods, 99"x50"x38" (251.5cm x 127cm x 96.5cm). Photographer: R. J. Muna.

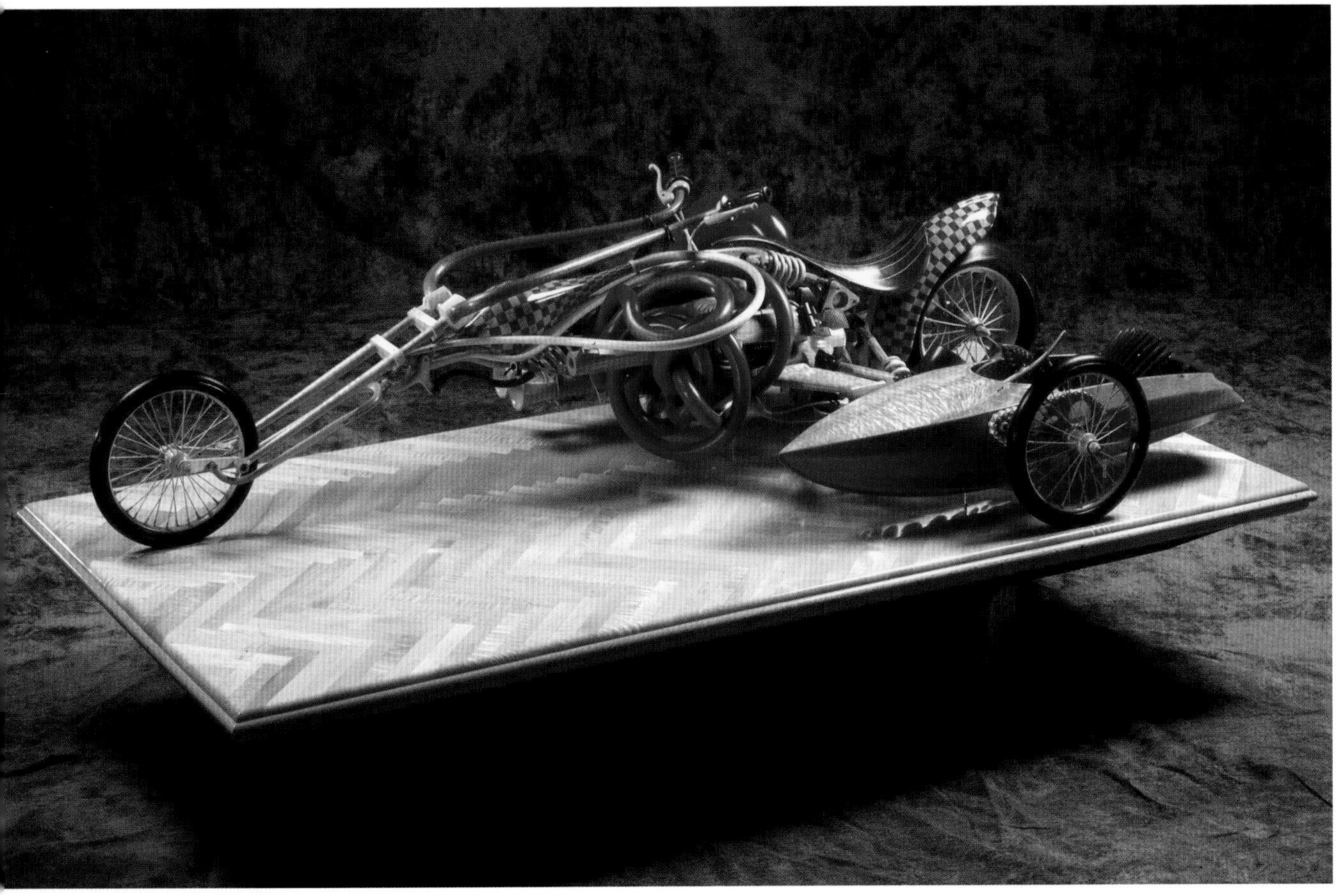

WOOD TURNING/WORKING

Details of *Gunshy*

by Michael J. Cooper

Rear chassis includes the rear tire (Wenge), wheel (Maple), chain (Maple), rear fender (checkerboard of Lacewood and Maple), seat (Walnut, Sycamore), and exhaust tip (Walnut).

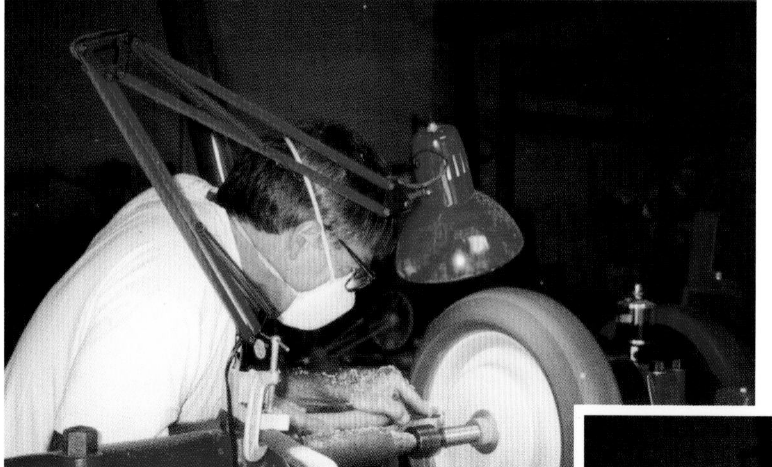

Turning the outer contours of the rear tires (Wenge) and wheel (Maple) on a large metal lathe.

Holes are drilled with a drill press for the nipple and spokes for each wheel with the wheel and tire assembly held in a rotating indexing fixture.

A detail of the Weber carburetor and exhaust pipe (Birdseye, Maple, Satinwood), turbo charger (Zebrawood, Bubinga) and exhaust pipes (Purple Heart).

Exhaust pieces of circular donut pieces (Purple Heart). One was cut within the other to save wood and sanded true with a disc and spindle sander. Afterwards, each corner was rounded over with a router in table jig.

Exhaust pieces were completed on a wooden fixture with inside and outside soft-jaws that held each donut part for sanding on a large metal lathe.

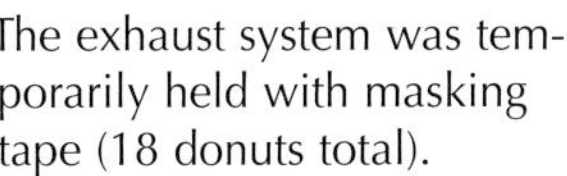

The exhaust system was temporarily held with masking tape (18 donuts total).

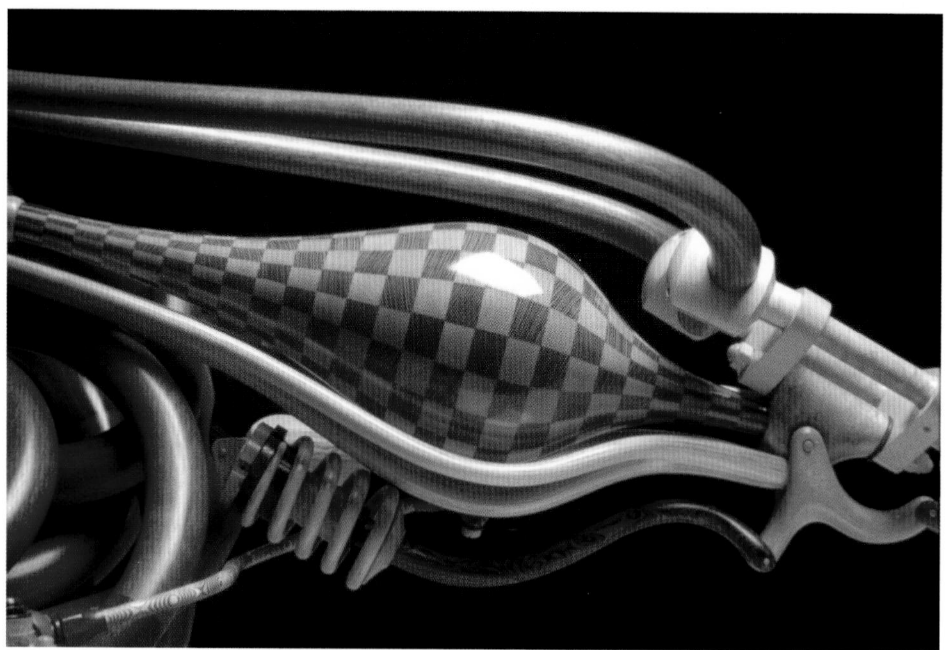

Bent laminated handle bars (Mahogany); gas tank (Lacewood and Maple); and front suspension (Ash, Maple, Cocobold).

Shaped pie sections (Lacewood and Maple) for the gas tank were cut and sanded very accurately.

Ring layers of glued staggered checker board pattern were clamped together with a threaded pipe.

The gas tank was turned on a metal lathe, sanded and then lacquered.

Michael J. Cooper, *Gunshy.* (rear view), 48 varieties of laminated hardwoods, 99"x50"x38" (251.5cm x 127cm x 96.5cm). Photographer: R. J. Muna.

Woodworker An individual who cuts, carves, saws and polishes wood. The resulting product may be furniture, cabinets, bowls or lamps, etc. *See* ***Woodcarver; Sculptor***.

Working model A model that is ready for use. It will be finished in another media or used for enlarging. When preparing for bronze casting, it is called the master copy. *See* ***Model***.

Workpiece lead The electrical conductor (line) of length necessary to reach the base metal torch. *See* ***Welding***.

Wrought iron Refined iron that is strong, easy to weld, very malleable and rust resistant, since it does not contain carbon. Blacksmiths use wrought iron for decorative metalwork. *See* ***Metals*** *(chart)*.

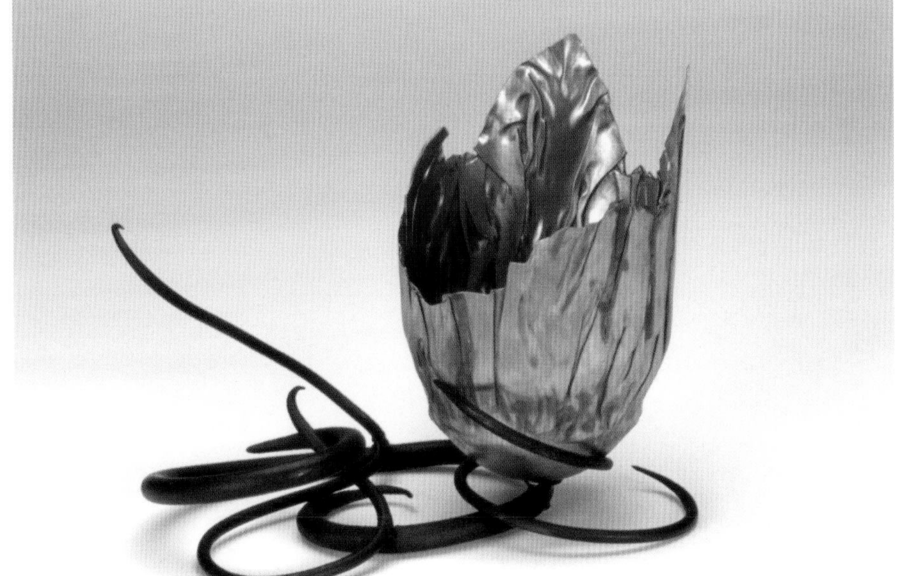

Dalya Luttwak, *From Many Spiral Branches.* Copper, steel, 10″x8″x9″ (25.4cm x 20.3cm x 22.9cm). Photographer: Elaine Mode.

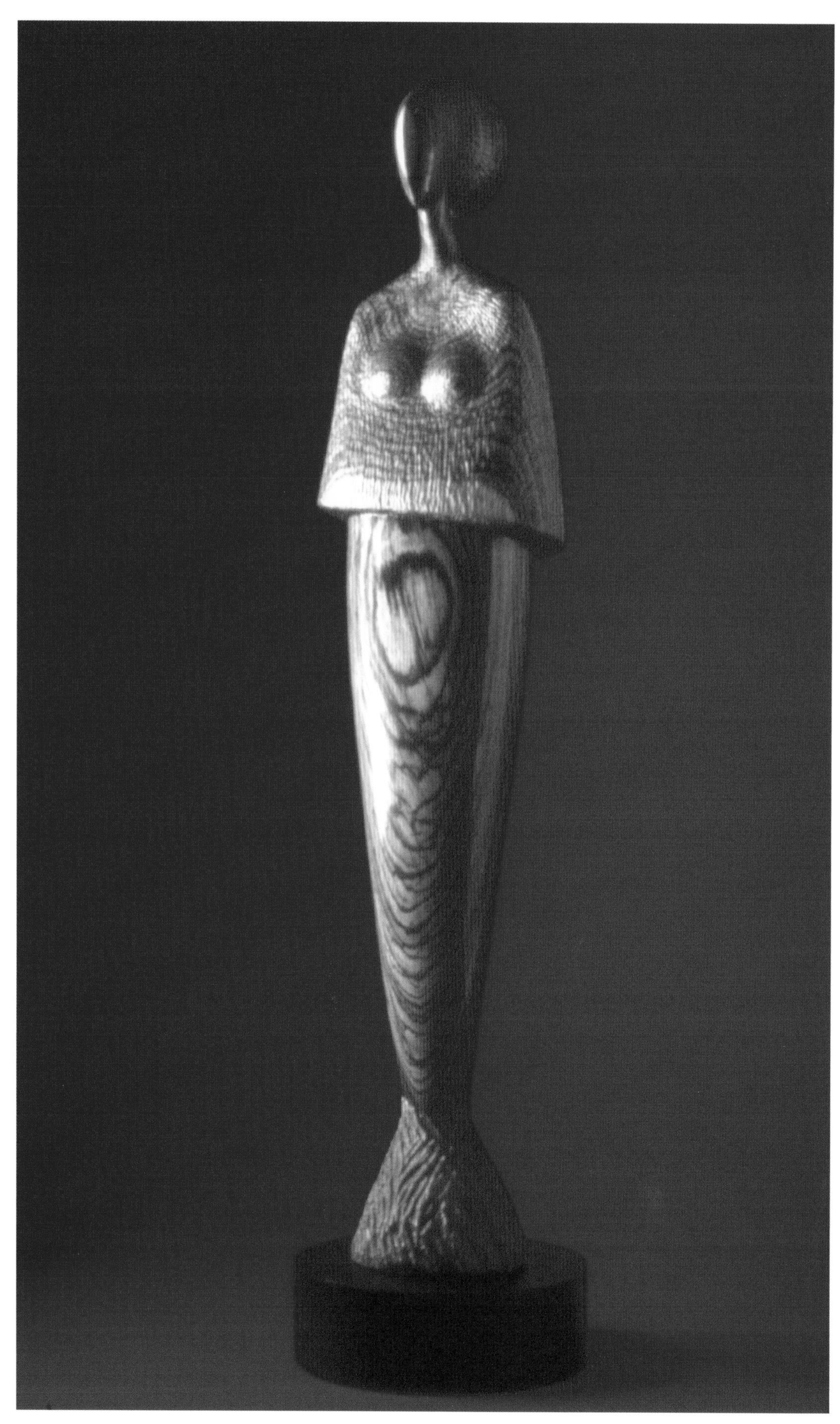

David Hostetler, *Ancestral Woman III*. Zebrawood, 72″ (183cm) tall.

X

X-acto™ (knife) A sharp, replaceable, thin bladed tool. Blades are available in many shapes for specific cuts. X-acto™ tools also include other small tools such as saws, etc.

Xylene A volatile (flammable) solvent made from wood and coal tar. It is used in the manufacturing of resins, rubber cements and lacquers. Sometimes it is called xylol. *See* ***Patina***.

Y

Yard A measurement of 36 inches, three feet or 0.9144 meters. It is also the measurement of a volume (not weight) of construction materials that equals 27 cubic feet (0.81m^3). The term is used for the volume measure of concrete, sand or dirt fill. The actual ground covering is nine feet by nine feet (2.75m x 2.75m) and four inches (10.16cm) in depth to equal a full yard of material (concrete). *See* ***Concrete***.

Yew An evergreen tree wood demonstrating a fine grain. It has been used for making cabinets and, in ancient history, for archery bows.

Yoke The Y-shaped support that holds the hot blowpipe end near the glory hole when glassblowing. It has ball bearings for better rotation of a loaded blowpipe. *See* ***Glass*** *(blowing);* ***Glory hole***.

Z

Zahn cup A small cup with a measured hole in the center for draining the liquid to test for the correct viscosity. The result is determined by timing the draining liquid's flow out of the cup. A timer is used from the start of the drain until it is completed for the number of seconds it takes to flow out. A No. 5 zahn cup is the one commonly associated with ceramic shell mixes. *See* ***Ceramic shell; Slurry; Viscosity***.

Slurry liquid pouring from a zahn cup while being timed to determine the viscosity.

Zebrawood A hard wood from a tropical American or African tree with a striped wood grain of a light, dull yellow color to a light brown with darker stripes of brown-black running parallel. *See* ***Wood*** *(chart)*.

Zinc Metallic element that is malleable when heated. It is primarily used as part of other alloys including bronze and brass. It can be used for galvanizing metals and plating metals to retard corrosion. *See* ***Metal*** *(chart)*.

Zircon (zirconium silicate) A hard, crystalline mineral and the source of zirconium. The term is used for zirconium when sold as a refractory material. *See* ***Zirconium***.

Zirconium A metallic chemical element primarily obtained from zircon. It is used in alloys, refractory kiln furniture and in fine milled powder as part of the metal casting slurry coating due to its high heat resistance. Mixed with colloidal silica, it can be used as a refractory coating in kilns. *See* ***Slurry; Zircon; Colloidal silica***.

ARTIST LISTING

John Sherrill Houser's *Don Juan de Oñate Monument* in progress.
Photographer: Ethan Houser. *See **Enlargement**.*

Artist Listings

Adams, Stephanie 448
Adamy, George E. 99,
Alquilar, Maria 53, 206
Amrhein, Dennis 86
Armstrong, Jane B. 34
Arns, Alan 182
Arvin, Jack Ransom 7, 15, 233, 235, 447, 465
Aurbach, Michael L. 379, 405
Azara, Nancy 191
Bailey, Barry 395
Balciar, Gerald 54, 159, 260, 271, 365
Baran-Mikle, William 146, 198
Barney, Christine 183
Barny, T 20, 21
Bartossik, Nikolai 274
Barwick, B.P. 25, 155, 156, 312
Baudoin, Ali 234, 424
Beailieu, Charlie 399
Beasley, Bruce 66, 67, 252, 253
Beatrice, Barbara 233
Becker, Travis 298
Beckwith, William N. 156, 265, 311, 331, 351, 352, 353
Belán, Kyra 318
Blocker, Annette 235
Blunk, Joyce 33
Boles, Shannon 346
Bollinger, Thomas Jefferson 479
Bolt, Gary 184
Boyd, Jim 363, 474
Brejcha, Vernon 177
Broderick, Geoffrey 73
Broussard, Wendel 197, 372
Brown, Bill 168
Buchanan, Sidney 254
Burch, G. David 63, 234
Butterfield, Deborah 381
Calhoun, Shannon 357
Campbell, Joe 139, 140, 141
Cappadonna-Nichols, Jean 86
Cardenas, Miguel 272
Castle, Wendell 152
Chabot, Aurore 114, 128
Chalke, John 411
Chase, Jack S. 475
Chatterley, Mark D. 196
Chen, J. Jaia 73, 319
Chrisman, Kathreen 285
Citrin, Ione 162
Clark, Kathryn 298, 299, 300
Cline, Lynden 129
Coffman, Brent 488, 489
Coffman, Ha Young 160, 161
Colson, Gary D. 72
Cooper, Michael J. 16, 19, 58, 84, 122, 229, 232, 381, 388, 463, 491, 492, 493, 494, 495
Cornell, Dee 348

Nan Hoeting-Payne, *Transitions*. Stoneware and spodeumene glaze, 36" (92cm) tall.

Costa, Jennifer 155
Cozzolino, Peter N. 54, 468, 469
Dawdy, Richard 197
de la Riva, Arturo 214
de la Riva, Lourdes 478
De Spain, Debbie 88
DeMoss, Max S. 407
Dial, Gail 190
Diduk, Barbara 37
Dowling, Rod 265
Driesbach, Walter 230, 486
Dudding, Jaymes 189
Eckmann, Leslie 115
Einfalt, Linda 273, 384
Ekstam, Keith 222
Emery, Lin 36, 227, 443
Endicott, Jodi 77
Engelhardt, Jason 142
Engler, Kathleen Girdler 302

Robert Pulley, *Canyon.* Stoneware, 20"x26"x18" (50.8cm x 66cm x 46cm).

Eriksen, Gary 247, 333
Etue, Don 80
Evett, Philip John 240, 487
Fall, Nicole 133, 309, 464
Fasnacht, Heide 459
FeBland, Harriet 170
Federighi, Christine 163, 459
Fenton, Gene 304
Ferris, Jr., Michael 213
Feuerman, Carole A. 13, 74, 174, 275, 280, 373, 470
Forbes, Wayne 228
Ford, Rochelle 290
Forman, Mark W. 442
Forsyth, Whitney 154
Fowle, Patz 87, 188, 223, 361
Fox, Michael David 360, 421
Franklin, Hannah 141
Fraughton, Edward J. 65, 269, 402

Friedly, Milt 221, 384
Gallia, Angela 122
Garrett, Eva 403
Ghirardo, Raymond 460
Gipe, Thomas D. 308
Gold, Elisha 47, 300, 338
Goodacre, Glenna 55, 306, 371
Graham, Boyd 134, 183
Granados, Juan 101, 116, 408, 409
Gray, Bruce 24
Greer, John 241, 245
Grimes, Bryan 240
Grygutis, Barbara 94, 97, 407
Gudjonsdottir, Kristin 185, 478
Gunderson, Barry 402, 490
Halldórsdóttir, Gudrún 224
Harper, Cynthia 145
Harrington, William 439
Hart, Forest 502
Harvey, Andrè 173, 266, 312, 400, 472
Haskell, Jane 165, 278
Herndon, Charles L. 242, 243
Herring, Connie 216, 477
Hill, Andrès 17, 329
Hiveley, Bryan 189
Hoeting-Payne, Nan 101, 499
Holen, Norman D. 59, 157, 203, 294, 322, 323, 347
Hoop 317
Hornecker, Mac 148, 249
Hostetler, David 220, 282, 360, 380, 417, 439, 481, 496
Houser, Ethan 136, 498
Houser, John Sherrill 2, 29, 135, 136, 137, 138, 272, 498
Huntoon, Abby 153
Jablon, Lorraine 423
Jackson, Jimmie 207
Jae 236
Jansen, Catherine 145
Jeffries, Paul 445
Jones, Carter 205, 351, 448
Joseph, Renè 10
Kaufman, Mico 246
Kelmenson, Lita 481
Kelsey-Mapel, Jane 348, 458
Kinard, Tim 35, 46, 64, 164, 231, 258, 354, 388
Klimek, Lylian 376
Kluge, Janice 53, 171, 462
Knapp, Stephen 178
Koehler, Ron 490
Koss, Gene 28, 73, 186, 187, 318, 380
Kostyniuk, Ronald 133
Kosuge, Michihiro 37
Kotkov, Ernest 274
Krentzin, Earl 406
Kretschmer, Melissa 39
Kronfield, Elizabeth 217, 384
Labadons, Lance 158
Larsen, Bruce 6, 83, 123

Tana Preminger, *Shield.* Wood, Glass, Skin, 13"x10"x 9" (32cm x 26cm x 22cm).

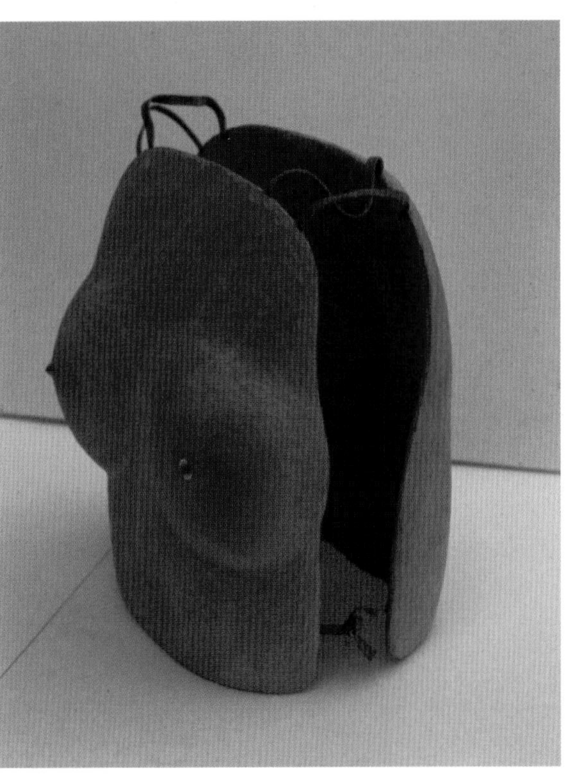

Lawton, James L. 279, 456
Leong, Lampo 281, 454
Lewis, Mary 197, 234, 371
Linn, Steve 180, 184, 387
List, Dawson 207, 208, 209
Little, Ken 216,
Littleton, Harvey 177
Lowenstein, Ellen 327
Luttwak, Dalya 495
McCreary, Susan Sasenick 438
Mader, Daniel E. 276
Maksymowicz, Virginia 301
Marinsky, Harry 450

Forrest Hart, *The Dominant One.* Cast bronze, 27"x27"x11" (68.6cm x 68cm x 27.9cm).

Mayhew, Elza 440, 466
McAllister, Mac 12
McDaniel, Harry 68, 69
McDonald, Thomas 171
McEneny, Brian 81
McRoberts, Sheryl 324, 372
Mellick, James 82, 120
Mendonis, Irene 374
Mensoff, Corrina 119
Minkowitz, Norma 148
Moczygemba, Cora 79
Mohr, Jeff 197
Mollet, Susan F. 476
Monteith, Jerry 305
Moran, Greg 166, 167, 199, 247, 355
Morin, Shawn Phillip 210, 229, 410, 433
Moroles, Jesús 176, 192
Mosley, Aaron Royal 51, 77, 321

Muench, Joe 32, 36, 100
Mulcahy, Kathleen 179
Muno, Rich 31
Myford, James 461
Nees, Sue 192, 433
Newkirk, Dale 93
Newman, Richard 263
Nickel, Lothar 117, 436, 437
Olson, Lynn 75, 76
Ott, Ron 351
Oxman, Mark 342
Parillo, Marlene Ferrell 477
Parish, Willie Ray 422
Parker, Herb 129, 277
Parrott, Melissa 189
Patrick, Deresa 102
Paxson, Duane 144
Pearson, Jan 173
Peden, Doñalee 52
Penteado, Duda 11
Phillips, Pamela 382, 412, 413
Pinardi, Enrico 239
Polenberg, Marcia 410
Polutanovich, Greg 85
Potratz, Wayne E. 110, 111
Poulton, Irene 237
Preminger, Tanya 501
Prent, Mark 149
Prince, Richard E. 150
Pulley, Robert 205, 441, 500
Quisgard, Liz Whitney 344
Ransdell, Michael R. 504
Reeves, Dianne L. 301, 503
Reichley, Karl 316
Remel, Melissa 143
Renninger, Lee 454
Richardson, Henry B. 90, 179
Richardson, John 475
Roberts, Megan 460
Robinson, Kelly 132
Rosen, Carol 263
Rotella, Joseph 90, 284, 307, 346, 455
Roussel, Claude 346
Rozinski, Richard 278
Ruby, Laura 216
Sakoaka, Yasue 297
Satin, Claire Jeanine 10
Sauder, Lee 218
Savoy, Chryl L. 303, 348
Sayre, Thomas 91, 127, 286, 467
Scaturro, BaBa 452, 453, 480
Schmuki, Jeff 143, 349
Seeman, Jon 426
Segal, Joe 121, 201
Segers, Pamela M. 15
Shaman, Floyd 295, 305
Shaughnessy, Sharon Dee 262, 284, 320, 369, 471

Dianne L. Reeves, *Depths of Rage.* Handmade ashe juniper jute paper, root, antlers, bones, 15"x24"x26" (38.1cm x 61cm x 66cm).

Sherman, Ira D. 319
Shipley, Roger 343
Siebert, Ted 399
Silverman, Arthur 24
Skoglund, Sandy 215
Skoracki, Reinhard 45, 394
Smith, Barbara 344
Snider, Shane 350
Sohikian, R. Mike 112,113

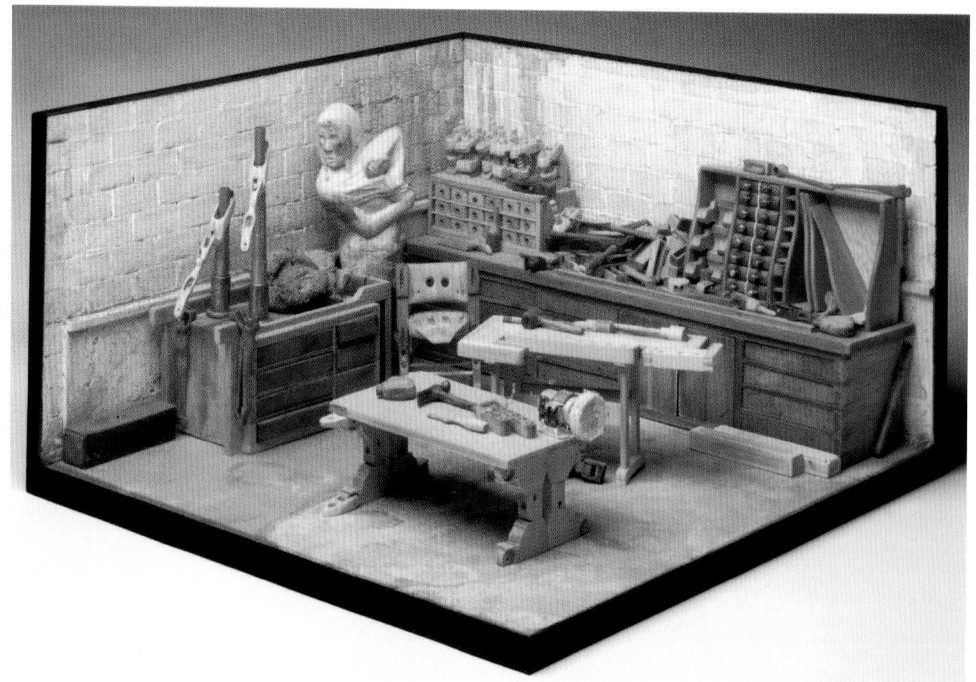

Michael R. Ransdell, *Figure in the Workroom.* Buckeye burl, found objects, metal, leather, woods, 9"x16 1/4"x16 1/4"x16 1/4" (22.9cm x 41.3cm x 41.3cm).

Spiczka, Sam 103
Stine, Jon M. 263
St. Pierre, Dennis 385, 476
Stubitsch, Dawn 151, 283, 296, 505
Sweetwater, Sarah 194,241, 310
Tadlock, Marvin 168, 293, 355
Taradash, Meryl 226
Thompson, Jack 14, 40, 336, 337, 358, 411
Thomson, Dahrl 365, 420, 449
Thrall, Leitha L. 41, 316, 404
Todorov, Todor 173
Torcoletti, Enzo 7, 18, 72, 118, 121, 193, 201, 345, 362, 363, 398, 434
Tsalikhin, Alexander 37, 105
Ullberg, Kent 266
van der Zanden, Diane 330, 471
VanGieson, Mary K. 372
Venhuizen, Von 295, 357
Verani, Patricia L. 19, 51, 304
Verbruggen, Marc 65
Vicini, Christopher 126, 286
Viviani-Finch, Gundi 91
Vivot, Lea 408
Vogler, Kathy 48
Volkersz, William 279
Volkin, Hilda Appel 342

Wald, Sylvia	302
Walsh, Suzanne Hauerstein	367
Weaver, John	439
Weidman, John M.	326
Weimer, Dawn	44, 250, 251
Weir, Matthew	212
White, Bruce H.	27
Wicker, Matthew C.	109, 219, 390, 391, 400
Wilkinson, Michael	9
Williams, Arthur	56, 57, 60, 61, 172, 194, 201, 211, 236, 238, 247, 254, 262, 267, 328, 346, 347, 356, 366, 375, 403, 425, 455, 484, 512
Williams, Kenyon	346
Williams, Remo	419
Woods, Ted	170
Wright, Shannon	41
Yokel, Fred	367, 438
Zajac, Jack	281
Zimmerman, Elyn	192
Zurko, Walter	125

Dawn Stubitsch, *Roy and Wednesday,* Cake Topper. Polymer clay, 7" (11.8cm) tall.

BIBLIOGRAPHY

The enlargers hold the white resin cast of the sword of Oñate. The sculptor, **John Sherrill Houser**, looks on. Photographer: Ethan Houser, *See **Enlargement***.

BIBLIOGRAPHY

Andrews, Oliver. *Living Materials: A Sculptor's Handbook*. Berkeley: California, University of California Press, 1988.

Barnsley, Alan. *Introducing Expanded Polystyrene*. London, England: B. T. Batsford, Ltd., 1973.

Barrie, Bruner Felton. *A Sculptor's Guide to Tools and Materials*: New York, New York, A.B.F.S. Publishing, 1996.

Barrie, Bruner Felton. *Model Making, Casting and Patina*. Princeton: New Jersey, Adams, Barrie, Felton and Scott Publishing, 1993.

Beazley, Mitchell. *Working in Wood*. London, England: Octopus Publishing Group, Ltd., 1999.

Bostrom, Antonia ed. *The Encyclopedia of Sculpture*. New York, New York: Fitzroy Dearborn, 2004.

Busse, Ronald A. and Robert Hund. *Dimension Stones of the World, Volume II*: Farmington, Michigan, Marble Institute of America, 1993.

Busse, Ronald A. and Robert Hund. *Dimension Stones of the World, Volume I*: Farmington, Michigan: Marble Institute of America, 1990.

Cami, Josepmaria Teixidó i and Jacinto Chicharro Santamera. *Sculpture in Stone*. Hauppauge, New York: Barron's Educational Series, Inc., 2000.

Caplin, Lee. *The Business of Art*. second edition. Englewood, Cliffs, New Jersey: Prentice Hall, 1989.

Cary, B. Howard. *Modern Welding Technology*, fourth edition. Upper Saddle River, New Jersey: Prentice Hall, 1989.

Castle, Wendell and David Edman. *The Wendell Castle Book of Wood Lamination*. New York, New York: Van Nostrand Reinhold Company, 1980.

Chaney, Charles and Stanley Skee. *Plaster Mold and Model Making*. New York, New York: Van Nostrand Reinhold Company, 1973.

Chappell, James. *The Potter's Complete Book of Clay and Glazes*, revised edition. New York, New York: Watson-Guptill Publications, 1991.

Chilvers, Ian. *A Dictionary of Twentieth-Century Art*. Oxford, New York: Oxford University Press, 1998.

Coleman, Ronald. *Sculpture, a Basic Handbook for Students*, third edition. Dubuque, Iowa: William C. Brown Publishers, 1990.

Duginske, Mark. *Band Saw Handbook*. New York, New York: Sterling Publishing Co., Inc., 1989.

Edge, Michael S. *The Art of Patinas for Bronze*. Springfield, Oregon: Michael S. Edge, 1990.

Edlin, Herbert L. *What Wood is That? A Manual of Wood Identification*. New York, New York: Viking Press, 1969.

Encarta World English Dictionary. New York, New York: St. Martin's Press, 1999.

Finch, Richard. *Welder's Handbook*. New York, New York: H. P. Books, 1997.

Finn, David. *How to Look at Sculpture*. New York, New York: Harry N. Abrams, 1989.

Gault, Rosette, *Paper Clay*. Philadelphia, Pennsylvania: University of Pennsylvania Press, 1998.

Geary, Don, *The Welder's Bible*. Blue Ridge Summit, Pennsylvania: Tab Books, Inc.,1980.

Giberson, Dudley F. *A Glassblower's Companion*. Warner, New Hampshire: The Joppa Press, 1998.

Grant, Daniel. *The Artist's Resource Handbook*, revised edition. New York, New York: Allworth Press, 1996.

Gregory, Ian, *Kiln Building*. London, England: A and C Black, 1995.

Gregory, Ian, *Sculptural Ceramics*. Woodstock, New York: The Overlook Press 1999.

Hall, Carolyn Vosburg. *Soft Sculpture*. Worcester, Massachusetts: Davis Publications, Inc., 1981.

Hamer, Frank and Janet Hamer. *The Potter's Dictionary of Materials and Techniques*. Philadelphia, Pennsylvania: University of Pennsylvania Press, 1997.

Hitchcock, Howard. *Out of the Fiery Furnace*. Los Altos, California: William Kaufmann, Inc., 1985.

Hoadley, R. Bruce. *Understanding Wood*. Newton, Connecticut: The Taunton Press, Inc., 1997.

Installation and Operating Manual. Danville, Illinois: McEnglevan, 1987.

Kipper, Patrick V. *Patinas for Silicon Bronze*. Loveland, Colorado: Path Publications, 1995.

Kipper, Patrick V. *The Care of Bronze Sculpture*. Loveland, Colorado: Path Publications, 1996.

Kirby, Ian. *Sharpening with Waterstones*. Bethel, Connecticut: Cambium Press, 1998.

Langland, Tuck. *From Clay to Bronze*. New York, New York: Watson-Guptill Publications, 1999.

Langland, Tuck. *Practical Sculpture*. Englewood Cliffs, New Jersey: Prentice Hall, 1988.

Lanteri, Edouard. *Modeling and Sculpting the Human Figure*. New York, New York: Dover Publications, Inc., 1985.

Leier, Ray, Jan Peters and Kevin Wallace. *Contemporary Glass*. Madison, Wisconsin: Guild Publishing, 2001.

Liebson, Milt. *Direct Stone Sculpture*. West Chester, Pennsylvania: Schiffer Publishing, Ltd., 1991.

Liebson, Milt. *Direct Wood Sculpture*. Atglen, Pennsylvania: Schiffer Publishing, Ltd., 2001.

Lincoln, William A. *World Woods in Color*. Fresno, California: Linden Publishing Co.,Inc., 1986.

Lindquist, Mark. *Sculpting Wood*. Worcester, Massachusetts: Davis Publications, Inc., 1986.

Lucchesi, Bruno.*Terracotta*. New York, New York: Watson-Guptill Publications, 1996.

MacCormick, Alex. *Paper Machè Style*. Iola, Wisconsin: Krause Publications, 1994.

MacIntosh, Hal. *Chainsaw Carving, The Art and Craft*. East Petersburg, Pennsylvania: Fox Chapel Publishing Co., Inc., 2001.

Magyszalanczy, Sandor. *The Wood Sanding Book*. Newton, Connecticut: The Taunton Press, Inc., 1997.

Mayer, Ralph. *The Artist's Handbook of Materials and Techniques*, fifth edition. New York, New York: Viking, 1985.

Mayer, Ralph. *The Harper Collins Dictionary of Art Terms and Techniques*, second edition, New York, New York: Harper Perennial, 1991.

McCreight, Tim. *Practical Casting*, revised edition. Cape Elizabeth, Maine: Brym Orgen Press, 1994.

Meilach, Dona Z. *Contemporary Art with Wood*. New York, New York: Crown Publishing, Inc., 1968.

Meilach, Dona Z. *Contemporary Stone Sculpture*. Atglen, Pennsylvania: Schiffer Publishing, Ltd., 1970.

Meilach, Dona Z. *Decorative and Sculptural Ironwork*. Atglen, Pennsylvania: Schiffer Publishing, Ltd., 1999.

Meilach, Dona Z. *Direct Metal Sculpture*, revised. Atglen, Pennsylvania: Schiffer Publishing, Ltd., 2001.

Meilach, Dona Z. *The Contemporary Blacksmith*. Atglen, Pennsylvania: Schiffer Publishing, Ltd., 2000.

Miller, Richard M. *Figure Sculpture in Wax and Plaster*. New York, New York: Dover Publications, 1987.

Mills, John W. *Encyclopedia of Sculpture Techniques*. London, England: B. T. Batsford, Ltd., 2001.

Mills, John W. *The Technique of Casting Sculpture*. London, England: B.T. Batsford, Ltd., 1967.

Mills, John W. *The Technique of Sculpture*. New York, New York: Reinhold Publishing Corporation, 1967.

Mills, John. *Sculpture in Concrete*. New York, New York: Frederick A. Praeger, 1968.

Narbury, Ian. *Relief Woodcarving and Lettering*. Fresno, California: Linden Publishing Co., 1987.

Nelson, Glenn C. *Ceramics, A Potter's Handbook*, fifth edition. New York, New York: Holt Rinehart and Winston, 1984.

Nigrosh, Leon I. *Low Fire, Other Ways to Work in Clay*. Worcester, Massachusetts: Davis Publications, 1980.

Olsen, Frederick L. *The Kiln Book*, third edition. Iola, Wisconsin: Krause Publications, 2001.

Olson, Lynn. *Sculpting with Cement*. Valparaiso, Indiana: Steelstone Press, 1997.

Padovano, Anthony. *The Process of Sculpture*. New York, New York: Da Capo Paperback, 1981.

Perryman, Jane. *Smoke-Fired Pottery*. London, England: A and C Black, 1995.

Peters, Rick, *Air Tools*. New York, New York: Sterling Publishing Co., Inc. 2000.

Plowman, John. *The Encyclopedia of Sculpting Techniques*. Philadelphia, Pennsylvania: Running Press, 1995.

Potratz, Wayne E. *Hot Metal*. Minneapolis, Minnesota: Turtle Sign Company, 1992.

Pye, Chris. *Woodcarving, Tools, Materials and Equipment*. Lewes, East Sussex: Guild of Master Craftsman Publications, Ltd., 1996.

Reiss, Julie H. *From Margin to Center*. Cambridge, Massachusetts: The MIT Press, 2001.

Rhodes, Daniel. *Clay and Glazes*. New York, New York: Chilton Book Company, 1973.

Rich, Jack C. *The Materials and Methods of Sculpture*. New York, New York: Oxford University Press, 1947.

Ritchie, Ralph W., *Burners*, second edition. Springfield, Oregon: Ritchie Unlimited Publications, 1999.

Rossol, Monona. *The Artist's Complete Health and Safety Guide*, third edition. New York, New York: Allworth Press, 2001.

Rothenberg, Polly. *The Complete Book of Creative Glass Art*. New York, New York: Crown Publishers, 1974.

Roukes, Nicholas. *Masters of Wood Sculpture*. New York, New York: Watson-Guptill Publications, 1980.

Roukes, Nicholas. *Plastics for Kinetic Art*. New York, New York: Watson-Guptill Publications,1974.

Schmid, Edward T. *Advanced Glassworking Techniques. Bellingham, Washington: Glass Mountain Press, 1997.*

Schmid, Edward T. *Beginning Glassblowing*. Bellingham, Washington: Glass Mountain Press, 1998.

Smith, Stan and H.F. Ten Holt, editors. *The Sculptor's Handbook*. New York, New York: Gallery Books, 1984.

Soft Sculpture and Other Soft Art Forms. New York, New York: Crown Publishers, Inc.,1994.

Sopcak, James E. *Lost Wax on Investment Casting*. Baldwin Park, California: Gem Guides Book Company, 1986.

The American Heritage Dictionary of the English Language, fourth edition. Boston, Massachusetts: Houghton Mifflin Company, 2000.

The Melting Pot Instruction Manual. Mitchellville, Maryland: Melting Pot International, Inc., 1997.

Toale, Bernard. *The Art of Papermaking*. Worcester, Massachusetts: Davis Publications, Inc., 1983.

Verhelst, Wilbert. *Sculpture, Tools, Materials and Techniques*, second edition, Englewood Cliffs, New Jersey: Prentice Hall, 1988.

Weygers, Alexander G. *The Complete Modern Blacksmith*. Berkeley, California: Ten Speed Press, 1997.

Widman, Lorraine Balmuth. *Sculpture, A Studio Guide*. Englewood Cliffs, New Jersey: Prentice Hall, 1989.

Williams, Arthur. *Beginning Sculpture*. Worcester, Massachusetts: Davis Publications, Inc., 2005.

Williams, Arthur. *Sculpture: Technique-Form-Content*, revised edition. Worcester, Massachusetts: Davis Publications, Inc., 1995.

Wolf, George. *3-D Wizardry, Design in Papier-Mâchè, Plaster and Foams*. Worcester, Massachusetts: Davis Publications, 1995.

Woodworking Machines, John Kelsey, editor. Newton, Connecticut: The Taunton Press, 1995.

Woody, Elsbeth S. *Handbuilding Ceramic Forms*. New York, New York: The Noonday Press, 1998.

Young, Ronald D. *Contemporary Patination*. Escondido, California: Sculpt-Nouveau, 1992.

Young, Joseph. *Mosaics: Principles and Practice*. New York, New York: Reinhold Publishing Corporation, 1963.

This is the author's third book. The first, **Sculpture: Technique-Form-Content**, was published in 1987 and has been through several printings and a revision in 1995. The second book, **Beginning Sculpture**, is a secondary text (2005).

The author has five college degrees including the Master of Fine Arts (University of Mississippi) and the Doctor of Arts (Carnegie Mellon University). He has been a Professor, artist-in-residence, a holder of an endowed chair, and a full-time sculptor. Over three hundred of his sculptures are located in more than twenty-five states, Canada and Mexico....

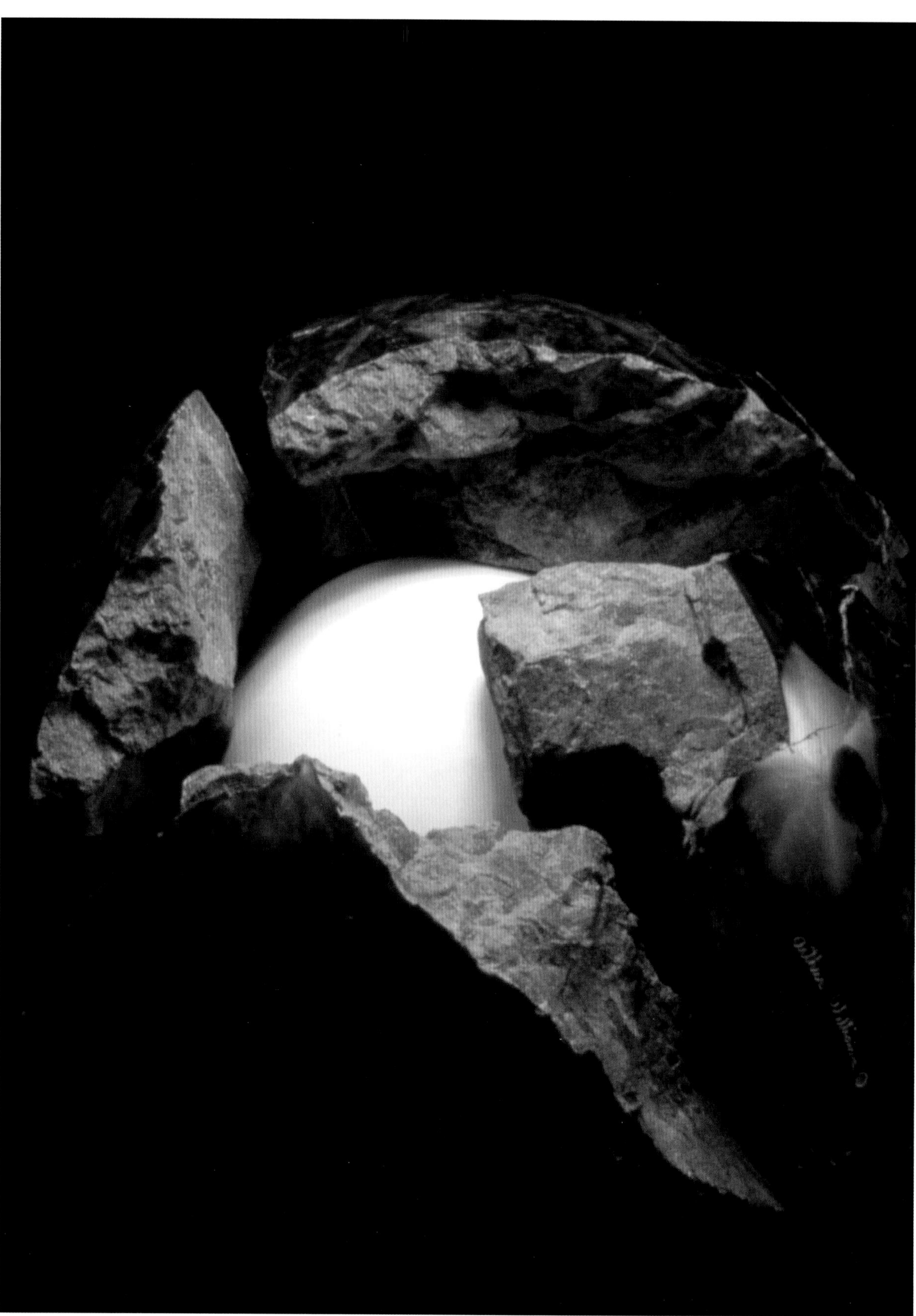